retailing management

RETAILING
MANAGEMENT

SECOND EDITION

Rom J. Markin, Jr.

Professor of Business Administration
Washington State University

Macmillan Publishing Co., Inc.
New York

Collier Macmillan Publishers
London

Macmillan Publishing Co., Inc.
866 Third Avenue, New York, New York 10022

Collier Macmillan Canada, Ltd.

Library of Congress Cataloging in Publication Data

Markin, Rom J
    Retailing management.

    Includes bibliographical references and index.
    1. Retail trade—Management. I. Title.
HF5429.M323   1977   658.8'7   76-26124
ISBN 0-02-376140-7

Printing: 1 2 3 4 5 6 7 8   Year: 7 8 9 0 1 2 3

preface

Retailing as an institution and as a category of trade is one of our most dynamic and expansive economic endeavors. In reflection of this fact, retailing has continued to gain greater standing as a part of the overall offering in professional schools of business administration, in community colleges, and in liberal arts institutions.

From the academic perspective, retailing is no longer looked upon as a small, unimportant vocational area, which, if taught at all, emphasizes only the how-to-do-it, mundane, routine orientation once so characteristic of the discipline. Instead, retailing, along with other offerings in the business and especially the marketing curriculum, is now an important subject, demanding high levels of understanding and skill, fully challenging the manager's and the decision maker's ability.

This revision retains the first edition's treatment of retailing management within the framework of general developments in the business curriculum and continues to emphasize company-wide management policies and the interrelatedness of the total company-environmental activities that characterize today's business organization. Furthermore, the revision continues to place a marked emphasis on analysis and decision making within the retailing organization. But the reader familiar with the earlier version will immediately recognize that this is a substantial revision. In what I believe is a successful effort to make the book more readable and accessible to the student, there has, for example, been a reduction in the use of "systems" terminology, and the interrelationships of decisions made in one area of retailing and their effects on the entire organization have been made explicit throughout. In addition to the translation of *retail management system* into *retail store*, there is less use of mathematical notation, greater simplicity in the examples given, and a good deal of reorganization and shortening to improve clarity.

The text is still for the undergraduate student at the beginning and intermediate stages of his business administration education. It attempts to synthesize and integrate the critical issues, processes, and techniques of the managerial function (the decision-making process) as it relates specifically to retailing.

My aims and hopes for the book remain what they were for the first edition: (1) to emphasize the *why* and not the *how to do it*; (2) to relate internal and external environmental factors into an integrated, interdependent whole; (3) to

v

present necessary descriptive information, on the assumption that before the retailing student can engage in anything approaching sophisticated analysis and decision making, he must have an adequate understanding of both the structure and the nature of the retailing enterprise; (4) to underscore the fact that retailing strategy involves the manager's attempt to build a comprehensive, dynamic plan of action in pursuit of company goals and objectives while anticipating environmental and competitive change; (5) to provide a comprehensive examination of the retailing mix, including the firm's decisions and policies relating to demand analysis, location decisions, product and inventory assortments, pricing, and promotional activities; and (6) to treat the retail manager as a decision maker, determining objectives and generating and evaluating courses of action.

The book now has two entirely new concluding chapters, discussing the dynamics of present-day retailing and its probable near-term future. Chapter 21, "The Changing Nature of Retail Merchandising," emphasizes franchising, nonstore retailing, thematic merchandising, automatic retailing, and the widespread development of boutique cluster shops. Chapter 22, "Retailing: What Lies Ahead," explores the significance of societal marketing, social responsibilities, and consumerism for the operations of the retail firm.

A textbook is the outgrowth of the labor of many people. My friends, colleagues, and students have contributed markedly. Like most professors, I am exceedingly grateful to my undergraduate students for their response to my classroom presentation. I thank the many authors who have permitted me to use their ideas and concepts. Two respected colleagues, Professor Marvin Jolson of the University of Maryland and Professor Walter Gross of the University of Georgia, read the entire manuscript. Their perceptive comments and suggestions were unusually helpful and have strengthened the resulting book. To still others I am most grateful: to my secretary, Mrs. Glenda Boone, and to my typist, Miss Linda Hastings, both of whom worked diligently in the preparation of this edition; and to my graduate assistant, Miss Debbie Ish, whose tireless efforts in our university library account for much of the basic research and updating upon which this effort is based. For all this I am most appreciative.

R. J. M.

contents

PART ONE

INTRODUCTION: RETAILING ACTION
AND TRANSACTION-ORIENTED ENTERPRISE

1 retailing perspectives: an overview   3

2 retail management strategy   24

3 financial analysis and retail
management decision making   44

PART TWO

ANALYZING AND ASSESSING
MARKET OPPORTUNITY

4 analyzing the market opportunity   73

5 major determinants of market
opportunity: population and income   94

6 understanding consumer behavior   120

PART THREE

LOCATION, SITE ANALYSIS,
AND STORE DESIGN

7 store location factors: community and
trading area analysis   143

8 store location processes   *164*

9 store design, layout, and
   space utilization   *192*

PART FOUR

THE RETAIL ORGANIZATION:
PATTERNS AND PROBLEMS

10 organizing the retailing effort   **223**

PART FIVE

MERCHANDISING: THE CRUX
OF RETAILING EFFORT

11 buyer role and behavior   **253**

12 merchandise assortment planning   **270**

13 merchandise management   **294**

14 models for merchandise management   **320**

PART SIX

PRICING POLICIES AND PROCEDURES

15 retail pricing: basic considerations   *351*

16 retail pricing: concepts, practices,
    and policies   *368*

PART SEVEN

RETAIL STORE PROMOTION

17 the role of promotion in
    retailing strategy   *393*

18 personal selling, store services, and
    credit: extensions of the retailing
    promotional effort   *420*

PART EIGHT

RETAILING AND MANAGEMENT
CONTROL PROCESSES

19 retailing management and control
procedures   449

20 retail control through additional
accounting techniques   475

PART NINE

RETAILING: INDUSTRY OF
FERMENT AND CHANGE

21 the changing nature of retail
merchandising   507

22 retailing: what lies ahead   533

INDEX   551

ONE

INTRODUCTION: RETAILING ACTION AND TRANSACTION-ORIENTED ENTERPRISE

1

retailing perspectives: an overview

The everyday lives of all of us are affected by retailing activities. The food we eat, the clothes we wear, the automobiles we drive, the services we consume—our total life styles are dramatically and positively affected by retailing and retail merchandising endeavors. It is difficult in this day and age to remove oneself from the presence of some sort of retailing activity. Naturally this is so because retailers must be located in close proximity to the customers they serve. Customers are strewn indiscriminately across the length and breadth of the land; therefore, retailers must be both widely dispersed and—in some instances—geographically concentrated in order to meet the needs of both the rural and urban customer.

Retailing is the act of selling goods or services to ultimate consumers. Thus, the *motive* of the consumer becomes the fundamental criterion for distinguishing sales at retail from other forms. Retail selling may be performed by a host of individuals, firms, or companies. Manufacturers may make sales at retail; so, too, can wholesalers or private individuals whose primary vocation is *not* retailing. Our concern, at this point, will be with sales and other activities of institutions that are primarily, as classified by the Bureau of the Census, *retail stores* or *retailing institutions.*

the transactional nature of retailing

Modern retailing is viewed as that set of human activities directed at and facilitating and consummating exchanges. Another way of putting it would be to state that retailing is an organized behavioral system of exchange. While such a statement sounds formidable, it is rather easy to explain and to comprehend. For example, just imagine trying to fill all your require-

3

ments for goods and services by buying directly from the individual producer, grower, or manufacturer. It would not be easy. At your given location, the assortments would likely be minimal, and because of the small scale that might be imposed on such direct selling businesses, prices would likely be high. The retailer facilitates your attainment of a wide variety of goods and services by collecting a diverse assortment of products that he anticipates you might need. The retailer offers you this rewarding service at a cost that is incorporated into the price of the merchandise. Hence, customers like you, and retailers, exist in a state of interstimulation and interdependence. Retailers depend on customers for sales and profits. Customers depend on retailers to supply a desired bundle of goods and services and certain psychological amenities. This is the exchange basis of retailing, and it underscores the transactional nature of retailing. Transactions are exchanges, exchanges of at least two things of value, and these are usually goods from the standpoint of the retailer and money from the standpoint of the buyer. Transactions imply a situation in which each party possesses things of value to the other (s) and a situation in which parties to the transaction are capable of communication and delivery. Transactions imply also that each party benefits from the exchange process so that the transaction has both economically and socially desirable consequences. In summary, an organized behavioral system of exchange states that people (customers) and organizations interact in such a manner as to maximize their rewards and minimize their costs. Typically, rewards are thought of as physical objects, psychological pleasure, or social gain. On the contrary, costs are thought of as noxious or stressful objects or as psychological and social punishments.

growth and development of retailing institutions

Much can be discerned about the nature of a nation's economic activity by examining the ways and means in which it trades. The sophistication evidenced by a nation in the techniques employed in marshaling and distributing resources is often a key to the overall sophistication of its political and economic system. The United States today demonstrates a unique capacity for meeting the needs of its retail consumers by possessing one of the most streamlined and efficient distribution systems in the history of all mankind. Such, however, has not always been the case.

The early forms of retailing were largely crude affairs but, generally speaking, were about as streamlined as the social, political, and economic systems could support. The earliest retail stores in the United States were the trading posts that sprang up along the trading and travel routes. Activities of these trading posts—where barter was as much the common form of exchange as money—were supplemented by Yankee peddlers who carried small packs of wares on their backs or in carts or horse-drawn wagons to the more remote sections of an exceedingly rural America.

In matters of economic development, it is generally assumed that specialization is limited by the extent of the market. For example, early rural, fractionalized, and decentralized America could support nothing more than the most rudimentary of retailing institutions. However, as cities began to replace the frontier outposts, general stores tended to replace trading posts. Necessarily and because of the economic supporting base, these stores carried broader assortments of merchandise in greater depth and varieties. Even as the economy expanded and as towns and cities became more populated, and further, as highways and other forms of transportation continued to develop and improve, thus making for more and greater mobility, retail stores became more and more complex. They increased the size and scope of their operations and began to develop along the lines required by large and diverse sections of the consuming population. The changing nature of the economy brought about such institutions as the department store, which served the needs of the urban and close-in rural consumer, and the mail-order house, which focused its services on the rural resident and which brought to him large selections of merchandise that his local area would have been unable to provide.

The impressive development of manufacturing and its ability to pour forth an unending stream of low-priced goods in turn helped to support the growth and development of such specialized retail institutions as the variety store (five-and-ten), specialty shops, supermarkets, and other modern forms of retailing institutions.

Improved methods of communication and improved managerial techniques are largely responsible for the development of the corporate chain organization—a development that tended to threaten the conventional pattern of both retailing and wholesaling activities, but which was stymied largely by the independent's capacity and flexibility for adapting to change.

The supermarket emerged in the early 1930s, largely as the result of the customer's increased mobility brought about by automobile ownership and his urgent desire to reap price advantages by performing certain of the marketing functions.

At least to date, it was one of the last great and significant retailing institutions to emerge. This institution with its emphasis on simplified selling and cash-and-carry merchandising has had a cataclysmic effect on the entire structure of retail distribution, leading to self-service merchandising strategies in many kinds of retailing institutions and to the widespread adoption of discount merchandising strategies.

The discount house is largely a post-World War II merchandising phenomenon. The many types of this institution are discussed in several places throughout this book. Basically, the *discount house* is a merchandising institution that attempts to expand sales by featuring low prices. As a matter of fact, the hallmark of discount store operations is that their prices are usually considerably lower than the prices of conventional retailers. Some would question if discount houses really represent a new way of retail merchandising or if they are simply retail institutions that adopt special merchandising tactics such as low prices and fast turnover as their modus operandi. Most authorities, however, treat discount houses as if they were a new and unique merchandising institution.

Retailing remains today an unsettled industry—an industry currently buffeted by distressed economic conditions, high unemployment, and unprecedented levels of inflation. The industry is dynamic and undergoing near-constant change; each year brings some new growth, expansion, and diversity. It is an industry of contrasts that features continued scrambled merchandising in some outlets while others strive to reduce inventories and operating costs by reducing the breadth of their merchandise lines. Energy shortages, the changing use of the automobile, the development of greater numbers of urban transit systems, the rebuilding of our central cities, and costs and profit squeezes are all manifestations and causes of the continuing turmoil in retail trade.

the structure of retail distribution

A fuller appreciation of the magnitude of retail distribution may be had by looking at some relevant statistics regarding the size and nature of retail distribution. Table 1-1 should facilitate this task. As shown in Table 1-1, over the decades covered by the *Census of Business,* sales volumes of retail stores are tied rather closely to the ebb and flow of general business conditions.

You will observe that retail sales in unadjusted actual dollars fell from 1929 to 1939. This was the period of the Great Depression, and in spite of

TABLE 1-1   Dollar Volume of Sales of Retail Establishments and Dollar Volume per Capita: United States, Census of Business for Years 1929–1972

YEAR	SALES (BILLIONS OF DOLLARS)	POPULATION (MILLIONS)	SALES PER CAPITA
1929	48,330	121.8	665
1939	42,042	130.9	664
1948	180,521	146.1	1,066
1954	169,968	161.9	1,122
1958	199,646	174.1	1,139
1963	244,202[a]	188.5	1,214
1967	310,214	199.9	1,552
1972	459,040	209.6	2,190

[a] Includes Alaska and Hawaii. These states are not included in earlier United States totals.

SOURCES: U.S. Department of Commerce, Bureau of the Census, Census of Business, U.S. Government Printing Office, Washington, D.C. Retail Trade Summary Statistics, 1948, 1954, 1958, 1963, 1967, 1972. Some retabulations have been made to make for greater comparability. The differences involve a small per cent of the total number of establishments and but a small fraction of the sales volume.

Population data are from U.S. Department of Commerce, Bureau of the Census, Population Estimates and Propensity, U.S. Government Printing Office, Washington, D.C., Series P-25.

small increases in the overall growth of the population, the severe economic and financial stresses were such as to drastically curtail most business activity. From 1939 to 1948, our economy was buoyed by the forces of economic recovery and World War II to the extent that this was a period of rapid growth and expansion of retail trade. Notice that retail sales during this nine-year period zoomed from $42 billion to $180 billion and that retail sales per capita increased from $664 to $1,066.

Retail sales have continued to parallel the growth and expansion occurring in the general economy. Sales volumes as well as sales per capita have mushroomed from 1967 to 1972. Much of this growth has occurred in terms of the real physical volume of goods. However, a large part of the growth of these figures must be attributed to inflation and increases in the general price level. Actual physical volume of goods has increased manyfold from 1929 to 1972. Much of the growth of retail sales can be attributed to increases in population, but a significant amount has resulted from actual expansion in the business economy. This expansion is reflected most significantly in the increases in levels of real per capita purchasing power.

number of establishments

From 1929 to 1939 there was a marked increase in the number of retailing establishments. In many respects this is a strange phenomenon. It is paradoxical that the number of retailing institutions would increase with a downturn in the business cycle. However, the explanation probably is that many who became unemployed from their regular occupations during a downturn invested small sums in retail ventures in the hope of maintaining some means of livelihood.

As can be seen from Table 1-2, the number of retail institutions remained relatively stable from 1939 to 1967. Yet to the extent that there were rapid and strong gains in sales volume during this same period, sales per estab-

TABLE 1-2   Number of Retail Establishments and Volume of Sales per Establishment: United States, Census of Business for Years 1929–1972

YEAR	NUMBER OF ESTABLISHMENTS	SALES VOLUME (BILLIONS)	PER ESTABLISHMENT
1929	1,476,365	$ 48,330	32,735
1939	1,770,355	42,042	23,748
1948	1,769,540	130,521	73,760
1954	1,721,650	169,968	98,724
1963	1,707,931[a]	199,646	111,638
1967	1,763,324	310,214	175,926
1972	1,912,871	459,040	239,974

[a] Includes Alaska and Hawaii. These states are not included in earlier United States totals.
SOURCES: Same source as Table 1-1.

lishment increased dramatically. During this period the size of the average retail store increased rather significantly.

From 1967 to 1972, the number of retail firms again showed a rather solid increase. In spite of the increased number of retailing institutions during this period, growth in sales volume continued apace. This means, of course, that sales per establishment continued to show marked increases. Once again, it must be pointed out that increases in overall retail sales volume as well as in retail sales per establishment reflect the general rising price level or the inflationary tendency manifest throughout this period. Nonetheless, these figures also reflect a great deal of real solid growth in the retailing sector of the overall economy. This persistent real growth, in part, has led to a marked increase in the size or scale of the individual establishments. Such a trend may reflect further the more efficient utilization of both physical and human resources in retail enterprise.

classification of retail stores

Space will not permit a complete analysis or discussion of the myriad ways in which retail stores are classified. The field of retail distribution is in many respects a hodgepodge of different kinds of establishments of different sizes, each possessing different and distinguishing characteristics. Table 1-4 may help to clarify the different classification schemes that may be employed. The listing here is by no means exhaustive.

Further, it might be pointed out that for most purposes the important criteria for classification center around (1) ownership, (2) extent and nature of lines handled, and (3) location. However, the Bureau of the Census does not gather information separately for single-line and specialty stores, but rather lumps both these institutional kinds into a category referred to as a *kind of business* grouping. Examples of this type of grouping are shown in Tables 1-3 and 1-5.

Another revealing and interesting classification of retail institutions is that of location (see Figure 1-1). Retail establishments and sales volume conform rather closely to the distribution of population and disposable income. Retail trade, although somewhat dispersed, has tended to become localized around major Standard Metropolitan Statistical Areas of the United States. The proportion of the total population residing in metropolitan areas has not increased at quite the same rate as the proportion of retail sales accounted for by those areas. Per capita retail sales have risen slightly faster in nonmetropolitan areas than in metropolitan areas, and nonmetropolitan areas have become relatively more important as retail distribution centers than would be expected on the basis of their population size.

To some extent, this condition may reflect the consumer's general dislike of the large downtown central shopping district and his preference for the generally more attractive, less congested, decentralized, planned shopping centers, many of which are located outside the boundaries of large metropolitan areas.

TABLE 1-3 Number of Retail Establishments and Per Cent of Total Retail Establishment Sales by Kind of Business, United States, 1948, 1958, 1963, 1968, and 1972

KIND OF BUSINESS	NUMBER OF ESTABLISHMENTS (THOUSANDS)					PER CENT OF TOTAL SALES[a]				
	1948	1958	1963[b]	1968[c]	1972	1948	1958	1963[b]	1968	1972
United States total	1,770	1,788	1,708	1,708	1,935	100.0	100.0	100.0	100.0	100.0
Lumber, building materials	99	108	93	93	77	8.5	7.2	6.0	5.6	5.4
General merchandise	74	87	62	62	76	13.1	10.9	12.3	16.0	14.2
Food stores	504	356	319	319	267	23.7	24.5	23.3	21.6	21.4
Automotive dealers	86	94	99	99	132	15.4	15.9	18.6	19.2	19.9
Gasoline service stations	188	206	211	211	227	5.0	7.1	7.3	7.2	7.2
Apparel, accessory stores	115	119	116	116	129	7.5	6.3	5.7	5.7	5.3
Furniture, home furnishings	92	103	94	94	117	5.6	5.0	4.5	4.9	4.8
Eating and drinking places	347	345	344	344	360	8.2	7.6	7.5	7.4	7.8
Drug, proprietary stores	56	56	55	55	52	3.1	3.4	3.5	3.4	3.3
Other retail stores	208	240	245	245	337	9.9	9.2	8.7	7.1	8.3
Nonstore retailers	n.a.	75	80	80	162	n.a.	2.7	2.5	1.9[d]	2.5

n.a. Not available.

[a] Total sales: 1948, $130,520,548,000; 1958, $199,646,463,000; 1963, $244,201,777,000; 1968, $339,710,000,000; 1972, $459,040,000,000.

[b] Includes Alaska and Hawaii. These states are not included in earlier United States totals.

[c] Same as 1963 figures.

[d] Estimated.

SOURCES: U.S. Department of Commerce, Bureau of the Census, Census of Business, U.S. Government Printing Office, Washington, DC, Retail Trade—Summary Statistics, 1948, Vol. III, p. 0.04; 1958, Vol. 1, pp. 1–7 to 1–8; 1963, Vol. 1, pp. 1–7 to 1–8; 1967, Vol. II, and the U.S. Census of Retail Trade, 1972, U.S. Summary, SC72-A-52.

TABLE 1-4 Classification of Retail Stores

I. On the basis of merchandise carried:
  1. General stores.
  2. One-line stores and specialty stores. One-line and specialty stores may derive the majority of their business from a single line of merchandise, such as groceries, shoes, filling station supplies, and so on, or from a number of lines of merchandise that are closely related.
  3. Multiple-line or convenience stores. This type is a limited edition of the old general store. It carries related merchandise but on a much wider base than the one-line or specialty store. Examples of such stores are those that carry all home-furnishing items, present-day auto accessory stores, drugstores, supermarkets, and so on.
  4. Department stores.
  5. Variety stores.
II. On the basis of functions performed or services rendered:
  1. Self-service stores.
  2. Cash-and-carry stores.
  3. Service stores.
  4. Supermarkets.
  5. Mail-order houses.
  6. Direct selling.
  7. Automatic vending.
III. On the basis of ownership:
  A. Extent of ownership.
    1. Independent retailers.
    2. Voluntary chains.
    3. Ownership groups.
    4. Chain stores.
    5. Branch stores.
  B. Character of ownership.
    1. Manufacturers' retail outlets.
    2. Leased departments.
    3. Company stores.
    4. Utility operated stores.
    5. State stores.
    6. Consumer's cooperative association.
    7. Franchising.
IV. On the basis of location:
  1. Neighborhood stores.
  2. Secondary shopping district stores.
  3. Shopping district stores.
    a. In shopping centers.
    b. In central downtown districts.
  4. Market stalls and stands.
  5. Roadside stands and markets.
  6. Mobile stores.
  7. Country stores.
  8. Pushcarts.

TABLE 1-5   United States Retail Trade: 1967 and 1972 (sales in millions of dollars)

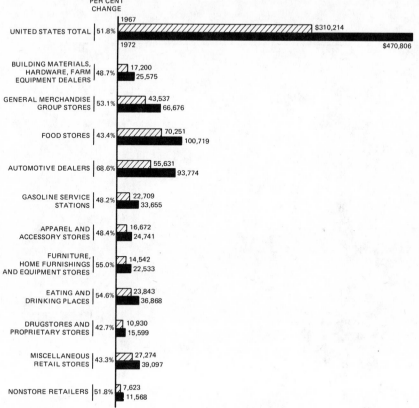

NOTE: DATA ARE BASED ON 1967 STANDARD INDUSTRIAL CLASSIFICATION.

SOURCE: U.S. Department of Commerce, Social and Economic Statistics Administration, Bureau of the Census.

a functional approach to retailing

Historically, there have been a number of approaches to the study of retailing-marketing systems. These approaches have been generally oriented around three patterns: the commodity, the institutional, and the functional. Many marketing studies focused on the marketing and economic activities involved in distributing certain commodities. As the number of these studies increased, attention began to focus on the principal institutions involved in distributing certain kinds or categories of goods. Thus, a fund of knowledge pertinent to both commodities and institutions was accumulated, and these studies led to salient generalizations that centered around the kinds of activities or functions involved in all areas of marketing-retailing activities. Although no one has come up with a list of marketing functions that is either limiting or exhaustive, the general consensus among

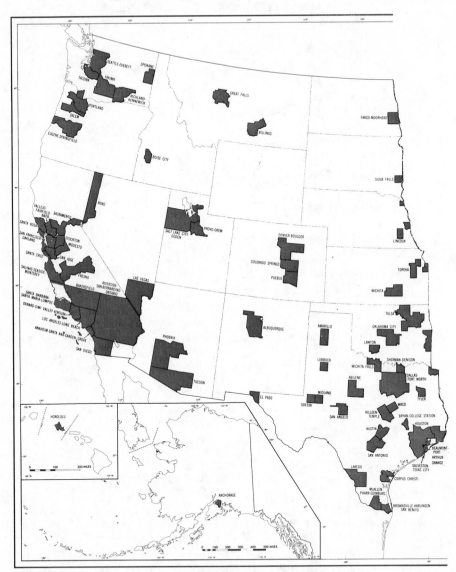

FIGURE 1-1 Standard metropolitan statistical areas of the United States. Areas defined by the Office of Management and Budget, January 1, 1974.

SOURCE: *Social and Economic Statistics Administration, Bureau of the Census.*

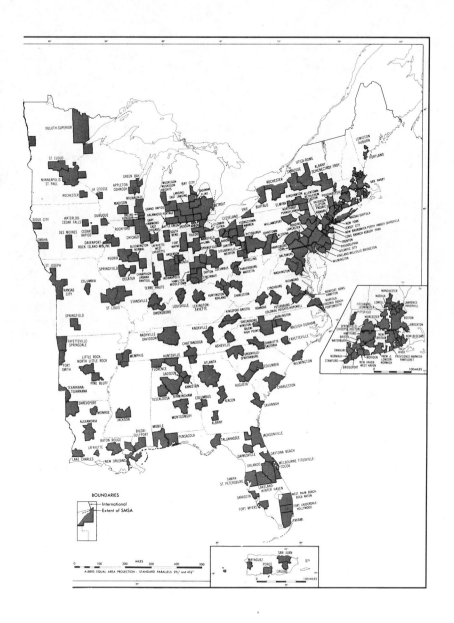

marketing authorities is that marketing functions cluster around the following kinds of activities:

1. Buying.
2. Selling.
3. Transportation.
4. Storage.
5. Risk taking.
6. Financing.
7. Market information.
8. Standardization and grading.

This really is a list of institutional functions and not necessarily a breakdown of managerial functions or activities. Our emphasis will be primarily on the latter. We are concerned with developing an understanding of managerial decision making within the retail firm. The retail manager will be viewed as a key organizational decision maker, or peak coordinator, who utilizes a management process to attain organizational and societal goals.[1] The functional emphasis of this point of view focuses on the management activities of planning, organizing, motivating, communicating, and controlling the organization's behavior.

Functionalism stresses the whole or the entire system, and it undertakes to interpret the parts thereof in terms of how they serve the system. Marketing-retailing is a very dynamic system: the foremost characteristic of the system is its tendency to change over time in order to serve the purposes for which it exists. As changes and developments occur in the external environment of retailing, then the retailing-marketing system is in turn forced to accommodate to these new environmental forces.

There are two fundamental concepts around which the functional approach to retailing is oriented. First, retailing exists within a framework of socioeconomic behavior, the principal component of which is the group. A group implies an interpersonal transaction—that is, a situation in which the action of one invokes a corresponding reaction from another, and vice versa. Therefore, a state of interdependency exists among the participants of the interpersonal transaction. This group behavior stimulates the development and operation of organized behavior systems about which we will now speak only briefly. An *organized behavior system* is a group taken in conjunction with, or related to, the environment in which it operates.

Such behavior systems emerge because of the practical exigencies of human existence and problem solving. Members of society must solve the problems that flow from, and are an attendant part of, that society. Basically conceived, the greatest problem confronting most individuals is that of fulfilling wants arising from a needs-wants hierarchy, ranging from basic physiological needs through safety, social, and esteem needs to the self-actualization needs of some individuals.[2] The important point is that needs

---

[1] See A. Papandreou, "Some Basic Problems in the Theory of the Firm," in *A Survey of Contemporary Economics*, B. F. Haley (ed.), Richard D. Irwin, Inc., Homewood, Ill., 1952, Vol. 2, pp. 183–219.

[2] These ideas are developed more fully in A. H. Maslow, *Motivation and Personality*, Harper & Row, Publishers, New York, 1954.

stem largely from an individual's existence, but the *means* for fulfilling the needs-wants hierarchy lie with collective or group action. Therefore, the tendency for individuals to act collectively and often in close harmony and cooperation leads to the formation of organized behavior systems. The marketing-retailing system is one such organized behavior system. The important point is that such systems come into existence in order to serve the wants and to facilitate the problem-solving needs of its members.

integrating retailing into the socioeconomic framework

The heritage and roots of retailing permeate many areas and stem from several disciplines; thus, retailing must be viewed as a part of a much larger whole. In the larger scheme of things, economics is typically considered the so-called mother science of business administration. And inasmuch as retailing is a part of the business administration curriculum, it too must look to economics as at least a partial source of generalization or principles.

Broadly conceived, economics historically has been the home of all inquiries concerned with the creation of utilities. *Utility* is the ability of something (usually a process of some sort) to satisfy a want or a need. Historically, economics has been concerned with the creation of several kinds of utility, namely, form, time, place, and possession utility. That is to say, economics had as its major concern the study and analysis of the processes or activities that lead to the creation of the utilities. For example, form utility principally resulted from two major kinds of economic activity: agriculture and manufacturing. In both these endeavors the task at hand is one of changing the form of goods or raw materials by processing or subjecting it to a particular production function. In agriculture, seed is purchased or obtained from previous crops; it is planted and cultivated, and—given a bountiful nature—it grows abundantly and is harvested as a marketable, valuable crop. That is, it possesses utility. In manufacturing, the process is somewhat similar. Raw materials, components, and fabricated parts are processed through a production function utilizing men, money, and materials (such as those mentioned), and the results are new cars, washing machines, and hair dryers. Both manufacturing and agricultural enterprise are called *production,* in the economic sense of the word, because their activities lead to the creation of utility. The utility that is created is *form utility,* so called because the processing has changed or altered the form of goods; which change presumably has, in turn, enhanced or added to the value or worth of the goods in question.

Changing the form of goods alone, however, is seldom enough to cause them to be demanded in great quantities or, in some instances, to be desired at all. In the economic sense, goods have value or utility only if they exist in sufficient short supply relative to the demand and, more importantly, if they are available at the right time, the right place, and if possession or ownership is transferable. These aspects or conditions are generated by distributive or marketing activities. Marketing then creates utility by facilitating the flow of goods from manufacturer-processor to resellers and to industrial and consumer buyers. Goods have a greater value to any potential user if they exist in the form he desires and are available at the time and place at which he wishes to take possession. If a seller approached you and offered a new, deluxe model color television set for $150 cash, you might be inclined to consider it a great bargain. But if you subsequently discovered that (1) the set was unassembled, consisting only of component parts; (2) the price was F.O.B. Camden, New Jersey, and you lived in Seattle, Washington; and (3) that the terms of sale called for delivery in 1985, the apparently good deal would suddenly sour because, subject to the conditions of sale, the utility or ability of the product to satisfy a want has drastically declined.

Both production and marketing, or distribution as it is sometimes called, have grown in complexity and sophistication to the point where, today, they are really no longer thought of in the strict sense as a part of economic analysis or theory. By specialization and growth each of these areas has to some extent spun away from the mother science to the point where it is considered a discipline in and of itself. However, it is important to remember that both still look to some extent to economics as a larger framework of analysis from which to draw meaningful insights regarding various facets of their operation.

The Marketing System

Retailing is a part of the marketing system, and we have just seen briefly how the marketing system is to some extent an integral part of our economic system. Marketing, as the term is currently and widely used, is concerned with the activities necessary to provide for the physical distribution of goods and to effect transfers in their ownership. To elaborate, marketing is further concerned with the processes and transactions by which the demand structure for economic goods and services is anticipated or enlarged and satisfied through the conception, promotion, exchange, and physical distribution of such goods and services.[3] In a strict academic sense, this is an appropriate statement regarding what marketing is. However, in the real expository sense, it misses much of the flavor and spirit of marketing activities. Another writer has defined marketing as "the response of businessmen to the need to adjust production capabilities to the requirements of consumers' demands."[4] In some ways this definition says less than the previous one, but in one important respect it says more. It implies and emphasizes the important key role of consumer demand and the necessity to adjust, coordinate, and accommodate the entire range of the firm's activities in both production and marketing to the needs of the market place.

Marketing might well be conceptualized as a gigantic network or pipeline

[3] Theodore N. Beckman, William R. Davidson, and W. Wayne Talarzyk, *Marketing*, 9th ed., The Ronald Press Company, New York, 1973, p. 4.

[4] E. Jerome McCarthy, *Basic Marketing: A Managerial Approach*, 5th ed., Richard D. Irwin, Inc., Homewood, Ill., 1975, p. 15.

through which the results of our productive-manufacturing enterprise flow to users and consumers. Marketing is therefore responsible for the establishment and development of this network and, furthermore, it is responsible for the undertaking of activities that will facilitate the flow of goods and services in order to meet the dictates of an ever-expanding economic system. This implies an Olympian task for our marketing system, a task that begins with the discovery of needs and wants and ends with the creation and dissemination of these want-fulfilling values or utilities.

More specifically, marketing creates values, and it implements these values through institutions, through the agencies or firms that perform marketing functions. These marketing functions are the activities endemic to the movement and distribution of goods and are the real value-producing mechanism or processes of marketing. Marketing managers are the key decision makers whose energies are devoted to the development of strategies consisting of plans and policies, the purpose of which is to assure the effective and efficient performance of marketing functions.

The Market System

The marketing system just described operates within a market system. Although this may appear a bit confusing, the marketing system is not the same thing as the market system, which may be defined as a means of allocating economic goods and services. Any number of systems might be adopted by a given economic-political unit to accomplish this end. In some countries, the allocating scheme is devised and administered by a central governmental authority or planning board. But what, specifically, is it that must be decided and administered? Every country or governmental unit must wrestle with the problem of how to resolve the following critical questions:

1. What goods will be produced?
2. Who will produce these goods?
3. How will they be produced?
4. In what quantities will they be produced?
5. How will the rewards or proceeds of production and distribution be shared among the contributors to the process?

In centrally administered countries emphasizing central planning, these questions are answered by a few authorities working through a bureaucratically structured hierarchy. Consumer choice in such societies is limited to choosing from among the products that the central planners have made available.

The market system is a means of allocating resources and answering the foregoing questions by way of the market mechanism. It is a decentralized system, instead of a centralized system. What this means, in effect, is that the decision centers are pushed out of a centrally administered bureau down to the level at which the action is occurring. The goods produced are those that entrepreneurs or marketing managers anticipate will be demanded. Who produces the goods and how they will be produced are determined to a considerable extent by existing technology and the efficiency of the various producers. Goods are produced in quantities that will clear the market and afford the seller some meaningful return on his investment.

Generally, the contributors to this process share in its rewards in direct proportion to their contribution or the degree to which they have enhanced the utility or value of the entire process. The central feature of the market system is the emphasis it places on what often is called consumer sovereignty. The consumer becomes the means of closing the loop between manufacturing and marketing. This system places the consumer in a vital decision-making role; when he enters the market place and casts his dollar votes, he decides the answers to the central economic questions. The consumer becomes the principal arbiter and decision maker in relation to the allocation problems.

Thus, marketing is focused or oriented around consumers. Why? Because marketing firms are anxious to win consumer favor, since favor means in turn more sales, and more sales are likely to mean more profits. More profits may lead in turn to greater investment, greater investment may mean more plants, more jobs, more purchasing power, and again more sales. Inasmuch as marketing creates values that are esteemed by the society of which it is a part, marketing contributes to the overall well-being of society.

The Retailing System

We have moved, you will observe, from the macroscopic to the more microscopic point of view. From the overall framework of economics, we have turned our attention to the marketing and market systems. We turn now to our primary area of concern, the retailing system.

The word *retail* comes from the French root *taillier*, which means to cut. Retail means literally to recut or to cut down, to reduce from a larger to a smaller whole. In the historical sense this was precisely the role or task of the retailer. The *wholesaler* was one who bought and sold in large or whole quantities and the retail function consisted of aggregating merchandise assortments and then cutting them down, so to speak, or making them available in smaller, more usable, quantities for ultimate consumers. To this day, this function remains the central task of retailing, i.e., aggregating assortments in anticipation of customer demand and having available this "concentrated variety" for the convenience of ultimate consumers.[5]

Retailing occupies a highly important role in the overall marketing system. Viewed in one light, retailing might be considered as the neck in the bottle of distribution. This is certainly true as far as ultimate consumers are concerned. For them, retailing ties them immediately to the distribution or marketing system. One study showed that of every dollar spent by consumers for goods and services, nearly 20 cents goes to pay for the cost of

---

[5] *Concentrated variety* is a concept of Seymour Baranoff's and can be more thoroughly explored by looking at Seymour Baranoff, "Retailing as an Operating System," in Reavis Cox, Wroe Alderson, and Stanley J. Shapiro (eds.), *Theory in Marketing*, Richard D. Irwin, Inc., Homewood, Ill., 1964, p. 161.

retailing activities.[6] This is in addition to manufacturers' marketing costs, transportation wholesale costs, and other miscellaneous marketing expenses.

Retailing facilitates the equalizing and dispersal activities required of a consumption-oriented economy. From Table 1-1, we discovered that consumers in 1972 purchased goods and services from retailing institutions in the amount of $459,040 billion through 1,912 million establishments (Table 1-2). This dollar volume amounts to billions of different items, manufactured by thousands of different producers. The presence of retail merchants and institutions in the form of specialized traders facilitates the marketing process immensely by reducing the number of transactions and, therefore, by reducing transaction time. The retail system acts as a gigantic screening, filtering, and facilitating mechanism in aggregating vast quantities of goods, anticipating consumer needs, and dispersing these goods throughout the consuming population. Retailing is a specialized kind of marketing activity concerned essentially with facilitating the matching and sorting process that emerges from consumer demand and manufacturer and wholesale supply.

The value of a retailing-marketing system is not necessarily a completely subjective intangible output, though in one sense it has a highly intangible aspect. Broadly conceived, the value of a retailing-marketing system is the degree to which it delivers the standard of living desired and supportable by a given society. If the system makes free choice readily available and effective, it is to this degree valuable. A more direct monetary measure of a marketing-retailing system is available, and is referred to as the *value added concept.*[7]

In generating data relating to government and business activity, manufacturing costs plus margins at the point of shipment are generally referred to as the *value added.* A similar measure can be undertaken for marketing or retailing activities. For example, examine carefully the following simple symbolic statement:

$$\text{Sales} - \text{Cost of Goods Sold} = \text{Gross Margin}$$
$$100\% - \qquad 76\% \qquad = \qquad 24\%$$

Assuming that for every dollar of retail sales, $.76 goes to pay for the acquisition costs of the merchandise, then $.24 remains as the gross margin. Using this figure as an average gross margin of all retail stores in 1972, the total value added by retailing activity for that year becomes

SALES	COST OF GOODS SOLD	GROSS MARGIN
(1972, Table 1-1, 100%) −	(76%)	= (24%)
$459,040	− $348,870	= $110,169

---

[6] Paul W. Stewart and J. Frederic Dewhurst, *Does Distribution Cost Too Much?* The Twentieth Century Fund, New York, 1939, pp. 117–118. For a further approach and breakdown of marketing costs, see R. S. Alexander, "The Distribution Machine and Its Costs," in C. F. Phillips (ed.), *Marketing by Manufacturers*, rev. ed., Richard D. Irwin, Inc., Homewood, Ill., 1951, p. 15.

[7] The *value added concept* for marketing has been refined considerably by T. H. Beckman. See "The Value Added Concept as Applied to Marketing," American Marketing Association, Chicago (Winter Meeting 1954).

Thus, the value added by retailing is something close to $110 billion. This figure represents or is indicative of the contribution generated by retailing and the performance of retailing functions. It is not the sole or exclusive indicator of the value of retailing activity. Real value is concerned not only with the economic but with the emotional and psychological satisfactions that are derived from a given activity.

Consumers in a competitive market-oriented system will buy goods only when the exchange value equated in dollars is equal to the pyschological and sociological expectations and utilities anticipated from the purchase.

Multiple Points of View

This leads us to the necessity of developing some relevant points of view. As it exists within the larger framework of marketing and economics, retailing must not be viewed solely within a framework of economic costs and efficiency. Consumers are not economic men any more than are retail managers and decision makers. Maximization of economic utility is not necessarily the foremost important criterion for decision making by either consumers or retail managers. Earlier, it was pointed out that retailing is an operating behavioral system. The study and analysis of an operating behavioral system requires several perspectives, only one of which is economic. However, retailing is like other areas of marketing and is most assuredly an interdisciplinary subject. Its analysis must be enriched and cross-fertilized by relevant applications of the behavioral sciences: especially psychology, sociology, anthropology, and mathematics and statistics. Therefore, as our analysis of retailing proceeds, these admonitions will of necessity underline our endeavor.

retailing: an interacting network of relationships

It is certainly no accident that our discussion has repeatedly emphasized *systems*. To repeat: The nature of the functionalist approach is to identify some *system* of action and then determine by study and analysis how and why it works as it does. Thus far, we have discussed the *economic system,* the *marketing system,* the *market system,* the *marketing-retailing system,* and the *retailing system.*

The emphasis on functionalism necessitates stressing the *whole* system and attempting to interpret the parts in terms of how they serve the system. Our discussion thus far has been an attempt to fit retailing into its larger contextual framework. From this point on, however, our attention will be more directly centered on our principal subject of inquiry and analysis—the retailing system.

Retailing organization and management are part of a man-made system that has a constant and dynamic interplay with its environment. The retail organization and its leaders must continually interact with competitors, customers, manufacturer and wholesaler suppliers, government, workers' representatives, and other agencies.

Within a systems framework the retailing process can be described both verbally and schematically. This process involves a continuous flow of consumer wants and needs into the system. The needs and wants act as signals to the retail managers throughout the hierarchy that action must occur in order to supply these needs and wants. The action consists of presenting a package of utilities (goods and services) to the customers. The firm's task is to present a bundle of desired expectations, consisting essentially of what might be called the firm's retailing mix, i.e., its total product offering—the price, promotion, and place aspects of its total offering—to consumers. This effort by the retail management system is designed to match the inputs of the system injected by consumers and the environment. The organizational output or effort is a solution to the organizational input or problem, and the result, we hope, is what one writer has called *matched parallelism*. "We hope" was used purposely. It is not likely that organizational solutions or outputs will *always* match organizational problems or inputs. The retail manager is continually faced with the challenge of bringing his firm's efforts into closer alignment with the needs of the customers within his environment. Also, the real task of the retailing manager often is that of deciding to what specific market or consumer segments he wishes to appeal. Most firms do not act in blanket fashion or attempt to appeal equally to all consumers. Instead, they attempt to match their particular bundle of unique skills and attributes with customer groups or target markets that appear in need of similar requirements. A model of the operating retailing system is shown in Figure 1-2.

The retailing management process is the accomplishment of *desired*

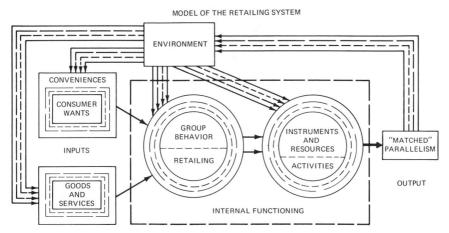

MODEL OF THE RETAILING SYSTEM

FIGURE 1-2 Visualization of the retailing system as a continuous process. The solid and dotted lines, respectively, indicate growth and expansion of the system. The lines emanating from "matched" parallelism show continuity and also that the satisfactions now become part of the environment. Note that the environment influences both the inputs and the internal functioning.

SOURCE: Seymour Baranoff, "Retailing as an Operating System," *in* Theory in Marketing, Reavis Cox, Wroe Alderson, and Stanley J. Shapiro (eds.), Richard D. Irwin, Inc., Homewood, Ill., 1964, p. 157. Reprinted with the permission of the American Marketing Association.

results through human effort and is responsible for the performance of at least three basic activities: [8]

1. *Anticipation-selection.* The retailing manager is responsible for correlating his goods selection with anticipated needs of the market place. His tools for accomplishing this correlation and coordination are market research, inventory systems and control audits, and other statistical record-keeping and planning devices. The relevant resources include finances, personnel, and education.

2. *Communication-information systems.* Communication literally means establishing a commonness between sender and receiver. The retailing manager must establish channels or routes through which information can flow from consumer-buyers to the firm and he must provide for feedback loops. Feedback is the process whereby a part of the original signal emanating from a communication system is recovered in order to correct, modify, or control the system. Both consumers and the firm operate on the basis of information established by the communication system. Effective system operation depends on proper linkage among components of the system. Communication/information is the adhesive that binds the components of the system into a cohesive whole.

3. *Convenience.* Consumer wants can be viewed within a structured framework of convenience. The merchandising function of retailing has historically conveyed the idea of the planning involved in having the right goods, at the right time, at the right price, etc. This is the true and literal meaning of the word convenience as it relates to the management of retailing systems. Consumers desire to optimize their shopping-purchase behavior by minimizing their shopping inputs, such as *time, money,* and *physical* and *psychic effort,* and by receiving a maximum output of shopping-purchase satisfactions.

The retail store has often been described as a machine for selling. Actually, it is a means of both generating and releasing a stream of customer satisfactions or convenience. It is the vehicle through which flow the processes and the outputs of the retail management system, a system that must structure a package or total bundle of customer satisfactions consisting of well-planned merchandise assortments; a range of fair and just prices, effectively promoted and communicated to relevant market targets; and goods offered in facilities and surroundings that enhance and contribute both to the customer's convenience and to the convenience and function of the total system.

QUESTIONS FOR STUDY, REFLECTION, AND REVIEW

1. What fundamental concepts are involved in the functional approach to retailing?
2. What are the main advantages of the market system that exists in the United States?

[8] Baranoff, op. cit., p. 156.

3. Describe some of the techniques utilized in appraising the value of a retailing-marketing system.
4. Define a systems approach as utilized in a retailing organization.
5. What are the benefits of utilizing the systems approach in the study of retailing?
6. Explain the meaning of a *matched parallelism* within a retail system.
7. What three basic activities are performed by the retailing management process?
8. Define and explain *utility* as used in economics.
9. What is the purpose of marketing functions or activities as related to marketing institutions?
10. What is the *functionalist point of view?*

2

retail management
strategy

The retailing management process is aimed at bringing about a total plan of action. It is not a piecemeal approach, nor is it an attempt to deal with every issue that arises on an ad hoc basis. Such approaches to operating a business firm are called many things, but they should not be called management. Instead of leaping adroitly from crisis to crisis, management connotes an attempt to lead the organization where it ought to go. In part, this is accomplished by managers who anticipate changes in their external environments and then set about to bring their units or systems into some kind of accommodation with this environment. Figure 2-1 illustrates the relationships of the firm to its environment.

The relationship between firm and environment creates the need for a retailing strategy. Basically, this need is brought about by the dynamic nature of the retailing environment, fast-paced, rapidly moving and changing. Retail institutions blossom and fade nearly every year. Our marketing system is flooded every day with thousands of new products, each competing for its niche in the overall retailing ecology. Each year, our federal and state legislatures enact thousands of new laws that affect the management and operation of the retail firm. Demand fluctuates with given changes in employment and consumer income. Surely, such a dynamic environment necessitates a constant alertness on the part of retail managers and an inclination (if not an urgency) to adjust their product and service offerings to the changing needs of the market place. A retailing strategy is a comprehensive plan of action. It involves the adjustment and accommodation of the never-changing elements of a firm's retailing mix, i.e., price, promotion, product, and place, to the ever-changing elements of a firm's environment. The retailing manager recognizes that in his strategy considerations there are certain elements over which he has little or no control. To some extent,

24

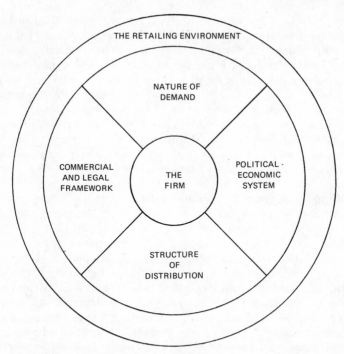

FIGURE 2-1 Schematic relationship of firm to environment.

though not always, a given firm's ability to change its environment is limited. A very large firm with vast aggregations of economic or market power may be instrumental in bringing about a change in its operating environment: A General Motors Corporation may affect the level or degree of federal safety standards for automobiles, or a Sears Roebuck, and Co. may affect provisions in federal legislation related to disclosure principles in consumer credit. However, this is not typical. The environmental factors that affect the operating and strategy considerations of a typical retail firm are considered by the retail strategist or planner as uncontrollable variables in his decision process. The decision theorist or operations researcher would label these uncontrollable variables as "states of nature" or "elements of the state of the world." The simple fact is that the uncontrollable variables exist, and the manager must contend with them in strategy formation.

Developing a retailing strategy is usually viewed as a two-part process: It consists of selecting a market target and of developing a retailing mix. Our efforts throughout later chapters will be directed toward expanding each of these aspects of retailing management strategy. However, a brief discussion of them would appear in order now.

The Market Target

Selecting the market target is a part of the major retail management task of appraising and developing the market opportunity. Generally speaking, no one store can be all things to all potential consumers. Appraising and developing market opportunity are really part of the matching and sorting process of marketing-retailing; there is hardly ever just one market opportunity for a firm, but usually several—if not thousands—of market opportunities. In light of a given firm's resources and abilities, the real question is its comparative advantage, what is the best market opportunity for which it should strive. This amounts generally to a scaling down of total market opportunity to something smaller, from the viewpoint of the individual firm, which is a market target. *A market target consists of a body of consumers or potential consumers whose perceived needs and wants appear to match a given firm's perceived ability to supply these needs and wants.*

Retailing management, therefore, determines its target market after analyzing the firm's capacities and objectives. Selecting market targets is an exercise in matching your firm's specific capabilities to a group of customers whose needs and expectations concerning goods and services square well with your abilities to supply these goods and services. Once again, this is related to what we discussed in the previous chapter under the topic of retailing as an organized behavioral system of exchange. Examples of given market targets, groups whose demand characteristics are somewhat similar, would be the "mod market," "the young sophisticates," "the teenage market," "the college market," "the young homemaker market," "the senior citizen market," and so forth. *It is important to realize that a market target represents a firm's appraisal of a market opportunity.* Another firm may not consider the same market target as a market opportunity. Why? Because its resources and abilities would not enable the firm to convert this specific market target into a market opportunity. Each individual firm is concerned with its differential advantage, the kind of advantage that gives an edge over competitors.

The search for differential advantage is really concerned with the activities involved in building strategies for differentiation of market position or opportunities. Viewed another way, it is the choice of elements that the company intends to combine in order to satisfy a target market. A firm can develop its differential advantage through the following means:

1. Market segmentation.
2. Selection of appeals.
3. Product improvement.
4. Service and process improvement.
5. Pricing.
6. Location and other spatial considerations.

Differentiation through market target selection or market segmentation has already been discussed. The essence of market segmentation is to select a customer or market target that has a relatively homogeneous set of demand characteristics. The remaining ways of achieving differential advantage fall largely under the concept of the retailing mix.

The Retailing Mix

The retailing mix is to a considerable extent the real heart of the retailing strategy. Retailing strategy has been characterized as

the utilization of analysis and foresight to increase the effectiveness of retail action . . . concerned with the objectives and goals that the retailing organization seeks to attain, the development of retailing systems, the operating system, through which retail management is attempting to achieve these goals, the availability of capacity and resources within the firm and existing facilitating agencies to exert the quality of effort necessary for their achievement.[1]

Figure 2-2 attempts to portray the various aspects of retail management strategy.

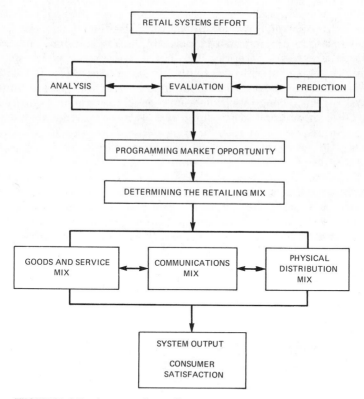

FIGURE 2-2 Aspects of retail management strategy.

SOURCE: *Adapted with slight modification from William Lazer and Eugene Kelley, "The Retailing Mix: Planning and Management," Journal of Retailing, Spring 1961, pp. 35–36.*

[1] William Lazer and Eugene Kelley, "The Retailing Mix: Planning and Management," *Journal of Retailing* (Spring 1961), pp. 35–36.

Recall that the retail system's effort is affected and conditioned by a set of external and uncontrollable variables. This necessitates, on the part of retail managers, the analysis, evaluation, and prediction of these uncontrollable states of nature in appraising and programming market opportunities. To program a market opportunity is to deliberately forecast, anticipate, and plan in terms of (1) the nature of the market opportunity, (2) its location, (3) its size, and (4) its special conditions. Once the market opportunity is decided upon in light of the firm's special resources and abilities, retail managers need to plan and develop a strategic retailing mix.

The retailing mix becomes that bundle of unique and special offerings of goods and services that the store offers to its market target (s). It is the total preconceived and programmed effort by managers to bring into adjustment the outputs of their retailing system with the demands perceived in their market opportunities.

The retailing mix is composed of a number of strategic elements. These are the firm's *prices,* its *product* or inventory assortments, its *promotional* activities, and its *place* or locational consideration. The retail system attempts to attain differential advantage by having unusually low prices or prices that represent exceptional values to customers; by having unusual or unique assortments of goods to offer for sale; by offering unusual services in connection with the sale of its products; by developing unusual or unique appeals through its promotional or selling programs; or by locating its facilities in unusual or unique places. It must be remembered that one firm's retailing mix may offer nothing unusual or unique to some market targets, and furthermore, that even a given target market is subject to change in terms of its wants and desires. This, of course, again underscores the vital necessity for firms to be constantly alert and to be ever ready to change their total retailing mix, or any part of it, to meet the demands of these changed market opportunities. Consumer satisfaction can be attained and maintained only through optimal submix blending.

Lazer and Kelley view the retailing mix in a slightly different sense than that just presented. They expand the mix from its simple components of price, product, promotion, and place to a series of what they call submixes. They list three submixes, and include the following activities in each of the various submixes:

A. Goods and service mix.
   1. Parking.
   2. Sales and service.
   3. Variety and assortment.
   4. Customer services.
   5. Credit and price lines.
   6. Guarantees and exchanges.
   7. Alterations and adjustments.
   8. Store image.
   9. Delivery.
B. Communication mix.
   1. Personal selling.
   2. Advertising.

    3. Internal displays.
    4. Public relations.
    5. Store layout.
    6. Catalogs.
    7. Telephone sales.
C. Physical distribution mix.
    1. Store location.
    2. Distribution centers.
    3. Warehousing.
    4. Transportation.
    5. Handling goods.
    6. Parking.[2]

This listing is more indicative of the wide range of activities undertaken by the retail system in developing its retailing mix, but it must be remembered that in the final analysis all these activities distill down to four principal items: price, promotion, product, and place.

recent factors affecting strategy considerations

Perhaps if some of the recent happenings and trends in retail merchandising are discussed briefly, it will serve to give the reader some flavor and understanding of the more significant meaning of retailing management strategy.

Retail management strategy can be more fully understood and appreciated when viewed within the competitive environment. As a matter of fact, it is competition that makes strategy such an important part of management. When demand exceeds available supply for a given class of commodities or services, the manager's task is simply one of rationing his goods out to whoever he feels should possess them. The principal rationing mechanism is usually price, and the retail manager has only to set a price that will clear the market of his goods. This is the typical condition in a sellers' market. In a buyers' market, the supply of goods and services exceeds the demand, and therefore, the manager is forced to compete among the existing suppliers for outlets for his product and service offerings. He competes by attempting to build a better bundle of satisfactions or utilities into his total product and service offering than his competitors. He strives for differential advantage, and he does this by shrewd, imaginative, creative development and implementation of strategy. The retailing system since just after World War II has been characterized by what might be called fiercely competitive activity. The market structure most characteristic of retailing activity is that of "monopolistic competition-large numbers." This means simply that the circumstances surrounding retail selling and the economic and market structure in which retail firms operate can be characterized by the following conditions:

[2] Ibid., p. 38.

1. There are a large number of firms.
2. Firms are all selling heterogeneous and, therefore, differentiated products.
3. Differentiation is achieved through strategic blending of submixes or product and service offerings.
4. There are many large firms and an unusually large number of smaller or marginal firms.
5. No firm is so large that it can appreciably affect the price or other aspects of total retailing strategy.
6. There is a degree of relative ease with which firms can enter or leave the market structure or the aggregate retailing system.
7. Competition is effectuated with both price and nonprice strategies.

A host of implications can be deduced from these characteristics. In the first place, it means that consumers have a wide range of choices in selecting stores and merchandise. Product (as well as store) substitution is extremely commonplace, and in order to maintain market share, firms have been faced with the perennial task of offering more and more by way of products, services, and appeals, and of waging an increasingly competitive battle via both price and nonprice competition. Also, this tendency toward continued escalation of stores' product and service offerings—or specifically their nonprice competitive activity—has put new pressures on the retail firm's cost-margin spiral. Essentially, the problem in retailing is one of productivity—or more correctly—the lack of it. Almost without exception, other industries have been reaping real economies or gains in productivity as a result of drastically altered capital/labor ratios. For example, agriculture, light and heavy industry, and to some extent in the distributive trades, wholesalers have substituted capital (machinery and improved technology) for labor in an effort to increase their productivity, i.e., their output per unit of input. Retailing has not stood still, but its attempts at increasing productivity in many instances are more feigned than real. Simplified selling—embracing self-service and self-selection—has resulted in considerable savings, but by and large, these have been strategies of larger stores.

Another factor has placed an increasing burden on retail managers in their efforts to maintain market share and thus spread their fixed costs over a larger sales volume, namely, the change in the consumer's propensity to consume. In times of economic uncertainty, characterized by the mid-seventies, which witnessed high unemployment, an above-normal inflation rate, and shrinking incomes, consumer expectations flatten and the demand for goods and services purchased through retail institutions declines. During such periods consumers spend somewhat less, and hence they save somewhat more. The difference between normal rates of expenditures of disposable personal income during more prosperous periods and the expenditure rates during recessionary periods often amounts to several billion dollars.

A continuing trend manifesting itself in retail merchandising is the growth or near explosion in expenditures for services. In 1967, consumers spent $107.2 billion for services. By 1973, this figure had increased to $310.9 billion, an increase of nearly 200 per cent.[3]

As the demand for goods decreases and the demand for services increases, the result must be a rethinking and reshuffling of the firm's total retailing strategy. Some firms (notably Sears) have reacted to these changes by rethinking, expanding, and altering their product and service mix to include insurance, service stations, auto repair centers, personal loans, and mutual funds.

Increased customer mobility, changes in the concentration and aggregation of retail firms into larger firms of greater economic and market power, and shopping center developments have all tended to bring about changes in retail management strategy.

A large portion of the activity involved with retail management strategy, such as changing the spatial location of retail clusters to controlled shopping centers, scrambled merchandising, and the striving for increased productivity through simplified selling and self-service, can be traced to the consumers' desire or even urgent need for one-stop shopping. This, in turn, has no doubt resulted in the following sequences of activities.

First, product lines have proliferated and in many instances the categories of merchandise carried have expanded, i.e., there are more shelf facings of specific categories of merchandise. Second, there has been the necessity for larger-sized units to house the greater merchandise assortments. Third, and very importantly, the tendency to larger establishments has resulted in what might be termed a new optimum-sized firm. Firms failing to attain this new optimum have simply found the sledding tougher, and to survive they have had to be increasingly alert and creative in their approach to retailing strategy considerations.

The nature of retailing competition, the ceaseless striving of consumers for something new or something better, the never-ending attempts of retail managers to attain a better differentiated advantage create a built-in dynamism or near disequilibrium, which constantly agitates for change in retailing management strategies.

Professor Malcolm P. McNair introduced the *wheel of retailing* concept to help explain the dynamics of institutional change within an overall or aggregate retailing system.[4] In this hypothesis, the wheel is always revolving and moving forward. The cycle begins because of a new innovation. These "innovators" enter the market as low-status, low-margin, low-price operators "in bad odor, ridiculed, scorned, condemned as 'illegitimate'." Gradually, they acquire more elaborate establishments and facilities with both increased investments and higher operating costs, and a top-heavy vulnerability. Finally, the cycle is completed when the new institutions mature as

[3] *Survey of Current Business,* United States Department of Commerce, U.S. Government Printing Office, Washington, D.C., Vol. 48, No. 2 (February 1968), pp. S-1, S-2; and Vol. 54, No. 12 (December 1974), p. 12.

[4] Malcolm P. McNair, "Significant Trends and Developments in the Postwar Period," in A. B. Smith (ed.), *Competitive Distribution in a Free High Level Economy and Its Implications for the University,* University of Pittsburgh Press, Pittsburgh, Pa., 1957, p. 17.

high-cost, high-price merchants, vulnerable to the newer types, who in turn go through the same pattern: "the next revolution of the wheel, to the next fellow who has a bright idea and starts his business on a low cost basis, slipping in under the umbrella that the old line institutions have hoisted."

This concept strongly implies that retail managers must be ever alert to avoid their own extinction mode: from lapsing into a mood of complacency and satisfaction; to guard against the tendency toward top-heaviness and vulnerability; to maintain a posture and to develop a frame of mind and retail management strategy that will assure flexibility, and competitive viability, which is most important. It must be emphasized that the real objective of business is survival. A firm that does not survive can have no expectations regarding other rewards such as profit.

The retail management system depends for survival upon its retailing management strategy—its comprehensive plan of action, its composite of activities related to store conduct in the market it proposes to serve. The retailing management strategy in today's competitive market system ought to be characterized by the following features:

Planning An emphasis on planning to achieve clearly defined retailing targets. Planning stresses that retailing objectives can be identified and that an integrated program of action be designed to achieve these objectives through orderly retail planning.

Customer Orientation The customer orientation is adopted as the focus for retail decision making. A philosophy of customer orientation is more important than any body of retailing techniques, personnel policies, or organizational arrangements. It insures that retail decisions are viewed through the consumer's eyes.

Systems Approach . . . In this approach, a retail organization is viewed as a total system of retail action. The interaction between the components of the retailing system is stressed, as is the functioning and structure of the whole organization. This approach focuses on the integrated use of all retail resources to satisfy current market needs and future opportunities.

Change Change is recognized as the "constant" in planning, organizing, motivating, communicating, and controlling retailing activity. The prime managerial responsibility is seen as that of adapting retailing organizations creatively to conditions of accelerating change. Retailing leadership's charge becomes that of planning for and managing change.

Innovation There is a new emphasis on research and innovation. Innovation is seen as the basis for retailing action. The important fact is that innovation is becoming programmed as a basic part of the retail management process. In short, research, a system of commercial intelligence, and innovation are becoming standard factors in modern retail action. This is resulting in the application of findings from the behavioral and quantitative sciences to retailing. The effect is new techniques of retail control, better management of inventories, improved communications, and a greater awareness of the usefulness of theory in understanding and solving retailing problems.[5]

[5] Lazer and Kelley, op. cit.

Our discussion of retailing management strategy and systems will proceed based upon these guidelines.

the basis for strategy decisions

One of the more difficult questions confronting the retail management decision maker is, "How should one evaluate his decision-making system or, for that matter, the organizational decision-making system?" It is not easy to answer this question. Therefore, in order for us to evaluate the output of our organizational decision-making system, we must know or posit what our organizational system is striving to attain. What are its goals and objectives? What are the so-called desired results? Up until quite recently, the conventional wisdom of business administration held that the major goal of business is to maximize profit. However, more recently, authorities in the area of business administration have begun to realize that the organizational system is like the individual person and has a hierarchy of needs or wants; this hierarchy calls forth a range of goals or objectives for which the organization strives. One research study generalized that organization goals and objectives, as manifested by the aims of management, consisted of the following:[6]

1. To make money or profits.
2. To pay dividends to stockholders.
3. To grow.
4. To meet or stay ahead of competitors.
5. To operate or develop the organization.
6. To provide good products: public service.
7. To contribute to the community: community relations.
8. To provide for the welfare of employees: a good living, security, happiness, good working conditions.
9. Miscellaneous.

This listing is as representative as any concerning the goals and objectives of the retail management system. From it we might conclude at least the following conditions:

1. There are multiple goals of a retail management system.
2. Since there are multiple goals, confusion is likely to develop in regard to the establishment of priorities among these goals and objectives, and confusion is likely to surround the criterion of choice when, given limited resources or numerous alternatives, there is conflict among a number of goals.

For example, the latter condition might be illustrated by a situation in which management wished (1) to make money or profits and (2) to con-

---

[6] James K. Dent, "Organizational Correlates of the Goals of Business Management," *Personnel Psychology*, Vol. XII, No. 3 (1959), pp. 365–393.

tribute to the welfare of employees—provide them with a good living, security, happiness, and good working conditions.

To minimize the conflict that is likely to result from situations such as this, the conventional decision rule regarding organization goals has been that the organization *should* or *ought to* strive to maximize its profits and it ought to undertake courses of action or make those decisions with respect to the alternatives that contribute the most to this singular organizational goal.

On the other hand, there is some evidence to suggest that profit maximization as the foremost organizational goal and criterion of decision making has some serious shortcomings. Simon states:

> In most psychological theories the motive to act stems from *drives,* and the action terminates when the drive is satisfied. Moreover the conditions for satisfying a drive are not necessarily fixed, but may be specified by an aspiration level that adjusts upward or downward on the basis of experience.
>
> If we seek to explain business behavior in the terms of this theory, we must expect the firm's goals to be not maximizing profit, but attaining a certain level or rate of profit, holding a certain share of the market or a certain level of sales. Firms would try to "satisfice" rather than to maximize.[7]

Throughout our treatment of retail management decision making we shall consider a satisfactory level of profit as the major objective of the retail management system and satisfactory profit or contribution to profit as the major criterion for choosing from among alternative courses of action.

profit as a criterion for decision making

Although profit or profit contribution is the ideal standard for choosing among alternative courses of retail management system action, this standard is difficult to apply in a realistic business setting. The reasons for this are allied to (1) the problem of defining profit—or what to include as current cost, (2) the problem of determining those costs that are affected by the decision, and (3) the problem of costs and revenues as related to time.

Profit from the economic point of view is not necessarily the same as profit in the accounting sense. Accounting costs are always historic or past costs, whereas economic costs are always future costs. If one assumes that the future is going to be much like the past, then some accounting costs may be used as valuable tools for decision making.

What Is Profit?

For the time being, let us ignore the theoretical problem of differentiating between economic costs and accounting costs to find profit and consider

---

[7] Herbert A. Simon, "Theories of Decision Making in Economics and Behavioral Science," *The American Economic Review* (June 1959), pp. 262–263.

that there is the basic problem of how one can evaluate a particular profit figure.

Profit is a word of many meanings. From the businessman's point of view, profit is viewed as a residual:

$$\text{Sales Revenue} - \text{Total Expenses} = \text{Profit}$$

For decision-making purposes in many instances, profit might be viewed as

$$\text{Sales Revenue} - \text{Direct Expenses} = \text{Contribution to Profit and Overhead}$$

Concepts of Profit

There are several concepts of profit used by the retail manager for decision-making purposes. Considerable ambiguity surrounds two of these concepts, but a few examples will make this point somewhat clearer.

Store A makes profits equal to 35 per cent of their sales. Store B makes profits of less than 10 per cent of their sales. Which firm is more profitable? Of course, the solution is indeterminate. Store A may be a small specialty shop (selling women's hats) whose annual sales volume is less than $10,000 per year. Store B may be the Safeway Stores Corporation with sales of nearly a billion dollars, or more. Profit stated *as a percentage of sales* is not the ideal standard for decision making. However, retail stores have historically relied on this measure of profit as a basic guideline for testing store operations. Profit as a per cent of sales used as a comparison figure for stores of similar size selling similar lines is only the crudest measure of the efficacy of a given store's operation.

Also profit *in absolute dollars* leaves a great deal to be desired as a measure of the firm's productivity, or as a measure of its profitability. An illustration may help to demonstrate this idea.

Store C earned a $200,000 profit last year. Store D made a $20,000 profit in the same year. Quite obviously Store C had more dollars left after deducting expenses than did Store D, but does that tell management or the stockholder anything about the success of the firms relative to each other? Obviously not. A $200,000 profit picture would not be the cause of elation at a board meeting of Allied Department Stores, but a $20,000 profit may provoke the owners of a small hardware store in Pullman, Washington, to proffer large Christmas bonuses to their two employees.

Thus, *profits as a percentage of sales and profits in absolute dollars are not very good measures of profitability.* Any given profit figure must be linked to some base in order to provide a meaningful concept of profitability, that is, a concept useful as a criterion for decision making. The difficulty with profit as a per cent of sales and profit in absolute dollars is that they are definitions of the counting house and they say little or nothing about relative profitability. A part of the confusion arises because there are several elements that interact to generate profits and most often, only one element receives consideration. The three main elements that contribute to profits are

1. Unit profit: the dollar-and-cents profit earned per item.
2. Volume of sales: the actual number of units sold.
3. Time: the actual period during which units are sold at the given price.

Thus, symbolically,

$$\pi = P \times Q \times T$$

where π = profits, P = unit profit, Q = sales volume in units, and T = time.

For example, a store or department has priced an item at $2.00 and sells 100 units of this item in a one-month period. After subtracting its expenses, which average $1.00 a unit, its profit equals

$$\$1.00 \times 100 \times 1, \text{ or } \$100$$

However, profit in the retail management sense is more than a dollar figure. It is the goal or objective of the enterprise sought at risk. This leads us to a most important concept of profit and one which we shall utilize extensively throughout our treatment—*profit as a return on investment.* Profit as a return on investment is expressed or related in terms of risk and uncertainty and this measure of profitability is expressed as

$$\frac{P \times Q \times T}{C}$$

where C = capital invested.

Profit, then, is the return on capital invested under conditions of risk and uncertainty; and profit as a return on capital investment is an effective index of how well the firm is utilizing its assets in relation to its market opportunity. This view of profit is in keeping with our economic philosophy, which holds that profits are the necessary payments to the entrepreneur in return for the services he performs in coordinating and controlling productive factors, and for engaging in uncertain but needed business enterprise. Profits are the rewards for successful entrepreneurship.

The various concepts of profit can be summarized more definitely and their implications more clearly understood by careful examination of Table 2-1.

TABLE 2-1 Profit and Loss Comparisons for Varying Sales and Net Profit Levels (in dollars and percentages)

	FIRM A		FIRM B		FIRM C		FIRM D	
	($)	(%)	($)	(%)	($)	(%)	($)	(%)
Sales volume	1,000,000	100	1,500,000	100	2,000,000	100	2,500,000	100
Total costs	700,000	70	1,125,000	75	1,600,000	80	2,125,000	85
Net profit	300,000	30	375,000	25	400,000	20	375,000	15

SOURCE: Thomas James Morelson, "How You Can Market for Profits," Printers' Ink, October 25, 1963.

TABLE 2-2 Concepts of Profitability, Opportunity Earnings, and Risk Return to Capital

	FIRM A	FIRM B	FIRM C	FIRM D
Capital invested	$100,000	$500,000	$1,000,000	$2,000,000
Opportunity earnings @ 6%	6,000	30,000	60,000	120,000
Risk return to capital = net profit — opportunity earnings	294,000	345,000	340,000	255,000

SOURCE: Thomas James Morelson, "How You Can Market for Profits," Printers' Ink, October 25, 1963.

Observe the following conditions:

1. The highest level of sales occurs in Firm D.
2. The highest net profit in absolute dollars occurs in Firm C.
3. The highest percentage of net profit to sales occurs in Firm A.

Let us look further in our analysis by introducing a few additional concepts. These can be found in Table 2-2.

Table 2-2 shows the dollar investment in each of the four firms whose sales volume, costs, and profits were shown in Table 2-1. It also shows *opportunity earnings* at 6 per cent. This term may require a comment or two of explanation. Opportunity earnings is an extension of the opportunity cost from economics. Whenever resources are scarce (like money), one of the costs of choosing a particular alternative is the cost of having to give up the profits from the alternatives you would, or could, otherwise have pursued. For example, the investments in the four firms, respectively, are $100,-000; $500,000; $1,000,000; and $2,000,000. Such resources have a basic earning capacity, or opportunity cost. For example, if the owner of Firm A placed his money ($100,000) in the local commercial bank, on the basis of the prevailing interest rate of 6 per cent, he would earn $6,000. Thus, in calculating his risk return to capital (Net Profit — Opportunity Earnings), he considers that his $100,000 should have earned him $6,000 at virtually no risk whatsoever: the $6,000 is the return to him for the use of his money or capital. His risk return to capital in a merchandising venture is $294,000, or the $300,000 profit as shown in Table 2-1, minus the $6,000 opportunity earnings shown in Table 2-2.

From Table 2-2, it can now be observed that the greatest profitability (earnings/capital investment) occurred in Firm A. This can be seen readily by examining the profit as a return on investment for each firm.

<table>
<tr><td align="center">Firm A</td><td align="center">Firm B</td></tr>
<tr><td>$\dfrac{\$294,000 \text{ earnings}}{\$100,000 \text{ investment}} = 294\%$</td><td>$\dfrac{\$345,000 \text{ earnings}}{\$500,000 \text{ investment}} = 69\%$</td></tr>
<tr><td align="center">Firm C</td><td align="center">Firm D</td></tr>
<tr><td>$\dfrac{\$340,000 \text{ earnings}}{\$1,000,000 \text{ investment}} = 34\%$</td><td>$\dfrac{\$255,000 \text{ earnings}}{\$2,000,000 \text{ investment}} = 13\%$</td></tr>
</table>

Profit as a return on investment is a nearly ideal criterion for decision making within the retail management system. However, in some instances the actual dollars of investment required to generate a stream of dollar revenues may not actually be known or readily available. What is important for decision-making purposes is some meaningful and unambiguous concept of profit. In the words of Howard:

> A clear-cut concept of profit is essential both in planning market research to obtain the information necessary for a decision and in making a decision. In so far as possible, the economists' definition of profit should be used, which for decision making purposes is contribution to profit. An estimate of the profit contribution is arrived at only by deducting only those costs affected by the decision. Profits have important time implications: (1) long term rather than short term profits are relevant; (2) current decisions determine, in part, the conditions under which future decisions will be made; (3) uncertainty is involved, since marketing decisions require a prediction of the future.[8]

Profit as a criterion for decision making has many important managerial implications. It partly assures the firm of having an objective criterion for decisions. It helps to minimize guesswork and it makes for greater efficiency. The profit criterion causes greater attention to be given to projects that actually tend to raise the profitability of the firm. When individuals and subordinates throughout the organization rely on the profit criterion for decision-making purposes, they have a tangible goal or target for which they should strive. Finally, profit as a return on investment criterion offers a much needed stimulus and reward for imagination and creative innovation within the entire retail management system.

the marketing concept and retailing

Retailing's origins in the marketing system were discussed at length in Chapter 1. It should be pointed out again that theoretical developments in marketing, generally, will almost always have ramifications for the retailing area.

Broadly conceived, the marketing concept is a management philosophy. It has been described as a "corporate state of mind" in which management requires that all marketing functions be integrated and that company policies be built on the basis that customer needs and wants are the starting point for all efforts.[9] A philosophy is an organized system of thought. More simply stated, philosophy is the way a man or a firm views tasks and responsibilities. The marketing concept was a way of rethinking the company's problems, which in turn resulted in a more unified and cohesive way of thinking about the company's tasks, its resources, and its objectives. The

---

[8] John A. Howard, *Marketing Management: Analysis and Planning*, rev. ed., Richard D. Irwin, Inc., Homewood, Ill., 1963, p. 23.

[9] Arthur Felton, "The Marketing Concept in Action," *Business Horizons*, Vol. IV (February 1961), pp. 14–21.

marketing concept emphasizes that the firm is inextricably linked to the market place. As one pair of authors put it, the firm takes its marching orders from the market.[10] And who is the market? In the case of the retail firm the market is the potential total of users for the firm's output of goods and services.

The firm and its management are charged with a specific set of responsibilities. "Business is a process which converts a resource, distinct knowledge, into a contribution of economic value in the marketplace. The [new] purpose of business is to create a customer."[11] Consequently, the focus and orientation of the firm becomes that of marketing.

The market concept (or marketing philosophy as it is oftentimes called) views the firm as innovative as well as adaptive. If the company designs a program or strategy to fit the forecasted conditions of its environment, its behavior will be characterized as adaptive. The future welfare of such companies is mainly a function of the predicted environment. However, a strategy or program of aggressive action in pursuit of predetermined goals and objectives is characterized as innovative, and the firm is viewed as shaping the environment instead of having its success or failure solely determined by environmental forces.

During the early 1950s, the United States economy began to witness a profound and fundamental change. Suddenly business firms began to realize that we were moving into an era of widespread affluence. Consumers, too, began to realize "no matter how little money [they] might have, that they are 'millionaires' compared to most people in the world."[12]

Given this new consumer affluence, which meant in turn new discernment, new and greater discretion and freedom of choice, marketing's task suddenly was focused on the need to produce markets, not necessarily on the production of goods. Firms whose previous orientation had been production or selling began—some suddenly, some unfortunately, not too suddenly—to realize that to survive in this new competitive environment they must drastically alter their business or management philosophy and pay more than lip service to the standard bywords of "competition" and "consumer sovereignty."

applying the marketing concept to retailing

Admittedly, retailing firms differ significantly in their orientation and operation from production-oriented firms or from manufacturers' field selling organizations. Certain phases or aspects of retailing and some retail managers have characteristically been more consumer-oriented than perhaps

---

[10] Wroe Alderson and Paul Green, *Planning and Problem Solving in Marketing*, Richard D. Irwin, Inc., Homewood, Ill., 1964, p. 5.

[11] Peter F. Drucker, *Managing for Result*, Harper & Row, Publishers, New York, 1964, p. 91.

[12] Steuart Henderson Britt, *The Spenders: Where and Why Your Money Goes*, McGraw-Hill Book Company, New York, 1960, p. 49.

other kinds of marketing firms. The maxim "the customer is always right" has been for many years a standard byword of retail sales management in training retail sales employees, although often it has been meaningless in its implications. These conditions hardly qualify retailers as strong advocates of the marketing concept, or as having been guided in their retail management strategies by the ideas that underlie the marketing concept.

The important point is that retail organizations are organs of society, and the basic reasons for their existence lie outside their own organizations.

One writer has observed that retail firms "exist to serve customers and therefore *must fully understand movements in customer wants.*" He writes further:

> Since there is this common element between retailing and manufacturing organizations, it can be concluded that retailers can focus on operating problems instead of on customer needs. . . . the former situation is the prevailing practice for the majority of retail organizations. In other words, retailers are defining their businesses too narrowly by stating that they are in the "retail business" when they should consider themselves to be in the business of "marketing goods and services to ultimate consumers."[13]

This condition, frame of mind, or philosophy can be demonstrated in a number of ways. The discount houses that emerged in the early 1950s began to siphon off large amounts of sales volume from department stores and such specialty outlets as furniture and appliance stores. To a considerable extent, many of the managers of these more conventional outlets simply ignored these new streamlined lower cost outlets, reasoning that they would not last and that they were not a viable form of retail distribution. It was some time before these managers became convinced that consumers were responding quite favorably to the newer institutions and that the conventional outlets were losing millions of dollars in sales volume and profit by not being more consumer-oriented and building their retailing programs or strategies around these changes in consumer wants.

By and large, some retailers constantly appear to lag behind consumer movements in developing and adjusting their retailing strategies. E. B. Weiss, a none-too-friendly critic of retailing, reported that throughout the late 1950s and early 1960s, chain stores had to be forced into major changes wanted by customers—more night hours, credit operations, catalog selling, and more in-the-home sales parties and demonstrations. Weiss argued that instead of taking their marching orders from consumer demands and movements, retailers spent too much energy imitating one another.[14]

He further alleged that had retail organizations been more attuned to customer movements and demand they would be in a better competitive and operational posture instead of in conditions that he summarizes as follows:

[13] Eugene H. Fram, "Application of the Marketing Concept to Retailing," *Journal of Retailing* (Summer 1965), p. 21.

[14] E. B. Weiss, *A Reappraisal of New Retail Trends*, Doyle, Dane, Bernbach, New York. 1964, pp. 9–10.

1. The traditional department store. Generally speaking, these institutions have been totally unable to reverse their ten-year downtrend in capital return percentage and net profit percentage.
2. The medium and larger sized food chains. This group—on balance—has shown a declining trend in these two critical measures for the better part of ten years.
3. The drug chains. Again, generally speaking, this group has fared even worse by these two critical yardsticks of business performance than the food chains.
4. As for the variety chains—their ten-year record by these two measurements, is even more dismal than that of either the food chains or the drug chains. Among the major variety chains, there is no exception to this consistent downtrend in net profit and capital return ratio.[15]

This is some evidence to support the contention that retail managers have not always looked to the market for guidance and direction in establishing their retailing programs and strategies. The marketing concept (especially the consumer orientation emphasis upon which the concept rests) underscores the importance of thinking in terms of the retailing management system. The breadth of our interest and inquiry does not encompass the retail firm alone, but instead the firm must be viewed in terms of its linkages, the components or sub-systems that comprise *the total system.*

Fram argues that the behavior of one of the principal retail managers or decision makers that affects the activity and operation of the retail unit within its system environment—the Buyer—testifies to the fact that retail firms are not overly addicted to the idea of customer orientation.[16]

1. The Buyer seeks products.
2. The Buyer relies on his records.
3. The Buyer uses buying office reports and talks with other buyers.

In addition to these things, he also states that the Buyer watches customers, but that the customers he watches are those already in the store. This kind of observation quite obviously is not enough because potential customers may be elsewhere, or regular customers may be shopping elsewhere because they are dissatisfied with the merchandise assortment or some other aspect of the merchandising or retail program or strategy.

It is not necessarily true that all Buyers or retail decision makers are so shortsighted that they overlook important movements in customer attitudes, habits, or trends. However, one research study concluded that 50 per cent of those who enter a given store with buying intentions never make a purchase and that walkouts occur because these potential buyers are dissatisfied with the store's merchandise, its salespeople, its prices, the store's layout and arrangement, or some other aspect of its total merchandise and service offering.[17]

To meet this challenge, retail managers are admonished to undertake a more concerted effort to learn more about the nature of their operating

[15] Ibid., p. 6.
[16] Fram, op. cit., pp. 22–23.
[17] "Retail Research Institute," *Stores,* Vol. XLVI (February 1964), pp. 15–18.

environment, their market opportunities, and to study and evaluate their own particular and unique comparative advantages. Specifically, to accomplish this, retail managers are encouraged to develop a new focus, orientation, or philosophy regarding their task, namely, to become more concerned about developing the marketing management point of view. A British economist once commented that in economics the gap between the toolmaker and the tool user is distressingly large.[18] Based upon this observation, a United States student of retailing management observed that retailing seems to be at the opposite extreme of such a trying situation. "Toolmakers are so few in retailing that their number is inadequate, relatively speaking, to create a gap."[19] Although it is a moot point as to how many "toolmakers" retailing might have, there is no debating the idea that the area has tools. And with these tools it should be possible for retailing systems to do a better job of matching inputs and outputs in a more efficient and effective manner, both from its own and society's point of view.

It has been suggested that in order for retailers to become more market-oriented and to build the marketing philosophy into their own retail management systems they[20]

1. Engage in more research.
2. Be more alert to changes in customer wants.
3. Consider market integration.
4. Alter the orientation of sales-supporting personnel.
5. Alter organization structure.
6. Engage in more long-term planning.
7. Charge top management with the responsibility of creating the proper atmosphere or state of mind.

What all this means is that retail managers must think in terms of a retailing management strategy—a comprehensive plan of action, the movement and counter movement in pursuit of system goals and objectives.

The retail management system is concerned with generating and delivering a stream of satisfactions or outputs that are desired by a certain societal or market segment. The incentive to the management system for producing this stream of satisfactions is the expectation of reward, profits, or other satisfactions. How retail managers perceive their market opportunities and respond to the societal demands will be determined largely by their management philosophies. Thus, management philosophies largely determine their behavior and reactions to market opportunities. Management is the art and science of accomplishing desired results through human effort, the major processes of which are planning, organizing, motivating, communicating, and controlling. Every manager of a retail system will desire to meet his market opportunity with a unique program or strategy.

---

[18] Joan Robinson, *The Economics of Imperfect Competition*, Macmillan & Company, Ltd., London, 1948, p. 1.

[19] John V. Petrof, "The Need for More Abstract Thinking in Retailing," *Journal of Retailing* (Summer 1965), p. 18.

[20] Fram, op. cit., pp. 24–26.

QUESTIONS FOR STUDY, REFLECTION, AND REVIEW

1. Discuss the meaning of the term *retail management strategy*.
2. Define the marketing concept and explain how it relates to retailing.
3. What are the main reasons that 50 per cent of the potential customers who enter a given store never make a purchase?
4. What can modern retailers do to become more consumer- and market-oriented?
5. Why is it important for a retailer to select a market target?
6. Define a market target.
7. What is the nature of the retailing mix?
8. The retail firm operates within a market structure of monopolistic competition. What are the conditions of this form of competition?
9. What is one of the main problems that has affected the retail firm's cost/margin ratio?

3

financial analysis and
retail management
decision making

The major criterion for retail management decision making is profit, but as has been suggested, there are several measures of profit. Some relevant questions thus arise. Which measure of profit do we wish to use? What do the various measures of profit tell us about the operating efficiency of the retail firm? Of what value for decision-making purposes is the profit margin? The retail manager is a highly eclectic creature, that is, from his environment he selects and chooses a range of ideas and concepts that he considers useful or practical for decision making. Thus, whatever measure of profits (under given conditions) appears useful to the retail manager is the measure he is likely to adopt. Profit as a criterion for decision making is both a planning and a control device. For either use there is the implication that profit standards or goals have been established, and inasmuch as they have, the problem is one of relating some past period or planned objective of performance profitwise to the existing standard.

Where profit standards exist or are available from trade association or other industry sources, the problem is not difficult. In the absence of standards, the decision maker is forced to create his own. One suggestion has been that

if we want to evaluate managerial performance, we might choose to do so by seeing how well management has used the assets at its disposal. In this situation, profit as a percent of investment would be the relevant form. If on the other hand, we wanted to determine whether our costs of doing business were in line with other firms similarly situated, we would probably use profits as a percentage of sales. In other cases absolute profits are a useful check against the distortions of percentage comparisons, since they give perspective to the magnitude involved.[1]

From this statement, one might conclude that the relevant question is not, "Which measure of profit shall I use?" but, "For what purpose do I intend to use profit as a criterion for decision making?" Once the latter question is answered, the former question becomes both more meaningful and less difficult.

The decision-making emphasis placed upon modern retailing operations naturally forces some focus on accounting and the financial implications of management. The retail system's profit or loss is determined by the relationship between total revenue and total cost. Therefore, the managerial decisions that concern us are those affecting revenue and costs. Interestingly enough, nearly all decisions within the system affect these two important variables and, therefore, there exists a high degree of interdependence among financial, merchandising, and organizational or personnel decisions. The principal task of the retail manager is to manage a profitable operation. He is entrusted with a set of assets, and he is expected not only to preserve those assets, but to increase their value as a result of all of his managerial decisions. Unless the manager accomplishes this, his operation will not be profitable and it will not survive.

We have all heard the adage, "It takes money to make money." It might better be stated, "It takes a knowledge of how to manage money in order to make money." Throughout the remaining pages of this chapter our task is to learn something of the financial implications of retail management. In short, we wish to acquire some knowledge of the finance function of business that entails "the task of providing the funds needed by the enterprise on terms that are most acceptable in light of the objectives of the business and with the effective utilization of funds in the business."[2]

Our treatment will necessarily focus more on the latter. One important point should be emphasized. Merchandising and financial results are inextricably bound together. Inventory decisions will necessarily affect working capital conditions, and vice versa. An increased effort directed toward credit selling will likewise affect working capital and cash flows. On the other hand, unless an adequate line of credit is obtained or existing funds are sufficient, the ability to buy and bargain judiciously in the market place will be hampered. Let us examine some financial planning concepts and techniques that will show more explicitly some of these many relationships.

the dupont schematic

The Dupont Schematic is a diagrammatic way of presenting the many variables of a firm's operation that contribute to and affect its return on

[1] Schuyler F. Otteson, William G. Panschar, and James M. Patterson, *Marketing: The Firm's Viewpoint,* Macmillan Publishing Co., Inc., New York, 1964, p. 37.

[2] Pearson Hunt, Charles M. Williams, and Gordon Donaldson, *Basic Business Finance,* Richard D. Irwin, Inc., Homewood, Ill., 1961, pp. 3–4.

investment.[3] Assuming that the retail firm is interested in maximizing profit or in receiving only a satisfactory target rate of return on its investment over time, then management must take cognizance of two distinct concepts. First, management must find some way of evaluating the worth of its present stock of assets, and secondly, management must find some way of measuring the flow of income and costs in order to determine the difference, which in the accounting sense is profit or loss.

The balance sheet is an accounting statement that presents a photograph (a static picture at a given instant of time) of a firm's stocks—assets, liabilities, and net worth. The profit and loss statement is the accounting record of the flow (a dynamic moving picture) of costs and revenues.

The Dupont Schematic utilizes these *flow* and *stock* data to give a meaningful blueprint of the interaction of changes in stock (e.g., inventories, new buildings, and so forth) on the flow (sales and expenses) of the firm. These stock and flow implications are then related to the ultimate objective function in this framework—the return on investment.

Financial and Merchandise Planning

The Dupont Schematic, shown as Figure 3-1, shows some of the relationships that exist between stocks and flows on the balance sheet and the profit and loss statement. You will observe that the information required for the entire lower half of the diagram relates to profit margin and would be taken from the firm's operating statement: a past statement to evaluate a past condition, or a *pro forma* statement to evaluate proposed operations. The information required for the upper portion of the diagram relates to investment turnover and would be taken from both the operating statement and the balance sheet.

As can be seen from Figure 3-1, return on investment has two determinants. Investment turnover multiplied by the profit margin gives the return on investment. Both investment turnover and profit margin have a number of determinants that can be seen by examining the schematic, and which we will subsequently explore.

Investment turnover is defined as the number of times investment (usually investment refers to total assets) can be divided into the current sales volume of a given firm. If a retail firm had total sales (sales of all product lines × unit prices for all the various lines) of $100,000 and total assets (current assets + fixed assets) valued at $50,000, then the investment turnover would be

$$\$100,000 \text{ sales} \div \$50,000 \text{ assets, or } 2$$

---

[3] The name Dupont became attached to this concept principally because of the I. E. du Pont Company's early use of the concept as a financial and planning device. For a description of how the concept has been used by this company, see C. A. Kline, Jr., and Howard C. Hessler, "The du Pont Chart System for Appraising Operating Performance," *Readings in Cost Accounting, Budgeting, and Control,* rev. ed., William E. Thomas (ed.), South-Western Publishing Co., Cincinnati, 1960, p. 799.

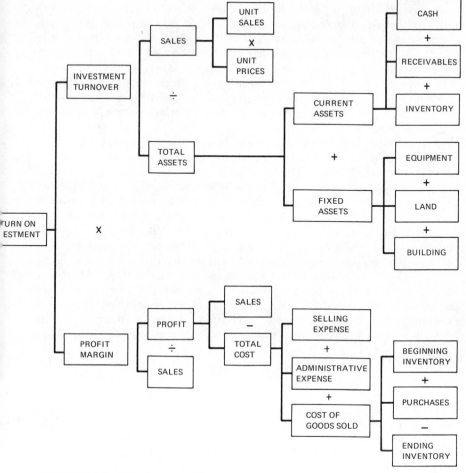

FIGURE 3-1   The Dupont Schematic: A framework for financial planning.

On the other hand, had investment been $100,000 and sales $50,000, then the investment turnover would be

$$\$50{,}000 \text{ sales} \div \$100{,}000 \text{ assets, or } .5$$

Investment turnover does not tell one much about the profitability of the firm, but it does tell one something about the relationship of assets to the flow of revenues. Stocks of assets are related to flows of income in the sense that the stock of one's assets generally is the means of releasing or generating a stream of income or revenue. The major assets of a retail firm consist of its inventory, or stock of goods that it has available for sales, and such other assets as land, building, and fixtures, which the firm uses to facilitate the sale of its merchandise inventory. Investment turnover is such an important determinant of return on investment that it must be managed carefully. Too small an investment turnover is likely to reflect too great an investment in assets in relation to the market opportunity for creating sales. In other words, the firm may be overcapitalized, meaning that some portion of the assets might better be used in some other venture.

On the other hand, an exceedingly large investment turnover may signify that you are not taking proper advantage of the given market opportunity, and that more inventory or other assets reflecting a larger scale of operations might be advisable.

Costs, profits, and revenues are interrelated under the lower portion of Figure 3-1 through the profit margin determinant: The profit margin is profit as a per cent of total sales revenue.

Profit in the accounting sense is the difference between total costs and total revenues. Therefore, to find profit, the analyst must first sum all the costs of his operation and subtract these from the sum of all revenues. We learned earlier that profit margins have characteristically been an important concept of profitability in retail management. However, the best measure of profitability—especially with regard to asset utilization—is one that is linked to investment turnover. Thus, an investment turnover of 25 on the part of a high-traffic, promotion-oriented, mass merchandiser with a profit margin of 2 per cent, would yield a 50 per cent return on investment. However, an old-line jewelry store may have an investment turnover of 2, offset by a 10 per cent profit margin, to give it a return on investment of 20 per cent.

The retail manager must be interested in the interrelated financial and merchandising aspects of the retail management system. The Dupont Schematic helps to spell out many of these relationships and ought to provide meaningful insight into the interdependent nature of financial and merchandising decisions.

Observe that the sales revenue figure plays a critical role in determining both investment turnover and profit margin. Sales are the crux of the business enterprise. Without sales, there can be no profits. In terms of both financial and merchandise planning, the sales forecast becomes the key to all integrated planning within the retail management system. All of the system's schedules and budgets are directly hinged upon the level of the sales forecast. However, it is not sales that we are attempting to maximize, or investment turnover, or profit margin, but return on investment. As we have seen, return on investment is affected by many interdependent variables. The effect of the retailing mix can be readily traced throughout the Dupont Schematic. It can immediately be discerned that price decisions will affect sales levels, and these will affect both profit margin and investment turnover. Product or inventory decisions will affect both total costs and levels of sales, and these in turn will affect profit margin and investment turnover. Inventory evaluation will also affect profit margin and investment turnover. For example, as we become more sophisticated in our knowledge and understanding of retail management systems, we will readily comprehend that to overvalue the firm's closing inventory is to overstate profits and to show too large a profit margin as a percentage of sales. Conversely, to undervalue the closing inventory is to understate profits, show too small a profit margin as a per cent of sales, too low a return on investment, and a distorted, unrealistic picture of the system's operation.

Promotion decisions reflect themselves in the Dupont Schematic through selling expense and profit margin figures and on through return on investment. Promotional expenditures are expressed in two principal ways, first, as increases in the overall cost structure of the firm. Promotion is not free, and therefore, promotional activities are bound to add to costs. Second, however, promotional expenditures are generally viewed as demand-creating activities. This means that the overall demand for the firm's output of goods and services ought to increase as a result of these activities. The fundamental decision rule for promotional decisions is to spend for these activities so long as the marginal, or last dollar spent, creates a marginal, or incremental, dollar of sales revenue.

Place and location decisions manifest themselves in the Dupont Schematic mostly as they reflect the firm's decisions in regard to certain kinds of fixed assets, namely, land, building, and equipment. In order to reduce their investment in fixed assets, many firms have more recently looked to leasing as a means of acquiring the needed facilities for conducting their merchandising operations. Such a move has the effect of reducing the firm's investment in fixed assets, which in turn can result in their markedly increasing their investment turnover and their return on investment. Generally speaking, the return from a dollar invested in merchandise inventory is greater than a dollar invested in fixed assets. That doesn't mean, however, that the retail firm can liquidate its fixed assets and convert all the funds into inventories and thus increase its return on investment.

Normally, to maximize return on investment, there is a necessity to maintain some balance or ratio between current and fixed assets. Given that the retail manager is profit-versus-sales oriented, this condition implies that he is interested in the effect of additional sales on profit.

If the retail firm is operating at or near capacity, additional sales may increase operating costs by requiring additional investment in equipment or buildings, which in the short run at least cannot be fully utilized. Increased volume could also result in higher labor costs or in a growing disaffection on the part of employees to the end of upsetting morale, causing a strike, with damaging results to return on investment.

Furthermore, the cost of acquiring the additional sales (more money for advertising, in-store promotion, selling salaries, and so on) may be greater than the contribution to profit from the realized extra sales. In short, it may cost too much in some instances to increase sales. This could and often does mean that a sophisticated retail manager who fully understands the implications of merchandising decisions on financial analysis and planning, and vice versa, could (and would) limit sales, with the result of increasing profits.

Accounting Costs and Decision Making

Earlier we bemoaned the fact that most cost data available for decision making within the retail system are accounting costs, and the costs examined in our Dupont Schematic have been accounting costs. But the retail manager is not necessarily limited to accounting costs in utilizing the Dupont Schematic for financial and merchandising decision making. Quite the contrary, inasmuch as planning is futuristically oriented, there is no reason why futuristic estimations of costs or opportunity costs could not be implemented in the schematic.

Accounting practices normally attempt to allocate full costs to all units. In other words, accounting costs are estimations of average cost, which includes both fixed and variable costs. Retail management decision makers should not be limited or forced to use only average costs for decision making. As was stated earlier, the only relevant costs for management are those that will change because of the decision. An illustration is offered here to demonstrate this point.

The controller's office of a retail firm informed a division manager that it was uneconomical to hire another salesman for a given department because the anticipated contribution to the firm's revenue was less than his fully allocated costs. The division manager correctly argued that the new salesperson's contribution would (1) cover his salary, (2) cover all his expenses, and (3) make some incremental addition to the company's profit. The controller corrected the division manager, indicating that the new salesperson must cover his fair share of the administrative and overhead costs. The division manager astutely replied with the rejoinder that these costs would have to be incurred whether the new man was hired or not and, therefore, administrative and overhead costs were not relevant for this decision.

The Dupont Schematic shows the interrelationship of decisions by relating flows of revenue to the firm's stock of capital. Retail managers can improve their decision-making skills if they fully understand the effects of their merchandising decisions on financial considerations, and vice versa. We shall continue with our treatment by examining other concepts and techniques designed for this purpose.

break-even point analysis

At this juncture, let us turn our attention to another widely used concept for business decision making. The concept in question is break-even point analysis and it can be developed either graphically, arithmetically, or algebraically.

It might appear that our discussion of retail management decision making has dwelled inordinately on profit as a criterion for decision making. But well it may, considering the crucial role of profits in business enterprise and in our economic system. We have also learned that profits result from operations; and in the case of the retail management system the specific and principal operation is merchandising. Merchandising operations generate sales revenue, and from sales revenue profits are ultimately derived. Earlier, we looked at a simplified model of the retail system in the following form:

$$\text{Sales Revenue} - \text{Cost of Goods} = \text{Gross Margin}$$
$$\text{Gross Margin} - \text{Expenses} = \text{Profit}$$

This concept is reintroduced once again because it reveals a great deal about the workings of the retail management system, especially the role of sales revenue.

You will observe that sales revenue eventually must cover or exceed three relevant items shown in the model: (1) cost of goods sold or the purchase price from suppliers of goods acquired for the purpose of resale; (2) all the firm's expenses, including expenses of administering the system, advertising, depreciation and so forth; and (3) profit, the amount left over after subtracting all expenses from sales revenue. Thus, a heavy burden rests on sales revenue because from it must essentially flow the funds to cover the costs of the firm's operation. Consequently, the term *break even* begins to take on a very significant meaning. The retail system is supposed to cover all of its costs for each operating period. When it does just cover its cost, the system is said to break even, and in terms of our previous statement, such a result would be viewed as follows:

$$\text{Sales Revenue} = \text{Total Costs}$$

On the other hand, when sales revenue is greater than total cost, shown as

$$\text{Sales Revenue} > \text{Total Costs}$$

the result or difference is profit. When sales revenue is less than total cost, shown as

$$\text{Sales Revenue} < \text{Total Costs}$$

the result or difference is loss. *The break-even point is that point or stage in a firm's operations where sales revenue just equals total costs.*

Elements in the Break-even Point Analysis

Break-even point analysis is a management decision-making tool that points up the relationship among several decision variables, namely, price, costs, and volume of sales.

Sales Volume. We have already explored the critical nature of sales volume in the firm's operation. It is generally understood that sales volume is a function of prices charged and quantity sold. Most of the firm's critical planning hinges around its sales budget, or what in the retail management system is called the merchandise budget.

Costs. Thus far we have discussed costs rather loosely as if there were only a single kind of costs for the system. In reality, there are several different kinds of costs but, for our purposes, we shall treat costs as if there were only two major kinds—fixed and variable.

Fixed costs are the costs of being in business. In this sense they are sunk or historical costs, and their real significance is that fixed costs (for a given level or range of operations) are fixed or constant at that level. Stated another way, fixed costs do not vary with the number of units handled but remain fixed or constant over a given range of output.

Variable costs (as the name implies) vary with the number of units produced and furthermore, for the purpose of break-even point analysis, the simplifying assumption is added that variable costs vary directly with the number of units produced. For example, if for every unit sold our variable costs are $1.00, then two units sold would mean a variable cost of $2.00, three units sold would mean a variable cost of $3.00, and so on. Variable costs are often considered the costs of running a business. Of course, there are other costs. For example, there are semi-variable costs, costs that vary not with output necessarily, but more with executive decisions. However, the two kinds of costs considered in break-even point analysis are fixed costs and variable costs.

Contribution. The concept of *contribution* is crucial to break-even point analysis; and now that the two major kinds of costs have been introduced and discussed, the contribution concept should be relatively easy to comprehend. If a retail merchant sells a man's shirt for $7.00 and his variable costs (consisting of cost of goods sold, $3.50, and his selling and other direct expenses of $1.50) equal $5.00, then his *contribution* to profit and overhead per unit equals $2.00. This figure was obtained by subtracting variable costs from sales revenue, which symbolically can be shown as

$$SR - VC = \text{Unit Contribution}$$

The contribution is an amount that when totaled from all sales must eventually be used to pay off fixed costs.

To further simplify our foregoing illustration, assume that our merchant sells only men's shirts, and that his total fixed costs are $10,000 per year. Every shirt he sells (he has a single price line and no markdowns) for $7.00 returns him (after paying his variable costs of $5.00 per unit) $2.00 as contribution. Obviously, when enough shirts are sold, he will eventually have enough money to pay his fixed costs of $10,000; after he sells exactly 5,000 shirts, or 5001 shirts, he will have made a profit of $2.00. Do you readily understand why?

The Graphic Approach to Break-even Analysis

Using the same example, we shall show graphically the essential elements of break-even point analysis. Recall that the principal elements of break-even analysis are

1. Sales.
2. Costs.
   a. Fixed.
   b. Variable.
3. Contribution.

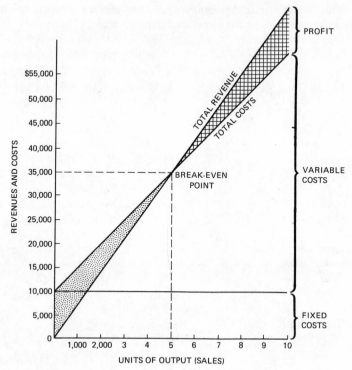

FIGURE 3-2   A graphic approach to break-even analysis.

Figure 3-2 is a graphic portrayal of break-even point analysis using the data from our previous example.

A great deal can be learned from this graphic analysis of the break-even conditions shown in Figure 3-2. The break-even point is 5,000 units of sales, or $35,000. We can check this figure by recalling that $7.00 is the selling price and $7.00 × 5000 units = $35,000. Observe that the fixed costs of $10,-000 do not vary with the number of units sold. Observe further that beyond the break-even point, profits are earned, and that to the left of the break-even point, losses are incurred. It is interesting to note that the level of sales can have a profound effect, given the relationship between fixed and variable costs. The fixed cost element of a firm's operation means that as more and more units are sold, the fixed costs can be increasingly spread over this larger output, a condition known as operating leverage.

The Arithmetic Approach to Break-even Analysis

The graphic approach is a more useful learning device than it is an analytical device for management decision making. Its greatest virtue is that it enables one to visually see the relationship among the break-even variables. Break-even points can be computed in a much simpler fashion by using either simple arithmetic or algebra. To demonstrate the concept of operating leverage, consider again our illustration in which

$$
\begin{aligned}
\text{Selling price} &= \$7.00 \text{ per unit} \\
\text{Variable cost} &= \$5.00 \text{ per unit} \\
\text{Contribution} &= \$2.00 \text{ per unit} \\
\text{Fixed costs} &= \$10,000 \text{ total}
\end{aligned}
$$

In symbolic form

$$
\begin{aligned}
\text{Selling price} &= SP \\
\text{Variable cost} &= VC \\
\text{Contribution} &= C \\
\text{Fixed costs} &= FC \\
\text{Break-even point} &= BP
\end{aligned}
$$

Therefore,

$$
BP = \frac{FC}{SP - VC} \text{ or } \frac{FC}{C}
$$

From the example,

$$
\frac{\$10,000}{\$7.00 - \$5.00} \text{ or } \frac{\$10,000}{\$2.00} = 5,000 \text{ units or}
$$

$$
SP = \$7.00 \times \text{units } (5,000) = \$35,000
$$

Table 3-1 continues our illustration with some further modifications. Thus, it is critical for the retail manager to generate sales beyond his break-even point. There are a number of other important considerations to be given to the factors that affect the break-even point. First of all is pricing. Under certain conditions a given retail manager may enjoy either spatial or temporal monopolies. That is, he may be the only one to have a given item

TABLE 3-1 Break-even Table for Retail Merchant at Various Sales Levels[a]

	LEVEL A	LEVEL B	LEVEL C
Revenue from sales	$21,000	$35,000	$49,000
Total variable costs	15,000	25,000	35,000
Total fixed costs	10,000	10,000	10,000
Profit or loss	($4,000) loss	0	($4,000) profit

[a] Given: Selling price per unit $= \$7.00$
Variable cost per unit $= \$5.00$
Total fixed costs $= \$10,000$

in demand at the *time* during which it is most wanted, or at the *place* in which it is most desired. Under these conditions he may set a price higher than would be the case under conditions of more rigorous competition. Promotion may enable you to significantly differentiate your product in the eyes of a particular group or market segment to the point where higher prices might be charged for these commodities. The retail merchant should be constantly alert to the possibility of reducing his costs for merchandise inventory, and he must wage a constant battle against the ever-increasing tendency for operating expenses to rise. For that matter, even fixed costs are not immune from the effects of good management. New systems of operation and innovation are constantly enabling some operators to reduce their fixed costs of operation and thus reach their break-even points more rapidly, with the end of generating more profits. From the data in Table 3-1 it can be seen that sales must be increased by $18,000 to move from a loss of $4,000 to a profit of $4,000.

The Special Case for Retailing

The retailer's use of break-even point analysis is complicated by the fact that he often has many product lines or even many departments. Break-even point analysis can still be a valuable tool for analysis and decision making, even under these conditions. A special way to use break-even point analysis for a particular department involves the following steps:

1. Determine the gross margin ratio for the department.
2. Determine the variable cost ratio for the department.
3. Subtract the variable cost ratio from the gross margin ratio, and divide the contribution ratio into total fixed costs.

Assume the following:

> The gross margin ratio of department B = 35%
> The variable cost ratio of department B = 25%
> The fixed costs for department B = $5,000

Therefore, the unit contribution ratio equals

.35 — .25, or .10
$5,000 ÷ .10 = $50,000, the break-even point for department B

To figure the break-even point for a number of product lines with varying gross margins, the analysis involves finding the average gross margin. For example, assume that in the home furnishings department of a department store these products were offered under the conditions in Table 3-2. Therefore, the average gross margin is found by multiplying the gross margin of each product line by the per cent of that product line's sales to the total department. For example,

TABLE 3-2

PRODUCT LINES	GROSS MARGIN (PER CENT)	PER CENT OF TOTAL DEPARTMENT SALES
a. Soft goods, sofas, chairs, etc.	50	40
b. Case goods, bedroom, occasional, etc.	50	35
c. Lamps and lighting	40	10
d. Floor coverings	30	10
e. Accessories	30	5

$$
\begin{aligned}
a.\ 50 \times 40 &= 20.0 \\
b.\ 50 \times 35 &= 17.5 \\
c.\ 40 \times 10 &= 4.0 \\
d.\ 30 \times 10 &= 3.0 \\
e.\ 30 \times 5 &= \underline{1.5} \\
&\ \ 46.0
\end{aligned}
$$

Thus, the average gross margin secured by the home furnishings department from all its product lines is 46 per cent. From this point the break-even analysis proceeds in the usual manner, i.e., subtract the variable cost ratio from the gross margin ratio $(GM\% - VC\%)$ to find the department's break-even point.

The Algebraic Interpretation of Break-even Point Analysis

For the reader with some knowledge of simple algebra, the break-even point concept is relatively simple. It is simply a means of examining the relationships between sales and expenses by means of linear models or equations. By letting y represent dollars of expense incurred when sales are x dollars, the linear relationship is

$$ y = mx + b $$

where

y = the value on the y axis or, as in our previous illustration shown in Figure 3-2, revenues and costs

x = the values of the x axis, or units of output where m is equal to the slope of the line and b is equal to fixed costs

From our previous example of the shirt merchant we have

$$ y = .713^*x + 10,000 $$

* .713 is unit variable cost/price $= \dfrac{\$5.00}{\$7.00} = .713$

which means that if sales were \$49,000, then expenses, y, are

$$y = .713(49,000) + 10,000 = \$44,837$$

You will observe that we still have the two major costs: variable costs of .713, which means that for every one dollar of sales we incur 71.3 cents of variable cost; and fixed costs, which are \$10,000.

The break-even point is the volume of sales that just covers total costs. If we let break-even volume be represented by x_e, then at break even, both x and y will equal x_e. For example,

$$x_e = .713x_e + 10,000$$
$$x_e - .713x_e = 10,000$$
$$.287x_e = 10,000$$
$$x_e = 34,843 \text{ or in rounded figures, } \$35,000$$

At \$35,000, x which is sales revenue $= \$35,000$, and y which is total cost also equals \$35,000. Hence, $x_e = y = x$.

Limitations to the Use of Break-even Point Analysis

Break-even point analysis is a simple, yet valuable tool for retail management decision making. It can be used for analyzing the financial and merchandising implications of many decisions. It is an especially useful device for pricing decisions, for use in inventory management and buying decisions, for appraising the value of increased promotional allowances, or in-store selling efforts. However, the simplicity of the device is to some degree its undoing, at least in terms of the simplicity of the underlying assumptions regarding cost. It is unrealistic to assume that fixed costs remain fixed at all levels of sales output. If sales volume falls in sufficient quantity, management is likely to have to react by drastic cuts in fixed costs, such as wages and salaries and promotional expenditures. As we have already learned, exceedingly high levels of sales activities are likely to push the firm beyond a given scale of operations onto a higher level of fixed costs. To continue using a given fixed cost figure for all levels of sales would be both foolhardy and naive.

The linearity assumption, which holds only for a very narrow and restricted range of output, is another weakness of break-even point analysis. The linearity assumption is weakened seriously as output (sales) is extended over a wide range. Break-even analysis holds only that *if* the cost-output relationship is linear, then certain interpretations and relationships present themselves.

The straight line total revenue curve is questionable in that it assumes that any quantity can be sold at that prevailing price. In effect, this ignores the concept of demand, which suggests that several prices and perhaps several total revenue curves may be needed, instead of only one.

Break-even point analysis is only as good as the data on which it rests. This means that good, relevant, and timely figures in terms of prices and costs are necessary, and that the decision maker must be supplied with good data from the firm's cost accounting department.

Finally, break-even analysis is a short-run tool or model. In an economic sense, all costs become variable costs in the long run. For this reason, break-even analysis is a most useful tool for short-run merchandising or budget periods, which usually in the retail system consist of six months to one year.

cash budgeting

A major part of the retail management decision maker's responsibility rests within the area of financial planning and analysis. Of the important factors to be considered within this framework, nothing looms larger than his responsibilities connected with acquiring and managing liquid or near liquid assets, especially cash. It is important to remember that Sales Revenue − Total Expenses = Profits, but that expenses of operation and the costs of acquiring a merchandise inventory must be paid with hard cash, and not necessarily with profits.

The retail management system's principal function is to generate a profitable merchandising cycle. Such a cycle is depicted in Figure 3-3.

‚ The retail management system begins its operation with cash resources, usually its own funds, some of which may be borrowed. Cash is converted into a merchandise inventory that the system hopes to sell profitably. In the case of credit sales, merchandise when sold becomes a different kind of asset. It now becomes an account receivable; and when it subsequently matures, it will be converted into cash again and, hence, the cycle is repeated over and over. Good management results in a profitable merchandising cycle.

One of the retail manager's more important responsibilities, then, is planning adequately for the cash needs of his business. He must be certain that

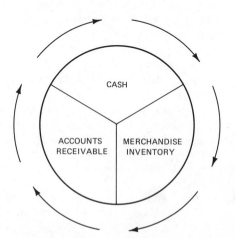

FIGURE 3-3 A retail firm's merchandising cycle.

he will have the necessary cash available to meet his bills as they come due, to take advantage of cash discounts for prompt payment to his suppliers, and to pay his employees' wages, as well as the other regularly recurring costs of operating his business.

In addition, he must anticipate probable future needs for cash so that bank loans can be paid at maturity, taxes and dividend payments can be met, and funds will be available for additional fixtures, delivery equipment, or store facilities.

An adequate cash balance is also necessary to ensure a good credit rating, but the astute manager realizes that there is as great a chance for error in holding too much cash in reserve as in holding too little. Idle cash—cash not needed to meet the current needs of the business—is making no contribution to the earnings of the business. On the contrary, holding reserves of excess cash during an inflationary period actually results in a purchasing power loss to the firm.

The management of cash resources, then, requires a forecast or projection of the expected cash inflows and outflows to and from the business, for a number of months in advance. The period covered by the forecast may vary from a few weeks to a year or more, depending on how accurately cash receipts and disbursements can be predicted.

Sources of Cash Receipts

Cash flows into the business from several sources. The most common in retailing are the sale of merchandise for cash, collections from customers of accounts receivable, and the liquidation of temporary investments.

In addition, the firm may receive cash from the rental of office or sales space, the sale of miscellaneous assets, the collection of service charges, and so forth.

Uses of Cash

The firm uses cash primarily to pay for purchases of merchandise inventory, for employees' salaries and wages, and for its usual operating expenses, such as heat and other utilities, advertising and promotion expenses, and so on.

Cash may also be needed to retire loan obligations, to purchase additional assets to be used in the business, and to make temporary investments.

Cash Budgeting Illustrated

The process of preparing a cash forecast, or budget, is illustrated in the following case.

Futura Shoppes' fiscal year ends on December 31. The following information related to Futura's operations is available for use in preparing a cash forecast for the first quarter of the company's operations during 1977.

1. Projected sales for the first six months of 1977.

January	$ 300,000
February	400,000
March	550,000
April	500,000
May	480,000
June	525,000
Total	$2,755,000

2. Actual sales for the fourth quarter of 1976.

October	$ 480,000
November	470,000
December	500,000
Total	$1,450,000

3. Selected account balances at December 31, 1976 are

Cash	$ 70,480
Accounts receivable	105,000
Accounts payable	260,000
Merchandise inventory	455,000
Notes receivable (30 day; 6%)	35,000

4. All of Futura's sales are on credit. A typical month's sales are collected as follows:

During month of sale	70%
During 1st subsequent month	20%
During 2nd subsequent month	9%
Uncollectible	1%

5. The company's cost of goods sold averages 65% of sales. Each month's merchandise purchases are paid for during the following month. The company policy is to have a two-months' supply of inventory on hand at the beginning of each month.

6. Monthly cash disbursements for operating expenses usually amount to 5 per cent of sales plus $15,000.

7. The monthly payment due on the firm's mortgage is $22,500.

8. Federal income taxes of $40,000 will be paid on March 15, 1977.

9. Cash dividends of $30,000 are paid the second month of each quarter.

10. Company policy requires an ending cash balance each month of at least $70,000. If cash on hand exceeds this amount, short-term investments are made in multiples of $1,000 for 30 days at 6 per cent interest.

If cash on hand is below $70,000 the firm borrows from the bank, giving its own 30-day 6 per cent note, in multiples of $1,000.

Cash Receipts from Sales

The first step in the preparation of the budget requires a forecast of expected cash receipts. Because Futura Shoppes is a merchandising firm selling to its customers on credit, most of its cash receipts will come from the collection of customer accounts. This means that there will be a lag between its expected sales and the time when the actual cash is collected from those sales.

Futura's sales projections are based on a careful analysis of past sales with appropriate adjustments for such factors as the expected sales trends within the company and the industry, and overall economic conditions.

After Futura's sales projections have been made, it is a simple matter to convert expected sales into expected cash receipts, using the company's past experience with the collection of customer accounts receivable; i.e., 70 per cent of customer accounts are collected in the month of sale, 20 per cent in the first month after sale, and 9 per cent in the second month after sale, with 1 per cent found to be uncollectible.

Projected cash receipts from sales are computed in Schedule 1 by this procedure. January 1977 is the second month after November sales of 1976; therefore, we can expect to collect 9 per cent of actual November sales ($470,000) in January, or $4,230. Similarly, January 1977 is the first month after December sales of 1976, and we can expect to collect 20 per cent of actual December sales ($500,000) in January, or $100,000; and we should collect $210,000 of January sales during January (projected January sales of $300,000 × 70 per cent). Cash receipts from sales to be collected in February and March are calculated in the same way as those for January, using the appropriate sales and percentage collection figures.

Cash Disbursements for Merchandise Purchases

In order to compute cash disbursements for merchandise purchases as in Schedule 2, we must first find the amount of merchandise purchases required each month. Futura's policy requires a two-month supply of inventory on hand at the beginning of each month. Thus, January's ending inventory (which is the same as February's beginning inventory) must be large enough to supply the merchandise for the expected sales during February and March. The amount of the required inventory at cost is calculated by multiplying this sales figure ($950,000) by Futura's normal cost percentage as given (65 per cent). The resulting ending inventory figure for January, $617,500, is added to the amount needed for January sales, $195,000 (January sales of $300,000 × 65 per cent = $195,000) to provide the total inventory requirements during January, $812,500. When we subtract goods on hand at the beginning of the month ($455,000) from our total inventory requirements during the month ($812,500), we have arrived at the amount of purchases required during the month ($357,500).

Because Futura pays for its merchandise purchases in the month following the actual purchase, there is a one-month lag between purchases and cash disbursements, as shown at the bottom of Schedule 2.

Cash Disbursements for Operating Expenses

Futura Corporation's normal operating expenses consist of a variable component, 5 percent of the monthly sales, and a fixed component of

SCHEDULE 3-1 Cash Receipts from Sales

	CASH RECEIPTS		
	JANUARY '77	FEBRUARY '77	MARCH '77
From sales in			
November 1976 (470,000 × 9%)	$ 4,230		
December 1976	100,000	$ 4,500	
January 1977	210,000	60,000	$ 2,700
February 1977		280,000	80,000
March 1977			385,000
Total receipts	$314,230	$344,500	$467,700

SCHEDULE 3-2 Cash Disbursements: Merchandise Purchases

MERCHANDISE PURCHASES	JANUARY '77	FEBRUARY '77
Desired ending inventory	$617,500[a]	$682,500[b]
Add: cost of goods sold during month	195,000	260,000
Total inventory requirements	$812,500	$942,500
Less: beginning inventory	455,000	617,500
Purchases required during month	$357,500	$325,000

SCHEDULED CASH DISBURSEMENTS—MERCHANDISE	JANUARY '77	FEBRUARY '77	MARCH '77
For merchandise purchased in			
December 1976	$260,000		
January 1977		$357,500	
February 1977			$325,000

[a] ($400,000 + $550,000) × .65 = $617,500
[b] ($550,000 + $500,000) × .65 = $682,500

SCHEDULE 3-3 Cash Disbursements: Operating Expenses

	CASH DISBURSEMENTS		
	JANUARY '77	FEBRUARY '77	MARCH '77
Variable:			
5% × $300,000	$15,000		
5% × $400,000		$20,000	
5% × $550,000			$27,500
Fixed:			
Total disbursements	15,000	15,000	15,000
	$30,000	$35,000	$42,500

$15,000 per month. Schedule 3 shows the computation of expected cash disbursements for operating expenses for the first quarter of 1977.

Other Receipts and Disbursements

As of December 31, 1976, Futura Shoppes holds a 30-day 6 per cent note receivable for $35,000 that will be collected during January ($35,000 + $175 interest).

Taxes, dividends, and mortgage payments are as given in the case illustration information.

The management of Futura Corporation, as a matter of policy, has decided to maintain a cash balance of $70,000 in order to meet the firm's operating cash needs. If the cash balance exceeds $70,000 at the end of a month, the excess, in multiples of $1,000, is loaned out on 30-day 6 per cent notes. If the cash balance is less than $70,000, the amount needed to reach the desired $70,000 level is borrowed from the bank in multiples of $1,000, 30-day 6 per cent notes. These notes receivable or payable are then collected or paid plus interest by the end of the following month.

Preparation of the Cash Budget

All of the information derived from the various schedules and other pertinent data is summarized in a projected schedule of cash receipts and disbursements, or cash budget, for the period (Table 3-3). Thus all of the

TABLE 3-3 Futura Corporation Cash Budget

FIRST QUARTER, 1977

Beginning cash balance	$ 70,480	$ 70,385	$ 70,070
Cash receipts:			
Collections from customers (Schedule 1)	314,230	344,500	467,700
Notes and interest receivable	35,175	37,185	
Total cash available	$419,885	$452,070	$537,770
Cash disbursements:			
Merchandise purchases (Schedule 2)	$260,000	$357,500	$325,000
Operating expenses (Schedule 3)	30,000	35,000	42,500
Installment on mortgage payable	22,500	22,500	22,500
Notes and interest payable			63,315
Federal income taxes			40,000
Dividends		30,000	
Total cash used	$312,500	$445,000	$493,315
Ending cash balance before borrowing or investing	$107,385	$ 7,070	$ 44,455
Short-term investment	37,000		
Short-term borrowing		63,000	26,000
Ending cash balance	$ 70,385	$ 70,070	$ 70,455

relevant information required for short-term investment and borrowing decisions is available to the managers of Futura Shoppes.

As in any budgeting procedure, the value of the cash budget is increased when actual performance is compared with planned performance. If differences exist, then the reasons for the variations can be investigated, and corrective action taken to change those factors that are within the firm's control. As new information becomes available, it should, of course, be incorporated into the preparation of succeeding forecasts.

Our discussion of tools and techniques for aiding the retail manager in his financial and merchandise planning will be concluded after we have briefly examined one final concept.

ratio analysis

In ratio analysis we are concerned with the effects of merchandising or financial operations on balance sheet and operating statement items.

These relationships among balance sheet and operating statement items resulting (at least from our point of view) from merchandising operations can be studied and manipulated for two major purposes: ratio analysis or trend analysis. In *ratio analysis* the decision maker or analyst computes certain ratios based upon data from the financial statements and compares them with standards established by financial analysts, trade associations, or those generally accepted as sound trade practice.[4] From these comparisons certain conclusions are drawn about the nature, strength, or weakness of the company's operation. In *trend analysis* similar computations and operations are made on a firm's financial statements for a current period of operation, and these results are then compared with similar computations for previous years. What is desired, of course, is an analysis that would reveal significant trends or tendencies within the business.

Our attention here will focus primarily on developing several useful and often used ratios or index numbers that purport to show meaningful insights into a firm's operation. Once the technique of developing the ratios is understood, and some understanding of the meaning and implications of the various ratios is presented, it is not a difficult feat to gather a historical sequence of a firm's financial statements and compute the ratios for various years in order to discern trends or tendencies.

The principal value of ratio analysis is that when computed and standardized (i.e., when a ratio has been built up from financial statements submitted by a large number of companies in the same line of business, with sufficient similarity in size, nature of business, and so on, to make it a homogeneous group), the ratio has considerably more usefulness than the raw data upon which it is computed. To illustrate, it is much more meaningful to compare current assets with (or against) current liabilities than it is to look at either of them without reference to the other. The reason,

---

[4] For a detailed discussion, see Herbert B. Mayo and Bert Rosenbloom, "Ratio Analysis for the Small Business," *Journal of Small Business Management*, Vol. 13, No. 1 (January 1975), pp. 9–11.

of course, is that current assets are the major defense or cushion against current liabilities. On the other hand, comparing notes payable with capital surplus is not only meaningless, but it is probably silly.

Before undertaking ratio analysis, there are several guidelines to be employed:

1. Ratio analysis must be based upon meaningful financial statements predicated upon sound and accepted accounting theory and practice.
2. Ratio analysis must be used in conjunction with reliable and accepted standard ratios in order that meaningful analysis, comparison, and interpretation can be undertaken.
3. Finally, the decision maker-analyst must know what ratios are worth computing and the relative strengths or weaknesses of the various ratios.

TABLE 3-4   Mark's General Merchandise Store Balance Sheet as of June 30, 1977

	1977
Assets:	
Cash and cash items	$ 19,242
Accounts receivable—net	252,171
Inventories	368,964
Other current assets	4,365
Total current assets	644,742
Investments	—
Property, plant, and equipment	326,142
Accumulated depreciation	156,006
Net property, plant, and equipment	170,136
Other assets	57,492
Total assets	$872,370
Liabilities:	
Notes payable	$ 18,000
Accounts payable	65,538
Accrued wages, taxes, etc.	41,742
Federal income taxes	8,874
Customer prepayments	38,574
Current portion long-term debt	12,663
Total current liabilities	185,796
Long-term debt	197,217
Deferred income tax	12,375
Reserve for retirement fund	450
Preferred stock (50) +	33,354
Common stock (5)	121,239
Capital surplus	152,838
Earned surplus	169,101
Total liabilities and net worth	$872,370

At most, ratio analysis offers a useful guide for financial and merchandising decisions. One must use ratio analysis with a great deal of discretion, recognizing that the ratios are only rough guides and indicate only loose approximations regarding trends in behavior, or deviations from standard acceptable ratios. It is important to realize that the real mettle of the decision maker comes not in computing ratios, but in astutely and judiciously interpreting the results and their significance.

The retail manager is concerned with several different kinds of ratios, and these kinds of ratios reflect several different areas of management decision making. The major ratios that we will examine fall into three principal categories:

1. Ratios concerned with liquidity and indebtedness.
2. Ratios concerned with turnover and funds utilization.
3. Ratios concerned with profitability.

With the usual exceptions, it is reasonable to say that the first set of ratios is probably more the concern of the retail management system controller or accountants, and that the second set of ratios is more the concern of the actual merchandise managers. The third set of ratios is the concern of all those in the firm who are both interested in and responsible for generating and maintaining profits.

TABLE 3-5   Mark's General Merchandise Store
Operating Statement (year ending June 30, 1977)

Net sales	$1,346,913
Cost of sales[a]	899,244
Gross profit	447,669
Selling and general expense	372,825
Net profit from operations	74,844
Other income	486
	75,330
Other deductions	
Interest	14,976
	60,354
Provisions for income tax	
Federal income tax	26,019
Net profit after taxes	34,335
Retained earnings on June 30, 1976	156,033
	190,368
Dividends	
Cash	5,940
Stock	15,327
	21,267
Retained earnings on June 30, 1977	$ 169,101

[a] Includes depreciation of $22,293.

We will examine several important ratios in each of these three categories. To facilitate our exposition we will use the data provided in Tables 3-4 and 3-5, the balance sheet and operating statement of Mark's General Merchandise Store.

1. Liquidity and Indebtedness Ratios
   a. The Current Ratio

$$\frac{\text{Current assets}}{\text{Current liabilities}} = \frac{\$644,742}{\$185,796} = 3.47:1$$

The current ratio is a means of estimating the ability of the firm to meet its debts promptly. For many years the acceptable and standard current ratio was 2 to 1. This rule is no longer applied indiscriminately. Current ratios will vary considerably in different lines of trade and for stores with varying lines of merchandise inventory. The current ratio is like all other ratios; it has more meaning when the analyst knows how it compares with the normal current ratio for companies similar to his own and with the current ratios of the same company in previous periods.

   b. The Liquidity Ratio

$$\frac{\text{Cash} + \text{Marketable securities} + \text{Receivables}}{\text{Current liabilities}}$$

$$= \frac{\$19,242 + 0 + \$252,171}{\$185,796} = \frac{\$271,413}{\$185,796} = 1.46:1$$

The liquidity ratio is sometimes called the acid test ratio and is used to test the firm's immediate ability to meet current liabilities. You will notice that inventories are omitted from the liquidity ratio. The reasoning is that inventories are not liquid assets. The acceptable or standard liquidity ratio is usually given as 1:1. However, there may be considerable variance around this standard. A liquidity ratio much less than 1:1 ought to be a red flag to management that all may not be well.

   c. Debt Ratios

   (1) $\dfrac{\text{Total debt}}{\text{Total assets}} = \dfrac{\$185,796 + \$197,217 + \$12,375}{\$872,370} = 45.32\%$

   (2) $\dfrac{\text{Long-term debt}}{\text{Capitalization}} =$

$$\frac{\$197,217}{\$197,217 + \$33,354 + \$121,239 + \$152,838 + \$169,101} =$$

$$\frac{\$197,217}{\$673,749} = 29.27\%$$

   (3) $\dfrac{\text{Total debt}}{\text{Net worth (equity)}} =$

$$\frac{\$185,796 + \$197,217 + \$12,375}{\$33,354 + \$121,239 + \$152,838 + \$169,101} =$$

$$\frac{\$395,388}{\$476,534} = 82.97\%$$

The various debt ratios are simply guides to decision makers and analysts as to the firm's ability to ride out a period of adversity, should such a period occur. The first ratio under this category reflects creditor leverage, i.e., the proportion of total funds contributed by creditors, as opposed to owners of the business.

2. Ratios Concerned with Turnover and Funds Utilization

   a. Accounts Receivable

$$\frac{\text{Sales}}{\text{Days}} = \frac{\$1,346,913}{360} = \text{Sales/day} = \$3741.43$$

$$\frac{\text{Receivables}}{\text{Sales/day}} = \frac{\$252,171}{\$3,741.43} = 67.39 \text{ days}$$

Total sales divided by the number of days in the business year would equal the average sales per day. By dividing accounts receivable by the average sales per day, we obtain the days' sales represented by receivables. In other words accounts receivable represent 67.39 days of sales activity.

These measures are useful when no detailed credit information pertaining to the age of accounts receivable is available. The 67.39 days represents an average collection period; and when compared with the average credit terms granted to customers, it can show any deviations that might indicate slow collection periods and a weakening in the value of accounts receivable. For instance, if the typical credit terms extended by Mark's were 60-day charges, then the 67.39 days means that they are carrying the credit of their typical customer for slightly more than 67 days.

  b. Inventories

(1) $\dfrac{\text{Cost of sales}}{\text{Average inventories}} = \dfrac{\$899,244}{\frac{1}{2}(\$366,471 + \$368,964)} = 2.45 \text{ times}$

(2) $\dfrac{\text{Sales}}{\text{Ending inventory}} = \dfrac{\$1,346,913}{\$368,964} = 3.65 \text{ times}$

(3) $\dfrac{\text{Sales}}{\text{Average inventory at retail prices}^a} = \dfrac{\$1,346,913}{\$525,311} = 2.56 \text{ times}$

(4) $\dfrac{\text{Inventory (ending or average)}}{\text{Sales}} = \dfrac{\$368,964}{\$1,346,913} = 27.39\%$

[a] We do not have an average inventory figure at retail for Mark's. However, we can easily compute one by assuming a 30% markup figure. Cost + Markup = Retail; therefore, Cost of 70% + Markup of 30% = 100% Retail. If the average inventory at cost equals $367,717.50, then the average inventory at retail would be found in the following manner:

Average inventory at cost $367,717.50 = 70%
Markup = 30%

Therefore: $x = \$367,717.50 + .30x$
$.70x = \$367,717.50$
$x = \$525,310.71$

The first three concepts related to inventory turnover, or the number of times (usually per year) that the inventory has been sold. The final concept (inventory/sales) is used mainly for forecasting merchandise requirements and for comparisons with other firms in similar kinds of merchandising operations. This ratio reflects the amount of inventory investment required to service a given level of sales.

All the ratios related to inventories are extremely valuable—especially to merchandise and departmental managers—in appraising past merchandising performance and for planning future merchandising operations. Later, in Chapter 13 on merchandise management, we shall look in much greater detail at the significance of the inventory ratios.

3. Ratios Concerned with Profitability
   a. Profit Related to Investment

$$(1) \quad \frac{\text{Earnings before interest and taxes}}{\text{Total assets}} = \frac{\$74,844}{\$872,370} = 8.57\%$$

$$(2) \quad \frac{\text{Net profit}}{\text{Total assets}} = \frac{\$34,335}{\$872,370} = 3.93\%$$

   b. Profit Related to Sales

$$(1) \quad \frac{\text{Earnings before interest and taxes}}{\text{Sales}} = \frac{\$74,844}{\$1,346,913} = 5.55\%$$

$$(2) \quad \frac{\text{Net profit}}{\text{Sales}} = \frac{\$34,335}{\$1,346,913} = 2.54\%$$

$$(3) \quad \frac{\text{Cost of sales}}{\text{Sales}} = \frac{\$899,244}{\$1,346,913} = 66.76\%$$

We have seen ratios related to profitability before, in connection with our analysis utilizing the Dupont Schematic, and the generalizations made in conjunction with the various concepts of profitability (especially profit as a percentage return on sales and profit as a percentage return on investment) would apply with equal meaning at this juncture.

Ratio and trend analysis can be greatly facilitated by the use of standard ratio figures. There is hardly any line of retail merchandising activity for which standard ratios cannot be obtained. The better sources are found within the trade associations of the various kinds of retailing business. For example, the National Retail Merchants Association, the National Retail Hardware Association, the National Retail Furniture Association, the Supermarket Institute, and many others collect and generate for their members and the public many useful statistics relating to operations. Banks, credit associations, and many other institutions also provide much valuable data relating to operating ratios, turnover figures, and raw financial information that can be used to facilitate financial analysis and merchandise planning.

Our discussion of financial analysis and retail management decision making has been concerned primarily with familiarizing the retail manager (whose primary focus is with merchandising) with the financial implications of his many merchandising operations. Retail management necessitates a real in-depth understanding of the interrelated nature of decisions made within the retail system. When viewed as an assemblage of operating units or subsystems, this interrelatedness underscores the interdependent nature of decisions made in all areas. The effective retail manager is one who understands and appreciates this interrelatedness and who coordinates and integrates decisions at all levels, in the best interest of the total system.

QUESTIONS FOR STUDY, REFLECTION, AND REVIEW

1. Describe one method of evaluating managerial performance.
2. What is the function of the Dupont Schematic model?
3. What two concepts must management be aware of in trying to maximize profit or to earn a target return on its investment?
4. Explain the relationship between assets and the flow of revenue.
5. Explain how the sales forecast is related to both financial and merchandise planning.
6. Explain how it is possible that increased sales may actually decrease profit and return on investment.
7. In the long run, sales revenue must cover three relevant items. What are these three items?
8. Discuss the role and significance of cash budgeting in retail management decision making.
9. How can ratio analysis help the retail management decision maker?
10. What are the principal categories of ratios, and for what purposes are they used?

TWO

ANALYZING AND ASSESSING MARKET OPPORTUNITY

4

analyzing the market
opportunity

Every retail firm must be linked successfully to its market opportunity. Such a linkage depends, of course, upon several factors, the foremost of which is a well-conceived and implemented retail management strategy. Strategy design, however, is largely a function of perceived market opportunity. Not all retail firms will attempt to link themselves to the same market opportunity. The basic reason for their different attitudes is that different retail firms will perceive different market opportunities and thus, in turn, develop and implement different strategies in order to best tap and cultivate these respective market opportunities. The small boutique in the upper-middle-class suburb has both a different market opportunity and a different retailing strategy than does the clothing store located in the low-income ghetto.

This chapter and the several that follow will focus on an analysis of the market opportunity, attempting to delineate some of its determinants and the means employed by retail managers to analyze and measure its size and other factors of significance.

the market opportunity

The traditional way of viewing the market has been to look at it as if it possessed two major sides or dimensions. The one side has characteristically been viewed as the *demand side* and the other has been viewed as the *supply side*. Wroe Alderson has offered the following observation of this existing situation: "From the standpoint of a marketing organization attempting to achieve its objectives in the market place, there appear to be distinct advantages in substituting the terms 'opportunity' and 'effort.' "[1] He reasons that these terms mean essentially the same as demand and supply but that *opportunity* and *effort* reflect a more dynamic view of the relationship as seen by the marketing organization itself. His argument that the term *opportunity* is more specific and more narrowly defined than the broad concept of demand appears well founded. Opportunity connotes demand for the particular and unique product or services that the individual firm stands ready and prepared to provide. On the other hand, effort fits well into our overall treatment of strategy discussed earlier because it designates the activities that a firm puts forth to serve its market. As you will discern, effort means more than merely offering a quantity of goods, but relates instead to *an entire set of activities,* which we earlier called the retailing mix.

Every business firm including a retail management system is most anxious to discover a market opportunity, for it goes without saying that the justification for the existence of the business enterprise is the parallel existence of a market opportunity. Two prevailing and generally valid points of view are that market opportunity exists and remains only to be discovered. On the other hand, the thesis that appears more in keeping with our fast-paced, dynamic approach to enterprise is that market opportunities are not just waiting to be discovered like the lode of gold a prospector looks for, but rather, they are created by imaginative innovation on the part of business management. Be assured that this is no easy task. One of the most important aspects of management and strategy design is that of defining the market opportunity.

Generally speaking, a market opportunity refers to a unique or specific situation in the market place, which includes the following important features:

1. Conditions that permit the firm to match its capabilities and resources with particular market requirements that fall within the general areas of market activity for the firm. Both market requirements and the capabilities of an individual firm to meet the requirements are essential elements.
2. Specific market requirements are those that the firm must meet, and which may have been shaped, for example, by the needs of buyers, the action of competitors, economic conditions, and government regulations.
3. The product of the matching process must hold the promise of improving the firm's position relative to profitable growth over the long run.
4. With respect to time, the situation may be in the present or any specific period in the future.
5. As to development, the specific situation may have been either brought about through deliberate action on the part of the corporate management of one or more individual firms, or it may have been cre-

---

[1] Wroe Alderson, *Marketing Behavior and Executive Action,* Richard D. Irwin, Inc., Homewood, Ill., 1957, p. 355.

ated by technological or environmental change, either internal or external to the firm.[2]

the nature of markets

The market opportunity concept is really just another way of looking at a more traditional marketing-retailing problem, namely, discovering and analyzing markets. Traditionally, markets have been viewed as having three major dimensions:

1. Markets are composed of people. Only people buy goods and services.
2. Markets are people with purchasing power *and*
3. A willingness or a propensity to spend and consume.

This tells us at least something about the nature of a market, but it still leaves a great deal to be desired. For example, if markets are people, it still remains to be discovered what people. Where are they located? In what numbers? What are the characteristics of these people? How much purchasing power do they possess? How do they earn their money? What is their style of life? What are their spending habits? Do they have a high or low propensity to save? What are their views and attitudes regarding credit? These are but a few of the many questions that arise and that must be explored and answered by the retail manager in his search for and delineation of markets and market opportunities.

Markets are a kaleidoscopic concept including such factors as geographic places, demographic characteristics, social-psychological descriptions of purchasers, and many other considerations.

Quite often, markets are identified with a generic class of products. For example, we hear discussions about the automobile market, the powerboat market, the beer market, and the cigarette market. This is not really a useful way to designate either a market or a market opportunity. Those who purchase the products would automatically be included in the market designation, and those who did not would be automatically excluded. When a previous nonpurchaser decided to purchase, he then would be included in the market designation. However, this purchaser would be a *new user;* his habits and attitudes concerning the product and the store from which it was purchased are likely to differ significantly from those of the *old user* of the product.

For these reasons, markets are often defined in terms of prospects or potential buyers rather than actual buyers. A generic classification of markets is little better than no classification at all. Most often, a really meaningful definition of a market is one that incorporates a host of considerations or characteristics and subclasses.

Once a market has been designated by generic product class, subclass, and

[2] Robert L. Clewett, "Market Opportunity and Corporate Management" in *Marketing and Economic Developments,* Peter D. Bennett, ed., Proceedings of the 1965 Fall Conference, American Marketing Association, Chicago, 1966, p. 187.

brand, potential purchasers or market opportunities can be analyzed by a number of means:[3] (1) the size of the market, (2) geographical locations of purchases, (3) demographic locations of purchases, (4) social-psychological characteristics, (5) reasons why products are purchased, (6) who makes the actual purchases and who influences the purchaser, (7) when purchases are made, and (8) how purchasing is done. At this juncture, a complete discussion of each of these factors does not appear warranted. However, we shall deal further with several of them in subsequent chapters.

market segmentation

There is seldom a single market opportunity for any individual firm. Or to put it another way, market opportunity does not necessarily consist of a single homogeneous market. What there is likely to be is a total market opportunity consisting in many instances of a series of somewhat diverse smaller markets—usually designated as *market segments*.

A market is composed of persons who have various needs and wants. But the needs and wants of consumers are many and diverse, which means that both the manufacturers who produce products and the retailers who distribute them must stand ready to supply a diverse product assortment in order to supply the needs of the market place and cultivate market opportunities. This implies that both market opportunity and retailing effort can be broken down into significant segments in an attempt to determine the optimum application of a given type of effort to a particular segment of opportunity.

The typical retail firm attempts to optimize its market opportunity by catering to a number of important and profitable market segments. Whenever the market for the products and services of a given retail firm is larger than two people, that market is capable of segmentation because (given the case of individual differences among people) the market is fragmented or different. A large department store sells goods and services to a wide variety of people with varying tastes, income, educational levels, styles of life, and so on. Yet, this department store probably does not view its market opportunity as consisting of a single market. Instead, the managers of this store logically and deliberately attempt to appeal to a number of profitable market segments with a whole series of strategic devices such as departmentizing, price lining, basement stores, branch and twig outlets, promotional appeals, and other significant strategy considerations.

Whenever the retailer attempts to seek out a particular consumer group or market segment and then proceeds to build some special retailing program to match the needs of this segment, the firm is practicing product differentiation and market segmentation as alternative marketing strategies.

Market segmentation is a fundamental part of the retailing strategy and has several benefits. First, it enables the retailer to better spot and compare market opportunities. Second, the retailer can use the knowledge of the

[3] Jack Z. Sissors, "What Is a Market?" *Journal of Marketing*, Vol. 30 (July 1966), pp. 17–18.

marketing response differences of the various market segments to guide the allocation of its total marketing budget. Third, the retail manager can make finer adjustments of his product and marketing appeals.

There are numerous criteria by which a market might be segmented. Examples:

1. Age.
   a. Preschool market.
   b. Teenage market.
   c. College age market.
   d. Senior citizen market.

2. Occupation.
   a. Blue collar versus white collar.
   b. Professional versus organizational.
   c. Skilled versus unskilled.

3. Income.
   a. Low.
   b. Medium.
   c. High.

4. Race.
   a. White.
   b. Nonwhite.

5. Religion.
   a. Protestant.
   b. Catholic.
   c. Jewish.

6. Region.
   a. Northeast.
   b. Southeast.
   c. Midwest.
   d. Northwest.
   e. Southwest.

Each one of these criteria potentially holds out the promise of becoming an important market segment or target of special market programs in terms of either the firm's goods or service mix, its communication mix, or its distribution mix. This is to say that the related needs of these various market segments may respond more readily to (1) product assortments or services especially tailored to meet their specific needs, (2) personal selling or promotion that incorporates special needs into effective appeals and message design, and (3) retail stores or branches that will reach these particular and unique market targets.

We are still faced with the very crucial question, "What is a market?" The answer is simple and straightforward: A market is a group of potential purchasers of a given product or service. A more fundamental question on which our attention will be focused subsequently is, "How does a retail manager locate, analyze, and measure the relative potential of markets and market segments?" The answers to this important question ought to lead to better decision making related to markets and market opportunity.

Figure 4-1 summarizes and focuses our attention on the many dimensions of a market. The market as depicted in Figure 4-1 has two basic dimensions: physical and behavioral. Each of these two dimensions has been further subdivided along the lines of our previous discussion. The magnifying glass in Figure 4-1 is used to both examine the market and to focus attention on the best or most profitable prospects. Furthermore, Figure 4-1 shows the need for considering all the many ramifications of the concept of a market. To view this concept too narrowly and look at a partial rather than a total market opportunity would limit the full perspective of the retail firm.

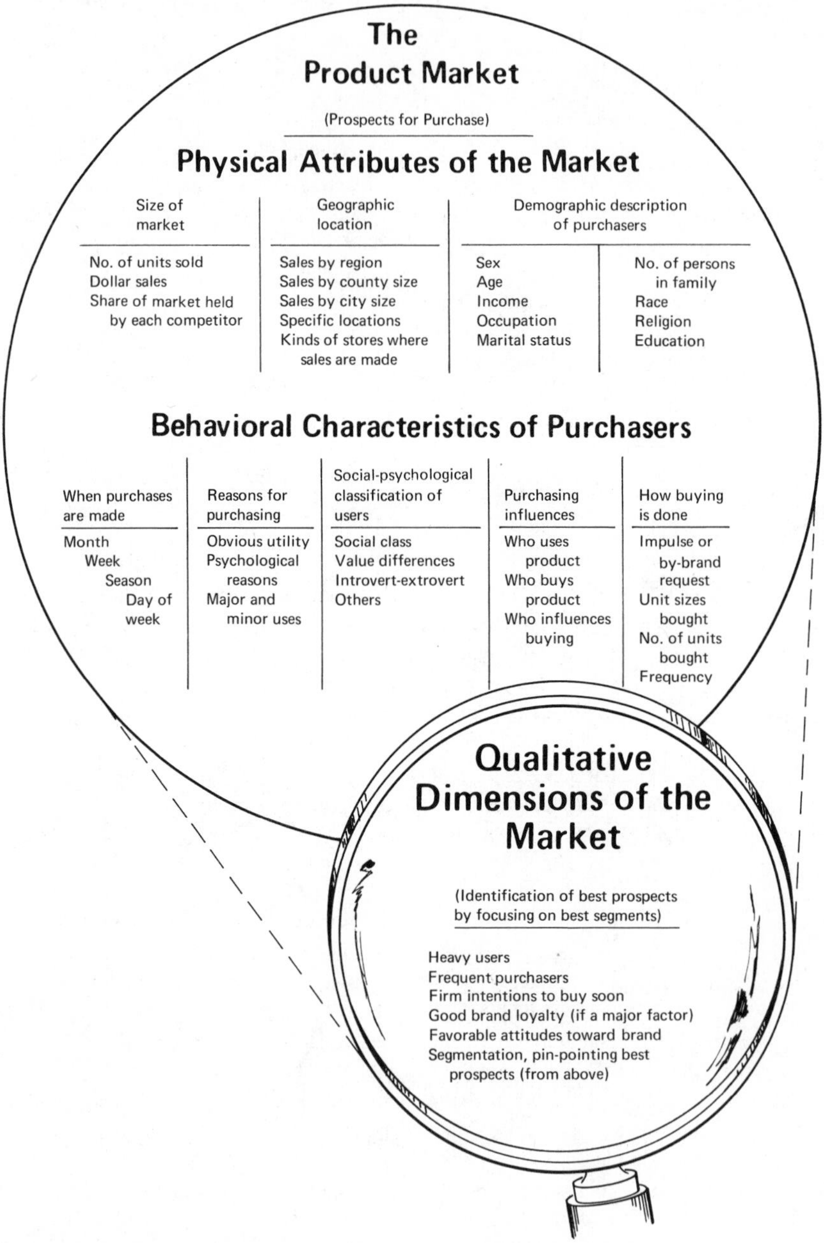

The Product Market

(Prospects for Purchase)

Physical Attributes of the Market

Size of market	Geographic location	Demographic description of purchasers	
No. of units sold	Sales by region	Sex	No. of persons
Dollar sales	Sales by county size	Age	in family
Share of market held	Sales by city size	Income	Race
by each competitor	Specific locations	Occupation	Religion
	Kinds of stores where	Marital status	Education
	sales are made		

Behavioral Characteristics of Purchasers

When purchases are made	Reasons for purchasing	Social-psychological classification of users	Purchasing influences	How buying is done
Month	Obvious utility	Social class	Who uses	Impulse or
Week	Psychological	Value differences	product	by-brand
Season	reasons	Introvert-extrovert	Who buys	request
Day of	Major and	Others	product	Unit sizes
week	minor uses		Who influences	bought
			buying	No. of units
				bought
				Frequency

Qualitative Dimensions of the Market

(Identification of best prospects by focusing on best segments)

Heavy users
Frequent purchasers
Firm intentions to buy soon
Good brand loyalty (if a major factor)
Favorable attitudes toward brand
Segmentation, pin-pointing best
prospects (from above)

FIGURE 4-1   A graphic picture of a market.

SOURCE: Jack Z. Sissors, "What Is a Market?" Journal of Marketing, Vol. 30 (July 1966), p. 21. By permission of the American Marketing Association.

the concept of the retail store image

In the relatively recent past an idea has emerged that has had a rather profound effect on retail managers' thinking regarding merchandising strategies and how they might perceive, analyze, and cultivate a given market opportunity. This idea is known as the concept of the retail store image or personality.[4]

This concept of store image as related to the problem of market opportunity warrants a rather full discussion at this juncture. Martineau argues that what causes consumers to buy where they do is not necessarily price, nor quality, nor service but the total personality or image projected by the institution. He asks

> What is it that draws the shopper to one store or agency rather than another? Clearly there is a force operative in the determination of a store's customer body besides the obvious functional factors of location, price ranges and merchandise offerings. I shall show that this force is the store personality or image—the way in which the store is defined in the shopper's mind, partly by its functional qualities and partly by an aura of psychological attributes. Whereas the retailer thinks of himself as a merchant concerned with value and quality, there is a wide range of intangibles which also play a critical role in the success or failure of his store.[5]

Thus, the store personality or store image is bound to play a highly important and significant role in the retail firm's effort to link itself successfully to the right market opportunity. The problem is two-edged. On the one hand, the market opportunity is likely to be limited by the store's image or personality. And on the other hand, the store image or personality may be determined or at least greatly affected by the way it perceives, analyzes, and cultivates its market opportunity.

Some stores are alleged to have dull personalities. In the eyes of many consumers these stores are nondescript. They lack an aggressive merchandising spirit. Their assortments are adequate but not broad. There is little or no spirit of enthusiasm or excitement which comes to one as a result of shopping in this institution. Surely, then, for those customers who are looking for these attributes—excitement, breadth of assortment, glamour, a sense of drama—in their shopping experiences, this store would appear lackluster and unappealing.

Customers very readily can and will describe their feelings and attitudes about the stores in which they do and do not shop. "I like that store. It gives me a feeling of satisfaction and pleasure to shop there." "That store has the warmest and friendliest salespeople in town." "Oh, I never shop _____ any more. That store really turns me off." Some stores make their

---

[4] The idea of store image or personality is attributed to Pierre Martineau. See "The Personality of the Retail Store," *Harvard Business Review*, Vol. 36, No. 1 (January–February 1958), pp. 47–55.

[5] Ibid., p. 47.

shoppers welcome and attempt to integrate them immediately into the social structure and the physical surroundings. Others impress many customers as being indifferent, if not actually hostile; as being cold and aloof, as when sales personnel look too critically at the shoppers' style of dress and manner. In some instances, customers have even reported sensing a feeling of outright snobbishness and rejection.

When shoppers are in the process of considering a new store or when they are evaluating their previous shopping experiences in anticipation of future shopping experiences, they frequently consider (most often unconsciously) four questions:

1. What is the status of the store? Is it high class or low class?
2. What can I expect of it in overall atmosphere, product quality, and personal treatment?
3. How interestingly does it fulfill its role?
4. How does this image match my own desires and expectations?

It is foolish for most stores to attempt to build a merchandising strategy based upon a mass appeal. Upon careful analysis of their sales records regarding customer location, income, education, occupation, and style of life, many merchants are astounded to learn that the store they had heretofore considered as catering to a large homogeneous mass market attracted from a wide range of the trading area actually turns out to serve a much more narrowly defined market segment, consisting of people largely in the same income group, with similar or at least closely related occupations and styles of life, and largely coming from the same part of the trading area. Such insight, of course, can have or ought to have a rather far-reaching influence upon the merchandising policies of the store.

To repeat what has been said before: No store can be all things to all people. Stores catering to people in the higher income brackets must be concerned with the symbolic meaning of the store in relation to its customers' attitudes regarding status and style of life. Stores catering to those in the lower-to-middle-income groups must concentrate increasingly on the more functional nature of the merchandise offerings, store layout, and physical facilities. Customers in this category are concerned with practicality and utility and above all the reputation of the store for honest values and dependability.

Customer attitudes regarding store images range along a rather wide continuum. Basic stores in many lines such as hardware, appliances, and medium-price apparel are usually most effective if they strive to avoid the extremes in store images. Middle-class respectability, cleanliness, honest value, fair and honest advertising, helpful and courteous service, and so on, are generally considered sound factors upon which to build a highly successful store image.

Considerable research has been done by way of testing the store image in department stores, although little sound research has been done on this concept as it relates to other institutions. Department store images have been found to fall basically into three categories: high fashion appeal, price appeal, and broad appeal. In one study of department store images, customer characteristics and customer shopping behavior were related to department stores falling into the three appeal categories in the following manner.[6]

Customer Characteristics

Generally speaking, the stores with a high fashion image are the ones most favored by the high income women. Conversely, the price appeal stores attract very few of these high income customers.

In terms of the total study, the middle income women represent the largest group for all three types of stores. The low income women shop mainly in the broad appeal and price appeal stores. However, some small percentage do patronize the fashion appeal stores.

Quite interestingly, it was found that age or the stage in the life cycle also to some degree affected the places where women shopped. The over-forty group tended more often to patronize the high fashion stores. This would indicate perhaps a higher rate of affluence among the older women, absence of children, and so forth.

The most prominent place of residence for the high fashion store customer tended to be in the suburbs. This was in contrast with the broad appeal stores and the price appeal stores, whose customers are much more likely to live in the city.

Customer Shopping Behavior

Three basic customer shopping behavior traits were investigated. These were the degree of interest shown in the changing fashions of women's clothing by respondents, the amount of bargain hunting they do, and, finally, whether or not they shopped at discount stores. The conclusions were that fashion appeal stores are the ones that generally attract the fashion-minded customer, but not exclusively. Even the price appeal stores were found to attract a sizable number of the fashion-conscious shoppers.

As would be expected, fashion appeal stores have limited appeal to the bargain-minded shoppers, and the broad appeal and the price appeal stores have the greatest attraction for the bargain-minded customer. As has been borne out in previous studies, even women favoring the high fashion stores also shop the discount stores.[7] Many of the customers who frequent the high fashion stores for their own apparel still go to the discount houses for merchandise such as children's clothing and appliances.

Store image is an important adjunct to the retail management system's strategy design. It is important for management to know something about its store's overall image as well as the image of its various merchandise categories or departments. Only when management is cognizant of the

[6] Stuart U. Rich and Bernard D. Portis, "The Imageries of Department Stores," *Journal of Marketing*, Vol. 28 (April 1964), pp. 10–15.

[7] For example, see Rom J. Markin, "The Omnibus Store: The Rise of Discount Merchandising," *Business Review*, Vol. 22, No. 1 (October 1962), p. 31, and Robert H. Myers, "The Discount Store Customer in Cincinnati," *Journal of Retailing*, Vol. 39, No. 4 (Winter 1963–64), pp. 36–44.

image its system is projecting can it hope to satisfy and bring into alignment its product and service offering with its store image and, in turn, to match these with its perceived market opportunity.

One writer has commented on the importance of the store image concept in this way:

> The closer management's image of its organization is to that held by potential customers, the more effective will be the store's communication through advertising and public relations. This sense of identity will affect the buying, pricing, and service functions of the store. It would be a mistake for management to try to implement such policies without a knowledge of the consumer image of the store. . . . It behooves management to measure its store image periodically to determine the framework within which it should operate.[8]

Retail managers, rather than viewing shopping in an atomistic way—in terms of how many items were bought, in what stores, and at what prices—must be reminded that such statistics on sales provide only a partial basis for intelligent decision making. There is something approaching a nonlogical basis for shopping behavior, and this is rooted in consumer motivation and psychology and manifests itself in such concepts as the store personality or image.

From this concept of store personality and image there emerges a host of strategic questions related to merchandising policy and overall store strategy.[9]

1. Does the store image as delineated register the same image as the management and promotion divisions have envisioned and upon which they are now operating?
2. Is net profit maximized most by better tailoring the store image to fit the image customers already have, or should those market segments that are not now shopping in the store be solicited?
3. If the image can be changed, how can it be accomplished, and how permanent will the change be?

forecasting the market opportunity

Businessmen and decision makers in general are always anxious to know as much as possible about the state of the external environment in which they must operate. Generally, we reflect on the future as a projection of trends now visible from the immediate past. This is certainly one of the important devices of the retail manager in his attempt to bring the firm into proper alignment with the conditions that are likely to prevail during some future period of time.

Earlier, we observed (1) that the retailing strategy is a comprehensive

[8] W. Bruce Weale, "Measuring the Customer's Image of a Department Store," *Journal of Retailing*, Vol. 37, No. 2 (Summer 1961) , p. 41.

[9] William J. E. Crissy, "Image: What Is It?" Michigan State University *Business Topics*, East Lansing, Mich. (Winter 1971) , pp. 77–80.

plan for bringing the retail firm into some kind of accommodation with its external environment and (2) that the external environment is composed of such uncontrollable variables as the nature of demand, competition, consumer tastes and behavior, the social and political structure, and the legal environment. It behooves the retail manager to observe these factors and forces diligently and systematically in order that he might better foretell what changes are likely to take place among these factors and how these changes are likely to affect his overall strategy and decision making. We will examine some of the considerations given to this problem in this section.

The Importance of Forecasting

The key to all integrated planning and decision making is forecasting. To forecast is to look ahead. *It is to anticipate and predict change.* It is not guessing; rather, it is the systematic analysis of trends projecting from immediate and past conditions. The importance of forecasting environmental conditions for the purpose of retail management decision making cannot be overstated. All of the retail firm's planning connected with scheduling and budgeting activities must be predicated on some kind of forecast.

Short-term forecasts are usually for a period of twelve to eighteen months and are used for the following purposes:

1. Regulating employment, inventories, and purchasing.
2. Setting sales quotas, directing the sales effort, and determining size and character of the advertising appropriation.
3. Estimating standard costs and setting budgets.
4. Budgeting and controlling expenses.
5. Planning cash requirements.

Intermediate and longer-run forecasts serve many useful purposes, including long-term financing, plant and equipment requirements, and merchandise and general operations planning. Forecasting facilitates both financial and merchandise planning, which we earlier learned to be the two principal areas of management decision making within the retail management system.

Later, we shall learn how the central planning activity of the retail firm (the merchandise budget) must be predicated upon a rather sophisticated forecast of the uncontrollable environmental variables. Managers cannot plan in a vacuum. Plans are based upon expectations about the future, and these expectations are based on either implicit or explicit forecasting endeavors.

All planners engage in some type of forecasting. Plans based on the general assumption that business conditions and other environmental forces will remain basically stable (without attempting to systematically assess the validity of this assumption) is an *implicit* forecast. On the other hand, a conscious and deliberate attempt to assess environmental conditions scientifically and systematically is an *explicit* forecast. Stable systems not subject to the ravages of a fast-paced, dynamic environment can generally survive on the basis of implicit forecasting. Retail management systems are not included in this designation.

What Shall We Forecast?

The retail manager is forced to forecast all those forces that constitute his uncontrollable external environment and that therefore affect his market opportunity. He must forecast his market opportunity and then set about to plan a strategy that will best enable him to cultivate that opportunity. Forecasting is a special kind of marketing research. Broadly viewed, forecasting activity first of all encompasses a wide range of environmental research activities, including such macroscopic forces as sociocultural changes, changing consumer tastes, consumer motivation and behavior, broad-gauge economic and demographic changes, and even changes in the political climate. From this level of forecasting activity attention is usually next turned to forecasting changes in the industry. From here the focus shifts to the individual company and then, perhaps in the case of a multiunit organization, to the individual unit, to departments and merchandise lines, and finally down to the individual product category.

Figure 4-2 depicts the kinds of forecasting activity that might be undertaken by a retail firm, and it shows also how as the forecasting activity progresses it becomes exceedingly more narrow and explicit in its orientation.

Forecasting Versus Measuring

You will observe from Figure 4-2 that environmental research and forecasting are concerned with the general recognition and assessment of trends, not with their precise measurement. It may be valid to generalize that as one moves from the more macroscopic to the more microscopic orientation he becomes better able to *measure* as opposed to simply *forecast,* or recog-

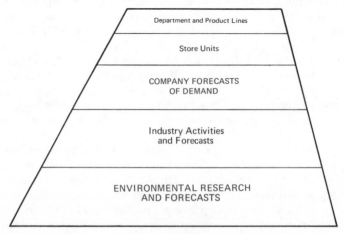

FIGURE 4-2 The types of forecasting activities.

nize trends or attitudes and subjectively evaluate them. However, our ability to measure with precision (given our current research methodology) is something of a handicap, although perhaps not so serious a handicap as we would imagine. Alderson and Green seem to have captured a significant marketing insight when they made the following observation:

> All marketing answers are approximations, and only rough approximations are required for planning and problem solving. "Is it a lot or is it a little?" is sometimes all the marketing executive wants to know, but he wants to know this much with a pretty high degree of reliability. He cannot afford to be caught on the wrong side of the issue as, for example, treating the market as if it were only a little market when it turns out to be a lot. The consultant learns that what he needs to tell his client is often very simple almost to the point of embarrassment. "Do this." "Don't do that.". . . The marketing organization which the executive controls does not respond to precise refinements. Once the actual is under way he gets a more sensitive feeling for market response.[10]

This statement appears to capture the essence and significance of forecasting environmental forces. It is presented in order to capture the nature and flavor of change, to recognize the significance of new forces at the turning point, and to assess and judge the general magnitude of markets and market opportunities.

Economic Forecasting and Demand Analysis

The retail firm, as we have seen, must anticipate and forecast a host of factors that affect its operations. In relation to the environmental research undertaken by many companies relating to such sociocultural factors as consumer tastes, attitudes, motivation and behavior, the central feature of most retail firms' forecasting activity is their interest and concern with economic forecasting and demand analysis.

Economic forecasting is concerned with anticipating and predicting changes in economic activity that conceivably would affect the sales and market opportunities of the retail firm. From a knowledge and understanding of economic conditions, the retailer turns to *demand analysis, which is a series of activities related to anticipating and forecasting demand for the industry of which it is a part,* for example, retailing, *and then proceeding to forecast demand for the particular individual system's output of goods and services.*

The range and extent of economic forecasting activities will vary widely from firm to firm depending upon size, merchandise lines, and management attitudes. As a matter of fact, some retail firms engage in little or no explicit economic forecasting and demand analysis, whereas others engage in considerable amounts.

By and large, economic forecasts of the general economy are undertaken by only a few of our larger retail organizations. In some instances, retail

---

[10] Wroe Alderson and Paul Green, *Planning and Problem Solving in Management,* Richard D. Irwin, Inc., Homewood, Ill., 1964, pp. 59–60.

firms contract with management consulting services such as RMS (Retail Marketing Services, Inc.), and for a service or consulting fee such firms supply ready-made sales and market forecasts for individual retail firms. Other firms build their sales and market forecasts around forecasting services such as Predicasts®, a firm that specializes in forecasting and projecting economic phenomena and business activity for a number of select trade and industry categories.[11]

Others simply take forecasts prepared by government agencies, such as the President's Council of Economic Advisors; or they consult such other sources as the Federal Reserve System, the *Fortune* poll, and the McGraw-Hill survey; or they study numerous industry and trade association forecasts and proceed to build their own company forecasts around these. In addition to providing general economic data, such economic forecasts and projections focus on such key economic indicators as Gross National Product, Personal Income, Personal Disposable Income, and, of course, Consumption Expenditures.

From such general forecasts, the retail manager at the firm or corporate level can obtain something of the big picture regarding general economic trends and opportunities. From here, the next step is a forecast of general industry trends and opportunities. Once again, this may not be done individually by many firms because of their lack of skill and expertise, size of the firm, or other factors. Numerous forecasts of general trends, opportunities, sales level, and so forth are available from sources such as those just mentioned. Probably the most important are those from trade associations such as the National Retail Merchants' Association, National Retail Hardware Association, and the National Retail Furniture Association, among others.

Learning the Terminology. To some extent, forecasting is a bit of an occult science and it is infused with a jargon known only to the initiate. To remedy this situation, we must discuss and define three terms that are relevant to our understanding of forecasting activity. These terms are

1. Market demand.
2. Company demand.
3. Sales forecast.

In referring to market demand, we have in mind projected or forecasted sales for a future period as contrasted with past or current sales. Market demand relates to the industry as opposed to the individual or firm level. It is not a simple concept. Kotler defines market demand as the total volume for a merchandise category or product class "which would be bought by a defined customer group in a defined location in a defined time period under defined environmental conditions and marketing effort."[12] This is a precise but weighty definition.

---

[11] See *Predicasts Annual Cumulative Edition,* published quarterly by Predicasts, Inc., Cleveland, 1974.

[12] Philip Kotler, *Marketing Management: Analysis, Planning and Control,* 2nd ed., Prentice-Hall, Inc., Englewood Cliffs, N.J., 1972, p. 195.

Company demand is the total projected volume of sales expected under given environmental conditions for a specific company or firm. Broadly, it is this company's share of total expected or forecasted industry sales.

The sales forecast is the expected or planned level of sales predicated upon a given retailing strategy and projected or anticipated environmental conditions. Figure 4-3 illustrates the relationship between company demand and the sales forecast.

The implication is rather clear that the sales forecast must be based on some level of proposed merchandising effort. The sales forecast at the limit could never be greater than company demand. However, the sales forecast will usually be somewhat less than the projected company demand.

This illustration further dramatizes the necessity for forecasting and projecting company or market opportunity. *Without some knowledge of the company's market opportunity there can be no intelligent basis for planning the level of the retail management system's marketing effort.*

Forecasting Company Demand. Because of the crucial role of forecasting company demand, we shall explain in brief detail some of the ways in which firms approach this problem. Much later, in our discussion of merchandise budgeting, we shall attempt to develop more fully the relationship between forecasted company demand and the sales forecast.

There are many ways by which companies attempt to develop projections and estimates of total demand for their products. Some of these techniques are extremely simple and are often labeled naive. Other approaches involve extremely sophisticated statistical-mathematical models.[13] Our task here is not so much concerned with developing skill in company forecasting and demand analysis but rather to review briefly some of the many approaches in order to develop some appreciation of the concepts as they would aid the retail manager in his analysis of market opportunity.

RETAIL MANAGEMENT SYSTEMS STRATEGY EFFORT

FIGURE 4-3 **Company demand and the sales forecast.**

[13] For more discussion on this topic, see "A Manager's Primer on Forecasting," *Harvard Business Review* (May–June 1973), pp. 6 ff.; and "How to Choose the Right Forecasting Technique," *Harvard Business Review* (July–August 1971), pp. 45–74.

Forecasting company demand can be oriented around three principal points of view: *what people say, what people do,* and *what people have done.*

Forecasting company demand based on *what people say* must focus by necessity on finding out what they are saying. This approach is therefore concerned with sounding out attitudes and opinions of customers, potential customers, sales personnel, in-store buyers, and experts such as fashion commentators or others possessing expert opinions.

Forecasts based on *what people do* are oriented around such activities as test markets, consumer panels, college fashion boards, and so on.

Forecasts based on *what people have done* are oriented around a systematic analysis of records and statistics related to past buying behavior and involve the use of classical time series analysis or statistical-mathematical demand analysis.

Forecasts Based on Attitudes and Impressions

There are principally two major sources of information on which a forecast of company sales or demand can be predicated. These are (1) consumers and potential consumers who are external to the firm and (2) such company employees as department and merchandise managers and buyers, who are members of the firm or who are members of the industry and therefore would presumably possess expert judgment.

Consumer intentions can be an excellent way of building a company forecast. However, several important questions do arise in connection with this technique: (1) Are consumers sufficiently aware of their purchasing intent to be reasonably able to predict their purchases in advance? (2) If they are, can they transmit this information to an interviewer meaningfully and accurately? There is considerable research that would suggest that intentions to purchase are related to purchasing behavior, but that this relationship is subject to many influences. The stated intentions of a group of individuals are a better predictor of buying behavior than those of an individual because within a group many of the deviations between planned and actual behavior will offset one another.

Department stores have successfully used another version of the consumer intentions survey to predict the particular style of clothing that will likely prevail during a future period. Customers are quizzed while in the store as to the characteristics of the dress they will buy next season. In spite of many obvious limitations, the technique has met with general effectiveness.

It would appear obvious that estimates of company demand based upon consumer attitudes and intentions should be used with a great deal of caution. Usually such approaches are combined with other techniques in order to broaden the base of the forecast and to temper the arbitrariness that usually pervades consumer behavior. A forecast based on consumer intentions is best used when the psychological attitudes of the consumer are the major marketing factor determining the demand for the product.

An often used source of information and base for projecting company demand by the retail firm is one that involves the expert opinion of the store buyers and department and merchandise managers. This technique is often called the composite method and begins by collecting from each buyer, department manager, or divisional merchandise manager his estimate of future sales of the various merchandise lines in his department or division. These estimates are often made in consultation with the general merchandise manager; thus total demand for the unit or store is then a composite of the demand for the various individual departments or divisions. Such a procedure has much to recommend it. Its principal outstanding feature is that since the experienced buyers and merchandise managers within the retail management system are basically responsible for merchandise planning, forecasting and demand analysis become integrated and coordinated with general merchandise planning and overall strategy formulation.

Several other advantages are that this method:

1. Uses the specialized knowledge of those closest to the market.
2. Places responsibility for the forecast in the hands of those who must produce the results.
3. Gives sales personnel greater confidence in quotas developed from forecasts.
4. Tends to give results greater stability and accuracy because of the training, experience, and judgment of the forecaster.

Forecasts Based upon Observable Behavior

If consumer intentions lack the necessary stability on which to base a firm's market forecast, then a better approach is actual observation of what consumers are doing, i.e., buying or not buying, under either a real or somewhat simulated shopping or buying experience. From these observations, the researcher then projects his findings to a larger body of consumers. Several techniques are available for observing or gathering information on consumer behavior.

Many retail firms engage in the test marketing of products in order to assess the relative strength of the product among various groups. Based on these reactions, the firms attempt to project their findings to larger market segments and ultimately incorporate these findings into an overall forecast of market demand.

Test marketing has limited applicability to market forecasting for the typical retail firm, however, because of its extremely wide assortment of product and merchandise lines. Stores with limited merchandise lines such as specialty shops having a well-defined and limited trading area might use test marketing very effectively for this purpose.

The use of consumer panels and fashion boards is becoming an increasingly popular method of forecasting demand and ultimately guiding merchandising and buying decisions.

Consumer panels and fashion boards reportedly perform a wide variety of services related to the task of forecasting market demand and opportunity. Wingate and Friedlander distinguish among five varieties of consumer panels: (1) the customer advisory group that makes suggestions concerning store policies, services, and merchandise assortments; (2) the consumer jury that expresses opinions on advertising, sketches of future styles, and buying intentions; (3) the consumer experience group that reports on performance of products in use; (4) the home inventory group that reports the goods they have on hand; and (5) the continuous-purchase-record group that records and makes monthly reports on family purchasing.[14]

The college fashion board is a special kind of consumer panel used to predict the tastes and demands of college students as well as to influence college students' taste and their store patronage behavior. College fashion boards are usually composed of social and fashion leaders from a number of colleges or universities.

Forecasts Based on Past Behavior

The more sophisticated and perhaps objective methods for forecasting market demand are involved with the systematic analysis of past behavior in relationship to some variable. This relationship is then projected into the future to produce an estimate of market demand. There are two basic techniques for undertaking such an analysis. The first is referred to as *time series analysis* and the second as *statistical-mathematical demand analysis*.

Time series analysis is a widely used method for projecting market or company demand into some future period of time. The calculation techniques are described at great lengths in all elementary textbooks on economics and business statistics and therefore need not be illustrated here.

A time series is a set of observations on the same variable, such that the observations are ordered in time. The data of the series is regarded as being composed of four elements: a secular trend (T), a seasonal variation (S), a cyclical movement (C), and an irregular variation (I). The most common practice is to assume that these elements are bound together in a multiplicative system so that the relationship is expressed by the formula $O = TSCI$. The relationship is also considered at some times to be additive, in which case the formula would be $O = T + S + C + I$. Figure 4-4 is a simple example of trend projection on the basis of time series data.

Sales figures for the Four State Distributors are shown for the years 1967–1977 plotted against time. A free hand line has been drawn from 1977 to 1980 to show what is hoped will be the future values of the variable. The more scientific approach would be to fit a line of "least squares" to our data.

The projection of trends from time series data assumes that conditions in the past will continue largely unchanged into the future. And surprisingly, this is often the case. The greatest danger of utilizing such a technique is that it is highly unreliable at the turning point. That is, when conditions underlying the relationship between sales and time do change, the trend projection that has not anticipated these changes will likely be quite erroneous and far off the mark.

[14] J. W. Wingate and J. S. Friedlander, *The Management of Retail Buying*, Prentice-Hall, Inc., Englewood Cliffs, N.J., 1963, p. 102.

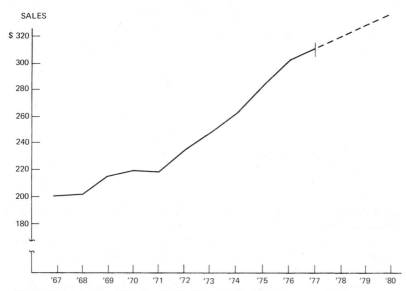

FOUR STATE DISTRIBUTORS

(000 omitted)

FIGURE 4-4   Retail sales, 1967–1977, and projections to 1980.

Time series analysis is a useful tool for forecasting retailing activity. However, it must be used with considerable caution and expertise. Trend, cycle, and seasonality factors all play important roles in forecasting sales and market activity for the retail firm. The fashion factor alone can be most upsetting in the use of time series projection techniques for most stores. The use of electronic data processing and computerized inventory systems permits rapid and accurate information retrieval and is tending to facilitate the increased use of time series techniques, as well as other statistical-mathematical techniques for forecasting and adjusting to perceived market opportunities.[15]

Probably the most widely used statistical-mathematical method for forecasting and projecting market and sales data is that of *correlation* or *regression analysis.*

Correlation analysis rests on the assumption that a dependent variable like sales is related to an independent variable like income. The relationship is thus expressed by a simple linear expression,[16]

$$y = a + bx$$

[15] See Warren H. Hausman and Richard St. G. Sides, "Mail Order Demands for Style Goods: Theory and Data Analysis," *Management Science,* Vol. 20, No. 2 (October 1973), pp. 191–202. Also see Sang Hoon Chang and David E. Fyffe, "Estimation of Forecast Errors for Seasonal Style Goods Sales," *Management Science,* Vol. 18, No. 2 (October 1971), pp. B-89—B-96.

[16] Not all the relationships, of course, are necessarily linear.

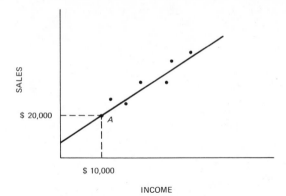

FIGURE 4-5 Regression relationship—Sales and income.

in which *y* represents the dependent variable, sales; *x* symbolizes the independent variable, income; *a* represents a constant; and *b*, the slope of the line. Values for *a* and *b* are estimated or discovered and by substituting values for *x, y* may be solved. Figure 4-5 shows a graphic representation between sales and income.

Point *A* represents the sales, $20,000, that would be realized when income is $10,000. As can be observed, the remaining dots represent other relationships between sales and income.

The purpose of regression analysis is to arrive at a mathematical equation (usually called a regression equation), which best discloses the nature of a relationship that exists between the dependent variable and an independent variable. Oftentimes the relationship is sought between a dependent variable and several independent variables such as income, population, geographic location, and so forth. In this case the technique is known as *multiple correlation analysis*.

The forecaster who uses regression analysis must be extremely careful in selecting or choosing from among the various determinants of demand. What we are dealing with is future sales. That is, our forecasting objective is either future industry or company sales; ideally, we are seeking a lagged relationship between sales and the independent variable. This is desired because we wish to use the current values of the independent variable in order to estimate the future values of sales.

The greatest danger of correlation analysis lies in the fact that the system that we are attempting to forecast is highly unstable and dynamic. There is real danger that an equation that has worked well in the past may not work well in the future. The forecaster must be alert so as not to allow himself to be mesmerized by the formula approach. No equation can ever be a complete substitute for imaginative and qualitative thinking.

a word about forecasting responsibility and methodology

Because of the diverse nature of retailing firms, it is difficult to generalize meaningfully about what kind of forecast is best suited to what system and who in the system at what level in the system hierarchy should be responsible for forecasting activity.

In the larger retail organizations such as department stores and in those organizations with numerous units such as supermarkets, variety, and general merchandise stores the most prominent approach to forecasting activities is known as the "right-angle method." With the right-angle approach, a committee of divisional and corporate officials working in many diverse company activities compares forecasts from a professional staff of economists or market researchers with the grass roots estimates of department managers and buyers. Via the right-angle approach, compromises are worked out, a sales or market forecast is agreed upon, and sales and merchandise budgets are then developed. This approach has the distinguishing and advantageous feature of incorporating data from many important operating, service, and administrative officials within the organization into the forecasting activity.

QUESTIONS FOR STUDY, REFLECTION, AND REVIEW

1. What has been the traditional way of viewing a market? According to one author, how should this view be changed?
2. What are the two prevailing points of view in analyzing a market opportunity?
3. Explain what is meant by "product differentiation and market segmentation as alternative marketing strategies."
4. Define and explain a market and the two dimensions of a market.
5. Explain the concept of the retail store image.
6. What are the types of department store images or personalities, and how do they relate to the customer?
7. For what purposes are short-term forecasts usually used?
8. Explain what an implicit forecast and an explicit forecast are.
9. Define and explain the major sources of information on which a forecast of company demand can be predicated.
10. Explain the forecasting technique known as the right-angle method.

5

major determinants of
market opportunity:
population and income

Two of the more critical factors that constitute the demand or opportunity side of a market transaction are population and income. We shall explore these two determinants of market opportunity in detail in order to assess their implication for retailing. In Chapter 6 we shall look at consumer motivation and behavior, a third critical factor in the demand or opportunity equation.

It must be remembered that it takes more than people with purchasing power in order to make an effective market opportunity. The consumer's psychological expectations must be favorably disposed toward the market situation. The retail firm must put forward a unique and attractive offer variation in order to favorably predispose the consumer and potential consumer toward the total market situation.

However, without a given population to generate a need for the commodities necessary to both sustain and embellish life, and without adequate income with which to purchase these items, we would only have the most rudimentary of marketing-retailing systems.

In the United States, as a result of our technological prowess, we have a generally literate and well-educated population that contributes to our ability to produce at a high level of productivity, generating a high level of income and wealth. Here we have at one and the same time perhaps the most demanding and the most potent of total market opportunities ever created.

The retail manager must be ever alert to the changing nature of market opportunities; to do so he must be ever aware of the changes taking place in the demographic and economic environment within which his system operates.

demographic forces affecting market opportunities

Rather remarkable changes have taken place in the postwar era in terms of overall changes in population growth, size and composition of families, and trends toward population decentralization; all these changes have fostered a favorable climate for many business institutions, especially those dealing with consumer durable and nondurable goods. The changes have benefited, generally, the whole range of retail firms by permitting them to sell more goods and to experiment with the wider and more diverse merchandise lines demanded by new and emerging age and life style groups.

The Growth in Population

A well-known industrialist is alleged to have once said that he would rather have a market than a mill.[1] In this day and age of the market concept, this statement is not at all hard to understand. Nothing about a mill necessarily suggests much by way of profitability, but a market connotes opportunity, and such an opportunity implies profit possibilities. As has been pointed out, the population of the United States is one of two key elements that stimulate the tone and vigor of the American market.

Table 5-1 shows the growth in the population of the United States from 1850 through 1970 and then projects total population figures from 1970 through 1980 and 1990. As can be seen from Table 5-1, the largest percentage increase in population from one ten-year period to another in the more recent past occurred from 1950 to 1960.

Between 1790 and 1950, the population of the United States doubled five times. Before World War II, it was generally conceded by most so-called prognosticators that the maximum population of the United States would be about 165 million people. However, as a result of postwar marriages and the baby boom, the United States passed the 165-million mark by 1955, and by 1975 was a nation of slightly less than 215 million people. Naturally this increase brought forth an increased demand for goods and services of all descriptions.

Population in the aggregate and the rate of population increase are two kinds of indices of market opportunities. As babies are born and move from infancy to adulthood, they generate a continuing need for various kinds of goods and services. Retailers in all lines of goods must plan their longer-term commitments in terms of the changing nature and composition of the population. Changes in the birth rate, the location of major living areas, mobility, and changes in the importance of various age groups relative to

---

[1] This statement is generally attributed to Andrew Carnegie.

TABLE 5-1   Growth of the Population of the United States (1850–1970) and Projections of Growth to 1990

YEAR	TOTAL POPULATION[a] (ROUNDED FIGURES)	INCREASE OVER PAST DECADE (%)
1850	23,261,000	35.9
1860	31,513,000	35.5
1870	39,905,000	26.6
1880	50,262,000	26.0
1890	63,056,000	25.0
1900	76,094,000	20.7
1910	92,407,000	21.4
1920	106,466,000	15.2
1930	123,188,000	15.7
1940	132,122,000	7.3
1950	151,683,000	14.8
1960	180,670,000	19.1
1970	204,879,000	13.39
1980 (projected)	224,132,000	9.39
1990 (projected)	246,639,000	10.04

[a] Includes members of the armed forces.
SOURCE: Compiled from U.S. Bureau of the Census figures.

total population must all be viewed as a complex barometer of economic opportunity and market demand.

The idea of an ever-expanding economy fueled by population growth is tightly entrenched in the minds of marketing retailers. Each new baby is viewed as a potential customer to stimulate an ever-growing economy. Retailers often feel gleeful at the thought that each American baby will consume in a seventy-year life span 21,000 gallons of gasoline, 10,000 pounds of meat, 28,000 pounds of milk and cream, $8,000 in school building materials, $8,500 in clothing and $8,000 worth of furniture. Of course, these are not nearly all of the expenditures, but they dramatically emphasize the magnitude of some of the more relevant categories.

Before we proceed further, however, some cautions may be warranted. Demography is one of the most mechanical of the social sciences. Yet, in many instances, its predictions are faulty. A great many population projections have been wrong. Sometimes these projections are not just a little wrong, but grossly wrong.

Not many anticipated the increased birth rate between 1947 and 1961, and not many anticipated the sharp decline in birth rate we are currently experiencing. In demographics you can get puzzling parametric changes almost overnight. For example, in the first nine months of 1971, Americans were having babies at a rate of 2.39 children for each family. However, since September 1972 through 1973 the birth rate has fallen below the replacement rate of 2.1 children per family to the all-time low of 2.08 children per family. Should this rate continue for a prolonged period of time, the American population would decline.

Other Population Characteristics

In 1900, 39.7 per cent of the United States population lived in urban places of more than 2,500 inhabitants, while the remaining 60.3 per cent lived in rural environments (places of less than 2,500 inhabitants). By 1960, these percentage relationships had reversed themselves, resulting in 69.8 per cent living in urban places as opposed to 30.1 per cent living in rural areas.

Much of this change resulted from the migration of people from farm to urban or suburban living arrangements. In 1970, only about 5 percent of the total number of families lived on farms, nearly 74 per cent of the total population resided in cities of more than 2,500 people, while the remainder lived in rural nonfarm communities.[2]

When large numbers of people left farming for urban residences, the result was an increase in demand for the goods and services of diverse kinds of retail stores. For example, such a movement placed a greater reliance on retail grocery stores to supply the food needs of these new city dwellers, and to a considerable extent the urban population constitutes the dominant market for both consumer durable and nondurable goods.

In many ways the interest in population changes is heightened even more when the changes in households, rather than in number of persons, are analyzed. From the point of view of retail management, the change in numbers of households (households include both families and individuals living alone) and the rate of household formations are of extreme importance. Certainly, the household remains the primary buying unit for many commodities including food, clothing, housewares, home furnishings, appliances, and a host of other general merchandise items.

The number of households in the United States has grown more rapidly than total population. During the first half of this century, for example, while the population doubled, the number of households almost tripled. In the decade since the close of World War II, households increased by 11 million units, more than twice as many as were ever previously added in a single decade. Between 1950 and 1970, the number of households in the United States increased by nearly 20 million, to a total of 63 million; or by 45 per cent.

The primary difference between the rate of growth of households and of total population is accounted for by the decrease in the size of households. At the first census (1790), there were some 5.8 persons per household; by 1966, there were only 3.3 persons per household. And if current low birth rates continue, some slight decrease in persons per household is likely to be evidenced by 1980.

The character of households in the United States is very likely to change significantly throughout the coming years. During the late 1950s, a high proportion of households were headed by women or men in their so-called middle years; over 57 per cent of the household heads during this period

---

[2] U.S. Bureau of the Census, *1970 Census of Population,* Vol. 1, *Characteristics of the Population,* Part A, Number of Inhabitants, U.S. Government Printing Office, Washington, D.C.

were between 25 and 54. During the present decade (1975–1985) this proportion will be reduced appreciably, for about three quarters of the increase in households will be accounted for by heads of households at the younger and older ends of the age continuum.

One type of household that grew rapidly during the 1955–1965 period, but which has remained at about the same size since 1965, is that category of households headed by men or women living alone. The growth of this household category has generally called forth an acceleration of activities on the part of many retail firms to meet the demands of these buyers— demands focused in large measure on such items as frozen foods, ready-mix preparations, health and beauty aids, special dietary foods, vitamins and other drug items, fast preparation items, and many other special classes of both merchandise and services.

The real thrust that threatens to swell the number of households in the United States will come in the category of husband-wife households. This category will increase about 8,000,000 to 53,000,000 in 1980 (in 1970 the figure was 44,728,000). These young married couples represent a very important market opportunity and in themselves constitute an important market segment with specialized needs for numerous merchandise lines and services. This young group is in the market for some products for the first time, and they confront the product-store search and the buying situation from a position of lack of experience and skill. Retail firms whose offer variation is especially designed to meet the needs of these young buyers are likely to find their efforts well rewarded by patronage and continued loyalty as young buyers move progressively through the life cycle.

Other demographic forces that foster growth, development, and market opportunity for retail institutions generally (and for some in particular) can be seen by looking at Figure 5-1. This shows that youngsters, teenagers, and oldsters will continue to increase their shares of the total population, while the middle-age group (20 to 64 years) will diminish proportionately. Many firms are already beginning to recognize the potential of catering to one specific age group by modifying facilities, offering extra services, and expanding product lines.

The Race for the Suburbs

Several root causes affecting the movement to and development of the suburban area and its consequent effect on the growth and development of retailing have been noted. By 1912, the expansion of electric street railways made it possible in many communities for at least the high-paid workers to escape from the gloom and shadow of the factory walls and the confinements of the dirty inner city. The success of the labor unions in securing shorter working days and better pay gave the laboring class reduced work schedules and more discretionary time.

The real impetus to this movement and race to the suburbs was the growing popularity of the automobile and the improvements in roads and highways. Industries, too, began to seek plant and factory locations outside of conventional city areas, for they realized that workers could easily follow them via auto, streetcar, and bus.

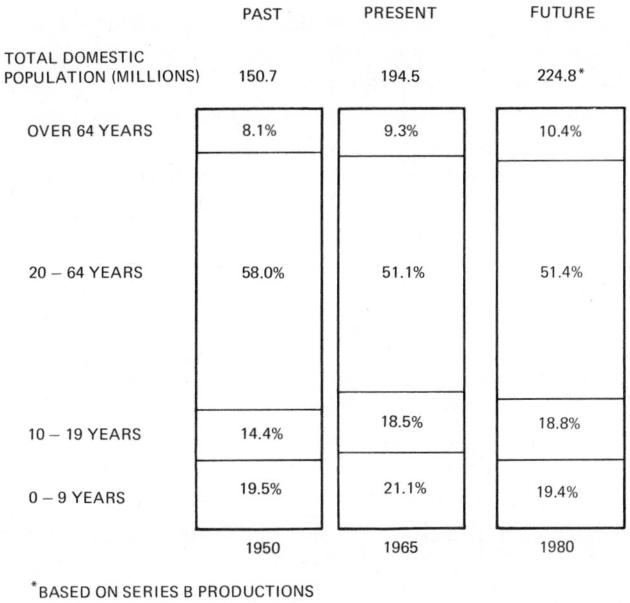

	PAST	PRESENT	FUTURE
TOTAL DOMESTIC POPULATION (MILLIONS)	150.7	194.5	224.8*

	PAST	PRESENT	FUTURE
OVER 64 YEARS	8.1%	9.3%	10.4%
20 – 64 YEARS	58.0%	51.1%	51.4%
10 – 19 YEARS	14.4%	18.5%	18.8%
0 – 9 YEARS	19.5%	21.1%	19.4%
	1950	1965	1980

*BASED ON SERIES B PRODUCTIONS

FIGURE 5-1 Domestic population trends by age groups (total United States).

SOURCE: U.S. Department of Commerce, Bureau of the Census, Current Population Reports, Series P-25, no. 329.

The changing structure of metropolitan and suburban areas brought important changes in retail store locations, in the merchandising strategies, and in the offer variations used to serve the merchandise and service needs of these new suburban dwellers. The following tables may help in part to underline the dimension and significance of these changes.

American consumer markets are located in urban places primarily, but the major place of residence of these consumers is not in the major central cities of America, but rather in the suburbs, the smaller central cities of urbanized areas, and the urban fringe that surrounds the major metropolitan central cities of the United States. This is supported by Table 5-2. The American central city is a place where Mrs. Middle Majority American consumer likes to shop but not live. The downtown urban area, while it possesses many desirable retail shopping facilities, is sometimes a difficult area to shop. There is a high incidence of crime, walking is hazardous, and conditions are often aversive because of traffic congestion and inner-city neglect. Consumers in suburban areas do, on occasion, shop downtown central trading facilities. However, their general preference tilts toward the outlying planned shopping center. If the downtown inner cities of America are rebuilt, if more mass transit systems are developed as is increasingly proposed, and if the automobile, because of continuously rising fuel costs, becomes less used as a major shopping vehicle, the downtown trading center may be revitalized as more people move from the suburbs back to the metropolitan inner-city areas.

As shown in Table 5-3, in 1970 almost twice as many people lived within Standard Metropolitan Statistical Areas as lived outside these geographic boundaries. Of the total SMSA population of 139.4 million, 116.9 million or 84 per cent lived in urbanized areas. One unexpected result of the use of SMSA for the portrayal of metropolitan data has been to exaggerate the impression of widespread area growth of American metropolitan centers and to give the impression that there is a heavy concentration of our population in inner cities. Despite emphasis on the fact that some SMSA counties unavoidably include extensive rural areas, there is a tendency to assume that most SMSA territory as shown in Table 5-3 is urbanizing, if not already urbanized. Strong evidence to counteract such an inference is the low average density of the portions of SMSA outside urbanized areas—64 per square mile, not much greater than the national average of 57. If the population and area of the remaining urban territory (places of 2,500 or more in SMSA but outside urbanized areas) were to be subtracted, the density of the rural SMSA population would drop below 50 per square mile.

If present trends continue, however, energy and capital shortages may curtail the shift in population to outlying suburbs. Rising costs of driving to urban places of employment combined with skyrocketing costs of new house construction may confine population shifts to close-in suburbs of standard metropolitan areas.

In summary, population has tended to move from rural areas, especially farms, to the large metropolitan areas located outside the major urban or central cities. These trends have significance for the retailer's market opportunity for several reasons. Basically, as population has tended to concentrate in the large metropolitan areas, it is probable that employment in retail stores has increased less rapidly than it would have had population

TABLE 5-2 Population by Selected Residence Categories: United States, 1970

AREA	POPULATION, 1970 (THOUSANDS)	PER CENT OF U.S. TOTAL
Total population	203,212	100.0
Urban population	149,325	73.5
Urbanized areas	118,447	58.3
Central cities of urbanized areas	63,922	31.5
Urban fringe:		
Places of 2,500 or more	38,612	19.0
Other urbanized territory	15,912	7.8
Places of 2,500 or more outside urbanized areas	30,878	15.2
Rural population	153,887	26.5
Nonfarm	45,591	22.4
Farm	8,287	4.1

[1] Nonfarm and farm populations are based on a 20 per cent sample and hence do not add exactly to rural population total.

SOURCE: U.S. Bureau of the Census, 1970 Census of Population, Vol. I, U.S. Summary, Tables 4 and 68.

TABLE 5-3 Population, Land Area, and Density of Standard Metropolitan Statistical Areas and Urbanized Areas: United States, 1970

AREA	POPULATION (THOUSANDS)	LAND AREA (SQUARE MILES)	DENSITY (POPULATION PER SQUARE MILE)
United States....	203,212	3,536,855	57
Inside SMSA...........	139,419	387,616	360
Urbanized areas.......	116,882	34,391	3,399
Other..............	22,537	353,225	64
Urban...........	6,125	(NA)	(NA)
Rural............	16,412	(NA)	(NA)
Outside SMSA.........	63,793	3,149,239	20
Urbanized areas.....	1,565	690	2,268
Other..............	62,228	3,148,549	20
Urban...........	24,753	(NA)	(NA)
Rural............	37,475	(NA)	(NA)
Urbanized areas.......	118,447	35,081	3,376
Outside urbanized areas	84,765	3,501,774	24

NA Not available.
SOURCE: U.S. Bureau of the Census, 1970 Census of Population, Vol. I, U.S. Summary, Table 17 and Appendix A, Table E; and Census Bureau records.

remained more dispersed. More retail stores are required per unit of population to serve smaller cities and rural areas than are necessary for larger cities. Moreover, sales volume in relation to population tends to be higher in the medium-sized and small cities than in the largest ones.

Consumer Mobility

A shifting population results in many changes in the composition of consumption expenditures. There is evidence to suggest that a move from farm to urban places is a force for a higher ratio of spending to disposable income, for example. Furthermore, a mobile population is, in itself, a factor which affects the demand characteristics of those who move or change their residences over time. Table 5-4 gives some indication of the percentage of the population that moves within a given period. Observe that "geographic mobiles," as they are sometimes called, are those basically in their early twenties to the early forties. This is the age period of upward economic progression, career establishment, household formation and consumer capital goods acquisition, i.e., housing, autos, home furnishings, major appliances, etc. Changing one's residence creates a need for goods and services and this in turn bodes well for the retailer's market opportunity.

To summarize our discussion concerning changing demographics, we should acknowledge that the adult population of the nation is becoming increasingly dominated by persons under 35 years of age. Such a shift has noticeable implications on consumption and spending habits. Very likely,

TABLE 5-4   Per Cent of Population Moving Within and Between Counties in 1
Year, by Age: United States, Average for 1966 to 1971

AGE	POPULATION (THOUSANDS)	PER CENT MOVING WITHIN COUNTIES	PER CENT MOVING BETWEEN COUNTIES
Total, 1 year old and over.........	195,703	11.8	6.7
1–4 years........................	15,084	18.0	10.2
5–9 years........................	20,677	12.1	7.0
10–14 years......................	20,177	9.4	5.2
15–19 years......................	17,092	11.7	6.0
20–24 years......................	14,621	25.0	16.7
25–29 years......................	12,593	20.6	12.5
30–34 years......................	11,104	13.9	8.5
35–39 years......................	11,315	10.6	6.3
40–44 years......................	12,134	8.7	4.4
45–49 years......................	11,964	7.6	3.6
50–54 years......................	10,904	6.7	3.0
55–59 years......................	9,722	6.4	2.7
60–64 years......................	8,208	5.6	2.8
65 years and over................	19,208	5.8	2.5

SOURCE: U.S. Bureau of the Census, unpublished data averaged from successive March Current Population Surveys, 1966–71. Survey questions referred to mobility status during preceding 12 months.

this shift could have a depressing overall effect on the demand for personal services. Young adults are more prone to goods than to services. The great increase in number of new households that will take place during the next ten years will create a demand for items for which the family is the consuming unit, such as housing, furniture, and other consumer durables. As we move along the time continuum, however, a more normal age distribution of the population will be achieved and past trends in consumption expenditures will probably be resumed.

market segments based on demographic characteristics

As we discovered earlier, there are advantages to segmenting a market opportunity. For that matter, the concept of market opportunity is meaningful only when viewed from a segmentation strategy point of view. It would be meaningless for most sellers to study every individual buyer or potential buyer in the market place and attempt to tailor an offer variation or total merchandising strategy to meet the needs of each individual buyer. On the contrary, the more efficient approach is for the seller to search for broad classes of buyers whose tastes and merchandise interests cluster rather closely, but differ from other broad classes whose merchandise tastes are dissimilar and subject to different appeals and motivations. Merchandise and marketing tastes are very likely to differ among different age groups or among those whose residences differ markedly, i.e., the rural versus the city dweller, or on the basis of some other demographic variable. Demographic and income variables are most often used by retail managers as a basis for segmenting their markets. They have generally been found to be a rather sound basis for market segmentation because they have proved to be good indicators of different degrees of buyer response. Two important new market segments have emerged as a result of the changing demographic structure of the United States; they are the teenage market and the senior citizen market.

The Teenage Market

Figure 5-1 indicates a great deal about the importance and significance of both the teenage (or youth market, as it is sometimes called) and the senior citizen markets. The growth in the 10- to 19-year segment of the total population will exceed that of the total population through 1980. Teenage expenditures for goods and services are expected to reach $30 billion by 1980, compared with $20 billion in 1970. Teenagers have a strong inclination to buy goods in addition to nondurables such as clothes, records, and other items of low unit-value. One study reported that nearly all teenage girls own a radio, 70 per cent own a phonograph, and nearly one third have their own personal television set.[3]

Much of the spending of the teenage market is, however, discretionary and is principally confined to nondurable goods. The teenage spender has often been associated with low-cost items such as soft drinks, phonograph records, home permanents, magazines, and lesser items of clothing and accessories. Many retail stores, however, are experimenting with teen centers in which the young customers are sometimes granted credit and exposed to a wider range of merchandising temptations. Retailers would be well advised to watch the spending movements and behavior of this young, yet reasonably affluent group.

The Senior Citizen Market

Some retail firms have found the senior citizen market a readily available and fertile field whose members are receptive to special and well-tailored product and service offer variations. A whole new class of product offerings, generally listed as geriatrics, has recently become available to be merchandised to this group. This product line includes general medicinal tonics, dietary supplements, digestive aids, cathartics, diuretics, oral and external analgesics and anti-rheumatics, and products for denture wearers.

Although population projections suggest that the proportion of old persons will remain relatively constant for the next quarter century (about 10 per cent of the total population), their absolute numbers will increase to about 27 million in 1990. In the future, an increasing number of older people will probably receive larger incomes through a widening participa-

---

[3] A study by *Seventeen* magazine, reported in *Merchandising Week* (August 9, 1965), p. 14.

tion in pension plans, social security, and other benefits. Health and medical plans such as Medicare will release savings and income for other consumption purposes. The upshot of all this is that these senior citizens will remain important customers for a longer period than was heretofore possible, and they will participate in consumption activities at a higher than subsistence level, which will therefore make them a market segment of continuing and increasing importance.

the hidden fallacy of population growth

There is no marketing magic in simple increases in population. As a matter of fact, the greatest problem facing the world today is the unchecked increase in population. Every economic and political system in the world is faced with the problem of how to feed and clothe its masses. The Western nations of the world with their sophisticated industrial and technological bases have not yet been confronted with the situation in which population increases have wiped out the productivity gains fostered by improved means of farming and industry in general.

If effective markets were only large masses of population, then China and India would be the largest and "best" markets in the world. However, most reasonably intelligent persons know that this simply is not the case. Every economy generates some measure—commonly known as GNP or Gross National Product—of its economic viability and virility. GNP is the value of all goods and services produced within a given economic system for a period of one year. The magnitude of a system's GNP will depend on many factors: the size and nature of the labor force, the use of capital, the kind of prevailing technology, and so on. The total GNP divided by the total population equals per capita GNP. Now, the point is that a rapidly expanding population can have a depressing effect on GNP if the system does not continue to increase its rate of productivity and therefore continually generate a higher level of GNP.

For example, if GNP had remained at the level of 1950, then with today's population per capita GNP would be much lower than would otherwise be the case. In short, increases in population do not automatically insure that prosperous business conditions will follow. Population, alone, does not create new markets, nor does it create the means of supplying the demand for the basic subsistence that the increase in population creates. The boon of most market situations is income, resulting from employment and productivity.

income and income-related factors affecting market opportunity

The economic changes witnessed in the United States during the last few decades have been phenomenal. The changes wrought, in turn, on the marketing scene have been no less amazing. The United States consumer

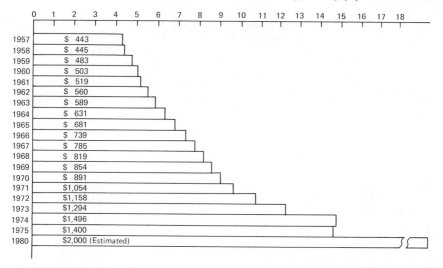

FIGURE 5-2   Trend of total business activity, Gross National Product (GNP). Seasonally adjusted annual rates.

Source: Compiled from U.S. Department of Commerce, Office of Business Economics, Survey of Current Business (Washington, D.C.: U.S. Government Printing Office). The 1980 figure is an extrapolation based upon the author's estimates.

for the most part is at an all-time high in terms of purchasing power and want-satisfying ability. During the 1950s the economy of the United States suddenly began to witness a profound and fundamental change.

Figure 5-2 is illustrative of the growth and dynamism of the overall economy and shows that the gross national product grew steadily during the 1950s, 1960s, and the early 1970s. In spite of the serious economic recession in late 1974 and 1975, the American economy shows every sign of continued growth, though such growth will in all likelihood not manifest itself in the same exuberant manner as it did during the decade of the "soaring sixties." Directly allied with this increase in overall economic activity is consumer buying power, which has also grown quite remarkably. Again, in spite of double-digit inflation in the mid-1970s and the economic recession that led to a rather dramatic dip in productivity, employment, and purchasing power, especially among the lower class, blue-collar segment of society, overall income and consumption levels have continued to show a vital buoyancy which, of course, bodes well for retail merchandisers. Table 5-5 depicts this growth in the consumer's ability to purchase goods.

From 1964 to 1974, disposable personal income increased from $436.6 billion to $966.5 billion. In other words, in just ten years, disposable personal income more than doubled. However, this was truly a remarkable growth period in the economy and, of course, in the market opportunity of retail merchandisers.

Personal consumption expenditures during this same period increased from $401.4 billion to $870 billion. Disposable personal income (DPI) is a very important barometer of marketing activity; it is of utmost significance

TABLE 5-5 Disposable Personal Income and Personal Consumption Expenditures for 1957 Through 1975 (seasonally adjusted annual rates)

YEAR	DPI[a] (BILLIONS OF DOLLARS)	PCE[b] (BILLIONS OF DOLLARS)	PCE/DPI[c] (PER CENT)
1957	308.8	285.2	92.35
1958	317.9	293.5	92.32
1959	337.3	313.8	93.03
1960	354.2	328.2	92.65
1961	363.6	338.0	92.95
1962	384.4	355.4	92.45
1963	402.6	373.8	92.84
1964	436.6	401.4	91.93
1965	469.1	431.5	91.98
1966	505.3	464.9	92.00
1967	544.7	491.7	90.26
1968	590.0	535.8	90.81
1969	634.2	577.5	91.05
1970	687.8	615.8	89.53
1971	744.4	664.9	89.32
1972	802.5	729.0	90.84
1973	903.7	805.2	89.10
1974	966.5	870.0	90.01
1975*	964.4	868.5	90.05

[a] Disposable Personal Income.
[b] Personal Consumption Expenditures.
[c] Personal Consumption Expenditures divided by Disposable Personal Income.
SOURCE: Compiled from data contained in the same source listed for Figure 5-2. * 1975 data are estimated, based upon tentative data.

in analyzing variations in total consumption over periods of time and the demand for various categories of consumption at any particular period of time.

Disposable personal income is the wherewithal that supports consumer expenditures, or what is more recently called *personal outlays*.[4] Personal outlays subtracted from disposable personal income equals personal savings. However, the major component of personal outlays is personal consumption expenditures. As can be seen from Table 5-5, personal consumption expenditures had been running about 92 per cent of disposable personal income. In the 1966–1967 period, however, there was some variation from the longer-run trend; and in 1967, the savings rate had risen to slightly over 7 per cent. This may seem insignificant, but it is important to realize that a change in the savings rate of one percentage point is roughly equivalent

[4] The concept of personal outlays was introduced for the first time in the revised computations of the national income and product accounts published in 1965. Previously, personal consumption expenditures plus personal savings equaled disposable personal income. In addition to personal consumption expenditures, the other items included in personal outlays are interest paid by consumers and personal transfer payments to foreigners, which basically include purchases of goods and services from foreign sources.

to 5.5 billion dollars in consumer spending. Thus, changes in the propensity to save and the propensity to consume can have serious effects on the level of spending and, therefore, on the market opportunity for retailers. When consumers choose to spend a larger amount of total current income, we say that there has been an increase in their average propensity to consume, which is defined as

$$\frac{C}{Y}, \text{ where } C = \text{consumption outlays, } Y = \text{income.}$$

The consumer has two major options to exercise regarding income: it can be spent or saved. If he chooses not to spend it, it automatically becomes savings. Therefore the average propensity to save is defined as

$$\frac{S}{Y}, \text{ where } S = \text{savings, } Y = \text{income.}$$

Very often a change in the average propensity to spend (or save) reflects a great deal about the emotional mood of a consuming group. That is, the average propensity to spend (or save) is affected by both economic and psychological expectations, and quite often psychological expectations are the real villain.

For example, in late 1974 and early 1975, confronted by both tapering incomes and other economic and political uncertainties, consumers cut back sharply in their spending. There was a precipitous cut in spending for automobiles. Sales of new cars plunged to a rate of about 7.5 million units in early 1975, down from the early 1974 rate of about 10.3 million units. The consumers' concern with unemployment and runaway inflation affects their psychological expectations and hence, their propensity to consume. Such a situation seemed to characterize the mid-1970s. The general effect was a considerable curtailment of expenditures for consumer durable goods. However, in an economy such as ours, characterized by a sizable portion of disposable personal income devoted to the acquisition of consumer durable products, the savings rate will show greater variability than in circumstances where durable goods purchases are of less importance. By the same token, the larger the stock of durables consumers have, the greater the variability of saving and spending behavior.

Major Consumption Categories Related to Disposable Income

Table 5-6 shows the major consumption categories related to disposable income for a series of years. Several important implications are shown and some general pattern in expenditures for various categories can be seen. It will be observed once again that durable goods manifest some volatility in terms of the percentage of income spent in this category. This would, of course, be in keeping with our earlier observations.

Another significant observation centers around expenditures for non-durable goods as a percentage of disposable income. You will notice that there has been a steady decrease in the proportions spent for food and beverages, and for clothing items including shoes. As is the usual case for

TABLE 5-6   Major Types of Personal Consumption Expenditures as Percentage of Disposable Personal Income, United States

ITEM	1950	1960	1964	1974
Disposable personal income[a]	100.0%	100.0%	100.0%	100.0%
Less: Savings	6.3	4.9	6.1	7.3
Personal consumption expenditures	92.3	92.9	91.5	90.0
Durable goods, total	14.7	12.9	13.5	13.3
Automobiles and parts	6.3	5.7	5.9	5.6
Furniture and household equipment	6.8	5.4	5.7	6.1
Other expenditures	1.6	1.8	1.9	2.0
Nondurable goods, total	47.4	43.2	40.7	38.8
Food and beverages	26.0	23.0	21.2	18.9
Clothing and shoes	9.5	7.8	7.6	7.6
Gasoline and oil	2.6	3.5	3.2	3.8
Other expenditures	9.3	8.9	8.7	8.3
Services, total	30.2	36.8	37.3	37.6
Housing	10.3	13.2	13.7	13.2
Household operation	4.6	5.7	5.6	5.6
Transportation	3.0	3.1	2.7	2.7
Other expenditures	12.3	14.7	15.4	17.3

[a] Personal consumption expenditures plus savings will not equal 100 per cent (total disposable income), for interest payments and personal foreign transfer payments are excluded from this analysis.

SOURCE: Survey of Current Business, *U.S. Department of Commerce, Office of Business Economics, Washington, D.C. 1951, 1961, 1965, and 1975.*

expenditures in these categories, when incomes go up, the percentage spent for these items tends to go down. A person can eat only so much food or wear so many garments. When incomes increase, the normal practice is for considerable "trading up" in these categories. That is, better and more expensive foodstuffs of higher caloric content are purchased, as well as more expensive items of clothing.

You will recall our comments in Chapter 1 about the current explosion in the service expenditure category. Table 5-6 more or less bears out this contention. During 1930, services as a per cent of DPI were at an all time high. After falling to a low of almost 30 per cent in 1950, the services expenditure category as a whole, however, had nearly regained its peak by 1964.

The Changing Distribution of Incomes

In addition to the quantitative changes in disposable income and personal consumption expenditures in the United States, another far-reaching and significant change has taken place in the distribution of income shares.

In the first three decades of this century, the United States began to develop its first so-called mass market. In 1900, almost half the family units in the United States had less than $2,000 of income in 1959 prices. During the 1920s, the most significant market development was the creation of a sizable lower-middle income class based on family units in the $2,000 to $4,000 income class. By 1954, over 40 per cent of all family units had an after-tax income between $4,000 and $7,500, and their income was about 40 per cent of the total.

In 1965, 66 per cent of all families had incomes in excess of $5,000 per year. By 1980, 82 per cent of all families will have incomes in excess of $5,000 annually. Another dramatic insight concerning the redistribution of income shown by Table 5-7 is the fact that in 1965, 22 per cent of families in the United States had incomes in excess of $10,000 per year. By 1980 the figure will approach nearly 30 per cent. Thus, the income revolution that began in the earlier postwar years will be essentially completed, with the income pyramid turned upside down. What we have typically called poverty will be virtually eliminated; only 6 per cent of all families will have incomes under $3,000—the government cutoff line for poverty—as against about 15 per cent today.

Helping to swell family income is the increasing incidence of working wives. In 1974, over 20 million wives were on the nation's payrolls; about 40 per cent of American families were characterized as having a working wife. In families in which the wife worked, about 40 per cent of the family spending power was attributable to her income. Interestingly, half of all families in the United States in the $10,000 to $15,000 income bracket have attained this level of income because the wife is working. These patterns of income and their resulting consequences to retailers will likely continue for these reasons: (1) Young families will become about half again as numerous as they are now and (2) the configuration of the prevailing income distribution curve indicates more young families will achieve higher income levels. Today, relatively many young families are clustered in the $7,000 to $10,000 income category. Given the overall improvement in earnings expected in the course of the next ten years, many families will be

TABLE 5-7   Per Cent of Families in Income Class (1965 dollars) and the Changing Income Pyramid

$10,000 and Above	2%	22%	28%			
7,500–9,999	3%	18%	27%			
5,000–7,499	11%	26%	28%			
4,000–4,999	7%	9%	8%			
3,000–3,999	14%	8%	6%			
2,000–2,999	21%	7%	2%			
1,000–1,999	24%	6%	1%			
Under $1,000	18%	4%				
	1930	1965	1985	1930		1985
					Income Pyramid	

SOURCE: Compiled from data from Survey of Current Business, U.S. Department of Commerce, Office of Business Economics, Washington, D.C. Figures from 1985 are estimated but based upon data from same source.

found in the upper income brackets. In summary, the general improvement in economic fortunes expected for the years ahead (in conjunction with population growth) will make for a pronounced increase in the number of young higher income families. By 1975, young and affluent homes—in which the head of household is under 35 and incomes exceed $10,000—will account for an estimated 15 per cent (based on present-day dollars) of total buying power. There is little doubt that this well-educated, mobile, and affluent group will comprise a very important market segment and market opportunity.

Family Expenditures for Major Categories of Consumption

Table 5-8 is an exceedingly rich source of information pertaining to expenditure patterns of families in the United States for various income categories. Our thesis has been that consumption is largely a function of income. Therefore, the way a family purchases goods and services and especially the "package" of goods and services it purchases generally ought to reflect that family's income bracket as well as certain other considerations related to income, such as life cycle, social class, and life style.

It appears obvious from the data that a previous generalization bearing on income and consumption for food would be borne out, namely, that as income increases, the percentage spent for food tends to decline. Notice, however, that the absolute amount spent for food increases rather significantly as we move from lower to the higher income families.

As family income increases, the percentage spent for occupancy and operation of households (when viewed in the aggregate) shows a pattern of consistent increase from the lowest to the highest income bracket. However, when related to total income, the percentage for this category declines markedly as each higher level is reached.

Clothing expenditures also reveal some interesting characteristics. Clothing expenditures are an increasing percentage of total expenditures. But in terms of income, once household income reaches $3,000 to $4,999, the relative amount allotted for clothing declines. As one might expect, when the higher income brackets are reached, a greater variety of clothing is purchased and the quality purchased tends to go up.

The automobile as the major form of family transportation tends to siphon off large amounts of family income. As a share of total expenditures, automobile expenses increase consistently until the $15,000 bracket is reached. But in terms of income, the relative amount spent for automobile transportation declines once an annual income of $3,000 to $4,999 is reached.

From our observations regarding expenditure patterns by American families for different income categories, it seems safe to generalize that *as income grows, there are marked shifts in the demand manifested for different categories of goods and services.* Expenditure patterns of families in different income categories have been observed for many decades, the earliest study possibly being that of Ernst Engel, a German statistician, who in 1857 compared the budgets of individual working-class families.

He observed that while rising family income meant generally rising spending in all categories, the following qualifications were to be considered:[5]

1. The proportion of income spent on food tended to decline.
2. The proportion of income spent on housing and household operation tended to remain constant.
3. The proportion spent on other categories, such as clothing, transportation, recreation, health, education, and savings tended to increase.

These generalizations are usually referred to as Engel's Laws of Consumption and have been generally validated in several subsequent budget studies.

It has been shown that income not only has an effect on the amount and kinds of goods purchased, but that the amount of income also affects shopping attitudes and frustrations. Higher income shoppers tend to put more emphasis on being able to get what they want, when they want it. Members of the upper-income group are more experienced in shopping and therefore more discriminating in their desires. These shoppers feel more secure in their knowledge and shopping experience, and are therefore less likely to rely on the retailer for advice. In short, upper-income shoppers are more independent, less loyal to a given merchant and to particular brands of merchandise, and they are more demanding in terms of store services.

Other Related Concepts

Income has been shown to be an important determinant of consumption, and consumption activities are the real crux of the market opportunity problem; it would therefore seem to behoove the retail manager to become as knowledgeable as possible concerning income groups and their respective consumption patterns. However, several other factors relate to income and when reviewed in this relationship help to refine our analysis of consumption-expenditure patterns, thus more sharply pinpointing the market opportunity. Income alone is not a totally sufficient indicator of consumption-expenditure patterns; for a really refined indicator, one must consider other relevant factors.

The Life Cycle Concept. To understand more fully an individual's consumption and buying behavior, it may be necessary to consider what stage in the life cycle he has reached, rather than his specific age. Family life cycle (FLC) is generally regarded as having more explanatory power than age or income alone. People have been observed to change both their attitudes and their behavior as they grow older, but these changes most often reflect not only increased age, but the influence of age upon the individual's family memberships.

One writer has described the importance and the effects of life cycle concepts in the following way:

[5] Ernst Engel, "Die Productions- und Consumptionsverhältnisse des Königreichs Sachsen," *Zeitschrift des Statistischen Bureaus des Königlich Sächsischen Ministeriums des Innern*, Nos. 8–9 (November 22, 1857), p. 8.

TABLE 5-8 Family Spending Patterns by Income Class for 1973–1974. Average Annual Expenditures, All Nonfarm Families and Single Consumers

ITEM	TOTAL	FAMILY INCOME					
		UNDER $3,000	$3,000– 5,000	$5,000– 7,500	$7,500– 10,000	$10,000– 15,000	$15,000 & OVER
Per cent distribution:							
All families*............	100.0	22.4	20.8	26.2	16.1	10.7	3.7
All persons.............	100.0	14.9	19.7	29.0	18.8	13.2	4.4
Total expenditures†....	100.0	8.9	15.6	27.1	21.2	18.0	9.1
Average family size....	3.2	2.1	3.0	3.5	3.7	3.9	3.8
				Dollars			
Total expenditures†........	5,152	2,043	3,859	5,315	6,788	8,679	12,687
Food...................	1,259	600	1,015	1,318	1,624	1,970	2,550
Prepared at home......	1,006	511	835	1,088	1,290	1,484	1,762
Away from home.......	253	89	180	230	333	486	788
Alcoholic beverages......	81	21	55	81	117	152	242
Tobacco...............	93	42	84	105	123	126	134
Housing, household operations....	1,236	620	968	1,263	1,552	1,889	3,002
Shelter...............	688	349	543	710	866	1,040	1,595
Fuel, light, etc........	250	153	208	263	311	348	448
Other operations......	298	118	216	290	375	502	959
Housefurnishings, equipment.....	269	83	185	284	376	476	690
Appliances...........	76	27	60	90	100	117	126
Furniture.............	78	19	53	81	116	146	192
Other furnishings......	115	37	72	113	160	213	372

Clothing and accessories	525	145	348	528	720	1,001	1,550
Men's and boys'	190	45	123	199	270	366	526
Women's, girls', etc.	266	81	177	259	358	509	833
Materials, services	68	19	48	70	93	127	189
Transportation	781	176	560	848	1,093	1,450	1,891
Automobile	700	143	501	783	1,005	1,293	1,541
Other	81	33	59	65	89	157	350
Medical care	342	174	269	350	425	539	771
Services	269	128	208	274	335	436	652
Supplies	73	47	60	77	90	104	119
Personal care	148	61	118	156	194	241	312
Services	67	26	50	66	86	119	179
Supplies	81	36	68	90	107	121	133
Recreation, equipment	205	48	133	201	291	419	597
Reading, education	100	26	55	88	126	215	440
Other expenditures	113	47	69	93	147	201	508

* Includes single consumers.
† For current consumption.
SOURCE: A Guide to Consumer Markets 1974–1975, The Conference Board, New York, 1975, p. 173.

The life cycle indicates temporality. Life is full of separate units of time. For example, in a family there is a period when there are no children and a period when children are growing up. There is a time when sons and daughters leave the home and a period characterized by the death of a spouse. Behavior patterns vary considerably as people pass through various temporal stages of the life cycle. The demand for various services and for durable and nondurable goods also varies with the stages. Durable goods are generally more important during the early stages of marriage while services take on increasing importance as children grow up and leave the home.[6]

Thus, the family life cycle concept has an important bearing on expenditure and shopping patterns. Households with young children are likely to reflect a much different pattern of expenditure than households in which the children have grown up or in which there never were children (sometimes called the empty nest concept). A family whose head is the male wage earner between 35 and 40, with three children, ages 10, 7, and 5 will probably have one pattern of expenditure; a household comprised of a man and wife 60 and 55 years of age, respectively, will have a different pattern of expenditure, as will a household composed of a man and wife 25 and 23, respectively, with an infant child—*even though the incomes of all three families are identical on nearly the same.*

Social Class. The Warnerian idea that six social classes constitute the basic division of American society has offered many attractions to market analysts and retail managers, who are dissatisfied with simple income categories or census-type occupational categories and feel a need for a more meaningful classification of categorizing and segmenting demand and analyzing market opportunity.

The six social classes referred to are those which W. Lloyd Warner and his associates observed in their analysis of such diverse communities as Newberryport, Massachusetts; Natchez, Mississippi; Morris, Illinois; Kansas City, Missouri; and Chicago, Illinois.

These social classes are groups of people who are similar to each other in many respects regarding prestige and community status. Supposedly, they are people who readily and regularly interact among themselves in both formal and informal ways; they form a class to the extent that they share the same goals and ways of looking at life. Warner's Index of Status Characteristics has been widely used in social research. In this index, Warner has selected four variables upon which class determinations are founded. These are source of income, occupation, dwelling area, and house type.[7] Around these criteria Warner presented a sixfold classification of social classes. Starting from the top down, they are

1. Upper-upper.
2. Lower-upper.
3. Upper-middle.

---

[6] Gerald Zaltman, *Marketing: Contributions from the Behavioral Sciences,* Harcourt Brace Jovanovich, Inc., New York, 1965, p. 12.

[7] Lloyd Warner, M. Meeker, and K. Eells, *Social Class in America,* Social Research, Inc., Chicago, 1949.

4. Lower-middle.
5. Upper-lower.
6. Lower-lower.

Social class concepts have been rather widely used as a means of analyzing consumer spending behavior and as a means of segmenting markets. Martineau has commented on the social class concept as a device for consumer analysis and research:

> The friends we choose, the neighborhoods we live in, the way we spend and save our money, the educational plans we have for our children are determined in large degree along social class lines. A rich man is not just a poor man with more money. He probably has different ideals, different personality forces, different church membership, and many different notions of right and wrong, all largely stemming from social class differentials. With its disciplinary pressures of approval and disapproval, belonging versus ostracism, social class is a major factor shaping the individual's style of life.[8]

Thus for a retail firm to operate effectively, it may be necessary to design a retail strategy around the social class that fits one's product and service offering. The many socioeconomic changes that have so recently taken place in our society (i.e., increased income, better education, more leisure time, and movements to suburbia), have cut across traditional class lines and some researchers have concluded that social class distinctions have been obscured by rising incomes and educational levels. Others, however, have found social class a significant factor in determining certain aspects of consumer behavior.

Life Style. Life style is another income-related concept that has been suggested as a valuable indicator of certain aspects of consumer behavior. The reader will notice also that *life style* is closely related to the concept of social class. For example, the fact that a person is a member of a certain social class may predispose him to possess a particular life style. Life style has been defined in the following manner:

> It refers to the distinctive or characteristic mode of living, in its aggregative and broadest sense, of a whole society or segment thereof. It is concerned with those unique ingredients or qualities which describe the style of life of some culture or group, and distinguish it from others. It embodies the patterns that develop and emerge from the dynamics of living in a society.
> Life style, therefore, is the result of such forces as culture, values, resources, license, and sanction. From one perspective, the aggregate of consumer purchases and the manner in which they are consumed reflect a society's life style.[9]

It would appear from the above statement that life style is a broader and much more comprehensive concept than either life cycle or social class. In

[8] Pierre Martineau, *Motivation in Advertising*, McGraw-Hill Book Company, New York, 1957, pp. 166–167.

[9] William Lazer, "Life Style Concepts and Marketing," in Stephen A. Greyser (ed.), *Proceedings of the Winter Conference of the American Marketing Association*, American Marketing Association, Chicago, 1964, p. 130.

our analysis of consumer behavior, as we concentrate more on the environmental and psychological forces that affect this behavior, we should develop a more refined understanding of life style concepts and their role as a predictive and explanatory device for understanding consumer behavior. This understanding should contribute greatly to a better matching of our product and service offering to perceived market opportunities. We shall explore the concept of life style, or what is more frequently referred to today as psychographic analysis, more fully in Chapter 6.

market segments based on income

Obviously, a retail management system might very well perceive its market opportunity within some kind of income or income-related framework. Several market segments based on income and income-related concepts have been suggested, some implicitly and some quite explicitly, the two most polarized being the high-income market and the low-income market.

Many stores throughout the nation have structured their merchandising strategies in an attempt to project an image compatible with and catering to the high-income recipients of their trading areas. Such stores as Gump's in San Francisco and Neiman Marcus in Dallas are good examples.

Market segmentation has been characterized as a situation in which differences in demand elasticity of buyers exist; therefore, it is possible to divide the market opportunity into smaller and smaller units. Income, of course, is one of the foremost determinants of market opportunity. Most stores do not attempt to cater to one specific income level alone, but rather, given the overlap in demand characteristics of various market segments based upon income, to merchandise to several related or clustered income groups.

In the United States today, one out of every four, or more than 17 million, households had earnings in excess of $15,000. Quietly and subtly, we are experiencing a realignment of income distribution of dramatic dimensions. This realignment will affect merchandising strategies and will work to cause retail merchandisers to modify their overall store images as well as their merchandising policies in order that they may stay abreast of their market opportunities.

Profiling the Income Class Markets

Income, as we have learned, not only is an important determinant of the absolute levels of consumption, but it affects the quality of consumption, i.e., the kinds of goods consumed, the kinds of stores patronized, the use of credit, and many other factors of concern to retail merchandisers. The income class markets can be briefly delineated and a few salient comments pertaining to each will be made.[10]

[10] See Fabien Linden, "The Characteristics of Class," *The Conference Board Record* (October 1973), pp. 61–64.

Household Income Under $5,000. One out of every four households is in this income bracket. It is a bracket in which many current social problems are encountered. Per capita income in this bracket is about $1,300. All told, this group accounts for 6 per cent of total income. Persons whose incomes fall into this category live at best a marginal existence. The major portion of their incomes is spent for food, clothing, and housing. In many instances, this category is composed of lone individuals, often female, and often over 65 years of age. Their incomes are spent for consumption maintenance largely related to survival. They shop neighborhood and ghetto stores, pay cash, shop frequently, and live virtually a hand-to-mouth existence.

Household Income $5,000 to $10,000. One out of every four households is in this earning bracket, but the characteristics of this group differ significantly from the previous group. Here the household in most instances is made up of a husband and wife, and in many instances, children. Per capita income in this bracket is approximately $2,600 annually. About 18 per cent of all spending power accrues to those in this bracket. The incidence of working wives is low. The educational level is also low, and most are employed as unskilled, blue-collar workers. However, some clerical and service personnel are also heavily represented here. There are few funds for discretionary expenditure. As in the previous category, expenditures for necessities such as food, clothing, and housing predominate. Shopping is confined largely to low-price, mass-merchandising institutions located in the immediate area. Much shopping is also confined to the neighborhood and ghetto store. When credit is extended, it is typically a time-credit or installment-credit plan, and usurious rates of interest are not unusual. It has even been suggested that in some instances higher prices are charged by stores in low-income trading areas than are charged in higher-income areas. For example, Caplovitz found that New York City poor families paid higher prices than the well-to-do for consumer durables.[11]

Household Income $10,000 to $15,000. Nearly a quarter of all homes are in this income class. There is a high incidence of working wives in this category. Most households in this category consist of a husband and a wife (45 per cent of whom are bringing home a paycheck) and children. The average age of this category is younger than the preceding two categories. The educational level is also higher. Half the persons in this category are blue-collar workers, but there is also an increasing incidence of better educated white-collar service workers. Persons in this earning bracket are more frequently found in the suburbs and the proportion residing in non-metropolitan areas is small. Shopping is done mostly in suburban shopping centers in mass-merchandising, largely price-oriented discount and general merchandise department stores. There is much emphasis on discretionary consumption and some expenditures are made less for products of instrumental significance than for symbolic significance. There is a higher incidence of both store-loyal and brand-loyal customers in this category than

[11] David Caplovitz, *The Poor Pay More,* The Free Press, New York, 1963.

in previous categories discussed. Store and bank credit cards that feature revolving credit are increasingly used. However, autos as well as most major durables are purchased on installment-credit plans.

Household Income $15,000 to $25,000. Some 13 million households, or about one out of every five of the nation's homes, are in this class. Per capita income now exceeds $5,000. Again, there is a high incidence of working wives; as a matter of fact, in well over half the homes the wife is employed. This is an extremely important income segment for retailers, for it accounts for almost a third of all consumer purchasing power. Most of those in this category are in the middle years of the life cycle. The educational level is relatively high; 40 per cent of all household heads in this category have had some college. White-collar workers constitute 55 per cent of this category, and blue-collar workers, about 28 per cent. As would be expected, about half of these homes are located in the suburbs. This category is the main quality market for most United States retailers. The major downtown department stores and their branches, the better specialty shops, and the better quality mass merchandisers such as Sears, J. C. Penney and others are most frequented by these shoppers. This category constitutes the major income category for items such as better clothing, fancy foods, appliances, and capital goods items such as color television sets, luxury autos, boats, and home furnishings.

Household Income $25,000 to $50,000. Less than 6 per cent of the homes are in this bracket, yet they have at their disposal 15 per cent of total earnings. The incidence of working wives declines in this bracket, and persons in this bracket are most frequently in their middle years, or between 45 and 64. In this category, 53 per cent of all households are located in the suburbs. Educational attainment is high, and employment is most likely to be in the managerial and professional occupations. In all, about 80 per cent hold white collar jobs. Consumption and expenditure patterns are not too different from the previous category. More money, of course, is likely to be spent on housing, automobiles, second homes, boats, and home furnishings. Invariably, purchasing is concentrated among better quality stores that emphasize assortments and services, as opposed to strictly price. Customers in this category are often image-conscious and brand-specific in their purchasing.

Household Income $50,000 and More. This is the rich or upper-crust segment of American society. It consists of about half a million homes, or less than 1 per cent of the nation's population. Just slightly over 4 per cent of total personal income flows to this group. The incidence of working wives drops to 29 per cent. There are comparatively few young households in this category. Among those in this category, there is a tendency to relocate in the big city. The proportion living in the suburbs declines to 48 per cent. About 54 per cent of all household heads in this group hold a college degree. Truly, this category is a market share comprised of affluent, aware, discerning consumers. They demand exceptional products and services and patronize those specialized retailing institutions that provide them. As would be expected, their consumption, while consisting of large amounts of high-quality goods, is highly service-oriented as well. They spend large amounts, as did the previous category, for travel and entertainment.

As we have seen, population and income are important determinants of consumption and hence, market opportunity. In examining the profile of market segments based upon income, as we have just done, it becomes rather obvious, however, that income alone is not the single most important determinant of consumption. Other behavioral factors, which transcend the basic demographic characteristics of consumer markets, must also be explored.

QUESTIONS FOR STUDY, REFLECTION, AND REVIEW

1. How do the increases in population present market opportunities for the retailing system?
2. In what way does the change from a rural to an urban economy affect the retailing system?
3. Why is the household considered an important part of the retail manager's total market opportunity?
4. What are some of the important factors that have caused the movement from the inner cities to the outlying centers or suburbs?
5. What is the relationship between market segmentation and factors such as population or income?
6. Why is the teenage market becoming an important market segment for some retailers?
7. Why is the senior citizen market becoming a more attractive market segment for some retailers?
8. What is the importance of disposable personal income as a barometer of marketing activity?
9. What are some important generalizations that can be made about family expenditures as related to income?
10. What effects do composition of family and occupation of head of household have upon family consumption patterns?

6

understanding consumer behavior

It is not enough for retail managers to study market opportunity on a nonpersonal basis, using such questions as How many people are there? Where do they live? How much income do they earn? *Instead, it is necessary for retail managers to study consumer behavior with a view toward gaining an understanding of consumer habits and motivations in order that management might be better able to predict changes in behavior, tastes, and attitudes and therefore build more effective and dynamic merchandising strategies.* A merchandising strategy built on assumptions pertaining to consumer tastes, motives, and behavior that are no longer true or operative is certainly not going to be an effective strategy in the sense that consumer needs are fulfilled and the market opportunity successfully tapped.

Because they stem largely from the existent social forces that surround them, consumer tastes and behavior are continually subject to change and modification. The retail manager cannot therefore treat consumer behavior as a constant in his decision processes, but instead must be ever aware of changes in taste and attitude. Only in this way can the retail firm serve its customers in the best and most profitable manner.

Years ago, when retailing was considerably less complex and of a much smaller scale, the individual merchant–decision maker was much closer to his customers, interacting with them on a face-to-face basis. This enabled him to have a firsthand knowledge of consumers. Today, given the much larger size of the average institution, the separation and specialization of activity, and the impersonal nature of some kinds of retailing operations, the key decision makers in the organization are far removed from their customers. Today's top retail managers have little opportunity to leave their offices and feel the goods or interact with customers on the sales floor. Nonetheless, the retailer must demonstrate his understanding of customer needs, motives, attitudes, and the other principal determinants of consumer behavior. The entire spectrum of the merchandising and marketing program depends on such an understanding. The effectiveness of merchandise selections, price and promotion policies, and location decisions hinges on how well the retailer understands his customers and how (on the basis of this understanding) he builds a total strategy to meet the needs of the perceived market target.

The retail manager must recognize at the outset that the success or failure of his merchandising strategy rests ultimately with the consumer or market for which his strategy has been designed. Consequently, most strategy formulations are based upon the assumption that consumer behavior can be either (1) analyzed and understood or (2) analyzed, understood, and modified. Both assumptions strongly dictate that the retailing manager know and understand what affects consumer behavior, i.e., how consumers learn; how impressions, opinions, and images can be modified; and how firms can successfully communicate their merchandising programs to the consumer.[1]

Most retailing programs and strategies continue to be built upon the seeming certainty of analysis regarding such consumer behavior as what they buy, when and how often, from what kinds of retailers, and how much they spend. These aspects of consumer behavior are generally referred to as buying habits. Many of today's retailers have a penchant for collecting market data; as a consequence, they have an overwhelming mass of data and information regarding the quantitative significance of certain markets. Although much of this demographic and descriptive information fills important gaps in the retailer's information structure, his retailing strategy continues to suffer from a lack of information related to the equally important psychographic dimension of customer analysis.

Too few retailers have come to realize that the American consumer can best be characterized in terms of these two important dimensions: demographic and psychographic. Increasingly, however, there is a growing recognition among retail merchandisers that consumers are affected by both their economic states, as signified by their income or buying power, and their social-psychological states, which are dictated by their occupation, their place of residence, and their life style. The retail consumer can be profiled neatly, as was done in the previous chapter, into categories of income, consumption, and occupation. We can describe markets in terms of numbers of people, where they live, how many families have working wives, and how many persons there are per household, but this is not a complete picture of the retail consumer, nor does it explain why he prefers particular items over others, or why he spends more for recreational equipment than for travel, or why the automobile is so central a feature in a given consumer group's purchasing-consumption behavior. Neat and precise statistical tables that reveal consumers' demographic characteristics will not tell the retailer much about his customers' buying habits, the influence and role of

[1] See Rom J. Markin, *Consumer Behavior*, Macmillan Publishing Co., Inc., New York, 1974.

emotions, bias, ideas, or value-orientation. Too much of the market research of retailers deals with only sterile reports that show where people are, what they do for a living, and the average age and earnings of the male head of the household. This information tells management little or nothing about why customers do or do not shop in his store, what new departments might be added or which ones dropped, why his customers prefer color and fashion dramatics in their goods acquisition, or why customers are trading up and demand better quality and more complete assortments of merchandise. Retailers need the answers to all these questions, and many of the answers lie in the realm not of demographics but of *psychographics,* which is concerned with an analysis of customers' activities, interests, and opinions. Retailers need a better understanding of consumer behavior. What is needed is an understanding of customer preferences and dispositions, attitudes, motivation, and other factors. Retailers need to understand all those broad spectrum economic, social, and psychological forces that affect consumption generally and retail merchandising specifically. In short, what is needed is a better grasp of the entire concept of consumer choice.

alternate theories of consumer choice

The problem of consumer choice (i.e., what products consumers buy, in what quantities, for what prices, when consumers buy, and most importantly, why consumers buy) has been studied by many different disciplines with varying results. In the following pages, several of these contributions of the various social sciences to the problem of consumer choice will be examined. In no instances are these solutions complete, but many of them offer models that are partial explanations of consumer behavior in regard to choosing products for consumption.

Most of the comprehensive theories of consumer choice have been built around concepts developed in the various fields of the social sciences, namely, economics, psychology, and sociology; therefore, an attempt is made here to relate an example of the type of thinking and the approach to problems which have been undertaken by each of these disciplines.

Economics

The economists have provided us with a rather widely adopted theory of consumer behavior based upon the concept of indifference curves, which represent different combinations of two goods, to which the consumer is indifferent. The consumer attempts to move to the highest indifference curve, limited by qualifying factors such as income and product price. The consumer is visualized as substituting one good for another until the highest level of equilibrium is achieved. Having reached this equilibrium point, he is spending his income in such a way that the last dollar spent on each kind of good results in the same additional satisfaction or marginal utility. Such an *economic man* employs the measuring rod of money as the psychic barometer of his consumption desires. Economic man is concerned with maximizing his utility, which he does by rationing his scarce economic resources over a number of alternative consumption options. Most of us are well aware of the shortcomings of this approach. It rules out the impact of motivation and social status of the consumer in question. Furthermore, it assumes that tastes are autonomous and that changes in taste may not occur, except those of an autonomous nature.

The main fact that emerges from a survey of the economic literature is the contrast between the detailed theory of the influence on demand of income and price in a static situation and the almost complete lack of concern with the way in which tastes and habits, as dictated by social status, affect consumer behavior.

Psychology

The psychologists have approached the problem of consumer choice and consumer behavior on the basis of observations and data usually subsumed under the rubrics of needs, desires, and motives. Such terms refer to something that apparently lies behind the observed behavior of people. The study of human behavior has characteristically been the domain of psychology; and inasmuch as modern psychology has been so profoundly affected and structured by the work of Sigmund Freud, it is small wonder that Freud's ideas have come to dominate almost exclusively the psychologists' thinking in regard to consumer choice behavior.

Freudian psychology orients itself around several key concepts. To a considerable extent it is a regressive psychology. It stresses man's hesitancy to grow up and mature. Its basic tenet is that man is largely ruled by the *id* facet of his personality, a facet that is infantile and impulsive. Freudian psychology is also a deterministic psychology, believing that the original cause of an act of behavior can be traced backward from the event itself. Finally, from the Freudian point of view, the basic motive force of human behavior is repressed guilt feelings related to unfulfilled or thwarted sexual desires.

The Freudian-oriented analyst of consumer choice most frequently views American consumers as bundles of daydreams, misty hidden yearnings, guilt complexes, irrational emotional blockages. We are image lovers given to impulsive and convulsive acts.[2]

As a result of Freudian insights, some rather strange explanations of consumer behavior have been postulated. For example, it has been suggested that

> Men want their cigars to be odoriferous, in order to prove that they (the men) are masculine.
>
> A woman is very serious when she bakes a cake because unconsciously she is going through the symbolic act of giving birth.
>
> A man buys a convertible as a substitute mistress.
>
> Men who wear suspenders are reacting to an unresolved castration complex.[3]

[2] Vance Packard, *The Hidden Persuaders,* David McKay Co., Inc., New York, 1957, p. 4.

[3] Philip Kotler, *Marketing Management: Analysis, Planning, and Control,* Prentice-Hall, Inc., Englewood Cliffs, N.J., 1972, p. 107.

One must seriously question the value of the Freudian approach in today's environment, because it largely ignores the factor of different existent situations, i.e., the role and influence of one's life style, place of residence, social status, and so on. Much of our recent investigation into behavior suggests serious flaws in the role of libidinous influences on behavior. Thus, in short, it is doubtful at best if we can generalize at all about overall consumer behavior on the basis and findings of Freudian analysis and investigation; furthermore, many of the basic premises of Freudian psychology are open to serious question and doubt.

Sociology

The sociologists have made many noteworthy contributions in terms of insights into consumer behavior. Several of these studies have been in connection with social stratification and reference groups as they influence buying, product, and store decisions.

Special attention should be called to a study that permits varying kinds of personal attitude. The popularity of a beverage among a man's friends can override his desire to stay slim and his moral objections to the beverage; but if he dislikes its taste, he is not likely to drink it, even if his friends do.[4]

Buying habits can also be used to characterize social position and conceptions of role. Thus, Stone has shown that isolated city dwellers prefer to buy in small stores because this provides them with personal contacts.[5] A number of activities are considered the sign of a good housewife by some women and old-fashioned by others: home sewing,[6] doing one's own laundering,[7] and shunning instant coffee.[8] Other sociologically oriented studies have focused upon the role of social class and the adoption of fashion merchandise, the comparative role of personal advice and influence versus advertising in affecting behavior, and the formation of attitudes and dispositions.

The sociologists have thus made some important contributions to the study and understanding of consumer behavior. However, many of the sociological studies (much the same as those of economics and psychology) have several important shortcomings. In many instances the methodology has inherent deficiencies. Terminology is often forced and without standards and little, if any, mention is made of the importance of the learning process as conditioned by personality and income over a period of time.

However, our knowledge of consumer behavior continues to grow apace. Marketers in general and retailers in particular have probably learned more

---

[4] Francis S. Bourne, "Group Influences in Marketing and Public Relations," in *Some Applications of Behavioural Research*, Rensis Likert and Samuel P. Hayes (eds.), Science and Society Series, UNESCO, New York, 1957, pp. 205–207.

[5] Gregory Stone, "City Shoppers and Urban Identification," *American Journal of Sociology*, Vol. 55 (July 1954), pp. 36–45.

[6] Joseph Newman, *Motivation Research and Marketing Management*, Harvard Graduate School of Business Administration, Division of Research, Boston, 1957, p. 313.

[7] American Marketing Association, *The Technique of Market Research*, McGraw-Hill Book Company, New York, 1936, p. 275.

[8] Mason Haire, Projective "Techniques in Market Research," *Journal of Marketing*, Vol. 14 (April 1960), pp. 649–656.

and acquired a better general understanding of the problem of consumer behavior in the past ten years than they had acquired in all the previous years of their inquiries. The reasons for this lie in the intensified effort and study given to the problem and in the more widespread use of the inter-disciplinary approach.

the social-psychological approach
to consumer behavior

As we have seen, there are many ways of looking at consumer behavior. Characteristically, it is viewed from the economic, sociological, and psychological points of view. Valuable insights have been obtained via each of these perspectives, and even more insight is to be gained by combining some of these approaches, e.g., the social-psychological approach, which looks at consumer behavior as a function of many factors. However, the central focus of consumer behavior, viewed in this context, is the concept of *motivation,* but in a social milieu. That is, motivation is a function of a host of individual drives or needs that result from several other factors such as *perception, cognition,* and *learning.* All these factors work interde-pendently within a social environment and affect behavior.

Social psychology is concerned with the study of the interaction processes of human beings. It recognizes that all people exist as a part of a dynamic and intimate transaction with their environment. This environment con-sists of all perceived things: other persons, objects, institutions, the entire psychological field as it is sometimes called, of the consumer. Social psy-chology emphasizes that persons exist within a social context and that all needs, motives, attitudes, values, interests, predispositions, and opinions are molded and shaped by the transactional nature of human beings living within the context of society. Furthermore, social psychology acknowledges that much behavior, including consumer behavior, results from a socializing process. Consumers are social beings who learn adaptive behavior as a result of being taught the ways of society.

Social psychology assumes two other major characteristics of human action. First, human action is motivated or goal directed; second, human action is integrated—that is, the individual's wants, emotions, perceptions, and cognitions operate in concert to influence his actions. It makes no difference whether we are studying the behavior of a man in the laboratory or the haberdashery or his performance on an intelligence test or his churchgoing habits; in effect, we are studying the behavior of a man as a participant in interpersonal behavior events. The effects of a man's past, present, and anticipated behavior events influence each of his activities, no matter how simple or apparently remote. What a man has been determines what he is. A consumer, like any man, is a product of his choices.

Social-Psychological Determinants
of Consumer Behavior

Consumer behavior within a framework of social psychology can be viewed largely as a function of four factors: cognition, perception, motivation, and learning. Let us briefly describe the first two of these factors and then spend somewhat more time in analyzing the role of the latter two in consumer behavior.

Cognition. Cognition is the process whereby we make sense out of what we see or perceive. Someone once said that, "We see only what we know." This reflects the role and importance of cognition—an organizing process of the mind. Cognition is the sum total of values, ideas, beliefs, and attitudes that we hold; and, when integrated into some meaningful pattern, it constitutes our total belief system. Cognitive processes are purposive in that they serve the individual in his attempts to satisfactorily achieve his needs. Cognitive processes are also regulatory inasmuch as they determine in large measure the direction and particular steps taken in the individual's attempts to attain satisfaction of the initiating need.

Perception. Perception is a phenomenon closely related to and dependent upon cognition. Perception is what we see, but it is not simply an experience requiring specific sense organ stimulation. Instead, it is the result of complex patterns of stimulation filtered through our own unique and individual cognitive processes. It therefore reflects our past experience and present attitudes and predispositions. Thus, when a customer enters a store she is likely to perceive things that she either does or does not see. What she sees (i.e., the physical stimulation bombarded toward her sense organs) are a building, people, merchandise, fixtures, and so forth. What she perceives may be a warm, congenial, friendly atmosphere, a place where she may wish to shop and linger. On the other hand, given a set of prior occurrences that may have affected her values, attitudes, or *cognitions*— say an unpleasant previous shopping experience—what she may perceive is a hostile, unfriendly environment from which she may wish to flee instantly.

The consumer's cognitive set or total belief system predisposes him to receive and retain perceptions that are compatible with this belief system. These phenomena are known as *selective attention, selective perception,* and *selective retention.*

For example, if a person is in the market for a new automobile and he characteristically drives Chevrolets, then his cognitive set which embraces strong favorable attitudes toward Chevrolet will likely be such that advertisements and other messages about Chevrolet are likely to gain his attention faster than messages, say, about Ford. By the same token, he is likely to perceive these messages more favorably and retain them longer than would be the case for messages about another make of automobile.

This really means that the consumer becomes, in turn, a gatekeeper and a decision maker regarding the communication process and its effects. In terms of various companies' communication efforts (especially in regard to advertising and personal selling) , the consumer *decides* what messages to receive by deciding to what kinds of communication messages or media he will expose himself. He, in turn, decides what messages to *perceive* and what messages to *retain* on the basis of certain social-psychological factors, such as group norms, attitudes, and culture, which in turn affect his cognitions.

Motivation. A great deal is known about motivation, yet only recently have we begun to link up some of the other relevant behavior variables with motivation. These efforts are beginning to pay off handsomely in terms of our overall understanding.

Though much is already known about these processes, there is still much insight to be gained. Marketers and retailers have been concerned with *motives* for many years. However, only more recently have we begun to place our study and interest in motives within a psychological framework of motivation. Motives are the drives, impulses, wishes, desires, or reasons that initiate the sequence of activities known as behavior. The retail manager is interested in several different kinds of motives that elicit various forms and degrees of consumer behavior and prompt the consumer to action. Basically, retail managers are concerned with *buying motives,* those reasons that impel consumers to buy goods. *Product motives* are those reasons that impel consumers to buy particular products or particular brands of products; *patronage motives* are those reasons that impel consumers to shop at particular stores.

Other aspects of motives that concern retailers are such factors as *primary buying motives,* the reasons that impel consumers to be interested in a general class of goods, say, women's suits. In contrast with primary buying motives are *selective buying motives,* i.e., the reasons that impel a consumer to be interested in a particular style or color of women's suit. It is quite obvious that some motives are innate, i.e., we are born with these basic motives. Innate motives mostly are concerned with physiological processes such as hunger, thirst, and perhaps sex. By and large, modern retailing is concerned with *learned* or *acquired motives.* It matters very little how needs that lead to motives develop, that is, whether they are innate or learned; the important point is that individuals (and consequently consumers) want their needs satisfied. The urges to satisfy these needs are called drives or motives, and it is the action that stems from these motives that is called consumer behavior.

Man is both an animal and a social being. Consequently, he is possessed with the classic needs of hunger, thirst, and sex, along with a list of other motivating needs. Maslow has supplied the following list of needs:[9]

1. Physiological needs.
2. Safety needs.
3. Social needs.
4. Esteem needs.
5. Self-actualization needs.

For retailers the most important insight stemming from a knowledge of man's need hierarchy ought to be that *retailing activity contributes to man's ability to help satisfy this range of needs.* That is, *retailing* is a means to the ends or goals sought by man as a consumer. Another important point revealed by current research is that a satisfied need is no longer an im-

[9] See A. H. Maslow, "A Theory of Human Motivation," *Psychological Review,* Vol. 50, (1943), pp. 370–396.

portant source of consumer motivation. In today's affluent society, the basic physiological needs have been met. Therefore, with some exceptions, retailers ought to focus their strategies on the upper ranges of the needs hierarchy; they should attempt to discern more about the needs of the self-actualizing personality—a label that might very well describe a whole range of consumers' personality types.

Learning. Learning is the organism's behavioral reaction to stimuli. In the case of consumer behavior, stimuli may be a product, a message about a product, a package, or a suggestion from a neighbor. The behavior reaction may be the inclination to buy the product, or simply to think favorably about it. It is generally recognized that the customer's thinking-reasoning process moves through a series of stages before a final purchase or decision is made. The progression from initial awareness to final adoption for example, is not instantaneous; there are a number of intermediary stages. During this reasoning or deliberating period, learning often occurs. This learning usually results in some kind of adaptive behavior.

The changing environment of the buyer over a sufficient length of time is made up of such things as new stores, new products, changes in tastes, and increased incomes or progression through the life cycle; buying behavior is largely learned from these changes in the buyer's environmental situation. Changes in behavior over time can be shown by the use of a *learning curve.* Figure 6-1 shows such a learning curve in the case of some new product.

The learning curve shown in Figure 6-1 would probably reflect some given level of retailing activity. Possibly the steepness of the slope along various segments of the curve might be increased if greater expenditures or more creative strategies were employed. Learning is generally a sequential kind of activity, moving (in the case of retail merchandising) from an awareness stage, in which a store and its product and service offering are discovered or brought above the significant or threshold level, through an interest stage, an evaluation stage, a trial stage, and finally, perhaps, an adoption stage. Of course, the process can be interrupted at any point along

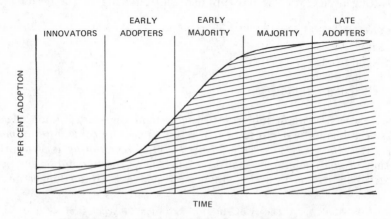

FIGURE 6-1 Learning curve for a new product.

the cycle. The very flat portion of the learning curve shown in Figure 6-1 reflects the difficulty of persuading people to change their habits or to alter established and previously learned relationships. The accelerated steepness of the curve for those in the early adopter stage represents a period of increasing returns, probably because the initial hard core of resistance has been broken and the innovators are now excited about possessing the product. In turn, as innovators or key influentials, they are convincing others of the merits of the goods.

Several relevant considerations bear upon the learning process from a retailing management point of view.

Goal Objects. The goal object, as defined in the marketing context, is any product or service that provides or is expected to provide the ability to reduce or eliminate a need. Stated another way, a goal object is a product that satisfies either or both physiological or psychological needs. Such products as goal objects become important reinforcing agents and are thus sought for their reward and reinforcement value.

The product functions as a goal object, and in the eyes of the consumer it is a bundle of expectations. Of course, these expectations will vary from consumer to consumer, depending upon their needs, the strength of those needs, and the consumer's expectations as to what the goal object will do for him (what satisfactions will be derived from its use). The obvious implication of this fact is that the product purchased by the consumer for the purpose of reducing a need had better live up to his expectations if repeat sales are to be expected. This idea ties in with the principle of reward, or reinforcement, which will be discussed as we proceed.

Cues. In the search for a goal object, the consumer must have some means of differentiating between products, or brands of products. Cues provide the means of differentiation. Cues are the product or store characteristics, or the characteristics of an innovation.

According to the usual economic demand theory, the consumer has a wealth of information concerning the markets, particularly about products. Unfortunately, this may be less true in the real world. Often the consumer faces a purchase decision with a notable lack of information as to the product characteristics. For example, when a product's quality is in doubt, the consumer may rely on its price to infer quality. In this case, the consumer is substituting one cue (price) for another (quality) and provides himself with a set of expectations regarding the goal object's quality.

One important thing to note about cues is that not only should they represent product differences, but that these differences do exist. For example, the act of changing the color of a product or changing the decor of a store creates a differentiation or different cue. However, an increase in consumer acceptance will depend upon the consumers' expectation of the ability of the product or store to reduce their need. If a change in color of the goal object does not add to the consumer's perceived value of the product, then theoretically, sales should not increase because of this perceived change. Cues direct the responses of the purchaser, but the ability to direct behavior will depend upon the relative strength and change in those cues. The expectations of the consumer will to some degree depend on the cue value and will thus influence the ability of cues to initiate the desired response.

Response. A response roughly is an organism's reaction to a cue. Therefore, the act of shopping or purchase is a response to the original stimulus or drive, and the choice of a specific store or a specific product or brand of product is a response to cues that guide the purchase behavior.

Reinforcement or Reward. Reinforcement takes place when the original drive is reduced or (in the case of drives such as prestige) is increased. This suggests that the purchase or shopping response must be rewarded or reinforced to provide a more adequate bond—an increased probability that the response will again be elicited when the stimulus conditions once again present themselves.

Generalization. Most of us generalize our learning. That is, what we discover to be true for a particular thing, we generally impute to be true for a class of things. Generalization, therefore, is the tendency to respond the same way to all situations or stimuli that are similar to the one for which the response was originally conditioned. For example, if a store successfully promotes children's shoes to the satisfaction of the family decision maker, say, the mother, then the decision maker is likely to view that store as a satisfactory source of many of the family's needs.

Since cognition, perception, motivation, and learning are all important determinants of consumer behavior, any theory of consumer behavior used for understanding and predicting the store and product reactions of shoppers would, of necessity, be oriented around these concepts.

an outline of consumer behavior and decision processes

Consumer behavior is viewed as a subset of the universal set of human behavior, and, as such, it is concerned with all the behavioral manifestations associated with the search, screening, and selection aspects of the purchase and use of manufactured products and services. Of course, this is the behavior that the retail manager is attempting to understand and influence in a way which will be most advantageous to his firm.

One important aspect of consumer behavior is shopping. Shopping, while admittedly a complex set of behaviors, is basically a process of searching for information that will enable a buyer to make a satisfactory and informed decision. The purchase decision is in many instances based upon the information and impressions generated during the shopping process. In other instances, shopping is a way of reinforcing or rejecting information or impressions obtained from past experiences. Admittedly, much is omitted in this brief sketch of the consumer shopping process. However, even if the mechanics of this process have not yet been thoroughly isolated, important *theories* to explain aspects of this phenomenon have been advanced. One general theory of consumer behavior that appears valid (perhaps because of its generality) holds that *needs* lead to *drives*. The drive condition or state is one of tension. That is, as needs arise, and as drives to satisfy these needs are intensified, the individual tends toward a state of disequilibrium—he becomes less and less content to remain in the unsatisfied state. If and when the drive is reduced as a result of the need being satisfied or sublimated, then the individual returns again to a state of mental or physical equilibrium.

Heuristic Problem Solving

Consumer behavior is a rather good example of heuristic problem solving. The consumer's behavior is goal directed (satisfaction of needs) and therefore purposive. His goal is often nonspecific; he is open to recommendation and suggestion. Thus, learning and communication can be considered as an important means for helping the consumer attain various levels of insight and consumption satisfaction. Consumer behavior is largely directed along the lines of search and discovery; therefore his behavior is *heuristic*. Inasmuch as it is heuristic, he develops certain rules of thumb that he utilizes as guidelines to shape and structure his behavior. What he learns later become programmed or habitual modes of reducing tension, and yet he also learns that some of yesterday's satisfactions become as useless as yesterday's newspaper. He looks for some excitement, though at the same time he is still interested in stability and variety. He learns to rely on dependable modes of reducing tensions, but he is constantly sloughing off old habits and taking risks in searching out new means of problem solving.

A set of general conclusions based upon these premises would be that (1) consumer behavior is an effort related to consumer problem solving; (2) behavior is therefore caused, the causes or reasons being the problems which confront consumers; (3) the satisfaction of needs and wants tends to remove the original causes of behavior; (4) behavior is affected by learning; and (5) adaptive social learning, a part of which is consumer behavior, is often a function of communication and of culture.

Post-Decision Dissonance

Our discussion has already recognized the fact that consumer behavior is something of a sequential (multistage) decision process. The generally recognized stages in this process are (1) the search stage, (2) the prepurchase evaluation and comparison stage, and (3) the post-decision use and judgment stage.

An overwhelming portion of the material relating to consumer behavior has focused on the first two stages of the process. More recently however, a phenomenon relating to the third stage of buyer behavior and referred to as *post-decision dissonance* has been treated rather extensively in marketing-retailing literature.[10] Post-decision dissonance is a kind of anxiety that arises in the customer after a purchase has been made. There is dissonance (incongruity) among the buyer's various cognitions about the product purchased and the other foregone opportunities. According to Leon Festinger, dissonance occurs after a decision, if a person is faced with doubt that he made the right choice.[11] He states further that "Dissonance then will be the result of the simple act of having made a decision. Consequently, one may expect to see manifestations of pressures to reduce dissonance after a choice has been made."[12]

Consumer behavior influenced by dissonance is likely to take one of two major forms. First, the consumer's anxiety will lead to guilt feelings of such magnitude that the purchase is returned or, second, the consumer who is striving for a feeling of internal and congruent harmony is likely to intensify his search for information that will bolster and support his original decision. The retail manager's best attack on the problem of dissonance will center around a strong program of personal selling and advertising in order to thoroughly convince the customer of the worth of the store and its products and services. Furthermore, the merchandising strategy is likely to be extended to the post-purchase decision period by follow-up communications that continue to stress the merits of the retail management system in question and especially the merits of the merchandise and services purchased by given customers.

Matching Images

From his life style, the consumer typically conceptualizes himself in terms of a self-image—the total sum of impressions that the consumer forms of himself—and his behavior is one which manifests or projects his self-image. The self-image is often likely to be a little distorted, inasmuch as the consumer seldom ever sees himself just as others see him. However, the consumer is a striver. His problem is one of purchasing goods with the thought of enhancing, increasing, or changing his self-image. He purchases goods in order that he might see himself becoming bolder, smarter, richer, more secure, or more socially acceptable.

To repeat, an image is a total conceptualization of a person or object. Images are formed via the cognitive processes that consist of perception, motivation, and learning; and the consumer-buyer's principal task is often that of securing a product or service whose image matches his own self-image. Sometimes, consumers discover that they simply like a certain product. In other instances, the consumer may discover that for some reason unknown to himself he simply avoids buying either a certain product or a certain category of products, or from a certain institution. In short, for some reason his image of these conditions is contrary to his existing self-image or total value system.

[10] For example, see Leon Festinger, *A Theory of Cognitive Dissonance,* Stanford University Press, Stanford, Calif., 1957; and Bruce Straits, "The Pursuit of the Dissonant Consumer," *Journal of Marketing,* Vol. 28 (July 1964), pp. 62–66.

[11] Ibid.

[12] Ibid., p. 35.

Psychographic Analysis

Throughout our treatment, it has been repeatedly emphasized that there are two basic dimensions to consumer analysis. In Chapter 5, we emphasized the demographic characteristics of customers and, in many respects, throughout this chapter we have emphasized the psychographic aspect of customer analysis. Astute retail management planning, analysis, and control efforts, of course, would underscore the necessity of combining both demographic and psychographic approaches. While demographics relates mostly to numbers such as how many, how much, etc., psychographic analysis seeks to describe the human characteristics of consumers that may have bearing on their response to products, packaging, advertising, public relations, and store choice. Such variables may span a spectrum from self-concept or self-image and life style to an in-depth analysis of attitudes, interests, and opinions, as well as perceptions of store attributes. Psychographics is, in many respects, a sophisticated attempt to match the store's total offer variation or store image to the life style or psychographic image or profile of the major market segments to which the store hopes to appeal.[13]

Psychographic variables, from the perspective of retail merchandising, fall basically into three classes:

1. Store attributes—as proposed by the retailer and as perceived by the customer.
2. Life style—manifested by behavioral variances illustrating the use of time, services, products, shopping, and living habits by the consumer.
3. Psychological—often expressed as self-concept, but oriented around the discovery and analysis of customers' attitudes, interests, and opinions.

The purpose of psychographic analysis is to pinpoint the relationships between the three classes of variables so that one can say with reasonable accuracy consumers in market segment A have the highest propensity or likelihood to purchase products from store B because store B's attributes fit the life style or psychographic profile that results from consumers in market segment A's self-concepts, interests, and opinions. Psychographics is an attempt to humanize data.[14]

To illustrate the fundamental differences between conventional demographic research and psychographic research, examine the two following figures (Figures 6-2 and 6-3).

Figure 6-2 is a page from a traditional questionnaire used in market research. Conventional demographic data are likely to reveal that an

[13] For more on store image, see *The Journal of Retailing*, Vol. 50, No. 4 (Winter 1974–1975). This entire issue was devoted to articles dealing with store image.

[14] There are several good primers on psychographics. For example, see Fred D. Reynolds, *Psychographics: A Conceptual Approach*, Research Monograph No. 6, Division of Research, College of Business Administration, University of Georgia, Athens, Ga., 1973. Also, see William D. Wells, *Life Style and Psychographics*, American Marketing Association, Chicago, 1974.

FIGURE 6-2   Page from a Traditional Questionnaire

1. What is the highest grade of school completed by the head of your household?
   - (1) under 7 years _____
   - (2) 7–9 years _____
   - (3) 10–11 years _____
   - (4) high school graduate _____
   - (5) 1–3 years' college _____
   - (6) college graduate _____
   - (7) postgraduate _____

2. What is the occupation of the head of your household? (Please write in specific description.)_____

   _____

   _____

3. Which of the following age groups are you in?
   - (1) under 25 _____
   - (2) 25–34 _____
   - (3) 35–44 _____
   - (4) 45–54 _____
   - (5) 55–64 _____
   - (6) 65 and over _____

4. What is the size of your household?
   - (1) total number _____
   - (2) number under 12 years _____
   - (3) number 12–18 years _____

5. Into which of the following categories does your total family income per year fall?
   - (1) under $3,000 _____
   - (2) $3,000–4,999 _____
   - (3) $5,000–6,999 _____
   - (4) $7,000–8,999 _____
   - (5) $9,000–10,999 _____
   - (6) $11,000–12,999 _____
   - (7) $13,000–14,999 _____
   - (8) $15,000 or more _____

SOURCE: Fred D. Reynolds, Psychographics: A Conceptual Approach, *Research Monograph No. 6*, Division of Research, College of Business Administration, University of Georgia, Athens, Ga. 1973, p. 4.

average customer of Store A is 32.4 years of age, has 12.62 years of schooling, has 2.1 children, earns $8,437 per year, and that 90 per cent of respondents are married. However, psychographic research, as revealed by the questions shown in Figure 6-3, is likely to show that customers of Store A are not particularly self-confident, are mildly concerned with fashion-consciousness, are price-sensitive, believe in shopping around, buy a considerable amount on credit with a bank credit card, and are relatively store loyal, but do some shopping around.

An Integrated Approach

The point to be emphasized is that retail managers need both demographic and psychographic information. Each tends to complement the other. A retailer who does not view his market as a large homogeneous mass of consumers, all of whom have similar demand characteristics, must therefore think of his market opportunity as a series of distinct market segments, each of which has unique demand characteristics. The retailer then presumes that the specific market targets to which he will cater will expect a tailored offer variation to meet the specific demand characteristics which these segments manifest. In other words, the retailer's market planning or

FIGURE 6-3   Page from a Psychographic Questionnaire

STATEMENT	DEFINITELY DISAGREE					DEFINITELY AGREE
I think I have more self-confidence than most people.	1	2	3	4	5	6
An important part of my life and activities is dressing smartly.	1	2	3	4	5	6
I find myself checking the prices in the grocery store even for small items.	1	2	3	4	5	6
I sometimes influence the types of clothes my friends buy.	1	2	3	4	5	6
I am more independent than most people.	1	2	3	4	5	6
I try to keep my wardrobe up-to-date with the latest fashions.	1	2	3	4	5	6
I usually watch the advertisements for announcements of sales.	1	2	3	4	5	6
My friends come to me more often than I go to them for information about clothes.	1	2	3	4	5	6
I enjoy looking through fashion magazines.	1	2	3	4	5	6
I think I have a lot of personal ability.	1	2	3	4	5	6
A person can save a lot of money by shopping around for bargains.	1	2	3	4	5	6
I feel that I am generally regarded by my friends as a good source of advice about clothing fashions.	1	2	3	4	5	6
I like to be considered a leader.	1	2	3	4	5	6
When I must choose between the two, I usually dress for fashion, not for comfort.	1	2	3	4	5	6
I can think of someone I have told about some new clothing fashion in the last six months.	1	2	3	4	5	6
Our family travels quite a lot.	1	2	3	4	5	6
Shopping is really a bother in any store.	1	2	3	4	5	6
I buy many things on credit or with a charge card.	1	2	3	4	5	6
I am an active member of more than one social or service organization.	1	2	3	4	5	6
When I see a new brand on the shelf, I often buy it just to see what it's like.	1	2	3	4	5	6
I do most of my shopping in the same stores I have always shopped in.	1	2	3	4	5	6

SOURCE: Fred D. Reynolds, Psychographics: A Conceptual Approach, Research Monograph No. 6, Division of Research, College of Business Administration, University of Georgia, Athens, Ga., 1973, p. 5.

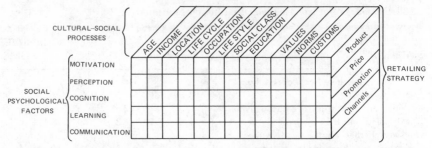

FIGURE 6-4 The relationship between demographic–cultural–social processes, social–psychological processes, and retailing strategy: An integrated approach.

strategy is tied specifically to how he perceives his market target. Of course, his market target consists of those clusters of consumers and potential consumers whose demand characteristics both demographically and psychographically match or fit the retailer's offer variation—his unique combination of store attributes, merchandise offering, promotional activities, and store locational features. Figure 6-4 conveys the relationships that exist between much of what we have discussed in Chapters 5 and 6. For example, retailing strategy, which is the outgrowth of the discussion related to the retailing mix, i.e., product assortment decisions, price, promotion, and place considerations, must be balanced and made to fit within the framework of the store's demographic-cultural-social processes and the social-psychological factors that affect purchase-consumption behavior.

In essence, Figure 6-4 suggests that retailing strategy in the final analysis is an outgrowth of the demand characteristics of specific market targets. These market targets, of course, are customers whose demand characteristics are a function of demographics—age, income, location, etc., but also of psychographic factors such as social class, values, and life styles. Furthermore, such an analysis underscores the notion that social-psychological factors such as motivation, perception, learning, and others must be looked at within the context of demographic-cultural-social processes. For example, what motivates a given customer will be affected by a host of other variables or considerations such as his income, his occupation, where he lives, his social class, his educational level, and other factors.

Other Aspects of Consumer Behavior

Although many dimensions of consumer behavior can only be briefly and superficially treated here, consumer behavior is a complex phenomenon, much broader in scope and complexity than our treatment suggests. Thus far in our treatment, we have attempted to weave a meaningful analytical and descriptive framework of consumer behavior and consumer decision processes that stem from social-psychological motivations.

Many other interesting and rewarding avenues remain to be discussed, but space will permit only a cursory treatment.

Different kinds of consumer behavior are likely to be manifested, depending upon the role or characteristic pattern of behavior imposed upon an individual because of his status or influence in the overall scheme of things. The effects of certain kinds of decision making in the buying, shopping, consumption complex will vary, depending upon the particular role being examined. Some behavior affecting a store's merchandising strategy may reflect only the role of *buyers*, i.e., those whose role encompasses the actual shopping and decision making. In other instances, the buyers may be less important in shaping store strategy than the users of a commodity. A food store's selection and assortment of breakfast cereals may reflect the influence of children 5 to 15 years of age, rather than the actual taste preferences of the adult purchaser. Some strategies may be more particularly aimed at opinion leaders or *key influentials* in recognition of the two-step flow of communication, which holds that influences stemming from the mass media first reach opinion leaders, who in turn pass on what they read and hear to those of their everyday associates for whom they are influential. This hypothesis has been called the two-step flow of communication, and as the reader would imagine, it has important implications for consumer behavior and for merchandising strategy.

As yet, there is not too much information to suggest that the decision-making process, as such, differs much for a family decision-making unit, as opposed to the individual decision maker.

There are interesting questions pertaining to family purchase behavior that deal with the effects of husband versus wife as family purchasing agent. Characteristically, the woman of the household has been given the role as the key family purchasing agent, but as more and more women take jobs outside the home and as store hours lengthen and night and Sunday shopping become more prevalent, the dominance of the wife in purchase decisions is open to more serious questioning. Purchase decision making is quite often a shared responsibility. In many instances, it has been shown that before making a purchase decision, as many as 80 per cent of the women check first with husbands. Some items are purchased more frequently by the husband and, hence, his influence is likely to be stronger. For example, the husband is usually the dominant factor in the decision making for such items as beer, liquor, automobiles, tires, life insurance, air conditioners, electric shavers, shaving creams, and outboard motors. It would appear that although the wife is still an important influence in family decision making regarding consumer purchases, the degree of her influence has probably been overstated.

Changing Consumer Shopping Habits. In discussing changes in buying habits, the concern is principally with the how, when, and where of customer behavior, rather than the why. The posing of these questions and the answers thereto can greatly aid a merchandiser in establishing and modifying store policies, methods, and procedures, in order that he might best meet the needs and wants of his customers and thus assure larger and more profitable sales.

A plethora of studies dealing with consumer buying habits has been conducted by advertising agencies, private research firms, universities, and the research departments of corporations, newspapers, and periodicals. These studies of customers have been undertaken for all lines and kinds of retail establishments. No attempt will be made here to discuss the merits or findings of all these studies. However, the *Progressive Grocer* studies that deal with supermarket shoppers are indicative of the kinds of information revealed. For example, a recent *Progressive Grocer* study in cooperation with the Home Testing Institute detailed several significant changes in supermarket shopping habits and attitudes. Here are several highlights of this study:[15]

1. Women alone still do in excess of 50 per cent of the family shopping in supermarkets. Two out of five shoppers are accompanied by men or children. Supermarket shopping continues to be a family affair.
2. Today's shopper is spending more time per shopping trip. However, in just one year, 1973–1974, the average supermarket shopper moved from 3.04 trips per week to 2.28 trips per week.
3. Currently, because of high prices, inflation, and unemployment, supermarket shoppers are more conscious of prices and "specials." This has resulted in smaller proportions of food budgets spent for meat and other higher-priced luxury items.
4. The gasoline shortage and higher gasoline prices have initiated a change in supermarket shopping habits. In early 1973 the regular supermarket accounted for 60 per cent of a shopper's supermarket trips and 72 per cent of her expenditures. This seems likely to change as "shopping around" becomes less of a habit, shopping trips become fewer, and the regular store gains in eminence.
5. There has been a slight rise in the percentage of family weekly income spent in supermarkets. This is attributable to higher prices and a larger proportion spent for non-food items. Supermarkets, with their expanded product lines, may get an increasing proportion of the consumer's dollar as the costs of shopping increase.
6. Supermarket shoppers may be becoming more discerning, since 74 per cent of all shoppers make a shopping list.
7. The bulk of today's customers are in the 25- to 40-year-old age group and have family incomes in excess of $8,000 per year.

Research that centers on customer buying habits can be an invaluable merchandising aid. The information just presented on supermarket shoppers is only a small sample of the kinds and range of information available. The American consumer is constantly changing and, as the consumer changes, his habits and attitudes regarding retail stores and their offer variations change also. Research has shown that retailers are not nearly so knowledgeable about consumers as has been assumed and that the retailers' misconceptions of consumers may lead to ill-conceived merchandising strategies.

The Role of Market Research.   We have emphasized that the retailer needs to know his market. Knowing his market entails making inquiries about consumers as dynamic, emotional, living organisms rather than just

[15] See "Consumers in Crisis," *Progressive Grocer* (April 1974) , pp. 45–54.

as bloodless digits. Such inquiries can be both diagnostic and predictive. The conventional statistical kind of nose counting is a needed and useful research tool that provides much insight into customer habits and shopping patterns. However, much consumer behavior research needs to concern itself not with when, how much, where, or how often. We need to know why the consumer prefers Store A to Store B; why multiunit priced items move at a faster rate than single-unit priced items; why merchandise located in one part of the store moves more rapidly than in another area where traffic flow appears similar. More sophisticated marketing research is being undertaken by retail merchandisers. The increasing use of psychographic analysis, store trade area studies, consumer image studies, site analysis studies, and social audits promises to provide an increasingly rich amount of new information related to consumers, upon which better merchandising strategies of the future will be built.

Consumer behavior is subject to a host of influences that have already been classified and discussed under the rubrics of psychology, sociology, and economics. Such a statement reflects the nearly boundless aspects of consumer behavior. The retail manager must therefore look at a multitude of contextual influences: life style, groups, role theory, psychology, and culture, as all bearing on the phenomenon referred to as consumer behavior.

QUESTIONS FOR STUDY, REFLECTION, AND REVIEW

1. Explain why it is important for the retail firm to study the consumer from a personal or behavior point of view.
2. What are some of the important retailing activities that are based upon a clear understanding of consumer behavior?
3. Explain some of the reasons why earlier attempts to understand consumer behavior have not yielded adequate answers to the question of why consumers act or buy in a certain manner.
4. Describe and explain some of the basic concepts on which the psychological approach to the study of consumer choice or behavior is predicated.
5. Define and explain the two classes of buying motives that suggest a more concise approach to the study of consumer behavior.
6. Explain what is meant by post-decision dissonance.
7. What two major forms of consumer behavior may result from dissonance? How can the retail manager attempt to reduce dissonant behavior?
8. Define and explain the hypothesis called the "two-step flow of communication."
9. What are some of the advantages and shortcomings of a theory of consumer behavior based upon the economic approach?
10. How does psychographic customer analysis complement demographic customer analysis?

THREE

LOCATION, SITE ANALYSIS, AND STORE DESIGN

7

store location factors: community and trading area analysis

Store location decisions are critical to the proper functioning of the retail management system, primarily for reasons of profit maximization. And in the aggregate, society demands an efficient network of retailing units in the overall interest of social and consumer welfare.

Choosing the location and the site for the retail unit is the final stage in the linkage between the firm and the market opportunity, which we have discussed so extensively. As we shall soon see, the many generalizations offered thus far in relation to market opportunity will take on clearer focus when viewed through the aperture of the retail store, placed in a given community and a particular geographic point in space.

Analysis of location and site is essentially a more refined study in analyzing the market opportunity: Retail store location and site analysis are market-oriented. That is, the principal determinants of both a good location and a good site center around such complex (but fundamental) considerations as people (buyers and users), income (purchasing power), and propensity to consume (attitudes, habits, and motivations). Where the store's product and service offering appears to be well matched in a spatial sense with a given or discovered market opportunity, then, it would appear that both location and site problems have been solved. The problem however is easier stated than solved.

Because of the increasing scarcity of unutilized sites and the extensive coverage of market opportunity in most communities by an existing network of retail outlets, every store manager will be forced to scrutinize each and every location decision with as much scientific determination as possible. The day has probably passed when a retail store executive could drive through the countryside and discover an untapped market opportunity, drive through the community and find a prime vacant lot available, or circle the square and find an empty building just suitable for his needs.

If anything, retail merchandising may be in for a period of contraction and consolidation. The actual number of retail firms—given the tightening of the economy and shrinking incomes, resulting from continuing inflationary pressure and serious levels of unemployment—may decline. In all likelihood, the trend toward increased average size of retail stores will continue. Such an increase in average size probably means some excess capacity in many units, which in turn, is likely to mean higher average costs and stringent competitive activity toward reducing these costs. The mortality rate of retail businesses is extremely high: between 15 and 25 per cent of the total retail stores go out of business each year. About one third of all retail stores have a life span of a year or less, and one half remain in business no longer than two years. Problems of overexpansion naturally bloat and contribute to the problem of excess capacity.

The problem of retail store location and site analysis is a critical part of the retail management firm's strategy. Locating a retail store or expanding the network of a firm's distribution pattern is much like drilling a well for gas or oil, or sinking a shaft for the purpose of mining precious metals. Out of all the possibilities, and given our limited resources, which one offers the best possibility for maximizing profits by releasing the optimum stream of income? Just as sinking a well or drilling a mining shaft is a means for releasing a stream of income, so too, is locating the retail store. The mining engineer and the geologist look for the area that shows signs of greatest promise, and within that area they search for the specific site in which they might tap the sought-after resources. The store location analyst is analogous to the mining engineer and the geologist. Naturally, in adding to the retail firm's distribution network, the store location analyst will proceed in as scientific a fashion as possible, for his task is to minimize— figuratively speaking—the number of dry holes. In short, scientific location and site analysis insures that the retail store, properly located, both releases and generates a stream of income from a given perceived market opportunity.

the nature of the location problem

The retail store location problem is one of properly locating the retail unit within the framework (boundary) of the discovered or perceived market opportunity. A market opportunity does not in itself assure a profit opportunity. A poorly located store, or one whose product and service offering does not match or is not accommodated to the market opportunity, will mean something less than full profit opportunity.

A sound location decision is a complement to—not a substitute for—a sound merchandising strategy. Location decisions must be continually reevaluated. New clusters of retail units are always emerging, population and trading centers are constantly undergoing some form of change, new forces and new competitors are continually upsetting the equilibrium of the market place or trading area. For these reasons, the location decision must be evaluated as often as are the store's product lines, or its pricing and promotion policies. However, it must be noted that once a store is located, the cost of changing its location (i.e., loss of established trade, as well as the physical costs of moving the inventory, fixtures, and so forth) may be greater than the opportunity cost of doing business in a less than optimum location.

The typical retailer owner or manager is not well versed in location theory, economic geography, or urban ecology; all are disciplines that contribute to an understanding of location and site analysis. Retailers most often are specialists in merchandising, not real estate; and for this and other obvious reasons the retailer faced with a location decision should study the problem most carefully and deliberately. When conditions warrant, as they almost always will, he would be well advised to consult a specialist who could assist him with his particular and unique location decision.

The problem of where to locate the retail store has several dimensions. First of all is the problem of whether our concern is with locating a new store, or re-evaluating the location of an existing store. Within another context, store location is a finer adjustment of the market opportunity concept. As such, it is first of all concerned with finding the market opportunity (i.e., discovering and evaluating the city or community within which to locate), then analyzing and delineating the trading area, and finally considering the factors that bear upon specific site analysis.

In this present chapter we shall examine the problem of community and trading area analysis, and in Chapter 8 we shall look carefully at the narrower and more restricted question of choosing a specific site within the community.

community analysis

The basis of the retail store location and site problem most logically begins with some discussion and analysis of community growth, function, and structure. We are today in the midst of vast changes in retailing and merchandising. The phenomenal changes and increases in technology, the population explosion, the movements from farm to city, and from city to suburb are producing changes of considerable significance and magnitude. Our forms and methods of distribution are catching up with our ability to produce goods. The emergence of the supermarket, the large discount department store, the shopping center, and the downtown mall reflect fundamental changes in both the structure and function of the American community. Until perhaps the early 1900s, communities and the retail establishments that served them remained basically as they had been for the past several centuries. As we have repeated so often, decision making in a stable, nonchanging environment is not so difficult as it is in a dynamic, fast-paced situation.

The retail store's existence depends almost entirely upon some kind of community. Community has been defined as "people living in one locality or region under the same culture and having some common geographical focus for their major activities. The distinctive characteristic of the community is that a constellation of institutional organizations have grown up around a particular center of specialized function."[1] To a great extent, the number and kinds of retail institutions within a given community will depend in turn upon the nature of the community in question, its size, character or function, and its ultimate structure. Thorstein Veblen has said

> Any community may be viewed as an industrial or economic mechanism, the structure of which is made up of what is called its economic institutions. These institutions are habitual methods of carrying on the life process of the community in contact with the material environment in which it lives. When given methods of unfolding human activity in this given environment have been elaborated in this way, the life of the community will express itself with some facility in these habitual directions.[2]

The general store is an example of a retailing institution that accommodated the needs and tastes of a given community's mode of functioning at a given point in time. By contrast, the supermarket today reflects the process of accommodation by a given economic institution to the so-called life processes or mode of living of a community at another point in time. The small Amish-dominated community of Millersburg, Indiana, will reflect economic institutions, especially the size and kinds of retailing establishments, that are far different from the swinging, swashbuckling community of Dallas, Texas.

Industry and Community

Any analysis of the structure and function of communities as they in turn shape and affect the market opportunity will involve an understanding of the effect of industry upon community size, type, structure, and function. As a matter of fact, the chain of analysis would be as follows:

Industry → Community → Market Opportunity → Location Analysis
→ Site Analysis

Thus, the size and nature of industry play paramount roles in determining the size and character of the community. Industry affects the location of cities, influences the size of the community, and shapes and structures the growth pattern of communities, because it differentiates the community by functional type and occupational composition, as well as affecting the power and social class structure and the basic community character.

[1] William H. Form and Delbert C. Miller, *Industry, Labor, and Community,* Harper & Row, Publishers, New York, 1960, p. 19.

[2] Thorstein Veblen, *The Theory of the Leisure Class,* Macmillan Publishing Co., Inc., New York, 1912, p. 193.

Communities and Commercial Centers

Different kinds of communities will naturally spawn different and specialized kinds of commercial activities. However, one central feature of all communities has characteristically been the market place—a center for the exchange of goods and services. In ancient times it was the open air markets of the central city sponsored by the community officialdom or the church. With increases in transportation and communication facilities, modern communities began to witness the emergence of unique and sophisticated trading centers largely dominated by retail enterprise. Our industrial system has introduced a large variety of commercial functions to the city or community that were never present in the simple communities of earlier times. Primarily four recognizable types of commercial districts have emerged in the modern community.

Every urban community dweller is familiar with the *downtown*. It is usually the center of financial and governmental enterprise, as well as the retail and wholesale trade center of the area. New York's Wall Street district and Chicago's LaSalle Street district lie at the heart of such downtown commercial areas. Generally, the commercial centers in the downtown heart of the community have not been planned, nor are they necessarily balanced and well integrated. Instead, they have simply grown by a process of creeping commitment outward and upward within a both existing and expanding network of streets, as the economic fortunes of the cities ebbed and fell. The central business district serves a vital and necessary function for the larger community as a whole. But dynamic and centrifugal forces are manifested by urban blight, congestion, pollution (such as noise, fumes, smog, and smoke), and greatly accelerated land values; these forces are tending to shift business enterprise to the outer fringes of the urban core.

Another type of commercial center within the urban community is the small, *central business district of the satellite community*. These districts form a continuing part of the ecological pattern that is emerging to meet the needs of the changing living and working patterns of their inhabitants. Such commercial centers in these communities are generally scaled down versions of their big city counterparts. Stores are often branches of larger parent organizations located in the downtown urban core.

Large financial and government centers are generally not existent in the smaller satellite community. The small city will contain the chain retail stores, professional offices, service supply enterprises, motion picture houses, branch banks, and small offices of stock exchanges.

The third, and one of the fastest growing commercial centers to be found as a part of the community complex, is the *outlying shopping area or center*. To some extent they may overlap or be well integrated with both the downtown commercial center and the commercial centers of the satellite communities. Oftentimes however the integration results more by accident than by design. Among the facilities found in the outlying shopping area are large food markets; discount department stores and large general merchandise stores; chain stores of various types; branch banks; telegraph, telephone, and postal service offices; and complex networks of medical, dental, and other professional offices.

The final type of commercial center is the *neighborhood center,* located primarily for the sake of convenience. Its assortment of merchandise and services of all types is generally limited. Such neighborhood commercial centers are designed to provide the day-by-day commodities for the immediate convenience of a limited population. These centers may have a grocery store, a meat market, a package liquor or beer and wine carryout store, a small restaurant, a bakery, a drugstore, a stationery store, and the ubiquitous barber shop and beauty salon.

A description of these commercial centers, largely on the basis of community size, reflects a fundamental economic dictum, namely, that specialization and division of labor are limited by the extent of the market. A given community of a given size and character can only support a kind of commercial activity that is balanced in relationship to the community's needs and resources.

Functional Classification of Communities

Given the many thousands of urban communities, it is no surprise that attempts have been made to order them into some kind of classification. We rather unconsciously classify many communities by one sort of device or another. Some communities we refer to as large, others small or medium sized. Some communities are classified as old, others young. We often subjectively classify communities as progressive or conservative, good or bad. Some communities swing, others are dull or square. As you would imagine, there are numerous ways of classifying communities.

However, from the retail manager's point of view, the market opportunity posed by a given community is probably best interpreted on the basis of the community's functional characteristics. Thus, the crucial question becomes, "How can cities be grouped or classified on the basis of the economic activities they perform?" The answer would of course center around an analysis of the most extensive yet basic activity of the community. As a matter of fact, most communities have multiple personalities, so to speak. That is, there is a multifunctional character to almost all communities. As we have mentioned so often, retailing institutions and some variety of retail trade are always found, to some degree, in all places where people live or congregate. And every community to some extent has a form of basic industry, whether it be educational or manufacturing. However, in spite of the multifunctional characteristic of most communities, some single function usually dominates; many a city has acquired a distinction for some one single dominant characteristic.

The most widely accepted functional classification of cities was made by Chauncy D. Harris.[3] Nine principal types of cities are recognized, and each type is designated by a letter and definition, as shown in Table 7-1.

The important insight to be gained from a functional analysis of communities is that a given functional type is likely to represent a different and unique market opportunity for the retail manager. The college town most

[3] Chauncy D. Harris, "A Functional Classification of Cities in the United States," *The Geographical Review* (January 1943), pp. 86–89.

TABLE 7-1 Criteria Used by Harris in Classifying Cities by Function

Manufacturing Cities M' Subtype:
   Principal criterion: Employment in manufacturing equals at least 74 per cent of total employment in manufacturing, retailing, and wholesaling (employment figures).
   Secondary criterion: Manufacturing and mechanical industries contain at least 45 per cent of gainful workers (occupation figures).
Manufacturing Cities M Subtype:
   Employment in manufacturing equals at least 60 per cent of the total employment in manufacturing, retailing, and wholesaling. The manufacturing and mechanical industries contain between 20 and 45 per cent of the gainful workers.
Retail Centers R:
   Employment in retailing is 50 per cent or more of the total employment in manufacturing, wholesaling, and retailing, and at least 2.2 times that in wholesaling alone.
Diversified Cities D:
   Employment in manufacturing, wholesaling, and retailing is less than 60 per cent, 20 per cent, and 50 per cent, respectively, of total employment in these activities. No other special criteria apply. Manufacturing and mechanical industries, with few exceptions, contain between 25 per cent and 35 per cent of the gainful workers.
Wholesale Centers W:
   Employment in wholesaling is at least 20 per cent of the total employment in manufacturing, wholesaling, and retailing and at least 45 per cent as much as retailing alone.
Transportation Centers T:
   Transportation and communication contain at least 11 per cent of the gainful workers, and workers in transportation and communication equal at least one third the number in manufacturing and mechanical industries and at least two thirds the number in trade.
Mining Towns S:
   Extraction of minerals accounts for more than 15 per cent of the gainful workers (applied only to cities of 25,000 and over for which data are available).
University Towns E:
   Enrollment in schools of collegiate rank (university, technical schools, liberal arts colleges, and teachers colleges) equal to at least 25 per cent of the city population.
Resort and Retirement Towns X:
   No satisfactory criterion found.

SOURCE: Chauncy D. Harris, "A Functional Classification of Cities in the United States," The Geographical Review (January 1943), pp. 86–89.

likely would support a larger aggregation of men's and women's fashion clothing stores than would, say, the mining community or the transportation center. The nature of the economic base (the basic employment opportunities) is likely to vary directly with the functional character of the community. The retail store manager contemplating the expansion of an operation or the opening of a new store would certainly be less than astute if he proceeded without fully analyzing the character and functional basis of the community or communities that he has under consideration.

Stages of Growth

Not only the functional character of the community, but its position in the life cycle should be explored. Communities, like products or people, emerge, develop, exist, and then expire. All cities are constantly expanding or contracting with the vicissitudes of geographic, biological, and social change. The history of some communities follows short cycles of life and growth, and others have very long lives.

Growth patterns of various communities differ significantly, and these growth patterns obviously would exert considerable influence on the retail market opportunity.

Over a span of time, growth patterns of communities may be of four major types. These include the pattern of rapid growth, the pattern of continuous growth, the pattern of relatively stable growth, and the pattern of decline. The rapid growth pattern can be found largely in communities located along the Gulf Coast, in the Southwest, and in the West. The continuous growth pattern is appearing in communities that are developing new industries and expanding established industries. The slow or constant level growth pattern can be found when a city has developed an established economy that remains in a relatively stable position. The diminished or declining growth pattern is often associated with the exhaustion of resources or a shift in technology.

The important point is that the growth pattern of any community can sometimes be affected positively by the climate of community attitudes engendered by the population and its leaders. Some communities refuse to die; as a result of community planning and initiative, a declining growth pattern might actually be reversed.

Community Structure

The problem of retail store location and site analysis leads one to a central and crucial question: Is there to some degree a common pattern or order that carries over from city to city and that implies similar processes of origin? Many students of the city and its resultant land use pattern have claimed that there is and have tended to follow one or another of the ideas that have been advanced.

Weimer and Hoyt contend that a community may expand (1) by growing vertically through the replacement of lower structures with higher ones, (2) by filling in open spaces between settled areas, or (3) by extending the existing settled area.[4] They argue that when the settled area is expanded, growth may take several forms. Given the market orientation of the retail location decision, it would appear that knowledge of community structure would be one of the first factors upon which a particular location decision would proceed. The three principal explanations of community structure have commonly been referred to as the *concentric zone theory,* the *sector theory,* and the *multiple nuclei theory.*

Concentric Zone Theory. According to Burgess, "In the absence of counteracting factors" the American city should take the form of five concentric zones. The characteristics of these zones designate both the suc-

---

[4] Arthur M. Weimer and Homer Hoyt, *Real Estate,* 5th ed., The Ronald Press Company, New York, 1966, p. 290.

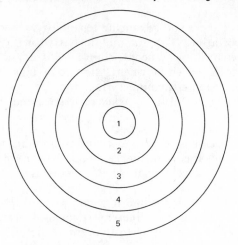

FIGURE 7-1 The concentric circle theory of community growth.
Key: 1. Central business district.
2. Zone of transition.
3. Zone of workingmen's homes.
4. Zone of middle-class dwellers.
5. Commuters' zone.

cessive zones of urban expansion and the types of areas differentiated in the process of expansion.

Burgess believed that each zone tended to invade the next one by a process called *succession*. At the heart of his model was the *loop* with the financial and office district at the center, and the retail district surrounding and penetrating it. Figure 7-1 shows a graphic sketch of the ideas involved in this theory.

As Burgess pointed out,

Encircling the downtown area there is normally an area in transition, which is being invaded by business and light manufacture. A third area is inhabited by workers in industries who have escaped from the area of deterioration but who desire to live within easy access of their work. Beyond this zone is the "residential area" of high class apartment buildings or of exclusive "restricted" districts of single family dwellings. Still further out, beyond the city limits, is the commuters' zone—suburban areas or satellite cities—within a thirty to sixty minute ride of the central business district.[5]

The Burgess theory has been a useful concept in explaining city form and structure. However, the complexity of the modern city has rendered it virtually useless today. His theory was made obsolete essentially by the automobile, but there have been other mitigating factors as well, including

[5] R. E. Park, E. W. Burgess, and R. D. McKenzie, *The City*, University of Chicago Press, Chicago, 1925, pp. 50–53.

rising incomes and advancing technology, especially in communication and transportation. The automobile has wrought profound and fundamental changes in the way people shop and live. The wide separation of workers from places of employment, the rise of planned shopping centers, the decentralization of manufacturing, and the more complex utilization of land resources have all to a greater or lesser extent been influenced by the automobile.

The Sector Theory. A second major theory of community growth and structure is the sector theory. It can be traced in part to the work of Hurd,[6] but Hoyt's development of the theory is based on a vast amount of empirical work.

Hoyt's analysis led him to generalize that if an entire city is thought of as a circle, and if the different residential areas are thought of as wedge-shaped sectors pointing to the center, the high-rent or high-priced areas of the city will tend over a period of years, to move outward toward the periphery in the path described by one or more of the sectors. If a certain sector develops originally as a low-rent or low-price area, the balance of that sector is likely to be occupied by low-rent or low-price residences, as expansion proceeds outward. The same generalization would hold for other sectors, whether they be intermediate or high-priced areas.

Hoyt based his sector theory on the following basic propositions:[7]

1. There is a grouping in the social order that occurs primarily as a result of incomes and social position.
2. High-income recipients tend to live in the areas that command the highest prices and rents, while the lower-income groups live in houses that are offered for lower prices and rents. Low-rent areas are located near the business and industrial center of the city and from here they tend to fan out, generally on one side or sector of the city.
3. The principal growth of American cities has taken place by new building at the periphery, rather than by the rebuilding of older areas.
4. High-grade residential areas tend to develop along the fastest existing transportation lines.
5. Trends of movement of office buildings, banks, and stores pull the higher-priced residential neighborhood in the same general direction.

Hoyt's sector theory offers considerable insight for the store location analyst. It underlines the importance of several features of a differentiated market opportunity. First of all, it suggests that the community structure in terms of residential neighborhoods is a function of several factors including income, social class, and perhaps even life style. It also suggests that community structure is a function of transportation axials and that roads, highways, rivers, or other factors either facilitating or inhibiting access or egress will affect the community structure. Finally, it suggests the concept of convenience and clustering (proposition 5) as a factor of location.

---

[6] R. M. Hurd, *Principles of City Land Values*, The Record and Guide, New York, 1924.

[7] Homer Hoyt, *The Structure and Growth of Residential Neighborhoods in American Cities*, U.S. Federal Housing Administration, Washington, D.C., 1939.

Residents and consumers are attracted to economic facilities that appear to match their particular needs.

It is generally true that high-rent areas are located in one or more sectors of a city, and usually these high-rent sectors do not form a complete circle around it. However, again the automobile has had a great impact on the structure of urban places. There exists great flexibility in urban growth patterns, which results from radial expressways and belt highways. The changing growth patterns would, in turn, exert a great influence upon the kinds of retail outlets in the community and the factors that one would analyze in order to assure a reasonably scientific approach to the location and site analysis problem. Figure 7-2 depicts the sector theory for several American cities.

The Multiple Nuclei Theory. This concept was developed by Harris and Ullman as a modification of the sector theory. They suggest that frequently the land use pattern of a city is built around several discrete nuclei, rather than around a single center such as is postulated in the concentric zone and sector theories. The term *nucleus* is used to refer to any attracting element around which growth—residential, business, industrial, or other—

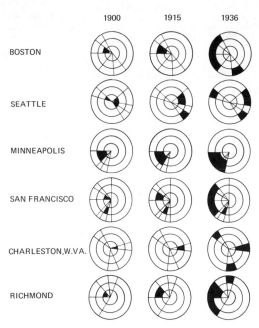

FIGURE 7-2 Sector theory of city structure, showing shifts in location of fashionable residential areas in six American cities, 1900–1936. Fashionable residential areas are indicated by solid black.

SOURCE: *After Figure 40 in* The Structure and Growth of Residential Neighborhoods in American Cities *(Washington, D.C.: U.S. Federal Housing Administration, 1939).*

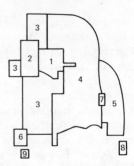

FIGURE 7-3 Multiple nuclei theory explanation of city structure. The diagram represents one possible pattern among innumerable variations. Numbers refer as follows: (1) central business district, (2) wholesale and light manufacturing, (3) low-class residential, (4) medium-class residential, (5) high-class residential, (6) heavy manufacturing, (7) outlying business district, (8) residential suburb, and (9) industrial suburb.

SOURCE: After C. D. Harris and E. L. Ullman, "The Nature of Cities," The Annals of the American Academy of Political and Social Science, Vol. 242 (November 1945), Fig. 5.

takes place. The rise of separate nuclei and differentiated districts reflects a combination of four factors:

1. Certain activities require specialized facilities. The retail district, for example, is attached to the point of greatest intracity accessibility. . . .
2. Certain like activities group together because they profit from cohesion. . . . Retail districts benefit from grouping which increases the concentration of potential customers and makes possible comparison shopping. . . .
3. Certain unlike activities are detrimental to each other. . . . The heavy concentration of pedestrians, [and] automobiles . . . in the retail district are antagonistic both to the railroad facilities and the street loading required in the wholesale district, and to the rail facilities and space needed by large industrial districts and vice versa.
4. Certain activities are unable to afford the high rents of the most desirable sites. . . . Examples are bulk wholesaling and storage activities requiring much room.[8]

[8] C. D. Harris and E. L. Ullman, "The Nature of Cities," *The Annals of the American Academy of Political and Social Science,* Vol. 242 (November 1945), pp. 14–15.

The multiple nuclei theory would appear to be a useful model to aid the retail manager in his analysis of store location decisions. Figure 7-3 graphically depicts the multiple nuclei concept of community growth and structure.

What conclusions can be drawn about the various theories of community growth and structure? In a most general sense, we can find considerable usefulness in each of the theories. For instance, hardly anyone can deny that the concentric zone theory applies in a very general way to the average city. Nor can one deny the usefulness of understanding the process of transition or succession that emanates from the theory.

Elements of the sector theory are evident in most expanding communities. This theory offers valuable insight into such factors as income and social class as determinants of location.

The multiple nuclei concept would appear to offer real promise as a guide or model on the basis of which a truly sophisticated approach to location decisions might be based. It is unquestionably a theory that fits the highly flexible modern urban scene. The widespread use of automobile traffic appears to weaken both the concentric zone theory and the sector theory; however, the multiple nuclei theory seems to accommodate even better as a result of this basic change in transportation.

trading area concepts and analysis

From our discussion of community function and structure, we turn our attention now to another most important concept related to the problem of store location and site analysis—the *trading area.*

The concept of trading area is intuitively rather well understood by both students and practitioners of marketing. Yet this intuitive understanding is difficult to apply to actual trading area analysis and delineation. The definitions committee of the American Marketing Association defines a trading area as

> a district whose size is usually determined by the boundaries within which it is economical in terms of volume and cost for a marketing unit to sell and/or deliver a good or service.[9]

This definition captures the meaning and essence of the trading area concept only in its broadest and loosest sense. Others have defined a trading area as "a spatially ordered framework within which a store gets its business within a given span of time."[10] Another has called the trading area "perimeters for consumer space preference";[11] still another has defined a trading area as

---

[9] Committee on Definitions of The American Marketing Association, *Marketing Definitions: A Glossary of Marketing Terms,* American Marketing Association, Chicago, 1960.

[10] William Applebaum and Saul B. Cohen, "Store Trading Areas in a Changing Market," *Journal of Retailing* (Fall 1961) , p. 18.

[11] Bernard J. LaLonde, *Differentials in Supermarket Drawing Power,* Bureau of Business and Economic Research, Michigan State University, Paper No. 11, East Lansing, Mich., 1962, p. 59.

a geographically delineated region, containing potential customers for whom there exists a probability greater than zero of their purchasing a given class of products or services offered for sale by a particular firm or by a particular agglomeration of firms.[12]

This last definition seems to offer the most useful framework within which to present our discussion of trading area concepts. The trading area consists essentially of the geographical space from which the retail store develops its market opportunity; it is generally bounded by zones, not fixed lines of demarcation. Another characteristic of trading areas is that they vary considerably in size, and this size variation is usually a function of the size of the community and/or the size of the store. As the last definition implied, a trading area will exist for a given store and a trading area will exist for a given aggregation of stores such as a downtown shopping district or an outlying planned shopping center. The city of Spokane, Washington has an extremely large trading area—extending from parts of Southern Canada in the north to Lewiston, Idaho in the south; as far east as Missoula, Montana, and generally as far west as the eastern slopes of the Cascade Mountains. Now, this does not imply that all persons living within this space perimeter shop for all their goods and services in Spokane, Washington. It does, however, bound an area that contains potential customers for whom there exists a probability greater than zero of their purchasing goods within Spokane.

It is probably true that the Crescent Department Store or the Bon Marche Department Store (each located in Spokane) have trading areas that are nearly coextensive with that of Spokane generally. However, it would be highly unlikely that a food store or variety store in Spokane would have an individual trading area anywhere nearly as large as these major department stores. Store trading areas and community trading areas often are not likely to coincide. Trading areas generally are the joint product of many simultaneously interacting factors. However, as a result of trading area studies, a number of important empirical regularities have been shown to exist:[13]

1. There is a maximum amount of mileage and time which consumers will invest in travel for a particular product.
2. Consumers generally purchase goods or services from the closest place that offers these goods and services.
3. Consumers oftentimes prefer to combine purchases on a single trip and may even go past a store offering the product if they can purchase several products at one stop where there is a greater variety of merchandise.
4. The distance consumers are willing to travel does not differ greatly between convenience and shopping goods.
5. The attitudes that consumers hold concerning the shopping alternatives around them markedly affect the size and shape of retail trading areas.

[12] David L. Huff, "Defining and Estimating a Trading Area," *Journal of Marketing* (July 1964), p. 38.
[13] Edward M. Mazze, "Determining Shopper Movement Patterns by Cognitive Maps," *Journal of Retailing*, Vol. 50, No. 3 (Fall 1974), p. 43.

Figures 7-4 and 7-5 are designed to show in hypothetical fashion several dimensions of the trading area concept. Figure 7-4 shows the general retail trading area of Spokane, Washington.

Figure 7-5 shows in hypothetical fashion the trading areas of various trading centers or retail clusters within the greater Spokane area. The reader should be aware that in the downtown central business district the trading area for some goods will be the same as the trading area shown for the city of Spokane in Figure 7-4. Other of the trading areas will be considerably less extensive. Also from Figure 7-5, notice that there is considerable overlap of the trading areas for the various major trading centers. This material is meant for illustrative purposes only.

Another refinement of the trading area concept has been added by introducing the concept of probability contours or demand gradients.[14] These gradients are expressed as probability contours ranging from $P > 1$ to $P < 0$. An example of how these contours look when mapped is illustrated in Figure 7-6, in which a partial retail trading area has been calculated for shopping center J_1.

Had the retail trading areas of shopping centers J_2 and J_{14} been calculated and superimposed over the trading area of J_1, the reader would observe that parts of each shopping center's trading area envelop parts of the others. It

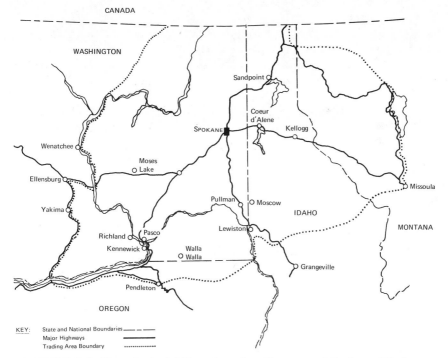

FIGURE 7-4 **Hypothetical delineation of trading area of Spokane, Wash.**

[14] David L. Huff, *Determination of Intra-urban Retail Trade Areas*, Real Estate Research Program, University of California, Los Angeles, 1962.

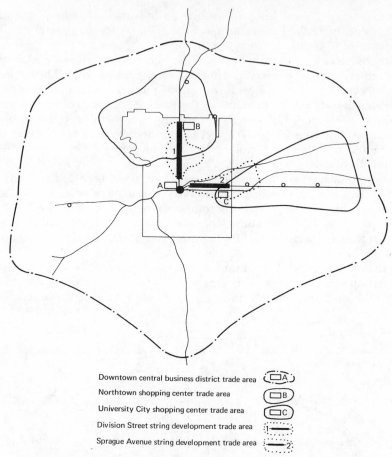

Downtown central business district trade area   A

Northtown shopping center trade area   B

University City shopping center trade area   C

Division Street string development trade area   1

Sprague Avenue string development trade area   2

FIGURE 7-5   **Hypothetical delineation of trading areas for retail clusters, Spokane, Wash.**

should also be pointed out that where these envelopments occur at intersections of contours having the same probability values, it would be possible to determine the breaking points between each of these competing centers. The following general conclusions can now be drawn concerning the nature and scope of a trading area:[15]

1. A trading area represents a demand surface containing potential customers for a specific product (s) or service (s) of a particular distribution center.

2. A distribution center may be a single firm or an agglomeration of firms.

3. A demand surface consists of a series of demand gradients or zones,

[15] David L. Huff, "Defining and Estimating a Trading Area," *Journal of Marketing* (July 1964), p. 38.

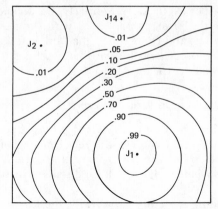

FIGURE 7-6 A trading area defined in demand gradients or probability contours.

SOURCE: David L. Huff, Determination of Intra-urban Retail Trade Areas (Los Angeles: University of California, Real Estate Research Program, 1962).

reflecting varying customer-sales potentials. An exception to the condition of demand gradients would be in the rare case in which only one distribution center existed in a unique geographical setting, thus representing an absolute monopoly in providing products and/or services that are of an absolute necessity. Under these conditions, no gradients would exist but rather a single homogeneous demand plane.

4. Demand gradients are of a probabilistic nature, ranging from a probability value of less than one to a value greater than zero (except in the complete monopoly situation in which the probability value equals one).

5. The total potential customers encompassed within a distribution center's demand surface (trading area) is the sum of the expected number of consumers from each of the demand gradients.

6. Demand gradients of competing firms overlap; and where gradients of like probability intersect, a spatial competitive equilibrium position is reached.

The concept of probability contours of demand gradients has been used by many location analysts in referring to such concepts as *core* or the *primary* and *secondary* trading areas. The primary trade area is usually referred to as a core or perimeter space from which a store gets most of its business. Consequently, a ratio of store sales from the core area to total store sales is arbitrarily set. In the example presented in Figure 7-6, the area encompassed by the demand gradient .70 might well be conceived as the store's *primary trading area*. This is the area generally closest to the store and with the highest density of customers to population and usually the highest per capita sales. Similarly, the *secondary trade area* is that area adjoining the primary trade area with the next highest ratio of customers to population and from which the store gets 15, 20, or 25 per cent of its sales. The *tertiary* or *fringe trade area* is defined as the residential portions of the store's trade area.[16]

Related Trade Area Concepts

An understanding of several other important concepts related to trade area analysis is vital to the retail management decision maker. These are (1) the size of the trading area, (2) trading area shape, and (3) trading area movement. Each will be discussed in turn.

Trading Area Size.   Basically, the size of the trading area is a function of store size and the size of the urban area in which the store is located. As a further generalization, the per cent of sales obtained from the more distant portion of the trading area varies inversely with the size of the city. In short, the trading area for a retail cluster (whether it be a downtown shopping district or a suburban shopping center) is said to vary directly with the distance between competing facilities, and inversely with the size of such facilities. We shall dwell further on this generalization later.

Large populations appear to attract or draw larger and greater numbers of the same type of stores to one central location area. When this occurs there is a multiplicative effect that results in a larger sized trading area for the given retail cluster, but this multiplicative effect is dampened by the friction of distance that serves to act as a counterforce and which diminishes the share of business that the retail cluster would obtain from the outer reaches of the trading area. Several other observations have been made pertaining to factors that affect trading area size. The higher the income of the population surrounding a retail cluster, the greater the size of the trading area. This probably reflects the increased mobility of the higher-income recipients and their greater tendency to travel longer distances in order to shop in areas with greater depth and assortments.

A trading area tends to increase in size as the means of access and egress are improved. This factor points up the importance of accessibility: natural or artificial barriers that impede the movement of goods to a central shopping place can greatly restrict the size of the trading area.

Shape.   Numerous shapes have been suggested as being more typical than others in defining and outlining the space perimeters of the trading area. For the sake of convenience, simple circles are sometimes drawn around a given store or trading center as lines of demarcation, or as suggested areas from which the store or center draws trade. Generally, however, the hexagon, triangle, or star shapes are more representative of the actual shape of trading areas.

Theoretically, where topography was uniform and consumers wished to

---

[16] William Applebaum, "Methods for Determining Store Trade Areas, Market Penetration, and Potential Sales," *Journal of Marketing Research* (May 1966), pp. 127–141.

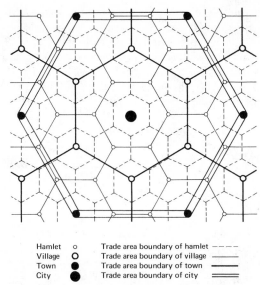

Hamlet	o	Trade area boundary of hamlet	– – – –
Village	O	Trade area boundary of village	———
Town	⬤	Trade area boundary of town	▬▬▬
City	⬤	Trade area boundary of city	═══

**FIGURE 7-7   Size and shape of trading areas:
The Christaller Hypothesis.**

minimize travel time, the trade area around each shopping facility nucleus
(either store or retail cluster) would be a circle, the radius of which would
reflect the optimum travel time for the customer. However, contiguous trade
areas circular in shape would, of course, produce overlaps or voids. Of all
geometric shapes, hexagons come the closest to circles, and still neither overlap nor leave voids when packed together (Figure 7-7). Therefore, it has
been postulated that trade centers would be located in hexagonal patterns
and their trade areas would be hexagons instead of circles.[17] This suggests
that a retail store or trade center will sell its products outward in all directions from its location to a point in each direction where it can compete just
as effectively, but no more effectively, than its competitors reaching the same
point.

At these points, buyers will be indifferent as to whether they buy from
one competitor or another who is equally and optimally well located. Under these conditions each firm or retail cluster will have a hexagon-shaped
market area, and these hexagons will absorb all space, giving the appearance of a segment of a honeycomb. When all space is not absorbed, new
firms or centers will enter the market area until the circular market areas
(which arise when companies have no immediate competitors) are com-
pressed into hexagons. Competitive effort would then tend to be optimal.

Some very interesting work, related somewhat to the concept just discussed, has been done in terms of measuring the breaking point, or pre-

[17] The Christaller Hypothesis is, as the name suggests, credited to a German geog-
rapher, Walter Christaller, *Die zentralen Orte in Süddeutschland,* Gustav Fischer Verlag,
Jena, Germany, 1933.

dicting the boundary line separating trade areas around two cities, or trade centers unequal in size. Assume that we have two cities, City Y and City Z. The distance between the two cities is 100 miles. City Y has a population of 10,000, and City Z has a population of 30,000. Where would the boundary line separating the trade area of City Y and City Z be?

Breaking point theory attempts to predict the location of this line by means of the following formula:

$$\text{Distance of breaking point from the smaller trade center} = \frac{\overset{\text{Ratio}}{\text{Distance between two trade centers}}}{1 + \text{the square root of population of larger city} \div \text{population of smaller city}}$$

In symbols, the ratio is

$$\frac{d}{1 + \sqrt{\text{pop Z/pop Y}}}$$

and by substituting the appropriate values from our knowledge of the distances and sizes relating to the two cities, we find

$$\text{Distance from Y} = \frac{100}{1 + \sqrt{\dfrac{30,000}{10,000}}} = 36.6 \text{ miles}$$

Quite realistically, however, we must consider that the position of a trade area boundary is influenced not only by the forces of distance and size of trade centers, but also by such factors as variations in land forms, nature of transportation routes, and political boundaries.

Trading Area Movement. As a basic generalization, trade areas are never neat geometrical forms such as squares, circles, or hexagons. Their shapes most often are erratic amoebae or star-shaped configurations most strongly affected by street patterns, irregular topography, rivers, and other transportation axials.

Most often, store trading areas are elongated in the direction of customer movement. Consequently, a super highway and a well-developed set of arterials into and out of a trading center will greatly affect the size and the market potential of the area. In such a case, the trading area is most likely to resemble a leaflike configuration with the roads and highway representing the skeletal framework.

One is cautioned also to consider that if the population tributary to the major highway is sparse, then in spite of heavy traffic, the store is not likely to draw much trade from this traffic flow.

Trading areas do change. They are not fixed and stable configurations over long periods of time. The stability of the trading area or its dynamics will reflect the economic, demographic, and other conditions affecting the entire general area. Rapid infusions of population with adequate purchasing power are likely to mean accelerated business opportunities generally, and this in turn is likely to mean disequilibrium in trading area patterns and networks. A single new store emerging in a long-established trading center is likely to have a profound effect on the trading area pattern for the entire center, as well as for the individual units.

The Importance of the Trading Area Concept

As retail firms become more sophisticated in their approach to market opportunity, they will of necessity be more concerned with acquiring a greater understanding of trading area concepts such as measurement, delineation, and evaluation. Trading area analysis deals with a special case of the larger problem related to the spatial dimension of demand. Knowledge of the spatial dimension of demand serves two fundamental purposes for the retailing executive: (1) it gives him a basis for planning and decision making and (2) it gives him solid information to use as a means for evaluating these decisions and for managerial control.

As mentioned at the outset of this chapter, trading area analysis fits hand in glove with our earlier treatment of market opportunity, our study of population and income, and consumer behavior. A study of trading areas reveals something about the consumer groups from which the store's customers are drawn. It also permits a more careful determination and analysis of the market segments to which the system is directing its merchandising efforts. If this is true, the system's output of goods and services ought to reflect a more precise adjustment and accommodation to the segments determined by its trading area analysis.

QUESTIONS FOR STUDY, REFLECTION, AND REVIEW

1. Explain the relationship between location and site analysis and that of market opportunity.
2. Why will store location and site decisions continue to be critical decisions for the retailing system?
3. Explain why store location decisions must be continually re-evaluated.
4. Retail store location begins with an analysis of the community. Define what is meant by a community.
5. Of the three community structure theories, which one offers the most promise for the retail manager? Why?
6. Define the trading area concept that offers the most useful framework within which to discuss the retail system.
7. As a result of trading area studies, a number of general regularities have been shown to exist. What are these regularities?
8. Explain the concept of probability contours or demand gradients as related to the trading area concepts.
9. Explain the concepts of primary and secondary trading areas.
10. Explain what the breaking point theory attempts to do. What are some of its limitations?

8

store location processes

The reader will have deduced by now that the store location problem is an optimizing problem, from the point of view of both the retail firm and the individual consumer. The retail unit seeks an optimum network or distribution pattern for its products and services, and the consumer seeks an optimum balance between his shopping inputs—time, money, distance —and his shopping outputs—satisfactions in the form of acquired goods and services.

The ability to locate retail trade centers or retailing systems in an optimum fashion is affected by such considerations as the nature and demand characteristics of the goods; the generative or pulling power of central place assortments; transportation costs and access facilities to and from central place assortments; and the organization or hierarchy of marketing-retailing establishments found in central place locations.

In Chapter 7 we looked broadly at some of these many factors related to store location or central place concepts. We shall continue our discussion by looking next at some of the key problems connected with delineating and then evaluating a retail trading area.

delineating the trading area

The importance of delineating or outlining the space perimeters of the trading area was spelled out in considerable detail in Chapter 7. However, we did not spend much time discussing the various means for accomplishing this important task. Delineating the trading area for existing stores presents considerably fewer problems than accomplishing the same thing for proposed stores. As a matter of fact, attempting to delineate the trading area for a nonexisting store is a problem of considerable magnitude and difficulty, and the help of a competent trained specialist is strongly advised.

Because of this difficulty, our discussion will focus on the problem from the point of the existing store or store network. Some of the generalizations can be loosely applied to the nonexisting store problem.

There are essentially two methods used to delineate or establish the trading area boundaries, space perimeters, or demand gradients for an existing retail store. One is an empirical approach, in which considerable field research is undertaken and data generated, from which conclusions are drawn regarding the trading area boundaries. The empirical approach can generate about any level of accuracy desired. That is, accuracy is largely a function of methodology, time, effort, and money spent. However, even a minimum level of accuracy will involve considerable sums of each of these elements, and when a fast and reasonably accurate measure is desired the alternative is to use a gravitational model that depends upon secondary, instead of primary data. The choice of approach or technique will depend upon a host of considerations, including the purpose of the delineation, the time and money available, and the degree of accuracy sought. We shall look first at the gravitational models and then turn our attention to several of the more popular empirical approaches.

The Gravitational Approach

The numerous gravity models take their name from their similarity to Newton's Law of Gravitation, which states that the potential power of attraction between two bodies increases with the product of their masses and decreases with the distance between them. The reader will recall that in discussing the breaking points between trading areas, this basic principle constituted the crux of our analysis.

The gravitational approach to trading area analysis was first suggested by William J. Reilly and was stated as follows:

> Under normal conditions two cities draw retail trade from a smaller intermediate city or town in direct proportion to some power of the population of these two large cities and in an inverse proportion to some power of the distance of each of the cities from the smaller intermediate city.[1]

From this verbal statement of relationships, Reilly developed his original formula:

$$\frac{Ba}{Bb} = \left(\frac{Pa}{Pb}\right)^j \left(\frac{Db}{Da}\right)^j$$

where

Ba = business which city A draws from intermediate town T
Bb = business which city B draws from intermediate town T

[1] William J. Reilly, *Method for the Study of Retail Relationships,* Research Monograph No. 4, University of Texas Bulletin No. 2944, Bureau of Business Research, University of Texas Press, Austin, Tex., 1929, p. 16.

Pa = population of city A
Pb = population of city B
Da = distance of city A from intermediate town T
Db = distance of city B from intermediate town T

With this formula, the retail store manager could determine where the trade of an intermediate town would go between two competing cities or retail trade centers. Paul D. Converse simplified the Reilly formula by assuming $Ba = Bb$ and thus used the concept to determine the breaking point for trade flow between two towns.[2] The reader will recognize the Converse formula as the one used in Chapter 7 to determine the breaking point between two trading areas:

$$\frac{\text{Breaking point between A and B,}}{\text{miles from B}} = \frac{\text{Distance between A and B}}{1 + \sqrt{\dfrac{\text{population of town A}}{\text{population of town B}}}}$$

In addition to breaking points between trading areas, the gravitational models can also provide a way to predict the volume of retail trade patronage that one city's residents will give to other cities. For example, recall the illustrative cities in Chapter 7, City Z with 30,000 population and City Y with 10,000 population. City X, with 20,000 population, is located 50 miles from City Y, and City Y is located 100 miles from City Z. What are the relative volumes of patronage that inhabitants of City Y will give to businesses located in Cities X and Z?

Using Reilly's gravitational model

$$\frac{\text{Volume of Y's patronage to X}}{\text{Volume of Y's patronage to Z}} = \frac{\text{population of X}}{\text{population of Z}}\left(\frac{\text{distance Y} - \text{Z}}{\text{distance Y} - \text{X}}\right)^2 =$$

$$\frac{20{,}000}{30{,}000} \cdot \left(\frac{100}{50}\right)^2 = \frac{2}{3} \cdot (2)^2 = \frac{2}{3} \cdot 4 = \frac{8}{3}$$

Consequently, for every three dollars of goods that City Y's inhabitants purchase in City Z, they will tend to purchase eight dollars worth in City X.

There has been considerable research and discussion related to the gravitational approach to retail trade area delineation and analysis. The general consensus among those who use such approaches to determine trade area boundaries is that, while in some instances this approach may not correctly predict trade flows among cities, by and large this procedure predicts such trade flows reasonably well and, compared to other methods, it is low in cost and easy to use.

Both Reilly and Converse have contributed significantly to a procedure for systematically estimating retail trade areas. Their work in providing a set of functional relationships and estimated parameters has provided precise and meaningful hypotheses for empirical testing and evaluation. Their

---

[2] Paul D. Converse, *Retail Trade Areas in Illinois,* Business Study No. 4, University of Illinois, Urbana, Ill., 1946, pp. 30–31.

contributions have been the springboard for further work toward developing more meaningful mathematical models for trading area analysis.

For example, Huff has worked productively toward developing a model that contains a parameter λ (lambda) that is estimated empirically to reflect the effect of travel time on various kinds of shopping trips.[3] This work has led to the concept of a trading area as a series of probability contours or demand gradients, as discussed in Chapter 7.

James W. Rouse has suggested and demonstrated the possibility of using Reilly's Law for estimating trading areas for planned shopping centers.[4] By substituting the retail presentation of shopping goods in square foot area for size of the city, and converting distance to driving time, Rouse has shown that the principle of retail gravitation could be applied in urban areas.

Leon W. Ellwood has refined the Rouse conceptualization by restating the principle:

> The principal retail districts within a metropolitan trading area attract trade from the residential sections of the area approximately in direct proportion to the size of the retail districts and in inverse proportion to the square of the driving time distance from each residential section to the retail districts.[5]

In essence, Ellwood's formulation is a modification of Reilly's Law, used to calculate pulling power as expressed by breaking points between competing shopping centers and proposed centers where the ratio is

$$\frac{\text{Distance from A to B}}{1 + \sqrt{\dfrac{\text{size A}}{\text{size B}}}}$$

The buying power within the generating or pulling range of the proposed site is then calculated and the optimum, relative size of the proposed shopping center is obtained.

Gravitational models have shown considerable validated predictive ability to determine the relative size of trading areas between competing communities, the breaking points between trading areas, and (to some extent) the optimum size for a proposed shopping center. However, in some instances hypothetical data are used and little or no evidence of reliability is presented. Further empirical research will be needed to more clearly establish the value and reliability of the various gravitational models for the many uses to which they are put in relation to questions pertaining to trading area analysis.

[3] David L. Huff, "Defining and Estimating a Trading Area," *Journal of Marketing* (July 1964), pp. 34–38.

[4] James W. Rouse, "Estimating Productivity for Planned Regional Shopping Centers," *News and Trends in City Development,* Urban Land Institute, Washington, D.C., 1953, pp. 1–5.

[5] Leon W. Ellwood, "Estimating Potential Volume of Proposed Shopping Centers," *The Appraisal Journal* (October 1954), pp. 581–589.

The Empirical Approach

A number of empirical methods have been devised for measuring and determining trade area boundaries. Generally speaking, the various empirical methods require the generating of primary data. However, it is sometimes possible to use secondary data in such a fashion that generally good trading area boundaries and other significant data can be established. Normally, the empirical methods require extensive use of customer or potential customer interviews, either at the store site or in what is perceived to be at the time the potential trading area, such as the customer's home or the retail trading center. Several of the empirical methods will be discussed briefly.

Customer Spotting. The customer spotting or interview technique generally involves a series of customer interviews, within or adjacent to the store, after the customer has completed her purchases. A detailed questionnaire is completed by a courteous, fast, and well-trained interviewer. The significant aspect of the interview concerns such questions as the kinds and amounts of goods purchased, the amount spent in this particular store, planned expenditures for the entire shopping trip, occupation of head of household, and the address of the respondent. From this information the analyst then proceeds to spot all the interviewed customers on a spotting map containing census tract information. From this effort, the location of customer residences can be established and trading areas delineated. The census tract data can reveal a wealth of information relating to the income and life style characteristics of the inhabitants of a particular tract. The customer spotting technique is used frequently and with generally good success. It has been especially favored by the supermarket industry as a reliable method of trading area analysis. However, its major disadvantage has two dimensions: (1) It is extremely costly if done correctly and (2) it is a lengthy and time-consuming method.

A slight variation of this procedure involves using maps of a given region and interviewing customers concerning the areas over which they shop. The maps are then overlaid with cencentric circles and the density of customer shopping in terms of dollar purchases is determined.[6]

License Plate Analysis. This method is very similar to the customer spotting technique, especially in its latter stages. With this technique, instead of an interviewer we have recorders, stationed at all the entrances and exits to the store's parking lot. Employee cars are recorded and excluded before the analysis is undertaken. All customer car license plates are then recorded. The next step is to obtain the addresses of the car owners from the state Motor Vehicle Bureau. From here the analysis proceeds just as in the customer spotting technique. This approach has considerable merit. It does not involve what can be an annoying disturbance to the customer while shopping—the interview. On the other hand, it has virtually no value for stores with no off-street parking facilities; and for stores located in a group

---

[6] Edward M. Mazze, "Determining Shopper Movement Patterns by Cognitive Maps," *Journal of Retailing*, Vol. 50, No. 3 (Fall 1974), p. 43.

or retail cluster such as a shopping center, it is most often necessary to follow up with a telephone call to request information pertaining to the exact store visited, the kinds of purchases made, and the amounts spent.

Credit Record Analysis. A great deal of information is available to a store manager whose store sells merchandise on credit. The credit application and the records of credit sales can be used to determine meaningful conclusions regarding the store's trading area and the nature of its customer clientele. The procedure involved is again similar to the customer spotting technique. The analysis is accomplished by listing the addresses of credit customers and plotting them on area maps. The greatest drawback to this procedure is the fact that, unless the store has a high ratio of credit sales to total sales, this procedure may not accurately reflect either the true status of the trading area, or any other of the store's customer characteristics.

One large retail organization successfully used samplings of customer credit accounts, an optical scanner, and a digital computer in a major empirical research program designed to delineate the trading areas of its stores and to obtain summary profiles of credit customer characteristics. The significant features of this approach were that no customer contacts were made, no key punching of data was necessary, nor were extensive manual computations and tabulations required. However, the results led to the determination of trading areas for 700 stores and the major demographic-economic characteristics of over 10,000,000 retail credit customers, summarized by store, by metropolitan area, by territory or region, and nationally.[7]

Other Empirical Methods. There are several other empirical methods useful for trading area determination and analysis. Information pertaining to entrants in store contests or sales campaigns is often recorded and used as a source of primary data for determining trade boundaries and customer characteristics. Telephone interviews are undertaken that utilize the cross-index telephone directory available in most large cities and the sampling procedure used in regular home interviews. After the telephone interviewing is completed, the study proceeds in the same fashion as in home interviewing. The data obtained from check cashing and clearing operations are also utilized as an important source of information on which to base trade area studies.

Once again, it should be mentioned that the kind of method employed to determine trade area boundaries and the characteristics of customers within these trade boundaries will vary with the more specific purposes of the investigation, the amount of time and funds available, and the frequency with which trade area studies are undertaken.

Customer Outshopping

The trading area represents a boundary of customer trade preferences. It does not mean that customers concentrate 100 per cent of their shopping

[7] Manuel D. Plotkin, "The Use of Credit Accounts and Computers in Determining Store Trading Areas," in Frederick E. Webster (ed.), *Directions in Marketing*, American Marketing Association, Chicago, 1965, pp. 271–282.

within this bounded space. As a matter of fact, consumers frequently shop outside their local trade area. This tendency is referred to as *outshopping* or intermarket patronage. Outshopping is a factor with which almost all small communities must wrestle. As our discussion has already indicated, larger trading centers often have the ability to siphon off significant amounts of trade from the smaller contiguous communities. However, even large communities, which would appear to be reasonably self-contained and self-sufficient in merchandise assortments and store choice considerations, are nonetheless affected by the outshopper problem. Outshopping creates a high dollar outflow or leakage as purchasing power is transmitted from one community to another. Many small town retailers suffer from low inventory and mix capabilities, which invite outshopping patterns on the part of small town residents.[8] Furthermore, as access to competing contiguous trade areas is facilitated by better highways, faster transportation, and other improving factors, the outshopping increases.

The reasons for outshopping vary. Some outshoppers are looking for economic gains resulting from lower prices in larger trading centers where assortments are better and the level of competition more intense. Some outshoppers simply seek the diversity of unfamiliar or more stimulating surroundings. One study showed that demographically outshoppers are younger (25–54-year age group), are relatively well educated (had some college), and the relative income is high. This same study revealed that psychographically outshoppers are active, on the go, urban-oriented housewives who are neither time-conscious nor store-loyal shoppers. They tend to manifest a distaste for local shopping and hence, a strong preference for out-of-town shopping areas.[9]

Outshopping tendencies need to be considered in trading area analysis. First of all, it should be noted that most retailers almost always overestimate the size of their trading areas and second, many fail to consider the leakage problem which results from intermarket patronage. This leakage problem, while of course not uniform from area to area, can be considerable. For some areas, it may run as high as 10 per cent of total trade area sales. Thus, for each $100 spent in the trading area, $10 is spent or leaked to some contiguous area whose offer variation is perceived as more attractive.

the trading area and the market opportunity

Several times in our discussion, it has been mentioned that trading area analysis is a way of further refining the market opportunity concept. For example, any retail store having even limited sales will have a trading area. But what about the nature of its market opportunity? How can the retail

---

[8] Charles M. Lillis and Delbert I. Hawkins, "Retail Expenditure Flows in Contiguous Trade Areas," *Journal of Retailing*, Vol. 50, No. 2 (Summer 1974), p. 30. See also A. Coskum Samli and Ernest B. Uhr, "The Outshopping Spectrum: Key for Analyzing Intermarket Leakages," *Journal of Retailing*, Vol. 50, No. 2 (Summer 1974), p. 70.

[9] Fred D. Reynolds and William R. Darden, "Intermarket Patronage: A Psychographic Study of Consumer Outshoppers," *Journal of Marketing*, Vol. 36, No. 4 (October 1972), p. 50.

manager utilize his knowledge of trading area analysis in order to judge the size and magnitude of his market opportunity? There are several concepts imbedded in trading area analysis that can aid in this determination. Market opportunity ought to be related to the goals and objectives of the retail management system. For example, an analyst might conclude that a market opportunity existed if sales per capita for the existing retail stores within a given trading region were unusually high. "Unusually high" might be interpreted to mean higher than national averages for such stores, as reported by trade association figures. A market opportunity might be thought to exist if sales per square foot of selling space for the existing stores were higher than average, or if the return-on-investment for stores in the trading area showed marked deviation, on the high side, from trade association figures. There are many indices, guides, or benchmarks to which the decision maker might look in order to examine and test the strength of a market opportunity thought to exist within a given community or trading area.

There are other ways of gauging the strength of a trading area or community, in order to judge the merits of a given market opportunity. The *Sales Management Survey of Buying Power* provides a wealth of useful information for the interested store manager and decision maker. This information is available by states, leading counties and cities, and metropolitan areas. Table 8-1 shows information pertaining to Washington State metropolitan areas.

For example, look at the metropolitan statistics shown for Spokane. One observes that statistics are provided on a host of relevant factors related to market opportunity. As a matter of fact, an index of market opportunity, called the Buying Power Index, is presented in column 13. This index translates the three basic factors—population, income, and retail sales—into a single measure of market strength or market opportunity. It is a balanced index made up of

> 5 points to % U.S.A. Effective Buying Income
> 3 points to % U.S.A. Retail Sales
> 2 points to % U.S.A. Population

By referring again to Table 8-1 and looking at column 13, you will notice that the Spokane metropolitan area has a buying power index of .1422 compared with a buying power index for the Seattle-Everett metropolitan area of .7058. Obviously, on the basis of this index, the Seattle-Everett area offers a total market opportunity greater than the Spokane area.

indices that reflect the nature of the market opportunity

There are several devices or indices that can be used to qualify the nature of the market opportunity within a given trading area. Such concepts are referred to as saturation, drawing power, and over- and understoring.

TABLE 8-1 Data Relating to Sales and Market Potential for Metropolitan Areas in Washington

WASH. POPULATION—12/31/73

METRO AREA	County	Total (thousands)	% of U.S.	% White	Median Age of Pop.	% of Population by Age Groups — 0-5 Yrs.	6-11 Yrs.	12-17 Yrs.	18-24 Yrs.	25-34 Yrs.	35-49 Yrs.	50-64 Yrs.	65 & Over Yrs.	Households (thousands)	% of Household Heads by Age Groups — Under 25 Yrs.	25-34 Yrs.	35-44 Yrs.	45-54 Yrs.	55-64 Yrs.	65 & Over Yrs.
‡ΔBREMERTON	Kitsap	103.4	.0490	95.7	29.6	9.0	10.1	11.2	12.8	14.9	15.8	15.9	10.3	35.3	10.2	19.8	15.6	18.7	16.7	19.0
ΔOLYMPIA	Thurston	83.7	.0397	97.8	28.7	9.4	10.3	12.4	12.5	13.2	16.5	15.0	10.2	29.2	9.2	20.6	16.4	19.2	15.1	19.5
RICHLAND-KENNEWICK		97.8	.0463	96.6	26.9	9.4	11.3	13.7	13.4	13.2	16.8	16.1	7.3	31.5	8.3	21.9	18.4	19.7	18.4	13.3
	Benton	70.1	.0332	98.1	27.2	9.0	11.5	13.8	13.0	12.1	17.1	15.9	7.4	22.7	7.5	22.5	18.9	19.4	18.5	13.2
	Franklin	27.7	.0131	93.7	26.1	10.2	10.9	13.3	14.4	11.9	16.3	15.9	7.1	8.8	10.2	20.5	17.0	20.5	18.2	13.6
SEATTLE-EVERETT		1,394.3	.6611	92.8	29.3	8.5	10.7	12.0	12.0	15.7	17.3	14.9	8.9	492.5	10.2	24.1	16.9	18.3	14.4	16.1
	King	1,127.6	.5346	92.7	29.8	8.3	10.4	11.6	12.1	15.8	17.3	15.3	9.2	405.6	10.4	23.7	16.5	18.4	14.7	16.3
	Snohomish	266.7	.1265	98.0	27.1	9.7	12.0	13.4	11.8	14.9	17.5	13.1	7.6	86.9	9.3	26.2	18.6	17.6	13.2	15.1
SPOKANE	Spokane	297.9	.1412	97.1	28.9	9.3	10.1	11.9	13.5	13.5	15.4	15.1	11.2	102.4	10.2	18.6	19.7	17.7	16.3	17.5
‡TACOMA	Pierce	403.8	.1915	92.7	27.3	9.1	10.2	11.5	15.4	16.2	15.9	13.3	8.4	128.2	11.7	21.8	17.1	17.8	14.1	17.5
YAKIMA	Yakima	150.5	.0714	94.8	28.2	9.7	10.8	12.7	13.0	11.7	15.2	15.5	11.4	50.8	7.7	17.9	15.4	17.7	18.3	23.0
TOTAL ABOVE AREAS		2,531.4	1.2002	94.4	28.8	8.9	10.5	12.0	12.9	15.0	16.6	14.8	9.3	869.9	10.2	22.4	16.6	18.2	15.1	17.5
STATE TOTALS		3,435.0	1.6285	95.1	28.9	8.9	10.4	12.0	13.1	14.5	16.3	15.0	9.8	1,179.2	9.9	21.5	16.0	17.9	10.7	16.7

WASH. EFFECTIVE BUYING INCOME—1973

METRO AREA	County	EBI ($000)	% of U.S.	Per Capita EBI	Median Hsld. EBI	Avg. Hsld. EBI	% of Hslds. by EBI Groups — $0-$2,999 Hslds.	$3,000-$4,999 Hslds.	$5,000-$7,999 Hslds.	$8,000-$9,999 Hslds.	$10,000-$14,999 Hslds.	$15,000-$24,999 Hslds.	$25,000 & Over Hslds.	Buying Power Index	Graduated Buying Power Indexes — EPP (Economy-Priced Products)	MPP (Moderate-Priced Products)	PPP (Premium-Priced Products)
‡ΔBREMERTON	Kitsap	521,044	.0592	5,039	10,944	14,760	10.0	6.2	14.7	14.7	23.5	20.5	10.4	.0517	.0457	.0488	.0559
ΔOLYMPIA	Thurston	409,568	.0465	4,893	10,893	14,026	11.2	7.2	14.3	12.7	26.3	19.2	9.1	.0428	.0381	.0430	.0424
RICHLAND-KENNEWICK		386,433	.0439	3,951	10,319	12,268	13.5	7.3	14.5	13.0	27.8	18.1	5.8	.0448	.0431	.0491	.0419
	Benton	281,487	.0320	4,016	10,604	12,400	13.0	7.0	14.3	12.2	28.8	19.0	5.7	.0307	.0300	.0338	.0306
	Franklin	104,946	.0119	3,789	9,668	11,926	14.4	8.1	15.0	15.1	25.8	15.6	6.0	.0141	.0131	.0153	.0113
SEATTLE-EVERETT		6,647,517	.7548	5,009	10,359	13,497	10.6	6.7	16.0	15.0	25.4	18.4	7.9	.7058	.6336	.7350	.6856
	King	5,647,935	.6413	4,768	10,694	13,925	10.4	6.3	15.2	14.5	25.7	19.3	8.6	.5991	.5101	.6119	.6035
	Snohomish	999,582	.1135	3,748	9,274	11,503	11.1	8.2	19.8	17.3	24.7	14.2	4.7	.1067	.1235	.1231	.0821
SPOKANE	Spokane	1,160,208	.1317	3,895	8,917	11,330	15.0	9.5	18.8	14.5	22.2	14.2	5.8	.1422	.1546	.1493	.1256
‡TACOMA	Pierce	1,639,845	.1862	4,061	9,810	12,791	11.4	8.2	17.2	14.6	24.6	16.8	7.2	.1221	.1711	.1075	.1729
YAKIMA	Yakima	490,832	.0557	3,261	7,628	9,662	19.9	12.3	20.5	14.1	18.7	10.2	4.3	.0617	.0810	.0646	.0484
TOTAL ABOVE AREAS		11,255,447	1.2780	4,446	9,909	12,993	11.9	7.5	16.5	14.6	24.8	17.3	7.4	1.2311	1.1693	1.2771	1.1727
STATE TOTALS		14,826,383	1.6835	4,316	9,680	12,573	12.7	7.9	17.1	14.6	24.2	16.5	7.0	1.6404	1.6285	1.7070	1.5269

SOURCE: "Sales Management Survey of Buying Power," Sales & Marketing Management, July 8, 1974. Reprinted with permission of Sales & Marketing Management. Copyright 1974.

Saturation

Saturation of a trading area indicates that market opportunity and market offering are in equilibrium. When a trading area is saturated, it implies that the market opportunity for a given kind of store or for all stores has been absorbed, that enough facilities exist to serve the population and needs of this market adequately, and that the store units are making only a satisfactory level of return on their investment.

One researcher has developed a rather unique concept to enable location analysts to evaluate given communities in terms of the saturation factor for supermarkets. The concept deals essentially with two main factors: the amount of food sales available in any geographical area and certain characteristics of supermarket facilities in any given geographical area. These two factors are then combined to form an index of supermarket saturation. This index can be defined as an index number providing a relative measure of supermarket saturation in any given trading area. Here it is expressed as a functional relationship:

Formula for Index of Supermarket Saturation

$$IRS_1 = \frac{C_1(RE_1)}{RF_1}$$

where

IRS_1 = Index of supermarket saturation for area one
C_1 = Number of consumers in area one
RE_1 = Food expenditures per consumer in area one
RF_1 = Retail facilities in area one

Consider the following example in analyzing supermarket potential in Market area A:

The 100,000 consumers in Market A spend an average of $10.50 per week in food stores. There are 15 supermarkets serving Market A, with a total of 144,000 square feet of selling area.

$$IRS_A = \frac{100,000 \times 10.50}{144,000} = \frac{1,050,000}{144,000} = \$7.29$$

The $7.29 per square foot of selling area measured against the dollars per square foot necessary to break even would provide the measure of saturation in Market A. The $7.29 figure would also be useful in evaluating relative opportunity in different areas.

For example, if a retailer was considering entering four different market areas and the *IRS* for each was calculated as follows: Market area A = $7.29; Market area B = $2.69; Market area C = $3.24; and Market area D = $4.50; his course of action would be reasonably clear.[10]

[10] Bernard J. LaLonde, "New Frontiers in Store Location," *Supermarket Merchandising* (February 1963), p. 110.

In summary, the concept of saturation and any such index that can measure saturation provide valuable insight for the store manager and location analyst in evaluating the potential of any market. The saturation index provides a superior measurement for the simple analysis of market opportunity because it takes into account both the demand side (potential) and the supply side (retail facilities) in evaluating a market.

Drawing Power and Market Share

The drawing power concept attempts to relate the per cent of sales that a store obtains from a specific area (trading area) of a community in relation to its total sales. Earlier, we mentioned that the per capita sales of a store (a store's retail sales per person by week, month, or annum) would be an index of the store's penetration of a given area, as opposed to its per capita sales for another area. This relative comparison is an indicator of a store's drawing power. A closely related measure is that of market share. Market share can be expressed as

$$\text{Market share} = \frac{\text{Store sales per capita}}{\text{Per capita sales potential}}$$

This is not necessarily an easy factor to determine. As the reader would surmise, the most difficult thing to determine in the equation is the denominator or per capita sales potential. However, the market share figure is a valuable index of the particular store's efforts in capturing or exploiting a given market opportunity. If market share in relation to potential is extremely low, an immediate action should be launched to discover why this is so, and efforts should be made to remedy the situation.

Overstoring Versus Understoring

A given trading area or community can only support so many stores. The principal index of an understored or overstored situation within a given trading area is return on investment. When return on investment is lower than industry or trade standards would indicate it should be, and all other things remain equal (i.e., when the total retail merchandising strategy is adequate), then an overstored condition exists. An overstored condition most likely would mean that all the stores within the trading area have lower than normal return on investment. This low return also indicates a saturation and an overexploitation of the market opportunity. Conversely, if return on investment for the stores in the trading area is higher than industry statistics indicate is normal, then a situation of understoring exists. This indicates that the market has too few stores to satisfy the needs of its customers.

accommodating the store to the trading area and community—site selection

It must be emphasized that the whole problem of store location and site analysis is essentially a sequential one. It begins basically (as our coverage would suggest) with an evaluation and selection of a community within which to establish a business, followed by an evaluation of the various trading areas, their size and potential within the community; then finally, it concludes with the actual determination of the store site within the community and within the trading area. However, it must also be mentioned that the entire issue of store location and site analysis is to a considerable extent interdependent. The choice of community will depend upon the relative merits of the trading areas involved, and if no suitable site is found within what is considered a very desirable community and trading area, then the entire analysis must be reiterated. When the community has been chosen, the trading area in which the final site is selected will depend upon many complex factors.

Store location decisions are generally predicated upon a set of generalizations related to certain customer convenience factors. For example, one writer has suggested that the study of retail location models is structured along these propositions:[11]

1. Consumers in their shopping behavior manifest an interest in both utility and disutility.
2. The distance that consumers are willing to travel to satisfy their need for goods and services purchased from retailing institutions is some measure of the extent of inconvenience or disutility that they are willing to undergo.
3. Some goods and purchases call forth much larger amounts of search and shopping time and this factor significantly affects the spatial distribution of retail outlets.
4. Consumer shopping behavior, attitudes, and habits do change over time and this, in turn, may affect retail area structure.

Throughout the discussion of retail store location, it has been emphasized that market coverage by the retail unit depends not only on the number of retail outlets within a given trading area, but on their location or total network in relation to the spatial distribution of market potential.

Aspinwall has provided a set of generalizations relating to the classification of goods purchased at retail, based upon shopping behavior. Obviously, shopping behavior is a key determinant of store location; therefore, his classification would warrant our examination. Aspinwall suggested five criteria as affecting or determining the basic characteristics of retail goods based upon shopping behavior:[12]

1. Replacement rate—the rate at which a good is purchased and consumed by users in order to provide the satisfaction a consumer expects from the product.

[11] These factors have been adapted with minor modifications from Donald L. Thompson, "Consumer Convenience and Retail Area Structure," *Journal of Marketing Research* (February 1967), pp. 37–44.

[12] Leo V. Aspinwall, "The Characteristics of Goods Theory," in William Lazer and Eugene Kelley (eds.), *Managerial Marketing: Perspectives and Viewpoints,* rev. ed., Richard D. Irwin, Inc., Homewood, Ill., 1962, pp. 633–643.

2. Gross margin—the money amount that is the difference between purchase or acquisition price and the final selling price.
3. Adjustment—services applied to goods in order that they (products) meet the exact needs of the consumer.
4. Time of consumption—the amount of time over which the good yields up satisfactions or utility to the consumer.
5. Searching time—the measure of average time and distance from the retail store and consequently the convenience the consumer is afforded by market facilities.

Upon these criteria Aspinwall based several conclusions regarding the location of retail establishments. For example, in the case of the location of establishments selling cigarettes, a convenience good, he concluded

> the amount of inconvenience suffered by the consumer is usually very low since the market has reacted to the fact that there is a wide and insistent demand for cigarettes. To meet this demand, points of purchase are established wherever large numbers of potential customers are to be found.[13]

Store Location and Customer Convenience

The discussion thus far leads us to one single, but meaningful, generalization—the central basis for store location decisions and site analysis is the crucial question of customer convenience. At best, however, customer convenience is a nebulous concept. A given retail outlet may have several different kinds of patronage. On the one hand, the store or the cluster within which it is located may have *generative business*. This is traffic and sales volume that stem from the efforts of the store or cluster as a result of deliberate strategy efforts such as heavy advertising, promotions, or unique merchandise assortments. Another kind of patronage is *shared business*. This is traffic or sales volume that redounds to a given unit or outlet as a result of the generative power of its neighbors. Finally, there are traffic and volume that are not generated by the store itself or its neighbors, but rather result from the fact that business and traffic come from people whose principal purpose in being at, or near the store, is something other than buying or shopping. This is called *suscipient business*.[14]

However, all three forms of patronage still reflect the concept of customer convenience, if convenience is thought of as having two major characteristics: (1) proximity or accessibility, i.e., putting the retail outlet in close and easy juxtaposition to consumers; and (2) compatible grouping or clustering, i.e., grouping retail outlets in patterns or clusters that facilitate

---

[13] Ibid.

[14] The terms *generative, shared,* and *suscipient* are from Richard L. Nelson, *The Selection of Retail Locations,* F. W. Dodge Corp., New York, 1958, p. 53.

consumer convenience in regard to reducing their search, shopping, and comparison activities for shopping and specialty goods.[15]

For example, in the case of suscipient business, the location of retail outlets is guided by the playing-purchase complex, the working-purchase complex, or the travel-purchase complex. These outlets are located around resorts, hotels and motels, theaters, transportation terminals and in the business and financial districts of communities in order to facilitate the attainment of certain consumption needs of those who work and function within these areas. Most of these outlets tend to specialize in the sale of convenience goods items. In terms of Aspinwall's criteria, these goods would have a high replacement rate, a low gross margin, require little or no adjustment, have a relatively short time span of consumption, and require little search time.

In the case of generative business, however, outlets are located so as to facilitate the shopping-purchase complex. These location decisions are guided by purchase criteria that are generally different from those relating to suscipient purchases. For instance, the replacement rate of products purchased may be slower, gross margins may be somewhat higher, and the product may require adjustment, i.e., servicing or alterations may be necessary. The time span of consumption may be longer, and the search time involved to find "just the right product" is likely to be greater.

Where Retail Stores Locate

As a simple generalization, retail stores locate at that spatial juncture where the market opportunity for their kind of establishment seems greatest. This idea is compatible with a concept that is often used in land resource economics, and is referred to as *highest and best use*. In general, the concept of highest and best use means the utilization of real property assets in such a way as to generate the greatest economic advantage over time. In the case of retail usage of real property, the highest and best use concept is reflected in the 100 per cent idea. In referring to site selection, frequent reference is made to the 100 per cent location concept. The essence of this idea is that there is a location that is the best possible (most optimum) site for every store within a given shopping district. Generally, this is the location with the greatest amount of the kind of traffic desired.

The concepts of both highest and best use and the 100 per cent location suggest that different types of stores have different site requirements. A location might have a 100 per cent rating for a supermarket and only a 20 per cent rating for a hardware store; a hardware store located on the 100 per cent supermarket site would be an obvious example of a location decision that has resulted in something considerably less than highest and best use. For that matter, this is the principal justification for continual reexamination of site decisions. Population changes, decentralization of trading areas,

---

[15] Peter Scott, *Geography and Retailing*, Hutchinson's University Library, London, 1970.

and deteriorating neighborhoods can all lead to something less than the highest and best use for a given site.[16]

Kinds of Locations

In the process of selecting a store site, the retail store manager or store location analyst can choose from among the following possible types of business areas:

1. *Central shopping district.* This is generally the downtown or primary shopping district. The area will include the financial and governmental units of the community and the principal shopping goods institutions such as department stores. The central shopping district is often coextensive with the *central business district* or CBD.
2. *Secondary shopping area.* This type of area is similar to the central shopping area with the exception that it is smaller. Central shopping areas are generally composed of a number of secondary shopping areas.
3. *String street developments.* These are minor shopping districts located along lines of radial and axial transportation routes.
4. *Neighborhood area.* This is a business area containing a cluster of convenience goods stores located within or adjacent to a small residential area.
5. *Free standing location.* A single store of either suscipient or generative character, or both. Its location may be the result of accident or design, but it exists as an independent, unintegrated retail unit.
6. *Shopping center.* This term is reserved for planned or developed centers in suburban residential neighborhoods.

Several important observations can be made regarding some of these types of business areas. The central business districts of most communities are not growing at quite the same rate as some of the other areas. In spite of a declining rate of expansion, however, they still continue to change and to move. There is nothing static about the downtown central business community. It has been observed that the main retail shopping center tends to move toward the best residential areas. The stores in New York City, for example, moved up Fifth Avenue, following the high-grade residential movement. The growth of Chicago, Washington, D.C., and Houston also illustrates movements of this type. By the same token, the development of Miami Beach and the northeast section of Miami has attracted the central business section of the city.

Core Versus Frame. One study analyzing the nature and composition of the central business districts (CBD) advanced the *core* and the *frame* concepts.[17]

The central business district *core* is defined as an area of intensive land

---

[16] David B. MacKay, "A Microanalytic Approach to Store Location Analysis," *Journal of Marketing Research*, Vol. IX (May 1972), pp. 134–140.

[17] Louis C. Wagner, "A Realistic Division of Downtown Retailing," *Journal of Marketing* (July 1964), pp. 34–38.

use characterized by offices, retail sales outlets, consumer services, hotels, theaters, and banks. Characteristically, the core is generally very compact and tends to be limited by pedestrian walking distances. Furthermore, the horizontal size of the core does not increase with the growth in the metropolitan area. As population increases, there is a tendency for the area to grow vertically, rather than horizontally.

As the core relates to retailing, it implies that the downtown core contains establishments able to support maximum rentals and to achieve highest sales per square foot. The stores with the greatest drawing power in the central business district core are the large department stores. These stores frequently occupy whole blocks, such as Macy's in New York, Marshall Field's in Chicago, and the J. L. Hudson store in Detroit. Many of these stores have two million square feet of space in a single building and have tremendously large annual sales volumes. Of course, such volume is necessary in order to generate the funds with which to pay the high costs of such sites.

Other kinds of retail stores—like furniture stores—with a relatively low volume of sales per square foot are located on the fringe of the core of the central business district where rents are somewhat lower. These areas are called the *frame*. The frame is an area surrounding the core and generally involves much less intensive land use. The frame area is not so compact as the core, since in the frame the movements of people are mainly vehicular. Within the frame area parking can be provided; this means that the area has greater appeal to automobile users than the core area. From a retailing standpoint, the frame contains the types of retailing and service establishments that are not able to command the high rentals necessary to secure locations in the core.

Many of the secondary shopping centers, string street developments, and even some neighborhood locations are found within the frame boundary of the central business district. However, the primary central shopping district would always be located within the core of the central business district.

The breakdown between core and frame is alleged to result in a more comprehensive picture of all retailing facilities attracting business from the entire metropolitan area. In addition, Wagner argues that the inclusion of the frame area in retail trade area and site analysis activities may make possible more uniform comparisons of downtown retailing facilities in one city, as compared to another.[18]

In summary, the kind of business area that emerges and develops, whether central shopping district, secondary shopping center, string street development, neighborhood area, free standing store, or planned shopping center, is caused by the purposes that the various areas serve. Each of the various kinds of areas represents a reaction to specialized market and consumer needs. The nature and extent to which such areas develop depends on the number of customers in the area, their current and potential purchasing power, and the specialized needs of the customers in the immediately surrounding areas. The locations of these various retail trading centers all reflect some special economic, geographic, or transportation problem. Out-

[18] Ibid., p. 38.

lying business centers have developed at or near intersections between radial and crosstown transportation lines, and at the intersections of main transportation arteries. Controlled shopping centers and free standing locations generally tend to emerge on the periphery of large cities, because it is difficult to reach the central downtown shopping area where traffic is usually congested.

The Decentralization of Retailing

The downtown central business district, including both frame and core areas, is not necessarily the most desirable, attractive, or convenient area for the consumer to shop today. While much of the aggregate city structure is undergoing considerable change, the downtown shopping district usually is not. The future of the downtown shopping district is uncertain; whole districts of the downtown CBD have deteriorated.

The downtown central shopping area has been hurt by a number of forces, but one of the major factors contributing to the decline of the downtown central or primary shopping area has been the vast migration of residents to the suburbs. It must be repeatedly emphasized that retail stores and trade centers follow the movements of the better residential areas; therefore, decentralization of retail shopping areas has been a natural evolution of urban expansion. Until the early 1930s, over 90 per cent of the general merchandise trade was concentrated in the central business districts. By 1954, the amount of trade outside the central business districts had surpassed the downtown area in all cities with more than a million people; and by 1958, it was nearly 20 per cent higher than that of the central business districts in 94 of the large metropolitan areas. As the rate of this increase continues to spiral, the dollar volume of trade in the central business district has been cut in half.[19]

The Suburban Shopping Center. The principal magnet that has tended to draw retail trade away from the central business district has been the suburban shopping center. Although a few of these centers date from thirty or more years ago, the majority have been built since World War II. From approximately 1,000 centers at the end of 1955, the number jumped dramatically to 4,500 by 1960, and to approximately 10,000 by 1970. It has been estimated that planned or controlled shopping centers now account for 25 to 35 per cent of all retail sales, and by 1980 their share may approach 40 to 50 per cent.[20]

The shopping center is a commercial development which is designed, developed, controlled, and operated by a single ownership with off-street parking at the site to serve jointly all establishments in the center. Shopping centers are directly related to the trading area through site location and the proper admixture of store types.[21]

[19] Homer Hoyt, *Urban Land,* Urban Land Institute, Washington, D.C., September 1961.
[20] Louis G. Redstone, *New Dimensions in Shopping Centers and Stores,* McGraw-Hill Book Company, New York, 1973, pp. 3–5.
[21] John Casparis, "Shopping Center Location and Retail Store Mix in Metropolitan Areas," *Demography,* Vol. 6, No. 2 (May 1969), p. 125.

The planned shopping center is built around the model of customer convenience mentioned earlier. That is, it is located as conveniently to large residential complexes as possible so as to facilitate customer convenience in terms of spatial movement (getting to and from the complex). On the other hand, the planned shopping center is also designed to meet the other dimension of convenience, namely, clustering. The planned shopping center aggregates large assortments into what has been called a pattern of concentrated variety. Such clustering facilitates consumer shopping convenience and makes possible what appears to be a most satisfactory and desirable feature, from the standpoint of many consumers—one-stop shopping.

Types of Shopping Centers. Planned shopping centers can be divided into three general categories:

1. *The neighborhood center.* The neighborhood center is the smallest of the three types. It is principally a convenience goods complex, the source for staple goods and daily services for a population of between 7,500 and 20,000 people. The typical neighborhood center has about 40,000 square feet of space, but it may vary between 30,000 and 75,000 square feet of gross floor space. The total site is usually 4 to 10 acres in area, and the principal tenant is usually a supermarket.
2. *The community center.* The community center is basically a convenience goods complex; however, some shopping goods lines are merchandised. The community center serves a population of between 20,000 and 100,000. Most often, it includes a variety store or small department store (sometimes a branch of a larger downtown parent store) as the principal tenant. The average size is 150,000 square feet of gross floor area, but the range is from 100,000 to 300,000 square feet. The site required for a community center ranges between 10 and 30 acres in size.
3. *The regional center.* The regional center is the largest of the three types. It carries vast amounts of convenience goods but it does offer the consumer a large nucleated shopping complex. Principal tenants usually include one and oftentimes two major department stores. The total complex offers the full complement of retail facilities usually found in a balanced, medium-sized CBD of a community. Such a complex serves a population ranging from 100,000 to 250,000 people. An average size is about 400,000 square feet of gross floor area, but in some centers 1,000,000 square feet is not unusual. A minimum site of 40 acres is required, but the large regional centers require as many as 100 acres.

Table 8-2 contains information concerning the various types of shopping centers and other related factors.

The trading areas of the various types of planned shopping centers are to some extent a function of their size. However, the trading area is likely to vary even among centers of similar size on the basis of such factors as accessibility, the goods available, and competition.

TABLE 8-2 Indicators for Types and Sizes in Shopping Centers

TYPE OF CENTER	NEIGHBORHOOD	COMMUNITY	REGIONAL
Leading tenant (basis for definition)	Supermarket or drugstore	Variety, discount or junior dept. store	One or more full-line dept. stores
Average gross leasable area	40,000 sq. ft.	150,000 sq. ft.	400,000 sq. ft.
General ranges in GLA*	30,000–100,000 sq. ft.	100,000–300,000 sq. ft.	300,000 to over 1,000,000 sq. ft.
Usual minimum site area	4 acres	10 acres	30–50 acres or more
Minimum support	5,000 to 40,000 people	40,000–150,000 people	150,000 or more people
Parking standard	5.5 parking spaces per 1,000 sq. ft. of GLA (see "Parking," as discussed later)		

* GLA stands for gross leasable area.
SOURCE: J. Ross McKeever, Shopping Center Zoning, Urban Land Institute, Washington, D.C., 1973, p. 12.

Research in one locality has shown that a shopping center's trading area is limited by the factor of driving time and that the most significant driving time dimension for trade area analysis is 15 minutes.[22] However, additional research is needed to ascertain the degree to which these observations are true for shopping centers in other communities.[23] The generally accepted rule of thumb is that the large regional centers may draw trade and attract customers up to 30 minutes' driving time away; community centers draw customers from up to 20 minutes' driving time away; and the neighborhood center would draw customers from a radius of up to 10 or 15 minutes' driving time away.

However, it has also been suggested that distance and driving time are both subjective factors. If the customer particularly likes a given center, she will probably perceive both the distance and driving time as shorter than they actually are.

Figure 8-1 shows schematically the usual relationships which prevail between shopping center success or effectiveness and customer driving. As was stated previously, the center's success is inversely related to the distance its customers must travel to shop its facilities.

Shopping Center Location Analysis

The location analysis problem for shopping centers is simply a more complicated exercise in the overall problem area of location generally. Each

[22] James A. Brunner and John L. Mason, "The Influence of Driving Time upon Shopping Center Preference," Journal of Marketing (April 1968), pp. 57–61.
[23] See William E. Cox, Jr. and Ernest F. Cooke, "Other Dimensions Involved in Shopping Center Preference," Journal of Marketing, Vol. 34 (October 1970) pp. 12–17.

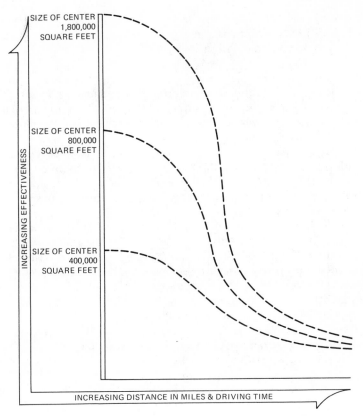

FIGURE 8-1 Hypothetical effectiveness of regional shopping centers in their trade areas.

SOURCE: Victor Gruen and Larry Smith, Shopping Towns, U.S.A. (New York, Reinhold Publishing Corp., 1960), p. 32. © 1960 by Litton Educational Publishing, Inc. Reprinted by permission of Van Nostrand Reinhold Co.

shopping center development is a case study in the dynamics of human enterprise. It is a complex tangle and network of decisions involving legal, political, economic, governmental, and social implications. Of course, in the final analysis the issue is still embedded within the merchandising framework of creating a desirable exchange or transaction process, a process related to the principles of the economic role of central market places and their relation to market opportunities.

While there are great differences in shopping centers throughout the country, the basic approaches and the salient factors concerning location and development are generally the same. Whether it be the Rouse Company's Perimeter Mall in Atlanta, The May Company's Great Lakes Mall in Cleveland, or Meier and Frank's South Center Development in Portland, shopping center development is based upon three principles: (1) location, (2) location, and (3) location. Now to assure the reader that he has not misread the last statement, let it be emphasized that location analysis is the *primary* orientation around which shopping center development is focused. This location analysis and other development issues are based upon the following kinds of activities:

1. *Economic and Feasibility Analysis.* Before any decisions are made, the developer must evaluate a community and measure its potential for new retail and commercial outlets. This includes measuring and estimating developmental costs, income, and revenues so that profitability estimates can be generated.
2. *Site Evaluation.* This phase involves the analysis of potential sites within the prescribed trading area. Sites are ultimately chosen which (a) are all in one piece, (b) have ample area, (c) have adequate soil base, (d) have utility and sewage facilities, and (e) have a favorable zoning atmosphere.
3. *Site Planning.* Site planning involves what to do with the site to best utilize its features in conjunction with the type of center proposed. Aspects of site planning include (a) parking; (b) division of movement between customers and service vehicles; (c) circulation and general traffic movement; (d) arrangement of stores in accordance with size, customer shopping habits, pulling power, and compatibility; and (e) an agreeable overall center design.
4. *Architectural Planning.* Such planning involves the harmonious blending of the topographical and other physical characteristics of the site with the functional and aesthetic demands of the potential consumer public.
5. *Management and Operation.* Finally, it should be understood that skillful center management will ultimately affect the success or failure of the overall developmental process. Such management activity includes the policing of lease clauses, which themselves are important performance standards that will benefit in the aggregate the tenants, the customers, and the community at large.

To the retail manager reconsidering a location decision or contemplating the opening of a new retail unit, the planned shopping center is an attractive alternative. Because of the glamor and customer drawing power of the controlled shopping center, many retail firms have rushed to take locations in these centers as they have been made available. There is a danger in this behavior, however. Shopping center locations viewed as location options by individual retailers or lessees should be given the same study and scrutiny as are given to all other location options. Above all else, the center developer should not be relied upon to make the trading area studies. The future of the suburban shopping center appears reasonably secure, yet the impact of a continuing energy crisis on shopping center operations has yet to be assessed. It should be further noted that in many areas shopping centers are performing less than optimally because they are overdeveloped and because the downtown shopping facilities are being revitalized.

Many problems affecting the downtown primary and secondary shopping centers are being overcome. Traffic congestion is being alleviated by such techniques as creating malls, closing off streets, and establishing one-way traffic. There is some evidence to suggest that much of the distasteful quality of the downtown commercial street would disappear if the shopper were converted from a driver to a pedestrian. Some even contend that the downtown trading center will once again gain pre-eminence over the suburban planned shopping center. This re-emergence of the downtown area will come about as a result of several factors:[24]

1. The urban renewal and redevelopment program.
2. A greatly expanded effort to increase public mass transit systems.
3. A concerted drive by downtown merchants to make the downtown area a less aversive and hence a more stimulating and reinforcing place to shop.
4. Some population movement back to core metropolitan areas by those disenchanted with suburban living.
5. The increasing tendency to ban the auto in inner-core cities.

Having taken this brief but important digression to examine the issue of shopping center location problems, let us return now to our analysis of store location processes from the standpoint of the individual retail store as opposed to the larger complex of stores—the shopping center.

Evaluation and Site Analysis

Site evaluation and analysis must combine techniques, concepts, and methodology from urban ecology, marketing geography, land resource economics, and city and community planning, as well as from other related disciplines. In the majority of instances, site selection is a highly personal and subjective retail management decision based upon intuition or feel of the situation.

The essence of good site selection centers around determining the point in space where the market offering can best be matched to market opportunity. There is no pat procedural technique or recipe approach that can be employed in site evaluation or analysis. It is the location or *situs* of urban land that is of primary importance in determining its income potential. However, the location of urban land for retail store sites takes its greatest importance from its *location in relation to a market opportunity*.

Therefore, in site analysis for retail stores, one of the central guiding principles is that the site ought to generate profitable levels of traffic for the goods and services that the proposed store will offer. This potential is usually determined by pedestrian traffic counts, or automobile traffic counts in the case of retail firms that depend on vehicular traffic.

Although there are many difficulties to be encountered in measuring the potential of a site from traffic counts, it remains a highly important part of the overall analysis.

Another principal component of site analysis and evaluation is concerned

[24] E. B. Weiss, "Downtown Areas, The Original Shopping Center to Become New Mecca of Retail," *Marketing Insights* (February 27, 1967), pp. 16–17.

with a knowledge of the circulatory system of a community, consisting of the roads and highways used by people to move about from place to place. Man's routes of travel have been the vital threads in his pattern of commerce, and his economic and social interaction. Because of the overwhelming use of the automobile, it must become the principal focus of the circulatory system and the sites that are created as a result of circulatory movements and patterns.

Mertes has discussed and categorized retail store sites, based upon analysis and evaluation of community circulatory patterns. His classification follows:

The Internal Site The internal site is a part of the downtown core or frame and as such can be characterized in much the same manner as the downtown central shopping district. The essential feature of the internal site is that the traffic, which becomes primarily pedestrian as soon as the customer reaches the area by rapid transit or automobile, is composed of workers, visitors, residents and suburbanites—some concerned with shopping and some not. The retail market area for the central business district is affected by a system of accumulator traffic arteries and an internal distributor system. In many instances these circulatory systems are inadequate to handle crushing volumes of traffic and the internal site is thus negatively affected.

The Axial Site The axial site, which is sometimes referred to as a strip development by real estate men, is located along the major traffic arteries leading out of the central business district toward residential districts. Axial sites generally serve as links between the interior site and the pivotal sites scattered throughout the city.

The Pivotal Site A pivotal site occurs at the confluence of two or more principal traffic thoroughfares. Such a site primarily attracts residential traffic from the surrounding area and today these are often the preferred locations within a community, especially in new residential areas.

Peripheral Sites These are sites located at the outer reaches of a community, often adjacent to the interchanges or access roads of the circumferentials being constructed around many communities.

The External Site The external site is one located along a high volume traffic artery in the hinterland between communities.[25]

One of the principal desirable features of any site—whether it be axial, pivotal, peripheral, or external—is its intercepting quality. The concept of interception involves two fundamental notions: a site has reference to an area *from* which customers are drawn, and a site has reference to an area *toward* which customers are drawn. For example, customers are drawn to primary and secondary shopping districts, planned shopping centers, and large free-standing discount department stores. They are drawn from residential areas and places of employment. The principle of interception is concerned with locating between a lodestone such as one of the areas to which customers are drawn and one of the areas from which customers are drawn.

[25] John E. Mertes, "A Retail Structural Theory for Site Analysis," *Journal of Retailing* (Summer 1964), pp. 19–31.

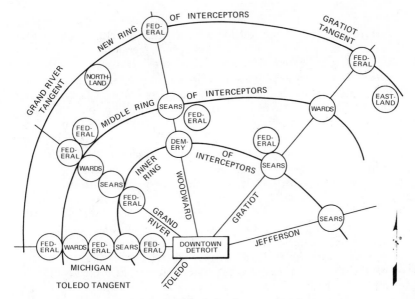

FIGURE 8-2 Interceptor rings and the interceptor site.

SOURCE: Richard L. Nelson, The Selection of Retail Locations (New York: F. W. Dodge Corporation, 1958), p. 27.

Figure 8-2 illustrates the principles involved with interceptor rings and the value of the interceptor site.

In Detroit the first ring of interceptors grew up around a series of Sears stores on radial streets such as Jefferson, Gratiot, Grand River, and Michigan. The middle ring of interceptors grew up around a Ward's store on Gratiot, a Sears store on Woodward, a Federal and Ward's store on Grand River, and another on Michigan. A third ring grew up largely around the shopping centers of Northland and Eastland.[26]

One of the really well-qualified experts on site analysis and location evaluation has commented as follows regarding the interceptor qualities of a site:

> People will rarely go through a business district or pass by a shopping center or store to get exactly the same product (in as pleasant an atmosphere) farther on. It is much easier to stop them en route, as it were, than to pull them off or away from a beaten path.[27]

The Theory of Cumulative Attraction and Compatibility. The great success of the planned shopping center and (to some extent) that of the primary and secondary shopping centers can be attributed to what Nelson has called "the theory of cumulative attraction," which holds that "a given number of stores dealing in the same merchandise will do more business if

---

[26] Richard L. Nelson, *The Selection of Retail Locations*, F. W. Dodge Corp., New York, 1958, p. 27.
[27] Ibid., p. 54.

they are located adjacent or in proximity to each other than if they are widely scattered."[28] When stores of a similar nature are clustered together, their cumulative drawing power as a retail center tends to increase. It is for this reason that we generally tend to find the large department stores clustered very close together in the downtown central shopping districts. It is for this same reason that today more and more of the large regional shopping centers have two or more department stores as principal tenants, rather than just one. Fundamentally related to the theory of cumulative attraction is Nelson's "principle of retail compatibility." It is a fact that in choosing a location, one can locate either adjacent to outlets that strengthen his total merchandising effort or adjacent to outlets that weaken his total merchandising effort. Stores are either compatible with other stores in terms of price policy, total store image, quality, promotional activity, and merchandise assortments, or else they are incompatible. Quite naturally, the retail store manager wishes to locate adjacent to outlets having maximum compatibility. The principle of compatibility states: "Two compatible businesses located in close proximity will show an increase in business volume directly proportionate to the incidence of total customer interchange between them, inversely proportionate to the ratio of the business volume of the larger store to that of the smaller store, and directly proportionate to the sum of the ratios of purposeful purchasing[29] to total purchasing in each of the two stores."[30]

The relationship is expressed much more succinctly by the following equation:

$$V = I(V_L + V_S) \times \frac{V_S}{V_L} \times \left(\frac{P_L}{V_L} + \frac{P_S}{V_S}\right)$$

where

V_L = Volume of larger store
P_L = Purposeful purchasing in larger store
V_S = Volume of smaller store
P_S = Purposeful purchasing in smaller store
V = Increase in total volume of two stores
I = Degree of interchange

Given the situation wherein two retail stores are located side by side and one customer in 100 makes a purchase in both, the rule suggests that together they will do one per cent more business than if separated by a distance that would restrict the interchange. On the other hand, if one customer in ten makes purchases in both stores, their total increase in business would be about 10 per cent.

[28] Ibid., p. 58.

[29] A purposeful purchase is one made by a shopper who, when interviewed, states that a visit to the store was a major purpose of the shopping trip. Total purchases, of course, include incidental and impulse purchases as well.

[30] Ibid., p. 66.

The principle can be used most effectively to demonstrate the effect of a large and small store in terms of the compatibility factor. A department store doing $5,000,000 worth of retail business per year is located next to a variety store doing $500,000 a year.[31] What is the effect of this relationship? If their customer interchange were on the order of 25 out of 100, the total increase in business for the two establishments would be directly proportionate to the interchange, or 25 per cent, but inversely proportionate to the ratio of their volumes, which is 10:1. Thus, the total increase would equal one-tenth of 25 per cent, or 2.5 per cent. If, however, interviews showed purposeful purchasing at the department store and the variety store respectively to be on the order of 90 per cent and 15 per cent of total purchasing, the 2.5 per cent increase would have to be multiplied by 105 per cent. Thus, these two stores together would show a business increase of 2.5 × 1.05, or 2.625 per cent of the total of $5,500,000—an additional $144,375. It is important to point out that this $5,500,000 + $144,375 is not a market potential. The compatibility determination assumes that an adequate market exists.

Parking. No treatment or analysis of location and site considerations would be complete without a careful evaluation of the role of parking. The value and stability of a given site or an entire trading center directly hinge in large measure on the adequacy and convenience of space for automobile parking available to customers. In large measure, the deficiency and the inconvenience related to parking may be measured by the exodus of retail trade centers to outlying areas of the community.

The cost of parking space dramatizes effectively the seriousness of the downtown parking problem. Land values in the downtown shopping districts are seldom ever less than $10 a square foot. And if one automobile requires 200 square feet of parking space, this means that parking space per car would average $2,000. However, land in the suburbs for a shopping center complex may be purchased at a cost of from $2,000 to $15,000 an acre, or at a per car cost of $10 to $75.

The amount of land required per car varies from store unit to store unit. The quick "in and out" drive-in markets (specializing in fill-in items rather than complete weekly food needs) generally require a smaller ratio of selling to parking space than their larger counterpart, the supermarket. The amount of parking space generally required varies with such factors as the frequency and length of the store visit, the kind of establishment, and the kind of neighborhood in which the establishment is located.

Shopping centers generally require a 4 to 1 ratio between parking and net selling areas. Parking adequacy is usually determined on the basis of normal or average selling seasons. To take care of peak loads at Christmas time or during other high-volume holiday periods would require parking lots that were at least 25 per cent empty during more normal selling periods. The large food supermarkets generally estimate that each parking space should generate about $25,000 in sales volume per year—$10,000

[31] The example is from Nelson, op. cit., p. 67. The reader is urged to work through the example, using the above equation.

of which is in general merchandise lines and $15,000 in conventional food lines.

In order to combat the effectiveness of the suburban shopping center, much of which is usually attributed to parking, many of the larger downtown stores have been attempting to reattract customers to their stores and their trading centers by building central parking garages in combination with retail shopping facilities that are usually located on the ground floor. The futuristic Parkade Center, a nine-story parking and retail facility in Spokane, Washington, is an example of such enterprise. Other large parking facilities have been developed by the Lazarus store in Columbus, Ohio, and by Foley's in Houston. Large and extensive parking garages have also been built in Chicago, San Francisco, Baltimore, Los Angeles, and other cities for the purpose of aiding the central retail districts.

To Buy or Lease.   Another critical aspect of the location and site problem is whether to buy outright or to lease the facility. Because of the dynamic feature of location problems, many retail firms will not buy property, and some will not sign leases longer than 20 to 30 years. They generally contend that they prefer to be merchandisers rather than real estate investors, and thus maximize their return on capital investment by increasing return on merchandise. As seen in Chapter 3, a dollar in merchandise investment generally brings a greater return than a dollar invested in real estate. Broadly speaking, leases are of two main types. One is the fixed percentage lease, which means that regardless of volume the amount of the rental fee remains a fixed cost. The second type of lease is a percentage of sales lease, in which the rental cost of the facility is determined on the basis of a percentage of sales, with some minimum guarantee. The percentage paid varies with the desirability of the location, the volume of sales generated per square foot, and the age and condition of the building.

Supermarkets usually pay only one per cent of sales as rent, but they have exceedingly high sales volumes, usually ranging between $1,000,000 and $2,000,000 per year and from $150 to $350 a square foot. On a square footage basis, this would mean a rental cost of $1.50 to $3.50 a square foot.

General merchandise and apparel stores usually pay 5 per cent of their gross sales as rent and have sales volumes ranging from $50 to $100 per square foot, which would mean a rental cost of $2.50 to $5.00 a square foot.

Some stores, especially appliance and furniture stores whose products are large and bulky and require large amounts of floor space for merchandise display, have a relatively low sales volume per square foot of selling space. Sales for these kinds of outlets usually do not exceed $30 a square foot, so that on a 5 per cent basis they would not pay much over $1.50 a square foot in rent.

The buy or lease question is best resolved after careful analysis of all relevant factors. The advice of a real estate broker who specializes in retail properties would likely contribute much to the decision process.

Site analysis thus involves a careful and astute evaluation of several relevant considerations, including a knowledge and understanding of circulation patterns, interceptor rings, cumulative attraction, compatibility principles, parking requirements, and the question of whether to lease or buy facilities.

Consequently, the site analysis and evaluation problem is the fine tuning involved in the final extension of the market opportunity question. Hence, firms that engage in location research are often hopeful of accomplishing at least these minimum objectives:

1. An evaluation of specific sites regarding their sales potential and the probability of the store's long-range success at the site.
2. A store location strategy plan or model that undertakes to select from among the location alternatives in a given geographic area those locations that will produce for the firm an optimum share of market potential, a minimum hazard for future sales erosion, and a maximum return on total investment over the lease period.

It is hoped that the material in the last two chapters will have provided at least the basic and broad-gauge framework within which such a location strategy plan or model could now be undertaken.

QUESTIONS FOR STUDY, REFLECTION, AND REVIEW

1. What considerations affect the optimum location of retail trade centers or retailing systems?
2. Explain and define the two methods used to delineate or establish the trading area boundaries.
3. Explain what the gravitational approach (model) to trading area analysis attempts to do.
4. List several of the empirical methods used in determining retail trading areas.
5. What are some of the factors that can be used to determine if a market opportunity exists in a given area or location?
6. In the *Sales Management Survey of Buying Power* of what is the Buying Power Index composed?
7. What is meant when we speak of the saturation of a trading area?
8. Explain the concept of drawing power.
9. What is the formula for computing market share? What is the significance of it?
10. Define and explain what is meant by overstoring or understoring.

9

store design, layout,
and space utilization

The retail store, as has been mentioned, has often been described as a machine for selling. What it really is, of course, is a means of both generating and releasing a stream of customer satisfactions or convenience.

The merchandising function—defined as the planning involved in having the right goods, at the right time and price, and in the *right place* —underlines the importance of store design, layout, and space utilization. "In the right place" connotes something more than simply a point or aggregation of space in a particular geographic surrounding. Instead, "in the *right* place" literally means not only in the best or most strategic geographic location, but in a building suitably accommodated to the needs of the customer groups intended to shop the institution's product and service offering. It must be attractively designed and styled to project the image of the store and its merchandise offering, and effectively laid out in order to facilitate *the flow* of the functions or activities intended to take place within the confines of its walls and the exterior space to which it is related. Finally, the right place implies that the utilization of the space will assure that standards of engineering economy and aesthetic sensibility are reasonably balanced. The problems and issues of store design, layout, and space utilization are a vital and integral part of the retail management strategy. Store design has become a major weapon in the war of commerce and industry, and, given the escalation of business rivalry and one-upmanship, designers and merchandisers are beginning to think more earnestly about the interrelationships between simply design on the one hand and merchandising on the other. As the competitive battle for the retail consumer continues to heat up, more and more stores will begin to recognize the importance of store design, layout, and proper space utilization.

We are all inclined to take the arrangement of space that surrounds us more or less for granted. But these arrangements, whether contrived by man or nature, affect the performance of our everyday lives, our moods, our movements, and our interactions with others. Hall has suggested that space and spatial arrangements are a part of an individual's culture and affect his perception of the world.[1] He further states that, "The important point about fixed feature space is that it is the mold into which a great deal of behavior is cast. It was this feature of space that the late Sir Winston Churchill referred to when he said, 'We shape our buildings and they shape us.' "

the role and importance of store design

Store design has considerable significance. In the first place, it strongly suggests a planned deliberate approach to the structuring, arrangement, and coordination of the store's physical facilities. Also, as the very essence of the word *design* is to plan and fashion artistically and skillfully, it would imply that the purpose of store design is to plan and fashion the physical facilities of a retail store in an artistic and skillful manner. Store design creates the setting for the retail firm's performance—buying, selling, and the ancillary supporting activities.

Store design is responsible for creating what one author has called the "agreeable environment."[2] From the standpoint of the retail firm, this environment is one that provides congenial, yet stimulating, surroundings for customers and salespeople through appropriate layout, fixturization, illumination, color, and space utilization. The task of good design, "in a store, a hotel, a motel, restaurant, theatre . . . may be to strike common denominators of public taste that will attract business by appealing to mass psychology—without confusing it or going over its head."[3]

There are at least three major dimensions to the store design problem. These are engineering economy, psychological aesthetics, and merchandising or store style, and they must be brought into some kind of meaningful balance. A store is not merely so much space to be manipulated and evaluated with the engineer's slide rule, nor is it a canvas for the modern designer-artist to fill with dazzling and bewildering colors. Instead, it is a place where buyer and seller must meet and operate under conditions that optimize their reasons for meeting. The store must be a place where customers wish to congregate and to transact those operations necessary to fulfill their desires for goods and services. From the standpoint of the retail store unit, design is a means of balancing all of these major dimensions. Siegel seems to capture the nature of the store design problem when he states that "when technical considerations are made part of a scale of

---

[1] Edward T. Hall, *The Hidden Dimension,* Doubleday & Company, Inc., Garden City, N.Y., 1966, p. 177.

[2] Faber Birren, *Color for Interiors,* Whitney Library of Design, New York, undated, p. 120.

[3] Ibid.

aesthetic values, questions of economy acquire enhanced importance."[4] Here, the word *economy* is used in a rather special way—not just in the sense of saving money, even though that may be the case—but to denote the maximum return, in an aesthetic as well as a material sense, for a minimum outlay. The real challenge of store design is to comply with what Van de Velde has defined as "the perfect harmony of means and ends"[5] or what Mies van der Rohe has described as "function is an art."[6]

Store design is a means and not an end. It is a means of harmonizing and coordinating the store's total market offering to its selected market targets. It is a means of shaping styles and attitudes, of accelerating the buying mood, and of providing for the efficient, economical distribution of goods in an atmosphere that is satisfying and aesthetically pleasing to customers. Store design is the visual projection of the store's merchandising style or image. Whatever the store wishes to be—whether a specialized boutique or a convenience superette for fill-in food items—it can become through the effective use of store design. Store design is a comprehensive concept. In the case of the large department store, it is a means of tying together and co-ordinating the entire merchandising effort into some kind of meaningful and related pattern. In the case of smaller stores, store design is an attempt to sensitize customers to their smaller package of merchandise and service assortments. However, for all stores, store design is simply an extension of what was earlier called enterprise differentiation: the attempt to reach a particular market segment or to cultivate a market niche through the principles of differential advantage.

Form Follows Function

Classical design has long followed the dictum that "form follows function." If the designer devoted taste to his endeavors, it was in the glorification of that which was prescribed by the customs and civilizations of his times. In this pursuit he was objective rather than subjective. Today, there is a new functionalism that arises out of the notion that there is more to function than meets the eye. It has been discovered that customers are not really interested in buying goods in machine-like buildings or warehouses, stark and unadorned, with wooden tables and pipe racks. Instead, consumers by and large are attracted to pleasant, bright, cheerful, congenial surroundings where the atmosphere creates a mood of relaxation, gaiety, and cheerfulness. Thus, design practices must follow these contemporary attitudes. Affluence, mobility, and mass communication have all tended to create a sophisticated and cosmopolitan consumer. For such a consumer, the retail store manager must provide sophisticated and cosmopolitan shopping environments. As the nature and behavior of retail consumers is changed and modified, one can witness the corresponding changes that transpire in store facilities and store design.

[4] Curt Siegel, *Structure and Form in Modern Architecture*, Van Nostrand Reinhold Company, New York, 1962, p. 7.

[5] Kunstgewerbliche Larenpredegten, see Henry Van de Velde, "Zum neuen stil," selected from his writings by Hans Curjel, Piper-Verlag, p. 125.

[6] Mies van der Rohe, *Baukunst und Werform*, No. 6 (1953) , p. 276.

Ever since peddlers settled down to fixed locations in some market place and started to deal with sidewalk traffic, shopping environment has played a vital part in the design of shops and stores. From then on store fronts have been built to provide, in varied ways, on the spot contact between the customers out front and the merchant inside. Their design has expressed the different ways of living, trading and building successive civilizations, but the basic solution has always been the same. The shops of ancient Rome, of medieval Europe, or of Colonial days are strikingly similar to those today in all except technical detail.[7]

Thus, the market place would appear to change more often than its cities and shops. However, it must be recognized that whatever changes are wrought in the market place are those which bring about the changes in store design and operation. Form *does follow function*.

Retailing Activities and Store Design

If form follows function, it would strongly suggest that retailing activities would largely dictate design practice and behavior. And such is the case. Essentially, most retail stores must provide for two major kinds of activity. First, they must provide for the complex and dramatic exhibition of goods, and second, this exhibition must be combined with the most efficient and workmanlike of warehouses. In short, retailing performs two vital and crucial marketing functions. One is the aggregation and dispersal of goods and could be called the physical distribution function. The other is the buying-selling function, or the function of exchange. *These two major functions largely dictate the conditions that surround the store planning and design activity.* Both the physical distribution function and the exchange function are such that large stocks (either in the warehouse or storage area, or stocks already moved to critical points of sale in merchandise departments or display areas) must be continually drawn down and replenished without causing major disruptions to the normal flow of retailing activity that centers around customer shopping.

These two major retailing functions affect design considerations relating to layout and space utilization and will be discussed in this context more thoroughly later. At this juncture, let us look briefly at several of the factors relating to store operation as they affect design considerations.

Comprehensive Planning

Store design is concerned with and related to overall or comprehensive store planning. Comprehensive planning must begin by setting up a program of overall requirements consisting of a study of the needs, habits, and buying potential of the public in the area; the ratio of dollar volume of yearly business to the sales area to be occupied by various types of merchandise within the store; and finally, the business background, philosophy, and attitude of the merchant who is to operate the store. Only then can

---

[7] Morris Ketchum, Jr., "Shops and the Market Place," in *Stores and Shopping Centers*, James S. Hornbeck (ed.), McGraw-Hill Book Company, New York, 1962, p. 13.

the designer plan the store and integrate this data into proper area and volume allocations, and make the necessary total design specifications. The designer must provide also for the nonselling functions that are essential to proper customer service, comfort, and store operation. All this includes both exterior and interior design considerations, fixtures, lighting, color, vertical transportation, total store layout, and space utilization.

Contemporary Trends and Influences in Store Design

In both the suburban shopping center and in the shopping districts of the downtown community, the basic aim of store design is the same: the facilitation of the shopping-buying complex, or the customer's search, evaluation, and decision relating to purchase needs. However, the means used to accomplish this objective will differ between the suburban, planned shopping center with its ample amounts of parking and the downtown store without adequate parking facilities. Store designers today are successfully solving the interrelated problems of the indoor-outdoor shopping street. The problems of sales and service, advertising and display, pedestrian and auto traffic walkways, and parking space are being approached in a satisfactory and sophisticated manner.

Most designers have come to realize that the basic fundamental of store design is to build flexibility into the overall design framework in the planning of the indoor space, especially in the behind-the-scenes, nonselling activities related to the physical and logistical movement of merchandise.

One of the currently emphasized design principles is to organize each sales floor for the flexible free flow of horizontal traffic, and for centralized vertical traffic. Flexibility must be an integral part of the total plan, including equipment and fixtures; many stock fixtures have interchangeable parts and uses. Sales space and sidewalk displays are being integrated by visually open store fronts that when the occasion warrants may become closed fronts, whenever modular window backgrounds are installed.

To attain maximum adaptability, most modern retail store buildings today are being designed with a minimum of fixed structural components such as columns, shaftways, and walls. The buildings consist of a fixed outer shell, inside which inner areas can be flexibly arranged via curtain walls, modular moveable panels, and mobile scenic backgrounds. Today's design emphasis is upon knock-down units capable of multiple use, providing flexible access to the space and equipment they enclose.

Other contemporary design influences will be discussed in terms of specific features of the design process.

Exterior Appearance.   The exterior of the store must be designed with a thought to aesthetics, but also with an eye to economy and ease of maintenance. One of the pleasing treatments of the modern store exterior is the glass wall. Its use allows daylight to accent interior lighting and breaks the monotony of masonry expanses. However, the glass wall makes interior display more difficult and imposes a costly maintenance factor. Snaith argues that the glass wall is appropriate only for restaurant, employee, and office areas. He says that "only two types of sales operations can live under glass: those wherein the merchandise itself has decorative value, as gifts; or those not requiring exposed stock, as a salon, which sells only by atmosphere and total image."[8]

The exterior of a store is much like a face. It must project several images:

1. Size. The building should convey visually something of the size of the establishment and the range and depth of its merchandise and service offering.
2. Permanence and institutionality. The store exterior is a facade which projects trust and dependability.
3. Definition from its neighbors. The store exterior ought to project an atmosphere of personality and individual differences.
4. The nature of merchandise and customer. The store exterior is a form of communication. Its front, signs, and window are cues and signs which ought to convey a meaningful message to consumers.
5. Store character.
6. Regional or community character.

Interior Appearance. The interior appearance of a store ought to take advantage of the full capacity of design ingenuity to project and complement the total store image. As we learned earlier, that image is a composite of the store's merchandise, its way of doing business, and its customer segments, all incorporated into a total comprehensive organization or corporate style. The principal means of projecting this total store image within the framework of the store's interior appearance is via the display of merchandise assortments. What is displayed, as well as how the displays are presented, is another form of meaningful communication. From the viewpoint of the customer shopping within the store, the store's image is largely determined by how she perceives the merchandise displays.

Fixtures. Fixturization is a complex task, almost always requiring the assistance of a trained expert. However, there are a few general principles to be observed. The fixture is a vehicle, the purpose of which is to sell merchandise, display merchandise, and store merchandise. Emphasis in terms of the latter consideration has changed dramatically over the past several years. Fixtures are no longer viewed as containers to conceal and protect merchandise but are chosen to reflect the character and basic appeal of the store and to complement rather than detract from the displayed merchandise. Quite naturally, the type of service offered by the store will affect the style and type of fixture chosen. Another major consideration in choosing and coordinating fixtures is the labor cost saving versus the display presentation. Snaith suggests:

> Labor is a store's most expensive commodity; retailing has been described as the last of the manual industries. If we plan fixtures to reduce

---

[8] William T. Snaith, "How Retailing Principles Affect Design," in *Stores and Shopping Centers*, James S. Hornbeck (ed.), McGraw-Hill Book Company, New York, 1962, p. 9.

the amount of sales help we save in operation cost, but this reduction automatically lowers the level of presentation. In fixture design we must seek some comfortable median between turning the store into a super-market (maximum self-selection and self-service) and a salon where the customer is individually helped at every stage of the sale. Personnel cost pushes up the merchandise price, and there is a point somewhere here of no return.[9]

Color. One of the most striking features of store design to emerge in the last 20 years is the greatly accelerated use of color as part of the decoration and design scheme. More can be accomplished with color, and more color can be used in stores than is generally realized. There are few rules to restrain the store designer in his use of color, but the basic principle is that store colors ought to suit the type of merchandise being sold.

Most retailers have long since learned this lesson: Good merchandising is not a matter of whim or accident. And in the case of consumer goods, right colors sell in profitable volume, while wrong colors lie dormant in unsold and expensive inventories. In the retail store, color is a means of brightening and highlighting the total package of store design and of making this total package more saleable to the public. But we must not forget that color can be a temperamental thing and must be handled correctly.

There are both emotional and functional reasons why certain colors are better than others. The most liked colors, in the psychological sense, are blue, red, and green. Yellow may also be accepted for its high visibility and compulsion. This would suggest that the primary hues and tints of these colors would be acceptable for walls, end walls, fixtures, displays, and backgrounds.

By and large, the most widely adopted colors in retail stores today are the pastel colors, which are used mainly on upper walls, while the darker colors are used mostly for accent purposes. Flamboyant use of color is not encouraged unless, of course, the total image of the store or shop is given to some flamboyance. An effective way to set off different departments is to use different colors in each area, with an off-white neutral as a foil. Such use of color generally suggests high attraction and emotional appeal, plus an interesting variety to invite greater store traffic. Oftentimes, very deep and dramatic colors are used at the store ends in order to pull customers to these areas.

Color is also important as a part of fixturization. Light neutral tones, such as sandstone, warm grays, and beige have been found to be useful fixture colors; they suggest warmth, quality and drama, without seriously detracting from the merchandise itself.

Lighting. Consumers are sometimes thought of as human moths because they appear to be highly attracted to light. The lighting levels in today's stores have been stepped up in intensity by 5 or 6 times over the pre-1950 era. Apparently, retail merchants are keenly aware of the selling power of light. However, as is often suggested, "Lighting, like any other

[9] Ibid.

creative effort must be interesting. To achieve this, it must be used with due consideration to contrast, perspective and color as well as foot candle power. In other words, there must be design as well as engineering."[10]

The advantages of proper lighting cannot be overemphasized. In addition to being a powerful force that affects the consumer buying mood, good lighting is also alleged to step up sales personnel productivity, increase merchandise turnover, facilitate self-selection, increase the effectiveness of displays, and reduce shoplifting.

Much is being written today about the intensity or level of light suitable for retail stores. It is well known that brightness attracts, stimulates visual and emotional response, and prompts action. Quite generally, the most pleasing qualities of light are found in the warm lights or incandescent sources, while the cold light of the fluorescents gives human color a cold, cadaverous look. Incandescent lighting is widely used, both for its warm tint and for the fact that it is more directional than diffuse, and thus gives form to merchandise displays by building up highlights and shadows. Warm incandescent light is almost mandatory for personal products such as women's fashions and cosmetics. However, in most stores the level of brightness or intensity sought can only be obtained with the use of the cold light fluorescents. The widespread use of the hotter incandescent sources actually raises temperature levels appreciably. A desirable solution is to attain a high level of light intensity via fluorescent lights and, in addition, to use incandescents for a softer outlining of certain store areas, departments, or displays.

Although impulse purchases seem to be stimulated by really bright light, the general illumination for the overall customers' benefit should be warm. Sources that more nearly approximate natural daylight can be specified for merchandise areas that demand more accurate color discrimination. In the final analysis, no one light tone is ideal; light color and intensity should be chosen to enhance the character of the particular merchandise.

In a conceptual way, we have treated many of the factors related to store design. This treatment has focused only upon the issues to which the general retail store manager should address himself. Many of the issues with which we have dealt have very definite technical implications and are best left to the technical specialist. Our interest has focused neither exclusively on engineering economy nor on psychological aesthetics. Instead, the intent has been that store design must be a balance of these factors, oriented primarily around customer convenience and total store style or image. Much can be summarized about the importance of store design. Most paramount, of course, is that a subtle dimension of in-store customer shopping behavior is the environment of the space itself. Retail space that surrounds the retail shopper is never neutral. The retail store communicates a number of significant messages to consumers: it creates mood, activates intentions, and generally affects customer reactions. It has been suggested that there is a social-psychological dimension of space, and that this space affects customers in the following ways:

[10] Abe Feder, "Store Lighting," in *Design for Modern Merchandising,* James S. Hornbeck (ed.), F. W. Dodge Corp., New York, 1954, p. 24.

1. Space is an important modifier and shaper of behavior. We shape people's future behavior by the environment we create.
2. Retail store space affects behavior because of its reinforcing or rewarding characteristics. If an environment is perceived as desirable, nonhostile, comfortable, and hence rewarding, we are inclined to perceive the activities which transpire in that environment as also desirable, rewarding, and reinforcing. With repeated exposure to such desirable environments, customers are soon likely to learn or sense that they belong to a given territory or space, and that this space in turn belongs to them.
3. The retail store is an important behavior-shaping instrument. The retail store shapes behavior via a psychology of stimulation and expectation. This is accomplished by the use of novelty, intensity, complexity, temporal change, surprisingness, and incongruity.
4. The retail store shapes and affects perception. Stores and store design in the form of atmosphere project massive amounts of information to shoppers. Space planners and designers should think of retail customers as surrounded by a series of expanding and contracting dynamic fields that provide information, all of which affects customers' perceptions. How a store is thus perceived will affect frequency of shopping, store loyalty, and other important patronage factors.
5. Retail store space and design affects customers' attitudes and images. Such attitudes and images, which consist of bundles of related attitude clusters, are behavioral predispositions. The usual assumption regarding psychological causality is that by creating favorable attitudes and images we have generated the first step toward creating actual shopping behavior. Via design features attitudes and images are created; that is, store personalities are created and shaped, and these personalities—friendly, upper-class, aloof, high-quality, low-priced, convenient, warm, inviting, cool, haughty, etc.—are in turn meant to affect customer attitudes and images and hence to shape behavior.[11]

There is today an increasing emphasis on store design, interior decoration, and overall environment programming by retail merchandisers to sell goods. This recognition has been described in a limited way in the literature. The use of atmosphere, a form of environmental programming, influences customer behavior in the following ways:[12]

1. As an attention-creating medium.
2. As a message-creating medium.
3. As an affect-creating medium.

The increasing use of atmosphere and environmental programming is an integral part of today's thematic merchandising, which means merchan-

[11] Rom J. Markin, Charles M. Lillis, and Chem Narayana, "The Retail Store: An Exploration into the Social-Psychological Significance of Space," *Journal of Retailing,* Vol. 52, No. 1 (Spring 1976) , pp. 43–54.

[12] See Philip Kotler, "Atmospherics as a Marketing Tool," *Journal of Retailing,* Vol. 49, No. 4 (Winter 1973–1974) , pp. 48–65.

dising in keeping with a theme. The themes—youth culture, ecology, health, vitality, back to nature, or nostalgia—are always emergent parts of the customers' culture and life styles. It is the behavioral sciences that bridge these emergent cultural developments to retail merchandising and other marketing developments.

approaches to store layout

Store layout refers to the location of the various merchandise assortments, their patterned arrangement, and their relation to each other within the confines of the total store space. It is a continuing part of the total store design problem. A layout is the physical arrangement of space and activities that require space into some kind of planned meaningful arrangement. The question arises, "Why plan the use of space?" The answer has economic, aesthetic, and merchandising implications. First, we plan space because it is a scarce resource and exists in short supply. The merchant must pay for every inch of space that he occupies. Therefore, because it is a scarce commodity, he must plan wisely for its use. Second, humans generally and customers quite particularly seem to have a penchant for neatness and order. Layout is the principal means of accomplishing this order, and the neatness which follows usually has a desired aesthetic value. Finally, layout facilitates the merchandising function from the point of view of both seller and buyer. The departmentalization, the planned arrangement of a store's merchandise, and the separation of selling and nonselling activities facilitate the work of store personnel and store customers. Record keeping, inventories, buying, and merchandise evaluation are all facilitated by store planning, and specifically, by layout procedures. From the standpoint of the customer, a sound layout facilitates the customer shopping process that consists of (1) the search for goods, (2) the evaluation of goods, and (3) the choice or decision relating to goods.

The Basis for Layout Procedure

Our basic dictum of "form follows function" is the basis for layout procedure, inasmuch as the layout selected is a function of the activity sequences that are to be undertaken by the facility. The objective of the space planner or the merchandiser responsible for layout is to make the proper evaluation of the work flows or behavior sequences and to arrange the space and determine the layout on the basis of these studied activities. The layout is thus predicated on a functional analysis of the given store's activities.

The principal activities of a retail store have already been discussed at some length. Primarily, however, the layout pattern of any retail store must provide for the utilization of space in terms of paths, along which either people or goods must move. However, not all layout is concerned with movement; much of the problem is concerned with providing fixed apportionments of space for a variety of purposes such as workrooms, personnel and customer rest areas, storage room, displays, and work stations such as cashiers and customer wrap stations. However, the essential factor is that the given layout must provide space in the form of paths or aisles that will permit the optimum functioning of these activities.

The layout of any given store must focus on two broad considerations: (1) How can the intended activities be carried out most efficiently? (2) How will the layout address itself to the customer group to which the store attempts to cater?

Narrowly conceived, the major function of a retail store is to sell. With this thought in mind, the layout and space-planning job becomes somewhat simplified. Total store space consists essentially of three areas: (1) a sales area where goods are displayed and sold, (2) a service or nonselling area where goods are received and dispersed, and (3) a store front used to advertise and project the store's merchandise and total image. The problem of layout and store planning is to arrange these three areas in such a way as to meet the needs of the sales and operating methods of the retailer, the buying habits of the customer, and the shopping environment in which the store is placed.

The interior of a store is much like that of a community. The aisles or customer paths are like streets or traffic arteries; some are accumulators and some are dispersal outlets. The store's various merchandise assortments should be arranged on the customer traffic aisles like shops along an outdoor thoroughfare. Starting at the store front, these merchandise assortments or departments are best located in a horizontal or vertical sequence of impulse, convenience, and demand goods. Most merchandise, in most stores, falls within the demand category; i.e., customers wish to undertake some amount of shopping and comparison activity for these goods. However, the real plus business of many stores comes from the impulse sale, or what might better be called the unplanned purchase. Good layout will facilitate the sale of impulse or complementary items by placing them in the proper relationship with other convenience or demand items. The major task of retail store layout is to locate and interrelate all types of merchandise for maximum impulse buying, and to take full advantage of every square foot of sales effort for selling functions. Finally, the selling area must be tied meaningfully to the nonselling areas.

The plan in Figure 9-1 illustrates rather well our preceding comments. It shows a sequence of customer traffic, starting near the highest traffic area with merchandise that has quick appeal, high unit profit, fast turnover, and is bought on impulse; then customer traffic proceeds with the location of merchandise lending itself to related selling or logical association; and then to areas that ordinarily get the least traffic, stocked with merchandise that is scarce, or staple, and therefore is bought on demand.

Locating Nonselling or Service Areas. Every retail store will have to devote some amount of its total space to nonselling activities. In small stores, the proportion of selling space to nonselling space is much larger than in larger stores, where there is considerably more specialization and division of labor. In a very large store such as a department store, 25 to 40 per cent of the total employees may perform jobs other than selling. This means that in large stores as much as 30 to 40 per cent of the total store

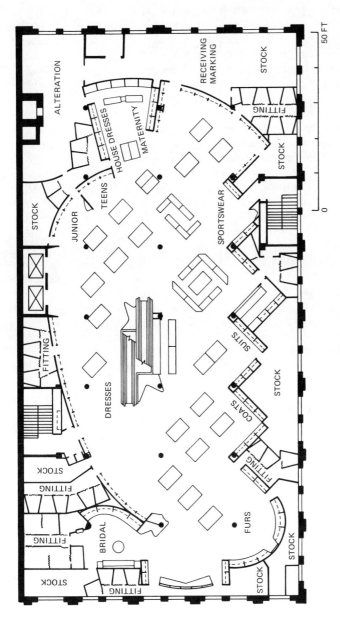

FIGURE 9-1 Merchandising sequence determines layout.

203

area may be used to perform nonselling tasks. The key to effective layout for nonselling activities is to use space that cannot be more effectively used for selling activities, yet which is located in such a way as to facilitate the major task of the store, which is merchandising. Good layout presumes a balanced and coordinated relationship between selling and nonselling activities.

A great portion of the nonselling space must of necessity be devoted to storage areas for back-up merchandise. The layout will affect the manner in which the store approaches the physical distribution aspect of its operation, and physical distribution will have a profound effect on the store's total efficiency. The method of handling goods spells the difference between an expensive and an inexpensive operation. Thus, careful planning can minimize the cost of handling merchandise. Each product inventoried has a handling cost associated with it, depending on its particular location in storage and its position in the selling area of the store. This cost is the expense incurred for routing the product through the warehouse or storage area; that is, the cost of moving the product from the receiving dock to the storage point or points, and from there to the selling area. The problem is one of evaluating and assessing the tradeoffs in handling costs among the various stock arrangements.[13]

The crucial factor of the nonselling layout and arrangement is how the service areas of a store are located in relation to the total work flow or circulation pattern. There are three ways in which such areas can be located. One is the *sandwich approach,* wherein one entire floor in a multi-storied building may be utilized for service activities. It is sandwiched between the other selling floors of the store in order to provide maximum convenience and minimum handling costs for merchandise storage, price marking, workroom, alteration activities, and so on. The May Company in St. Louis has used the sandwich floor approach in locating its major service areas.

A second approach to locating service or nonselling areas is the *internal core.* In this method, selling areas evolve and operate around an internal core of centralized space devoted to merchandise storage and other non-selling activities. The most outstanding example of the internal core service facility is the J. L. Hudson branch at Northland, in Detroit.

The most accepted practice regarding the location of major nonselling and service areas is the concept of *peripheral service.* The most promising feature of this concept is that customer circulation is centralized and allowed to fan out in all directions on the floor. Also, peripheral service means that incoming merchandise is routed from the outer edges of the building to the inside shops or departments so that merchandise circulation and customer circulation do not cross.

Major Layout Patterns.　There are basically two major patterns used for store layout arrangements. Of course, by combining the two in one store

---

[13] For a discussion of the principles involved in warehousing and storing goods, see Ronald H. Ballou, "Improving the Physical Layout of Merchandise in Warehouses," *Journal of Marketing,* Vol. 31 (July 1967), pp. 60–64.

or one department, a third variation or pattern comes into use. The two
major patterns, however, are the *grid pattern* and the *free form*.

The similarity between travel paths in retail stores and city streets has
been frequently observed. There are a series of major aisles or pathways,
which are analogous to the major traffic arterials of a city or community. At
right angles to these major aisles are a series of smaller aisles, used both as
accumulators and dispersals.

The grid pattern of store layout no doubt reflects the merchants' earlier
interest in engineering efficiency. However, the grid pattern makes many
stores look like warehouses, with aisles and pathways laid out in military
precision, with fixtures that often resemble bunkers. Figure 9-2 shows a
layout based upon the grid concept. As can be observed, the regimentation
of customer traffic patterns is not quite so compelling as that found in most
supermarket layout arrangements. However, customer movement is directed
by the aisles and fixtures, which are usually arranged at right angles to each
other.

The free-form pattern is sometimes called the free flow of layout pattern
and is perhaps a realization on the part of store designers and management
that customers by and large like to form their own traffic patterns within
the retail store or, at least, they do not wish to feel quite so compelled by
right angles to move in predetermined directions. The free-form pattern
is a more casual and relaxed approach to layout, resulting from what
amounts to a more relaxed and casual approach to customer shopping.
The grid pattern is perhaps more efficient in the simple engineering sense;
more fixtures can usually be placed in the same given amount of space by

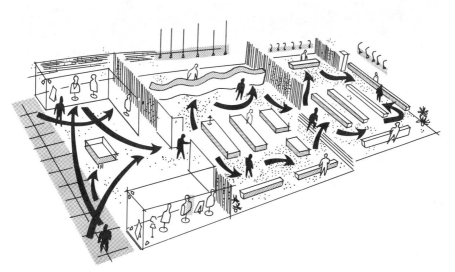

FIGURE 9-2   The grid pattern of layout and resulting customer traffic patterns.

using the grid pattern instead of the free form. Where shopping and customer needs prescribe traveling in a given path in order to fulfill sequential requirements, such as weekly food shopping, the grid pattern may also result in the greatest convenience to the customer. However, in shopping goods stores and in specialty stores where the customer is interested in prolonged and relaxed shopping, comparison and evaluation of products, the free-form pattern of store layout is much to be preferred.[14]

The reader is cautioned to remember that the layout pattern chosen is a part of the total store planning and design responsibility, and as such it must be consistent with the overall store design. This means that the layout pattern must complement and facilitate the overall merchandising approach of the particular store. It must be consistent with the overall store image, accommodated to the shopping habits and preferences of the store's customers, and suitable for merchandising and displaying the kinds of merchandise sold. Figure 9-3 illustrates the free-form pattern of store layout in use in a Northwest department store. Notice how uncompelling the arrangement appears. Instead of definite, prearranged customer travel paths, the pattern is conducive to relaxed, informal, and unregimented browsing among the various merchandise assortments.

It is small wonder that in larger stores, especially department stores, a variety of layout patterns is used. This results from the different types of merchandise being sold, with the resultant varying needs for merchandising and displaying these assortments, as well as from the fact that there are many diverse customer types who visit the various departments.

Departmentizing. In larger stores it has long been recognized that certain merchandising and operating advantages stem from departmentalization. That is, by aggregating homogeneous merchandise collections into concentrated assortments, record keeping and merchandising are greatly facilitated. Separate records of stocks, purchases, and sales are kept for each concentrated assortment, or department; in many instances operating expenses are separately recorded and allocated to departments, making these departments profit centers for purposes of management planning and control.

Departmentizing has a special significance to store planning, design, and layout. An integral part of the layout responsibility is concerned with classifying and grouping the merchandise into homogeneous categories and then placing these assortments within the overall layout plan. There are several bases for departmentizing. Often, concentrated assortments are determined on the basis of the generic kinds of goods. For example, footwear, underwear, outerwear, or headgear might be the basis for determining merchandise classifications and departments.

Other bases for determining departmental classifications are trade practice, market targets, or customer segments, the method used for storing or

---

[14] See "Making Waves in Store Design," *Chain Store Age* (January 1972), pp. E30–34. Also, "Consumer Life Styles Change Store Design," *Chain Store Age* (August 1972), pp. E21–23.

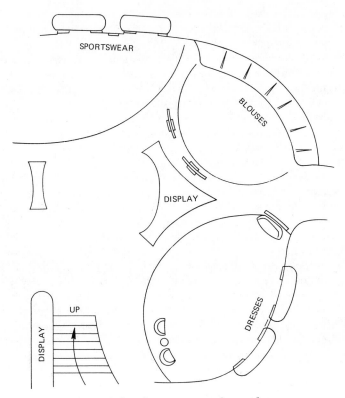

SPORTSWEAR

BLOUSES

DISPLAY

DISPLAY

UP

DRESSES

FIGURE 9-3   A free-form pattern of store layout.

displaying the goods, and the consumer's motive of purchase.[15] The major point to consider is that the store's approach and attitude relating to departmentizing will seriously affect layout decisions in such critical considerations as (1) Where in the overall layout plan should various departments be located? (2) How much space should the separate departments be allocated? Consideration of the latter question will be taken up in the final section of this chapter.

Factors Governing the Location of Departments.   The location of departments will be affected to a considerable degree by the number of departments established and the total amount of space available. In smaller stores with fewer departments the location decision may be easier to approach. However, in very large stores there may be as many as 100 or 200 departments, and the proper location of these departments will focus on such considerations as (1) the size and shape of store space, (2) customer clientele and customer shopping habits, (3) the nature and breadth of

[15] See "How Will the 'New Retailing' Affect Store Design?" *Chain Store Age* (January 1973), pp. E29–33.

merchandise assortments, (4) the value of store space, (5) the number of floors available, and (6) the desire to maximize customer traffic and exposure to merchandise.

These considerations require little further discussion, although (4) and (5) warrant some elaboration. As has been frequently mentioned, store design is largely concerned with the optimum use of space. Not all space however is of equal value. In the single-floor store, the front of the store immediately adjacent to the entrance is the area of greatest value, because it is here that foot traffic is highest and the greatest dollar sales per square foot of selling space are generated. Distance creates an inertia or friction in terms of customer traffic. *As a generalization, the further a given unit of space lies from the main point of customer egress or entrance into the store, the less the value of that unit of space.* Furthermore, this means that customers must be pulled or attracted to these more remote spatial areas by high demand or shopping items. Thus, in the single-floor store, as one moves back from the customer entrances to the rear of the building, the space has less and less value, and in the multifloored building, as one moves from the main floor upward, the space has less and less value. For example, merchandisers often will conclude that in the case of a single-floor store, four zones of productivity or value can be established. In zone 1, the area immediately adjacent to the customer entrance, 40 per cent of the store's volume (in some cases criteria other than volume may be established) will be generated. In zone 2, the next zone in a progression from front to rear, 30 per cent of the volume will be generated. Zones 3 and 4 should therefore generate 20 and 10 per cent of store volume, respectively. A similar basis is often established for rent-paying purposes in multifloored stores. For example, a six-story building with a basement might be costed out for rent-paying purposes in the following manner:

FLOOR OR AREA	ALLOCATION OF OCCUPANCY COSTS TO EACH AREA (%)
Basement	6
1st floor	34
2nd floor	18
3rd floor	14
4th floor	10
5th floor	8
6th floor	4
All service areas	6

Departments are located within a particular unit of space on a particular floor in accordance with certain prescribed merchandising tendencies and customer shopping habits and attitudes. As a general rule, a particular merchandise department will be located according to its sales-generating capacity in relation to the value of the space occupied. Items that are purchased infrequently, have a low unit value, and are poor generators of store traffic generally are given the less-favored positions in the total store layout arrangement. On the other hand, items that are purchased frequently and thus generate adequate contributions to profit and overhead are likely to be given the most-favored positions or space allocations.

The nature of the goods also plays a role in determining the location of departments within the total store layout. Impulse and convenience goods must be located in areas of greatest customer density and traffic; customers will not travel far nor expend much energy by way of search to locate these items. Demand items, the term for items of high unit value where purchase intent is well established and deliberate (as in the case of home furnishings, appliances, or furniture) can usually be located in the farthest regions of the total space arrangements. The reason of course is that these demand items will pull traffic to these remoter regions.

Departmental location is also a function of other factors, such as the need to locate some departments in close proximity to others for purposes of complementary selling. For these reasons, draperies and home furnishing accessories are frequently located next to furniture departments in large department stores. Items with a high replacement rate that are purchased frequently must be located in positions that strategically intercept the customer as she enters or leaves the store. For example, women's hosiery is almost always located at points of high traffic density on the main floor next to entrances, rather than on upper floors where other items of women's apparel are usually found. Finally, seasonal items are located in space areas that permit flexibility and accommodation to seasonal selling patterns.

A more recent departmental concept that is affecting conventional layout considerations is the "shoppe concept," which is also referred to as "category selling." The basis of the shoppe concept is that merchandise is related and grouped according to use, rather than in accordance with the more conventional basis of grouping such as generic similarity. One successful Northwest department store has recently opened an "Answer Shoppe." This is a department of rather expensive gift items for women to be purchased by men. Heavy emphasis is placed upon sales person assistance and suggestion. Other category or shoppe departments are related to recreation, such as camping centers or ski shoppes, and some are related to occasions such as weddings and showers.

Departmentalization in the final analysis must be approached from the consumer's point of view, as is the total approach to store planning, design, and layout. As one team of researchers put it, the key to successful design, layout, and departmentization

lies in *current* information on the activity patterns of the *store's clientele*. Activity patterns differ among income groups, age groups, occupational, educational and other socioeconomic categories. To consider seriously the [proper approach to space planning] requires that retailers make a commitment to research their customers.[16]

Layout and Selling Method. Store layout will depend to a considerable degree on the type of selling method or methods employed by the store. Selling methods basically range across a continuum from total salon selling to complete self-service. In the total salon the layout may feature no

---

[16] Montrose S. Sommers and Jerome B. Kernan, "A Behavioral Approach to Planning, Layout, and Display," *Journal of Retailing* (Winter 1965–1966), p. 62.

displayed merchandise whatsoever; in appearance it may resemble a fashionable Fifth Avenue living room with fixtures consisting of sofas, chairs, cocktail tables and accessories, and it may be decorated in an expensive motif. Customers do virtually no moving; the merchandise is brought to them. However, in many of these stores, layout is used as a means of routing customers to the merchandise assortments in which they are interested and in facilitating the customers in their search-evaluation-and-decision process. Even in the so-called better stores, emphasis is being placed on simplified selling techniques based upon layout, display, and fixturization that facilitate the merchandising activity and reduce the store's operating costs, a large part of which historically has been salary cost. Many stores, especially those of a mass merchandising character, have followed the examples of the large food supermarkets and gone exclusively to self-service merchandising techniques. Such has been the case for drugstores, variety stores, and large soft-goods discount stores.

Whatever the selling method, whether it be extreme clerk-service such as salon selling, clerk-service with simplified selling techniques, or complete self-service, the point to be considered is that it will have a profound effect upon the planning of total store systems such as cashier stations, checkout stands, sales personnel stations, and department locations, as well as the layout of the store's total space facilities.

Store Layout in Food Supermarkets. Many of the generalizations discussed thus far in relation to store layout procedures can be applied in a special way to the food supermarket. The supermarket really began as a warehouse where the public was permitted to shop. There were and continue to be acres of aisles and vast assortments of merchandise. Although today's supermarkets are far more attractively designed than their early counterparts of the 1930s, they remain the best example of what we earlier described as a machine for selling. Today's average supermarket shopper spends approximately 29 minutes in the store per shopping trip. During this time she (54 per cent of the shoppers in supermarkets are women) purchases 14 items and spends approximately $17 per visit. To accomplish this, she must travel over nearly 20,000 square feet of floor space and search among approximately 9,000 different items to find those in which she alone is interested. This brings up a dramatic point: The average time for selling impact per item in a modern supermarket is from 0.15 to 0.20 seconds! Consequently, the layout must maximize the visibility and accessibility of the display for almost instantaneous purchase decision making. Thus, the supermarket shopper must behave much like an order picker in a warehouse. She must be presented with rather well-defined travel paths; assortment locations must be fairly well standardized; and related items ought to be featured in relatively close proximity. Layout must facilitate the ease and convenience of customer shopping, promote maximum exposure to merchandise selections, stimulate impulse sales, and minimize customer travel and search time. Figure 9-4 represents a well-designed and effective layout for a modern supermarket, promoting these objectives. The plan contains a total area of 25,000 square feet, of which the selling area accounts for 18,500 square feet. Visibility is facilitated by the openness of the aisles and the low gondolas. Dry groceries are located in the center areas, adequate back storage is provided at the rear, and vegetables and produce are located around a peripheral wall. General merchandise accounts for a sizable proportion of total supermarket sales and is strongly emphasized; however, the overall image conveyed by the layout arrangement is still that of food and food-related items.

Layout and Operating Efficiency. Efficiency refers to the ratio of output to the units of input. Much of our discussion of store layout has focused upon objectives greater than efficiency, e.g., aesthetic appearance, customer convenience, and merchandise characteristics; nonetheless, efficiency *per se* is a highly important criterion for judging the merits of any layout arrangement. Because space is such a scarce and therefore costly commodity,

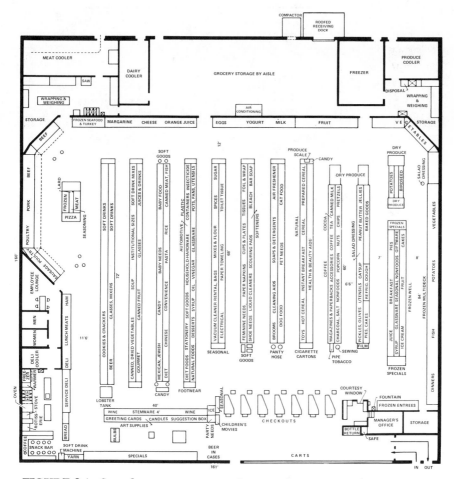

FIGURE 9-4 Store layout arrangement for a modern supermarket.

SOURCE: Progressive Grocer, Vol. 54, No. 2 (February 1975), p. 45.

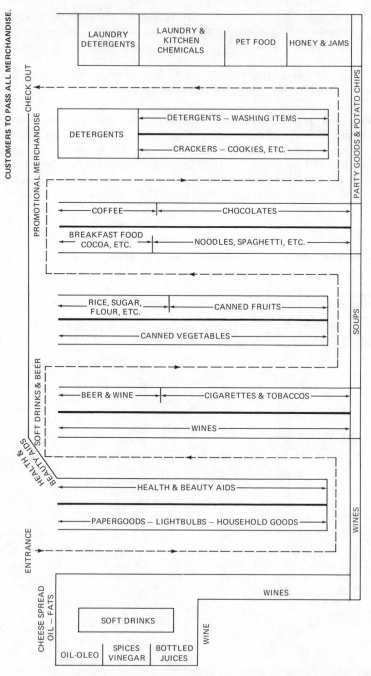

FIGURE 9-5 Layout pattern of limited-assortment discount food store.

SOURCE: Progressive Grocer, Vol. 54, No. 1 (January 1975), p. 85.

it is wise to use it efficiently. Furthermore, the efficient use of space can lead to savings and economies in other resources, namely, the human resources of store personnel and store clientele. In the previous section, it was shown why a particular layout arrangement in a food supermarket focused on customer shopping convenience or efficiency. The principal goal of the food supermarket is to maximize the customer's exposure to the merchandise while minimizing her travel paths.

Figure 9-5 shows the layout and traffic plan of what is known in Europe as a limited-assortment discount food store. These kinds of stores are emerging rapidly in the United States as well. Such layouts are models of productivity and efficiency and can result in greatly reduced operating expenses, with one third the payroll expenses of conventional supermarkets, faster turnover, and better gross margins.

space allocation

Before concluding this chapter, one final concept known as space allocation remains to be discussed. In many respects, our analysis of store design and layout has already touched upon the concept of space allocation. But the issues that remain to be discussed here center primarily around the question, "Given our entire merchandise assortment (or the total number of departments), how much space should be allocated to each product line (or department) of our total assortment?" The answer to this question is not necessarily easy to obtain, nor is it simple.

The retail manager's interest in such a question is justified by the necessity to utilize resources (space) in an efficient and productive manner. The tendency to exploding, ever-widening product lines through product innovation, the scrambling of product lines resulting from competitive pressures, and the price-cost-margin spiral demand that every merchant utilize his selling and display space in the most efficient and productive manner possible. It is imperative that space be used skillfully, because the way space is utilized will affect sales and it will also affect operating expenses, inasmuch as space is both costly to provide and expensive to maintain.

Unfortunately, not too much is known about how the size of the assortments stocked affects both sales volume and the cost of maintaining displays. Procedures relating to methods for allocating space are usually predicated upon the following basic assumptions:

1. All space is limited in extent and surrounded by some degree of inflexibility as to how it might best be used.
2. The amount of space allotted to a given product line or merchandise department will be a function of several factors including (a) the merchandise characteristics; (b) customer shopping habits such as frequency of purchase, importance of impulse buying, and hence, display; and (c) the problems relating to the physical distribution or handling of the merchandise such as the pattern of sales over time and the frequency of restocking.
3. The basic criterion used for space allocation is the contribution of

profit and overhead made by an item in relation to the amount of space occupied.

Space allocation, then, centers around a critical analysis of the above considerations. No truly satisfactory model for space allocation has yet been determined, even though some rather interesting approaches have been attempted. One of the major difficulties of devising and utilizing a model for determining optimum space allocation lies with the problem of developing accurate criteria for allocation decisions. For example, assumption 3 in the previous list poses several difficulties. First, in terms of contribution to profit and overhead there is the perennial question of what determines contribution and what costs one should consider in making the contribution decision. Should only net profits be considered? Are we concerned with full costs, or only incremental or marginal costs in our consideration? Second, another problem arises in determining with what unit of space we shall be concerned. Most models and especially those used for allocating space in supermarkets advocate using linear feet of shelf space. However, some argue that cubic feet of shelf or gondola space would result in an optimum utilization of space.

Unfortunately, the body of knowledge available to guide retail management in this decision area is indeed meager. However, several heuristic approaches are rather well known and utilized and the *theory* of space allocation has been rather well formulated. Let us look at two of these heuristic methods and conclude with a rather elaborate treatment of the theory of space allocation.

Heuristic Approaches to Space Allocation

These approaches are called heuristic because in essence they are rules of thumb or management guidelines that have been arrived at by trial and error, and they appear to produce reasonably satisfactory (not necessarily, however, optimum) results.

Space Productivity Ratios. A space productivity ratio is a rule that stipulates a desired or expected amount of dollar sales per square foot of selling space. Practically all trade associations for various classifications of retail stores generate data that relate to space productivity ratios and sales per square foot of selling space.[17] This information is utilized for space allocation decisions in this manner. First of all, the decision maker must find out from existing published sources what the typical sales per square foot of selling space are for stores of his type and size category. For example, if a new women's specialty store is proposed, with projected sales of $500,000, and with departmental sales as a per cent of total sales as follows:[18]

[17] For example, the *Journal of Retailing* frequently carries articles that deal with retail operating ratios. Other sources can be found in specific trade association materials, such as the National Retail Merchants Association's MOR, the National Retail Hardware Association, the National Retail Furniture Association; *The Lilly Digest* for drugstore firms, and *Progressive Grocer* studies for retail food stores.

[18] Data taken from *Departmental and Operating Results of 1964 Controllers Congress*, 1965 edition, National Retail Merchants Association, New York, p. 41.

1. Women's and Misses' Accessories, 5.4 per cent.
2. Shoes, 10.7 per cent.
3. Women's and Misses' Outer Apparel, 21.6 per cent.

then the amount of space for these departments in the new store can be determined by the following procedure:

1. For a given department, say, shoes, multiply the planned total store sales by 10.7 per cent. The result is $53,500—the amount of sales that will likely be generated by the shoe department.
2. Now, by using the typical specialty store's sales per square foot of selling space in this sales category, the amount of space to allocate to shoes can be determined. (The data for sales per square foot of selling space can be found on page 38 of the MOR figures for department and specialty stores with sales under $1,000,000. The figure is $70.83.)
3. If the sales per square foot of selling space are $70.83, then the amount of space to allocate to shoes would be

$$\frac{\$53,500 \text{ planned sales for shoe department}}{\$70.83 \text{ the sales per square foot of selling space allotted to shoes in comparable stores}}$$

The result is that approximately (recall that our procedure does not produce optimum results, but is only a heuristic or crude approximation) 754 square feet of selling space should be allocated to the shoe department. Similar computations would be made for the other departments, until the entire amount of floor selling space was allocated.

The use of space productivity ratios as a basis for allocating store space varies with the nature of the merchandising establishment. For example, in soft goods stores, such as wearing apparel and general merchandise, sales per square foot of space are the standard criterion used. In food stores, variety, and hardware stores, sales per square foot of linear shelf space are the standard criterion. For frozen food items, sales per cubic foot of freezer cabinet may be the established criterion.

In spite of the crudeness of this method, it can lead to improvements in space allocations, and consequently, increased total store sales, margins, and profits.

The Model Stock Procedure. A model stock is an ideal stock in terms of the composition or assortment of merchandise to be carried: the proper mix or assortment of styles, colors, sizes, price lines, materials, and other factors.

The *model stock* concept usually applies to fashion or style goods, while the concept of the *basic stock* is used to refer to the same considerations in regard to basic or staple merchandise. Included are (1) a basic list of the items to be carried in stock, classified by size, color, price lines, and so on; (2) the minimum quantities to have on hand for any one period of time, especially adjusted for seasonal needs; and (3) the amount or quantity to reorder when reordering is necessary.

The use of the model stock or basic stock concept as a basis for allocating store space is perhaps even more arbitrary and subjective than the procedure involving the use of space productivity ratios. Essentially, the procedure involves these essential steps:

1. On the basis of past experience predicated upon the careful use of store records relating to sales and stocks, the proper balance between sales and stocks is established. For example, if the operating history revealed that $2.00 of inventory in retail prices were necessary for each $1.00 of sales generated by a store, then this would be a stock sales ratio of 2 to 1. By determining the amount of inventory required to generate a given level of sales, the merchant has at least the beginning knowledge required for space allocation decisions.

2. Next, on the basis of his store's own operating historical data, or based upon standards established by similar stores (found in trade association literature or sources such as those previously mentioned), the store manager must determine the amount of space, either in square feet or linear feet, required to house a given merchandise assortment or a given department. For example, assume that a food supermarket experience shows that a stock sales ratio of 3 to 1 is required for canned pet foods. If sales for this particular merchandise category in an average supermarket amount to 250 units per week and the retail price per unit is $.20, then sales would equal $50.00 per week (250 units × $.20). With the established stock sales ratio of 3 to 1, $150 in total inventory is required; 750 cans ($150.00 ÷ $.20) must be stocked. If one linear foot of shelf space will hold 10 cans, then 750 cans will require 7.50 linear feet of shelf space.

Thus, the model stock and the basic stock concepts utilizing established stock sales ratios and standards of space utilization for various merchandise classifications can be used in the total store space allocation decision.

Both the space productivity ratio and the model stock approaches are fraught with many difficulties, yet they do provide some basis for handling the crucial economic question of effectively utilizing the scarce resource of store selling space. They are rules of thumb, and as such their widespread use must be tempered with the judicious use of experience and judgment. At best, they help to minimize the problems of out-of-stock situations, slow turnover, overinvestment in merchandise inventory, and the general and widespread problems generated by the inefficient and unproductive use of a valuable resource.

The Theoretical Approach to Space Allocation

The *theory* of space allocation has been rather well developed. However, as is sometimes the case, the developed theory cannot always be applied to the existing practice. Theoretical as well as the more practical and heuristic space allocation models postulate the maximization of store profits as their basic objective.

The theoretical approach to space allocation decisions is based upon this same consideration with several qualifications. As we learned earlier, gross profit or gross margin is the difference between selling price and acquisition cost. During a period of time, if operating expenses remain constant, then the retailer will maximize his net profit by maximizing his gross profits. There will therefore be one level of gross profit that represents a break-even point (sales revenue = merchandise costs + operating expenses). This means that any additions to gross profit (sales revenue) will result in increases to net profit (remember that our operating expenses are constant over the range of sales being considered).

The space allocation problem can now be cast within this framework. It amounts to using and allocating space in such a way as to maximize gross profits. The assumption is that the retailer has a fixed amount of space available and that this space is homogeneous; i.e., any one unit of space is as good as any other unit. This means simply that the rate of sale for a particular item is unaffected by the unit of space to which it is assigned.[19] This is a simplistic assumption, but it results in directing the problem to the question of *how many* units of space to assign rather than to *what* units of space to assign.

The problem of how much space or how many units of space to assign depends for its solution upon two major factors: (1) the gross margin contribution of each item as qualified by the earlier discussion and (2) the rate of sale for each item, given as a function of the amount of space the item is assigned.

In order to arrive at a solution, space is assumed to be all allocated to the total product assortment at a particular time. Each item in the assortment would therefore be making some contribution. All the contributions from all the commodities would be arrayed from highest to lowest. *Now the objective would be to increase total store profits by withdrawing the items rendering the least amount of contribution and replacing these commodities with those making a higher contribution.* When total store profits could no longer be increased as a result of substituting products with higher contributions for those with lower contributions, space would then be allocated optimally.

The theoretical approach to space allocation cannot yet be practically implemented, as such. The necessity for oversimplifying the model in order to make it produce results negates its use as a practical model for decision making. However, the value of the theory is that it shows rather dramatically just what it is we are trying to accomplish. Thus, it clarifies our objectives in space allocation, even though it does not provide us with a suitable means for accomplishing our objective. There is considerable evidence to suggest that the theory of space allocation and the practice (as described in the previous examples) are highly compatible. As a matter of fact, the heuristic approaches involving space productivity ratios and the model stock approach each deal with a practical way of developing contribution standards. When products are found not to be generating contributions up to a suitable standard, they are then replaced with more profitable products in order to raise overall profitability.

[19] The discussion in this section is based upon James P. Cairns, "Allocate Space for Maximum Profits," *Journal of Retailing*, Vol. 39, No. 2 (Summer 1963), pp. 41–45 and 52.

Is Store Space Homogeneous? The reader will have observed that one of the greatest deficiencies in the theoretical model for space allocation is the simplifying assumption that all selling space is homogeneous. In other words, the rate of sale for a commodity is a function of how much space it is allocated, rather than where the space is located within the total configuration. This assumption does not square well with our intuitive understanding of space and store layout. There are "hot spots" in layout arrangements. Some areas have a greater traffic density than others. The intersection of aisles and entrances often results in customer interceptor rings where sales per square foot of certain commodities skyrocket.

The constant conflict among many resellers and manufacturers to secure the most favorable shelf position for their products—on the assumption that shelf position will affect sales—is well known. For these reasons, it is probably safe to generalize that *what space* can have as important an effect on sales as *how much space*. Yet, the relationship is not yet clearly established.

One researcher, however, using rather refined statistical techniques for analyzing the relationship between shelf space and product sales in supermarkets, concluded that the hypothesis that product sales would increase if the product were given more shelf space did not hold in three out of the four situations tested.[20] Quite obviously, this is a question of considerable concern to the retail store manager; and until more conclusive evidence is produced, he will have to continue making his space allocation decisions on the basis of his own experience and that of other similar stores by using the methods that appear to produce the best results, given his store, his customers, and his total design, layout, and space allocation objectives.[21]

QUESTIONS FOR STUDY, REFLECTION, AND REVIEW

1. What are the three major dimensions of the store design problem, and how do they relate to the seller-buyer relationship?
2. Explain how retailing activities and store design are related to the concept that "form follows function."
3. What are some of the images that the exterior appearance of a store should project?
4. Why is it important for the retail manager to plan the use of space in relation to design problems?
5. Explain the major concepts and ideas related to the grid pattern of store layout.
6. What is the special significance of departmentizing in relation to store planning, design, and layout?

[20] Keith K. Cox, *The Relationship Between Shelf Space and Product Sales in Supermarkets,* University of Texas, Bureau of Business Research, Austin, Tex., 1964; and Keith Cox, "The Responsiveness of Food Sales to Shelf Space Changes in Supermarkets," *Journal of Marketing Research* (May 1964), pp. 63–67.

[21] For more on this topic, see Robert A. Petersen and James W. Cagley, "The Effect of Shelf Space upon Sales of Branded Products: An Appraisal," *Journal of Marketing Research,* Vol. X (February 1973), pp. 103–104.

7. What are some of the factors that govern the location of departments? Explain the role that distance plays in locating different departments.

8. Why does store layout depend to a large degree on the type of selling method or methods employed by the store?

9. What are the basic assumptions upon which the methods for allocating space are usually predicated?

10. What are space productivity ratios, and how do they aid in the allocation of store space?

FOUR

THE RETAIL ORGANIZATION: PATTERNS AND PROBLEMS

10

organizing the
retailing effort

Retail managers are charged with the continuing responsibility of developing a total retail management system that will effectively tap a given market opportunity. No small part of this assignment is the task of welding together an organizational whole from many diverse elements, individuals, talents, and resources. In the small retail store with informal relationships and face-to-face contacts, there is the usual tendency to underorganize; there is not likely to be any formal organization structure or chart. Duties and responsibilities are often assigned on the basis of "Say, Bill, you're not busy right now. How about giving some thought to what we might run in Friday's newspaper ad." The greatest danger in underorganizing is that all responsibilities or duties will not be covered evenly and that the store manager or owner will give careful attention only to those activities in which he has a special interest.

In some stores, especially in the larger retail management systems, the reverse is quite likely to take place. That is, instead of underorganizing, there may be far too much emphasis placed upon establishing elaborate or overorganized systems. Overorganization can have serious detrimental effects, both on store management and on the young individuals striving to work their way to the top of a complex organizational hierarchy.

The moral is simple. Organization is a means and not an end. If it becomes an end, it probably at the same time becomes an encumbrance. Lack of organization can impede performance; too much organization can just as surely impede performance, affect morale, and hamper productivity. All stores have some degree of organization. Patterned ways are established by which large numbers of people, engaged in a complexity of tasks, relate themselves to each other in the conscious, systematic establishment and accomplishment of mutually agreed purposes.

The Small Store Organization

The organizational requirements for small stores differ from those of large stores only to the extent that size and complexity of functions are different, not necessarily because there is any difference in basic functions. Remember that function determines structure and the basic organizing principle dictates that functional analysis ought to precede decisions relating to organizational structure; therefore the task of organizing the small store ought to proceed along these lines. Drucker has stated that there are three ways to determine the kind of structure needed in a specific enterprise: activities or functional analysis, decision analysis, and relations analysis.[1] *Functional analysis* is concerned with the activities performed by the enterprise. *Decision analysis* determines what kinds of decisions are needed, where in the organization structure they should be made, who should be involved in the decision process, and to what extent. *Relations analysis* means knowing with whom each person is to work, what contributions to programs and performance each must make, and what contributions the various members of the organization make to each other.

The organization patterns for small stores are likely to vary widely, if for no other reason than that there are so many small stores. By and large, the small store organization structure can be characterized as simple rather than complex. Organizational patterns are likely to be based on decision analysis and relations analysis rather than on functional analysis, simply because a small number of employees does not permit a high degree of specialization along functional lines.

The formal organization of the small store with ten employees or less will probably consist solely of a *line organization*. The line organization is that part of the total structure that possesses the power to act and is dedicated to getting the work out. As organizations grow, they often do so by adding *staff* specialists with the ability and power to think, plan, and advise the operative workers in their task of accomplishing the primary objectives of the enterprise. Under normal circumstances, staff does not have the power to act, i.e., to issue orders or take direct action. In some larger retail stores, although the primary function of staff is advisory, the concept of functional staff capacity is now widely used.

The typical functional approach to division of labor and organization is derived from the endemic functions or activities related to retailing. Retail stores do two major things: They buy goods and they sell goods. However, they also perform a host of other activities. Goods are displayed, employees are hired and trained, merchandise is stored and moved from warehouse to sales floor, and merchandise is sold and delivered. The store itself must be cleaned and operated. All these functions are related to retail store selling. In the smaller stores where there is usually evidence of some division of labor, this organization is more likely to be separated along product lines or merchandise classifications than functional specialization. Such division is shown in Figure 10-1, which illustrates that total responsibility

[1] Peter Drucker, *The Practice of Management*, McGraw-Hill Book Company, New York, 1964, pp. 194–201.

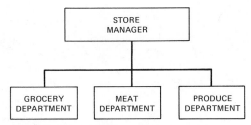

FIGURE 10-1 Organization of a retail food store based upon product classification.

is based upon product or merchandise characteristics rather than upon any functional specialization.

Product classification implicitly reflects that the store manager probably does all the major work of management, i.e., planning, organizing, motivating, communicating, and controlling, and that the other members of the organization are charged with completing responsibilities as they are outlined and defined by him. Those within the various merchandise departments are probably responsible for keeping the departments clean and well stocked and for performing customer service activities, but they probably have little or no voice in buying, pricing, or other merchandising decisions. When the smaller retail store begins to think about its organizational structure in terms of a more functional division of labor, the result is likely to be a two-functional arrangement as shown in Figure 10-2.

The basic organization shown in Figure 10-2 is still a rather simple line organization. Although there are only two boxes (divisions) shown, however, there may be several employees in any of the areas below that of the store manager. In Figure 10-2, the two major divisions are based upon the functions related to the physical store operation and to merchandising or the buying and selling of goods. Merchandising would include all those activities related to the merchandising function such as inventory collection and assortment, pricing, display, advertising, and perhaps personal selling. Store operations would pertain to store building operation and maintenance, design, layout, fixturization, housekeeping, security, and personnel. Figure 10-3 shows the same basic organization structure as Figure 10-2, but now two staff specialists have been added and the functional specialization has been carried a further step down through the organization. The duties

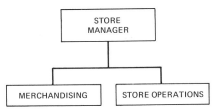

FIGURE 10-2 Retail store organization: Two-functional basis.

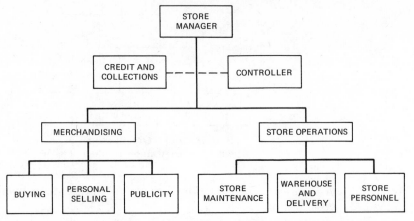

FIGURE 10-3 Retail store organization functionally oriented with staff specialists.

of the controller in this organization relate to financing and capital resource utilization and are a staff adjunct to the general store manager.[2]

The credit and collections function is a staff activity designed to facilitate the use of credit as a sales and merchandising device and is not included as a part of the controller's activities as a matter of management policy. Controller's activities are often aimed at controlling and reducing the store expenses. Such an attitude in relation to credit and collections would likely be restrictive and not in harmony with the practice of viewing credit selling as an extension of the merchandising function.

As the size of the retail management system increases, the likely result will be increased organizational complexity and a concomitant increase in organizational responsibility. For that matter, one survey has shown that as retail organizations increase in size, organizational planning receives more attention as a separate and specific function. A growing number of companies assign that function to a specific department, group, or individual for special and continuous attention.[3]

The usual result of increased size is a greater recognition of the more specialized functional activities within the firm. For example, the two-functional scheme shown in Figure 10-2 is likely to grow to at least a three-functional classification, with *control* becoming the third functional line activity. As we shall soon see, in larger stores, there are likely to be four, five, or even six or seven major functional line activities that will form the basic structure of the organization pattern.

[2] The duties of the controller are very often found as a part of the line organization, especially in the larger-sized retail firm. For example, see Erich A. Helfert, Eleanor G. May, and Malcolm P. McNair, *Controllership in Department Stores,* Division of Research, Graduate School of Business Administration, Harvard University Press, Boston, 1965.

[3] J. K. Bailey, "Organizational Planning—Whose Responsibility?" *Stores* (September 1964) , pp. 49–53.

The Larger Store Organization

The large store with its multitude of talent and activities can support a rather high degree of functional specializaticn, while often the case in the smaller store is that no single functional activity is so demanding as to require the services of a full-time functional specialist.

The Department Store. The department store really began to emerge as a distinct and viable institution in the United States just after the end of the Civil War. This institution offers an interesting and intriguing set of problems for the organization analyst. Its very structure (departmentation) means that it is already organized to some extent along departmental lines based upon merchandise classification. For many years, very little attention was paid to the value of organization in terms of improving or increasing the store's productivity or in terms of enhancing the store's competitive position. Retail store organization just grew haphazardly, without much conscious or deliberate attention. As new departments were added, they were simply appended organizationally to the overall formal organization structure.

From its early inception, the department store had been organized as an assemblage of shops under one roof, with a division of responsibilities by merchandise departments, and this came to be the all-important merchandising pyramid of the organization. As the store's volume increased and more merchandise lines and departments were added, further division of labor appeared within the merchandising pyramid. Instead of reporting directly to the general merchandise manager, the departmental buyer might report to a divisional merchandise manager or supervisor, who likely in turn would report to a merchandise vice-president in charge of a broad commodity grouping, such as soft goods or hard goods. Such thinking led to unusual amounts of responsibility handled by the department buyers. Oftentimes their word was final, even in such matters as store operation, accounting, and total sales promotion.

In 1927, there appeared a book, written by Paul Mazur, a partner in a New York investment banking firm, which was to have a profound impact on department store organization.[4] Mazur's book took a strong stand against checks and balances or duality of supervisors, and he urged that a department buyer-manager exercise individual profit responsibility. Mazur described his organization plan as follows:

a theoretical plan of organization was created. . . . Three factors were used in the determination of the structure which seemed to offer the most adequate machinery for the effective execution of the job. First, existing practices were analyzed and compared. Second, predominance in the character of existing forms of organization was given careful consideration and was a basis of influence. Third, emphasis was placed upon the application of these principles of organization which seem to have

[4] Paul Mazur, *Principles of Organization Applied to Modern Retailing,* Harper & Row, Publishers, New York, 1927.

stood the test of logic and experience. Only one plan of organization is presented as the ideal form of structure . . . one plan forced itself upon me as the only logical structure for the most effective execution of the requirements of department store success.[5]

The Mazur Four-Functional Plan, as his organizational scheme came to be known, was based upon functions and activities that he saw as falling into the following categories or divisions:

1. Merchandising, including such activities as:
   Buying.
   Planning and controlling stocks.
   Planning of sales promotional events.
   Selling.
2. Publicity, including such activities as:
   Window and interior display.
   Media advertising.
3. Store management, including such activities as:
   Care of merchandise.
   Customer services.
   Personnel.
   Store building and maintenance.
   Operating supplies and equipment.
4. Finance and control, including such activities as:
   Control and controllership.
   Credit.
   Stock and store record keeping related to merchandise and general store expenses.

The Mazur plan of department store organization is shown in Figure 10-4. In his strenuous objections to the duality of supervision existing between the department manager and the section manager over the selling function, Mazur contended that the duality was permissible (and his plan supported this) if the section manager's responsibility was related to customer service and not to selling. However, such a separation is not easy to accomplish. The necessity of supervising and controlling the sales function remains one of the most crucial issues relating to department store organization today. The critics of the Mazur plan argue that the four-functional plan fails to place proper emphasis on and allocate responsibility for *selling* —one, if not *the most* important, function of retailing. In the usual case using the four-functional plan shown in Figure 10-4, selling is divided among at least three of the four divisions, namely, the merchandise division, the publicity division, and the store-management division. This factor led one critic to argue, "Beyond a certain point, overall productivity fails to increase. The effort to specialize functions has made it necessary to create new positions to coordinate activities."[6]

As a result of such criticism, there have been created many variations and alterations in department store organizational patterns. Several of these

[5] Ibid., p. 7.
[6] Maxwell Kaufman, "Department Store Organization," *Harvard Business Review,* Vol. 2 (January 1933), p. 244.

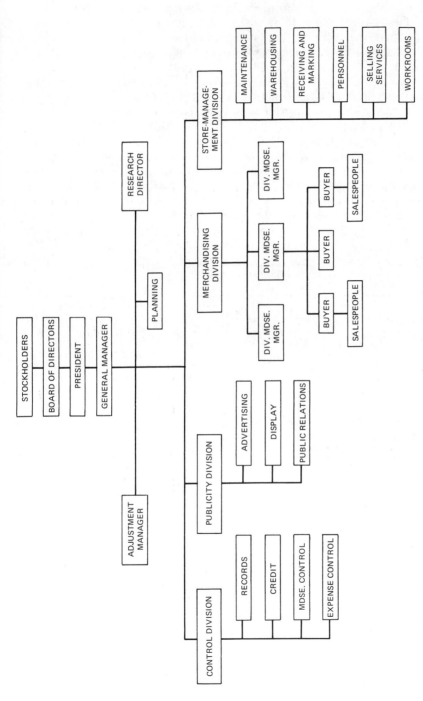

FIGURE 10-4 Mazur's four-divisional plan of department store organization.

SOURCE: Paul Mazur, Principles of Organization Applied to Modern Retailing (New York: Harper & Row, Publishers, 1927); see especially Chap. 2.

variations are shown in Figure 10-5. Plan 1 represents the organizational plan of Edward A. Filene.[7] In 1937, Filene undertook to devise a plan for retail department stores by "applying the general principles of organization which have proven sound in industry." The broad result was that he created a generally confusing seven-division plan. However, his plan did emphasize the selling nature of the department store, rather than the buying nature on which Mazur concentrated. In total, although Filene's plan was considered "interesting and provocative," it was commonly considered impracticable and seldom applied in large department stores.[8]

Plan 2 of Figure 10-5 is built basically around the four functions of Paul Mazur, but a fifth function to reflect the growing importance of personnel relations and activities has been added. In Plan 3, a more streamlined form of organization is shown, with buying and selling both concentrated in the merchandising function. Such a relationship would appear natural and in keeping with the logical dictates of the *marketing concept*. A retail

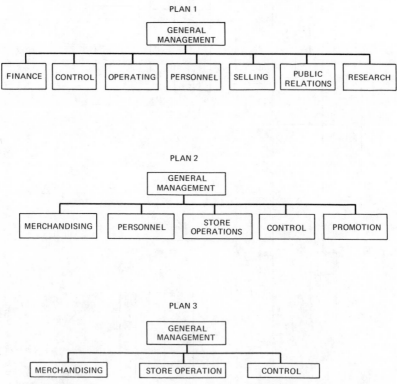

FIGURE 10-5 Variations of the four-functional form of department store organization.

[7] Edward A. Filene, et al., *Next Steps Forward in Retailing*, Harper & Row, Publishers, New York, 1937.

[8] David Carson, *The Organization of Commercial Functions in European Department Stores*, University of Pittsburgh Press, Pittsburgh, 1954, p. 16.

firm is a *marketing* organization with its primary activities being *both* the buying and selling of goods. Buying and selling should *not necessarily* be viewed as different functions but, instead, especially for a retail store, they most likely ought to be viewed as different sides of the same coin. It has often been argued that the illogical splitting of the buying and selling functions is a basic organizational weakness of retail stores.

It would appear that specialization does not require the separation of buying and selling activities. Actually, in the interest of the philosophy of decentralized management in many retail firms with a desire to push authority and responsibility as far down the organization hierarchy as possible, it would appear that such separation could add materially to the cost of coordination and adversely affect employee productivity and morale. Some department stores have gone to a type of profit center operation, in which merchandise departments are allocated resources and held accountable for a contribution to the overall profitability of the store.[9] In such cases, it becomes imperative that the department buyer-manager have complete responsibility for both the buying and selling functions, if he is to be responsible for merchandising his department or division at a profit.

Figure 10-6 shows an organization chart for a department or specialty store in which buying and selling responsibilities are combined at the buyer level. Such an organizational arrangement should enhance the ability of smaller department stores to provide customers with more personalized buying and selling service, thus increasing their effectiveness in competing with chain store units. In the final analysis, however, it must be repeatedly emphasized that no single plan will meet the needs of all stores, but these

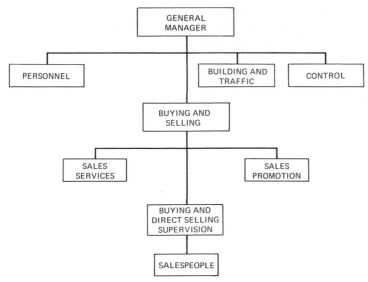

FIGURE 10-6 Department store or specialty store organization with buying and selling functions combined at the level of buyer.

[9] Such an arrangement is usually referred to as the *Lazarus Plan*.

plans are offered here as concepts or models that can be applied with appropriate analysis, tailoring, and adjustment, to individual stores.

Organizing the Department Store Branch. In the broadest sense, the organizational problems relating to branch store operations center around *coordination* and *communication*. Also, as department store growth continues primarily through increases in the number and size of branch units, the problems of coordination and communication will remain paramount.

Department store management has approached the task of branch store organization primarily by three avenues with little or no agreement as to which approach is most effective. The first branches to emerge were most often treated as subunits or satellites of the larger parent store. Their organization and operation was simply an appendage to the parent organization, and the status of each branch was similar to that of a unit of a large retail chain. Its character was highly standardized, with merchandise, services, and operations controlled by the central operation. This approach to branch organization is sometimes referred to as the "brood hen and chick" approach and has been classified by the National Retail Merchants Association as the *Basic Main Store System*.[10]

Some retail managements have approached branch store organization from the standpoint of much greater decentralization, and as a result branch units are viewed as autonomous units with established management and merchandising structures that completely parallel those of the parent store. This organization is referred to as the *Multiunit System,* and under this arrangement the usual case is that some of the branches have reached or are approaching the sales volume of the original parent store.

In branch store organizational planning, as is the usual case elsewhere, there are those who would strive for the best of all possible worlds. As a consequence, many retail managers have adopted a compromise attitude or solution to branch store organization, by charging an officer in the parent store with the responsibility for branch operations. This is referred to as the *Advanced Main Store System,* and under this arrangement each department head in the branch reports directly to this office. Another feature of this arrangement is that a common inventory is often used, with the buyer in the parent store being responsible for the merchandise in both his own department and in corresponding departments of the branches. Very often there is an elaborate committee structure used to coordinate some of the activities between parent and branch units.

Figure 10-7 (on pp. 233 and 234) shows the organization charts upon which these three approaches to branch unit planning and control are based. But, which approach is better? Unfortunately, there is no determinate answer to this question. Each approach has been widely employed, with varying results reported from each of the arrangements. However, the prevailing trend among department stores with suburban branches is to make some

[10] See *Survey of Organization of Multi-Unit Department and Specialty Stores Conducted for the Retail Research Institute,* National Retail Merchants Association, New York, February 1959.

attempt to tie these stores into the main store organizations. Consequently, the Basic Main Store System approach has been widely favored.

In summary, branch store merchandising organization is far from standard. As in the case of organization for other kinds of retail firms, each plan for branch store organization must be tailored to the individual needs and requirements of the particular firm. Management's answers to the following series of questions may help point the way to the best organizational arrangement for its own purposes.[11]

1. Which of your main store buyers are capable of handling another branch department?
2. In the case of those who are now carrying as heavy a load as they can, will the addition of capable selectors in the branch fill the need?
3. Who will control and coordinate overall branch merchandising?
4. Which branch departments, if any, will need and can afford experienced buyers? Can several branch departments be merchandised as one to allow this step?
5. Will branch merchandising be closely similar to the main store's, or did your market study show that you expect sales variations?
6. In view of the size and character of your branch store, the availability of competent buyers, and the need for close supervision, what would be the extra cost of a completely separated buying staff?
7. Are you planning branch operations of such an extent that an investment now in the development of people will bring heavy returns later?

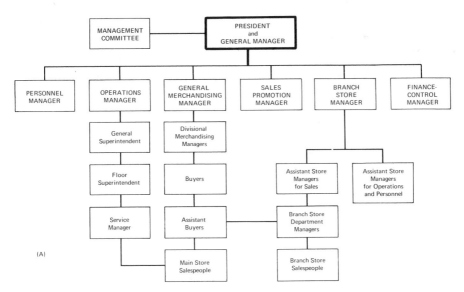

[11] For more on the topic of organization in retailing, see A. Thomas Hollingsworth, "Applying Organization Theory to Marketing Channels," *Journal of Retailing,* Vol. 49, No. 2 (Summer 1973), pp. 51–64, and also, Dennis J. Sutherland, "Managing by Objectives in Retailing," *Journal of Retailing,* Vol. 47, No. 3 (Fall 1971), pp. 15–26.

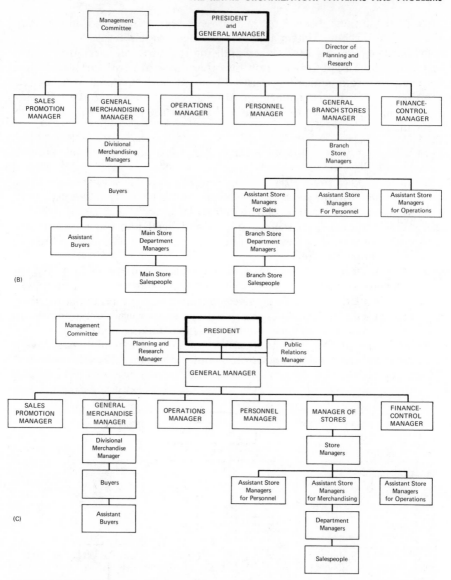

FIGURE 10-7 Organization arrangements for branch department stores.

Organizing the Chain Store System. Chain store systems manifest many different characteristics and yet, many of the basic organizational principles and concepts already discussed in relation to organization for single-unit systems, department stores, and branches are equally applicable to retail chain store systems. Chains can be found in nearly all lines of retail trade and in many of the numerous market segments—from stores selling such low-margin, fast turnover items as apparel and other soft goods lines to the high-margin, low turnover of jewelry and salon furs. The organization structure adopted for chain store selling will vary significantly, depending upon considerations relating to the nature of the system and its size: local, regional, or national chain, the merchandise lines handled, and the operating and organizational philosophies of top management.

However, chain store organization does have several unique features that warrant the attention of the serious student of retail organization. The major organization problem of chain systems is that management must tie together a vast bureaucratic network of decision centers, economic resources, personnel, and other related factors into a smooth-working, harmonious, coordinated, total *system* for effective action. This is no easy task. Historically, chain systems were organized along highly centralized and autocratic lines of authority. The chain system was a hierarchy of superordinate and subordinate relationships. Almost all management prerogatives relating to planning, organizing, and control were centralized in the top management echelons. Individual store managers were considered doers, not thinkers, whose only responsibility was to sell merchandise and to supervise the store's operations. Their duties and behavior were carefully monitored by the central management organization through elaborate procedures of reporting via the submission of numerous memoranda, checklists, schedules, and other reporting devices.

A second basic feature of chain store organization has been the almost total separation of buying and selling. The reasons for this division were to be found primarily in the operating characteristics of many of the early chains. They were almost totally mass merchandising institutions dealing in rather stable merchandise lines of low-unit value. Style and fashion were considered relatively unimportant to the low-income shoppers who constituted the basic market targets of these establishments. As a consequence, quantity purchases at low prices became the major focus of the merchandising function, with the result that buying became a highly specialized kind of activity requiring skill and centralized administration. The buying function was therefore concentrated in a central management headquarters from which the managers of individual store units could only requisition items, although in some chain units they were not even given this limited prerogative. It is probably fair to say that one of the greatest weaknesses of the chain store system was that it did not develop a high degree of competence, self-reliance, or creativity in its individual managers.

One final characteristic of retail chain store organization is the much larger number of functional management specialists found in the central organization. Such departments as real estate and location analysis, store maintenance and operations, warehouse and traffic, merchandising controls, sales promotion and publicity, and especially large personnel departments are among the functional specialties to be found in many chain organization structures. The nature, size, and complexity of managing a large retail chain no doubt accounts for the addition of these many functional specialists.

Figures 10-8 and 10-9 illustrate two rather elaborate chain organization charts. The Great Atlantic and Pacific Tea Company chart shown in Figure 10-8 readily demonstrates several of the generalizations just mentioned regarding chain store organization. Notice the large number of functional

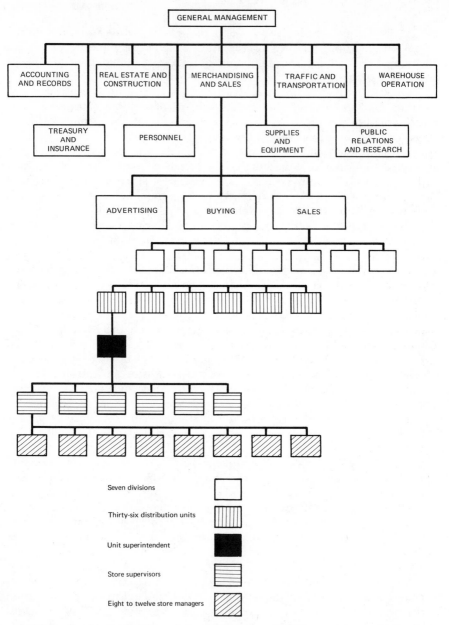

FIGURE 10-8 Organization chart of The Great Atlantic and Pacific Tea Company.

SOURCE: Business Week, June 13, 1964, McGraw-Hill Book Company.

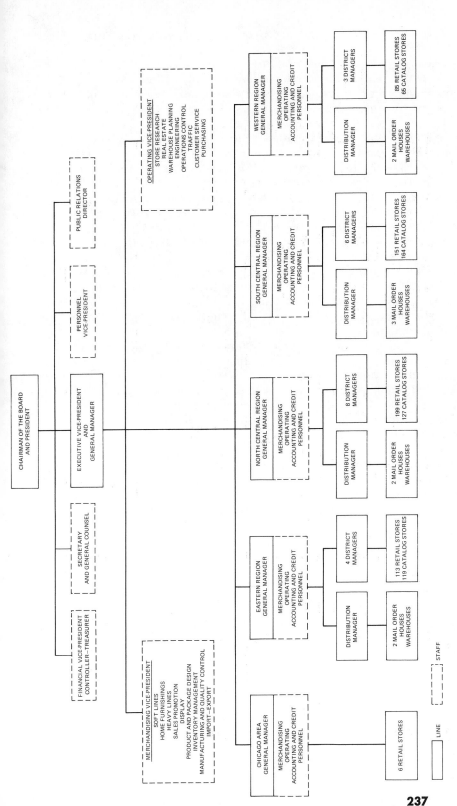

FIGURE 10·9 Organization chart of Montgomery Ward and Company.

CHAIRMAN OF THE BOARD AND PRESIDENT

FINANCIAL VICE-PRESIDENT CONTROLLER–TREASURER

SECRETARY AND GENERAL COUNSEL

PERSONNEL VICE-PRESIDENT

PUBLIC RELATIONS DIRECTOR

EXECUTIVE VICE-PRESIDENT AND GENERAL MANAGER

MERCHANDISING VICE-PRESIDENT
SOFT LINES
HOME FURNISHINGS
HEAVY LINES
SALES PROMOTION
DISPLAY
PRODUCT AND PACKAGE DESIGN
INVENTORY MANAGEMENT
MANUFACTURING AND QUALITY CONTROL
IMPORT–EXPORT

OPERATING VICE-PRESIDENT
STORE RESEARCH
REAL ESTATE
WAREHOUSE PLANNING
ENGINEERING
OPERATIONS CONTROL
TRAFFIC
CUSTOMER SERVICE
PURCHASING

CHICAGO AREA GENERAL MANAGER
MERCHANDISING
OPERATING
ACCOUNTING AND CREDIT
PERSONNEL

6 RETAIL STORES

EASTERN REGION GENERAL MANAGER
MERCHANDISING
OPERATING
ACCOUNTING AND CREDIT
PERSONNEL

DISTRIBUTION MANAGER

2 MAIL ORDER HOUSES WAREHOUSES

4 DISTRICT MANAGERS

113 RETAIL STORES
119 CATALOG STORES

NORTH CENTRAL REGION GENERAL MANAGER
MERCHANDISING
OPERATING
ACCOUNTING AND CREDIT
PERSONNEL

DISTRIBUTION MANAGER

2 MAIL ORDER HOUSES WAREHOUSES

8 DISTRICT MANAGERS

199 RETAIL STORES
127 CATALOG STORES

SOUTH CENTRAL REGION GENERAL MANAGER
MERCHANDISING
OPERATING
ACCOUNTING AND CREDIT
PERSONNEL

DISTRIBUTION MANAGER

3 MAIL ORDER HOUSES WAREHOUSES

6 DISTRICT MANAGERS

151 RETAIL STORES
164 CATALOG STORES

WESTERN REGION GENERAL MANAGER
MERCHANDISING
OPERATING
ACCOUNTING AND CREDIT
PERSONNEL

DISTRIBUTION MANAGER

2 MAIL ORDER HOUSES WAREHOUSES

3 DISTRICT MANAGERS

85 RETAIL STORES
65 CATALOG STORES

LINE

STAFF

management specialists and the unusual number of layers in the organization. Observe, also, that on moving down through the line organization, spans of control generally become somewhat broader. Each store in this system is visited at least once a week by a store supervisor whose task is to help the local manager run a better store.

Figure 10-9 is an especially interesting organization chart. It depicts the Montgomery Ward and Company organization and shows the intracompany relationship between store selling and catalogue selling, both of which are central features of this firm's merchandising strategy. The line of authority, responsibility, and accountability runs directly from the chairman and president through the executive vice-president to the field organization and the individual managers of stores, mail order houses, and warehouses. This, of course, is the line organization which is the skeleton of the entire organization.

Vital staff functions bolster the line organization at each management level. Notice that the executive vice-president is supported by a merchandising vice-president who is responsible for all merchandising functions, and an operating vice-president who is responsible for all operating and service functions.

With a line organization of four regional managers and one area manager, the executive vice-president is responsible for directing the merchandising and operating functions of over 1,000 stores and 9 mail order distribution centers. This highly compact management group with its attendant staff is responsible and accountable for the growth of Montgomery Ward's sales and for the achievement of the profit objectives in their respective geographic areas.

Updating the Chain Store System of Organization. No form of retail merchandising has cornered the market on modern organization theory and practice. The major effort of retail chain store managements in this area has been to focus on decentralized management philosophies, better systems of communication, and flatter organization structures. As the problems of coordination and communication continue to mount, we can expect to see new ways of reducing complexity and streamlining operations through changed organizational structure and more contemporary management philosophies.

Some chains and especially many of the large discount department stores such as Zayre's remain rather tightly structured, highly centralized operations. Store managers have the distinction of "carrying the keys," but they actually make few decisions in regard to the store's operating and merchandising policies. In such units, the separation of buying and selling remains virtually complete.

In ownership groups such as Federated Department Stores and Allied Stores there is a great amount of decentralization. Each store unit is considered a large profit center with a large amount of managerial autonomy. It must be pointed out, however, that ownership groups differ significantly from the regular type of chain organization. Many stores belonging to an ownership group began as autonomous department stores, and they joined the federation for increased financial strength and managerial and merchandising skill. Although buying to some degree is centralized, the individual buyers for the various merchandising divisions are also held responsible for the selling activities of those divisions.

In many medium- or popular-priced chain organizations such as Sears, Roebuck and Co., Montgomery Ward and Company, and the J. C. Penney Company there have been concerted efforts to decentralize some of the buying, selling, and sales promotion activities. Sears has broken up its operation into 5 major territorial groups, each of which has considerable autonomy and represents a basic profit center operation.

The Colonial Stores food chain has followed a similar pattern. After a recent reorganization effort, division managers are not held responsible for the profits of their divisions, and the job of store manager has been upgraded to one of real managerial responsibility.

Other firms, as well, have recognized the need to elevate the job of store manager. Many chain systems are beginning to look upon the store manager not as a mere operating and personnel store unit manager but as a *manager* with a much wider range of functional responsibility and autonomy with which to accommodate his store to a greater merchandising responsibility.

Retail chain store systems will continue to experiment and innovate in terms of their organization structures. The use of corporate level management committees, the greater use of advisory and functional staff services, and management philosophies reflecting a greater belief in the democratization of the organization through greater amounts of subordinate participation are all features that will likely characterize the organization structure of the retail chain stores of the future.[12]

special problems affecting retail organization considerations

The special nature of retailing and the environment in which it operates tend to make the effective design of retail organizations and their operation more difficult. In the first place, retailing is not a homogeneous industry. It is a diverse industry, both in terms of size and in terms of character of operations. Such diversity makes for lack of uniformity in practice and theory of organization. There are stores of great size and complexity, and there are stores of unusual smallness and simplicity. Stemming from this diversity and related to the special character of retailing is the vast range of talents and abilities required to make these diverse retail systems operate. Small stores have very little specialization of effort. A person of reasonable ability and very little training can be an effective retail merchandiser. On the other hand, larger stores are the epitome of specialization and division of labor and require a multitude of skills in order to successfully compete in a dynamic market place. The major problem of the manager is how to effectively put together a system, a balanced network of

[12] See M. J. Etzel and J. M. Ivancevich, "Management by Objectives in Marketing, Philosophy, Process, and Problems," *Journal of Marketing*, Vol. 38, No. 4 (October 1974), pp. 47–55.

wheels within wheels, when the components of this system are so different in terms of skills and abilities, and *when the components are not inanimate machines, but human beings.*

In the second place, one must consider the cyclical (if not weekly) fluctuations in retailing activity. Retailing is not a continuous flow type of economic activity, but instead a form of intermittent processes. The work flow is uneven because the demand for retail services is linked to the demand for retail goods. If only a small volume of business occurs one week, the sales personnel cannot wait on nonexistent customers, nor can the cashier wrap stations service nonexistent buyers.[13] Retail services must be provided in direct relation to the demand for such services. Over a period of time, the retail management system is expected to be able to expand to meet the increased demand brought about by longer run increases in population and income. Also, since retailing is a cyclical and seasonal business, store services and facilities must oftentimes be expanded and contracted with a very short lead time. A strike or work stoppage in a community's basic industry can mean a virtual drying up of consumer demand, with the resultant necessity to greatly contract and curtail the size of the retail facilities and level of service offerings. By the same token, in the thirty-day period preceding Christmas, many stores sell in excess of 25 per cent of their total annual volume, necessitating the building up of sales and services staffs as well as inventories. In fact, a great expansion in the store's total system must be created in order to meet this seasonal need. It can be readily seen that these factors greatly affect the store's organization, staffing, and personnel problems.

Finally, there is a host of other considerations, not necessarily of lesser importance, which compound the organizational difficulties of retail stores. Many employees are "in-and-outers." That is, they are students or young people in a trial work period whose expectations are not to remain in retailing. They may plan to go on to school, military service, or to get married and leave the work force entirely. Others may be older women who look to jobs in retailing as a temporary means of supplementing the family income in order to help defray college costs or build up a financial reserve for future retirement. The number of part-time workers continues to increase in all retailing establishments.[14]

Other factors complicate retail organization design, staffing, and personnel. A large part (as many as two thirds in department stores) of total employees are women. This fact means there must be special considerations relating to hours worked, physical duties, and physical facilities. Another factor complicates retail store organization policies relating to hiring and maintaining a satisfactory work force consistent with the needs of the organization, namely, the low prevailing wage rate paid to operative level retail employees. Finally, the overall effect of several of these conditions is that the retail store organization is usually faced with a very high employee

[13] Dale Vonriesen, "Toward Staffing Optimality in Retail Selling," *Journal of Retailing,* Vol. 49, No. 4 (Winter 1973–1974), pp. 37–47.

[14] For a discussion of this problem, see William B. Werther, Jr., "Part-Timers: Overlooked and Undervalued," *Business Horizons,* Vol. XVIII, No. 1 (February 1975), pp. 13–20.

turnover rate—in many stores as much as two to four times a year. This means, in the extreme, that in order to cover one job on an annual basis, four people must be recruited, trained, and integrated into the total organization. Conversely, for each person who stays to perform the work, three have come into and left the system.

retail personnel management

Much of the responsibility for maintaining a healthy organization, especially relating to such tasks as recruiting, training, and maintaining an effective work force falls within that purview of retail management known as personnel management. Broadly viewed, retail personnel management is concerned with the whole spectrum of management activities as they relate specifically to the personnel function. These would include planning, organizing, motivating, communicating, and controlling. More specifically, however, personnel management is concerned with the operative duties related to the procurement, development, compensation, integration, and maintenance of the personnel of an organization for the purpose of contributing toward the accomplishment of that organization's major goals or objectives.

In an effort to harmonize the interests of workers and management and deal effectively with union demands and other problems related to worker adjustment and conflict, the retail management system is placing more and more emphasis on personnel work. Its importance is emphasized by the fact that wage costs are one of the largest expense items on the retail management system's operating statement. Employees also contribute to many less obvious costs of the system such as employee recruiting, training, and absenteeism. The system's employees affect its ability to function effectively in relationship to its customers and competitors, and as a valuable human resource their use should be carefully administered. In the pages to follow, the scope of personnel work in the retail store will be examined. Our discussion will follow the accepted divisions of personnel management: procurement or hiring of workers, development and training, compensation, assimilation into the organization, and, finally, maintenance. Space limitations permit only a cursory discussion of these major areas.

Procurement and Employment

Retail store systems spend unbelievable sums searching the markets of the world for exotic merchandise to please their customers, and yet, paradoxically, they will often hire a person off the street, without training, experience, or aptitude to sell this merchandise. The result is often disastrous. Dissatisfied customers react by seeking outlets whose employees are better qualified to suit their needs and requirements. In spite of the tendency toward self-service and simplified selling, retail employees are becoming increasingly more important in determining the success of a given store.

Retailers' complaints about their inability to attract and retain effective retail employees usually attribute their lack of success to low starting salaries, long hours, and the low status or esteem of retail employment. Much of this is true. *However, if retail stores are to recruit effective employees in competition with other industries, they must seek increases in productivity through improved system design in order to offset these factors.*

The range of abilities required of retail employees varies widely from firm to firm. The talent required by a particular store will determine to a considerable extent the kind of employment procedure used. Sales personnel in variety stores, supermarkets, and general merchandise stores require only elementary skills, or those provided by high school training. Again, it must be emphasized that employment requirements should be based upon a functional analysis of the work to be done. This means that a careful job analysis ought to precede the development of the job description. Once these activities have been completed, an employment procedure should be adopted to match the level and sophistication of the job in question. Normally, for operative workers who are not especially destined for management responsibilities, the employment procedure consists of the completion of an application blank and a personnel interview. In the case of employment of management level workers, the employment procedure is likely to include in addition a battery of tests designed to evaluate the applicant's personality, his intelligence, and his managerial potential. Although some improvements have been made in the use of tests for predicting performance, their use in retailing has not yet become widespread.

Perhaps the paramount task of retail personnel management in the future will be the recruiting of capable employees into the field of retail merchandising. Failure in this respect can only mean a diminution in the effectiveness of all retail systems.

Development and Training

Retail employees are seldom ever recruited in exactly the stage of development preferred by the recruiting institution. Usually after being hired, personnel must be trained to some degree. The degree, of course, will again depend upon the nature of the job for which the employee was recruited and his previous experience and training. Some of the recruits will have had no previous training in retail work of any kind. Some will have had previous experience, but will need to be retrained and familiarized with the policies and routines of the new establishment. Some recruits, destined for almost immediate placement into management positions, will require management training differing in scope, content, and intensity from that of other recruits. The training program will vary from firm to firm. In smaller and medium-sized stores, training will likely consist of a brief indoctrination period, after which the new personnel are usually assigned to *sponsors,* older employees with a demonstrated success in their specific functional duties and the capacity for patience and understanding in dealing with new, inexperienced personnel.

This early period of employment is usually a vital period, of unusually high stress, in the indoctrination of the personnel into the operation of the system which usually appears to him as a vast and complicated network of rules, policies, and systems. For this reason, it is imperative that the new employee be treated with kindness and understanding. This is the critical period in terms of developing both competent and loyal employees.

Methods of training retail employees range from the very informal *sponsor technique, sink or swim,* or *Cook's Tour* through the more sophisticated and formal techniques such as the group or seminar training, using *case studies,* the *incident method,* and *role playing.*

Of late, many retail stores, sales personnel, buyers and non-selling employees are benefiting from a continuous type of training made possible by the use of teaching machines and programmed instruction. These self-teaching methods require a minimum of both training time and cost.

Retail stores are valiantly attempting to fill and maintain their executive positions with well-qualified management trainees. To accomplish this end, many stores are sending employees with management skills and aptitudes to participate in management development programs carried on by major universities. These programs are designed to round out and develop executive talent by increasing the trainee's capacity and appreciation for understanding (1) the special problems related to retailing, (2) the role of the executive in the top management hierarchy, and (3) the improvement of general decision-making skills.

Compensation

People work in order that they might obtain the wherewithal to purchase what they consider to be the necessities of life. Work is a means of earning a living and of purchasing a standard of living. The amount of one's wage is also often construed as an index or measure of one's value or esteem. This means that there are both economic and psychological factors at work that will affect worker attitudes regarding salary, while the manager often looks upon salaries as just another factor cost to be considered in his overall costs of operation.

Compensation is no panacea; it is no substitute for effective organization leadership; it cannot make for a healthy organization in the face of poor organization structure or low employee morale stemming from poor working conditions. Compensation can not be treated as a bribe, or a way of enforcing conformity to what would be otherwise considered undesirable or repulsive conditions of employment. On the other hand, compensation policies can have a salutary effect on the organization if they are fairly and wisely conceived and administered as a part of a total enlightened management process.

There are three major criteria that all compensation plans in retail stores must meet. It should also be pointed out that meeting these criteria is not an easy task. For the most part, compensation plans throughout all levels of the retail management system must (1) be satisfactory to the store in terms of its wage cost structure and its competitive position, (2) be satisfactory to employees in terms of their economic and social-psychological requirements, and (3) provide for a high level of motivation and incentive for all workers and managers.

Compensation plans designed in whole or in part to accomplish these ends center around three basic plans: (1) straight salary, (2) straight commission, or (3) some mix of salary and commission. Straight salary is the plan most usually adopted for most nonselling employees and for new trainees. It provides for a known wage without uncertainty. However, it does mean that wage costs as a percentage of sales are likely to fluctuate considerably from period to period. Most stores would find that a straight commission plan would actually meet their requirements for financial control better than a straight salary plan because such a plan means that selling costs as a percentage of sales remain constant. For example, assume that figures compiled by the National Retail Merchants Association show that wage costs as a per cent of sales equal eight per cent for stores whose volume ranges between $500,000 and $1,000,000 per year. If average salaries for employees in this size and kind of store are $450 per month, then sales per employee for this store should be $5,625. If a sales person on straight commission sells less than $5,625, his earnings are accordingly less; if he sells more, then his earnings are accordingly more. Thus, if a store pays its employees on the basis of straight salary, their sales over the year ought to average about $5,625 per month in order that the store's selling costs remain competitive with other stores in the area. Straight commission is not a popular way of compensating the typical retail sales employee and is used most frequently to compensate skilled sellers of "big ticket items" such as furniture, appliances, or automobiles.

To provide a high level of incentive for retail employees, many compensation plans feature a basic salary plus extra commissions or bonuses, once the quotas determined by management are reached. To refer to our earlier example, if the sales of some employee exceed the $5,625 (which is management's established quota), then a commission of some predetermined percentage would be paid on all sales exceeding this amount.

Compensation plans and policies are of great importance to management as well as to operative level employees. In an effort to stimulate management to a higher level of performance, many firms have adopted profit-sharing plans, executive bonuses, and stock option plans. Psychologists in industry have conducted many studies asking workers what they want from their jobs. These surveys usually reveal the following results: In order of importance the items most wanted are steady work, opportunity for advancement, good supervision, desirable work groups or companions, good pay, and desirable types of work, working conditions, hours, and benefits.

Good pay is included as one of the critical factors in job satisfaction but is not listed at the top of the rankings. Retail managers and especially personnel managers must be admonished to continuously monitor the motivation-money dyad. They must be especially sensitive to the role of compensation and its motivational impact throughout the organization. The following questions are basic to their continuing analysis:

1. How well are the system's various compensation plans working to attract, retain, and motivate our store's personnel?
2. Are our compensation plans successful? Are their returns greater than their costs to the retail organization?
3. How can our overall system of compensation be improved?

Unless personnel and retail managers are satisfied with their answers to these questions, then existing compensation plans ought to be carefully reevaluated.

Integration and Maintenance

Integration and maintenance is a double-barreled personnel management function. Integration is concerned with assimilating the worker into the overall organizational framework. It does not mean that the worker must give up his own identity, becoming only a small cog in a large, impersonal, corporate machine, but it does mean that personnel management must play the lead in working toward effecting a reasonable reconciliation of both individual and organizational interests.

No manager should ever be so naive as to believe that all workers are the captives of their employing organizations. At any given time, most workers have a central life interest focused in one or, at most, a few institutional settings. Although workers belong to many organizations, their degree of commitment will vary considerably among them. In our society, work does not appear to be a central life interest for a substantial proportion (perhaps a majority) of our citizens. This, no doubt, accounts for the apathy and indifference of many workers in the retail organization. *However, this does not necessarily mitigate against their effective performance as workers, so long as their required behaviors are adequately set forth for them and the incentives in the form of compensation and other payoffs are calculable.*

Although it is probably true that work is not a central life interest for a large number of workers within the retail firm, the job can be made meaningful to their existence, and their performance can be improved by sound personnel management procedure. A basic part of this procedure, in addition to the functions already discussed, is that relating to personnel maintenance. It would seem only natural that once we have recruited, selected, trained, and integrated the worker into the overall social system of our retail organization, a large part of the attention of personnel management would focus on maintaining a high state of organizational readiness, i.e., high performance through high morale. Worker morale has to do with worker attitudes, and favorable worker attitudes are affected by personnel policies and practices focused upon worker welfare. Such programs are usually oriented toward recreation, health and safety, and educational programs related to self-help and improvement. Such ordinary factors as providing clean, comfortable, and well-lighted employee lunchrooms or cafeterias, rest rooms, and lounge areas are all directed toward creating a favorable state of worker satisfaction, reducing turnover, increasing productivity, and avoiding general worker discontent.

government activities and retail organization performance

As has been the case in many other industries, government has attempted to restrain retailing management and sometimes workers in their efforts to bargain directly over factors pertaining to working conditions, compensation, hours worked, and other management-worker situations. Both federal and state governments have interceded in worker-management conflicts in retail store organizations, often to redress grievances or to temporize the power or strength of either workers or management.

Prior to 1935, the attempts of workers to band together in union organizations were generally construed as unlawful agreements in restraint of trade and enterprise. Oftentimes, the sympathy of the courts was clearly on the side of management. However, with the passage of the 1935 National Labor Relations Act, employees were given the legal right to self-organization. The terms of the Act prevented employers from interfering in any way with unions or discriminating against union members. If a majority of the employees chose to unionize, then the company was forced to bargain with the union representatives.

Along with other conditions affecting both labor and management, these rights were reaffirmed in the passage of the Taft-Hartley Act of 1947. This act, however, was designed at least in part to protect employees from certain union abuses. The provisions of the Taft-Hartley Act (or the Labor Management Relations Act of 1947, as it is more correctly known) were expanded in the Labor-Management Reporting and Disclosure Act of 1959. This Act prohibited such unfair labor practices as

1. Restraint, interference, or coercion of employees in the exercise of their right to organize freely.
2. The interference and domination in the formation or administration of a labor organization.
3. Acts of encouragement or discouragement of membership in a labor organization by discrimination in regard to hiring or tenure.
4. Any discrimination against an employee because he has filed charges or given testimony under the act.
5. Refusal to engage in collective bargaining with properly chosen representatives of the employees.

In effect, most of this legislation was designed to promote the strength of employees and organized labor interests. Government's role in labor-management relations has generally been aimed at promoting the rights and welfare of the individual, by sponsoring legislation relating to the rights of employees to organize and bargain effectively, as well as placing a floor under wages, establishing minimum working ages and working conditions, and guaranteeing fair employment practices relating to sex and race.

The Fair Labor Standards Act was originally passed in 1938, with amendments in 1949, 1955, 1961, and 1964; it established a minimum wage of $1.25 per hour and a maximum 40-hour regular work week, with provisions for time-and-one-half pay for any hours worked in excess of 40 hours. Under the early provisions of the law, retail establishments were exempted because of their small size and nature of their operation. Under the 1964 amendment, however, retailing establishments are no longer exempt, with the exception of certain specified types of employees, such as executive, professional, outside field salesmen, handicapped workers, students, and learners.

Many retailing managers viewed the inclusion of retailing under the provisions of the Fair Labor Standards Act as a major crisis. Faced with industry-wide spiraling costs, management predicted that markons would have to be increased by 5 to 7 per cent, sales staffs would have to be trimmed, and marginal and losing locations would have to be closed. No doubt, in many stores these things did happen. Earlier the minimum wage was $1.25 per hour; it was later raised to $2.00 per hour. In 1965, the minimum wage provisions applied only to retailers with at least $1,000,000 in total annual sales volume. But by 1971, the $2.00 minimum wage applied to all retailers, including those whose annual volume is less than $250,000 per year. In January 1976, the minimum wage increased to $2.20 per hour.

Although numerous problems related to ambiguity of coverage and record keeping have arisen, there is little evidence to suggest that the retailing industry will not be able to continue to compete under the provisions of the law.

Another major effort to legislate a part of the firm's retail personnel policies can be seen in the Employment Section of the Civil Rights Law, which was designed to become sequentially effective in 1965 and 1968. The essence of Title VII of the Civil Rights Act of 1964, succinctly stated, is the banishment of discrimination in employment because of race, color, religion, sex, or national origin in the following situations: hiring and firing, compensation, work assignments, terms, and working conditions, thereby establishing equal employment opportunity as a *civil right*. It is important to point out that this Act applies to the employment practices of employers, labor organizations, and employment agencies.

Unionization and Retailing

There were several attempts aimed at developing union organizations as bargaining units for retail employees prior to the passage of the Wagner Act in 1935, although they had only limited success. Such labor and union efforts date back at least as far as 1850.

At first blush, retailing would appear to be fertile ground for union organization. In comparison to other industries, wage rates have always been low, the work week has been unusually long, and working conditions —while not as arduous as some occupations requiring physical labor—are nonetheless strenuous. In spite of these conditions, however, the spread of unionism into the field of retailing has been relatively slow—only about 5 to 10 per cent of the sales personnel in retailing are union members. Union membership is much higher (perhaps as much as 25 to 50 per cent) among nonselling personnel, especially in such categories as warehouse workers, truck drivers, elevator operators, and maintenance and janitorial staffs.

Until rather recently, sales personnel in retail stores have not adopted union membership to deal with their grievances and complaints against retail management. There are, perhaps, several reasons which support this behavior.

1. Retail salespeople have viewed themselves as white-collar workers and have identified more with management interests than with blue-collar unions.
2. A large per cent of retail sales personnel are "in-and-outers," or have a short-run point of view. Considering the short time they plan to work, they feel that union membership would not justify itself.
3. Workers holding these low-paying retail selling jobs are not anxious to have their earnings further dissipated by union membership dues.

By the mid 1970s it was estimated that there were slightly more than one million members of retail or retailing-related unions. This figure includes 428,000 members in the Retail Clerks International Association; 167,000 in the AFL-CIO Retail, Wholesale and Department Store Union; and 341,000 who belonged to the Amalgamated Meat Cutters and Butcher Workmen.[15] Union membership drives are becoming increasingly more aggressive, and membership figures are expected to climb. The Retail Clerks International Association bills itself as "the fastest growing union in the world" and has become particularly active in its recruiting drives in the California area.

The efforts of unions in retail stores parallels their efforts in other industries; that is, they desire to gain union recognition, shorter hours, better worker conditions, more fringe benefits, and extra pay for overtime work, obtain established grievance procedures, and assure workers of job security and seniority rights. Management stands together as a cohesive bargaining unit; workers generally have stood alone, with little countervailing bargaining power. The union, from the worker's point of view, is a means of redressing this unequal balance of power. Certainly not all union demands are justified and not all managements have been remiss in their obligations and responsibilities toward workers. But all too often in the past, management policies toward workers have been guided too much by the logic of cost and efficiency instead of the logic of human values and sentiments.

The effect of increasing unionization on retail management and retail organization will be profound and far reaching. Communication and decision-making centers within the retail management system will be greatly affected by increased unionization and merchandising policies.

QUESTIONS FOR STUDY, REFLECTION, AND REVIEW

1. From the point of view of the retail firm, what is an organization?
2. Define and explain the three ways that can be used to determine the kind of structure needed in a specific enterprise.
3. What are the functions and activities that the *four-functional plan* is based upon?
4. How does the profit center concept operate within the retail firm?
5. What are some of the organizational problems relating to branch store operations?

[15] U.S. Department of Labor, *Directory of National and International Labor Unions in the United States, 1974,* U.S. Government Printing Office, Washington, D.C., 1975.

6. Explain the multiunit system approach to branch store operations.

7. Explain the concepts that underlie the advanced main store system approach to branch store organization.

8. What are some of the complaints cited by retailers regarding their inability to attract and retain effective employees? What can be done to offset these factors?

9. What are some of the retail stores doing to produce well-qualified management personnel?

10. There has been a great deal of debate concerning what workers want from their jobs. Discuss some of the findings.

FIVE

MERCHANDISING: THE CRUX OF RETAILING EFFORT

11

buyer role and behavior

Another of the critically important tasks of the retail firm is that of acquiring and maintaining a balanced assortment of merchandise and service offerings to meet expected customer demand. In the narrow sense, this is considered *the merchandising function.* In the broader sense, merchandising characteristically has been an ambiguous term concerned with the "planning involved in marketing the right merchandise or service at the right place, at the right time, in the right quantities, and at the right price."[1] Within this context, very little activity could be carried on within the retail firm that was not merchandising; retailing and merchandising would therefore be synonymous terms. Efforts to restrict the term merchandising to a narrower range of retail activities have met with only mixed success. Wingate and Schaller defined retail merchandising as "the planning done by retailers to assure an assortment of merchandise balanced to customer demand and offering a profit potential."[2] Malcolm McNair, a leading authority in the retailing field, has defined merchandising as a term "used to describe the whole group of decisions and tasks involved in determining what merchandise is to be offered, pricing it and acquiring it."[3]

The broader definitions of the term appear almost too inclusive and seem to invite confusion. The retail management strategy, as we learned earlier, is the comprehensive management plan developed in order to facilitate the behavioral and operating goals of the system. Included in this strategic plan are the activities related to product, place, pricing, and promotion decisions. *Within this framework, merchandising is considered as a*

[1] "Report of the Definitions Committee," American Marketing Association, *Journal of Marketing* (October 1948), p. 211.

[2] John W. Wingate and Elmer O. Schaller, *Techniques of Retail Merchandising,* Prentice-Hall, Inc., Englewood Cliffs, N.J., 1950, p. 1.

[3] Malcolm P. McNair, et al., *Cases in Retail Management,* McGraw-Hill Book Company, New York, 1957, p. 32.

set of activities related to product assortment decisions. Therefore it would include not only the *planning* involved in aggregating a balanced assortment of merchandise offerings, but also the *control* procedures that are developed and implemented to facilitate this process. Although pricing and promotional activities are generally inferred as being a part of the merchandising activity, they are considered outside the realm of merchandising, *per se,* in this treatment. These activities are part of the retail management strategy along with *place* decisions, but they are not considered an integral part of the merchandising function. Such a treatment of merchandising relates this concept to that of product planning for the manufacturing-oriented organization.

Merchandising, therefore, within the scope of this treatment, is concerned with the acquisition of merchandise resources and the balancing of these resources with the firm's market opportunity. Broadly conceived, merchandising is concerned with the integration of effort in the process of meaningfully relating (1) the firm, (2) the firm's supplier resources, and (3) the market opportunity. Such a meaningful integration subsumes profitable results.

developing merchandising or product assortment policies

With this background, it is now possible to proceed toward more specific delineation of merchandising or assortment decisions. From our previous statement, it becomes clear that merchandising decisions involve a thorough understanding of the retail firm's overall corporate strategy. Merchandising decisions must be predicated upon the buyer's or merchandise manager's understanding of the firm's goals and perception of its market opportunity. Merchandising decisions then become nothing more nor less than an extension of the firm's total strategy. In short, merchandising policies must be consistent with the retailer's total operating or management philosophy— the embodiment of the firm's policies. Robert H. Johnson suggested that sound retail policy should include the following:[4]

It should facilitate attainment of the firm's objectives.
It must be a planned development rather than the result of opportunistic decisions.
It should be clear and definite.
It should encourage consistency in the operation of the business.
It should lead to the development of a clear-cut character, or personality, for the establishment.
It must have a certain degree of flexibility.

Thus, merchandising policies, the firm's predetermined guides to action and behavior in relation to what goods to buy, in what quantities, from

---

[4] Robert H. Johnson, "Retail Policies: Their Selection and Application," in Max D. Richards and William Nielander (eds.), *Readings in Management,* South-Western Publishing Co., Cincinnati, 1963, pp. 345–350.

what suppliers, and how frequently must be compatible with the firm's total merchandising strategy as determined by its management philosophy and the market opportunity that presents itself.

Chapter 12 on "Merchandise Assortment Planning" is concerned with the development and implementation of merchandising policies. In this chapter the focus will be primarily on the role and behavior of the buyer. Chapters 13 and 14 will be concerned with a slightly more analytical treatment of the planning and control activities related to managing merchandise assortments.

The Importance of Buying Decisions

The importance of certain merchandising decisions (including buying) has been referred to before. The analysis of the major determinants of market opportunity—population and income, the material relating to the financial operations of the retailer, the interdependent nature of financial and merchandising decisions, and finally, the material related to consumer behavior—all dealt rather directly with the importance of matching retailing strategy to market opportunity, at least in part through the merchandising or buying function. It has long been a retailing axiom that "goods well bought are half sold." That is, well-bought goods [those having a high preference probability and matching the want characteristics of the firm's market target or segment(s)] will be readily cleared from the market. They will require minimum promotion and selling effort, will suffer minimum markdowns, will experience faster turnover, and hence, in general, will produce increased profits.

Most retailers are well aware of the importance of buying and merchandising decisions and their impact on customer patronage. For example, one study that attempted to assess the factors which consumers perceive as important in terms of where they shopped ranked such factors as (1) price/value relationship, (2) store specialization, and (3) quality of merchandise in this order out of a total of 14 factors.[5]

These factors are closely related to the merchandising function; for that matter, they constitute the very essence of merchandising and they underscore the critical role and importance of buying and buying policies.

Given the price-cost-margin squeeze confronting most retailers today, any saving in merchandise acquisition costs that can be effected through buying practices and procedures will redound to the profit opportunity of the firm. Table 11-1 shows median profit figures by kind of business for 1967 and 1973. The data in this table suggest that while profits on net sales continue to fluctuate among various kinds of retail enterprise, a continuing downward drift in overall profits as a per cent of net sales is manifested.

Recall, however, that profit as a per cent of sales is not necessarily the best barometer of merchandising or business efficiency. In Chapter 3 we learned that profit as a return on investment might constitute a better measure of

[5] Marvin A. Jolson and Walter F. Spath, "Understanding and Fulfilling Shoppers' Requirements: An Anomaly in Retailing," *Journal of Retailing*, Vol. 49, No. 2 (Summer 1973), pp. 38–50.

TABLE 11-1   Net Profits as a Percentage of Net Sales (by kinds of business)

TYPE OF STORE	1967 MEDIAN FIGURE	RANGE	1973 MEDIAN FIGURE	RANGE
Children's & Infants Clothing & Furnishings	2.24	0.93–4.34	1.67	0.55–4.52
(Men's & Boys')	2.47	1.11–4.62	2.30	0.91–4.38
Department Stores	2.08	0.95–3.26	1.89	0.77–3.32
Discount Stores	1.87	1.04–3.00	1.35	0.62–2.52
Family Clothing	1.79	0.70–3.46	1.99	0.73–4.55
Furniture	2.16	0.69–4.86	2.37	1.09–4.82
Grocery Stores	1.05	0.58–1.75	0.89	0.39–1.68
Hardware Stores	1.82	0.52–3.87	2.73	0.94–5.06
Lumber & Building Materials	1.86	0.39–3.10	2.69	1.61–4.26
Shoes	2.28	0.44–4.90	1.65	0.08–3.20
Variety Stores	2.23	1.27–3.76	2.07	1.30–3.96
Women's Ready-to-Wear	2.00	0.85–3.57	2.05	1.04–3.64

SOURCE: "*The Ratios of Retailing,*" Dun's Review, September 1967 and September 1974.

profitability. Figure 11-1 illustrates, however, that profit as a per cent of sales does have an impact on profit as a return on investment.

As the diagram in Figure 11-1 suggests, return on investment as a profitability index will fall as profit margins fall if investment turnover remains constant. However, it is possible to increase return on investment at the same time profit margins are falling *if* investment turnover is increased by a large enough amount.

Different retail merchandising institutions use different approaches to attain their profit goals. For example, a major medium-priced department store group might generate a profit ratio of 5 per cent of sales and an investment or capital turnover ratio of 3. Conversely, a major discount merchandiser may have a profit ratio of only 2 per cent and a capital turnover of 9. As you can determine, the product of these two figures would produce a return on investment capital of 15 per cent for the department store group and 18 per cent for the discounter. Thus we see that adequate, satisfactory returns on investment can be achieved by either high profit margins or high capital turnover.

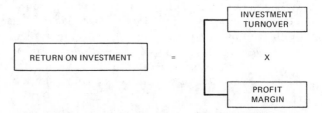

FIGURE 11-1 Relationship between profit margin, investment turnover, and return on investment.

The point to be emphasized is that in the light of stringent competitive activity profit margins are becoming increasingly difficult to maintain at a high level. Effective retail management is thus becoming more dependent on increasing capital turnover in order to generate sufficient returns on investment. Increasing capital turnover largely means increasing merchandise turnover, or the number of times per year that the average inventory is sold. Shown symbolically, where

$$TO = \text{Merchandise turnover}$$
$$S = \text{Sales at retail prices}$$
$$AI = \text{Average inventory at retail}$$

then

$$TO = \frac{S}{AI}$$

Average inventory is found by adding a number of BOM (beginning of the month) inventories and dividing that figure by the number of months or periods considered. A more elaborate discussion of the importance of turnover as it relates to merchandise management will follow in a later chapter. At this juncture, the intent is to illustrate simply that a key part of the capital turnover figure is determined by the stock turnover figure. Stock turnover can be increased with the sound buying decisions that result in a well-balanced assortment of goods to meet expected customer demand.

The problems related to capital turnover are becoming increasingly important to the retail firm. The comparatively small improvement in capital turnover may be a major reason why some retailers have failed to improve their returns on capital.

The counterpoint of this analysis is that buying decisions can have a profound effect on the merchandising operations of the retail firm. As a generalization, it follows that carefully conceived and well-executed buying decisions most often can lead to increased sales.

To illustrate, good buying can and often does lead to increased sales and reduced cost of goods sold as a percentage of sales which increases gross margin. Furthermore, if inventories can be lowered in relation to sales, turnover increases. The ultimate consequence of these actions is increased profitability.

Consider one more illustration of the effect of buying decisions on store operations. If buyers were to succeed in reducing the cost of goods sold via astute purchasing behavior, what would be the effect on profits? Assume the following situation:

A retail firm has

$5,000,000 sales volume
  3,500,000 cost of goods sold
$1,500,000 gross margin
  1,250,000 operating expenses
$ 250,000 net profit

If buyer behavior could lead to a 2 per cent reduction in the firm's cost of goods sold, the effect would be to increase profits as follows:

$5,000,000 sales volume
  3,430,000 cost of goods sold
$1,570,000 gross margin
  1,250,000 operating expenses
$ 320,000 net profit

Thus, we see that a 2 per cent decrease in the firm's cost of goods results in a $70,000 increase in profits. At a 5 per cent profit margin, sales would have to be increased by $1,400,000, or 28 per cent in order to attain a comparable gain. In other words, each $1 reduction in the cost of goods sold has about the same effect on profits as a $20 increase in sales.

With increases in sales volume so difficult to attain, it is easy to understand why retail management systems are increasing their emphasis on the buying function and other behavior related to the management of merchandise inventories.

Admittedly, there are many factors which contribute to the successful operation of a retail enterprise, but in many instances, the success or failure boils down to the question of who does the buying and what they buy. In simple terms, if the store doesn't have the goods the customer wants, success is jeopardized. What a store has to sell—the nature and desirability of

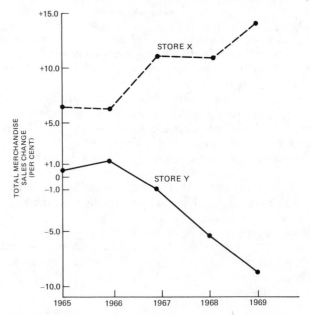

FIGURE 11-2 Sales trends—total merchandise, 1965–1969.

SOURCE: Claude R. Martin, Jr., "The Contribution of the Professional Buyer to a Store's Success or Failure," Journal of Retailing, Vol. 49, No. 2 (Summer 1973), p. 71.

its inventory assortment—makes a major contribution to the sales success of that store. This conclusion was borne out dramatically by a study that analyzed the results of two department stores in the same state. Although they did not compete with each other, they shared the details of their operations with each other through a common information sharing facility.[6] Figure 11-2 shows the sales trends of these two stores during the period 1965–1969.

The significant conclusions of the study relate again to the critical role and importance of buyer performance. It was found that the buyers for the successful store (store X) were more aggressive, more self-confident, and showed a greater tendency for leadership in new merchandise trends than the buyers for the failing (store Y) institution. The major argument is that these traits have contributed to the more successful pattern of sales growth for store X, while the follower behavior, the lack of aggressiveness, and the lower self-confidence of Y buyers have made a significant contribution to the store's sales decline. These findings may appear even more significant as we proceed in our discussion and as we attempt to more fully circumscribe buyer behavior.

Buying and the Marketing Concept

It is important that the retail store buyer as well as the divisional and general merchandise managers be thoroughly familiar with the *marketing concept* and its implications for the retail firm. Perhaps more than any other retailing activity, buying must be customer-oriented. The buyer is the consumer's purchasing agent; in the final analysis, it is the consumers who dictate *what* goods will be purchased.

The successful buyer learns readily that no store can be all things to all people. After studying the firm's target customers and the *market segments* that the store is attempting to serve, the buyer must formulate a buying plan with the aim of producing an *assortment differentiation* based upon the overall customer profile of the market segments to which the firm hopes to appeal.

The buying behavior of the firm is an extension of its overall retailing strategy. Sound buying decisions must be predicated upon the sound assumptions of the marketing concept—customer orientation, profit or contribution to profit as a criterion for decision making, the importance of market demand analysis, and the critical role of the sales forecast as a basis for operating decisions.

Circumscribing Buyer Behavior

The buyer's role is that of a critical decision maker whose behavior can lead to growth and profit—both valued goals of the retail management system. However, his decision making is affected by many factors, including such considerations as the nature of his role, his position in the organization hierarchy, the nature of the firm by which he is employed, and many other

[6] Claude R. Martin, Jr., "The Contribution of the Professional Buyer to a Store's Success or Failure," *Journal of Retailing,* Vol. 49, No. 2 (Summer 1973) , pp. 69–80.

considerations.[7] Buyer decision making is subject to the same constraints and conditions of uncertainty as decision making generally.

Another circumscribing characteristic of buyer behavior is that it generally involves planning and/or decision making toward predetermined goals. Higher-level authority figures are responsible for establishing the firm's overall goals and objectives. Thus, it becomes the buyer's responsibility, as well as that of his immediate superiors, the merchandise manager and the divisional merchandise manager, to interpret these higher-level goals and to respond with the purchasing behavior that is compatible with these goals. Most often buyer behavior is a form of phase planning under fixed goals, or the preparation of plans in terms of periods of time, application of degrees of effort, utilization of particular facilities, or movement in a given direction involving the establishment of subgoals.

To some extent at least certain dimensions of buyer behavior have already been delineated. Earlier, in the material dealing with store organization, the role of the buyer in certain kinds of organizational arrangements was discussed. In the small store, the buyer and store manager/owner roles may be coexistent. In the large store, the buyer's role may be well defined. The range of his behavior may be limited as in the case of the department manager/buyer of a retail system with a highly centralized management philosophy in which buying is restricted to requisitioning fill-in requirements from central merchandise headquarters. In other instances, the buyer role may be a highly autonomous one, characterized by a wide latitude of freedom of behavior.

Our next objective is to outline some of these determinants of buyer behavior—the behavior connected with the buyer's role as store purchasing agent. The attempt is made in order to more fully understand this behavior, its motivation and its overall impact on store operations, but, more specifically, as it affects the retail management system's ability to aggregate a balanced assortment of goods to meet expected or anticipated customer demand.

The Buyer as Gatekeeper. The retail store buyer has been characterized as a "gatekeeper."[8] The bureaucratic nature of the retailing institution underlines the constraints placed upon buyer behavior. Each level of authority is circumscribed or limited by the rules, regulations, and procedures outlining the responsibilities and roles of all the members of the organization. Supposedly, behavior is largely routinized as a result of this socialization.

Kurt Lewin first popularized the term *gatekeeper*, in referring to the person who has the power to make a decision that allows some item to enter or not to enter a channel.[9] Thus, the buyer as gatekeeper can allow an

[7] C. B. Saunders and C. T. Deeble, "The Personality Structure of a Group of Chain Store Buyers, with Implications for Management," *Journal of Retailing*, Vol. 41 (1965–1966), p. 44.

[8] See Edwin J. Gross, "Bureaucracy, the 'Gatekeeper' Concept, and Consumer Innovation," *Journal of Retailing* (Spring 1967), p. 9.

[9] Kurt Lewin, "Group Decision and Social Change," in T. M. Newcomb and E. L. Hartley (eds.), *Readings in Social Psychology*, Holt, Rinehart and Winston, New York, 1947.

item (merchandise selection) to enter a channel (the merchandise selection process and, ultimately, the merchandise assortment) by his favorable or unfavorable reaction to vendor or supplier offerings. It has been pointed out that the retail buyer is more of a negative gatekeeper than a positive one. Given the bureaucratic nature of many retail systems and the multiple purchasing influence, the buyer can usually veto a product by virtue of his authority role. Most often, however, he cannot insist on buying the product if there is opposition from other buyers or the merchandise manager.

Gatekeeper Psychology. What rationale or psychology underlies the retail store buyer's gatekeeper behavior? Regarding the buyer's receptivity toward product offerings, Gross conjectures that his perception of his status and/or role may be innovatively or noninnovatively oriented:[10]

Innovatively Oriented. The buyer gatekeeper may encourage his resources to develop and bring new products to his attention because he (a) interprets this as part of his management's marketing philosophy or (b) sees his association with successful innovations as a means of hastening his upward mobility through the organization.

Noninnovatively Oriented. The buyer may discourage or reject innovations, either because he (a) perceives the organization's philosophy as being noninnovative or (b) does not want to jeopardize his future in the organization with failure (s).

Quite interestingly, in the same way that buyers can be innovatively or noninnovatively oriented, so, too, can retail management systems. Thus, some retailers may be innovatively oriented and others may be more noninnovatively oriented. A typology of bureaucracies and gatekeepers would therefore result. For example:

BUREAUCRACY ORIENTATION	BUYER ORIENTATION	
	Innovative	Noninnovative
Innovative	I	II
Noninnovative	III	IV

On such situations the buyer's behavior would be circumscribed in the following manner:

1. *Bureaucracy and buyer orientation innovative.*
   Such a situation results in a progressive kind of merchandising institution. This is the type of retailer to whom a manufacturer will first present his new product idea. The policy on innovation is open, with the buyer allowing most reasonably good ideas through the gate to the buying committee.
2. *Bureaucracy innovative, buyer noninnovative.*
   This combination is generally rare because the buyer does not wish to

[10] Gross, op. cit., p. 14.

buck the trend. Management expects the officeholder to open the gate for innovations, and the buyer will generally comply.

3. *Bureaucracy noninnovative, buyer innovative.*

This amounts to an incongruent situation. One interpretation of this counterbureaucratic behavior is that the individual is attempting to make his mark and accelerate his upward climb. This is possible because he may be one of the very few to encourage innovation.

4. *Bureaucracy and buyer orientation noninnovative.*

This is often the situation which results in a conservative, tradition-bound institution. The buyer's position is reasonably secure. In many situations without his active intervention, his department will show increases from year to year simply because of population growth or overall organizational sales increases, on the order of 2 or 3 per cent annually.

This analysis is considerably simplified. Buyer and institutional behavior are both subject to a wide range of behavior characteristics; therefore, classifying all behavior or attitudes regarding their roles as either innovative or noninnovative does not do justice to the complex problem of circumscribing buyer behavior. However, the gatekeeper role of the retail buyer does pose some interesting considerations for possible further analysis.

The Buyer as Gaming Strategist. Another interesting view of retail store buyer behavior is one which characterizes the buyer as a strategist in a game situation.[11]

Dickinson defines a game "as a situation in which the individuals involved are attempting to gain some goal or goals in which their success or failure is dependent not only upon their strategy choices, but upon the strategy choices of the other individuals in the situation."[12] According to this definition almost all business situations are games. The buyer is competing in a strategic sense with the abilities of vendor suppliers, other competitors, other buyers, and perhaps even with a higher-level authority, such as a divisional or general merchandise manager. The point is that although buyer behavior is not directly amenable to game theory, the buying situation to some degree parallels what has been called a "mixed motive" game, in which mixed motives refer to the ambivalence of the relationship between the players. In the mixed motive game there is a mixture of mutual dependence, conflict, partnership, and competition.

The buyer as gaming strategist is consistent with the theory of buyer decision making under conditions of uncertainty. The environment faced by the retail store buyer is one of decision making, i.e., choosing from among numerous alternatives. There is usually some degree of conflict; buyers wish to purchase merchandise at low prices and sellers wish to sell at high prices. However, a degree of mutual dependence must exist between buyer and vendor seller, for the buyer (it is presumed) needs goods and the ven-

---

[11] The material relating to this concept is from Roger Dickinson, "Game Theory and the Department Store Buyer," *Journal of Retailing* (Winter 1966–1967) , pp. 14–24.

[12] Ibid., p. 14.

dor needs to sell goods. Therefore, bargaining and negotiation serve both their self-interests. Negotiative behavior is the essence of the buyer/seller dyad[13] and is built upon such factors as the commitment to role of both buyer and seller, i.e., the degree to which each is pledged to carry out the policies or proscribed behavior of his respective institution. Both buyer and vendor attitudes regarding their market power or strengths will affect their willingness to bargain, or engage in splitting the difference. Splitting occurs often in many negotiative processes, either because there is some ethical appeal in our culture to divide rewards, or because not splitting would result in psychological defeat for one of the bargaining members.

The use of a third party can also be an effective device to improve the bargainer's position in the negotiative process. Merchandise managers or other members of a buying committee may be called in to add strength to the buyer's arguments for bargaining concessions. As in most situations, a two-party game does not become a three-party game when joined by another member. Instead, a collusive agreement generally continues the two-party aspect, but amounts to a situation of two against one.

The buyer as a gaming strategist is an interesting analogy and much of his behavior can be fruitfully analyzed within such a framework. It must be pointed out that the buyer's role behavior will be affected by rational opponents. The rational opponent gives careful attention to what he expects the buyer-decision maker to do before he selects his own strategy. As defined earlier, strategy involves movement and countermovement in pursuit of goals. The essence of the game of strategy is that a degree of conflict of interest exists between opponents. Yet they are assumed to be rational and, therefore, economics and survival dictate that they continue to interact, even though some of their behavior is designed to frustrate their opponent's wishes.

Another point which must not be overlooked in evaluating and discussing buyer role and behavior is that buyers in the main operate under conditions of great stress. Retailing might best be described as a "disturbed environment." Retail stores, especially the more dynamic and successful ones, are pressure cookers. There exists in many instances an atmosphere of near panic and confusion. The pressures are of great magnitude: time constraints, frictions, and conflicts among personnel. This high-pressure atmosphere of the buyer appears especially conducive to greater feelings of frustration and dissatisfaction. Buyers often exist in a state of barely controlled agitation as they battle for better positions on the floor, higher advertising allocations, more travel money, and increases in their merchandise budget allotments (open to buy). All this of course suggests several things.[14] First, the retail manager should be aware of the possibility of high levels of frustration and dissatisfaction among buyers. Second, given that such possible levels of dissatisfaction conceivably exist, the retail manager should

[13] A *dyad* is a social-psychological concept that portrays interpersonal behavior, a situation wherein the behavior of one member of the dyad is in turn affected by the behavior of the other.

[14] Jacob P. Siegel and Dennis P. Slevin, "Need Satisfaction and Performance of Department Store Buyers and Department Managers: Implications for Management," *Journal of Retailing*, Vol. 50, No. 1 (Spring 1974), pp. 67–89.

seriously consider approaches to both monitoring attitude and reducing dissatisfaction among the buyer corps. Finally, more attention should be given within the retail store organization to the problem of communicating performance standards to buyers to the end that need satisfaction and buyer performance are more closely aligned.

A Model of Buyer Behavior. Buying behavior in at least its broader dimensions can be conceptualized into a model wherein the basic operant determinants of behavior can be pinpointed and characterized.

Buying has been defined as being concerned with the range of activities related to selecting materials or goods of the right quality, in the right quantity, at the right time, at the right price, from the right source, with the delivery at the right place.[15]

Kernan and Sommers have suggested that such a definition focuses any analysis of buyer behavior upon the notion of *rightness* from the standpoint of propriety for purposes of the buyer's role fulfillment.[16] Their model of buyer behavior is predicated upon a few simple but salient propositions regarding the buyer's role. First of all, the buyer is viewed as an advocate, or one who represents a principal. This proposition emphasizes that both buyer and seller (although subject to their own respective idiosyncrasies) are acting in behalf of their principals. Thus, their negotiating behavior is guided by the purposes of their respective institutions, rather than simply their own. Second, this model treats products or the objects bought as conceptualized symbols. In their roles as advocates buyers must view products in terms of what they are capable of doing, not only operationally or in terms of the physical performance of the product, but also in terms of the product's social and psychological interpretations.

Kernan and Sommers' role-taking model is oriented around the symbolic interactionist approach to buyer behavior, and much like the model of Gross outlined earlier, it circumscribes the buyer's behavior in terms of his role, his commitment to role, and the effects of institutional commitment. Buyer behavior is thus seen as a function of the interaction among these variables. The variables outlined here will explain the interaction of the model organized in Figure 11-3.

I_t: Institutional Role Type

I_c: Institutional Commitment

INNO: Innovative Institution (suggesting generalized weak commitment)

ADAP: Adaptive Institution (suggesting generalized moderate commitment)

LETH: Lethargic Institution (suggesting generalized strong commitment)

---

[15] Adapted from J. H. Westing and I. V. Fine, *Industrial Purchasing*, 2nd ed., John Wiley & Sons, Inc., New York, 1961, p. 7.

[16] Jerome B. Kernan and Montrose S. Sommers, "Role Theory and Behavioral Style," *Journal of Purchasing*, Vol. 3, No. 4 (November 1967), pp. 27–38. Also see their article, "The Behavioral Matrix: A Closer Look at the Industrial Buyer," *Business Horizons*, Vol. 9 (Summer 1966), pp. 59–72.

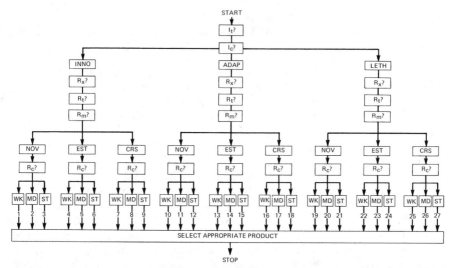

FIGURE 11-3 A role-taking model. Identification of the symbols on this model is made in the text.

SOURCE: Jerome B. Kernan and Montrose S. Sommers, "Role Theory and Behavioral Style," Journal of Purchasing (November 1967), p. 35.

R_x:	Role Interaction (occupational with nonoccupational)
R_t:	Occupational Role Type
R_m:	Maturity of Occupational Role
NOV:	Novel Role
EST:	Established Role
CRS:	Crystallized Role
R_c:	Occupational Role Commitment
WK:	Weak Commitment to Occupational Role
MD:	Moderate Commitment to Occupational Role
ST:	Strong Commitment to Occupational Role

The model in Figure 11-3 depicts the buyer initiating behavior as a result of ascertaining both his institution's role type and commitment. He is then led to one of three branches of the model: innovative, adaptive, or lethargic. He next turns to the individual principal for whom he is to negotiate an acquisition. To do this he must ascertain, to the degree he is able, what significant nonoccupational roles the principal plays. Then he must determine a clear understanding of the principal's occupational role type, the maturity of his role, which leads him to one of the three secondary branches. Finally, the buyer makes a judgment regarding the occupational role commitment of the principal, the accuracy of which tends to be a function of his previous experience with the principal. This decision leads to one of three tertiary branches of the model: weak, moderate, or strong. The buyer's behavior again becomes a function of his *strategic* interpretation of three elements: the principal's commitment to role, his institution's commitment, and the modal commitment occasioned by the maturity of the principal's role type. Kernan and Sommers suggest that buyer strategy ought to be based upon three normative propositions relating to both the firm and the buyer.

1. The [buyer] is a creative advocate. His function is not merely to facilitate his principal's behavior style. Rather it is to influence that style by providing appropriate products and services.
2. Creative, or at least progressive, behavior is preferable to inflexible behavior in an organization. There is a limit to behavioral mutation, of course, generally imposed by the institution's role type. Within this constraint, however, the [buyer] functions to encourage creative or progressive behavior by acquiring, for his principals, products and services which symbolize creative or progressive behavior.
3. In descending levels of significance, there are three categories of influence which affect a principal's occupational behavior—his own commitment to role, his institution's commitment, and the modal commitment of those not a part of the institution, but in like occupational categories. In an effort to influence creative behavior by principals, therefore, the most effective strategy for [buyers] is to encourage the principal's self-generated creative behavior. That strategy being unavailable, a more creative institution (preferably), or a more creative professional mode can be offered as reference points to the principal.[17]

Having thus circumscribed at least some dimensions of buyer strategy and psychology, our attention is turned now to an analysis of the buying process and a review of some of the problems that complicate buyer activity.

the buying process

The merchandise management function along with its related buying process is concerned with the primary administrative responsibility of relating the firm's merchandise resources to merchandise sources and to potential customer demand. This is done, of course, within the framework of the entire management system's merchandising policies.

Figure 11-4 relates buyer behavior that includes buyer and institutional role factors to the buying process. Observe that the model consists of three phases. *Phase 1* relates to the perceived role of the buyer, taken from his environment. His role conditions his purchasing activity, which relates to the actual buying process shown in *Phase 2*. Quite obviously, the buying process is related to the two major activities of merchandise management decisions—merchandise planning and merchandise control. The model is designed to illustrate the interacting nature of buyer behavior and the entire merchandising function. Such interaction is stimulated by a continuous feedback of information through the described system. Up to this point we

---

[17] Ibid., p. 36.

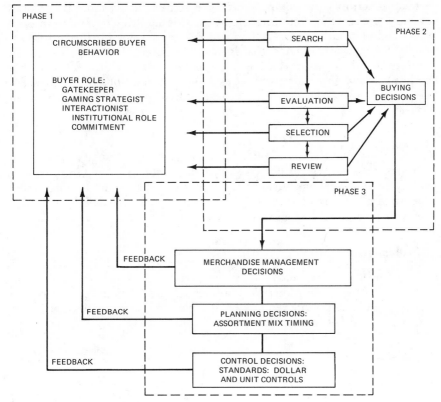

FIGURE 11-4   **A model of buyer behavior and the merchandising function.**

have dealt extensively with *Phase 1* activities; our attention now will be devoted to analyzing the buying process depicted in *Phase 2*. Activities related to *Phase 3* are merchandising management decisions and will be treated extensively in subsequent chapters.

The buying process (*Phase 2*) is comprised of a number of functional activities. One conceptual view holds that buying consists of responding to a series of planning questions relating to

1. What merchandise should be purchased.
2. From whom the merchandise should be purchased.
3. In what quantities it should be purchased.
4. How it should be purchased.
5. When it should be purchased.

Viewed from another perspective, buying can be seen as a process of decision making related to (1) determining what to buy, (2) locating sources of supply, (3) judging suitability of goods, (4) negotiating terms of sales, and (5) transferring title of goods. It would appear that while each of these ways of describing the buying process has some merit, a more behaviorally oriented sequence of activities might provide additional insight into this vastly complicated process. As shown in Figure 11-4, the buying process consists of four major sequences that in turn ultimately lead to a decision concerning the three major buying questions of *what to buy, when to buy,* and *how much.* As a matter of fact, each of these questions is approached by the store buyer as he proceeds through *search, evaluation, selection,* and *review* processes.

Search

Search activities relate principally to the problem of determining what to buy and from whom, by asking: What are the alternative sources of information regarding what to buy? and Once the needs have been established, how can they be related effectively to vendor availability and service?

Evaluation

The buyer/decision maker must continually evaluate the product and service offerings with which he is presented. Evaluation consists of comparing merchandise and vendors on the basis of predetermined values relating to quality-service-price considerations.

Selection

Selection consists of the actual choice from among available alternatives after the evaluation of these alternatives on the basis of some cost-benefit analysis. It is at this juncture that merchandise purchase decisions are actually made. Of course, decisions are of either the go or no-go variety, which means merchandise is either purchased or it is not purchased. The decision not to purchase usually triggers a reiterative process that results in further search and evaluation procedures.

Review

The review stage of buyer decision making is concerned with the buyer's continuing reappraisal of his entire search, evaluation, and selection activities. Review activities guarantee a kind of final control and reevaluation of the entire buying process. Hopefully, this review would tend to inhibit or prevent the ritualization and routinization of the buying function. It demands a perennial accommodation of buying activities to the ever-changing needs of the buying process.

QUESTIONS FOR STUDY, REFLECTION, AND REVIEW

1. Define the term merchandising. What are the central concepts of this definition?

2. How does merchandising relate to the goals and objectives of the retail firm?
3. What are merchandising policies? How do they relate to the overall retail policies of the firm?
4. Why is the retail firm becoming dependent on increasing capital turnover in order to generate sufficient return on investment?
5. How do merchandising decisions affect return on investment?
6. Explain the effect that good buying decisions have on the cost of goods sold and ultimately on net profit.
7. One view holds that the buying process consists of responding to a series of planning questions. What questions would facilitate this view of the buying process?
8. Explain and define the stages in the buying process.
9. If we assume that well-executed buying decisions lead to increased sales, explain what effect this will have on the rest of the financial elements in the income statement.
10. How does the concept of market segmentation relate to the buying process?

12

merchandise
assortment planning

The assortment mix problem has several dimensions. First of all, the buyer and the other members of the merchandise management unit must decide the issues relating to the *width* or *breadth of* their *assortment* mix. This problem relates to how many different merchandise lines are to be found within the retail firm. A merchandise line is a group of products that are closely related because they satisfy a class of needs, are used together, or are sold to the same basic market targets. It is made up of a series of demand-related merchandise items, which are specific versions of a product that has a separate designation. A merchandise item is unique and identifiable as a merchandise entity. The assortment mix is the entire aggregation of merchandise, by item and by merchandise line. Therefore, in a supermarket's merchandise assortment consisting of the sum total of its item and merchandise line composite, canned peaches would constitute a merchandise line, while a No. 10 can of Del Monte peach halves in syrup would constitute a merchandise item. A food supermarket would, therefore, have hundreds of merchandise lines, made up of the nearly 9,000 different merchandise items stocked by the average supermarket.

In addition to problems relating to the breadth of assortments are problems concerned with the depth of assortments and the balance or compatibility of assortments. *Depth of assortment* relates to the average number of items offered by a store within each merchandise line. *Compatibility of assortments* refers to how well the various merchandise lines complement each other in terms of the store's total effort to match its market offering to the market opportunity.

It would go without saying that assortment mix problems are related to such factors as the market opportunity and the store image that management wishes to project. By and large, full-service merchandisers are those who generally wish to offer complete merchandise assortments. That is, a heavy emphasis is placed upon having merchandise assortments of unusual breadth, depth, and compatibility.

Other retail firms have attempted to find a niche in the market by streamlining merchandise assortments. The breadth of their merchandise lines is reduced substantially, usually to the most popular or faster-moving items, and the depth of each line is carefully adjusted so as to minimize investment in inventories and facilitate store turnover. For example, if the management of a store discovers that 80 per cent of its sales in a given merchandise line stem from only four of the ten merchandise brands carried, they are likely to conclude that the benefits reaped from stocking and maintaining the additional six merchandise brands do not warrant the extra merchandising effort and expense. In marked contrast, and for entirely different management reasons related to image and competitive philosophy, another store is likely to conclude that it is essential to carry a full line. All ten brands would be stocked, even though six of the brands were contributing only 20 per cent of the sales volume for the entire merchandise line. Merchandise assortment problems must be analyzed in light of company goals and objectives and consumer preferences. Questions relating to merchandise compatibility are not easily answered. Given the tendency toward scrambled merchandising, the question in assortment planning is not so much whether the item or merchandise line fits the total store's offering in terms of store image and market segments, but whether it can be merchandised at a profit. With the buyer's and merchandise manager's interest in complying with the profit objectives of the system, it is small wonder that profitability and assortment mix decisions are so interrelated. Also, it must be remembered that profitability might be enhanced by either adding or dropping a product from the total assortment mix. However, in a marginal sense, it must be remembered that the profitability of a given item is not limited to the difference between that item's sales revenue (unit price × units sold) and its expenses. But rather, in the broader economic sense, profitability of an item is related to the difference in total department or store profit resulting from the decision to carry or not carry the item. Many assortment decisions relating to breadth, depth, and compatibility are based upon this sound managerial concept.

The role of profitability in the merchandise assortment decision process is not generally well defined or understood by many retail decision makers. Quite often, the decision to add or drop products to or from the assortment mix depends on the criterion of customary behavior, competition, or simple intuition. Yet, it is not to be inferred that profitability should be the sole criterion on which the decision rests. What is implied is that assortment mix decisions must be evaluated on a balance scale, with appropriate weights being given to such factors as compatibility among lines and items, competitive and customary behavior, sustainability and growth potential, and profit.

In department stores, the more conventional ways of determining an item's profitability in relation to the assortment mix problem most generally involve a series of judgment methods or techniques relating to such indices as turnover rates, dollar margins, and dollar margins per linear shelf fo ɔt, or per cubic foot of shelf space. A Harvard research study has attempted to treat the assortment mix problem and the profitability concept in a more spohisticated manner. In a pilot study based upon the concept of "direct product profit," four hypotheses were tested:[1]

1. If shelf space is shifted from an item with a relatively low rate of "direct product profit per cubic foot" (DPP/CF) to an item with a relatively high DPP/CF, total profit for the product will increase.
2. If an item with a relatively low DPP/CF is eliminated, and if the space released by the elimination is assigned to a relatively high-profit item, then total profit for the product family will increase.
3. The *relative* profitability of items within each product family is similar for all stores in a given chain or voluntary group.
4. There are no differences in the relative performance of items within a product family as measured by DPP/CF, on the one hand, and by (a) gross margin percentages or (b) gross margin dollars, on the other hand.

Direct product profit (DPP) is found by determining specific product revenues and specific product costs that result from and are affected by merchandising decisions.

The research findings of the Harvard study supported the first two of these hypotheses, and the authors conclude that the direct product profit method of measurement is a better indicator of profitability than such methods as the gross margin percentage, the rate of movement of each item, and even gross profit per cubic foot of shelf space. Therefore, the results suggest that retailers could increase profit for a merchandise line, or a product family, by shifting space from historically less profitable to more profitable items, and by eliminating items with low profitability.

Dropping Items from the Assortment Mix

Most often the approach to the assortment mix problem is focused upon what products, brands, or lines to add. However, such attention often leads to a failure to recognize that balanced assortments depend not only on adding products but on dropping products as well. For example, a typical supermarket may be offered 125 new or improved items a week, or about 6,500 a year. From these offerings, 800 may be added to the super's inventory mix. In the course of a year, however, the same store would typically drop 600 items, for a net gain of 200 items. Firms are faced with the product or brand deletion problem as a result of many factors. The shortened life and profit cycles of many product lines result from the concern of manufacturers with bringing forth a constant stream of new products and, hence, profits, from their enterprise point of view. Second, competition itself continues to threaten changes in the product and assortment mix *because merchandising assortments are an extension of the firm's overall strategy considerations.* Thus, competition forces the expansion and continuing reappraisal of the assortment mix problem.

[1] Robert D. Buzzell, Walter J. Salmon, and Richard F. Vancil, *Product Profitability Measurement and Merchandising Decisions,* Harvard University, Division of Research, Graduate School of Business, Boston, 1965.

The product deletion dimension of the assortment mix problem can also be approached from the profitability criterion. It is wise to remember that other factors must be considered here also. Alexander states that profit considerations must be evaluated in relation to the deletion problem in the following ways:[2]

1. The profit on no individual product or product line should be allowed to fall below some minimum standard related to overall company target profit in dollars or rate of return on investment.
2. The argument that certain products, while not profitable, still contribute to joint costs or help to defray overhead and thus should remain in the assortment should be evaluated judiciously.
3. However, it must be recognized that overhead costs will have to be charged against some products. Such costs are "sticky" but every effort should be used to find ways to reduce them.
4. If the deletion decision involves a product or merchandise line which accounts for a large proportion of total overhead or joint costs, then before the decision to delete is made, the effects, on a *pro forma* basis, should be forecast on the firm or department's operating statement. Thus, the effects of the deletion decision can be readily foretold and appropriate action considered.

The assortment mix problem of whether to add or delete products is also concerned with the question of brands, i.e., how many brands of each item should be included in the assortment mix and what brands should be added or deleted? The usual approach to these questions relating to brands is much the same as that relating to merchandise items and merchandise lines. That is, the decision will be affected by the store's merchandising philosophy, its image, the behavior of competition, and the effect of brand merchandising policies on the profitability and growth of the retailer in question. The increasing number of new brands within the existing merchandise classes plus the magnitude of new merchandise classes in all kinds of stores only add to the difficulty of economically allocating space among the various merchandise offerings. However, new merchandise lines and new brands within these lines can only be ignored at the risk of losing sales to specialized consumer groups. The choice amounts to a decision between carrying a given number of brands in each merchandise category and evaluating each of these on the basis of customer preference or profitability, or reducing the number of brands within each product class and using the available space to increase the product or merchandise class offerings. In a limited study, Munn has suggested the latter alternative as the most feasible. His findings support the contention that regardless of demographic characteristics consumers will give brands of consumer goods within specified merchandise classes similar price and quality ratings.[3] He therefore con-

[2] R. S. Alexander, "The Death and Burial of Sick Products," *Journal of Marketing*, Vol. 28 (April 1964), pp. 1–7.

[3] Henry L. Munn, "Should Retailers Reduce the Number of Brands Stocked?" *Journal of Retailing*, Vol. 38, No. 4 (Winter 1962–1963), pp. 1–6. See also Norman D. French, William A. Chance, and John J. Williams, "A Shopping Experiment on Price–Quality Relationships," *Journal of Retailing*, Vol. 48, No. 3 (Fall 1972), pp. 3–17.

cludes that it may be smart merchandising strategy to select one or two brands in each product class that consumers perceive as high in quality and low in price, and to discard the rest. Quite obviously, the discount merchandisers in food, drug, and general merchandise lines have adhered to this policy.

buying, and the product and fashion cycles

The major buying problems of what, when, and how much to buy and the buying goals of profit and growth are affected by the behavior or consequences of both product and fashion cycles. Much emphasis has already been placed upon the role of profit as a criterion for many buying decisions. However, it must be remembered that other goals of the retail management system are those of survival and growth. The firm must buy and manage its merchandise assortments in order to assure itself a continuing place in the distribution network.

Oftentimes, retail management becomes too obsessed with recognizing the profit implications of price reductions, new style changes, and product obsolescence, rather than buying and merchandising from the more comprehensive and integrated point of view of the product life cycle. Some products are designed and marketed for only a brief period. Consumer tastes change, and the product is psychologically—if not technologically—obsolete. Other products are brought forth that are considerably longer-lived.

The Product Life Cycle

The product life cycle is a rather simple concept. It suggests that products move through a series of stages and growth, and that conditions in each of these stages markedly affect both sales and profits. An understanding of the three rather basic assumptions upon which the product life cycle rests ought to facilitate the buyer's efforts toward aggregating the proper assortment mix to meet balanced and expected customer demand:

1. The speed with which products move through the various phases or stages in the product life cycle (i.e., introduction, growth, maturity, and decline) varies from product to product. Some move through very rapidly; others never even successfully move through the introductory stage to reach a growth period; while still others move through each stage in a strong and persistent manner.
2. Profits (per unit) rise steadily in the growth phase and start to decline during the maturity phase because of competitive pressures. During the later phases of the maturity stage, volume increases are most likely to outstrip profit increases.
3. The merchandising emphasis required for successful exploitation of the product life cycle concept will vary, depending upon the nature of

the retail management system, and at what phase the system attempts to enter the merchandising effort as it relates to the product life cycle.

In order to visualize the behavior of the product life cycle, consider Figure 12-1.

The product life cycle gives a view of the profit and volume relationships in each phase of the cycle. Losses frequently occur in the early phases of the cycle because, from the merchant's point of view especially, there may be great risks associated with products at this stage; prices are generally high, and the item may be merchandised only by the more exclusive stores. Some stores attempt to adjust their merchandising strategies to the various stages in the cycle by purchasing small amounts of the product during the introductory phase. As the product catches on and demand for it subsequently increases, assortments are broadened and promotional efforts increased. On moving through the maturity phase, the item is likely to become price sensitive and therefore subject to price discounting. As the product moves through the decline stage, it may be closed out or relegated to a basement store location.

Most retail stores adjust their buying and merchandising efforts in the growth and maturity stages. However, the style or image of other stores dictates a different kind of behavior. Thus, some stores would wish to buy more goods in the introductory phase of their cycle. This behavior enhances the image of the store as a front runner or innovator. Many higher-priced apparel stores, shoppes, or salons would fall into this merchandising category. Other stores may adjust a large part of their merchandising effort toward the maturity and decline stages of the product life cycle. Their buying efforts would therefore center around locating assortments of distress merchandise, manufacturer close-outs, odd lots, and other situations in

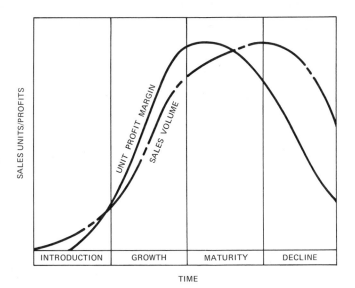

FIGURE 12-1 A product life cycle chart.

which price concessions and bargain merchandising might be emphasized.[4]

The buyer's behavior must be coordinated with the conditions that characterize each of the various stages of the product life cycle. For example, in the uncertain *introductory stage* in which there are generally low sales, with losses or low profits, relatively few vendors, and when the product is vulnerable to other competitive new offerings, the buying and merchandising policies would probably reflect the following considerations:[5]

1. A relatively low inventory of this product would be incorporated into the assortment mix.
2. Knowledgeable suppliers would be sought who could provide good merchandising service and assistance.
3. Suppliers would be patronized who could provide this merchandising service, and have, at the same time, the potential to grow with the product's expected growth, but who would also be patient enough to supply the small quantities needed at the outset.

The *growth stage* is characterized by a rapid rise in sales during the brief period when profits are beginning to emerge or increase and the number of vendors handling the product has begun to increase. In this phase buying and merchandising behavior ought to reflect efforts designed to

1. Provide the products in larger quantities with the full range of colors and other design features.
2. Develop new sources of supply in order that merchandising continuity be maintained.
3. Insist on rapid and frequent deliveries and make provision for this with merchandise suppliers.
4. Develop critical buying controls and be especially careful to continuously evaluate merchandise offerings.
5. Build larger inventories in order that stock-outs are avoided and no sales missed because of assortment imbalances.

During the *maturity stage,* the rate of growth in the new product's sales begins to decline, and there may be increasing sales but at a decreasing rate. But competition begins to stiffen in relation to the product, and prices and profits begin their downward spiral. In this phase buyers should

1. Begin to look for price concessions at the vendor-supplier level.
2. Start eliminating weak suppliers and remain alert to supplier merchandising plans regarding the product.
3. Begin balancing inventory levels very carefully in order that the absolute minimum investment is made in this product.

[4] John's Bargain Stores is an example of a merchandising effort directed along these lines. See Frank Schlesinger, "John's Bargain Stores," *The New York Retailer* (April 1963), pp. 10–19.

[5] Adapted from Conrad Berenson, "The Purchasing Executive's Adaptation to the Product Life Cycle," *The Journal of Purchasing*, Vol. 3, No. 2 (May 1967), pp. 62–68.

4. Capitalize on the product differentiation and packaging innovations of leading suppliers.

Finally in the *decline stage,* the product is making a smaller and smaller contribution to the department or firm's profit and overhead. Suppliers are discontinuing the product, and store buyers are reviewing the product's proper role in the store's continuing merchandising effort. At this stage, buyer behavior is concerned with

1. Re-examining and revising required inventory levels.
2. Closing out remaining stocks of the product.
3. Reassessing and reappraising the entire merchandising behavior of this product over its complete life cycle.

It can thus be appreciated that the concept of the product life cycle provides some insight and guidelines to store buyers and merchandise managers. The merchandising effort must be keyed (where appropriate) to the conditions implied by this cycle.

The Fashion Cycle

The merchandising and buying of fashion goods to a considerable degree is affected by many of the same factors considered in the discussion of the product life cycle. That is, fashion goods often represent new product developments and as such would be subject to a life cycle consisting of growth, development, maturity, and decline phases. In the retail store, one of the basic means of distinguishing between different classes of merchandise is to relegate goods or products to either the *staple* or the *fashion* category. Today, admittedly, with the heavy merchandising emphasis on new products, colors, and distinctive and unique design, it is no longer easy to distinguish between fashion and staple items. Staple items are those items to which customers attach little or no fashion importance. By and large, staple items are necessities, and rather standardized items are offered to meet this area of customer demand. Thus, a staple item is a standardized item that changes (if at all) only slowly over time. Fashion items are highly infused with style, color, and design characteristics. And as these characteristics are incorporated into product items, they usually do change markedly over time. Style and fashion are not synonymous terms. Nystrom defined style as "a characteristic or distinctive mode or method of expression, presentation, or conception in a field of some art."[6] Fashion, therefore, is a style that is popular at any given time.

There are many theories regarding fashion, the fashion cycle, and the ways in which fashions are adopted. The sociologists contend that fashion change and adoption is a discrete solution to conflict between the individual and the society to which he belongs. In a bureaucratic and technological society that perennially threatens the individual's ego, an individual can

[6] P. H. Nystrom, *Economics of Fashion,* The Ronald Press Company, New York, 1928, p. 3.

assert and rediscover himself by departure from standardized norms. The behavior thus affected is the desire for change in manner of dress or style of living. In short, fashion is a means of rebellion, and the individual concerned with ego identification sometimes uses it as a subtle means of "product differentiation."[7] Barber and Lobel argue that clothing fashions in all societies are a means of identification and ordering within the status or class system.[8] They attempt to show the relationship between the role symbolic functions of clothing and fashion and the utilitarian and aesthetic functions. They also allege that fashion is one of the means used by consumers to solve the dilemma of equality and difference in the American class system. They contend, further, that a trickle system exists in fashion—that a new fashion starts in the couturier collections and then slowly trickles down through all the social class strata, and thus, through various types of retail stores, from the exclusive designer-original shoppes to mass merchandising institutions.

Psychologists have analyzed fashion as a means of sexual expression. They argue that fashion in women's clothing is essentially a game of hide-and-seek and that it requires two players, prudery and fashion. The psychologists' theory of fashion deals with the concept of the "shifting erogenous zone." The object is to draw attention to this zone, to emphasize it in every possible way. In women's clothing fashion, the shifting erogenous zone moves from bust to bustle and from legs to back. This theory holds that once the erogenous capital of a given area is exhausted, then the zone will shift to another area.[9]

An economist once lamented that "no explanation at all satisfactory has hitherto been offered of the phenomena of changing fashions."[10] Veblen, like others today, attributes fashion change to conspicuous waste, the desire for differentiation through adornment, and the restless, ceaseless, search and striving for something new and different to satisfy our aesthetic senses.

However, the buyer does not necessarily have to have an elaborate theory of fashion in order to adjust his buying and merchandising activities to this phenomenon. That is, it is not imperative that we know *why* fashion cycles exist. Rather, it is imperative that we know that they *do* exist and that buying and other merchandising activity will be affected by the fashion phenomena.

The concept of the fashion cycle implies several things. On the one hand it implies a cycle or rhythm in the life of a given fashion innovation. This cycle is analogous to the phases of the product life cycle mentioned earlier and can be shown diagrammatically as in Figure 12-2.

Both fashions and fads are successful new product introductions. The basic distinction between the two is generally related to the respective ac-

[7] Edward Sapir, "Fashion and Sociology Theory," in Edward K. Borgatta and Henry J. Meyer (eds.), *Sociology Theory,* Alfred A. Knopf, Inc., New York, 1956.

[8] Bernard Barber and Lyle S. Lobel, " 'Fashion' in Women's Clothes and the American Social System," *Social Forces,* Vol. 31 (December 1952) , pp. 124–131.

[9] James Laver, "What Will Fashion Uncover Next?" *This Week Magazine,* December 10, 1961.

[10] Thorstein Veblen, *The Theory of the Leisure Class: An Economic Study of Institutions,* The New American Library, New York, 1953.

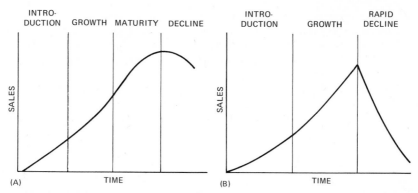

FIGURE 12-2 Fashion cycle and fad cycle. (A) Fashion cycle growth curve; (B) fad cycle growth curve.

ceptance rates. Fashions are thought to have an initially slower rise to popularity, a plateau of continuing popularity lacking in most fads, and a slow decline, rather than the abrupt decline typical of the fad. One would conclude, therefore, that the acceptance rate or cycle of a fashion is considered the same as the accepted theoretical course of the normal or average product life cycle. This concept of a fashion cycle is the one most considered when making buying and merchandising decisions.

There is another concept of the fashion cycle in which the curve is seen as a continuous repetition over time. That is, the decline phase is only temporary, followed by an upswing, or re-emergence of the same style, which once again becomes fashionable. There is some evidence to suggest that once popular styles do achieve a status of permanency that fact is reflected in their return to popularity after many years. After an exhaustive study of women's dress styles, Agnes Brooks Young concluded that there are three basic styles of dress, each of which has been fashionable for periods of 30 to 40 years.[11] These styles date back to the late 1700s in this country, and appear to re-emerge at regular intervals. The fashionableness of each style lasts approximately one generation, then gives way to the second. One style continues to replace another in successive generations, and the fashion wheel continues to revolve. This concept is based upon an analysis of drawings and photographs of dress styles from the 1700s to the present. One authority, reacting to this version of the fashion cycle, asserts:

> There are revivals of style from time to time, but the fashions of another day never come back in their entirety; neither history nor fashion plays itself back to us unchanged. Fashions are cyclical, however, to the extent that they go through stages of increasing and decreasing popularity.[12]

[11] Agnes Brooks Young, *Recurring Cycles of Fashion,* 1760–1937, Harper & Row, Publishers, New York, 1937.

[12] Rita A. Perna, "Analyzing Fashion Trends," in *Inside the Fashion Business,* Jeanette A. Jarnow and Beatrice Judelle (eds.) , John Wiley & Sons, Inc., New York, 1966, p. 5.

Merchandising with the Fashion Cycle. The fashion cycle is an important concept around which many successful buying and merchandising programs can be built. Changes in the fashion cycle reflect changes in fashion merchandise offerings, technological progress, and social movement. No retailing institution today is entirely immune from the fashion implications of goods, design, or packaging. The consumer's concern with style and fashion and his ever-increasing taste and discernment pose some rather difficult problems in selecting and merchandising items in all stores. There are fashion cycles and fashion influences in cars and clothing, hardware and appliances, houses and home furnishings.[13] Merchants and store buyers must anticipate the length of time from the creation of a new style to its arrival at the peak of the fashion cycle and then to its eventual decline and ultimate extinction.

Merchandising and buying activities must be coordinated to the fashion cycle and both in turn adjusted to the store's customer clientele in terms of its income groups and other customer characteristics. For example, a popularly priced mass merchandising system cannot take on the function of introducing new high-fashion items to its customers. The buying motives and the life styles of this store's market targets are such that they are usually prone to imitate others, rather than be style leaders. Thus, this store's customers can best be approached with the appeal that the particular style is already fashionable. On the other hand, some customers (i.e., the basement store customers of Filene's) are interested in both fashionableness and price, but their interest is undoubtedly price first, and fashionableness second. Low-income customers are often forced because of economy motives to buy merchandise that has passed the peak of its popularity and is no longer in great demand.

There are appropriate stores for merchandising a given fashion through each of its various stages. It is imperative that buying and merchandise policies reflect the store's efforts to time its acquisition and balance its assortment mix of fashion items to its customers' shopping and purchase habits and attitudes. In this way, the fashion cycle can be related to a kind of merchandising cycle, as shown in Figure 12-3.

Fashion and the Diffusion Process. It may well be that fashion sells more merchandise in many lines than any other factor. The American consumer, by and large, does not buy clothing, automobiles, and refrigerators because he has exhausted his stock of these commodities, or because his stock has been worn out through technological obsolescence. Instead, more often, his purchase motives have fashion implications. That is, he buys clothing, automobiles and major appliances because he wishes to have products that are new, or of the latest design, color, or style. Given the importance and role of fashion merchandising in so many lines of retailing enterprise, it has become essential that fashion be totally incorporated and coordinated with the other dimensions of the firm's merchandising strategy.[14]

---

[13] See L. Baltera, "Fashion Trends Loom Large in Ads for Growing Variety of Products," *Advertising Age,* March 26, 1973, pp. 100–101.

[14] See Edith F. Hayter, *Fashion Merchandising*, Pageant Press, New York, 1965. See also S. Mitchell, "Managing Fashion Merchandising," *Stores* (August 1974), p. 16T.

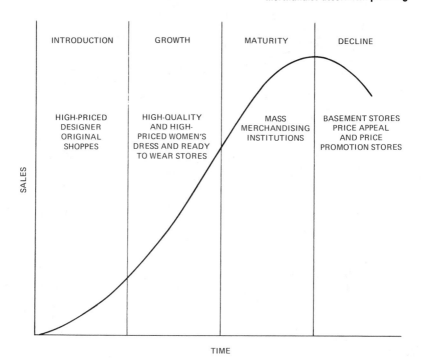

FIGURE 12-3   Fashion and merchandising cycles for women's apparel.

The beginning of such fashion coordination must start with an under-standing of how a new fashion is diffused through the population, how and to what extent it is accepted by the various segments of the consuming population, and the rapidity with which fashions are accepted or rejected. Such activity is referred to as the *diffusion process.*

A new style can be considered an innovation. Innovation is usually con-ceived as a process whereby a new "thought, behavior or thing, which is qualitatively different from existing forms is conceived of and brought into reality." Fashion is an obvious form of *programmed innovation.* That is, fashion changes are planned and merchandising efforts are designed to promote the fashion innovation. However, this is not to say that sales of fashion items are automatic, once the new style or innovation is created. In the final analysis, the consumer is the gatekeeper who decides the fate of all fashion innovations. But the buyer and the merchandising manager are anxious to learn as much as possible about the diffusion process *in the hope that such an understanding might lead to prediction, and perhaps ulti-mately, to the control of the process.* For example, they are interested in such questions as[15]

1. Does diffusion occur in a predictable manner?
2. Is there such a person as a consumer innovator?

[15] From Thomas S. Robertson, "The Process of Innovation and the Diffusion of Innova-tion," *Journal of Marketing,* Vol. 31 (January 1967), p. 16.

3. How are people persuaded to adopt new innovations?
4. How might the firm's activities be better coordinated with the adoption and diffusion process?

The Diffusion Process. Sociologist Everett M. Rogers views the diffusion process as an orderly sequence of activities.[16] He proposes a diffusion curve, which is essentially a normal curve of distribution. Such a curve is shown in Figure 12-4.

Such a curve suggests that innovations (which may be nothing more than "an idea perceived as new by the individual")[17] are diffused through the population in a sequence that amounts to minor innovation adoption by the early adopters—a very small percentage of the total population—proceeding to accelerate in magnitude through the early majority and late majority categories, and finally tapering off as it moves through the final category, referred to as laggards. Thus, diffusion begins slowly, snowballs, and then subsides.

The interesting question now arises, "Given such a diffusion process, so what?" The first point of significance is, "Who are the early adopters?" In the case of fashion clothing items for women, Barber and Lobel have argued that they are women in the lower-upper social classes and that fashions then "trickle down" through the other social class rankings.[18]

Social scientists, by and large, have viewed the trickle effect as a battle of wits between upper-status persons who attempt to guard their symbolic treasure and lower-status persons (and mass producers and mass distributors of goods) who attempt to devalue the status-symbolic currency. Others have viewed the trickle effect as a mechanism for maintaining the motivation to strive for success, and hence for maintaining efficiency of performance in occupational roles, in a system in which differential success is possible only for a few.[19]

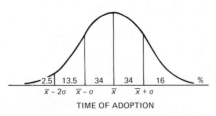

TIME OF ADOPTION

FIGURE 12-4 A diffusion curve and the adopter categories.

SOURCE: Everett M. Rogers, Diffusion of Innovations (New York: The Free Press, Macmillan Publishing Co., Inc., 1962), p. 162.

[16] Everett M. Rogers, *Diffusion of Innovations,* The Free Press, Macmillan Publishing Co., Inc., New York, 1962, p. 162.

[17] Ibid., p. 13.

[18] Barber and Lobel, op. cit., pp. 124–131.

[19] Lloyd A. Fallers, "A Note on the 'Trickle Effect,'" *Public Opinion Quarterly* (Fall 1954), pp. 314–321.

From a fashion merchandising point of view, the trickle effect, especially as it relates to social class, may be a most invalid concept. For high-fashion women's ready-to-wear, it may be that the early adopters are fashion-minded women in the lower-upper social class and that fashion innovations in the high-fashion category do trickle down through the various socio-economic classes. However, for most other goods (television as an example) the early adopters were not people in the upper socioeconomic rankings. Clothing for young people, the mod look, and other fashion innovations have been diffused, not by a trickle down effect, but rather, they have been more generally diffused through a given consumer group of persons having similar orientations and life styles. The success of a new product innovation or fashion will depend upon a number of considerations, a very important one of which is the role of the early adopter. Someone has to be the first adopter. The number of these early adopters and their influence within the community or within their peer groups will have a profound effect on the diffusion of the innovation. It has been postulated that the degree to which the early adopter is socially integrated—that is, those best accepted by their peers—will increase the success and degree of total adoption of the innovation.[20]

It has also been suggested that diffusion is affected by opinion leaders at all levels of the socioeconomic scale. Thus, the mass media are viewed as a means of reaching the opinion leaders or key influentials; then these opinion leaders are expected to affect the tastes, adoption, and purchase behavior of those within their particular reference groups.

The behavior of the early adopter in the fashion process is extremely critical. The buyer's efforts to coordinate fashion merchandising via fashion boards, consumer advisory panels, fashion counts, pre-season vendor and fashion shows, and central market buying trips are all to a degree related to discovering attitudes and propensities as they relate to opinion leaders and other early adopters. King has described the role of the early buyer in the adoption process in the following manner:[21]

1. The innovator initiates the adoption cycle within the season through her early purchases.
2. The innovator is the earliest visual communicator of the new season's styles for the mass of fashion consumers.
3. The innovator provides the first consumer feedback to the mass fashion industry on reactions to the new season's offerings and potential fashion trends. Based upon this early feedback, fashion manufacturers and retailers make major decisions on the season's product lines.
4. The innovator's early selections and reactions to the fashion inventory often give certain styles "legitimacy" in the mass consumer market. The early buyer displays the appropriateness of the season's offerings in various social settings to her social network. Because of the fashion

[20] For more relating to the issue of fashion merchandising, see R. A. Dickinson, "Fashion Management: Ways and Means," *Stores* (November 1974), pp. 8–9.

[21] Charles W. King, "The Innovator in the Fashion Adoption Process," in *Reflections on Progress in Marketing*, L. George Smith (ed.), American Marketing Association, Chicago, 1964, pp. 325–326.

industry's merchandising strategies, strong early sales of a style almost guarantee that style a major position in the inventory and merchandising program. Conversely, poor acceptance by the early buyers may doom a style or silhouette, particularly because of the reduced support by manufacturers and retailers.

5. In addition, in some social networks, the early buyer may also be a fashion influential or opinion leader. In this dual role, the innovator or early buyer would display the season's offerings early in the season and would define the broad fashion standards for her particular social network.

There is no denying the role of fashion in buyer and merchandising behavior. An orientation toward the diffusion process and the early buyer is merited, inasmuch as the fashion minded consumer represents a prime sales target for the retail industry. The dollar sales potential of each retail firm may hinge upon its understanding of the diffusion process of fashion and other innovations.

managing the negotiation process

The interest of this chapter has been directed primarily toward an analysis of several of the major problems affecting buyer behavior in relation to his assortment planning considerations. The emphasis has centered around the fundamental buying problems of what to buy, when to buy, and how much to buy. In Chapter 13 we shall once again look at this major problem, but primarily from a different perspective. It remains the task of this chapter to look further at some of the more prominent buying problems, namely, the problems related to such considerations as negotiation or vendor-buyer interaction, terms of sale, the question of number of vendors, and the role of central market facilities in the overall retail buying process.

Vendor-Buyer Interaction

The buying process or function is a part of the merchandise management activity and as such is concerned with the decision making necessary to have a balanced assortment of goods on hand to meet expected customer demand. The effectiveness of the buying process to a large extent will depend upon the effectiveness of the buyer as a negotiator. Negotiation is concerned with those activities that arise between two parties incident to the making of a contract. Successful negotiation implies that a contract may have been agreed upon. However, it does not always follow that success has characterized the behavior of each of the participants. Quite often, such is not the case at all. Negotiation implies a kind of fair and just bargaining, not "the barnyard scrap of two highly dissident game cocks . . . [where] the gain of one is the loss of the other."[22] Negotiation implies some conflict (the seller wishes to sell at a high price and the buyer wishes to buy at a

---

[22] John J. Kennedy, "The Management of Negotiation," *The Journal of Purchasing,* Vol. 3, No. 3 (August 1967), p. 43.

low price), but it also assumes reasonable compromise. Negotiation is the process whereby mutual agreement is reached on conflicting positions; buyers and sellers resolve conflicts and differences of opinion regarding terms of sale and other bargaining factors via negotiation. Negotiation requires skill and foresight. In a give-and-take bargaining situation, negotiation will be affected by the strength, i.e., the bargaining power of the negotiator, as well as by the individual's negotiating skill.

Negotiation is affected by what has been called *channel control,* which signifies "the ability of one member of a marketing channel for a given product (or brand) to stipulate marketing policies to other channel members."[23] Quite often, though certainly not always, the retailer is the weak member in the marketing channel, and when this is the case his ability to negotiate from a position of strength is seriously hampered. However, a knowledge of what is involved in negotiation and a deliberate plan on the part of the buyer to improve his negotiative skill can strengthen his position in the overall marketing channel relationship, as well as improve his overall buying performance. Figure 12-5 shows the various basic factors or variables involved in the negotiation process.

As Figure 12-5 illustrates, in a broad sense negotiation includes (1) the definition of objectives, (2) the analysis of facts, (3) the identification of the issues, (4) the development of positions relative to the issues, and (5) the planning of an overall negotiation strategy.

The virtue of such a model is that it provides a procedural point of departure for an analysis of the decision process within the negotiation. Probably its greatest benefit is that it provides a basis for planning and evaluating negotiation behavior based upon a conceptualization of the variables involved and the interrelationship of the impact of these variables on the entire process.

Terms of Sale. Specifically, what can be negotiated? There are many things, including prices, delivery dates, method of shipment and costs, the opportunity to participate in factory closeouts, special merchandise offerings by vendors, discounts, promotional allowances, and almost any other factor related to the buying-selling process. Negotiative constraints surround these various factors and are often proscribed by legal authority. For example, the Robinson-Patman Act [especially Section 2 (f), the main section applying to buying behavior] sets forth a considerable number of constraints that ought to affect the buying-negotiating process. Yet, quite often, both buyers and sellers behave in an extralegal sense as if the Robinson-Patman Act did not exist. However, the point of view advocated herein is not that the buyer engage in these extralegal efforts to secure concessions via negotiation, but rather that he bargain hard and effectively, so as to secure every concession to which he is legally entitled.

Successful negotiation thus involves a thoroughgoing understanding of the law that affects the negotiation process, and an understanding and appreciation of the major *terms of sale* under which goods are sold. Terms of

[23] Louis W. Stern, "The Concept of Channel Control," *Journal of Retailing* (Summer 1967), p. 14.

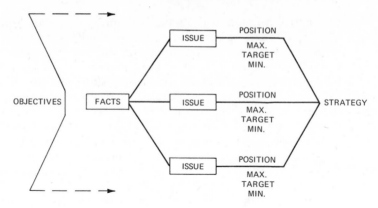

Facts: 1. Classify by issue and strategy
            2. Catalogue by degree and method of supportability

Issues: 1. Rank of importance
            2. Use—non-use
            3. Catalogue for strategy use
            4. Real—apparent

Positions: 1. Classified by importance
            2. Facts catalogued by issue and related to positions
            3. Maximum, minimum, and target positions

Strategy: 1. Analysis of procurement situation
            2. Use of issues
            3. Positions
            4. Human behavior
            5. Timing
            6. Organization

FIGURE 12-5   The negotiation process.

SOURCE: John J. Kennedy, "The Management of Negotiation," The Journal of Purchasing, Vol. 3, No. 3 (August 1967), p. 45.

sale refer to two categories of negotiative effort: (1) discounts and (2) dating periods.[24]

Discounts. Discounts are deductions from the billed or invoice price that are allowed under certain conditions. The most frequent forms of legal discounts are trade discounts, quantity discounts, and cash discounts.

Trade discounts are reductions from the list price given to all buyers in a certain class or category. They are sometimes referred to as "functional discounts," the logic being that they are given to cover a trade member's cost of performing his part in the distributive or trade channel effort. Manufacturers, therefore, are likely to give retailers a certain trade discount, and wholesalers another. For example, a manufacturer with a list price of $5.00 for a man's shirt, selling to either, or both, retailers and wholesalers, might

---

[24] A more basic treatment of discounts and dating periods can be found in the very excellent work by John Wingate, Elmer O. Schaller, and Irving Goldenthal, *Problems in Retail Merchandising*, Prentice-Hall, Inc., Englewood Cliffs, N.J., 1961, especially the supplementary section XXVI, "Invoice Mathematics," pp. 277–292.

grant trade discounts of 30 per cent and 20 per cent. A wholesaler's purchase cost would be $5.00, less 30 per cent ($1.50), less 20 per cent ($.70), or $5.00 − ($1.50 + .70), or $2.80. If a retailer purchased this item direct from the manufacturer, he would pay $5.00, less 30 per cent, or $3.50. The 20 per cent margin granted to the wholesaler is an acknowledgment of his channel or functional contribution.

Quantity discounts are deductions from the billed or list price based upon the amount purchased. Quite naturally, there are economies of scale that accrue to a seller when selling in large quantities. Quantity discounts are either cumulative or noncumulative in nature. Cumulative discounts are based upon the total amount purchased during a particular period, and noncumulative quantity discounts are based upon the amount purchased at a particular time. Once again, it must be emphasized that quantity discounts are limited to the actual saving that the quantity purchase makes possible. Although discounts have often taken the form of free goods, this form of discounting is subject to the same provisions of the Robinson-Patman Act as an outright price concession.

Cash discounts are deductions from the list price granted by a vendor to a buyer for the prompt payment of the net amount of the billed invoice. Cash discounts can be taken by any buyer who wishes to pay the invoice on or before the stipulated period allowed for taking the discount. It should be added that cash discounts are an important source of "other income" for most retailers. For example, a buyer may be offered terms of 2/10, n30 which means a 2 per cent discount can be deducted from the list price of the invoice total if the bill is paid within 10 days after the date of the invoice, or the net amount is due 30 days after date of the invoice. If he fails to take the discount, he is missing the opportunity to earn 36 per cent on his money in terms of an equivalent annual rate of interest.[25]

Datings. Dating refers to the time period within which payment is mandatory in order to obtain cash discounts (if offered) and to the time at which payment for the goods eventually falls due. Many considerations affect a seller's attitudes regarding the dating factor. Competitive conditions are the most important consideration, and it is the buyer's usual responsibility to negotiate for favorable dating provisions as a part of his purchase behavior. Business conditions, the nature of the goods, the marketing features that affect the sale of the goods, physical distance between buyer and vendor, and transportation facilities available will all affect the kinds of dating provisions provided and the negotiation that surrounds these dating provisions.

The most popular dating provision is that known as *ordinary dating*. This means that the credit period is based upon the date of the invoice, which usually coincides with the date the merchandise is shipped. For example, if the terms are 2/10, n30, and the invoice date is April 14, the buyer may deduct 2 per cent from the amount of the invoice if he remits payment

---

[25] This conclusion is reached in the following way: There are 360 days in the business year. The buyer earns 2 per cent for paying 20 days early. There are 18 such 20-day periods in a year, thus $2\% \times 18 = 36$ per cent, the equivalent annual rate of interest.

on or before April 24. If he chooses not to take advantage of the discount, he has until May 14 to pay the full amount.

There are many other often used dating periods. *Advanced dating* is used to induce the buyer to place early orders. *Extra dating* is another way of deferring the date on which credit terms begin to apply. *R.O.G. dating* means receipt of goods and is used to give more reasonable treatment to buyers whose stores are located at great distances from the supplier's shipping points. In this instance, credit terms apply from the date of the receipt of the goods, rather than from the date of the invoice. *E.O.M. dating* (end of the month) provides that credit terms date from the end of the month in which the goods were purchased, rather than from the date of the invoice, and this is another popular dating provision.

It would appear obvious that buyer-negotiative behavior presumes a thorough understanding of both discount and dating provisions and their particular implication to the buyer's merchandise management behavior.

vendor analysis: how many and how to evaluate

The buyer must also decide the most critical question, "How many vendors should I patronize?" The buying process, described earlier as a search, evaluation, selection, and review procedure *for goods acquisition,* could very well be used to describe the buyer's behavior in regard to *vendor selection.* It is generally well known that many retailers (especially the smaller-sized independents) do not pay careful attention to the number of vendors patronized. Larger retailing systems (especially the larger retail chain systems) have begun to recognize the need for limiting the number of vendors with whom they deal, as well as the necessity of objectively evaluating vendor offerings and behavior.

The concentration of purchases among a properly selected and evaluated group of vendors is generally said to have several salutary effects on the part of the purchasing firm. All too often, many buyers have fallaciously reasoned that buying from many suppliers assures a wide variety of styles and models, builds in assurance against missing new offerings, and provides the opportunity to play off one supplier against another.

However, sound reflection raises serious questions about this reasoning. Crooks argues that benefits do not exist, and that patronizing an overly large number of vendors can hurt profits through higher costs, higher markdowns, and lost sales.[26] For these reasons, he argues, every merchant should be concerned about the number of vendors from whom he regularly buys and should consider the adoption of a policy of concentration of purchases with a smaller number of vendors.

Concentration of purchases does not mean that a buyer should not or would not "shop the market." The wise buyer *views* the merchandise of

[26] Edwin W. Crooks, "The Case for Concentration of Purchases," *Journal of Retailing* (Summer 1966), pp. 14–18.

many vendors, to be sure that he does not miss desirable items, particularly in fashion merchandise, but he rarely needs to *buy* from many vendors.[27]

The greatest dangers affecting the merchant who buys from many vendors are that his operating costs will increase because of high per unit order costs so that the actual unit cost of the store's merchandise will be increased, markdowns will increase because of poor assortments, and the store's status will be dissipated for lack of prestige among the better vendors. The question of "how many vendors?" cannot be answered determinately. It is a question that must be researched and analyzed by each buyer in relation to the image and requirements of his store, within the total framework of the merchandise management process.

Vendor Analysis and Evaluation. The number of vendors with whom to deal and the ultimate question of which specific vendors to deal with can only be determined if adequate and objective methods of vendor analysis and evaluation are undertaken by the buyer and his firm. The buying plan and the assortment mix of inventories often must be altered because of a failure on the part of suppliers or vendors to conform to buyer expectations in regard to vendor behavior. Supplier failures often mean that inventories are different from those approved by the buyer or the buying committee. However, because the buyer chooses the supplier, he cannot escape responsibility if the vendor fails to deliver goods of the desired quality and quantity at the time that was stipulated in the buying contract. For this reason, many retail firms and their buyers attempt to measure supplier quality and delivery performance objectively. To accomplish this end, they develop numerous systems and techniques. Two of the more frequently used devices for generating information about vendor services are the (1) Buyer's Fast Selling Book and (2) The Vendor's Diary.

The Buyer's Fast Selling Book is a means of recording the fast-selling items in men's, women's, and children's apparel and accessory departments. However, for that matter it can be used effectively in most departments. It rates not only the supplier, but also each item according to style, color, pattern, and size. It is basically a qualitative kind of rating device.

The Vendor's Diary is a record book containing up-to-the-minute information on vendor performance in regard to quality, delivery schedules, merchandising assistance, and other factors. This record is kept by the buyer and is used by him and his superiors. Periodically, the Vendor's Diary is updated and, on the basis of performance, decisions are made to drop certain vendors.

The greatest difficulty in evaluating vendor behavior is in the selection of the criteria to be used in evaluating vendor performance. A second problem, of course, is concerned with how to actually implement some sort of evaluation procedure. Quite naturally, these procedures will vary considerably from institution to institution. Several companies now use electronic data processing equipment to measure supplier performance.

[27] Ibid., p. 16.

The value of good suppliers is inestimable. They do much more than simply fulfill the conditions of their purchase orders regarding quality, delivery, and terms of sale.[28] Their other contributions (such as merchandising assistance, assistance with market information, and operating problems) cannot always be easily measured. However, it is the totality of the supplier's performance that demands good supplier relations be included as a part of every buyer's activities. At the very least, the buyer is responsible for developing some program or set of procedures by which supplier contributions to the buying and store program are periodically summarized and evaluated.

Central Buying and Resident Buying Offices.   In many kinds of retailing systems (the multiunit chains in such lines as women's, men's, and children's apparel, automobile accessories, food, and other general merchandise lines), buying is not done by the individual unit managers, nor by buyers assigned to the individual units of the operation. Instead, buying is largely done by buyers located at either central or divisional headquarters. This transfer of authority over the buying function from the local to the central level is done for the purpose of achieving certain buying economies, which have essentially two dimensions. On the one hand, any retailing system wishes to develop buying skill, that is, the ability and capacity to know the market—what is available, from whom, and with what array of services, to know a great deal about product and fashion developments, to know delivery possibilities, and to know all the other factors that allow a firm to fulfill its buying function or prevent it from doing so. The other side of the buying economy is referred to as buying power, or the ability of a retail firm or system to bargain and negotiate from a position of size and strength. This is a kind of countervailing power that permits the retail system to bargain against concentrations of economic power within a large manufacturer-supplier complex. A well-known political and economic axiom is "In size there is strength." A vendor is likely to provide more favorable treatment to a buyer who represents ten retail units than he would to a buyer for one unit whose requirements were only one tenth of those of the greater unit buyer.

One of the most dramatic and discernible trends in retailing today is the effort of many retail management systems to centralize many of their buying functions. Both the increased size of the retail unit and the increased size of the manufacturer-supplier are forces that augur for this continued movement.

In order that central buyer activities do not completely emasculate the authority of the buyer or store manager, many of the larger medium price, mass merchandising systems, such as Sears, Roebuck and Co., Montgomery Ward, and the J. C. Penney Company, allow their store managers (or the department heads, in particular lines) to make some decisions regarding the buying activities. Central buyers are thus charged with the responsibility of screening manufacturer and other supplier offerings, and supply-

[28] See Marshall G. Edwards, "Supplier Management Evaluation," *Journal of Purchasing,* Vol. 3, No. 1 (February 1967), pp. 28–41.

ing a list of acceptable items to local store and department managers. These people at the local level can then select the items that they deem most appropriate, in light of local market conditions and demand. This procedure really amounts to more of a requisitioning process than an actual buying process. However, it does provide some form of buying training to those people on the local level, and (more important, perhaps) it helps to defray the frustration that sometimes arises in chain unit operations when local managers are charged with the responsibility of selling merchandise that they had no participation in buying.

Resident Buying Offices.   Both local and central buyers have need of great amounts of information, both in relation to fashion and staple merchandise. The number of new products, the myriad number of suppliers, and the criss-crossing trends that are so much a part of the retail store buyer's operation are often too much for a single buyer or store system to contend with successfully. Sometimes, it is necessary to seek highly specialized expertise in regard to particular buying problems or special merchandise needs. This specialization is available in the form of *resident buying offices,* which perform many functions for their clients. Essentially, however, the resident buying office sells skill. It functions much like a merchandise manager or a merchandising consultant, usually at a relatively modest fee. Resident buying offices have intimate market contacts, daily market trips, and generate a nearly continuous flow of market information. For these reasons, the resident buyer is in a most favorable position to help individual store buyers achieve better stock assortments, higher turnover, and usually improved departmental profitability. Perhaps the key role of the resident buyer for many stores is the role he plays in coordinating the store's fashion merchandising effort—although his role in facilitating the purchase of more staple lines should not be overlooked, either.

There are several varieties of resident buying offices. Figure 12-6 is one convenient way to depict these various classifications.

The independent resident buying office is an independent or autonomous

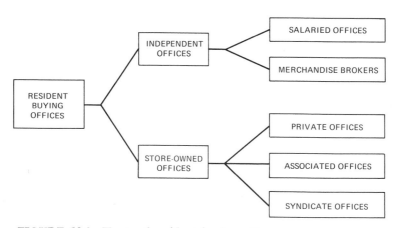

FIGURE 12-6   Types of resident buying offices.

operation, separate and apart from the clients whom they service. These are private companies that provide merchandising services to other independent companies. The relationship between the *salaried offices* and the clients that they serve is a contractual one, with a minimum fee varying considerably from office to office. However, some salaried resident buying offices offer their services for as low as $100 per month. By and large, fees do range somewhat higher than this, and stores with an annual sales volume of less than $100,000 can seldom afford the services of such a facility. However, the *merchandise broker* is a convenient kind of resident buyer for the small store because he receives his payment, usually a commission ranging between two and four per cent, from the seller or vendor, rather than from the buyer. This means that any buyer can receive *free* a great deal of buying assistance from the merchandise broker form of resident buying office.

Store-owned offices, as seen in Figure 12-6, take three major forms. The *private offices* are owned outright by a single store. For example, Neiman Marcus of Dallas, Texas owns such an office in New York City, as do several other retail management systems. If the resident buying office is owned by several different ownership interests, or by an ownership group such as Federated Department Stores, it is called an *associated office*. Finally, there is the *syndicated office*, representing the chain store system, or the ownership group situation. In the case of the associated office, buying power and authority are largely concentrated in the individual units or buyers who use the service, but the syndicated office is able to demand that its purchase recommendations be adopted. One example of the syndicated type of resident buying office is the Allied Purchasing Corporation. This office serves 100 or more stores of the Allied Stores Corporation. It maintains buying offices in New York, Chicago, Dallas, and Miami; it also does considerable foreign buying through facilities established in several foreign countries.

The resident buying office performs a range of functions and activities to help solve the buying and assortment mix problems related to the overall merchandise management task of given retail management systems. For example, buying offices

1. Interpret market trends.
2. Shop the market for new items and resources.
3. Look for improved quality and new styles.
4. Train local store buyers via example and precept.
5. Shop with local buyers when they come to market.
6. Follow up on orders and expedite deliveries.
7. Give help in planning promotional events.
8. File orders and requisitions forwarded by local buyers.
9. Give detailed information on style, business, and economic trends.
10. Act as clearing house between local buyers and central market resources and vendors.

This is an impressive array of services, and it strongly suggests that retail store buyers, no matter what their size or the nature of their operations, ought to at least explore the possibility of utilizing a resident buying office to aid them with their buying and assortment mix problems—the range of which, as has been outlined in this chapter, is both wide and complex.

QUESTIONS FOR STUDY, REFLECTION, AND REVIEW

1. Define the terms *depth* and *compatibility* as related to the assortment problems of the retail firm.
2. Why are many firms faced with the product or brand deletion problem? Explain the factors that have increased this problem.
3. How does the deletion problem relate to the profits of the retailer?
4. What is the rationale of the product life cycle?
5. What are the basic assumptions upon which the product life cycle concept is predicated?
6. In relation to the product life cycle concept, how does the style or image of the store influence its buying behavior?
7. Explain what is meant by a fashion item. Differentiate between a style and a fashion.
8. Explain what is meant by the "trickle system." How does it relate to the sociological interpretation of fashion?
9. It has been pointed out that the role of the early adopter in the fashion process is an extremely critical one. In light of this finding, describe the role of the early buyer in the adoption process.
10. What are the basic factors or variables involved in the negotiation process?

13

merchandise management

Within a retail firm, the central and most crucial task of the buyer and merchandise manager is that of merchandise management. This is a far more comprehensive task than simply buying; yet, buying is a critically important part. Merchandise management is concerned with the planning and control procedures related to the task of having a balanced assortment of merchandise to meet expected or anticipated customer demand. Both parts of this definition warrant some elaboration. For example, merchandise management is concerned with *balancing stocks and the assortment mix* (merchandise departments, lines, and items) in relation to expected or *anticipated customer demand*.

It must be repeated and continually reemphasized that store planning in total—including merchandise management—begins with a forecast and assessment of the firm's market opportunity. In the case of merchandise management, it becomes necessary to appraise this market opportunity, to define it in terms of market targets or segments, and then proceed to build an assortment mix with characteristics that parallel those of the market opportunity.

The explicit assumption upon which merchandise management activities are predicated is that specific and detailed procedures for *planning* and *controlling* inventory assortments will be established and that these devices will enable the buyer, store manager, or merchandise manager to routinize much of the behavior related to these activities. The store image, profits, and other measures of the retailer's general well-being will be affected by the finesse with which merchandise management activities are carried on. Our concern in this chapter will center around several of the more conventional approaches to merchandise management, i.e., the merchandise budget, dollar and unit control devices, and stockturn. In Chapter 14, our emphasis will be focused on some newer approaches to merchandise planning and control, i.e., inventory models, capital budgeting, and other approaches.

the merchandise budget

Good managerial results seldom occur solely by accident. The essence of management is that the manager designs a system of action or a framework for behavior and then proceeds to bring about the kind of desired behavior within that framework that will assure him of the desired results. This is certainly the case, as it pertains to merchandise management—the planning and controlling of inventories in accordance with predetermined objectives. These predetermined objectives relate to sales, profits, turnover figures, and return on investment. In order to bring about these desired objectives, the retail decision maker (whether he be an owner/manager in a small or medium-sized store or a buyer or merchandise manager in a large, complex retail firm) must plan and control sales efforts, markdowns, shortages, purchases, initial markups, and gross margins. An often used device to attain these ends is a planning and control procedure called the *merchandise budget*. The merchandise budget details both expected sales for a given period and then on a monthly or even weekly basis, details the amount of stock planned for the beginning of each of these periods, and the planned amount of reductions. From this information, the decision maker can determine the amount of purchases that must be made in order that assortments and stocks are adequately balanced in relation to anticipated sales. The merchandise budget is both a planning and control device. It enables the retailer to make better merchandising decisions and at the same time provides a method for more completely integrating the effects of merchandising decisions within the overall framework for financial planning and control in the retail system. Therefore, the merchandise budget is not solely a device to aid in making merchandising decisions, but it is an important financial planning and control device as well. It indicates the amount of funds necessary to support a given merchandising program for a period, or how much money will be required to acquire and carry an inventory that is balanced in relation to expected customer demand. On the other hand, the merchandise budget reveals important sources of cash flow. It provides retail decision makers in many areas and at several different levels throughout the organization with a fairly definite idea about the financial income and outgo that can be expected during the indicated period. This information is very valuable because it enables the finance and control divisions of the store to relate many of their financial decisions to the appropriate phases of the merchandise budget, to gauge more effectively the working capital requirements, and to coordinate the overall store or system's behavior in the interests of better profit margins and total expense and capital management.

The Nature of a Budget

In numerical terms, most frequently financial accounts, a budget expresses the anticipated results of operations in some future period.[1] Budgets are more than mere predictions. As a matter of fact, a budget is a device for reflecting actual plans for each of the activities covered; and once prepared, it constitutes a goal toward which efforts and energies are directed. Furthermore, it inherently provides the essential bases upon which control is ultimately established. Therefore, budgets are planning devices in that they are used as an aid for deciding in advance what needs to be done; and second, budgets are control devices upon which standards of performance are established, comparisons between actual and planned performance are made, and corrective action is taken. One writer has further characterized the budget by stating, "The budget . . . is the vehicle for communicating the plans of the organization to each level of the organization in sufficient detail to guide activities and serve as a frame of reference for decisions and for evaluation of effort."[2] The budget's role as so important a communicative and reporting device is often overlooked. In many different ways, budgets have been viewed as devices to *limit* the expenditures of funds to approved functions; to *restrain* subordinates by requiring approval of superiors for expenditures; to *impose clerical control* by which spending was compared with available balances; to *impose communicative control* through circulation of interim reports to department heads; and, finally, to provide *benchmark* numbers that allow flexibility within a range of contemplated activity.[3] The merchandise budget is designed to be used for all these purposes. However, the fundamental purpose of the budget as it relates to an inventory planning and control device is to fix responsibility for performance in accordance with plans.

As a means of scheduling or programming activities, there are two major dimensions to the planning aspects of a budget. First of all, it must outline and detail *what activities* are being planned. Second, but very important, it must outline and detail *when* these activities are supposed to occur, and in what sequence. This aspect of the budget is concerned with timing those activities that are a critical part of all administrative planning, and which involve establishing time goals in the form of deadlines. A detailed budget is like a merchandise budget in that it requires a whole series of deadlines. Of necessity, these deadlines must be related to each other so that preliminary steps are completed before succeeding steps must start. Of course, all the steps must be integrated with the major date or relevant time period as it applies to the budget situation.

Finally, it must be pointed out that a budget as a plan must make some provision for a margin of error. Budgets are costly because they require

[1] For more about budgeting, see Jerry D. Dermer, "Budgetary Motivation of Retail Store Managers and Buyers," *Journal of Retailing*, Vol. 50, No. 3 (Fall 1974), pp. 23–33.

[2] I am indebted to my colleague, Professor John Fertakis, for this idea. A more comprehensive statement by him on the budget problem has been outlined in an unpublished paper entitled, "The Positive Side of Budgetary Controls."

[3] Selwyn Becker and David Green, Jr., "Budgeting and Employee Behavior," *Journal of Business* (October 1962), pp. 392–402.

time and energy in their preparation and implementation. Naturally, the payoff of a good budget is that it leads to better decision making. If it does not, then the budget ought to be abandoned in favor of some other device or the budgeting procedure should be re-evaluated and improved.

Components of a Merchandise Budget

No merchant would argue the fact that his basic goal is to have what customers want, when they want it, and in the proper assortments, which means minimum stock outs and minimum inventories. The inventory is the most important nonhuman resource found in any retail management system, and as such its proper management becomes imperative in terms of the general well-being of the system. A good merchandise budget must provide a realistic guide to merchandising behavior in terms of a comprehensible and meaningful format, with sufficient flexibility in order that unanticipated contingencies can be accommodated to merchandise planning, and finally, it must have the cooperation of all those individuals within the system whose behavior it constrains or affects. The budget's success will vary almost directly with the degree to which all those affected by the budget were allowed to participate in its formulation and implementation. Budgets that are developed by top management and then handed down by way of management edicts or decrees are seldom very effective in terms of stimulating responsible and purposive behavior.

The major components of a merchandise budget (that is, the basic items that are to be planned and controlled) are (1) sales, (2) stocks, (3) reductions, (4) purchases, and (5) markup. Of course, many other items can be included in more sophisticated merchandise budgets. For example, the budget may treat such factors as inventory shortages, alteration costs, cash discounts, and other forms of nonoperating revenues. Some budgets also attempt to treat variables below the level of gross margins or maintained markup, by attempting to plan and control selling and nonselling expenses. Such a budget would then be related to total revenue and expense planning.

The Merchandise Budgeting Procedure—
A Case Study

To facilitate the reader's understanding of the merchandise budgeting procedure, an illustrative case study approach dealing with the merchandise budget, its development, components, and other features will be outlined in considerable detail in this section. Quite naturally, this case study cannot possibly detail all the features of every merchandise budget. Detail, as well as procedure, methodology, and format will vary from retail system to system; however, the general principles employed in merchandise budgeting are generally quite similar. One such general format for a merchandise budget is shown in Figure 13-1.

The merchandise budget is the end result of much planning, coordinated among the merchandise manager, the controller, and the individual store buyers. A merchandise budget for an individual department is usually the

MERCHANDISE BUDGET

PERIOD FROM _____ Aug. 1, 19 _____ TO _____ Jan. 31, 19 _____   DEPT. NO. _____ 11 _____

KIND OF GOODS _____ Silks, Velvets, and Synthetics _____

	AUG.	SEPT.	OCT.	NOV.	DEC.	JAN.	CURRENT SIX MONTHS TOTAL
SALES							
2 YEARS AGO							
1 YEAR AGO							
PLANNED							
ADJUSTED PLAN							
ACTUAL SALES							
TO DATE LAST YEAR							
TO DATE PLANNED							
TO DATE ADJUSTED PLAN							
TO DATE ACTUAL SALES							
RETAIL STOCK E.O.M.							
LAST YEAR							
PLANNED							
ADJUSTED PLAN							
ADJUSTED PLAN							
ACTUAL STOCK							
OVER OR UNDER PLAN							
STOCK SALES RATIO							
LAST YEAR							
PLANNED							
ACTUAL							
RETAIL PURCHASES							
LAST YEAR							
LAST YEAR % TO TOTAL							
PLANNED % TO TOTAL							
PLANNED							
ADJUSTED PLAN							
ADJUSTED PLAN							
ACTUAL RETAIL PURCHASES MO.							
– – – – – – – TO DATE							
COST PURCHASES							
LAST YEAR							
PLANNED COST INV. REQ.							
ADJUSTED PLAN							
ADJUSTED PLAN							
ACTUAL COST PURCHASES MO.							
– – – – – – TO DATE							
** OPEN TO BUY							
MARKUPS							
LAST YEAR % TO DATE							
PLANNED % TO DATE							
ACTUAL % TO DATE							
MARKDOWNS							
PLANNED MONTH							
ACTUAL MONTH							
LAST YEAR % OF SALES MO.							
PLANNED % OF SALES MO.							
ACTUAL M.D. % OF SALES MO.							
ACTUAL M.D. % OF SALES TO DATE							
GROSS MDSE. MARGIN							
LAST YEAR TO DATE %							
PLANNED % TO DATE							
ACTUAL GROSS MARGIN % TO DATE							

** UNFILLED ORDERS AND MERCHANDISE INVOICES NOT INCLUDED IN YOUR LAST MONTHS BOOK INVENTORY
MUST BE DEDUCTED FROM THE AMOUNT "OPEN TO BUY" OR ADDED TO THE AMOUNT "OVER BOUGHT"

FIGURE 13-1   A sample merchandise budget format.

result of build-up or composite planning undertaken for each of the individual merchandise classifications that make up that particular department.

Wilston's Men's Shoppe.   Wilston's Men's Shoppe is a medium-priced store that carries a broad assortment of men's and boys' merchandise. As a matter of fact, its three principal merchandise classifications are men's clothing, men's furnishings and accessories, and boys' wear. Wilston's is located in a community that has a higher per family income among its local residents than the per family income on a national average basis. The community's principal industries are education—Broadmore University, with a current enrollment of about 12,000 students—and light, research-oriented, manufacturing. Wilston's attempts to appeal basically to the university student trade, the high school trade for young teenage males, and to the community's young businessmen.

Sales last year were in excess of $700,000 and are estimated for the succeeding year at $800,000 because of a large increase in forecasted enrollments at B.U., and a new science-based industry that will employ 1,000 highly skilled and trained research workers and operatives.

On the basis of a market research study utilizing sales tax expenditure figures, Wilston's discovered that they have an 80 per cent competitive pressure against them. That is, Wilston's accounts for 20 per cent of the total sales of men's and boys' clothing within their competitive trading area. Relatively speaking, this is a rather mild competitive pressure. Research has shown that competitive pressure for stores of this size often exceeds 90 to 95 per cent.[4] An 80 per cent competitive pressure means that Wilston's will receive about $.20 of each dollar spent for men's and boys' clothing within their trading area.

Wilston's plans its merchandise budget and its merchandise calendar in two periods:[5] February 1 through July 31, and August 1 through January 31. These termination dates mean that inventories are then usually at their lowest point and, consequently, the firm's cash position is at its highest. Sales for the first six months have historically averaged about 40 per cent of the year's total sales because of (1) the summer vacation period, when large numbers of students are not on campus; (2) the large number of adult residents and workers who are away during the summer for vacations; and (3) the lower unit price of summer merchandise, opposed to the higher unit price of fall and winter lines. For merchandise budgeting purposes, three departments are considered. These are men's clothing, men's furnishings and accessories, and boys' wear. Historically, sales have been divided among these three merchandising classifications in the following proportions: 40 per cent, men's clothing; 40 per cent furnishings and accessories; and 20 per cent, boys' clothing. It is assumed that these relationships will prevail for the first six-month period of Wilston's merchandise budget.

Sales. Wilston's sales have been estimated for the year at $800,000 and for the first six-month period at $320,000 ($800,000 × 40%). The forecasted

---

[4] For more on the idea of competitive pressure, see Jerold S. Meyer, "Dollar and Unit Merchandise Planning and Budgeting," The Merchandising Division, National Retail Merchants Association, 1960, p. 4. Competitive pressure would be the reciprocal of market share, which is discussed in Chap. 4. For example, a 20 per cent market share would mean an 80 per cent competitive pressure. Conversely, a 97 per cent competitive pressure would imply a 3 per cent market share.

[5] The merchandise budget and the merchandise calendar are two ways of looking at the same thing. The budget is a schedule or plan in terms of merchandise units expressed in dollars. The merchandise calendar is a schedule of specific events and activities related to merchandising performance for particular periods of time.

sales figure is the key to an effective merchandise budget. If sales are grossly misjudged, then the entire merchandise budget will suffer ill effects. It should be remembered that sales forecasting is an integral part of determining the overall market opportunity, and unless this opportunity is correctly perceived and analyzed, all management efforts to guide and coordinate the efforts of the system are likely to be misdirected.

Once total sales are forecasted for the period, the figure must then be broken down into merchandise classifications by months, weeks, or even sometimes by days. Usually the selling period is analyzed carefully in terms of special selling occasions, such as Christmas, Easter, or other important holidays or seasonal events. Forecasts of sales by merchandise classifications and time periods must incorporate such factors as trends in sales by merchandise classifications, general business conditions, changes in the general price level, changes in competitive conditions, and any changes or alterations in planned levels of merchandising support for particular departments. Quite often, sales are broken down by merchandise classifications and by months on the basis of historical operating results. Such a breakdown is shown in Table 13-1.

Only a brief explanation of Table 13-1 is required. Wilston's has discovered from analyzing previous sales that the above relationships are indicative, and therefore suitable for planning purposes relating to breakdowns of sales by merchandise classifications and by months. In other words, historical analysis shows that of total period sales, 40 per cent will be contributed by men's clothing sales, 40 per cent by furnishings and accessory sales, and 20 per cent by boys' wear. Furthermore, an analysis of historical records shows that of total store sales 14 per cent are obtained in February, 16 per cent in March, 17 per cent in April, and so forth.

Therefore, to plan sales by merchandise classifications and by months, it is necessary only to multiply the appropriate sales figure (i.e., total store, $320,000, men's clothing, $128,000, men's furnishings and accessories, $128,000, or boys' wear, $64,000) by the appropriate percentage normally attained during the period. Table 13-2 shows the results of such an exercise. So that no confusion is likely to persist as to where the data in Table 13-2

TABLE 13-1 Wilston's Men's Shoppe: Monthly Percentage Goals

	STORE TOTAL	MEN'S CLOTHING	MEN'S FURNISH-INGS AND ACCESSORIES	BOYS' WEAR
SALES	$320,000	$128,000	$128,000	$64,000
February	14.0	10.0	14.0	16.0
March	16.0	15.0	16.0	17.0
April	17.0	21.0	20.0	20.0
May	20.0	19.0	17.5	17.5
June	18.0	19.0	16.5	16.5
July	15.0	16.0	16.0	13.0

TABLE 13-2 Wilston's Men's Shoppe: Monthly Sales Forecast by Merchandise Classifications

MONTH	STORE TOTAL	MEN'S CLOTHING	MEN'S FURNISHINGS AND ACCESSORIES	BOYS' WEAR
February	$44,800[a]	$12,800	$17,920	$10,240
March	51,200	19,200	20,480	10,880
April	54,400	26,880	25,600	12,800
May	64,000	24,320	22,400	11,200
June	57,600	24,320	21,120	10,560
July	48,000	20,480	20,480	8,320

[a] All figures throughout the discussion have been rounded to the nearest even dollar.

comes from, two cells of this table have been outlined with a heavy black line. For example, the figure $44,800, in the first cell of the first row and column of Table 13-2, was obtained by multiplying $320,000 (total estimated store sales for the first six-month period) by 14 per cent, the estimated per cent of total store sales for February. A similar procedure was used to find the value entered in the last cell in the last row and column, i.e., $8,320, the estimated sales figure for boys' wear for the month of July.

The reader is cautioned that such a procedure must never become perfunctory, nor should historical percentages be used if present conditions appear to suggest a breakdown in known historical relationships. However, historical relationships can be used to advantage if research suggests that they are both valid and stable.

Retail Deductions. There are two basic kinds of retail deductions other than sales. These are markdowns and shortages. A retail inventory can be viewed as a stock of assets. These assets (inventory) have a value or worth that is determined in terms of retail dollars if the store uses the retail inventory method of accounting,[6] as almost all stores do. The value of the inventory changes as it is increased or decreased. For instance, purchases add to the value of the inventory. As more goods possessing value are added to our stocks, the value of those stocks increases. Conversely, sales tend to reduce the value of our inventory,[7] because as sales are made we are moving out goods, or reducing the stock of this particular asset. Inventory values are decreased as a result of markdowns and shortages as well. Markdowns reduce the value of our inventory in the following way: Assume that we have an inventory evaluated at $1,000 in retail prices. If it is discovered that this inventory will not move, or that competitors have lower prices

[6] The retail inventory method of accounting is discussed at length in Chap. 21.

[7] The reader should be aware, however, that although sales reduce the value of one asset (inventory), they increase the value of other assets, namely, cash or accounts receivable.

than our store and we are thus forced to mark down our inventory by 10 per cent, then it is now worth only $900. We may still have the same number of units in our inventory as previously, but nonetheless, it is worth less money.

Shortages affect the value of our inventory in a somewhat different manner. Again, assume an inventory valued in retail prices at $1,000. If an item worth $100 is lost to a shoplifter, dishonest store employee, or through any form of negligence, our inventory is now worth $900 and the store system has suffered a shrinkage in inventory *value,* as well as in the actual number of units that make up the total inventory.

It is incumbent upon every store manager, buyer, or merchandise manager to plan total deductions from inventory in order that these figures can be incorporated into total merchandise budgeting procedures as they relate to stocks, markups, and purchases.

Markdowns occur for many reasons. Buyer enthusiasm for a product may lead him to overbuy. Consumer taste and reaction to new products can never be anticipated with 100 per cent accuracy. Buying mistakes thus have two basic aspects: (1) buying the wrong goods and (2) buying in too large quantities. These conditions mean that markdowns must be taken and it is usually best that they be planned or anticipated in the total merchandise budget. Planning markdowns leads to developing a markdown sensitivity on the part of buyers and managers, which may lead to a better understanding of markdowns, i.e., why they occur and how they might be eliminated. Second, planning markdowns may lead to the practice of taking markdowns early, which may lead in turn to fewer markdowns and an overall faster moving stock of goods.

Markdowns are usually expressed as a percentage of retail sales. For example, if Wilston's has a $5.00 shirt that it marks down to $4.00 and then sells, the markdown is $1.00 or 25 per cent, determined as follows:

$5.00 original retail
4.00 actual retail
$1.00 the amount of the reduction

$$\frac{\$ \text{ markdown}}{\$ \text{ actual selling price}} = \frac{\$1.00}{\$4.00} = 25\%$$

However, the usual case is that markdowns must be planned not on the original retail price, but on the actual retail price at which the goods will finally be sold. How can the decision maker determine how much of a markdown must be taken on the original retail price in order to arrive at a given markdown in terms of actual net sales? Again, assume that a Wilston's buyer had a shirt with an original retail price of $5.00. He wishes to take a markdown on that shirt which will amount to 10 per cent of the sales price. Therefore,

If 100% = the sales price, and the
markdown = 10% of the sales price, then
100% + 10% = 110%, or the original retail price

In terms of the original retail price of the shirt, the markdown becomes

$$\frac{10\%}{110\%} \text{ or } 9.09\%$$

By substituting the actual figures into this formula, we find that the result is

$$9.09\% \times \$5.00 = \$0.4545 \text{ markdown}$$
$$\$5.00 - \$0.4545 = \$4.55 \text{ sales price}$$

Shortages have two basic causes: dishonesty and employee or system failures. Laxity on the part of store employees results in many shortages. Untold amounts of merchandise are thrown away each year as a part of workroom trash deposits. By and large, however, most of the shortages result from thievery on the part of either employees or customers.[8] The tendency toward self-service merchandising, larger store units, and open fixtures and displays has generally aggravated the shortage problem in retail stores. These shortages take a drastic toll in terms of the profitability of the retail store system. For example, assume that a store has merchandise shortages of $10,000 a year. That is, in terms of retail values, the firm has lost $10,000. If the firm has profits as a per cent of sales of 5 per cent, then the stolen goods have caused a loss of $500 in the form of foregone profits, alone. But the loss is really much greater. If the store has a gross margin of 40 per cent, then $6,000 of the $10,000 shortage represents a direct out-of-pocket loss to the firm. With profits as a per cent of sales at 5 per cent, the firm will have to increase sales by an additional $120,000 in order to make up the loss of $6,000 in stolen merchandise.[9]

To return to our example, Wilston's plans markdowns and shortages as a part of its total merchandising budgeting procedure. Table 13-3 shows Wilston's markdowns and shortages for the six-month budget period. These figures assume an 8 per cent markdown figure and a 2 per cent shortage figure, which experience has shown is about the same as the average figure for stores of a similar size and line of trade.

The sales figures are taken from Table 13-2 and the figures in the remaining cells are found by multiplying the sales figure by the percentage for markdowns or shortages. Column 5 shows total retail deductions, and Column 6 is simply a running (cumulative) total figure. Figures for markdowns and shortages are not shown here by merchandise classification. However, most stores would make this additional determination.

---

[8] Shortages resulting from both employee and customer dishonesty is a burdensome, profit-draining problem of retail merchandisers. Not only must buyers take shortages into consideration when planning their merchandise budget requirements, but many other aspects of retailing management such as layout, store design, electronic monitoring systems, and other efforts are geared to the reduction of these losses. For more on this problem, see Amin El-Derghami, "Shoplifting Among Students," *Journal of Retailing*, Vol. 50, No. 3 (Fall 1974), pp. 33–43. Also in this same issue, "Employee Views on Theft in Retailing," by Ronald L. Tatham, pp. 49–56.

[9] $6,000, cost value of the goods and the amount of the out-of-pocket loss $\div 5\%$, the store's profit margin $= \$120,000$.

TABLE 13-3   Wilston's Men's Shoppe Markdown and Reduction Planning

MONTH	SALES	8% MARK-DOWNS	2% SHORTAGES	TOTAL RETAIL DEDUCTIONS FOR MONTH	TOTAL RETAIL DEDUCTIONS SEASON TO DATE
February	$ 44,800	$ 3,584	$ 896	$ 4,480	—
March	51,200	4,096	1,024	5,120	$ 9,600
April	54,400	4,352	1,088	5,440	15,040
May	64,000	5,120	1,280	6,400	21,440
June	57,600	4,608	1,152	5,760	27,200
July	48,000	3,840	960	4,800	32,000
Total	$320,000	$25,600	$6,400	$32,000	

Planned Stocks.   The next critical element in the merchandise budget is planning stocks with the objective of having a balanced assortment of goods in order to meet expected or anticipated customer demand. Several alternative ways of determining stock needs are available. Each of these alternatives is briefly described and two of the techniques are generally illustrated. The formal ways of deciding on stock levels are

1. *Stock-Sales Ratio Method.* A stock-sales ratio is a ratio between the stock on hand at a particular time during the period and the sales for the period. In formula form:

$$\text{Stock-sales ratio} = \frac{\text{Retail stock for a given period}}{\text{Sales for the period}}$$

Stock-sales ratios are usually beginning of the month stocks and are designated B.O.M. However, end of the month stocks can be used and, if so, they are designated as E.O.M. stocks.
2. *Weeks' Supply Method.* With this method, stock is planned in terms of a predetermined number of weeks' supply, based upon some stock turnover goal. For instance, if 3 stock turns are planned during a six-month or 27-week selling season, 27 would be divided by 3, which shows that a 9-week supply must be carried. The sales for the upcoming 9 weeks are then forecasted to determine the amount of stock needed at the beginning of the period.
3. *The Percentage Deviation Method.* In formula form:

$$\text{B.O.M. stock} = \text{Average stock} \times \tfrac{1}{2}\left(1 + \frac{\text{Sales for the month}}{\text{Average monthly sales}}\right)$$

This method is not really so formidable. It means simply that stock fluctuations from the average stock are 50 per cent of the sales fluctuations from the average monthly sales. If sales in February are 50 per cent higher than the average monthly sales for the year or selling period, the stock on February 1 is established at a point 25 per cent higher than the average retail stock for the year.

4. *Basic Stock Method.* This method is suitable for stores or merchandise classifications that have a stock turn of six times a year or less. B.O.M. stock is determined by adding a basic stock figure to the planned sales for the month. In formula form:

B.O.M. stock at retail = Sales for the month + (Average stock at retail — Average monthly sales)

Wilston's determines its B.O.M. stocks by using the stock-sales ratio method. By analyzing its own past stock-sales ratios and comparing them with the stock-sales ratios of retailers in similar lines of trade and similar size,[10] Wilston's has determined its stock-sales ratios used for planning stocks as illustrated in Table 13-4.

It is important that the reader understand that these stock-sales ratios have been determined by analyzing previous relationships between the stock on hand at the beginning of a period in terms of retail prices, and the sales for that period. From these relationships and the resultant stock-sales ratios, Wilston's has arrived at the planned B.O.M. stocks for each of the months of its current budget period.

Planned B.O.M. stocks, as shown in Table 13-5, are found by multiplying the appropriate stock-sales ratio by projected sales for the particular month. For example, the planned B.O.M. stock of $183,680 , found in the first cell of the first row and column of Table 13-5, was determined by multiply-

TABLE 13-4 Wilston's Men's Shoppe Planned B.O.M. Stock-Sales Ratios

MONTH	STORE TOTAL	MEN'S CLOTHING	MEN'S FURNISH-INGS AND ACCESSORIES	BOYS' WEAR
February	4.1	5.2	3.8	4.0
March	4.0	3.9	4.2	3.7
April	3.4	3.5	3.5	3.1
May	3.6	3.7	3.6	3.5
June	3.6	3.5	3.7	3.5
July	3.9	3.8	3.9	4.0

[10] Stock-sales ratios for selected departments by store size are provided regularly in such sources as *Departmental Merchandising and Operating Results of Department and Specialty Stores*, National Retail Merchants Association, New York.

TABLE 13-5   Wilston's Men's Shoppe
Planned B.O.M. Stocks (by merchandise classification)

MONTH	STORE TOTAL	MEN'S CLOTHING	MEN'S FURNISH-INGS AND ACCESSORIES	BOYS' WEAR
February	$183,680	$66,560	$68,096	$40,960
March	204,800	74,880	86,016	40,256
April	184,960	94,080	89,600	39,680
May	230,400	89,984	80,640	39,200
June	207,360	85,120	78,144	36,960
July	187,200	77,824	79,872	33,280

ing total store sales for February ($44,800) by the February total store stock-sales ratio of 4.1, as shown in Table 13-4.

The *basic stock method* of planning B.O.M. stocks is another widely used method. Although it is not used by Wilston's, an illustration of its possible use follows:

1. Average monthly sales are computed by dividing the total sales of the budget period by the number of months in this period.

$$\$320,000 \text{ budget period sales} \div 6 = \$53,333$$

2. The average value of the stock is found by dividing period sales by the appropriate stock turn rate. For example, period sales = $320,000, and the stock turn rate = 3 times annually. However, for our purposes, the stock turn rate is 40 per cent of 3, or 1.2, which is the relevant six-month turnover figure, since only 40 per cent of sales are really attributable to the six-month budget period in question. Working from the basic formula,

$$\text{Stock turnover} = \frac{\text{Retail sales}}{\text{Average inventory at retail}}$$

$$1.2 = \frac{\$320,000}{x} \qquad \begin{array}{l}(x = \text{average inventory at retail or} \\ \text{average value of stock})\end{array}$$

$$1.2x = \$320,000$$

$$x = \$266,666 \text{ (average inventory at retail)}$$

3. Subtracting average monthly sales ($53,333) from average inventory at retail, or average value of stock ($266,666) = $213,333, which is the *basic stock* figure.

4. B.O.M. stock is computed by adding the basic stock to the sales

planned for the month. For example, the B.O.M. stocks for Wilston's are found by adding each month's sales to the basic stock of $213,333. The results are shown in Table 13-6.

It should be pointed out that the value of the B.O.M. stocks calculated under the basic stock method will vary with the stock turn rate used in the calculations. It will also be observed that B.O.M. stocks calculated via the basic stock method are considerably higher than the B.O.M. stocks planned via the stock-sales ratio method. This is the usual case for merchandise classifications of this type.

Further, it must be emphasized that no single method should be adopted and employed automatically. Instead, each method should be judiciously and critically evaluated and tested in terms of the results it produces for each specific situation. The results, of course, relate to customer satisfaction with stock levels, turnover rates, the absence of stockouts, and satisfactory profit levels.

Planning Purchases. One of the principal objectives of merchandise budgeting is to provide a guide, or aid to decision making, for the buyer or store manager in his purchase planning. Knowing *what to buy* has already been pinpointed as one of the critical buying problems.[11] However, knowing *how much to buy* is nearly as critical. Although it is true that buying the right quantity of the wrong merchandise will earn buyers no accolades, it is equally true that buying the wrong quantities of the right merchandise is nearly as serious a problem. Purchase quantities are an important facet of buyer behavior and merchandise management. Determining the right quantity to purchase becomes a somewhat easier task *if* the previous steps in the merchandise budgeting procedure have been undertaken carefully. As a matter of fact, determining the amount to purchase is a matter of relatively simple calculations based upon the following known relationships:

TABLE 13-6 Wilston's Men's Shoppe
Planned B.O.M. Stock (using the basic stock method)

MONTH	BASIC STOCK	+	SALES FOR THE MONTH	=	B.O.M. STOCK
February	$213,333		$44,800		$258,133
March	213,333		51,200		264,533
April	213,333		54,400		267,733
May	213,333		64,000		277,333
June	213,333		57,600		270,933
July	213,333		48,000		261,333

[11] For a general discussion of the critical role of buying, see Philip Kotler and Sidney J. Levy, "Buying Is Marketing Too!" *Journal of Marketing*, Vol. 37 (January 1973), pp. 54–59.

Planned purchases = Planned stock at end of a period + Planned sales + Planned reductions — Stock at the beginning of a period

Once again using data from our case illustration, Wilston's, these relationships can be shown quite easily. For example, consider determining planned purchases for Wilston's for March.

Planned stock at end of a period (B.O.M. stock for April) $\boxed{\$267,733}$ + Planned sales for March $\boxed{\$51,200}$ + Planned reductions $\boxed{\$5,120}$ — Stock at beginning of period (B.O.M. stock for March) $\boxed{\$264,533}$ = Planned purchases for March $\boxed{\$59,520}$

Wilston's could now proceed to determine their planned purchase requirements for each of the months and for each of their merchandise classifications, on the basis of these relationships. It should be emphasized that the $59,520 planned purchases figure for March is stated in terms of retail selling prices. Should the buyer wish to convert this to a cost or wholesale basis, he would only have to multiply this figure by the cost complement of the markup percentage.

The O.T.B. or *open-to-buy* concept, is another useful device, helpful to buyers and store managers in planning merchandise requirements and other aspects of the merchandise management task. Open-to-buy refers to the amount of merchandise that the buyer may order for delivery during the remaining part of any merchandising period. This device aids the buyer-decision maker to determine how much merchandise he is open to buy at any particular time during the purchase period, whether it be the beginning, middle, or very near the end of the month. At the beginning of a period, the open-to-buy is the difference by which planned purchases exceed the outstanding orders. When the buyer is computing the open-to-buy at a particular time during a period, he subtracts from the planned purchases for the period the total of all merchandise received thus far during the period and the sum of all merchandise that has been ordered for delivery before the end of the period. Once again using data from the Wilston's illustrative case, the open-to-buy for March is determined. This illustration is based upon these factors:

March	
Actual stock, March 1	$204,800
Planned sales for the month	51,200
Planned retail deductions, markdowns, and shortages	5,120
Planned stock, March 31	184,960
Planned markup	40%

Sales are brisk during the first half of March, net sales were $29,700; markdowns and shortages $2,250; and receipts of goods $20,000. On March 15, goods on order for March delivery amount to $15,000 at current retail prices. The amount that Wilston's is open-to-buy may be calculated in the following manner:

STOCK REQUIREMENTS		CURRENTLY AVAILABLE	
Planned stock, March 31	$184,960	Actual stock, March 1	$204,800
Planned sales for remainder of		Plus receipt of goods	20,000
month $51,200 — $29,700	21,500	Total stock handled	$224,800
Planned markdown and		Markdowns and shortages	
shortages for remainder of		to date	$ 2,250
month $5,120 — $2,250	2,870	Sales to date	29,700
		Total deductions	$ 31,950
		Stock on hand at present	
		= Total stock handled	$224,800
		— Total deductions	31,950
			$192,850
		Goods on order for March	+
		delivery	15,000
Totals	$209,330		$207,850

Stock requirements $\boxed{\$209,330}$ — Stock available $\boxed{\$207,850}$ = the open-to-buy at retail $\boxed{\$1,480}$. The open-to-buy at cost is $1,480 \times$ 0.60 (the cost complement of the markup per cent) = $\boxed{\$888}$

It would appear that Wilston's buyers have nearly committed their purchasing budget for the month. However, there remain some funds with which to buy fill-ins of fast-moving stocks, should such a need arise, or to purchase a very unusual buy should one present itself. It must be pointedly emphasized that the O.T.B. is only an aid to decision making, and its use should not supplant buyer judgment. It would be ridiculous to forego a sales opportunity for lack of sufficient merchandise assortments or depth of assortments, simply because the O.T.B. was fully committed for a period. In most stores the merchandise manager usually attempts to have some reserve in order that no real buying opportunity or bargain purchase will have to be foregone because of a lack of sufficient funds.

Planning Markup Requirements. Merchandise budgeting and expense planning and control necessitate planning initial markup requirements. It must be realized that initial markup must ultimately cover all expenses or costs, plus profits. Several different kinds of markup are normally involved in markup planning requirements. Initial markup is of primary importance in markup planning, however, and can be illustrated as follows:

$$\text{Initial markup } \% = \frac{\text{Maintained markup} + \text{Reductions}}{\text{Sales} + \text{Reductions}}$$

Maintained markup = Gross margin − Cash discounts earned + Alteration costs

Gross margin = Maintained markup + Cash discounts earned − Alteration costs

To facilitate an understanding of the markup planning process, consider once again the hypothetical data from Wilston's case study. Assume that operating expenses for the store for the six-month planning period will average 30 per cent of planned sales. Markdowns have already been planned at 8 per cent and merchandise shortages at 2 per cent. The planned sales for the period are $320,000. If a net profit of 6 per cent for the period is desired, what markup, in dollars and in percentage, should be planned for the period?

Expenses	30% of $320,000 =	$ 96,000
Markdowns	8% of $320,000 =	25,600
Shortages	2% of $320,000 =	6,400
Profit	6% of $320,000 =	19,200
		$147,200

The dollar markup required is therefore $147,200 for the six-month period. The task now is to relate this dollar markup figure to the original price of the retail merchandise. The original retail value of the merchandise equals the retail sales $320,000 + the retail deductions of $32,000, or $352,000. By dividing the dollar markup, $147,200 by the original retail value of the merchandise, $352,000, the initial markup is found to be

$$\frac{\$147,200}{\$352,000} = 41.8 \text{ or } 42\%$$

This method of calculating the initial markup per cent can be determined by using the following formula:

$$\text{Markup \%} = \frac{\text{Expenses} + \text{Profits} + \text{Reductions}}{\text{Sales} + \text{Reductions}}$$

Substituting the percentages, the results are

$$\frac{30\% + 8\% + 2\% + 6\%}{100\% + 8\% + 2\%} = 42\%$$

Markup without question is an exceedingly important concept in retailing and it is important that the term be used correctly. Markup should normally be considered in terms of *initial markup*. Markup in dollars is the difference between original retail value and the cost of the merchandise. The markup percentage is the markup in dollars divided by the original retail value of the merchandise.

Markup formulas often can be confusing, especially if one does not understand or know how the formula was derived, and if one does not understand the relationship among the variables or components of the formula. Another way of looking at the problem just presented in a somewhat less confusing way is presented below. For example, using the same data where

Operating expenses	=	30%
Markdowns	=	8%
Merchandise shortage	=	2%
Net profit	=	6%
And $ sales for period	=	$320,000

determine what markup in dollars and percentage of original retail value should be planned for next year. Table 13-7 can be used in a diagrammatic way to replace the formula approach previously utilized.[12] The values given in the problem are shown in the outlined boxes, such as $\boxed{30\%}$ for operating expenses and $\boxed{8\%}$ for markdowns. Notice that since operating expenses and profit percentages are given, line 5 should be completed first.

Now, remembering that gross margin = expenses plus profits, the cost of merchandise can be calculated (sales − gross margin = cost of merchandise). The value of cost of merchandise, $204,800, can now be transferred to line 1. Original retail value is, of course, planned sales ($320,000) + markdowns ($25,600) + shortages ($6,400), or $352,000. Cost of merchandise subtracted from original retail value equals dollar markup $147,200, and markup as a percentage of original retail value is $147,200/$352,000,

TABLE 13-7   Diagrammatic Presentation of Markup-Related Variables

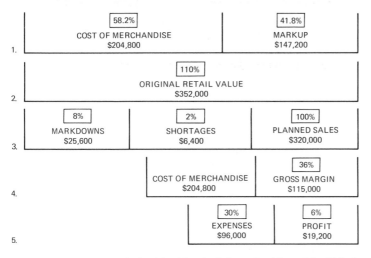

[12] This method was devised by Marvin Jolson. See his article, "Markup Calculations— Still a Fuzzy Area?" *Journal of Retailing,* Vol. 49, No. 3 (Fall 1973), pp. 77–80, and "A Diagrammatic Model for Merchandising Calculations," *Journal of Retailing,* Vol. 51, No. 2 (Summer 1975), pp. 3–9 and 92.

or 41.8 per cent. Cost + markup = retail; therefore, cost (58.2 per cent) + markup (41.8 per cent) = retail 100 per cent.

Of course, our two methods yield the same result, and whether one is superior or less confusing than the other is a debatable point. Perhaps the latter diagrammatic method serves its best purpose in illustrating the relationship among the various component concepts which tend to affect the issues concerned with markup planning requirements.

The store manager or buyer should always strive to attain his planned markup goals. If expenses rise, profits must inevitably fall *if* markups are not increased. When confronted with a situation wherein planned markup goals are not being met, it becomes imperative that the retail decision maker analyze his operations to find out what is happening and what needs to be done to correct the situation.

The merchandise budget procedures just described are of great service to managerial decision making within the retail management system. The merchandise budget is a valuable planning tool and *if used* as a set of standards or goals by which to compare actual performance with planned performance, then the merchandise budget is also an effective merchandising *control* device. It is not enough simply to implement merchandising budgeting procedures within a system. They must be used as a guide to *future* merchandising decisions, as well as a yardstick for analyzing and appraising *past* performance.

dollar and unit control systems

The merchandise budget has been described as a management device for both *planning* and *controlling* inventories. By and large, most merchandise management devices possess these dual characteristics; that is, they are used both for planning and control purposes. However, the dollar and unit management devices about to be discussed are most frequently referred to, simply, as *merchandise controls*.[13]

Merchandise planning and control devices must be designed in terms of two major characteristics. First of all, they must relate to overall merchandise values or *dollars;* and second, they must also often relate to physical characteristics, as they pertain to the quantity of goods in *units*. Because merchandise is sold to customers in units and bought by the buyer in units, many of the retail management system's control mechanisms must be designed in terms of units. On the other hand, invoices are paid for by the store in dollars, and store sales, operating expenses, merchandise acquisitions, and all other financial receipts and disbursements are paid for and accounted for in dollars; therefore merchandise buying plans and controls must also be made in dollars. The important point is that dollar control is the usual basis for beginning systems of merchandise planning and control

[13] An excellent basic work in dollar and unit control devices can be found in Jerold S. Meyer, *Dollar and Unit Merchandise Planning and Budgeting*, The Merchandising Division, National Retail Merchants Association, New York, 1960.

and is oftentimes complemented by the use of unit control systems. Many
retail management systems are not content to know only how much goods
they have sold. A sales total of $1,500 in a particular merchandising depart-
ment or particular merchandising classification is in many ways a relatively
meaningless bit of information. What the decision maker needs to know
is what merchandise is selling, what sizes are selling, what colors, styles, and
so forth, and what price merchandise is selling. The source of such information is to be found in both dollar and unit control systems. In smaller
stores such information is readily available. The appropriate information
can be gained by analyzing the day's sales slips and by tallying or tabulating
the needed information. However, in larger, more complex, and sophisticated stores more complex and sophisticated systems or procedures for
establishing and reporting dollar and unit performances are required.

The basis of both dollar and unit control systems can be found in the
tendency of most retail management systems to break up their total merchandising effort into a series of subefforts related to specific and particular
merchandise classifications. Thus, a department store begins to orient its
control procedures around departments. Specialty stores may orient their
control procedures around merchandise lines. Food supermarkets and hardware stores orient their control procedures around merchandise classifications. Still other stores direct dollar and unit control activities to price
lines, or other means of merchandise classification.

Dissection Control Activities

This basic prerequisite to merchandise control by dollars or units is
called classification or dissection control. It implies that the basis of control
is the classifying and categorizing of total merchandise selections into sub-
assortments. The logic is straightforward: what is large and differentiated
is not as easily analyzed as that which is smaller and more homogeneous.
Dissection control activities therefore consist of classifying merchandise
into categories of similarity, and then establishing data collection and reporting systems that center around value (dollar information) or physical
characteristics (unit information). Most generally, the principal means of
facilitating such systems are split total cash registers.[14] The split total cash
register provides a means of recording a large number of classifications or
dissections within a department, with complete totals at the end of the day.
All sales are registered, thus insuring complete accuracy. Stores using the
floor audit system obtain their classification totals at the end of the day as
a by-product of the sales register operation. The totals can easily be posted
to merchandise control records from the cash register tape. In a men's department, for example, the classification or dissection for men's dress shirts
might appear as follows:

[14] In many large stores today these cash registers are linked to electronic computers
and result in very sophisticated systems relating to total inventory management and
control procedures. The use of EDP equipment for managing inventories will be discussed in Chap. 14.

Types of material:
1. Broadcloth.
2. Oxford cloth.
3. Nylon.

Prices:
1. Under $6.50.
2. $6.51 to $7.99.
3. $8.00 to $10.99.
4. $11.00 and up.

It is possible to make an even finer breakdown than this: colors and collar styles such as regular tab, button down, or pin collar could be included as a basis for further dissection. The point is that when an item is sold, it is carefully identified by using the appropriate key on the cash register. This is the most simple method of handling classification control now in use. Stores with a large number of classifications often control the most active classifications on the cash register, and they use a split price ticket or tally card for controlling the others.

Dollar Control

Classification or dissection control is the basis for establishing systems of either (or both) dollar and unit control. Dollar control, as has been stated, is concerned with controlling inventories in terms of dollars or values. The retail store manager or buyer attempts to control inventory values because he wishes to keep his stocks well balanced in relation to sales; to minimize stock shortages and to prevent excessive markdowns; to know in what merchandise departments he has the largest investments in merchandise inventory, and from what departments or classifications he is deriving the greatest dollar sales. With such information, the decision maker can proceed to plan and control all the dimensions of the firm's merchandising behavior. *However, the retail decision maker cannot plan or control any dimension of merchandising behavior unless he knows or can determine at any point of time the value of his inventory.* Without this information he cannot plan purchases, he cannot determine his cost of goods sold, he cannot determine his gross margin, or his profits. Therefore, dollar control is principally concerned with determining for any point in time, the value of the firm's inventory. Two techniques for making this determination are used: the perpetual inventory method and the periodic inventory method.

The Perpetual and Physical Inventories. The perpetual inventory method is a book inventory. It results not from an actual counting of physical merchandise, but rather from recording all purchases and sales in a ledger, at retail prices. Present inventory value is then determined by adding to beginning inventory the firm's purchases in retail prices, and then subtracting all deductions by way of retail sales. In formula form, the perpetual inventory is determined as follows:

Beginning inventory + Purchases − Sales = Present inventory

Furniture and appliance stores, automobile dealers, and other systems that feature big ticket items usually find a perpetual inventory system quite adequate for determining—on a frequent basis—the value of their inventory. However, variety stores, department stores (at least many departments), and food stores cannot effectively use perpetual inventory systems because of the record keeping and burdensome detail involved with such a large and diverse merchandise assortment. Retailers are required by law to take a physical inventory at least once a year, but this annual determination would not provide sufficient information for the control and planning purposes of most retailers. The only exact way to determine the value of an inventory is to analyze and count the actual physical goods. This is an exceedingly costly and time-consuming process, however; given the nature of the task, most firms simply cannot afford to take a physical inventory each time they wish to know the approximate value of their inventory. Thus, some way of estimating inventory values or levels is required. It should be pointed out that the perpetual inventory is an estimate: the actual inventory can only be determined by a physical count of the merchandise. For instance, shortages resulting from thievery or other forms of negligence or dishonesty do not show on the perpetual inventory. The physical inventory, used in conjunction with the book inventory, permits the decision maker to determine (among other things) the amount of *overage,* the amount of *shortage,* and the *derived sales figure.*

Overage is the difference between the book and the physical inventory when the latter is the larger. *Shortage* is the difference between the book and the physical inventory when the former is the larger. Shortages are caused both by clerical errors and physical merchandise losses, but overage is almost always the result of clerical error. In formula form, the physical inventory produces a *derived sales figure.*

Beginning inventory + Purchases − Ending inventory = Sales +
Retail deductions (markdowns and shrinkage)

Beginning inventory was determined by an earlier physical count and evaluation. Purchases is the amount added to inventories; and ending inventory represents another physical count and evaluation. The taking of a physical inventory is admittedly time-consuming and costly; however, it does give the retailer a familiarity with and appreciation for his inventory that he might not otherwise have. It permits him to evaluate each piece of goods on the basis of its present market value and saleability, and it often turns up items that need to be reduced in price and closed out. It sometimes turns up items that need to be cleaned up and repromoted or revitalized.

In any event, both book and physical inventories are important and integral parts of many stores' dollar control processes.

Unit Control

The objective of merchandise control is to make possible the maintenance of ideal assortments. Unit control is designed to *help* bring about this objective, but it is not a substitute for dollar control in any sense of the word. Instead, it is a tool designed to help facilitate the complete merchandise control process. Unit control is concerned with the recording and reporting of quantities on hand and on order—of individual items and their respective rates of sale.

Such information is necessary in order to accomplish the following merchandising objectives:

1. To know what merchandise items, lines, or classifications are selling best. A system of unit control reveals the number of each item sold and therefore immediately indicates to management decision makers what items ought to be reordered and what items ought to be discontinued from merchandise assortments.
2. To optimize the investment in merchandise inventory. Investments in merchandise inventories are not without costs. Too large an investment in relation to sales would mean a reduced merchandise turnover with a subsequent reduction in capital turnover and lower profits. It also would mean higher operating expenses, especially in terms of inventory carrying costs. Therefore, in order to have an optimum investment in merchandise inventory, it is often necessary to design and implement a unit control system.
3. To implement sound buying practices and procedures. Buyers and store managers must approach their buying function on the basis of an objective knowledge of what is needed and what has been selling. Merchandise controls, *per se,* are not just sterile statistical and accounting records, but if used properly, they are dynamic and valuable *aids to decision making.* Buyers must base their judgments and decisions on objective records of past sales and other devices. Unit control procedures should be designed in order to facilitate the overall buying function.

Unit control procedures are based upon the same general concepts as dollar control procedures. That is, unit control systems begin by implementing some form of classification or dissection control. Then they establish the model stock, which is the list of total items that make up the assortment on which the unit control system will be based. The model stock is an ideal stock in terms of the composition or assortment of merchandise to be carried; it contains the proper mix or assortment of styles, colors, sizes, price lines, materials, and other factors. Problems related to inventory assortments must always be framed within the analysis of what products to carry, i.e., fashion items, staple items, new items, conventional items, and so on. Furthermore, inventory assortments are generally planned on the basis of model or basic stock requirements in units. For this reason, considerable care must be devoted to the establishment of these lists and to such factors as the rate of sale for each item or classification, the delivery period, the quantity required, the amount of safety stock needed for each item or classification, at what point merchandise should be reordered, and the amount to be reordered. These are the crucial problems for which unit control systems are adopted.

These systems require the same general kind of information as a dollar control system. It is necessary to know inventory levels at any particular period of time, not in dollars or value, however, but in terms of units. Thus, both perpetual and physical inventory systems must be established.

In addition to the cash register systems discussed earlier, another method of implementing unit control procedures involves the use of perforated price tickets. When the item is sold, one part of the ticket is torn off and deposited in a container that later is sorted and totaled by classification. This procedure can be done manually, but it is rather expensive and inefficient. Figure 13-2 illustrates simply but dramatically a system of unit control that is mechanically implemented and therefore requires considerably less human effort. However, the initial cost of implementing a mechanical or electronic system is usually much higher than the less sophisticated systems. Some stores, and especially the smaller ones use a tally card system that requires the salesperson to write the coded information on a tally card each time a sale is made. Records are then made by posting from the cards. Of course, unit sales information can also be obtained directly from sales checks. This method requires that a sales check be made out for every sale, and that unit sales information be written on each sales check. Later, the sales checks are analyzed in order to compute unit sales data.

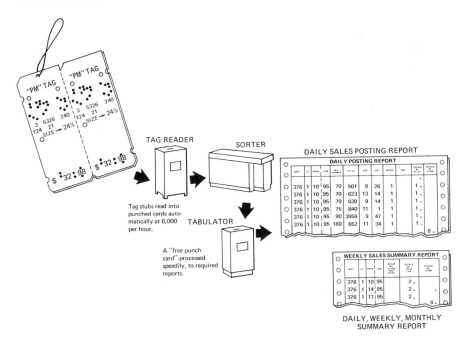

FIGURE 13-2   An illustrative unit control system.

Unit control systems are designed in order to minimize lost sales caused by merchandise being out-of-stock, and they propose careful observation and analysis of inventories at all times, for all merchandise lines and classifications. In addition to the physical inventory and the perpetual inventory, retail management systems have adopted many unit control procedures utilized by manufacturers and wholesalers who must manage large multi-inventory assortments and who have found such unit control devices as Requisition Stock Control, Tickler Control, Warehouse Control Systems, Checklist Systems, and Nomographs useful to their operations.

Unit control generally is most useful and beneficial to the retail management system, but it is not without drawbacks. Its basic shortcoming is that it can be very costly to design and implement. Any system is valuable and useful only as long as the benefits it creates outweigh the costs of their generation. Some retail stores have discovered that unit control systems do not materially contribute to the decision maker's ability to make better merchandising decisions. In some stores unit control devices have been resisted by store buyers who viewed them as another of management's methods of examining their operations. Buyers often feel that their expertise lies with merchandise and markets, not with accounting and statistical devices. However, as the use of EDP (Electronic Data Processing) equipment becomes more widespread in connection with merchandise management problems, perhaps buyers and store managers generally will develop a deeper appreciation of reporting and control systems as the bases for sounder management planning.

QUESTIONS FOR STUDY, REFLECTION, AND REVIEW

1. Briefly describe the merchandise budget and give the areas of application or usability of such a budget system.
2. What are the two major dimensions of the planning aspects of a budget?
3. A budget as a plan has two dimensions that must be considered when forming and evaluating its usability. How do these two factors (error and costs) affect the decision maker's use of budgets?
4. What are the two basic kinds of retail deductions other than sales, and how do they affect the value of inventories?
5. Markdowns occur for many reasons; but, generally, buying mistakes have two basic aspects. Name these two areas of mistakes, and state how markdowns are related to the merchandise budget.
6. If you have a shirt for $5.00 which is marked down to $4.00 and sold, what is the dollar markdown and per cent markdown?
7. If a store wishes to take a markdown on a $5.00 shirt that will amount to 20 per cent of the *sales price*, what will be the dollar value of the markdown and what is the sales price?
8. Knowing how much to buy is a critical problem that can be made easier if the proper merchandising budgeting procedures have been undertaken carefully. If these procedures have been followed accurately, how can the planned purchases be determined?

9. Planned markup must consider several planning and control areas. What are the major variables in determining the markup percentage? Express the markup percentage as a formula.
10. Dollar control and unit control are two systems designed to aid the merchandise manager. How do these two systems aid merchandise planning and control?

14

---

models for merchandise management

Throughout this text, various decision-making models have been introduced and their relevance to retailing strategy decisions has been demonstrated. The activities of the retail decision maker, whether he be owner/manager, merchandise manager, buyer, or sales supervisor can be treated on essentially three levels. First is the *content* level. That is, his efforts can be described in terms of what he does, what jobs he performs, and his role behavior in relationship to the content of his work. Second, the retail decision maker's work can be treated in terms of the *method* (the conceptual bases) on which his work is carried out. Finally, the retail decision maker's activities can be analyzed in terms of the *techniques* he employs in order to aid him in solving his decision problems. The treatment used in this text embraces all three levels of analysis; where possible it departs from the basic description of content and emphasizes a discussion and analysis of method, i.e., the conceptual or strategic consideration of retail decision making. In many instances, it moves to the level of techniques, where procedures, tactics, and decision models are used as a framework for analysis and decision making. A model has been defined as "a representation of a system which is used to predict the effect of a change in certain aspects of the system on the performance of the system."[1] In this chapter several analytical models will be presented, which are unlike the many other models previously discussed in relation to merchandise planning and control in that they are neither widely adopted, nor is their potential as yet fully realized. By and large, the models to be discussed in this chapter are outgrowths of management science, that discipline concerned with

[1] William R. King, *Quantitative Analysis for Marketing Management,* McGraw-Hill Book Company, New York, 1967, p. 84.

decision theory, which uses mathematics and the high-speed computer. Such approaches have a two-pronged value. On the one hand, they often lead to valuable decision rules that can be adopted and implemented as practical guides to action. On the other hand, even if actual decision rules are not forthcoming, *the use of highly analytical mathematical models can be a valuable tool that enables the retail decision maker to perceive relationships and thus gain a fuller understanding of the system that he is trying to manipulate and control.*

The models presented in this chapter are designed more to facilitate the latter objective than to present a set of pat decision rules or formulas, which through manipulation would produce instant answers to complex decision situations.

the merchandise management problem

The coming decade will undoubtedly be marked by an increasing sophistication and complexity of retail management systems, with a more widespread use of computer technology and science instead of hunch and intuition. Thus, the retail decision maker ought to be familiarizing himself with the techniques for more scientific decision making.

The merchandise management problem has been characterized as the attempt by the retail decision maker—owner, manager, buyer—to plan and control a balanced assortment of merchandise offerings to meet expected or anticipated customer demand. The complexities of such an assignment have already been spelled out in considerable detail, and the *conventional* approaches to merchandise planning and control have been discussed and analyzed. However, as one writer has stated:

> The complexity and size of modern business operations, even in many so-called small organizations have reached such proportions in our high-technology, management science age, that it is no longer advisable to make inventory decisions unaided by quantitative evaluation of the factors involved.[2]

Without a careful evaluation of the quantitative factors involved, all too often inventory management problems are routinized and treated in a perfunctory manner—one that usually perpetuates a series of built-in errors related to inventory management.

Part of the merchandise management problem, as Padley has suggested, is that the majority of inventory troubles are rooted in the following causes:[3]

1. Unworked or unworkable systems for controlling unit inventories.
2. Failure to tailor the number of items stocked to one's pocketbook.
3. Use of dollar sales and inventory budgets for inventory control.

[2] Norbert Lloyd Enrick, *Management Operations Research,* Holt, Rinehart and Winston, New York, 1965, p. 151.
[3] John T. Padley, "Inventory Management Increases Store Profits," *Journal of Retailing,* Vol. 39, No. 2 (Summer 1962) , p. 1.

It should be pointed out that nonquantitative inventory or merchandise management systems *per se* do not necessarily lead to problems in merchandise management. What should really be said is that errors related to the use of these pragmatic or rule-of-thumb systems are the principal causes of merchandise management difficulties. The mistakes that result are errors related to order quantities, errors in estimating delivery times, errors related to levels of safety stock, errors related to estimating the rate of sale, and errors related to overall inventory levels based upon faulty turnover rates and stock sales ratios. Figures 14-1 and 14-2 depict the differences between the management intuition and the management science approaches to inventory management.

It must be carefully pointed out that the management science approach cannot avoid losses from errors related to anticipating and forecasting market demand or requirements. No matter how sophisticated, a model or quantitative approach cannot produce meaningful answers on the basis of meaningless or unsophisticated raw data.

By and large, as has been repeated so often, effective merchandise management begins with a careful and sophisticated forecast and analysis of

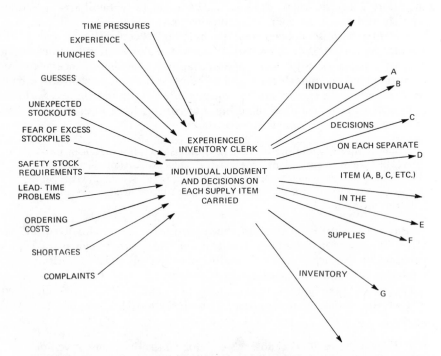

FIGURE 14-1 Management-intuition approach. Each individual item requires a separate decision on reordering point, lead-time allowance, and quantity to order. Conflicting and below-optimum decisions will occur.

SOURCE: From Management Operations Research, by Norbert L. Enrick, p. 152. Copyright ©
1965 by Holt, Rinehart and Winston, Inc. Reprinted by permission of Holt, Rinehart and Winston.

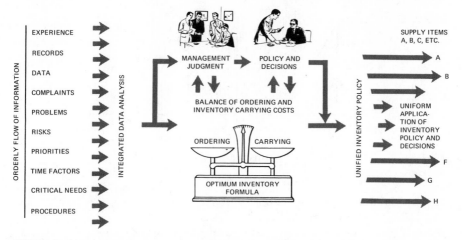

FIGURE 14-2 Management science approach. Inventory policy is laid down by management once, based on integrated data analysis, optimum inventory formula, and managerial judgment. Management experiences fewer stockouts and overstocking; management personnel is freed to devote time to more meaningful tasks and decisions.

SOURCE: From Management Operations Research, by Norbert L. Enrick, p. 152. Copyright © 1965 by Holt, Rinehart and Winston, Inc. Reprinted by permission of Holt, Rinehart and Winston.

the firm's market opportunity.[4] The principal advantage of the management science approach to merchandise management is the possibility for management decision makers to obtain useful information, abstracted and summarized from the mass of operating data that accumulates in the retail management system. By utilizing this information via simple formulas for weighing and evaluating the cost factors, and by combining this cost analysis with management judgment, a comprehensive management science approach can be incorporated into the merchandise management decision process. Such an approach can enable a system to reduce the risks and costs of decision making and in turn lessen the possible errors in planning and controlling inventories.

Inventory Levels and Time Considerations

From the supply point of view, merchandise management is largely concerned with managing inventory levels. The point has been made that this does not mean keeping the inventory level extremely low. Such a decision (one could reckon intuitively) would mean frequent stockouts and lost sales. Conversely, it would be unwise to build up inventories to exceedingly high levels, because again intuition would suggest that such a policy would

[4] See Ross W. Ritland, "New Methods of Estimating and Forecasting Retail Sales," *Journal of Retailing*, Vol. 39, No. 3 (Fall 1963), pp. 1–9.

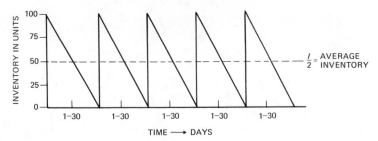

FIGURE 14-3 A theoretical inventory cycle.

lead to an uneconomic investment in merchandise inventory and a corresponding need for an unlimited amount of costly display and storage
space. What is desired is an optimum inventory level consistent with customer demand as it relates to rates of sale and other factors such as safety
stocks and reorder lead times. For example, the relationship between inventory level and time can be shown graphically in Figure 14-3.

In Figure 14-3 inventory in units is shown on the vertical axis and time
in days is shown on the horizontal axis. Several assumptions are basic to
Figure 14-3. At the beginning of each monthly period, 100 units of the item
in question are ordered into stock, and it is assumed that delivery is
instantaneous, i.e., there is no waiting time required to replenish inventories. The rate of sale is constant and continuous: At the end of the thirty-
day period the inventory is exhausted, and immediately upon exhaustion
is automatically and instantaneously replenished. The illustration further
assumes a perfect accommodation between inventory level and demand.
There are never any stockouts, and average inventory for any period is
found by dividing 100 by 2. Of course, such a depiction is unrealistic for
many reasons, which will be discussed shortly. Before proceeding, however,
observe that changing the order period used in Figure 14-3 from thirty days
to fifteen days results in a reduction in the size of the average inventory. A
policy of more frequent reordering would mean that reordering costs would
go up, while costs associated with carrying inventories would decline. Fig-

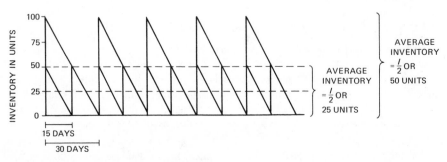

FIGURE 14-4 A theoretical inventory cycle.

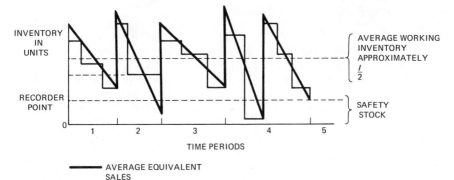

FIGURE 14-5 **A more realistic inventory cycle.**

ure 14-4 is predicated on the same *unrealistic* assumptions as is Figure 14-3, namely, that there is a constant rate of sale, demand has been forecast perfectly, so that inventories are automatically replenished when the last unit is sold, and that replenishment or reorder time is instantaneous. In actual practice these conditions would never prevail. Inventory cycles are generally quite erratic and sales rates are discontinuous stair step curves, rather than smooth straight lines. Several more realistic conditions are used in characterizing the inventory cycle shown in Figure 14-5. Most importantly, perhaps, are the factors that the sales rate and the receipt of new merchandise into inventory assortments will vary, and that new merchandise seldom ever arrives at just that instant when old stocks are sold out. Furthermore, Figure 14-5 shows an erratic sales rate, in the form of a discontinuous stair step reduction in inventories. The smooth line shows only an approximate average equivalent sales rate. This chart also illustrates that a safety stock is needed because of variations in the rate of sale and in the time required to receive shipments of new stocks (lead time for receiving new orders). Without safety stock, several stockout situations would have occurred. Observe, also, that the peaks and troughs of the inventory cycle are no longer symmetrical. For example, in period (1) slow sales permitted a stock build up. In (2) a late shipment depleted stocks; in (3) there was a deceleration in the rate of sale; in (4) accelerated sales because of peak seasonal demands necessitated a rapid reorder; and in (5) an early receipt of merchandise on order brought inventory levels back to normal. Figure 14-5 also shows a reorder point, which is selected in the following way: If the planned sales rate during reorder lead time is 5 units per day, the reorder lead time is 15 days, and inventory policy calls for a 15-day supply, then the reorder point would be $(15 \times 5) + (15 \times 5) = 75 + 75 = 150$ units. Thus, given a particular rate of sale and the delay between placing and receiving an order, the order for additional units would be placed when stock reached a minimum level of 150 units.

Based upon an understanding of these factors, the analysis can now move toward a discussion of how to determine the proper inventory planning and control devices to be employed to best manage the various kinds of inventory and to determine the most optimum economic ordering quantity.

The Classification of Inventories

In Chapter 13, the idea of classifying inventories was proposed, as the first step toward establishing inventory planning and control. Yet, at that point, the discussion purposefully skirted the issue as to explicitly *why* inventories should be classified, and, furthermore, it did not discuss the *basis* on which inventories could be most productively classified. It would appear that the reason for classifying and segregating inventories lies with the advantages to be gained from developing specialized planning and control procedures for the various classifications or segments of merchandise. One of the tasks of the retail decision maker is to choose the appropriate tool for each particular job. In the discussions thus far, it has been shown that there is a multitude of different merchandise planning and control devices, procedures, or tools. Merchandise classification can lead to the more effective choice of procedures and thus to more effective total merchandise management. It is small wonder that much attention and care should be devoted to the establishment of a balanced system of inventory planning and control devices, when one considers that thousands of items are typically merchandised in most retail stores. Such a balanced system has been characterized in the following manner:[5]

1. *It is selective.* Energy, time and money are channelized to control items with the highest dollar sales.
2. *It includes ordering rules* to determine when and how much of an item to order.
3. *It is economical to operate.* That is, it minimizes inventory carrying and ordering cost.
4. *It prevents stockouts,* aging of merchandise, and the resulting necessity for markdowns.
5. *It is flexible,* or easily adaptable to changing conditions.
6. *It is easy to operate,* both on the sales floor and in the stockroom.

A system incorporating these features for planning and controlling inventories is the *inventory management model,* or what is sometimes called the *economic ordering quantity model,* or E. O. Q. However, its effective use depends on a careful and systematic evaluation and classification of total inventory into several classifications based upon *inventory value.* A retail manager would know almost intuitively that there are some items of inventory that are of extreme importance because of their high value. These may be the 10 per cent of the total items in your assortment that account for 70 per cent of the total value of the total inventory. Another 40 per cent of the total items may account for only 20 per cent of the total value of the inventory. Finally, there may be 50 per cent of the total items in the inventory that account for only 10 per cent of total inventory value. The conclusions appear obvious. The merchandise manager *ought* to develop and implement planning and control devices for merchandise management that are balanced in relationship to the appropriate merchandise

[5] Padley, op. cit., p. 2.

classification based upon value. For example, low value items require only loose and inexpensive planning and control procedures such as would be found in order point review, bin systems, tickler files, and requisition stock room methods. On the other hand, high value items require a very careful and meticulous kind of planning and control activity, such as would be found in *order cycling methods* with a close personal inspection of inventories on a frequent periodic (hence the term *cycling*) basis. Medium value items would then require some system that is not as low cost, impersonal, or automatic as low value items, nor as expensive, personal, and frequent as high value items. Effective inventory planning and control calls for (1) the segregation of all inventory items into classifications based upon value and (2) the development and implementation of the proper planning and control procedures for each category. Merchandise management, then, suggests selective planning and control activities.

Classification Procedures.   The procedure for classifying inventory items into high, medium, and low value categories, is essentially uncomplicated and straightforward.

1. Determine the expected average cost per unit for each item inventoried or stocked during the period. This can be accomplished by relating inventory items needed to the forecasted sales for each item for the period.

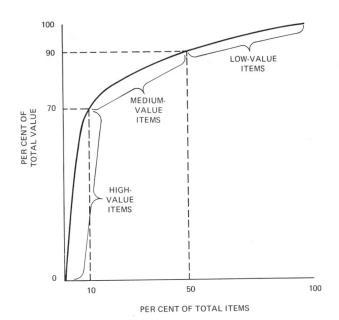

FIGURE 14-6 Inventory classification by value distribution.

2. From (1), determine the total requirement for each inventory item over the relevant period of the merchandise budget, i.e., one year, six months, a selling season, and so forth.
3. By multiplying average cost per inventory item by the forecasted requirement for this item over the relevant merchandise budget period, the total value of that item to the merchandising operation for the period is determined.
4. When this is done for all items, rank the items in order of value from highest to lowest.
5. These figures can then be converted into percentages.
6. Finally, the percentage of total items can be plotted against the percentage of total value, as is shown in Figure 14-6.

Figure 14-6 shows graphically and demonstrates more dramatically the consequences of inventory classification and the resulting possibilities for instituting more selective inventory planning and control procedures. On the basis of the value analysis and placement of inventory items into high, medium, and low value classifications, it is now possible to summarize the requirements of planning and control procedures, especially in terms of the time and talent involved. Table 14-1 presents such a breakdown and shows several interesting relationships.

Controls Based upon Classification. From the analysis thus far, several relationships ought now to be generally well understood. For example, low value items do not tie up large amounts of funds in investment in inven-

TABLE 14-1 Allocation of Time, Talent, and Control Effort Related to the Value of Merchandise Items

MERCHANDISE PLANNING AND CONTROL CHARACTERISTICS	HIGH VALUE ITEMS	MEDIUM VALUE ITEMS	LOW VALUE ITEMS
Merchandising talent required	Very best available	Average	Low
Merchandise records needed	Very complete	Simple	Not essential
Reorder point and order quantity use	As guides, or adjusted frequently	Adjusted less frequently	Adjusted infrequently, strictly used
Number of orders per year	Generally high	Two to four a year	One or two a year
Replacement time length	As short as possible	Normal	Can be long
Amount of safety stock	Low	Moderate	High
Turnover	High	Moderately high	Low

SOURCE: John T. Padley, "Inventory Management Increases Store Profits," Journal of Retailing, Vol. 39, No.2 (Summer 1962), p. 4. The headings have been altered in order to make them more consistent with the total presentation.

tories. Therefore, they are generally ordered in large quantities, and large safety stocks are carried economically. The number of orders placed during a merchandising period is thus rather small, and reorder points and order quantities are adjusted only infrequently. *The essential point in relation to low value items is that since investment in inventory is small, the costs associated with carrying a merchandise inventory consisting of large amounts of low value items is minimal.*

At the other extreme are high value items. Because of their critical nature, the merchandise records and controls needed must be very complete, the number of orders placed during a merchandising period must be high, safety stock is kept low, reorder points and order quantity use are reviewed personally, and adjusted frequently. The reason is that because the items are of high value, the cost associated with carrying such a merchandise inventory is exceptionally high. To lower this cost, it is necessary to minimize the investment in high value items by ordering in smaller quantities and placing more frequent orders. However, because of the critical nature of high value items, it is incumbent upon the system that out-of-stocks for these items be avoided. Therefore, selective control devices that carefully monitor the item-by-item flow or movement of this merchandise classification are usually implemented.

The control procedure for medium value items should be less rigid than for high value items, but not perhaps as inexpensive and fully automatic as for low value items. From the discussion of inventory cycles earlier in the chapter, the reader will recall that more frequent ordering leads to lower average inventory costs. *In selective merchandise management planning and control activities it is desirable to strike a balance between costs associated with ordering merchandise and costs associated with carrying a merchandise inventory.* This is known as the *Economic Ordering Quantity.* An approximate E. O. Q. can be found by utilizing a rather simple tabulation process. For example, assume that in some given department, total merchandise requirements for the period of the merchandise budget have been forecast at 2400 units. Assume, further, that each time an order is placed for any quantity of this item, from one to 2400 units, it costs $6.00

TABLE 14-2   Approximate E.O.Q. by Tabular Determination

	(A)	(B)	(C)	(D)	(E)	(F)
ORDERING CHARACTER-ISTICS	ORDER SIZE	NUMBER OF ORDERS 2400 ÷ (A)	AVERAGE INVENTORY (A) × $4.00 / 2	TOTAL ORDERING COST (B) × $6.00	TOTAL CARRYING COST (C) × 6%	TOTAL VARIABLE COST (D) + (E)
	200	12	$ 400	$72.00	$24.00	$ 96.00
	400	6	800	36.00	48.00	84.00
	600	4	1,200	24.00	72.00	96.00
	800	3	1,600	18.00	96.00	114.00
	1,200	2	2,400	12.00	144.00	156.00

to write and process the order. The wholesale cost of the item to the retailer is $4.00, and the inventory carrying cost as a per cent of inventory value, is six per cent. Table 14-2 shows several different order sizes and the consequent relationships that develop between ordering cost and inventory carrying costs. You will observe that as the order size increases, the ordering costs decline, but that inventory carrying charges rise directly with increases in the order size.

The data calculated in Table 14-2 show that total cost is Ordering cost + Inventory carrying cost; and given the merchandise requirements and the other relevant constraints pertaining to ordering and inventory carrying costs, this total cost is minimized with an order size of 400, which requires the placement of six orders. Therefore, minimum total cost is $84.00, or $36.00 (ordering cost) + $48.00 (inventory carrying costs). This is an approximate solution, because ordering costs and carrying costs have not been evaluated for order sizes between 200 and 400 units. If such an evaluation were undertaken, it might be discovered that there was a combination of ordering costs and inventory carrying cost lower than $84.00 and, if so, then 400 units would not be the E. O. Q.

A Graphic Approach to E. O. Q. The rationale of the *Economic Ordering Quantity* model can be demonstrated readily via the use of a graphic analysis. First, however, it is necessary to develop and explain several important concepts. The E. O. Q. model assumes that the decision maker wishes to minimize the total variable costs associated with inventory management. Fixed costs are disregarded, because as emphasized in the discussion related to profits and decision making in Chapter 3, the only relevant costs for decision making are those that are affected by the decision (variable) costs. It should be borne in mind, however, that the objective of minimizing total costs *may not necessarily* be the optimum criterion for decision making from the standpoint of the retail management system.

Furthermore, the E. O. Q. model assumes certainty where certainty may not actually exist. For example, sales and/or demand are given, and the data pertaining to ordering costs and inventory carrying charges are considered certain or accurate to the degree necessary to produce meaningful conclusions.

With these understandings, it can be postulated that the inventory manager/decision maker wishes to minimize total variable costs associated with inventory management and that total variable costs consist of two costs, inventory carrying costs and ordering costs. Furthermore, the decision maker wishes to determine the optimum order size, the optimum number of orders, and optimum turnover that in turn will result in maximizing the objective —to minimize total variable cost.

Before proceeding to the mathematical application of this model, several of the more important elements can be demonstrated graphically. For example, Figure 14-7 shows the variable cost for the period plotted against order size (which is labeled Q). Graph A shows ordering cost for period (A) declining as a function of order size (Q). Graph B shows inventory carrying cost for period (B) increasing as a function of increased order size (Q).

These curves could be shown another way by plotting ordering costs and

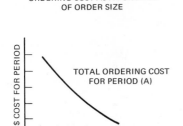

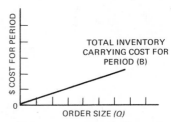

FIGURE 14-7 Graphic relation between ordering costs, inventory carrying costs, and order size.

inventory carrying costs against orders per year, instead of order size. The difference would result from the fact that orders per year are the converse of order size; or stated another way, order size varies inversely with the number of orders placed. However, by plotting each of these elements of total variable costs associated with inventory management against order size (Q), the slope of each of the curves and the behavior that leads to their respective slopes can be more fully understood and appreciated. Before proceeding further, each of these elements of total variable costs will be more fully explained.

Ordering Costs. From Figure 14-7 you will observe that order costs decrease with increases in order size. It must be understood that placing an order for merchandise costs money. Each order requires the actual requisitioning, preparation of the purchase order, order placement and follow-up, receiving and processing assistance, and accounting activities. The important point is that ordering costs are a function of the number of orders placed, rather than the value of the merchandise ordered.

Inventory Carrying Costs.[6] No merchant maintains an inventory of any size without incurring costs in connection with carrying this inventory. One of the major costs is an opportunity cost, which is an amount foregone by not having the money invested in some other income-earning asset such as stocks or bonds, or, for that matter, foregoing the interest paid by a commercial bank for a time deposit. For example, if a merchant has an inventory investment of $100,000 and a commercial bank was paying six per cent interest on time deposits, then *if* the merchant had his money in the bank instead of in inventory investment, he could earn 6 per cent on $100,000, or $6,000 on an annual basis. Therefore, the opportunity cost of his investment in merchandise inventory would be (at a minimum) 6 per cent, or $6,000. In some instances, costs other than opportunity bank earn-

---

[6] Students and other noninitiated readers usually understand the concept of ordering costs rather well, but have considerable difficulty grasping the logic of inventory carrying costs. It is hoped that the discussion of this section will help clarify this situation.

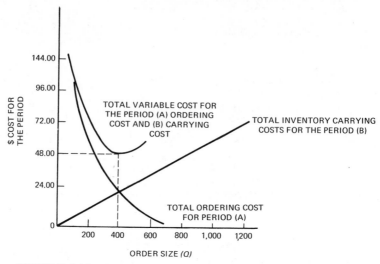

FIGURE 14-8   A graphic E.O.Q. model.

ings are included in inventory carrying costs. Such costs as obsolescence, depreciation, storage, handling, insurance, and taxes are oftentimes considered. Where this is the case, inventory carrying costs may vary between 10 and 20 per cent. It has been argued that a six per cent cost of capital for inventory—given an inventory which is a composite of short-term and long-term funds and other factors—is entirely satisfactory for most retail firms.[7] You will recall that this was the figure employed in computing carrying costs in Table 14-2.

With this background, the elements of total variable costs associated with inventory management can now be meaningfully put together into a single figure.

Figure 14-8 is based upon the data used in Table 14-2, our earlier tabular E. O. Q. model. It shows what is already known, namely, that given ordering costs (A) and inventory carrying costs (B), total variable cost (A + B) is minimized where these two curves intersect.[8] The graphic E. O. Q. model in Figure 14-8 minimizes total variable costs and determines the economic order quantity, i.e., that quantity or purchase order size which minimizes total variable costs. It could be used further to show the optimum number of orders. Recall that requirements $(R) = 2400$ units, and if optimum order size $(Q) = 400$ units, then the optimum number of orders to be placed during a period (N) would be

[7] Roger A. Dickerson, "Department Stores Should Retain a 6 Percent Imputed Interest on Inventory," *Journal of Retailing*, Vol. 42, No. 1 (Spring 1966), pp. 8–12, and 61.

[8] A technical note: Where the two curves or lines representing ordering costs and carrying cost in Fig. 14-8 intersect, the curve expressing the sum of the two is at a minimum if the carrying cost function is linear. It has been pointed out that this is seldom the case in retailing. See Marvin Jolson, "The Assumption of Linear Carrying Costs in the E.O.Q. Inventory Model," *Akron Business and Economic Review* (September 1972), pp. 25–28.

$$\frac{R}{Q} \text{ or } \frac{2400}{400} = 6$$

The E. O. Q. Formula. However, the easiest way to use the E. O. Q. model is not by the tabular or the graphic method (merchandising decisions are seldom so simple that they lend themselves to either of these approaches), but by a formula, which will now be briefly developed. The value of the tabular and graphic methods is that they build and develop our understanding so that the formula approach will not appear as a mysterious "black box," which cranks out useful but little-understood answers.

The objective is to develop a formula that expresses the order size (Q) in terms of the other variables involved in the problem in such a way as to result in minimum total variable cost for the period. The following legend will be used to develop the formula:

Q = order size
R = requirements of the item
    for the period
S = ordering cost per order

C = cost per unit of the item
I = inventory carrying cost as a
    per cent of inventory value
TVC = total variable cost

Intuition would tell us that what is desired is to minimize total variable cost where

$TVC = A + B$ (where A = ordering cost, and B
                                     = inventory carrying cost)

$A = \dfrac{R}{Q} \times S$ (where $\dfrac{R}{Q}$ = number of orders placed during the period)

$B = \dfrac{Q}{2} \times C \times I$ (where $\dfrac{Q}{2}$ = average inventory)

The formula now is

$$TVC = \left(\frac{R}{Q} \times S\right) + \left(\frac{Q}{2} \times C \times I\right)$$

Remember that it is our objective to choose a value for Q that minimizes total variable costs. In order to get the formula for E.O.Q., the differential calculus is used.[9] By setting the first derivative of the total variable cost function equal to zero and solving for Q, the new formula becomes

$$\text{E. O. Q.} = \sqrt{\frac{2 \times R \times S}{C \times I}}$$

[9] The calculations are not shown here. However, what is involved is the taking of a first derivative. Reference to any elementary treatise on the calculus would explain this operation.

Thus by knowing (R) requirements, (S) ordering cost per order, (I) inventory carrying cost as a per cent of inventory value, and (C) cost per unit, the E. O. Q. (economic order quantity) can be obtained.[10]

The E. O. Q. model has further possibilities. For example, the optimum number of orders (N) would be

$$N = \frac{R}{E.\ O.\ Q.} \quad \text{(where } R = \text{requirements, and } E.\ O.\ Q. = \text{economic ordering quantity)}$$

By substituting the formula for E. O. Q. in this equation and then simplifying, the following expression is obtained:

$$\text{Optimum } (N) = \sqrt{\frac{R \times C \times I}{2 \times S}}$$

Now it is possible to calculate the optimum turnover of an item for a period by dividing the figure for optimum (N) by the requirements for the period (R), or

$$\text{Optimum turnover} = \frac{N}{R}$$

The E. O. Q. model is a powerful aid to decision making by a buyer, merchandise manager, or anyone concerned with making rational decisions about inventory. Its use is becoming more widespread in spite of the shortcomings of the model, which we mentioned earlier. The E. O. Q. model should never be used indiscriminately. It is only a guide to decision making, and when used it must always be tempered with the judicious wisdom born of merchandising experience. Oftentimes, an economic ordering quantity arrived at by calculation or the use of a formula will be altered in order that quantities purchased will be in rounded figures, or consistent with the quantities characteristically used by the sellers, e.g., dozens, grosses, cases, and so on. Economic ordering quantities are often modified to conform with standardized units of shipment, e.g., carload or truck load lots. Finally, the economic order quantity may be changed in order to qualify for quantity or trade discounts. However, the important point is that any model (including the E. O. Q.) is an aid to judgment and a guide to decision making—not a magic wand that produces instantaneous solutions to complex business problems.

merchandise management as a capital budgeting exercise

Merchandise management is the planning and control of merchandise assortments for the purpose of assuring a balanced stock and mix of goods in order to meet expected customer demand and can be treated within the

[10] It should be pointed out that slide rules and nomographs are available from which an E. O. Q. can be obtained without calculation.

framework of a capital budgeting process. Like other problems in retailing, the merchandise management problem is an allocation process where limited resources such as space and investment funds are divided among alternative uses such as products and merchandise lines or departments, in such a manner that profits are maximized.

Merchandising and Capital Budgeting

The major merchandising decisions are what goods to buy and in what quantities and can be approached from the standpoint of capital budgeting. The general answer would be to buy those goods in the quantities that maximize return on investment. Holton has built a model that permits the merchandise management problem to be treated as a capital budgeting exercise.[11] The essence of Holton's model is that it creates an index that makes possible the ranking of products, merchandise lines, or entire departments in terms of their ability to generate profits. Such a model makes it possible to incorporate such ambiguous but related factors as sales, merchandise costs, gross margin, expenses, and turnover into a single index—percentage contribution return on investment. Retailers have been perennially plagued with the issues of how to allocate space or build a merchandise assortment consisting of products falling essentially into two categories: (1) products that have a low gross margin but a high turnover; and (2) products that have a high gross margin and a low turnover, in addition to the categories of products that fall between these two extremes.

Percentage contribution return on investment integrates these two elements (margin and turnover) in a rather neat manner. The index is relatively easy to calculate. However, two distinctions will be made: the case of an individual item and the comparison of two or more similar items. In the first instance, one need only relate dollar contribution to investment in order to yield a percentage return. To illustrate:

$$C = 100 \times (S - W - D)/I$$

where

$C =$ the item's contribution as a percentage return on inventory investment
$S =$ the item's sales volume
$W =$ net invoice cost of goods
$D =$ direct expenses for the item
$I =$ average investment in inventory at cost

Several interesting relationships can be discerned from the formula itself. First of all, it reflects a host of important retailing variables in one formula; the rate of sale, the turnover rate, the gross margin percentage, the direct handling (controllable) costs, and the average investment tied up in inventory. The interaction of these variables produces the decision criterion (index), percentage contribution return on investment.

[11] Richard H. Holton, "A Simplified Capital Budgeting Approach to Merchandise Management," *California Management Review* (Spring 1961), pp. 82–99.

Observe that

(1) $S - W$ = gross margin
(2) Gross margin $- D$ (variable costs) = contribution to profit and overhead

Furthermore,

$\dfrac{W}{I} =$ turnover, where W = merchandise cost, and I = average inventory at cost

And

$\dfrac{S}{I \times (100\% + C_2)}$ also = turnover, where S = sales and I = average investment in inventory at cost, and C_2 = the supplement of the markup

With these relationships in mind, several points become apparent.[12] If turnover increases, the contribution return on investment is increased. If the gross margin is increased and the number of units sold per time period remains unchanged, the contribution-return is increased. When sales are increased, the contribution-return is not altered unless the sales increase proportionately more than the average investment and the direct costs of selling the merchandise. Finally, as selling costs rise, the contribution-return on investment falls.

In the second case, that of two or more similar products, additional refinements must be made to take into account the differences in stock turnover rates and cost patterns among products. These are incorporated into the formula that follows, where

C = contribution return on inventory investment
C' = contribution per unit in dollars
T = stock turnover rate per annum
S = selling price per unit
W = net purchase price per unit
I = average inventory investment computed as one half the purchase price plus one half the cost of getting the merchandise into selling position
D_1 = direct costs, in dollars, per unit handled
D_2 = direct costs that vary with dollar sales, expressed as a per cent of the selling price

Thus, the contribution percentage is

$$C = \frac{C'}{I} \times T \times 100$$

[12] Ibid., p. 85.

And because

$$C' = S - (W + D_1 + D_2S)$$

And average investment is

$$I = \frac{1}{2}(W + D_1 + D_2S)$$

Then,

$$C = \frac{100\,T[S - (W + D_1 + D_2S)]}{\frac{1}{2}(W + D_1 + D_2S)}$$

which reduces to

$$C = 200\,T\left[\frac{S}{W - D_1 + D_2S} - 1\right]$$

With this formula and certain assumptions (i.e., that investment funds are fixed in the short run, that each investment return schedule is close to the point of diminishing marginal return, and that the demand for any given product is independent of the demands for all others), the criterion for merchandising decisions is the equimarginal principle,

$$MC\%_{oa} = MC\%_{ob} = MC\%_{oc} \ldots MC\%_{ok}$$

where the marginal contributions of all products are equal.[13] At this point, profits will be maximized.

Economic and business logic that dictates profit maximization calls for maximizing return on a given merchandise inventory investment. The usual criteria for merchandise investment or such inventory decisions as percentage gross margin, sales per square foot, and rate of stock turn are all inherently inadequate when used alone. When the merchandise manager is faced with the dilemma of expanding his assortment mix, he no longer has to rely solely on either gross margin or turnover, but he can now combine these measures into a more meaningful index (decision rule) that is economically both sound and practical to implement. Gross margin—long a desired criterion for decision making in regard to product decisions—has the shortcoming that it really reveals nothing about *profitability*. The same is true of turnover. Although many merchants would add to a merchandise line those items that they knew had a high turnover rate, they frequently knew little or nothing about the item's profitability. Sales per square foot has also been used as a criterion for decision making in regard to merchandising and space allocation problems. However, the essential shortcoming of each of these criteria is that they fail to recognize that different amounts of investment in inventory are required for different product lines or departments, and that different levels of costs are required to generate differ-

[13] Holton, op. cit. The relevance of these assumptions and their limitations are discussed in this article. See pp. 96–99.

ent levels of sales and gross margins per item, line, or department. All this would suggest that the dollars of contribution (expressed as an annual percentage return on the inventory investment) may be currently the best available general criterion of performance for a range of merchandising decisions.

GMROI

As suggested in the previous discussion, the retail decision maker must work to identify those merchandising decision variables which have the greatest influence in the firm's financial performance and when possible, the decision maker must work to develop experimental techniques for identifying the probable effects of utilizing alternative merchandising decision rules.

Another model or conceptual approach to focusing the decision maker's attention to these problems is a technique known as GMROI, or gross margin return on investment. GMROI attempts to sensitize management decision making to the critical importance of evaluating merchandising performance in terms of a ratio of net profits produced per dollar of assets committed or return on investment. Throughout earlier parts of this text, the importance of utilizing just such a decision framework has consistently been emphasized. And, of course, this notion is the essence of merchandise management within the context of a capital budgeting framework.

Gross margin return on investment is simply

$$\text{GMROI} = \frac{\text{Gross margin dollars}}{\text{Average inventory investment (cost)}}$$

Using average inventory as a concept for investment is a simple, easy to use, noncomplicated way of assigning responsibility for a given asset management for which buyers, department managers, or merchandise managers can be held exclusively accountable. On the other hand, return as represented by gross margin dollars is an equally simple, unambiguous and readily measured variable which selectively reflects only the effects of merchandising decisions.

Because retail values as opposed to cost values for inventories are more frequently used by most retail firms, gross margin return on investment can be readily calculated also as

$$\text{GMROI} = \frac{\text{Gross margin dollars}}{\text{Net sales}} \times \frac{\text{Net sales}}{\text{Average retail inventory investment}}$$

Gross margin dollars divided by net sales represent, of course, the familiar gross margin ratio or per cent, and net sales divided by average retail inventory investment is the reasonably familiar concept of stock turnover.

This suggests much about the use of the concept of GMROI. For instance, two of the more critical aspects of merchandising management are

(1) gross margin ratio and (2) the stock turnover. Thus, an index such as GMROI which combines the use of these two crucial factors can be an important managerial tool to aid retail decision makers in their planning and control activities and to focus their efforts on factors which critically impact on both the interrelated merchandising and financial aspects of their decisions. Other important aspects of the concept of GMROI have been acknowledged.[14]

1. It is an operationally meaningful measurement device for evaluating the buyer or other merchandising executive.
2. Because it parallels the basis for evaluating other aspects of retail managerial performance such as ROI (see Chapter 3), it is consistent with the newer concepts of decentralized management, profit center evaluation, and in some respects an ideal basis for implementing a management by objectives philosophy for merchandising operations.[15]
3. GMROI is not necessarily a method for evaluating past performance, but would be best used as a planning device which forces managers to think and plan in terms of desired combinations of target gross margins and target turnover figures, both of which would be reflected in their overall merchandising decisions and produce the desired GMROI.
4. Utilizing a composite index such as GMROI permits and facilitates comparisons of merchandising results from department to department or even from merchandise line to merchandise line. Hence, GMROI is an evaluative measure of performance which is objectively applicable across different merchandise groupings.
5. Finally, GMROI is a decision rule of merchandise management which utilizes readily available data from the store's reservoir of MOR, or merchandising operating results. Furthermore, a given store's results can be readily compared with other stores' experience by utilizing the available MOR figures from such trade associations as the National Retail Merchants Association.

As retailers attempt to stem the decline of their falling financial fortunes resulting from lowered gross margins, rising operating expense ratios, and declining turnover figures, concepts such as GMROI can demonstrate that their best managerial efforts should be devoted more to managing gross margins and turnover, and not necessarily to efforts devoted primarily to increasing sales volume and markups.

stock turnover

In both the capital budgeting model and the GMROI model, the concept of merchandise turnover was seen to be a critical variable. Thus, it would

---

[14] Daniel J. Sweeney, "Improving the Profitability of Retail Merchandising Decisions," *Journal of Marketing*, Vol. 37 (January 1973), pp. 60–68.

[15] Dennis J. Sutherland, "Managing by Objectives in Retailing," *Journal of Retailing*, Vol. 47, No. 3 (Fall 1971), pp. 15–27.

appear fitting that an extensive and detailed discussion of this concept be developed at this juncture.

Maintaining the proper turnover while at the same time maintaining adequate profit margins is in essence the real crux of the merchandising problem—it might very well be called the key or central task of retailing management. If proper turnover and profit margins are being maintained, it can be fairly well assumed that both buying and selling activities are being carried out effectively. The role of stock turnover has been discussed earlier, in relation to the Dupont Formula and profit as a criterion for decision making. It has also been pointed out that stock turnover is an important part of investment turnover. With the exception of land and buildings, inventories are likely to constitute the single largest investment (asset) of the retail merchandiser. If inventory turnover can be accelerated, quite likely the effect is to accelerate investment turnover. If this can be accomplished without reducing the operating profit margin, the result in turn is an increase in return on investment.

Measures of Turnover

There are several measures of turnover employed by retail decision makers as criteria for evaluating certain aspects of their operations. Earlier, the concept of *investment turnover* was used.

$$\text{Investment turnover} = \frac{\text{Sales at retail}}{\text{Total assets}}$$

Investment turnover shows the number of times during a period (usually one year) that total assets are converted or turned over into sales. Such an index is a measure of the firm's efficiency in utilizing total assets in relationship to the production of sales. You will recall that investment turnover is the principal turnover index used in the Dupont schematic in calculating return on investment.

Capital turnover is an important financial index, measuring the number of times during a year that the cost of the average investment in inventory is returned in sales.

$$\text{Capital turnover} = \frac{\text{Sales at retail}}{\text{Average inventory at cost}}$$

Finally, there is an index called *stock turnover* or *stock turn,* which is the number of times that the average stock is sold during a certain period of time, usually one year. There are several ways to figure stock turnover. It can be computed on the basis of dollars, at either retail or cost; or it can be figured on the basis of units. For example:

$$\text{Stock turn in dollars at retail} = \frac{\text{Net sales at retail}}{\text{Average inventory at retail}}$$

$$\text{Stock turn in dollars at cost} = \frac{\text{Cost of goods sold}}{\text{Average inventory at cost}}$$

$$\text{Stock turn in units of merchandise} = \frac{\text{Net sales in units of merchandise}}{\text{Average number of units in stock}}$$

It is immaterial which basis for figuring stock turnover is used. What is most important is that the same procedure be used on a continuing basis, especially if comparisons are to be made from one period to another. Furthermore, when comparing one stock turn rate with another, it is most important to be sure that the stock turn figures were determined on a similar basis. A stock turn rate figured at retail will not compare favorably with a stock turn rate figured at cost. When it is necessary to compare one incompatible stock turn figure with another, it is a relatively easy matter to convert them to the same base.[16]

One other caution is offered in connection with using stock turn ratios: the ratio (stock turn index) is only as good as the data from which it is determined. The denominator of the ratio is an average, and like any average it can be very misleading. For example, if average inventory is figured by utilizing the results of a physical inventory taken once a year, two yearly inventories are simply added and divided by two. Since physical inventories are often taken only after stocks have been sold down in prep-

---

[16] For example, by dividing its sales by its average retail stock, Store A computes its turnover to be 6, but it wishes to compare this figure with a stock turn of 6.5 reported by Store B which computes stock turn at cost. The markup on sales in the first store is 36 per cent, and its average markup on the inventories used in its stock turn calculation is 40 per cent. In the second store the markup on sales is 35 per cent, and the markup on cost is estimated to average 38 per cent of retail. To convert,

(a) Express the stock turn rate of the first store on a cost basis, or
(b) Express the stock turn of the second store on a retail basis.

Solution:

(a)

$$\text{Let sales in Store A} = \$60$$

$$\text{stock turn at retail: } \frac{\$60 \text{ (sales)}}{\$10 \text{ (average retail stock)}} = 6$$

$$\text{Cost of merchandise sold: } \$60 \times 64\% = \$38.40$$

$$\text{Average cost stock: } \$10 \times 60\% = \$6$$

$$\text{Stock turn at cost: } \frac{\$38.40}{\$6.00} = 6.4$$

(b)

$$\text{Let cost of merchandise sold in Store B} = \$65$$

$$\text{stock turn at cost: } \frac{\$65 \text{ (cost of sales)}}{\$10 \text{ (average cost of stock)}} = 6.5$$

$$\text{sales: } \frac{\$65}{65\%} = \$100$$

$$\text{Average retail stock: } \frac{\$10}{62\%} = \$16.13$$

$$\text{Stock turn at retail: } \frac{\$100}{\$16.13} = 6.2$$

Note: This example is used by permission and is from John W. Wingate, Elmer O. Schaller, and Irving Goldenthal, *Problems in Retail Merchandising*, 5th ed., Prentice-Hall, Inc., Englewood Cliffs, N.J., 1961, pp. 143–144.

aration for the inventory, a stock turn figured on such a basis is not likely to be representative, nor a very good criterion for any sort of decision making. A better way to determine the value of the average inventory is to find the summation of the book B.O.M. inventory records for each month, plus the physical closing inventory and divide this figure by 13. The result is a much more representative and (therefore) accurate stock turn index.

Turnover as a Criterion for Decision Making

Historically, stock turnover has long been an important criterion for merchandise planning and control procedures. However, there is some evidence to suggest that the role of stock turnover in merchandise management decisions has either begun to wane, or has been neglected by retail managers. In conventional retail stores and especially in department stores turnover rates have been allowed to fall to their lowest level in 20 years. Two explanations can be offered for this phenomenon. First, it might very well be that proliferating product lines, scrambled merchandising, increased number of branch store openings, and increasing emphasis on non-price competitive activities have resulted in operating pressures that prevent the attainment of stock turn levels characteristic of historical levels of operation. Second, it has been suggested that many department store managers and decision makers neglect the use of stock turn as an effective criterion for decision making. In a study by Douglas Dalrymple, department store executives were asked to rank the goals of their operations, and they listed proper stock turnover 16th.[17] Such things as profits, sales growth, customer service, fashion emphasis, and so forth were all ranked ahead of stock turnover. This might well have been expected. Stock turnover is a criterion for decision making. It is a yardstick that indicates efficiency in certain aspects of the firm's operation, such as level of sales and the management of inventories.

Dalrymple has offered the explanation, also, that the retail method of inventory focuses attention on the production of profits rather than the maximization of stock turnover.[18] This is probably as it should be. The retail firm is interested in attaining a satisfactory rate of return on its investment. Therefore, stock turn is a means, not an objective to be sought at either the expense of lost sales or increased expenses resulting from hand-to-mouth buying with more frequent purchasing and larger ordering costs. If the firm's objective is simply to raise stock turnover, it could be attained quite easily, but not without incurring certain high costs. For example, sales might be increased by large expenditures for advertising and promotion. However, if revenues were not increased by an amount sufficient to offset the additional costs for this advertising and promotion, it would prove to be an uneconomical move, even if stock turn were increased. Selling more merchandise via the price reduction route would also increase the

[17] Douglas J. Dalrymple, *Measuring Merchandise Performance in Department Stores,* Retail Research Institute, National Retail Merchants Association, New York, 1964, pp. 19–61.

[18] Douglas J. Dalrymple, "How Important Is Stock Turnover?" *Journal of Retailing,* Vol. 40 (Winter 1964–1965), No. 4, pp. 1–5.

stock turn rate. But, unless demand were quite elastic and the resulting total revenues after the price reduction were equal to (or greater than) total revenues before the reduction, this technique also would be an uneconomic form of merchandising behavior.

The point to be stressed is that the stock turnover index used in connection with total merchandise planning and control can be an effective criterion for decision making, which will contribute to the overall economic well being of the firm or department.

Attaining the proper turnover rate means maintaining a rate of turnover that optimizes the relationships between profit margins and investment turnover, as shown in the Dupont schematic. Specifically, this statement means that a proper turnover rate leads to a smaller capital investment in proportion to the volume of sales obtained, or a more effective utilization of capital in the business. Merchandise taxes, insurance, interest, and rent are reduced in relationship to sales; buyers are in a better position to buy clean, fresh new merchandise; and markdowns as a percentage of sales are likely to be reduced.

A proper turnover rate means a marked improvement in profits, especially profit as a return on merchandise investment, which can be determined by using the following formula:

$$\frac{\text{Profit as a return on}}{\text{merchandise investment}} = \frac{\text{Dollar profit}}{\text{Average investment in inventory at cost}}$$

To illustrate, consider the following situation. An automobile dealer stocks a car selling for $4,000, and makes a net profit of $200 (5 per cent of sales). Now consider that another dealer buys, stocks, and sells a similar car for $4,000, makes a $200 (5 per cent) profit, and repeats the process another time during the year. The dealers each made a profit of $200 on the $4,000 cars. However, the second dealer made two turnovers, while the first dealer made only one. Their net profit as a percentage of sales was the same. Dealer A sold one car at $4,000 and made $200 (5 per cent profit). Although Dealer B sold two cars ($4,000 × 2) for $8,000 and made $400 profit, his profit ($400) as a per cent of sales ($8,000) was still 5 per cent. The net profit on the average investment was different, however, for the two dealers.

Assume that the dealers' cost of acquiring the cars was $2,800 each (this assumes a markup of 30 per cent). The first dealer made $200 net profit as a return on merchandise investment of 7.1 per cent ($200 ÷ $2,800). With a stock turn of two, the second dealer obtained an $800 profit on the same average investment of $2,800. This is a return on merchandise investment of 14.3 per cent ($400 ÷ $2,800). Thus, by increasing turnover, profit as a return on merchandise investment can be markedly improved.

Improved Merchandising Performance Through Increased Stock Turn

The proper stock turn has already been defined as one that reflects the optimum relationship between investment turnover and profit margins.

Thus, it would follow that when profits as a return on investment are inadequate, a symptom of this condition would be an improper turnover figure. Such a revelation may encourage the firm to analyze its operation with the goal of improving profits through an increase in stock turnover.

Turnover can be increased in three ways. One way is to reduce the size of the average stock without proportionately reducing sales. Another way is to increase sales without proportionately increasing the investment in the average inventory; and finally, stock turnover can be increased by obtaining a larger sales volume with a proportionately smaller average stock. The latter way would represent the best of all possible worlds, and although it is conceivable, it is also difficult to attain.

The value of using stock turnover as a criterion for decision making in relation to merchandise planning and control is that in order to increase turnover—or simply to manage turnover by attempting any one of the three alternatives mentioned—the decision maker must scrutinize almost every dimension of the firm's total retail merchandising strategy. *Buying* errors are thus often discovered to be a major cause of slow turnover and increased markdowns. *Pricing* decisions that fail to consider the nature of demand or customer buying attitudes also are likely to be implicated in the problem. *Promotion* that is ineffective and based upon poor appeals or carried in inadequate media might be found as the major cause for poor customer traffic, low sales, and slow turnover. Poor *location* decisions likewise might affect low turnover ratios.

An inadequate or slow rate of merchandise turnover is a symptom that is likely to indicate a number of causal factors. It is reasonably certain that a continuing and prolonged low rate of merchandise turnover is indicative of ineffective merchandising behavior and should be interpreted as a signal to trigger a determined attitude toward the establishment of formal merchandise controls, or an exhaustive evaluation of those merchandise planning and control devices already implemented.

merchandising and the computer

The planning and control of merchandise inventories has always amounted to a complex, time-consuming task, involving considerable amounts of man hours and great expense. What is more, the value of an inventory planning and control system is usually directly related to its cost. In other words, a good system—one that generates a generous amount of meaningful information—costs large amounts of money. The expense arises because an inventory planning and control system is *an information system*. And as most business-oriented readers know, information on which to base sound operating decisions is not cheap. As a matter of fact, it is quite dear, because it is difficult to obtain. Any merchandise planning and control system must consider at least the following factors:

1. What information is desired?
2. Where should the information be obtained?
3. When should the information be gathered?

4. Who should gather the information?

5. How should it be utilized, reported, and disseminated?

The problems associated with many merchandise planning and control systems relate to the tremendous bulk of paper work, tabulating and classifying of information, incorporating this information, and disseminating it at the right time to the decision makers charged with the critical responsibility of merchandise management decisions. This problem has two major dimensions. On the one hand, the sheer bulk of information to be processed, tabulated, and worked up into a meaningful report form adds a burden of paper work not easily managed by the average retail firm. On the other hand, this factor generates another: By the time the information is available, it is a collection of obsolete operating statistics, rather than a set of timely and meaningful data, thoroughly analyzed and ready for management utilization. To a considerable extent, the electronic computer and a complementary assortment of hard- and software packages have eliminated these problems.

Computer Applications

The electronic computer is providing assistance with merchandise management problems in several areas. For example, buyers and merchandise managers often wish to know how their operations compare with others. To make these comparisons they have relied heavily on MOR (Merchandising Operating Results) figures made available by the National Retail Merchants Association. Unfortunately, these figures were never as timely as the decision maker would have preferred. However, with EDP (Electronic Data Processing) equipment, the NRMA is now making MOR figures available much faster; in some instances, even monthly reports are being made available. The classifications reported and the speed of these reports, made possible by the computer and a new format, are bringing increasing benefits and opportunities for better decisions to retailers throughout the country.[19]

When computerization of business began to take on the look of a practical reality, retailers initially looked on the computer as a tool to accelerate the velocity of the rather traditional methods of handling data. The computer was viewed as simply another labor-saving device. Given its ability to process staggering amounts of information and to print out useful summaries and records, it was seen as a means of freeing human personnel from much of the drudgery of information gathering, processing, and record keeping.

However, as retailers became more familiar with the electronic computer, they began to see its capabilities and the potential for handling new forms of data processing, for providing more detailed processing using more sophisticated techniques, with an end result of furnishing more useful information. Today, new forms of electronic data processing equipment specifically designed for retailing and used in conjunction with new programs to direct the equipment speed processing of vital reports offer capabilities for

[19] See "Retail EDP Costs to Hit $800 Million," *Chain Store Age*, Executive's Edition, (February 1971), pp. E17–E22.

more useful reports and make automatic reordering a routine possibility for retailers.[20]

The computer offers almost unbelievable assistance in terms of inventory planning and control activities for both the individual store and the chain operation. In the chain operation, EDP systems form the basis of an information network that makes it possible to tie the inventory management, physical distribution, and merchandising activities of all the units into a centralized information management system, resulting in better overall planning and control.[21]

The typical computer installation, designed as a merchandise management information system, is based essentially on a process of classification or dissection control. As an adjunct, the employment of special cash registers makes possible the handling of a much larger number of classifications. These cash registers punch out a special computer tape that contains the department number, amount of sale, identification of the sales clerk, classification of item, the specific item number, and sometimes even the code number for an individual customer. After hours, the tapes are fed into a battery of equipment that includes optical scanners, and then on into the computer. By the next morning, buyers and merchandise managers receive flash reports on the preceding day's total sales, and immediately thereafter they are given detailed reports broken down by department, subdepartment, and buyer. On a periodic basis, usually weekly, unless special reports are called for, an analysis between inventory and sales is generated. Using input item numbers, very specific reports as to inventory balances and movements can be generated. Some stores are now attempting to input customer numbers, and by doing so, they will eventually build a profile of each individual family's purchasing habits. Information on fashion item movements have been difficult to obtain in the past, but the computer in an EDP system can now send up warning signals indicating whether a line should be reordered or discontinued.

The computer not only offers valuable assistance in terms of managing existing inventories, but in some instances computers are being tested to prepare purchase orders based upon the buyer's forecast of sales potential. The equipment is also being used to predict future sales on the basis of past sales performance.

The computerized grocery store has already arrived. The key to this development is the computerized cash register or check out. Built into each counter is a laser beam scanner. The scanner reads a "Universal Product Code" which consists of a series of vertical bars which are symbols for numbers that identify manufacturers, products, size, or quality. The check out clerk simply slides the products purchased by the consumer over the scanner which instantly looks up the price of the coded commodity and prints it on the customer's receipt along with a description of the item. This price

[20] S. B. Smith, "Automated Inventory Management for Staples," *Journal of Retailing,* Vol. 47, No. 1 (Spring 1971), pp. 55–62.

[21] "Kresge Counts on Computers in Distribution," *Women's Wear Daily,* April 27, 1970, p. 32.

also flashes on a small window so the customer can see the item and the price recorded.

Produce is placed on a computerized scale, a code number is pushed by the clerk, and the produce weighed far more accurately than can be done with the human eye. The weight is translated into price, and then weight, price, and name of the product will be printed on the customer's sales receipt. Finally, the computer-register will then add the bill, figure the applicable taxes and such matters as coupon rebates or the value of food stamps, and print a summary of the entire transaction along with the date and exact time of purchase. At the same time a system-linked computer will keep track of the diminished number of items on the shelves and prepare the necessary data for instant reordering. Such a system may mean a reduction in operating costs of as much as 5 percentage points. Naturally customers are anxious to receive the benefits of these new systems if it means a substantial savings in their costs of purchasing. However, some customer groups are already organizing their resistance to the innovations, stimulated largely by the fear of new systems, the perceived threat imposed by increased impersonalization, and the apprehension that their costs of purchasing will not actually decline.

Computer Costs and Availability

EDP equipment and systems are not inexpensive, yet some type of EDP system for merchandise management operations is generally available to all sizes of retailing institutions. The larger department stores usually own their own systems. However, both larger stores and smaller ones should not overlook the possibilities for leasing such services.[22]

The advent of the time-sharing computer and the remote terminal unit offer unusual opportunities for multiunit operations. With such a system, the main computer can be housed in the centralized merchandising headquarters, and each unit of the system (or the branch stores) can both make inputs and receive outputs at stores located hundreds of miles away. Such a system also greatly facilitates centralized merchandise planning and control and decentralized buying and assortment planning.

The NRMA has recently begun offering a computer service through a contract with Retail Electronic Systems, Staten Island, New York. On a fee basis, each subscribing member can obtain weekly reports on sales, monthly sales and inventory reports, shortages and turnover, open-to-buy, unit control, and other relevant merchandising data.[23]

The computer as a merchandising aid is a valuable tool for decision making. However, the application of the computer to merchandise management requires careful and deliberate thought. The computer is no panacea and should not be viewed as a mysterious but omniscient machine to which

[22] "Does Computer Leasing Hold Any Advantages for Your Company?" *Stores* (October 1967), pp. 37–38.

[23] "Are You Inventorying Less and Enjoying It More?" *Stores* (January 1968), pp. 41–43.

all problems are turned over for instantaneous solution. Quantitative approaches to merchandise management that rely on computer utilization do offer real promise toward the solution of historically sticky merchandising problems. However, computer scientists and operations researchers have a dictum that says, "Garbage in means garbage out." An elaborate formula or a sophisticated computer program and an IBM 360–40 are no assurance whatsoever of sound operating results if the data (the assumptions on which the formulas or programs are based) are inadequate or logically faulty. Models for handling merchandising decisions and/or the computer are not about to replace the merchandise manager. However, they can provide him with meaningful merchandising assistance and free him from an unlimited amount of routine operations.

QUESTIONS FOR STUDY, REFLECTION, AND REVIEW

1. How can the use of analytical models by merchandise managers aid the management process?
2. Why is it helpful to classify and segregate inventories?
3. What is the procedure for classifying inventory items into high, medium, and low value categories?
4. Economic ordering quantity is a merchandise management planning and control activity that desires to balance what two inventory variables?
5. How is merchandise management (the planning and control of merchandise assortments for the purpose of assuring a balanced stock and mix of goods in order to meet expected customer demand) treated within the framework of a capital budgeting process?
6. Of what value to merchandising management decision making is the GMROI concept?
7. Explain the statement, "Stock turn is a means, not an objective, to be sought by the retail firm." Relate your explanation to decision making and cost considerations.
8. If the decision maker uses stock turnover as a criterion for decisions, he must scrutinize almost every dimension of the firm's total retail merchandising strategy. What are some of the possible trouble areas that will be scrutinized if the turnover rate is inadequate or too slow?
9. Gross margin, turnover, and sales per square foot have all been used as decision criteria in regard to product decisions. What are the general shortcomings of these criteria?
10. "The computer offers a valuable aid to merchandise management but is not without areas of limitations." Discuss this statement.

SIX

PRICING POLICIES AND PROCEDURES

15

retail pricing: basic considerations

Price probably has a multiple role in any particular retailing strategy. A retailer may use price to convince customers that the quality of his merchandise is high, or that he is a medium-priced merchandiser, or that his merchandising and pricing program is fair or reasonable.

A given retailer may also use price as a promotional device, as the thrust of his major merchandising appeal. Price might also be used to suggest or project a strong snob appeal or aura of exclusiveness. The role of price is not only multifaceted, but, more importantly, it is also a function of the overall merchandising strategy and goals of the particular merchandising institution.

In the economic sense in our system of market-oriented behavior, price has been delegated the role of market arbitrator. Price is the mechanism for allocating all scarce resources, namely, land, labor, and capital. Price is the mechanism for clearing markets. That is, when oversupplies exist, prices are bid down to the point where the market is cleared. On the other hand, if scarcity of a commodity prevails, price is the mechanism for rationing the scarce supply over the available purchasers; and if too many purchasers exist in relation to available supply, the price is correspondingly bid up until the market forces of supply and demand reach some equilibrium.

From the standpoint of the retail firm, price continues to act as the mechanism that leads to optimal input and output decisions in the system. Decisions relating to what goods and assortments to stock, i.e., the merchandising function, are affected by decisions related to merchandise prices. Decisions relating to price will also affect the decisions of how, where, and to what extent to promote, and what appeals to use. Furthermore, price decisions will affect store location decisions. The decisions about merchandise assortments, promotion, and place in turn will have a strong bearing on the decisions relating to price.

Price decisions also have strong competitive overtones. How decisions are made and what importance is given to price as an active competitive tool are both functions of how the decision maker views his competitive situation. Of course, price differentials affect consumers in many ways and in varying degrees, depending on the product in question, the consumer's relative income position, and the status image of the store and its products. However, no retailer can hope to have considerations such as these compensate for a large price differential for any period of time successfully—more likely than not he will experience some loss in patronage and will eventually find it necessary to take some retaliatory action to meet the competitive situation. In this respect, one writer has dramatized the role of price in the overall strategy of the firm, in the following manner:

> Pricing, and pricing alone, more than any other single decision making activity, is responsible for most of the profit differences among similar firms. . . . How order or product is priced will in itself determine the product mix (that will be offered). The pricing action will make the product more or less attractive to the buyer; the major factor which determines the buyer response. To the extent that costs of the mix produce both profit contributions and favorable responses from buyers, the volume sold will be profitable. The sales revenue, then, is a mixture of the various prices of the different products or orders, and the resultant period profit is a mixture of their profit contribution.[1]

The focus of this chapter to a great extent will be to analyze and to challenge the validity of this set of propositions. First, however, it will be necessary to explore the dimensions of the question, "What is price?"

Price Defined

From an economic standpoint the price of a good or service is derived from its exchange value; that is, value is considered as the command one good or service has over others, and the price is simply that value restated in terms of monetary units. The price of a good or service is an expression in terms of monetary units of the command which that good or service exercises in exchange on the market.

In brief, a price is based upon some assortment of goods and services and is probably easiest to visualize in terms of a simple equation: Money or price (i.e., list or quoted price less deductions—discounts and allowances) equals something else (i.e., a product or service with an attendant bundle of expectations that may include extra services, quality, delivery, credit, and other factors). Thus, in structuring and understanding retailing price policies and decisions, it must be borne in mind that pricing includes dimensions other than just dollars and cents. Price is a figure that equates a given amount of money to some total bundle of satisfactions or expectations.

[1] Spencer A. Tucker, *Pricing for Higher Profit,* McGraw-Hill Book Company, New York, 1966, p. 4.

If the price in terms of dollars and cents is altered, it is likely that the other side of the equation, i.e., the bundle of satisfactions and expectations will likely be altered also. As our discussion will consequently reveal, there are dimensions to price decisions that fall beyond simple accounting and economic calculations.

Price Decision Making Throughout the Channel

The retailer is a member of a distribution network and as a consequence his price decisions are never made in a vacuum. In addition, of course, to his competitors whose prices will in turn affect his, the retailer must also price his merchandise in accordance with factors and conditions relating to other members of the channel network, for example, the manufacturers and, if one is present in the network, the wholesaler. Too many people are under the impression that large profits are always forthcoming from merchandising activities and that a given price for a commodity almost always contains a large amount of both dollar and percentage profit. In reality, however, this is not the usual case. Of course, it is true that all business firms are operated with the expectation that prices will cover operating costs and generate a profit, but the actual amount of profit is usually surprisingly small.

For example, consider the following situation. The P & M Hardware Store stocks and sells a small electric-powered, portable hand mixer that retails for $12.95. P & M Hardware buys the mixer in relatively small quantities from The Empire Distributing Company, a medium-sized specialty line wholesaler. The Empire Distributing Company buys the mixer directly from the manufacturer, The Acme Manufacturing Company.

Let us examine the cost and markup figures in each of these transactions:

Step 1. P & M Hardware Selling Price to Consumer = $12.95
   Markup on Selling Price = 40% or $5.18
   Retail Price − Markup = Cost
   $12.95 − $5.18 = $7.77
   $5.18 Markup = Profit $1.04 (8%) + Expenses $4.14 (32%)

What is revealed is that given a $12.95 selling price, a markup of 40 per cent yields a dollar markup of $5.18, of which 8 per cent or $1.04 is profit and 32 per cent or $4.14 is operating expenses.

Step 2. P & M Hardware bought the mixer from Empire Distributing Company.
   P & M's Purchase Price = $7.77
   Empire Distributing Company's Selling Price = $7.77
   Empire Distributor's Markup (20% of Selling Price) = $1.55
   Price $7.77 − $1.55 = $6.22
   Markup $1.55 = Profit 8% or $.62 + Expenses 12% or $.93

What is revealed in this transaction is that the Empire Distributing Company received a price of $7.77 for the hand mixer, and with a markup of

20 per cent after covering operating expenses of 12 per cent or $.93 per unit, made a unit profit of $.62 or 8 per cent of its selling price.

Step 3. Empire Distributing Company purchased the mixer from Acme Manufacturing Company.

Empire's Purchase Price = $6.22
Acme's Selling Price   = $6.22
Acme's Markup
   Manufacturing Cost per Unit (45%) = $2.80
   Marketing Cost per Unit (40%)   = 2.49
   Profit per Unit (15%)   =   .93
   Selling Price per Unit $6.22

Looking at Step 3 shows that Acme Manufacturing made a profit of $.93 or 15 per cent on a selling price of $6.22 after covering costs of manufacturing and marketing. Finally, what this illustration shows in a rather dramatic way is that no one member of the channel is making a singularly large profit and that in each instance the selling price must cover (1) the acquisition cost of the goods, (2) the operating expenses, and (3) some amount for profit. One additional observation would appear pertinent. Considering that this commodity was sold by three sellers, the manufacturer, the wholesaler, and the retailer, only $2.59 in profit was earned by all three. Again from the above examples, notice that the profit figures are

Retailer $1.04
Wholesale Distributor $ .62
Manufacturer $ .93
                    $2.59 or as a percentage of final retail selling price,

$$\frac{\$2.59}{\$12.95} = 20\% \text{ profit}$$

The important points are that profits by most entrepreneurs, retailers, wholesalers, and manufacturers are usually not excessive and that the selling price must cover a great deal of expenses before profits actually occur. Determining the idealized or right price that will cover these expenses and generate a profit is, for retailing managers, a difficult question, the answer to which involves both the application of art and science.

pricing goals: normative versus realistic considerations

The real question confronting the decision maker is "What price to charge?" In terms of the price equation discussed earlier, it really means, "How does the price decision maker determine the basic list price for his commodities?" *The goal of the price decision maker in the retail firm is to choose a price that in the long run will assure the system of gaining the greatest net return on the total assortment mix.*

To accomplish this end in light of the fact that the costs of a retail management system are nearly all fixed in the short run, the decision maker's approach to price is to choose a level of prices for the total merchandise mix so as to maximize sales or total revenue. Now, total revenue is price × quantity. The sticky point is that often the price that can be received is a function of the quantity offered, and conversely, the quantity that can be sold is a function of the offered price. Furthermore, the price and resulting output sold will affect unit costs, given various sales levels.[2] Thus uncertainties surrounding price decision making begin to mount, preventing or impeding the price decision maker from setting the idealized, right price. Lacking perfect information, the decision maker is forced, therefore, to engage in a combination of conjecture and science in order that he might reduce these states of uncertainty to states of risk. Before proceeding further, it is necessary to outline, more explicitly, the types of uncertainty facing the price decision maker and to explain why these uncertainties impede his pricing objectives and behavior.

Broadly conceived, these uncertainties amount to the following:

1. The price decision maker is uncertain about the nature of the competitive environment within which he operates. Quite simply, he no doubt recognizes that he has some discretion in setting the prices for his products, but, lacking perfect knowledge, he doesn't know clearly either the upper or lower bounds of his pricing freedom. It would thus follow that he does not know the price to charge in order to maximize total revenues or profits.

2. Because of his ignorance about the nature of his competitive environment, the price decision maker does not know what the reaction of his rival sellers will likely be to his price decision. Given the nature of most market structures, price decisions will not go unobserved by competitors, and therefore the price behavior of one seller is likely to be constrained to some degree by his rivals. The degree of constraint will depend upon the nature of the competitive market, i.e., the number of sellers, the nature of the product, and so on.

3. Finally, the typical retail price decision maker is relatively ignorant (or uncertain) about the nature of the demand for the specific products in question. He does not know what the effect of a price decision on sales is likely to be. He does not know if the demand for a given commodity is elastic or inelastic, and therefore his ability to determine the optimum price for his assortment mix is severely limited.

What Relevant Economic Model for Retailing? An analysis of retail pricing decisions and the formation of price policies must give some consideration to organizational objectives, particularly the forces that influence the formulation of these ends. The most obvious and important of the external forces in this respect is market structure. The retail market structure

---

[2] However, given the nature of costs in a retail store, the consequences of this effect are less severe than in some other type of enterprise.

has been called "a complex form of a specific type of nonperfect competition; namely, differentiated oligopoly."[3] According to one authority:

> By oligopoly is meant a situation in which the seller, in determining his price and output policy, takes into account the probable reactions (of competitors) to changes in his policy.[4]

The important point to be emphasized is reflected in this definition, namely, the small number of sellers, the strong interdependence among them with respect to changes in price or any other competitive policy, and the distinction each has, based on real or consumer-perceived differences in the store's products or image.

Although the oligopoly model appears to be a fairly realistic abstraction of retail markets, a number of writers, including Hood and Yamey,[5] Holdren,[6] and Baumol[7] contend that retailers are monopolistic competitors. For example, Baumol states quite forthrightly:

> Competing neighborhood retailers of all sorts are typically monopolistic competitors, each with his corps of more or less loyal customers and locational and personality differences which make his products and services at least somewhat distinct from those of his competitors.[8]

Hood and Yamey continue by stating:

> The use of an oversimplified theory of oligopoly is . . . unrealistic. Freedom of entry and chain linking of markets make it unwise to rely upon a mere counting of numbers. Tacit or formal agreements are not the simple arrangements some theories suggest.[9]

The summary of these positions seems to be that (contrary to the theory of oligopoly) retail monopolies are limited with respect to location, in the sense that firms in juxtaposition with one another are competitively linked with those around them, and this linking by markets continues practically *ad infinitum*. Second, the high degree of entry freedom and lack of price interdependence also give evidence that favors the monopolistic competitive model.

Monopolistic Competition and Price Determination. The general theory of price determination under conditions of monopolistic competition can

---

[3] Ralph Cassady, Jr., *Competition and Price Making in Food Retailing*, The Ronald Press Company, New York, 1962, p. 56.

[4] Margaret Hall, *Distributive Trading*, Hutchinson's University Library, London, 1949, p. 38.

[5] Julia Hood and B. S. Yamey, "Imperfect Competition in the Retail Trades," *Economica*, Vol. 18, No. 70 (1951), pp. 119–137.

[6] Bob R. Holdren, *The Structure of a Retail Market and Market Behavior of Retail Units*, Prentice-Hall, Inc., Englewood Cliffs, N.J., 1960, p. 182.

[7] William J. Baumol, *Economic Theory and Operations Analysis*, 2nd ed., Prentice-Hall, Inc., Englewood Cliffs, N.J., 1965, p. 182.

[8] Ibid.

[9] Hood and Yamey, op. cit., p. 136.

be sketched briefly. Figure 15-1 represents the demand and cost structure of a retail firm in a monopolistic, competitively structured market.

The retail firm in the monopolistic, competitively structured market has a degree of monopoly power because of its ability to differentiate its product assortment or its store's total offer variation in the eyes of some buyers. Therefore its demand curve or its average revenue curve slopes downward and to the right (a negative slope), which indicates that at higher prices the firm loses some sales, but not all. Recall that the seller in pure competition has a perfectly elastic demand curve—a demand curve that is a horizontal straight line at the level of the going market price. From the demand curve, the marginal revenue curve (MR) that represents the change in total revenue resulting from a unit change in output is derived. The average total cost (ATC) curve and the marginal costs curve (MC) are then drawn; and in terms of the conventional decision rule of economic analysis, price is set at the point on the average revenue curve where (MC) marginal costs $= (MR)$ marginal revenue. This is the point at which the rate of change in total costs equals the rate of change in total revenues. From Figure 15-1 the observation can be made that the optimum output is ON units that will be sold at a price, OP. Total revenue is the price times the quantity sold, or the geometric area of the rectangle $OPRN$, and total cost is the geometric area $OTSN$. Net profit (total revenue $-$ total cost) would be the area of the rectangle $PRST$. Net profits are only maximized when price and output are established where $MC = MR$.

As a matter of fact, the decision rule for price and output determination under each of the economic models discussed is the same, namely, set price and determine output at that level where $MC = MR$. It is a normative decision rule, inasmuch as it tells the decision maker what he *ought* to do. However, in actuality, economic price decision making has several serious

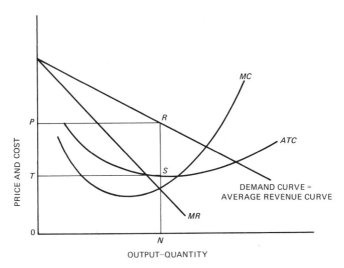

FIGURE 15-1 Price determination for a retail firm in a monopolistic competitive market structure.

shortcomings that limit its usefulness for the retail management decision maker. The economic decision rule to set price where $MC = MR$ contains the following implicit assumptions:

1. At any point in time, the business firm desires only to maximize total profits; other business goals are not considered. From earlier discussions we have learned that this is not a likely condition. The retail manager/decision maker is probably much more of a satisficer than a maximizer.
2. Marginal analysis is a static concept; therefore, it ignores the time dimension of decision making. The $MC = MR$ decision rule applies only to a given *point* in time, and the decision maker may be quite willing, when considering his entire planning horizon, to choose a price that does not equate MC to MR.
3. Finally, the most serious limitation is that in order to derive both marginal cost and marginal revenue, the demand at various prices and total costs at various outputs must be known.

It should be pointed out that fulfilling these assumptions is at least as difficult as completing the twelve labors of Hercules. This is not to say that there is nothing of value for the retail price decision maker regarding economic analysis or demand-oriented pricing. Quite the contrary, as has already been shown, economic analysis provides considerable insight into the whole problem of price determination. However, it does not provide determinate answers or solutions to pricing problems, unless the pricing problem is structured quite simply with simplifying assumptions relating to demand and costs underlying the pricing situation.

Retail Price Determination: Upper and Lower Bounds

No firm can charge more for its commodities or services than is justified by demand considerations. On the other hand, no retail firm should charge less for a commodity or service than its incremental costs of producing and/or selling that commodity or service. Somewhere between these upper and lower bounds (i.e., the level of demand and the level of the firm's relevant costs) lies the right price for each of the firm's individual products or services.

Earlier, it was stated that the pricing goal of the retail decision maker was to choose a price that in the long run would assure the firm of gaining the greatest net return on the total assortment mix. This is an ideal goal, because such a price would be optimum; that is, it would maximize profits and would equate marginal costs to marginal revenue. Given the difficulties of using and implementing marginal analysis in his price decisions, the retail manager is more concerned with obtaining a satisfactory return (profit). This means setting his prices so as not to price above the level of demand or price himself out of the market, and not setting a price below his variable or incremental cost in the short run, which would mean a direct out-of-pocket loss on all the units sold for this particular commodity. Therefore, demand is the upper bound or constraint on the price decision maker, and a price that exceeds this upper bound can be ruled as too high. Conversely, costs are the lower constraint on the pricing decision, and in the short run no price should be lower than the incremental or variable costs associated with the product. In the long run, of course, all costs become variable costs; therefore price must exceed total costs.

The realistic goal of the retail price decision maker is to know when a price is either too high or too low. If he can make this determination, he should thus have some insight as to when one price is better or worse than another.

Administered Pricing Models

Like most businessmen confronted with pricing decisions, the typical retail manager argues convincingly that he knows considerably more about the nature of his costs of operation than he does about such nebulous and esoteric concepts as demand. As a result, his pricing behavior tends to reflect this attitude, and the effect is a great emphasis in retailing on cost-oriented decisions. Bear in mind that retailing is characterized as an industry in which administered pricing is the norm. The retailing manager is a satisficer rather than a maximizer. Demand is too difficult to estimate to come up with determinate demand equations. Because of these factors, cost-oriented pricing decisions appear not only likely but highly probable. There are two widely used and standard cost-oriented pricing approaches: average cost pricing and target-rate-of-return pricing.

Average Cost Pricing. Average cost pricing is a cost-oriented pricing system whereby a reasonable or standard markup is added to the cost per unit to determine the retail selling price. Both average cost pricing and target-rate-of-return pricing must rely on cost figures that are sometimes nothing more than crude estimations. Because of the large number and variety of products carried, most retailers find that it is difficult to allocate costs accurately to specific products. Merchandise acquisition costs are the only costs that can be treated with certainty.[10] The allocation of other costs to particular products is done on a largely arbitrary basis. In addition, as discussed in Chapter 3, retailers are often more interested in the overall gross margin of the entire store or of a major department than in the gross margin or contribution margin earned by any single product. For this reason, exact costs associated with particular products are not always considered crucial to a particular decision, and retailers are therefore willing to rely on average cost concepts as guides to price decision making.

However, even average cost estimates can be improved by the use of distribution cost analysis, which involves essentially the identification and classification of costs into functional cost groups. Such a classification might include selling space costs, the costs of space for merchandise display and storage, inventory costs, and movement costs; or the costs of customer and

---

[10] William E. Arnstein, "Relating Price to Costs," *Management Review*, Vol. 61, No. 3 (March 1972), pp. 27–30.

service area space and clerk time, and sales volume costs; or costs emanating from such activities as trading stamps, contests, or other forms of special promotions. Distribution cost analysis can thus lead to better price decision making on the basis of a better understanding of costs. It assists in the identification and measurement of distribution costs and thereby permits the firm to price more wisely. Furthermore, distribution cost analysis provides information on the probable results of alternative prices, helps to determine when price adjustments are required by pointing up profitable versus unprofitable products, and finally, it can provide concrete supporting evidence that can be used to persuade suppliers to make price and margin adjustments.[11]

Average cost pricing methods can best be illustrated by using a simple example. The essence of average cost pricing is to determine the cost base for a recent period or for a forecasted period by dividing total costs by the number of units sold or anticipated to be sold. To illustrate, assume that the total costs for a toy department during a given period (the last Christmas season) amounted to $25,000. Of this $25,000, $10,000 was allocated to fixed costs, and variable costs amounted to $15,000. For the sake of simplicity, assume that 2,500 units of toys were sold during this period. The average cost per unit was thus $10 ($25,000 total cost divided by 2,500 units sold). The next step is to determine the amount of profit that would appear reasonable and, if 15 per cent was deemed so, then take 15 per cent of $10 = $1.50, which, when added to the cost of $10 would result in a chosen price of $11.50. However, retail profits seldom reach much over 5 per cent of the sales dollar on an after tax basis. In the case of supermarkets, both chain and independents are likely to report profits of only one or two per cent of sales. The critical point is that average price is closely related to the cost of goods sold and the level of expenses incurred; that is, price is closely related to total costs, plus the desired profit margin. Another important point in regard to average cost pricing is that specific prices may be above or below the average, depending upon local market conditions, the specific price policies of the retailer, or his estimate of the rate of sale of a particular commodity at various selling prices.[12]

Average cost pricing can be summarized as a method whereby an attempt is made to forecast costs and then to choose a price that at a given volume will generate sufficient sales revenue to cover all costs and provide a margin of profit.

Target-Rate-of-Return Pricing. Target-rate-of-return pricing is another form of average cost pricing with which the price decision maker attempts to receive some percentage of, or total dollar return on, his investment, which is the capital required to service or support a level of sales activity. For example, assume that in a luggage department of a department store 500 units of a given size bag were sold last year, and it is anticipated that the same number will be sold again this year. If fixed costs allocated to the line

[11] Alfred R. Oxenfeldt, "A Decision-Making Structure for Price Decisions," *Journal of Marketing*, Vol. 37, No. 1 (January 1973), pp. 48–53.

[12] Otto L. Hall, "Markup—Based on Assets Employed," *Management Accounting*, Vol. LII, No. 8 (February 1971), pp. 48–49.

are $5,000, $15,000 is the total investment in assets required to service and support this line, and a 20 per cent return on investment (R.O.I.) is desired, then, fixed costs plus investment return are determined as follows: $5,000 (FC) + $3,000 ($15,000 investment times 20 per cent, or R.O.I.) = $8,000, or total fixed costs plus the target-rate-of-return. This figure divided by 500 (the units anticipated to be sold) = $16.00. If the variable cost per unit equals $12.00, then the retail selling price that covers all costs and generates a 20 per cent return on investment would be $16.00 + $12.00 = $28.00.[13]

Shortcomings of Average Cost Pricing. The shortcomings or failings of average cost pricing apply with equal strength to the target-rate-of-return model just described. Both rely on average cost determinations, which in turn have two critical requirements. The first is the necessity to forecast sales with reasonable accuracy. During such constant growth periods as the last eight to ten years, this has not been too difficult a factor. However, because average costs are a function of a particular sales level, any sales level that deviates widely from that which is anticipated can throw pricing accuracy completely out of kilter. If actual sales do not vary too much from the previous period, average cost pricing methods will produce reasonably good results. If actual sales are much lower than anticipated, then losses will be the likely result. Conversely, if actual sales are much higher than anticipated, then large windfall profits are likely to be the result.

There is a considerable amount of circular reasoning involved in average cost pricing. For instance, the decision maker must forecast sales to determine his prices. Yet, intuitively, one knows that the level of sales actually achieved will be a function of the level of prices set. Certainly there is no guarantee of good results with average cost methods of pricing because sales may fluctuate either way. Therefore, when market conditions are changing rapidly, average cost methods of pricing leave a great deal to be desired. Given the favorable climate of rapid and steady growth that has characterized the economy for the past several years, however, average cost pricing methods continue to be widely used.

The second critical requirement of average cost pricing methods is that costs must be analyzed and carefully allocated to the various products in the total assortment mix. Most retail firms use some sort of worksheet to develop an expected cost per unit for each particular product, when evaluating individual product prices. Yet a great deal of guesswork and judgment must go into the actual determination of costs as they apply to each specific product pricing decision. Economic analysis would dictate that demand (rather than cost) should be the principal determinant of prices. Yet the uncertainties relating to demand conditions, a multiproduct line consisting of hundreds and thousands of different products, and the complexities of demand-oriented pricing models generally bode against the adoption of demand-oriented pricing models by the practical retail decision maker. Simplicity of understanding and ease of use and implementation may mean

---

[13] For more relating to this topic, see George C. Cutler, "Developing the Selling Price," *Management Accounting,* Vol. LIII, No. 2 (August 1971), pp. 41–42.

that in the final analysis average cost pricing models are most efficient and effective from the standpoint of the retail price decision maker.

average cost pricing
and markup policies

A knowledge of average cost pricing methods greatly facilitates a more thoroughgoing understanding of retail markup policies. The typical retail decision maker using average cost pricing methods, determines the retail selling price for each item in his assortment mix by adding some markup (either in dollars or percentage) to the cost price of the item. Thus, Retail selling price is Cost + Markup, where cost is defined as acquisition cost (landed cost) of the merchandise, and markup is the amount added to cost in order to cover expenses and to generate some reasonable profit. These relationships are shown schematically in Figure 15-2.

Figure 15-2 shows exactly what has been shown before, though in slightly different fashion, namely, that Sales − Cost of goods = Gross margin, and Gross margin − Expenses = Profits. Figure 15-2 has simply summed these elements, i.e., Net profit + Operating expenses + Cost of goods sold (acquisition costs) = Selling price.

Average cost pricing is a method of determining prices by adding an average margin or markup to average costs. One of the interesting issues that arises in retail price determination is whether the decision maker should always add the same standard or uniform percentage margin to merchandise cost in order to determine the retail selling price. Practice varies among retailers in regard to this question. For many years it was characteristic for retail management systems such as department stores, furniture stores, and jewelry stores to follow the practice of adding standard or uniform percentage margins to merchandise costs. For instance, it was long common practice in department stores to have a uniform gross margin of 40 per cent on all commodities. Retail prices in furniture stores were determined for all commodities by doubling the cost of the commodity and adding 10 per cent. Jewelry stores followed similar uniform percentage or gross margin pricing practices. However, two factors that are probably re-

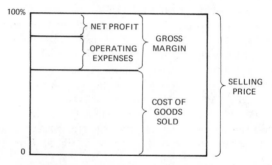

FIGURE 15-2 A schematic composite of retail selling price.

lated have led to an increasing departure from this practice. One is the greater understanding of the concept of price elasticity, and the other is the demonstrated use of this concept by certain retailing institutions, foremost of which is the discount store. This practice of applying uniform set markups to cost almost automatically left some types of retailers extremely vulnerable to the new competition of discount and other low-margin operators who were more carefully examining such factors as cost, demand, and elasticity considerations.

The first major introduction of the reader to the concept of markup came in Chapter 13, "Merchandise Management." In that chapter it was emphasized that merchandise budgeting and expense planning necessitate planning initial markup. Because it is so central a management responsibility, merchandise budgeting actually touches upon the whole range of strategy decisions including promotion, place, and *price* decisions. As has been learned, initial markup must ultimately cover all expenses (costs) plus profits. It was also shown earlier that several different kinds of markup must be considered in markup planning requirements. Usually, it is *initial* markup that is of primary importance in markup planning. The reader should understand that markup planning is a form of pricing decision, inasmuch as retail prices most often are simply average costs plus markup.

Initial markup and its relationship to both the important retailing decision concepts of maintained markup and gross margin can be illustrated as follows:

$$\text{Initial markup} = \frac{\text{Maintained markup} + \text{Reductions}}{\text{Sales} + \text{Reductions}} \qquad (1)$$

$$\text{Maintained markup} = \text{Gross margin} - \text{Cash discounts earned} + \text{Alteration costs} \qquad (2)$$

$$\text{Gross margin} = \text{Maintained markup} + \text{Cash discounts earned} - \text{Alteration costs} \qquad (3)$$

You can readily acquire an understanding of these concepts by examining their interdependence. In the initial markup formula (1) for example, by substituting the information to the right of the equal sign in formula (2), both the concept of initial markup and maintained markup become clearer in terms of their relationship to gross margin (3).

To illustrate the relationship between markup planning and retail pricing decisions, consider the following situation: A small store has a budgeted sales figure of $100,000 for the next six-month planning period. Its operating expenses are expected to equal 30 per cent of sales, markdowns to equal 8 per cent of sales, shortages to equal 2 per cent of sales; and it wishes to attain a profit of 6 per cent of sales. Therefore,

Sales = $100,000	$30,000 = expenses
	8,000 = markdowns
	2,000 = shortages
	6,000 = profit
	$46,000 = dollar markup required to bring about these conditions

The original retail value of the merchandise equals the budget sales figure of $100,000, plus the retail reductions ($8,000 markdowns + $2,000 shortages) or $110,000. Therefore, the $46,000 (dollar markup) ÷ $110,000 = 41.8 or 42 per cent, which is the initial markup. Determining the initial markup is thus an exercise using average costs to determine markup and therefore pricing decisions, because the markup percentage is found by using the following general formula:

$$\text{Initial markup} = \frac{\text{Expenses} + \text{Profits} + \text{Reductions}}{\text{Sales} + \text{Reductions}}$$

It will be observed that in this formula Expenses + Profits = Gross margin. Thus, the formula could be stated as

$$\text{Initial markup } \% = \frac{\text{Gross margin } \% + \text{Retail reduction } \%}{\text{Sales } (100\%) + \text{Retail reduction } \%}$$

From the foregoing example

$$\text{Initial markup } \% = \frac{30\% + 6\% + 10\%}{100\% + 10\%} = \frac{46\%}{110\%} = 42\%$$

This example is intended to show that a merchant who wishes to price his merchandise and service offering in order to yield an average gross margin of 36 per cent would require an initial markup of 42 per cent.[14]

Markup is the difference between retail price and the cost price of the merchandise. However, retail price can be a rather nebulous and confusing term. Ordinarily, when speaking about markup what is really meant is initial markup that is based upon the original retail price. Cost also can be a confusing term. For markup purposes, Cost = Merchandise cost + Freight-in. Cash discounts are ordinarily not deducted from the billed cost of the invoice, but are treated as other income, because they are a financial earning rather than a merchandise earning.[15]

By formula:

$$\text{Markup} = \text{Retail} - \text{Cost}$$

Or, solving for retail:

$$\text{Retail} = \text{Cost} + \text{Markup}$$

Or solving for cost:

$$\text{Cost} = \text{Retail} - \text{Markup}$$

[14] Two excellent treatises on markup determination and related concepts are B. P. Corbman, *Mathematics of Retail Merchandising*, The Ronald Press Company, New York, 1952, especially Chaps. 1, 2, 3, and 4; and John W. Wingate, Elmer O. Schaller, and Irving Goldenthal, *Problems in Retail Merchandising*, Prentice-Hall, Inc., Englewood Cliffs, N.J., 1961, especially Chaps. 5, 6, and 7.

[15] Quantity or trade discounts are considered merchandise earnings and not financial earnings; therefore these discounts would be deducted from the billed cost of the invoice in order to determine the net price of the merchandise.

Often what is desired is to compute the markup percentage on either the retail price or the cost price of the merchandise. To illustrate, assume that an item selling for $1.00 carries a $.40 markup. The markup on retail equals

$$\frac{\$\text{ Markup}}{\text{Retail price}} = \frac{\$.40}{\$1.00} = 40\%$$

The markup on cost equals

$$\frac{\$\text{ Markup}}{\text{Cost}} = \frac{\$.40}{\$.60} = 66\tfrac{2}{3}\%$$

How was the cost determined? By using the formula above; namely, Cost = Retail − Markup. Therefore, Retail = $1.00, and Markup = $.40, so the cost of the merchandise is $1.00 − $.40 = $.60.

Two other formulas are useful in markup and pricing decisions. As is often the case where markup is figured as a percentage of the retail selling price, the decision maker may wish to compare his markup with a markup figured on cost. Or, conversely, a markup on cost might be compared to a markup on retail. Thus,

$$\% \text{ Markup on Selling price} = \frac{\% \text{ Markup on Cost}}{100\% + \% \text{ Markup on Cost}}$$

or

$$\% \text{ Markup on Cost} = \frac{\% \text{ Markup on Selling price}}{100\% - \% \text{ Markup on Selling price}}$$

Some examples might serve to illustrate the use of these two formulas. Assume that markup on cost in a given store equals 50 per cent. What is the equivalent markup as a percentage of the retail selling price? The solution is as follows:

$$\begin{aligned}
\% \text{ Markup on Selling price} &= \frac{50\% \text{ (Markup on Cost)}}{100\% + 50\% \text{ (Markup on Cost)}} \\
&= \frac{\$.50}{\$1.50} \\
&= 33\tfrac{1}{3}\%
\end{aligned}$$

In another instance, suppose John Jackson, Jr. runs a retail store inherited from his father. John, Jr.'s average markup percentage on retail is 40 per cent. John's father always figured markup per cent on cost, and he argues that John, Jr. is not as good a merchant as he was in his day, because he was always able to realize an average markup on cost of 50 per cent. How would you settle the argument? The solution is as follows:

$$\begin{aligned}
\% \text{ Markup on Cost} &= \frac{\text{Markup } \% \text{ on Selling price (40\%)}}{100\% - \% \text{ Markup on Selling price (40\%)}} \\
&= \frac{.40}{.60} \\
&= 66\tfrac{2}{3}\%
\end{aligned}$$

Actually, therefore, John, Jr. is receiving a higher equivalent markup than his father did, because a 40 per cent markup on retail selling price is equivalent to a 66⅔ per cent markup on cost.

Table 15-1 is a table of equivalent markups.

By using similar though somewhat more detailed tables, buyers, department managers and others concerned with pricing decisions can readily compare markup percentages on retail with markup percentages on cost, and vice versa. The standard procedure for using markup tables is to first determine the desired markup percentage on retail and then in the parallel column to find the markup percentage on cost. By multiplying the markup per cent on cost by the actual cost price (merchandise cost plus freight-in), the actual retail selling price of the item can be determined. The markup determined as a percentage of the selling price is always less than the markup determined on cost. This is so because of the following relationships: If retail price is always equal to 100%, then Retail = Cost + Markup; Markup = Retail − Cost; and Cost = Retail − Markup.

To summarize:

Markup	$ .40 =	40% of Cost or 28.5% of Selling price
+ Cost	$1.00 =	100% of Cost or 71.5% of Selling price
= Selling price	$1.40 =	140% of Cost or 100% of Selling price

Consequently, if selling price is the base, then Cost + Markup will never exceed 100%. However, if merchandise cost is chosen as the base for figuring markup, the selling price will equal 100% (the cost base) plus the markup percentage on cost.

TABLE 15-1   A Table of Frequently Employed Markups: Retail and Cost

MARKUP % ON SELLING PRICE	MARKUP % ON COST	MARKUP % ON SELLING PRICE	MARKUP % ON COST
20.0	25.0	34.0	51.5
21.0	26.6	35.0	53.9
22.0	28.2	35.5	55.0
22.5	29.0	36.0	56.3
23.0	29.9	37.0	58.8
23.1	30.0	37.5	60.0
24.0	31.6	38.0	61.3
25.0	33.3	39.0	64.0
26.0	35.0	39.5	65.5
27.0	37.0	40.0	66.7
27.3	37.5	41.0	70.0
28.0	39.0	42.0	72.4
28.5	40.0	42.8	75.0
29.0	40.9	44.4	80.0
30.0	42.9	46.1	85.0
31.0	45.0	47.5	90.0
32.0	47.1	48.7	95.0
33.3	50.0	50.0	100.0

It matters relatively little whether markup is figured as a per cent of the retail price or the cost price of the merchandise. The important points are that the decision maker understands the difference between the two markup bases and that he is consistent in his use of one or the other. Historically, markup was more frequently based upon cost. However, there now is an almost universal adoption of the Retail Inventory Method of Accounting in which sales equal 100 per cent and expenses are related to sales as a percentage of sales. Consequently, profits are obtained by selling merchandise, and thus quite appropriately, profits are figured as a percentage of sales. If expenses and profits are thought of as percentages of sales, gross margin likewise would be determined as a percentage of sales. Thus, markup was gradually converted to a retail sales basis from a cost basis.

In summary, an understanding of the various markup concepts is absolutely fundamental to the understanding of retail price decision making. It should be thought of as a valuable retail tool—as a control and planning device by the buyer's superiors, as a negotiation instrument with suppliers, and as a decision tool by the buyer.[16] Our attention will be directed in Chapter 16 to a discussion and analysis of actual retail pricing behavior, policy, and procedures.

QUESTIONS FOR STUDY, REFLECTION, AND REVIEW

1. What is price?
2. What are the relevant factors that need to be considered in retail price decision making?
3. What three primary areas of uncertainty does the retail price decision maker face?
4. Discuss the usage and limitations of the economic decision rule to set price where $MC = MR$.
5. Retail price determination can be viewed within upper and lower bounds. What are these bounds and what implications do they have regarding pricing?
6. Describe the average cost pricing method for decision making.
7. Describe how to determine a price by the target-rate-of-return pricing decision criterion.
8. What are the major shortcomings of the average cost pricing decision?
9. What arguments could you advance that would support the notion that supermarkets are oligopolists?
10. What should be the relationship between the product's selling season, the product's life cycle, the markup that is added to cost, and the price elasticity of demand?

[16] Roger Dickinson, "Markup in Department Store Management," *Journal of Marketing*, Vol. 31 (January 1967), p. 34.

16

retail pricing: concepts, practices, and policies

In Chapter 15 some theoretical considerations for understanding retailing price practices and policies were laid down. The material of that chapter dealt basically with the major determinants of retail pricing decisions, namely, demand and cost considerations. The treatment was undertaken within a framework of economic analysis, but it was learned, also, that retail price decision makers usually have some freedom or discretion to administer prices. By definition administered price means that price is not determined solely by impersonal market forces, as would be the case of a firm operating in a purely competitive environment. Instead, administered price suggests that the price maker has options or freedom to choose from among a range of prices that price which he believes is best for his pricing situation. Sometimes the range from which the price decision maker must choose is very narrow, given a thin demand for the product, a number of sellers, similar cost structures, and relatively little product or enterprise differentiation. In other instances, the range may be quite large, which would suggest a number of possible conditions: brisk demand, a limited number of sellers, product or enterprise differentiation, or possibly different cost structures.

In Chapter 15 we learned that retail prices usually are determined more on the basis of costs than on demand. The usual and more pragmatic explanation for this determination is that demand is both complex and highly uncertain and therefore difficult to analyze, understand, and use as a basis for retail pricing decisions. Yet, demand is reflected in pricing decisions that are predicated on such other concepts as turnover and variable markup formulas.

Retail price decisions therefore are usually based upon costs. They are influenced by competitive conditions, or what might be called economic factors, and they usually are set at an odd figure ($1.98), rather than at even dollar figures ($2.00). The two principal forms of administered pricing approaches utilized are average cost pricing and target-rate-of-return pricing, and the former is much more popular than the latter. Most firms (smaller ones, especially, use standard gross margin or markup pricing, while some firms (usually the larger and more sophisticated ones) recognize the importance of demand considerations (if only intuitively) and therefore use flexible markup systems.

In this chapter, our interest will center more closely around the pragmatic retail pricing concepts, practices, and policies that actually influence or affect the retail pricing decision. The different kinds of retail pricing decisions will be more completely analyzed. A range of frequently practiced and implemented pricing policies will be examined and finally, a series of external constraints placed upon the pricing decision maker (e.g., legislative prohibitions) will be treated.

programmed or routinized price decisions

Many of the price decisions made by retail managers are programmed decisions. The term *program* has been borrowed from the electronic computer industry and is used here in largely the same way as it is used in that context. A *program* is a detailed prescription or strategy that governs the sequence of responses of a system to a complex task environment. It should be pointed out that most of the programs (deliberate plans or schedules) that govern the retail management system's organizational response are not as detailed or precise as computer programs. However, their purpose is largely the same, namely, to permit an adaptive or accommodative response to a dynamic decision situation. Programmed decisions are repetitive and routine, and for this reason, definite procedures have been worked out for handling them. Nonprogrammed decisions are novel, unstructured, and consequential; there is no readily available cut-and-dried method for handling them.[1] In actuality it is possible to work out deliberate, preplanned, programmed procedures for handling the preponderance of pricing decisions in most retail firms because of their repetitive and routine nature. Such a condition facilitates the operation of the retail firm in several ways. First, it enables the members of the decision-making system to understand the basis on which prices are often determined. Second, it often makes it possible for superiors in the system to study the nature of the pricing problem and then build or program a procedure for handling all the pricing problems fitting this particular classification. Third, having programmed or routinized certain pricing problems, managers can then delegate the actual price making to lower level subordinates throughout the system.

The usual pricing models of economic analysis are prescriptive rather than descriptive. That is, they tell the decision maker that he *ought* to set

[1] Herbert A. Simon, *The New Science of Management Decision,* Harper & Row, Publishers, New York, 1960, p. 6.

price where marginal cost equals marginal revenue. But he often doesn't know how to determine either his marginal cost or his marginal revenue. Thus, economic analysis offers no real or useful explanation of actual price behavior. It assumes an economic rationale, perfect information, goal consistency, and profit maximization. Yet, a more careful examination of programmed pricing models reveals that factors such as personal biases, conjectural interdependence, imperfect competition, and organizational influences may more realistically depict real price decisions in a realistic setting.[2]

Programmed pricing decisions are generally based upon models of a particular pricing situation. More generally, the models used to depict pricing decisions in realistic settings are *descriptive;* they represent attempts to describe what is, rather than what should be. Furthermore, these models are based upon direct observation and testing rather than on abstract or theoretical principles, and for this reason, the models are said to be empirical. Thus far, the reader of this text has been exposed to several different classes of models such as verbal models and mathematical models. The programmed pricing models about to be introduced are what one set of writers has called "logical flow models." They are sometimes called simply flow charts. Logical flow models use three kinds of language:[3]

1. Everyday language—to describe questions asked and actions taken by the subject of the model.
2. Circles, diamonds and squares—to enclose physically the sets of questions and actions described by the model.
3. Arrows—to indicate the flow of questions and actions: the sequence in which questions are asked and actions are taken.

Figure 16-1 shows verbal, mathematical, and logical flow models. The logical flow model is constructed from the verbal or prose model by describing the questions asked and by describing the action taken. The statements that flow from the action taken are set down in the logical sequential fashion in which they appear in the behavior process and by simply using geometrical shapes and arrows (which depict the direction of behavior), there emerges a picture of relationships that describes all the behavior sequences.

Logical flow models are generally constructed with the aid of three kinds of data. First, interviews are usually held with the decision maker, in which the interviewer attempts to assess how the decision maker performs his job. Second, the interviewer attempts to observe the decision maker as he makes current decisions, and third, the analyst attempts to gain access to the department's or firm's written records that summarize the results of a host of past decisions.

[2] Leonard J. Parsons and W. Bailey Price, "Adaptive Pricing by a Retailer," *Journal of Marketing Research,* Vol. IX, No. 2 (May 1972), pp. 127–133.
[3] William F. Massy and Jim D. Savvas, "Logical Flow Models for Marketing Analysis," *Journal of Marketing,* Vol. 28 (January 1964), pp. 30–37.

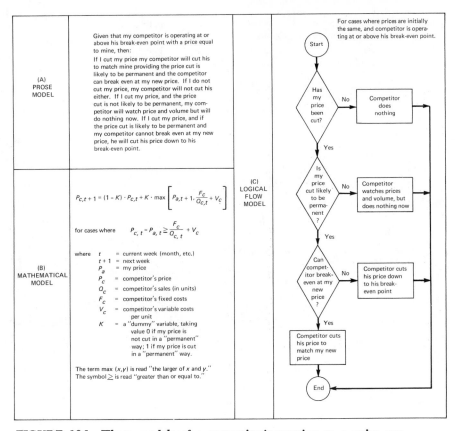

FIGURE 16-1 Three models of a competitor's reaction to a price cut.

SOURCE: William F. Massy and Jim D. Savvas, "Logical Flow Models for Marketing Analysis," Journal of Marketing, Vol. 28 (January 1964), p. 32.

Kinds of Programmed Pricing Decisions

There are essentially three major kinds of programmed pricing decisions made by retail stores: (1) regular price decisions, (2) sale price decisions, and (3) markdown pricing decisions. Not all stores, of course, will generate all three kinds of programmed decisions, but, generally, most stores from time to time will generate all three.

Regular Price Decisions. Regular price decisions are by far the most normal and therefore most routine price decisions made by the retail firm. Although they are affected by a host of pricing determinants or policies, the essence of the regular pricing decision is concerned with what original price to place on the merchandise or services for sale. As was shown earlier, the preponderant method of determining retail prices centers around some average cost formula converted to a markup base. By firm policy, standard or regular prices usually end in $.95. Thus, in a store whose normal markup

TABLE 16-1 Regular Prices from Standard Markup Program

STANDARD COSTS ($)	PLANNED PRICE ($)	EFFECTIVE MARKUP (%)
3.00	5.00	40.0
3.75	5.95	37.0
4.75	7.95	40.2
5.50	8.95	38.5
6.75	10.95	38.3
7.75	12.95	40.1
8.75	14.95	41.5
10.75	17.95	40.0
11.75	19.95	41.0
13.75	22.95	40.0
14.75	25.00	41.0
18.75	29.95	37.4

SOURCE: Richard M. Cyert and James G. March, A Behavioral Theory of the Firm, © 1963. Reprinted by permission of Prentice-Hall, Inc., Englewood Cliffs, N.J., p. 138.

is 40 per cent, the standard programmed decision rule for determining the price of regular merchandise would be

Divide each cost by 0.6 (1 — markup) and move the result to the nearest $.95.

Using such a rule, the effective markups are shown in Table 16-1.

By policy edict, this programmed pricing routine may be altered. In the case of exclusive items or other special purchases which might represent exceptional values, the standard procedure would be used, but with instructions to use the next highest price on the standard schedule.

Sale Price Decisions. Both regular price decisions and sale price decisions ought to be considered as normal programmed pricing situations. That is, they are a part of the firm's normal operation. On the other hand, markdown pricing is a form of *exception principle pricing*, which means that determining markdown prices arises from the fact that mistakes have occurred within the system (goods were originally overpriced, buying mistakes were made, e.g., wrong colors, sizes, styles, amounts), or conditions have changed outside the system that have altered the demand characteristics of the goods, e.g., a change in a competitor's price, change in a supplier's price, and so on.

Sales events are promotional activities designed to stimulate sales revenue by tempting consumers to visit the store and buy the sale-priced item plus other items and/or to arouse consumer interest that will eventually shift the demand curve to the right. Sale pricing can be a highly effective form of creative decision making in the retail management system.[4]

[4] See David B. Gardner, "An Experimental Investigation of the Price/Quantity Relationship," *Journal of Retailing*, Vol. 46, No. 3 (Fall 1970), pp. 25–41.

Once again, it should be emphasized that programmed decision rules for sale pricing events stem from the store's general pricing attitudes and policies. In one study, sale pricing decision rules were as follows:[5]

1. If normal price falls on one of the following lines, the corresponding sales price will be used:

NORMAL PRICE ($)	SALE PRICE ($)
1.00	0.85
1.95	1.65
2.50	2.10
2.95	2.45
3.50	2.90
3.95	3.30
4.95	3.90
5.00	3.90

2. For all other merchandise, there must be a reduction of *at least* 15 per cent on items retailing regularly for $3.00 or less, and *at least* 16⅔ per cent on higher-priced items.
3. All sales prices must end with 0 or 5.
4. No sales retails are allowed to fall on price lines which are normal for the product group concerned.
5. Whenever there is a choice between an ending of 0.85 and 0.90, the latter will prevail.

Once general decision rules of this nature are laid down, they are then usually subject to the general policy constraints of the given department within the total store system. As we shall learn subsequently, policy constraints cannot cover all contingencies and therefore prescribe pricing behavior in complete detail. However, from general store or departmental decision rules usually flow the basic determinants of sale pricing considerations.

Markdown Pricing. The reasons for taking markdowns were discussed in Chapter 13, "Merchandise Management." The adaptive nature of the retail firm has been mentioned before; however, it should not go unmentioned that price is one of the principal adaptive mechanisms of the retail firm. It is certainly one of the quickest ways—sometimes the surest—for the firm to trigger an adaptive response to its own goal-oriented behavior. Stocks are lowered via price decisions, traffic may be generated via price decisions, departmental or store operating goals of all kinds *can be* more readily attained by implementing the *right* price decision. However, as discussed earlier, choosing the right price may be as much of an art as a science. In some instances, the right price may be one that is adjusted to within a few cents, or a penny. In other cases the right price may be one that is within a rather wide range or zone of acceptable prices. Variations from this zone may be tolerated if justified in terms of location, services offered,

[5] Richard M. Cyert and James G. March, *A Behavioral Theory of the Firm*, Prentice-Hall, Inc., Englewood Cliffs, N.J., 1963, pp. 139–140.

or store image.[6] There are some decision rules that can guide the decision maker in programming price decisions for products that are critical and therefore must be priced as right as possible. For example, critical pricing decisions are usually involved for items meeting these characteristics:

1. Well-known or well-advertised brands.
2. Products that are exceptionally price sensitive.
3. Products that are central items in the consumer's expenditure budget.
4. Products with a high frequency of purchase.

Many times, regular pricing or sale pricing decisions are inadequate to meet the critical adaptive needs of the retail enterprise. When this occurs, special or markdown prices are employed. It should be emphasized that all pricing decisions are designed to sell or move goods. The usual expectation is that regular pricing and sale pricing decisions will move goods at a profit, i.e., return some margin over cost. However, the normal expectation in markdown pricing is to move the goods, with profit or contribution considerations not necessarily paramount. What is desired is to convert the slow-selling items in inventory to cash, or near cash that in turn can be reinvested in a more dynamic and viable part of the assortment mix.

A general model for markdown pricing is shown in Figure 16-2. The general rule for the first markdown is to reduce the retail price by one third and carry the result down to the nearest markdown ending (0.85). In this study, although the department did not seem to follow any specific explicit rule with second or third markdowns, the higher the first markdown value, the greater tended to be the reduction to the succeeding markdown price. The authors observed that this relationship seemed to follow the top half of the parabolic curve

$$y^2 = 5(x - 2)$$

where

y = succeeding markdown price
x = initial markdown price

As a result, the following empirically derived rule appeared to work well with second or higher markdowns.

Insert the value of the initial markdown price in the parabolic formula, and carry the result *down* to the nearest $.85 ($.90).

Interestingly enough, when this logical flow model of programmed markdown prices was tested by comparing its results with actual results in a department store, it predicted 88 per cent of 159 markdown prices exactly to the penny.[7]

It should be pointed out that occasions do arise when regular price de-

---

[6] Alfred R. Oxenfeldt, "Developing a Favorable Price-Quality Image," *Journal of Retailing*, Vol. 50, No. 4 (Winter 1974–1975), pp. 8–15.
[7] Cyert and March, op. cit., p. 143.

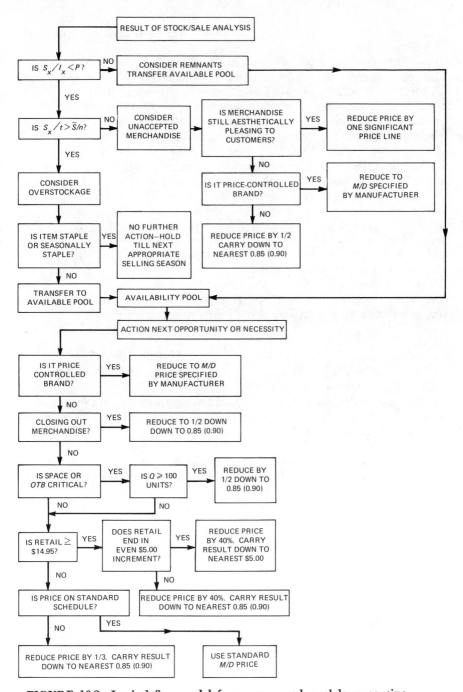

FIGURE 16-2 Logical flow model for programmed markdown routine.

SOURCE: Richard M. Cyert and James G. March, A Behavioral Theory of the Firm. © 1963. Reprinted by permission of Prentice-Hall, Inc., Englewood Cliffs, N.J., p. 145.

cisions are found to be too low, and are thus hurting the sale of the goods. This phenomenon may be related to a condition known as psychology pricing, which will be discussed subsequently. However, the point is that prices can be cut too much or set too low originally. One situation developed in which a store had two major price lines for hosiery—$1.00 and $2.00. A special purchase of the $2.00 line was made at a cost of $.65, but when it was offered as a special at $1.00 per pair, it moved poorly. When they were marked up to $1.14 a pair and could be differentiated from the regular $1.00 hose, they sold quite well. It was suggested that at the higher price they represented a higher value, and thus moved more rapidly.

The programmed approach to price decision making holds much promise. The analysis of positive or descriptive models can lead to the development of better normative or prescriptive models. Perhaps soon, as more such procedures are developed, computers will be programmed in a complete sense to make many retail pricing decisions. However, the need for decision rules on which to base the logical flow models (and ultimately the computer models) still remains; thus the essentiality of management judgment endures as a critical part of the retail pricing decision.

retail price policies and decision making

The kinds of decisions made by a business organization and its approach to decision making in any area will depend to a great extent upon the organization's goals, its style or image, and its operating policies. In the concluding paragraph of the last section an important statement was made regarding the relationship between retail price decisions and the essentiality of management judgment. This point needs amplification. Pricing decisions based upon a stated markup rounded off to the nearest acceptable odd figure (or any form of programmed price decision) will be based on, or supported by, a host of managerial policies.

A policy is a guide for decision making—a general plan of action that directs members of an enterprise in the conduct of its operation. Decision rules that result in what have been called *programmed* decisions are never made without reference to the firm's policies. Even nonroutinized or nonprogrammed decisions must be handled within the framework of the firm's operating policies; and in some instances where situations are novel, it may be necessary for the firm to make policy decisions before making operating decisions. Pricing decisions are no exception, and strategic considerations with respect to price necessarily are a part of and derived from the organization's price policy.

Many business firms including many retailers do not explicitly state their pricing objectives or even what means (policies) are to be used to achieve them; yet all firms have such a policy, simply because they do not price their merchandise intentionally or unintentionally in a manner similar or dissimilar to that of their competitors. Even the fact that prices remain unchanged over long periods of time as in the case of *administered prices* does not preclude the existence of a price policy; instead it implies that by rational processes or in some cases simply as a matter of oversight the firm has chosen to do so as a part of its policy. Hence, a price policy effectively means reasons for changing or not changing prices when the management of the firm considers price to be an active, dynamic variable in the total marketing strategy.

The retail firm's price policies (i.e., its predetermined attitudes regarding certain pricing practices or alternatives) determine and shape the firm's actual pricing decisions. For this reason, it is necessary to analyze and understand a whole range of retail pricing policies, in order more fully to understand and appreciate the retail firm's actual pricing decisions.

A Survey of Retail Pricing Policies

The paths of retail business progress and history are strewn with the debris of outworn management devices and gimmicks that once were called policies. It is well known that systems, plans, concepts, and policies become obsolete and worn out just like machinery and other equipment. Policies that at one time may have been fresh and constructive sometimes become encrusted with habit and tradition to the point where they deter and impede decision making rather than facilitate it.

At this juncture, several of the more viable and dynamic retail pricing policies will be examined. At this very moment, some are in a state of flux and their future remains uncertain. Some may at this very moment be destined for the garbage heap of retailing history. No doubt new conditions and new factors are right now at work, fermenting and agitating for change and accommodation in the pricing policies and behavior of the retail firm.

Pricing and Competition. The pricing policies of any specific retail firm are likely to be influenced by the pricing policies and behavior of its competition. Therefore, price policies are to a great extent influenced by competitive activity.[8] Most firms must reckon with their competition and must modify their own pricing behavior in light of the behavior of the other firms in the particular market area. There are several policy postures that any firm can consider in relation to its price decisions and those of its competition. In some instances, a given firm may decide to follow the policy of *pricing at the market*. That is, it develops a programmed approach to pricing, and its decision rule in relation to pricing might be, loosely, as follows:

What is our principal competitor charging for this item? Match his price.

Such a price policy has obvious disadvantages. First, it really means that the follower firm is abandoning its management prerogative of decision making—choosing from among alternative courses of action. The barometric firm (the price leader) may not be setting prices that are optimum or near optimum for the price follower. Yet, price emulation (pricing at the market) is a frequently practiced price policy of many retail firms.

[8] See Walter J. Primeaux, "The Effects of Consumer Knowledge and Bargaining Strength on Final Selling Price: A Case Study," *The Journal of Business,* Vol. 43, No. 4 (October 1970), pp. 419–426.

A firm choosing not to price at the market has two remaining options: pricing *above the market* or pricing *below the market*. A specific firm may adopt either of these two alternatives as a blanket measure, each for good reasons.

A store such as Tiffany's may consider itself such an arbiter of taste and such a prestigious establishment that prices that are not above the market might detract from its overall image. On the other hand, Macy's has virtually guaranteed to sell merchandise at 6 per cent less than the price offered in charge account stores. For example, socks that sold for $1.00 in other stores became 94 cents at Macy's. Such pricing behavior accentuated the odd-pricing policies that Macy's had begun earlier, and its claim to undersell competition started what has become another widespread industry practice, that of comparison shopping, which Macy's needed in order to verify the claims of its customers in regard to competitors' prices.[9]

Choosing a price policy either above or below the market is not quite so clear cut as choosing to price at the market. Because even after the general policy is decided upon, it still must be decided how much higher or how much lower to set the level of general prices.

What is often the case is that firms do not choose deliberately to set prices at, above, or below the market for their entire general price levels. Instead, there is usually considerable price variation among the prices charged for different merchandise items within different departments.[10]

Percentage Markups Versus Dollar Contribution Margins.　The retail manager must often decide whether to adopt a standard markup policy, a variable markup policy, or a pricing policy that strives for a dollar contribution margin. As stated earlier, a prevalent practice among retail firms is to adopt a pricing policy based upon a stated standard markup percentage. As was also stated, some firms that recognize the importance of demand considerations and different levels of cost incurred in selling different merchandise lines have adopted variable markup policies. In other words, the markup per cent used to determine the selling price is varied from product to product as a function of cost and demand factors.

Some merchants have abandoned the concept of percentage markups altogether. Their contention is that markups should be based upon dollars, not percentages; in pricing goods, if dollars are considered, the percentages will look after themselves. There is much evidence to suggest that some price decision makers were developing a near fetish in their slavish attention to markup percentages. No doubt, much of this attitude resulted from the great deal of attention focused on markup percentages by the *retail method* of *accounting*. In fact, the retail method has supposedly led to the following conditions:[11]

[9] Tom Mahoney and Leonard Sloane, *The Great Merchants*, Harper & Row, Publishers, New York, 1966, pp. 162–163.

[10] See Allen F. Jung, "A Different Retail Price Pattern: The Case of Carpeting," *Journal of Business*, Vol. 38, No. 2 (April 1965), pp. 180–185.

[11] Adapted from McNair and May, op. cit., p. 108.

1. Decision makers not fully understanding the retail method of accounting have focused on the gross margin percentage and the planned markon percentage as the major operating tools or criteria for decision making.
2. Too little attention is paid to differences in the costs associated with the merchandising of particular items.
3. Demand considerations are almost fully disregarded in determining markup policies.
4. Too much emphasis is placed on the final departmental net profit percentages after expense allocation.

In short, too much attention is focused on ratios to sales, rather than on dollars; the percentages have become crutches and obstacles to sound pricing decisions.

The markon percentage profit is based upon the following previously discussed standard relationships:

Sales (100%) − Cost of goods sold (60%) = Gross margin (40%)
Gross margin (40%) − Operating expenses (35%) = Net profit (5%)

Dollar markon pricing is based upon similar relationships, but with a different underlying philosophy. Goods must be priced not to produce *percentages* but to produce *profits*, which are measured in dollars. Thus, $ Sales − $ Cost of goods = $ Gross margin and, $ Gross margin − $ Direct expenses = $ Contribution to Profit and Overhead.

Carlos B. Clark, a pioneer in the development of retailing management, recognized 44 years ago something that some price decision makers have yet to realize:

selling departments are not parallel businesses producing net profit, but are like streams pouring each its contribution into a common reservoir. That contribution consists of the gross margin on its sales less its direct expenses. What are direct expenses? They are those expenses which would not exist if the department were discontinued, and therefore are almost directly controlled in relation to that department alone. . . . So net profit can be built up either by increasing the flow into the reservoir or by decreasing the outflow.[12]

Pricing policies built upon the concept of dollar markups are known as *contribution pricing*. It implies that what is sought is profit, and profits are dollars, not percentages. It assumes further that prices will be set that maximize not necessarily net profits but dollars of contribution to overhead and profits. The department store characteristically has been a prime offender in the charge of percentage markup pricing, but has modified its approach, especially in light of the success of the discount store and other low-margin sellers, and now looks increasingly to markup dollars instead of only percentages.

[12] Carlos B. Clark, " 'Reservoir Concept' Is Keynote to Future Profits," *Retail Ledger* (December 1933) , p. 13.

Negotiated Prices Versus One-Price Policy. Every retail firm must decide whether to negotiate its prices with consumers, or whether to post its prices and charge all consumers the same price, regardless of who they are, the quantities purchased, or individual bargaining ability. Such alternatives are sometimes referred to as varying price policy and one-price policy. With the exception of what might be called consumer capital goods, i.e., big ticket items such as automobiles, appliances, television sets, and furniture, most retailers follow a one-price pricing policy. Such a policy offers several advantages to store and customer. It simplifies the pricing and selling situation. Since the price is determined and placed on the merchandise, there is no need for haggling between buyer and seller and no need to train the sales personnel in the negotiative tactics of price bargaining. Customers benefit, too, in one sense of the word. In one-price stores customers have the comfort and security of knowing that the price they pay will be the same as the price paid by all other buyers; thus their ability to purchase good value merchandise is not necessarily dependent upon their bargaining or haggling ability. No doubt, a one-price policy streamlines and facilitates the buying-selling transaction and adds considerably to an already efficient distribution mechanism. These policies save time and much administrative effort. Yet, today, there still remain vestiges of an earlier era when haggling and negotiation were a normal part of every consumer's shopping routine.

Negotiative prices are a regular part of big ticket merchandising in at least two respects. First, it appears a normal part of consumer psychology to want to bargain and negotiate price for large expenditure items. Given the size of the expenditure, this is not an unusual phenomenon. A $2.98 item is hardly critical to a consumer's budget and a 10 per cent concession from bargaining would save about $.30, hardly enough to warrant the effort, considering the value of one's time. However, a $298 refrigerator is another matter. It may constitute the biggest single expenditure in the consumer's entire yearly budget, and a 10 per cent concession resulting from negotiation is $30 saved, enough for one month's payment, or enough to buy a second small appliance, such as a toaster or blender. A $30 savings for haggling that takes perhaps as little time as ten minutes represents an hourly earning of $180 (6 × $30).

In addition, negotiated prices often result from the necessity to figure the value of trade-ins. And in some instances, trade-in allowances are simply a fictitious way of permitting a retailer to deviate from a one-price pricing policy.[13]

It would appear safe to generalize that one-price pricing policies are the normal rules of the game in the case of the typical retail firm selling consumer shopping and convenience goods.

Odd Versus Even Dollar Pricing. The practice among many retailers of setting prices in such a way that they end in an odd number just under a round number is well ingrained. This practice is alleged to have begun in the china department of Macy's Department Store, in New York.[14]

[13] The author recalls one advertisement for electric carpet sweepers in which the seller was granting a $25 trade-in allowance for the customer's old broom!

[14] Mahoney and Sloane, op. cit., p. 160.

The original aim of odd pricing was twofold. Undoubtedly, the practice was partially based upon the idea that odd prices led the customer to believe that she was getting more for less—a real bargain. However, the merchant's original interest in odd prices was not all customer-oriented. At least a part of this interest was motivated by the desire of the store's owner/manager to force clerks back to the cash register to ring up every sale in order to make change, thus foreclosing on the possibility that a clerk might make an even dollar sale and pocket the money from the transaction.

Odd pricing is a form of *psychological pricing*. It has been observed in some pricing experiments that a change in price has little effect over certain ranges of demand. Thus the average revenue curve is viewed as a step-down curve with critical points located at prices that are psychologically significant to buyers. Pricing experiments at Macy's Department Store revealed such step-shaped demand curves, suggesting that the demand curve has considerably different elasticities at different points.

Actually, although some studies have been made, the real effect of psychological phenomena on price decision making has not yet been fully determined.[15]

Surely, attitudes, perception, communication, culture, and group membership all play important roles in price decision making, and in particular in the consumer's reactions to price decisions.

Odd prices are commonplace among most retail firms. It has been shown that prices ending in 9 are commoner than those ending in other numbers. One researcher points out that 64 per cent of retail processed meat prices end in the digit 9 and 69 cents is a much more common price than 70 cents or 68 cents.[16]

Figure 16-3 shows the type of demand curve implicitly assumed by the seller who uses the odd number rule to set prices. Obviously, the decision maker *believes* that sales are larger when the price ends in an odd number than when it ends in the next lower even number. The reader will observe that the quantity demanded is believed to be greater at $.99 than at $.98, and greater at $.97 than at $.96.

It should be mentioned that no conclusive evidence exists to support the contention that an odd price policy actually results in larger sales when it is employed. Twedt argues:

> Experimentation is clearly called for to determine whether the popularity of odd numbers, and "9 fixation" in particular, really represent

[15] The reader might begin with at least these materials: Harold J. Leavitt, "A Note on Some Experimental Findings About the Meaning of Price," *Journal of Business,* Vol. 27 (1954), pp. 205–210; A. Oxenfeldt, D. Miller, A. Shuchman, C. Winick, *Insights into Pricing,* Wadsworth Publishing Co., Inc., Belmont, Calif., 1961, especially Chap. IV, "Perception and Pricing," and Chap. V, "Attitudes and Pricing," pp. 66–102; Chester R. Wasson and David H. McConaughy, *Buying Behavior and Marketing Decisions,* Appleton-Century-Crofts, New York, 1968, especially Chap. 15, "The Dynamics of Competitive Pricing," pp. 298–327.

[16] Dik Warren Twedt, "Does the '9 Fixation' in Retail Pricing Really Promote Sales?" *Journal of Marketing,* Vol. 29 (October 1965), pp. 54–55. Also, see Jan Stapel, "Fair or Psychological Pricing," *Journal of Marketing Research,* Vol. IX, No. 1 (February 1972), pp. 109–110.

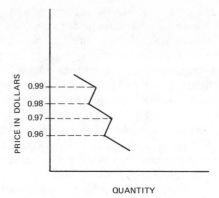

FIGURE 16-3 Assumed demand
curve for odd number pricing.

"magic numbers" that promote sales. Or are they only "sticky prices"
that hinder scientific pricing decisions and optimum profits?[17]

Price Lining. Another common pricing policy among retailers, most
notably among department stores and apparel shops, is that of price lining.
Price lining consists of offering merchandise in a limited number of price
lines, e.g., women's street dresses at $24.95, $28.95, and $32.95. The price
lines supposedly are based upon differences in workmanship, materials, and
design, which are cost considerations, and upon consumer expectation,
which is a demand consideration. In short, price lines are based upon both
cost and demand considerations. Many different classes of goods are subject
to price lining; among the most frequent are dresses, suits, hosiery, some
jewelry, furniture, appliances, and other household items. Price lining is a
means of exploiting quality differentials; and because quality differentials
must be greater than the consumer's j.n.d. (just noticeable difference), it
usually means that prices for different quality goods must be spread by
several dollars.[18] When price lines are established they usually remain fixed
for long periods of time. But problems arise when supplier prices are increased. Usually this necessitates moving or shifting the price lines up one
level. Price lining means that retail prices for some lines are always predetermined, and the decision burden now shifts to the store buyer, who
must seek out merchandise at appropriate cost price levels to afford the
store its regular markup goals when sold at the predetermined price line
level.

[17] Ibid., p. 55.
[18] The relationship which governs the size of the j.n.d. is known as Weber's law:
j.n.d. $= Kx$ (the intensity of the initial stimulus) , where K is some specific constraint for
each of a given individual's senses. The concept of j.n.d. applies to all sorts of perception
situations including visual, tactual, olfactory, and taste. For instance, the j.n.d. concept
in relation to price would work as follows: A difference between a $24.95 dress and a
$25.95 dress is not perceived as significant by a customer; the figures are different but not
perceptually significant. However, the difference between a $24.95 dress and a $27.95
dress would be considered perceptually significant by a large number of customers.

The usual practice is to offer three price lines for the various classes of merchandise. This is done in order to give the consumer several alternatives in the range of good, better, and best merchandise price levels. Another prevalent practice is to offer price lines that are really a range of several prices—called price zones—according to differences in customer tastes and preferences.[19]

Because of the fact that merchandise in the particular price lines is purchased at different landed costs, the practice of price lining results in a variable markup policy for that department or merchandise classification. Price lining is a mixed blessing for most retailers. It compounds the inventory mix problem; for example, three price lines with 24 items and a range of 3 basic colors means 216 items $(3 \times 24 \times 3)$ for the basic inventory. On the other hand, it appears to simplify certain inventory control problems by reducing the number of prices and groups of products that conceivably could emerge. Price lining is alleged to facilitate the customer's decision processes by the convenient grouping of the total merchandise assortment, and it supposedly facilitates the sales personnel training process inasmuch as store clerks are not required to learn many different prices.

However, the two most frequently mentioned advantages are that price lining simplifies the pricing structure, and that it avoids the need for making frequent pricing decisions after the original establishment of the price lines. These are probably overpromoted advantages and certainly not substantiated by any hard core evidence. In addition, the major reason for adopting any price policy (including price lining) ought to be whether it increases sales and results in a higher level of profit. Like so many ingrained pricing practices and policies, price lining has not been subjected to much scientific scrutiny based upon these criteria.

Price lining can sometimes lead to the establishment of customary prices, i.e., the 15 cent and 20 cent candy bars, the $10.50 men's shirt, the $19.95 pantsuit, or the $7.98 men's work overalls. Hence, the repetitive practice of offering merchandise at fixed levels may lead consumers to associate merchandise of a particular character with particular price levels. At prices above the customary $19.95 for women's pantsuits, sales would fall off rapidly, suggesting high elasticity above the customary price. Below the customary $19.95 price, sales would increase less than proportionately, suggesting relative inelasticity.

During periods of relatively stable prices, price lining is a fairly safe and effective price policy for a retail firm to follow. However, in recent periods of constantly rising prices, price lining presents considerable managerial difficulties.

Leader Pricing Policies. In an attempt to increase profits for the store as a whole or to convey an impression of overall low store prices, some store operators follow a practice known as leader pricing. Leader merchandise pricing has been explained in a number of ways. The practice is gen-

[19] See Kent B. Monroe, "Buyers' Subjective Perceptions of Price," *Journal of Marketing Research*, Vol. X, No. 1 (February 1973), pp. 70–80. Also, James R. Bettman, "Perceived Price and Perceptual Variables," *Journal of Marketing Research*, Vol. X, No. 3 (August 1973), pp. 100–102.

erally defined as knowingly and intentionally marking a part of the stock at prices that will not yield the greatest dollar profit return on these particular goods. Articles that are selected for special price emphasis are identified as *leaders*. Loss leader pricing is the practice of marking goods for sale with a retail price that does not cover costs. Loss leader pricing is construed by many states as being an unfair method of competition, and sales of this type are prohibited by unfair sales practices acts.

The term *loss leader* is in reality a misnomer. In all instances, intelligent price setters hope to increase their total profits by the careful selection and use of price leaders. Given the prices of other products, a change in the price of the loss leader produces larger sales of all products. The fact that the cost of the leader is greater than its marginal revenue is somewhat irrelevant. The true marginal revenue of the leader is the change in the firm's total revenue, with other prices remaining constant.[20]

The use of price specials (leaders) as a promotional and pricing device appears to create less disturbance among competition than do general price cuts. This is largely because of the fact that price specials (leaders) are considered within the normal rules of the game and often result, not just from price-cutting decisions by the retail operator, but also result from price cutting and special discounts granted by manufacturers and other suppliers.

Leader prices usually are placed on high-frequency traffic items. The general characteristics of a good price leader are as follows:

1. It is well known, widely used, and appeals to many customers.
2. It is priced low enough so that many persons can buy it.
3. It is not so low in price that reductions will arouse no interest.
4. It is not usually bought in large quantities and stored.
5. It enjoys a high price elasticity of demand.
6. It does not compete closely with other products in the retailer's assortment of merchandise (in which case it would destroy sales opportunities instead of creating them) .

Leader pricing is practiced widely by many kinds of retail institutions in the belief that the practice pulls customers into the store, thus increasing store traffic and exposing more customers to a greater number of conventional and higher markup impulse items. The food supermarket practices leader merchandise pricing policies extensively, and their weekly food ads usually feature such effective leader items as meat, detergents, and coffee.

Unit Pricing. Unit pricing is hardly a means of determining price at all. Instead, unit pricing involves placing some indication of the cost per ounce or some other standard measure on the actual product itself. Unit pricing is an attempt by the retail store (the supermarket is the main institution where unit pricing has been widely adopted) to eliminate much of the confusion which arises from various package sizes. Unit pricing prices the commodity as a total package, but it also provides a price per ounce so that

[20] For an elaboration of this argument, see Lee E. Preston, "Markups, Leaders, and Discrimination in Retail Pricing," *The Journal of Farm Economics,* Vol. 44 (May 1962) , p. 294.

customers can decide for themselves which package size offers the best value. Some states have passed unit pricing laws making such procedures mandatory. In other states, many retailers have voluntarily implemented unit pricing procedures.[21]

governmental constraints on pricing behavior

The size or the amount of the retailer's margin does not really indicate the range of the retailer's price discretion or freedom. Some retail prices are the result of decisions made at other levels and by authorities other than those of the retail firm itself. This would imply that in some cases the retailer's influence upon price is smaller than his margin would indicate. This problem presents itself to the retail manager and to the student of retail decision making as one of inhibitions upon retailer pricing behavior. There are many such constraints placed upon pricing decisions, i.e., situations whereby the price decisions are made by authorities other than those of the retail firm. For example, liquor sales are usually controlled by state liquor boards of control and retail prices of liquor are set by these authorities. Milk-marketing agreements are found in most states, and under milk-marketing orders the government directly sets the price of fluid milk marketed at retail.

In some instances, though rarely documented through empirical evidence, horizontal price-fixing agreements probably do exist, with some impairment of individual price-fixing authority and responsibility. Although the amount of overt horizontal price fixing in retailing is doubtlessly limited, the prevalence of price leadership by particular firms in many communities suggests a degree of tacit horizontal price fixing.

Vertical pricing is a situation whereby a given channel member assumes or takes the responsibility for setting prices at other levels in the distribution channel. When a manufacturer or supplier of a well-known, branded, and advertised product suggests to his resellers, wholesalers, and retailers that they sell the product at a price that is supplier-determined, and threatens to withhold his product from them if they do not comply, then price making for this product at retail has been removed from the retailer's jurisdiction and shifted to the manufacturer or supplier level. In an effort to more fully control the total marketing effort designed for their products, suppliers and manufacturers will sometimes franchise dealers (retailers) to represent them in a particular market area.[22] By franchising, the manufacturer restricts his product to one or a few outlets and supplies considerable merchandising assistance, but expects certain controls in return, one of which is control over the retail selling price of his commodities. Without franchising, manufacturers and sellers will sometimes pre-ticket their

---

[21] For a broader discussion of unit pricing, see Robert E. Wilkes, "Consumer Usage of Base Price Information," *Journal of Retailing*, Vol. 48, No. 4 (Winter 1972–1973), pp. 72–85.

[22] We shall explore the issue of franchising more fully in a subsequent chapter.

products with suggested retail prices. It is not necessarily mandatory that the retailer sell the item at the supplier's suggested retail price, but in the interest of maintaining harmonious dealer-supplier relationships, or for the sake of convenience (not having to re-mark the merchandise) the retailer often does.

The retailer's price discretion is often constrained by governmental authority. That is, some branch of state or federal government will sanction vertical price-fixing agreements or directly impose floors below which prices are not permitted to gravitate. These two situations take the form, respectively, of resale price maintenance and unfair sales practices acts.

Resale Price Maintenance

Resale price maintenance is a situation involving vertical price fixing between manufacturer-supplier and retail outlets that is specifically sanctioned by law. When a manufacturer-supplier wishes to control the price at which his goods will sell at retail, he often suggests a retail selling price as a guide to the retail firm. In addition, under resale price maintenance agreements, the manufacturer-supplier can actually determine the retail selling price of his commodities and insist that they be sold at this price. Both state and federal laws exist that sanction resale price maintenance agreements, or fair trade laws, as they are sometimes euphemistically labeled by their proponents. Resale price maintenance is an arrangement under which the seller of a product that is identified by a brand name or trade-mark sets a minimum price below which the retailer may not go in making a subsequent sale, or prescribes the exact price at which the commodity will be resold. The price setter may be the producer or the supplier of the product in question. Prices are thus controlled for those who sell the product at retail. Retail price maintenance laws apply only to branded goods that are in fair and open competition with other commodities of the same general class, produced or distributed by others.

Prior to the 1930s, resale price maintenance had repeatedly been condemned by the courts, both as behavior that violated the Sherman Act and as an unfair method of competition under the Federal Trade Commission Act.

Resale price maintenance agreements are state acts, the first of which emerged in California in 1931. The most successful of these acts contains a so-called *nonsigner clause,* which states that if a manufacturer is able to sign a resale price maintenance agreement with one retailer in the state who agrees by contract to sell at the prices recommended by the manufacturer, then all other retailers, after receiving due notification of this condition, are bound by that agreement. The first nonsigner clause provision was passed in California in 1933, and resale price maintenance acts containing nonsigner clauses were subsequently passed in many states.

In 1936, the Dearborn case tested the state nonsigner clause in resale price maintenance agreements, with the resultant court ruling that the nonsigner clause did not violate the due process clause of the Fourteenth Amendment to the Constitution. In 1937, the Miller-Tydings Act was passed, which was a federal enabling act legalizing resale price maintenance in interstate as well as intrastate commerce. In a case in 1951, a major setback to resale price maintenance occurred as a result of a court case in which the non-signer clause was ruled invalid. Once again, however, the proponents of fair trade prevailed; and in 1952, Resale Price Maintenance came back when Congress passed the McGuire Act, which upheld the rights of the states to pass fair trade laws with nonsigner provisions.

Today, however, the status of resale price maintenance is at a general all-time low. Fewer than 30 states have resale price maintenance laws. And only 13 states have nonsigner clauses. In 1975, Senator Edward W. Brooke of Massachusetts introduced a bill (S. 408) to repeal exemptions in the antitrust laws relating to fair trade laws. This bill was passed and signed into law by President Ford in 1976. Even at its peak, it is doubtful if more than 10 per cent of the goods sold at retail came under the impact of resale price maintenance agreements. Many states have now held that such agreements are either illegal or so difficult to enforce that they are unconstitutional. Manufacturers who once advocated resale price maintenance agreements no longer seem much concerned. The impact and volume possibilities of low-margin or discount sellers now appear more in the form of a market opportunity than a market threat.

Resale price maintenance is an inhibition on retail management behavior. It means that the freedom of the retail price decision maker to choose from among a range of prices in order to attempt profit maximization or other pricing goals is seriously restricted. The economic effect of resale price maintenance is that it subsidizes the high-cost, inefficient operator and penalizes the low-cost, efficient operator who wants to sell his goods for less than the fair-traded price. The general effect is a redistribution of sales revenues and profits.

From the consumer's point of view, resale price maintenance (though the evidence is hardly conclusive) generally leads to a higher general level of retail prices. One study suggested that a general federal fair trade law would increase the consumer price index by one to ten points, depending upon the extent to which fair trade currently prevailed.[23] Numerous examples of the ill effects of fair trade pricing laws abound. In Maryland which has fair trade, Bayer aspirin sells for $1.48 for a regular-size package. In Washington, D.C., where no fair trade laws are in effect, the same size package of Bayer aspirin sells for $.99.

Most marketing authorities would contend that resale price maintenance from the point of view of manufacturer, retailer, or consumer is unsound legislation, poor economics, and a weak merchandising and pricing policy.

Unfair Sales Practices Acts. Unfair sales practices acts or unfair trade practices acts, unfair sales acts, minimum price laws, or minimum markup laws (as they are sometimes designated) are designed principally not to set specific prices at which goods will sell at retail, but to place floors under prices for certain commodities. Advocates of unfair sales practices acts argue

---

[23] Unpublished study done by the Economics Division of the Library of Congress for Senator Edward W. Brooke. Fair Trade, according to this study, costs the consumer approximately $2.1 billion every year.

that the merits of such legislation relate to its tendency to stop predatory price cutting. Most specifically the laws are designed to restrict and prohibit loss leader pricing. Usually they take one of two forms: either the minimum specific markup above cost at which goods can be sold is specified, or they specify that the markup must cover the *cost of doing business,* which is then spelled out as specifically as possible—usually very ambiguously.

Unfair sales practices acts are state laws. Currently, about 25 states have unfair sales practices or similar acts to regulate loss leader pricing. During the 1930s when such acts were most popular, about 30 states had such legislation. State unfair sales practices acts do not make sales below cost illegal, per se. What they do is to declare it unlawful to advertise, offer to sell, or to sell goods below cost when the only intent or effect is to injure competitors and destroy competition. The rationale most frequently employed by the courts is that injury to a competitor is tantamount to injuring competition.

Unfair sales practices acts were a part of the early attempt by small-scale independent merchants to restrict and restrain the growth and development of chain stores and other large-scale retailers. Such legislation was conceived out of the logic of some retailers who expound the merits of competition but decry the agony of competing.[24] The advocates of unfair sales or minimum markup laws argue that such legislation curbs predatory price cutting and the loss leader, which to their notion is an unfair method of competition, injurious both to the legitimate merchant (one who does not cut prices) and to the consumer, who is deceived into patronizing the store with cut or slashed prices, when in reality only a few items to which the customer is price-sensitive have been cut, and other prices may actually have been raised above their normal level. While conceivably true, it is doubtful if this is the prevailing situation. As any astute merchant would testify, consumers are not quite so easily deceived.

From the merchant's point of view, and because of considerable weakness in the language of the acts and the lack of a suitable means of enforcement, unfair sales acts are a pricing nuisance and management hindrance. The laws make no provision whatsoever for enforcement, except to state that it is the burden of the injured party to seek satisfaction from the offender in a civil suit. As every reader knows, such litigation is always costly and uncertain.

The general effect of unfair sales practices acts is similar to that of resale price maintenance agreements. Such acts restrict the price maker's authority, subsidize the inefficient, and penalize the efficient operator who strives to lower the cost of distribution through economy and innovation.

Nonetheless, the perennial (though limited) agitation for price-fixing legislation supports the earlier contention that nonprice competition is usually more desirable to retail sellers generally than outright price competition. Next, we will therefore focus on aspects of nonprice competition —advertising and personal selling as parts of the retail management system's overall promotional strategy.

---

[24] For a highly readable account of this subject, see Jack Anderson, "State Laws That Create Higher Prices," *Parade, The Spokesman Review,* April 6, 1975, pp. 7–10.

QUESTIONS FOR STUDY, REFLECTION, AND REVIEW

1. How can the operation of the retail firm be facilitated by working out deliberate, preplanned, programmed procedures for handling the pricing decisions?
2. What are the three alternatives for pricing policy decisions under a competitive situation?
3. What is the basic difference between standard markup percentage and variable markup policy?
4. Explain the statement that "net profits can be increased by pricing below total costs for some products and above total costs for other products."
5. The original aim of odd pricing was twofold. Briefly describe these two desired objectives.
6. Describe the price lining pricing policy used by retailers, and discuss some of the limitations and advantages of using price lining policies.
7. Define leader pricing policies, and discuss the rationale for following such policies.
8. What are some of the factors that you would consider when selecting a product to use as a leader item? Explain why.
9. Briefly point out the possible areas of constraint that can be imposed upon retail pricing policies.
10. Discuss the usage of retail price maintenance laws from the manufacturer's, retailer's, and consumer's viewpoints. Point out the motives for wanting such practices and the legal nature of retail price maintenance.

SEVEN

RETAIL STORE PROMOTION

17

the role of promotion in
retailing strategy

The retailing strategy has been defined as a comprehensive plan of action designed to facilitate the attainment of the goals and objectives of the retailing firm. By manipulating elements of the retailing mix—that blend or combination of price, product, place, or promotional activities—the retailing management system adjusts and accommodates to its marketing environment. It is the purpose of this chapter and Chapter 18 to examine and discuss in detail the role of promotion in the overall retailing strategy. The elements of the retailing mix constitute the controllable variables over which retail managers exercise control; collectively they are the essential ingredients with which retail managers strive for enterprise differentiation. If all retail firms carried the same products, priced at the same level in very similar stores, promoted these products through the same media, and used the same appeals, then indeed, retail firms would project an image of great sameness and monotony. Yet, because there is so much variation in the range of goods sold by various firms, the prices charged, the types of stores and facilities utilized, and the promotional methods employed, what prevails is not sameness and monotony but a great diversity and range in store types, product offerings, promotional appeals, merchandise assortments, and prices. In short, it is possible to create a veritable multitude of store types simply by permuting and combining different approaches and combinations of the four basic P's—price, promotion, product, and place.

Perhaps more so than any other element in the retailing mix, promotional activity has the power to create a range of favorable or unfavorable store images. Prices may be fair and equitably determined, merchandise assortments broad and in depth, store location acceptable, and store facilities and design modern and appealing, but without an effective promotional program, the total store effort may fall far short of its market potential. A potent and well-planned promotional program may prevent the store from being lost in the scramble of competition.

Promotion is designed to promote. The term *promotion* comes from the Latin verb, *promovere,* which means to move forward. More loosely defined, it means to advance an idea, a thing, or an institution. It implies that advancement is caused or brought about by persuasive communication. People need to know of an institution's existence. They need to know where it is, what merchandise it carries, how its merchandise is priced, what range of special services it offers, and why some particular institution can serve their needs better than another. The essential thrust of promotional activities is directed at such questions as these. Promotion is unique in the sense that as a part of retailing strategy, its basic purpose is to direct attention and generate interest in some one or all of the remaining elements of the mix, namely, the firm's products, its prices, and its place considerations. To be sure, promotional activities wisely conceived and executed have the capacity to convert the whole into something that is actually greater than the sum of the parts. Promotional activities have the potential capacity to move forward, to enlarge and enhance the store's total offering into a pleasing, harmonious image that can appeal to a market segment far larger than its actual size or location might warrant.

A store's promotional activity to some extent will be a function of its overall merchandise strategy, its corporate philosophy, and most importantly, the market segments to which it strives to appeal. Furthermore, a given store's promotional activity ought to be predicated upon some understanding of the behavior of the consumers that make up the store's market opportunity. Such an approach would appear to simplify not only promotional undertakings, but other merchandising activities as well. In the treatment of consumer behavior in Chapter 6, the problem-solving nature of retail shopping-purchasing was emphasized. As we learned, consumers desire to buy goods for problem-solving purposes.

There is an attraction-repulsion principle at work in nearly every sales transaction. Consumers are *attracted* to purchase situations because of their needs hierarchy. They need food, clothing, shelter, comfort, and relief from monotony. Furthermore, higher on their needs hierarchy, they manifest a desire for goods that have social and psychological manifestations. Make no mistake about it, consumers want to buy goods—more goods and better goods. Their desire for goods is practically infinite. However, consumers are *repulsed* from buying goods because of constraints imposed by income and budget. The very fact that needs or wants are unlimited and financial resources almost always are limited means that consumers have to ration their available wherewithal over some developed or arranged priority system. Thus, the essential consumer problem is, "What goods should I buy in order to best fulfill my own personal needs hierarchy?" Such a question stimulates the consumer into a series of activities, i.e., awareness of need or want, search, evaluation, and finally choice or decision. Collectively all this behavior is sometimes referred to as search activity that emanates from the consumer-buyer.

promotion as communication

The retail firm promotes by communicating information about its total offering to its perceived market opportunity. In turn, the retail firm attempts to gather information from its customers and potential customers via its marketing research activities, customer want slips, employee suggestions, consumer panels, and comparison shoppers. What is desired is a two-way flow of information both to and from the firm and to and from the consumer market segments.

Kinds of Retail Promotional Activities

Two authors, in summarizing the importance of communications to marketing-retailing activity, stated:

> Marketing effectiveness depends significantly on communication effectiveness. The market, in reality, is energized (or activated) through information flows. The way a buyer perceives the market offering of the seller is influenced by the amount and kind of information he has about the offering and his reaction to that information.[1]

The firm is confronted with the competitive necessity of developing a retailing strategy, which was defined earlier as a comprehensive plan of action. The retailing mix consists of those elements or activities around which such a systematic plan can be formulated. However, the implementation of strategy requires information flows that may be channeled through any of a number of communication alternatives, as shown at the bottom of Figure 17-1. Put another way, the firm is an isolated organism until it both sends and receives information. In short, until communication takes place, the firm is not triggered into any kind of purposeful behavior. The market-oriented firm takes its marching orders from the market. Once the market communicates its needs to the firm (you will observe that the arrows in the diagram are shown with bi-directional thrust), the firm responds to this environmental stimulus with some aspect of its retailing mix —product, price, promotion, place, or some combination thereof.

Advertising, personal selling, publicity, sales promotion, and packaging are ways of projecting values, ideas, expectations, and so forth, to consumers. Market research is a set of techniques used by the firm to perceive and receive values, ideas, and expectations of customers or potential consumer groups. Although all these activities constitute efforts toward communication, usually only advertising, personal selling, publicity, sales promotion, and packaging are considered strictly *promotional* devices. A brief description of the promotional activities would appear warranted.[2]

[1] Thomas A. Staudt and Donald A. Taylor, *A Managerial Introduction to Marketing,* Prentice-Hall, Inc., Englewood Cliffs, N.J., 1965, p. 353.

[2] These descriptions and definitions follow closely those adopted by the Committee on Definitions of the American Marketing Association.

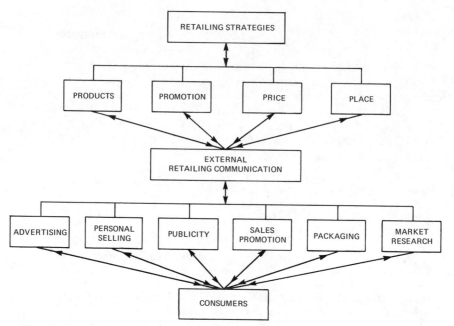

FIGURE 17-1 **Relationship between retailing strategy and communication strategy.**

Advertising. Advertising is any paid form of nonpersonal presentation and promotion of ideas, goods, or services by an identified sponsor.

Personal Selling. Personal selling is a direct face-to-face relationship between sellers and potential buyers. Telephone selling is considered a form of personal selling.

Publicity. Publicity is free promotion of a firm's products, ideas, or services.

Packaging. Packaging consists of the containerization activities designed to protect the product and to facilitate its sale.

Sales Promotion. Sales promotion activities consist of many special purpose and nonrecurring promotional activities such as the design and distribution of novelties, store signs, catalogs, trade shows, premiums, contests, and trading stamps.

The Place of Advertising and Personal Selling in the Retail Organization Structure

Before proceeding with the managerial analysis of retailing promotional activities, let us examine where the responsibility for these activities lies within the organization structure.

In order to achieve its greatest impact, retailing promotion demands effective coordination of promotional activities. Advertising and personal selling activities must be planned, implemented, and controlled as an integral package and mix of activities. Yet such is not always the case in retailing. All too often in retailing firms, there exists a schism between the persons responsible for advertising and those responsible for managing the personal selling operation. In the department store, advertising and publicity are often the concern of an advertising manager while personal selling activity is directed by either the department manager or the buyer, depending upon the prevailing type of organizational philosophy. Studies have shown an appalling lack of coordination between advertising, window display, product assortments, adequate sales personnel to handle special sales events, and other related factors.[3] The typical store does less than a commendable job in the following instances:

1. Merchandise assortments are often inadequate to meet the demand created by promotional activity.
2. The store fails to locate special promotion merchandise for the convenience of its customers.
3. The customer seldom receives adequate point-of-sale information from sales personnel.
4. Window displays and in-store displays are seldom adequately coordinated with print and broadcast media advertising in order to assure maximum sales impact and customer service.

Employment of the marketing concept and the systems approach to retailing management dictates better organizational treatment and cohesiveness among all of the firm's promotional activities.

retail advertising

Advertising is a most popular form of retailing promotion and a valuable means of communication for the retailing firm. Earlier, during our discussion of retail pricing, the importance and popularity of nonprice promotional activities was discussed. It should be reemphasized at this point that nonprice promotional activities such as advertising and display are effective means of competition and enterprise differentiation. Advertising increases the scope and dimensions of the retail firm's total competitive strategy, because it enables the firm to reach out to inform and persuade customers, thus greatly extending the sphere of influence of the firm far beyond the mere physical boundaries of the store.

Advertising continues to become more and more popular as a means of competing on a grand scale. With improvements in transportation came new customer mobility, with advertising as the principal means of activating

---

[3] For a detailed presentation and continuation of this argument, see John D. Whitney, "Better Results from Retail Advertising," *Harvard Business Review,* Vol. 48, No. 3 (May–June 1970), pp. 111–120.

this mobility. The mass media have made advertising an even more potent tool for the modern merchandiser. Also, the increasing use of advertising by the retail store stems in part from the emphasis of manufacturers and retailers on *pull* instead of *push* merchandising (selling strategies). Pull strategy attempts to create a strong demand for products at the consumer level by direct consumer advertising, sales promotion, and branding. What is attempted by the manufacturer-marketer is to develop some degree of either (1) brand or product insistence, (2) brand or product preference, or at least (3) brand or product recognition. When (1) or (2) is attained, the customer is presold, and upon entering the store she requests a given product or brand, requiring very little in-store selling. In effect, such strategies really mean that the point-of-purchase (at least in terms of the mental commitment to buy) has shifted out of the store and into the home or other places where media and message effects are felt.

Push strategy is still employed by many sellers for many different kinds of products and is oriented primarily around a highly persuasive personal sales presentation. Instead of attempting to pull the product through the channel via advertising, the product is literally pushed from one consecutive station (reseller) in the channel to another. Quite obviously, many marketing programs are built around both push and pull considerations. Advertising is used to entice customers to visit the store and shop the merchandise offerings, and then, personal selling is used to push products after the customers have arrived. However, because of the increasing tendency toward self-service and simplified selling, advertising (preselling) is used today to shoulder more and more of the actual selling responsibility.

Advertising without doubt is a very important part of the retailing strategy. It is persuasive activity designed to promote the store and its products by providing needed and worthwhile information to the potential consumer-buyer. It must be strongly emphasized, however, that advertising is not a panacea or a cure-all for all the company's ills. *Instead, as a form or kind of communication, advertising is most effective as a reinforcer of favorable attitudes, values, and dispositions already held by consumer-buyers.* When customers, as a result of unfavorable experiences, have already decided that they do not like a store, its merchandise, or its policies, advertising is found to be least effective. A prolonged advertising effort, in addition to changes in store methods, policies, merchandise assortments, and personnel is usually required in order to bring about a change of heart (conversion).

It goes without saying that a store's advertising must be congruent with its basic merchandising policies and procedures. Advertising is a form of propaganda, but that is not to say that it should be false and misleading. Quite the contrary, the most successful advertising campaigns are those that are consistently up to the high standards of honesty and integrity found in most business enterprises today.

Advertising effectiveness is the result of many factors, including how much is spent, where the money is spent, what is said, to whom, and what appeals are utilized. No amount of advertising can successfully sell unwanted or shoddy merchandise, or merchandise that is not backed up by the other merchandising and selling divisions of the store. Finally, no retailer should expect unusual results from advertising unless it is used on a more or less continuous basis.

The Costs of Advertising. Poor advertising is costly. Yet, good advertising is relatively cheap. However, it is never easy to distinguish between good and poor advertising. By definition, good advertising is effective when it accomplishes what has been established as the firm's advertising goals. The goal of advertising is multidimensional. It is designed to inform, persuade, and remind customers about the store and its total offerings. What is more, advertising should facilitate the firm's profit objectives. If it does not, it is probably wasteful and ineffective.

In the face of increased competition and sluggish consumer purchasing, advertising expenditures in the United States continue to rise. These expenditures approached $24 billion in 1974 and by 1976, total expenditures for advertising were expected probably to reach the $26-billion mark, which means that retail advertising—which typically amounts to about one third of this total—would account for about $8.66 billion. The amount spent by different kinds of retailers varies widely according to size, location, merchandise lines handled, and the nature of local and regional competition. Small stores tend to spend very little for advertising. Some funds are expended for an occasional direct mail piece, or a listing in a local newspaper directory; oftentimes these expenditures amount to no more than $50 to $100 per year.[4]

However, larger stores with their high fixed costs structure and the necessity for attaining large sales volumes and the resulting economies of scale spend considerably more in an effort to generate large amounts of store traffic and volume. It is not unusual for advertising expenditures to be the second largest expenditure category after wage costs, or to be the third largest item of operating expenses after wages and occupancy costs. Advertising expenditures for Sears, Roebuck and Co. soared over $100 million for the first time in 1966, which gives the firm the distinction of being one of the biggest spenders for advertising in the retailing industry.

Average expenditure figures for advertising among all stores are not available, but the best estimate is that the most modal figure would be somewhere in the range of 2.5 to 3.5 per cent of sales. Department stores, supermarkets, and conventional general merchandise soft goods sellers' expenditures would fall closer to the 2.5 per cent level. Stores such as discount food supers and promotional general merchandise stores would more nearly approach the 3.5 per cent figure.

Kinds of Retail Store Advertising

Broadly defined, there are two basic kinds of retail store advertising. These two are normally referred to as *promotional* or *direct action adver-*

[4] For a discussion relating to how small-scale retailers improve their advertising effectiveness, see Thomas H. Waltz, "How to Get Best Ad Results," *Editor & Publisher*, Vol. 106, No. 3, June 20, 1973, p. 18.

tising and *institutional advertising.* Given a considerably subtle and so-phisticated approach to advertising by many retail stores, the result often is a combination of these two kinds into a third. category—*promotional-institutional,* which is actually no more than an amalgam of the two basic kinds.

Promotional-Direct Action Advertising. This type of advertising is the one most frequently used by retail stores. Such advertising features specific products or services and usually (though not always) makes some specific reference to the price of the product (s) or service (s). It is *promotional* in the sense that it attempts to promote or push specific products or services; and it is called *direct action* because the advertisement often makes some direct bid for consumer action, namely, to come into the store and buy the product, to fill out the coupon and send for the product by mail, or to purchase it immediately by phoning the nearest retail outlet.

Promotional-direct action advertising is widely used by the entire range of retail store types, yet it takes many forms even among similar kinds of institutions. It may focus upon only the daily or regular season merchan-dising events and feature products at regular prices. At other times, and by some institutions, such advertising may be the vehicle for pushing special promotional events such as January White Sales, or it may be used for clearance activities such as pre-inventory clearance sales.

Institutional Advertising. The counterpart of promotional-direct action advertising, *institutional advertising* might easily be called the soft sell approach to advertising. There is often no bid for direct action; instead of promoting specific product offerings, institutional advertising stresses ap-peals that center around such factors as the convenience of the store loca-tion, its long existence in the community, the general high quality of its merchandise assortments, the competitive nature of its prices, the con-genial and friendly nature of its store personnel, the wide range of cus-tomer services offered, and so forth. Accordingly, the general goal of in-stitutional advertising can be seen to consist of an attempt to build good will for the store and thus assure it of continued loyal patronage.

In summary, institutional advertising works to

1. Dramatize the diversity and depth of the store's merchandise assort-ment.
2. Sensitize customers to the vast array of services offered by the store.
3. Build its prestige and hence its image by supporting worthy causes.
4. Communicate an awareness to the general public of the firm's mer-chandising policies.
5. Work over a period of time to systematically educate the consumer.

Cooperative Advertising. Cooperative advertising is less a different kind of retail advertising than it is a means of shouldering the responsibility of paying for the advertising. As its name suggests, cooperative advertising implies a degree of financial cooperation among the persons or firms spon-soring the ad. Such advertising is usually sponsored by a manufacturer or wholesaler of nationally branded products carried by retail firms. This cooperative arrangement is undertaken because it enables the manufacturer to take advantage of the lower rates brought about by the actual insertion of the ad by the local firm, and in turn such cooperation is a means of enabling the local retailer to stretch his advertising budget further. Manufacturer-wholesaler and retailer cooperation is referred to as *vertical cooperative advertising*.

Another form is known as *horizontal cooperative advertising*. This type of cooperation exists when units of a voluntary or cooperative chain organization collectively pool their resources and advertise for the mutual benefit of each member. It is called horizontal cooperative advertising because the resources emanate from firms operating on the same plane of distribution, whereas in vertical cooperative advertising the resources flow from firms operating on different (vertical) planes of distribution.

Under the stipulations of the Robinson-Patman Act (1936), such advertising allowances as take place under vertical cooperative advertising arrangements must be given to like purchasers of like quantities for like merchandise in interstate commerce. However, the enforcement of this provision has been far from uniform. In order to fulfill the provisions of the Act that require that promotional allowances be made available on a proportionally equal basis to all buyers, smaller stores (which spend relatively little for advertising) are often granted outright price concessions in order to equalize the effects of the promotional allowances granted under cooperative advertising arrangements.

A Two-Pronged Approach. Today some stores attempt to combine elements of both the direct action form of advertising and those of institutional advertising. Because of the similarity existing among the products handled by different stores, the prices at which these goods are merchandised, and the general similarity and attractiveness of the physical surroundings of most stores, it has become necessary for each store to attempt to differentiate itself in some way from the mass of competitive offerings. Many of these efforts revolve around an attempt to create a distinctive store image, which is often accomplished in part by a skillful blend of advertising and other merchandising efforts. Even when featuring specific merchandise at specific or special prices, store ads are likely also to emphasize the distinct institutional features of the outlet in an attempt to create an overall favorable merchandising image.[5]

The Advertising Spiral

The approach of a given retail firm to advertising is also very likely to be affected by what has been called *the advertising spiral*. This theory (Figure 17-2) suggests that, as a new business begins or as a new product

[5] Using both promotional and institutional advertising has a synergistic effect. That is, each tends to complement the other and thus result in overall greater benefits to the firm. For more information relating to how and why advertising functions, see Stephen Unwin, "A Synchronistic Theory of Advertising," *Journal of Marketing*, Vol. 36, No. 4 (October 1972), pp. 16–21.

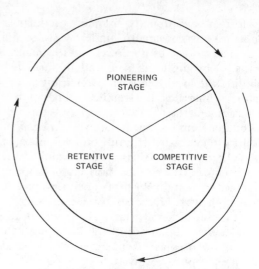

FIGURE 17-2 The advertising spiral.

is introduced, the store or product undergoes a change in the mind of customers.[6] Initially, the product or store is new and unknown. At this time the advertising is pioneering, and this particular period is called the pioneering stage. Later, if the firm or product survives, it moves into competition with other firms or products and the effort becomes one which is directed toward establishing a competitive niche, i.e., a given level of sales or some market share. At this stage, advertising must of necessity focus upon both direct action and institution appeals. Finally, some products or firms (though admittedly a very small number) move into a position of relative competitive security. These become the standard products or the established firm. Advertising for these products or firms may become lower-keyed attempts to remind customers of the product or firm's continued existence or availability. However, in the competitive environment of today, no firm or product is completely insulated against the rigors of competition or innovation. The retentive stage of advertising should not suggest that the firm begin to rest on its laurels.

One story of unknown reliability relates the response of a very successful product and firm that had virtually captured the market in its industry. When the chief executive was asked why, in light of all their success and market dominance, they continued to spend more for advertising than any other firm in their industry, he responded by saying, "Once you get an airplane up in the air you don't necessarily cut the engine."

Advertising and Consumer Reaction

Whether the firm is primarily using promotional-direct action advertising or institutional advertising, or whether its advertising is in the pioneering,

[6] Otto Kleppner, *Advertising Procedure*, 4th ed., Prentice-Hall, Inc., Englewood Cliffs, N.J., 1950, pp. 7–31.

competitive, or retentive stage, it must be designed to inform and therefore persuade the customer convincingly to buy the firm's products, to visit the store and shop its assortment, or at least to harbor favorable attitudes and expectations about the store. To accomplish these broad objectives, retail store advertising must be harmoniously related to the stages in the learning and consumer decision processes. It must be pointed out, however, that the phenomena related to consumer learning and decision making resulting from communication and advertising are not yet thoroughly understood.

One authority has suggested four variables that are involved, namely, Attention, Interest, Desire, and Action; and this scheme is usually referred to as the AIDA model. From this model comes the suggestion that several critical responses to advertising by consumers are likely, namely:[7]

1. *Stopping power* brought about by the initial discovery of the message.
2. *Holding power* brought about by the continuing perusal of the message.
3. *Sending power* that is associated with the message.

Robert J. Lavidge and Gary A. Steiner have generated another series of consumer reactions that they label as awareness, knowledge, liking, preference, conviction, and purchase.[8] Table 17-1 presents their model and indicates these steps in relation to the dimensions of psychological involvement pertaining to the consumer reaction.

It is important that retail advertisers attempt to coordinate their advertising and promotion to such known and understood consumer reactions. However, once again it should be pointed out that not all consumers move through this sequence with the same speed, nor do all consumers react in the same way to identical advertising. Each firm will therefore be forced to experiment to some degree with different approaches, different appeals, and different media.

Advertising Media

Any sound retail advertising program must be based upon a thorough understanding of the characteristics of the various advertising media. This understanding would then become the basis for managing, i.e., planning, organizing, implementing, and controlling the activities related to the retail advertising strategy. It has been discovered that media have unique characteristics or personalities, much the same as retail stores. W. M. Weilbacher has stated that descriptions of the audiences attracted by the media are of importance for a limited number of advertised brands or institutions that themselves have specific and limited characteristics. Added value (he suggests) is gained from studies dealing with the personalities of the individual

[7] Clark Leavitt, "The Application of Perception Psychology to Marketing," in *Marketing Precision and Executive Action*, Charles H. Hindersman (ed.), American Marketing Association, Chicago, 1962, pp. 430–437.

[8] "A Model for Predictive Measurement of Advertising Effectiveness," *Journal of Marketing* (October 1961), pp. 59–62.

TABLE 17-1   Advertising and Its Related Consumer Reactions

RELATED BEHAVIORAL DIMENSIONS	MOVEMENT TOWARD PURCHASE	SOME TYPES OF PROMOTION OR ADVERTISING RELEVANT TO VARIOUS STEPS	SOME RESEARCH APPROACHES OF GREATEST APPLICABILITY RELATED TO STEPS
	PURCHASE ↑		
CONATIVE—the realm of motives. Ads stimulate or direct desires.		Point-of-purchase; retail store ads; deals; "last-chance" offers, price appeals; testimonials	Market or sales tests; split-run tests; intention to purchase; projective techniques
	CONVICTION ↑		
	PREFERENCE ↑		
AFFECTIVE—the realm of emotions. Ads change attitudes and feelings.		Competitive ads; argumentative copy; "image" ads; status, glamor appeals	Rank order of preference for brands; rating scales; image measurements, including check lists and semantic differentials; projective techniques
	LIKING ↑		
	KNOWLEDGE ↑		
COGNITIVE—the realm of thoughts. Ads provide information and facts		Announcements; descriptive copy; classified ads; slogans; jingles; sky writing; teaser campaigns	Information questions; playback analysis; brand awareness surveys; aided recall
	AWARENESS		

SOURCE: Robert J. Lavidge and Gary A. Steiner, "A Model for Predictive Measurement of Advertising Effectiveness," Journal of Marketing (October 1961), p. 61. Reprinted from Journal of Marketing, Published by the American Marketing Association.

media—"the overt characteristics of the medium or vehicle itself and the way they are perceived by its audience."[9]

The list of alternative media available to the retail firm for advertising is extensive. The advertiser must choose among the available media for ones that best fit his merchandising and promotional objectives, in light of his individual needs. The combination chosen will constitute his advertising mix. The alternatives or ingredients for this mix are as follows:[10]

[9] W. M. Weilbacher, "The Qualitative Values of Advertising Media," *Journal of Advertising Research* (December 1960), p. 13.

[10] This list is adapted with minor changes from the excellent work of John S. Wright and Daniel S. Warner, *Advertising*, McGraw-Hill Book Company, New York, 1966, p. 166.

1. Printed media.
   (a) Direct advertising (direct mail).
   (b) Publication advertising.
       Newspapers and magazines.
2. Broadcast media.
   (a) Television.
   (b) Radio.
3. Position media (Outdoor advertising, transportation advertising).
4. Point-of-purchase media.
   (a) Point-of-purchase materials.
   (b) Specialties.
   (c) Film clips.
   (d) Directories, yellow pages, and so on.

Complete and exhaustive analysis and description of the characteristics of each of these media is considerably beyond the scope of this presentation. However, an effort to succinctly describe some of those most often used will be undertaken.

Primary emphasis in this discussion will therefore focus on characteristic advertising for out-of-store promotions and in-store promotional activities such as mass displays, point-of-purchase materials, contests, premium plans, and trading stamps. These two forms are frequently combined for greater emphasis, such as a newspaper ad featuring a particular article plus an in-store mass display of the article. Trading stamps are another example of a promotional activity that is both outside the store, i.e., a newspaper ad featuring and promoting a stamp plan, and in-store displays, as well as check-out personnel pushing the stamps.

Newspaper Advertising. Newspapers are the principal advertising medium for many retail stores. Realistic decision making by consumers requires specific facts, accurate descriptions, reason why copy, clear product representation, and opportunity to compare. Newspaper advertising meets these conditions quite well for most retailers and hence, such advertising is the consumer's primary source of competitive merchandise information. Among retail stores generally, newspaper advertising is exceedingly popular. The reasons for this are apparent. From the consumer's point of view, the newspaper is a valuable means of comparing and contrasting item prices, a particularly important practice in the case of many convenience and shopping goods items. Of the households in the United States, 85 per cent are reached by the 1,750 daily newspapers, whose combined circulation is now approximately 65,000,000.[11]

The popularity and effectiveness of newspapers can be attributed to their availability at the time of decision and purchase, and the believability of their factual reporting. This in turn makes newspapers appropriate for reporting information about new products, for telling about current availability and sales, the actual prices of products, and where to find things. The aim of most newspaper advertising focuses on how to satisfy the desires one

---

[11] These figures are approximate estimates compiled by the author from various resources.

already has. A limitation of the medium is that because there are so few newspapers with such widespread daily consumption, it is perceived by some audience members as a mass medium with little individuality.

Radio. Radio is not considered a primary advertising medium for many retail stores. Retailers generally differ markedly in their opinions on the effectiveness of radio advertising. One study—although somewhat dated—indicated that radio is considered ideal for promoting mass-consumer goods of low unit price whose sale may be motivated by the use of emotional appeals. Such items as food, drugs, soaps, cosmetics, and detergents fit well into the emotional appeal category.

> While the radio does not seem to be particularly well fitted for retail advertising, it can be used with some effectiveness, evidently, for the publicizing of retail institutions which feature low price merchandise, even of a durable type; or which stress easy payment, and can be used even to some degree to promote a limited number of specific items of merchandise.[12]

However, radio does lend itself quite well to some retail store advertising in a number of respects. The medium is quite adaptable and flexible. The advertising message can be changed readily without undue delays or lead time. Radio is especially effective for plugging special in-store promotions and for institutional spot announcements. Nevertheless, the character of radio has changed remarkably over the years, and these changes are causing many advertisers to reappraise their plans so as to include less radio.

A typical criticism of radio advertising is that since the advent of television and the disintegration of network radio, radio stations are nothing more than broadcasters of news and music and that the principal listeners are commuters and, all too often, young adolescents. This is not necessarily the market audience desired by many advertisers.

Radio has recently, however, shown a marked capacity for revitalization by programming innovations such as talk shows, the all-news format, and rock music programs. Furthermore, the transistorized radio is a highly portable instrument for people of all ages. Radio, much to the same extent as magazines, has become more specialized by serving well defined segments of the population. Also like newspapers, it is being perceived as an increasingly better medium for retail advertising. The number of radio sets has tripled over the past two decades to the point where there are now more than 300 million in the United States.[13]

In conjunction with other media, radio will undoubtedly remain an important and integral part of the retail firm's advertising mix. For instance, radio and newspapers work very well as complementary media for reaching customers and for reinforcing appeals. Donald F. Cox describes two types of reinforcement as follows:

---

[12] R. Cassady, Jr. and R. M. Williams, "Radio as an Advertising Medium," *Harvard Business Review* (January 1949), p. 62.

[13] David A. Aaker and John G. Myers, *Advertising Management,* Prentice-Hall, Inc., Englewood Cliffs, N.J., 1975, p. 13.

By *mutual* reinforcement I refer to the added effectiveness which results when the same appeal is transmitted to the same audience via several different media. For example, we might predict that if the same audience were exposed to the same appeal on TV, on radio, and in magazines, the effect would be greater than that of triple exposure to any one of the media.

Complementary reinforcement may occur when two or more media transmit appeals or otherwise perform different functions for the same product in communications directed to the same audience.[14]

Television. Television advertising has been looked upon by many retail store operators with a great deal of trepidation. The high cost of the medium has caused many to adopt an attitude of "wait and see." Television advertising can be a most expensive form of retail store advertising. The trading area of an independent or single unit store is seldom ever as large as (nor does it necessarily coincide with) the telecasting area of the television station. Thus, the advertiser is frequently paying for much waste circulation. For this reason, the independent operator has often avoided the extensive use of television advertising.

Trends appear to indicate that television advertising is growing in importance for many retail store operators, especially those belonging to chain organizations that can spread the cost of a syndicated program or series of spot commercials over a large number of stores.[15] However, several limitations of television as an advertising medium are reported by Settel:[16]

1. Multiple item advertising on television is too difficult.
2. TV best lends itself to institutional advertising, and institutional advertising cannot be evaluated effectively.
3. Most desirable time periods on television are not available to retailers.
4. Too much planning and time are involved to produce effective programs and commercials.
5. Local shows produced by retailers cannot compete with network shows.
6. Other forms of advertising—radio and newspaper—offer more to the retailer than does television.
7. Newspapers reach the largest audience for every advertising dollar spent.
8. Most store operators consider the cost of television too high and feel the money spent cannot produce as many customers as other alternative advertising media.

Handbills and Direct Mail. For the smaller independent retail store operator and even for some large national chains, handbills and direct mail circulars are rapidly becoming the second most important medium for advertising. This medium appears to possess almost the ideal combination of qualities sought by retail store managers. First, the cost of direct mail or

[14] "Clues for Advertising Strategists," *Harvard Business Review* (September–October 1961), p. 160.

[15] Dorothy Cohen, *Advertising*, John Wiley & Sons, Inc., New York, 1972, p. 499.

[16] Irving Settel, "Why Retailers Bypass Television," *Journal of Retailing* (Winter 1955–1956), p. 181.

handbills can be tailored readily to the desired amount of expenditure by the store. Second, the retail store can advertise, via circulars or direct mail, directly in the trading area that surrounds the store. Waste circulation is thus largely eliminated. Third, many retail stores have customer lists or mailing lists, generated by credit and other sales records, around which the direct mail campaign can be organized.

Rather astounding results from retailers' use of circulars and handbills are often claimed. But, as in the use of all media, the effectiveness depends upon the strength of the appeal, the choice of items advertised, the quality of the production, and other factors.

In-Store Promotional Activities. There are a wide variety of in-store promotional activities used by retail management systems. Those that are most frequently employed are in-store displays, premiums, contests, and trading stamps.

Special Displays. The logic and success of special displays are predicated on two factors. First, and perhaps most importantly, is that many retail stores are self-service stores. The customers are encouraged to shop the aisles and display counters for items of their choice. Second, the rate or incidence of impulse purchasing is extremely high. Therefore, given these two factors—self-service merchandising and a high rate of impulse purchasing—there would appear to be a strong incentive for the store operator to use a large number of special displays. The effectiveness of special display has long been evident. One study reports that 5 per cent of total supermarket sales are the result of special displays.[17] These displays take the form of end displays, slot displays, mass displays, and unusual window displays.

There are many reasons why retail stores generally are using more special displays. Several of these reasons are

1. To increase store sales and profits.
2. To increase sales of related line products (shoppe or cluster selling) .
3. For decorative purposes; enhance appearance of the store.
4. To create a buying psychology on the part of the customer through psychological techniques of mass, color, and arrangement.
5. To create a price atmosphere.
6. To stimulate impulse buying.
7. To alter or influence customer traffic patterns.
8. To move out dead or slow-moving merchandise.

In addition to simply using more displays, the retail store operator must understand and use to his advantage the technique of making special displays more effective. Dr. Ernest Dichter, president of the Institute for Research in Mass Motivations, Inc., has stated that "displays must sell the customer immediately because the customer is not in a reasoning mood. All

[17] See "Improving Sale Item Display: The Display and Merchandising Workshop," *Chain Store Age* (January 1965) , p. 64.

the customer can do is react emotionally and quickly, and you have either made your point or not."[18] Dichter argues that there are three prime purposes of displays and an awareness of these will make the display more effective in terms of increased sales and profits:[19]

1. To climax the conditioned reflex of advertising, where such advertising has been proved effective in making up the consumer's mind.
2. To break the conditioned reflex when another product may have had more or equal effectiveness in influencing the buying public.

And when one is dealing with new products or the objective is to stimulate a latent desire to splurge, there is a third objective:

3. Why not? . . . Why not try something you have never tried before? Why not pamper yourself? Why not get a luxury item you did not dare buy until now?

Undoubtedly, much research remains to be done in terms of analyzing and evaluating the effectiveness of various techniques of displaying merchandise. Most merchants are uncertain about what will happen to the sales volume of an entire department if the display space is increased or decreased, or if the location of the display within the store is changed. Aside from a few limited studies in the grocery field, the problem has seen little orderly investigation. One researcher in this area, commenting on the need for further study, stated:

> Just as items vary in their price elasticity of demand, they also vary in their display elasticity of demand. Since the retailer may have more control over the display policy within his store than he does over the prices placed on certain classes of items, this would be a highly profitable area for careful study.[20]

Because of the inherent features of their operations, supermarkets, variety stores, general merchandise stores, and others using self-service and simplified selling lend themselves well to the opportunities presented for capitalizing on the psychological effects of displaying products.

Premiums. Many retail stores have long used premiums as a means of increasing store traffic, developing customer patronage, and (of course) increasing store profits. However, premium promotion is not without its problems for the retail store operator. Most premium promotions are undertaken as a result of manufacturer initiative rather than the initiative of the individual store. Evidence suggests that many stores are beginning to rebel against the practice of acting as clearing houses for manufacturer premiums. Much time and expense are expended by the retailer in such processing, and

[18] Ernest Dichter, "The Point of Point of Purchase," *Food Marketing* (May–June 1954), p. 1.

[19] Ibid.

[20] Edgar A. Pessemier, "Applying Supermarket Techniques to Non-Food Retailing," *Journal of Retailing* (Summer 1960), p. 110.

unless manufacturers can find ways of overcoming these problems or compensating the retailer for his effort, the use of manufacturer-sponsored premiums is likely to decline.

trading stamps

Although somewhat complex, the economics of trading stamps can be understood in terms of the way in which stamp plans operate. Trading stamps are purchased by the retailer from trading stamp companies. In some instances, however, retail systems have developed their own trading stamp plans. The retailer distributes the trading stamps to the customers at the rate of one stamp for each 10 cents' worth of consumer purchases. The rate of distribution is such that the stamps cost the retailer about 2 or 3 cents for each dollar of sales. After the consumer accumulates a large quantity of stamps (the minimum usually is referred to as a book), they are redeemed for merchandise premiums at a redemption value which is about two thirds of the cost of the stamps. Thus, about one third of the stamp cost goes to the stamp company to cover the costs of its operation and to provide it with a profit.

The popularity of trading stamps as a promotion device has varied from store type to store type and even from region to region. Although their greatest popularity has been with food supermarkets, their use by these stores appears to have peaked in about 1966, when at year's end approximately 42 per cent of independent supermarkets and over 60 per cent of chain supermarkets were offering trading stamps.

The intense interest in trading stamps manifested during the 1950s and 1960s seems to have largely abated. Rising prices, depressed incomes, unemployment, and increased store competitiveness seem to have focused the customers' and the store's attention on more aggressive price competition. Stamps have been discontinued by a massive number of food retailers, gasoline service stations, and a wide variety of other kinds of merchandising institutions. Discount merchandise may have rung down the death knell of trading stamp usage. Many a homemaker, however, still appears to like trading stamps—not because she thinks she is getting something for nothing when she receives and pastes stamps, but because she thinks that what she is getting is of value. The stamps she saves—whether green, gold, blue, or plaid—can still be a powerful attraction to pulling her back into the doors of a stamp-giving store.

Contests. Contests have grown to such magnitude that the contest design, rules, procedures, judging, and so forth are usually turned over to a special contest company. As a promotional device a contest is expected to accomplish a promotional goal, i.e., increase traffic, sales, or profits, in order to justify the contest. Currently, one of the most used contests is one that requires the entrants to do nothing but sign their names and leave the rest to fate. Retail stores and especially food supermarkets are finding this type of contest to be an effective promotion. As promotional devices contests are considerably more popular among food supermarkets and gasoline service stations than among most other retailers.

As the interest in trading stamps declines, it is conceivable that there will be an accelerated interest in games and contests as substitute promotional devices. However, many retail stores are encountering considerable opposition from customers to promotional activities and gimmicks that add to the purchase price of the commodities. In view of this reaction, some members of the industry are trying to get away from games, contests, and trading stamps, and are turning to discount pricing as a sales stimulus.

Changing Attitudes Regarding Promotion

Faced with shrinking margins and rising expenses, the retail store operator is becoming ever more concerned with getting full value from his promotion dollar. Retail stores no longer can afford to promote for the sake of promoting, but instead must choose their promotional mix, their media, and their promotional appeals, with an eye toward increased volume of business and better profits. Many retail firms seem to feel that there are advantages to using multiple media. However, the newspaper continues to be the nucleus around which retail store advertising and promotion are built. The increasing rigors of competition at the retail level and the sky-rocketing costs of advertising and promotion are causing retail store managers to view promotional and advertising activities in a more serious light. Retail managers are concerned with learning how to communicate, promote, and advertise more effectively. They are placing less emphasis on canned ideas, and are stressing the need for innovation and creativity in advertising programs. Many retailers are playing down the gross exaggerations that have always tended to characterize much retail advertising. In short, retail managers are becoming increasingly interested in the management aspects of advertising and promotion—a topic to which our attention is now directed.

advertising management considerations

Emphasis throughout this text has focused upon the necessity for *managing* retailing activities, that is for determining objectives and planning, organizing, and controlling processes in order to improve performance, increase efficiency, and assure the effective utilization of resources. One of the first prerequisites for the effective management of a system of activities is the understanding of that system. Hence, much of the attention of this chapter has been aimed at creating an understanding of the communication process and its role in retailing promotion, the nature and role of retail promotion within the framework of the retailing strategy, the kinds of retailing advertising, the role and influence of the various alternative media, and the nature of the retailing mix.

At this juncture some exploration of certain retail advertising management considerations would appear warranted. Two of the more relevant and more difficult issues relating to advertising management will be explored. These are the two key questions of advertising management: (1) How much should the firm spend for advertising? (2) Where should the money be spent for maximum sales-profits benefits?

Broadly conceived, advertising management is concerned with a host of management decisions, beginning, of course, with the most fundamental question, which is, "What are, or should be, the firm's advertising objectives?" The answer to this question lies in the nature of the firm, its market opportunity, the overall retail store image, and the nature of the goods or services merchandised. In addition to determining advertising objectives, advertising management is then confronted with the necessity for planning, organizing, and controlling the system's retail advertising effort. Appeals must be chosen, copy or continuity written, layouts determined, media selected, and the program constantly reveiwed and evaluated. In the smaller store, responsibility for this activity falls to the store manager. In the larger store, advertising specialists are usually a part of the overall management team. The local media such as newspapers, radio, and television stations often provide some assistance; in the case of larger stores with more substantial budgets, the advertising agency would play an important role in the management and implementation of the store's advertising program.

Determining the Size of the Advertising Appropriation

Deciding how much to spend is one of the very perplexing questions confronting the management of a retail store system. No really good operational method has yet been found to aid in the decisions relating to this important problem. Economic or marginal analysis would suggest that the firm allocate resources or continue to spend for advertising to the point where the last marginal dollar spent brings in one additional dollar of revenue. Operationally, this decision rule offers little value because of the difficulty of determining the sales-advertising relationship. In short, marketing science has yet to come up with a determinate advertising-sales curve whereby it is known what the response of sales is to the stimulus of advertising. Far too many factors affect this relationship: the kind of appeal, the media effectiveness, and the propensity of the audience to buy and react. It is difficult to conjecture about the shape of the firm's sales response function in relation to its total retailing effort, let alone only advertising. Several assumptions are usually made when discussing a firm's sales response function. First, increases in the firm's retailing effort will produce increases in company sales, and second, the relationship between the sales volume and retailing effort is not usually linear throughout. Two different versions of the possible shape of the sales response function are shown in Figure 17-3.

It is important to point out that these curves are hypothetical only. In curve A, it is assumed that the first dollar spent for retailing effort will be spent in the best possible way and that the second dollar spent will be spent in the second best way, and so on.

Dollars spent for retailing effort will continue to be spent in successively less productive ways (the more productive ways are exhausted with each

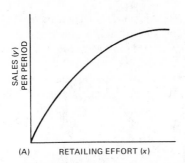
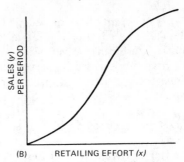

FIGURE 17-3   Two hypothetical sales response functions. (A) Sales increasing at a decreasing rate; (B) sales increasing first at an increasing rate, then at a decreasing rate.

successive expenditure), which accounts for the persistently diminishing rate of sales increase.

In curve B, the first small amounts of retailing effort are not very effective in terms of sales response. Perhaps because of the small dosage, the expenditures are below the threshold or impact level. However, it is assumed that additional doses of retailing effort will activate demand and capitalize on the preconditioning and thus precipitate substantial buying action. Both curves suggest that after successive increments of retailing effort, a diminishing rate of sales growth can be expected. This simply underlines the stiffer resistance that manifests itself after all the easier customers have been affected.

Several points need to be emphasized in relation to these curves. Retailing effort is the total effort made to attract customers and it is not advertising effort alone. Personal selling, store design, layout, and all the merchandising and promotional efforts collectively constitute retailing effort. Yet, it is usually impossible to net out the effect on sales of a single kind of retailing effort such as advertising. This presents a considerable burden when it comes to determining the size of the advertising budget, because, "How can a manager decide how much to spend if he doesn't know what the impact of that expenditure will be on his sales revenues?" Of course, the answer is that he cannot determine the size of the advertising budget in relation to its determinate impact on sales. Determining the size of the advertising budget thus becomes an exercise in good judgment tempered with vast amounts of experience.

The Per Cent of Sales Method.   One of the frequently employed rules of thumb or heuristic decision rules used to determine the size of the advertising appropriation is the percentage of sales method. As the name suggests, for reasons of habit, custom, or good judgment, some percentage of either past sales or forecasted sales is decided upon, and this is the figure appropriated for current advertising expenditures. For example, if 3 per cent of sales is the figure selected, and sales last year were $500,000, then the amount budgeted for this year's advertising would be $15,000. If a per cent of forecasted sales were used, again say 3 per cent, and sales were forecast for the coming year at $550,000, then advertising expenditures would be $16,500. There is an alarming fallacy in each of these techniques, namely, sales are determining advertising, and it should be the other way around. In the case as it exists, it is perverse to let sales determine the amount spent for advertising, when it is advertising which ought to be the independent variable and sales which is the dependent variable. Yet, because of the inability to determine the advertising-sales response, the percentage of sales method continues to be widely used.

Counter-Cyclical Advertising. Another concept is known as counter-cyclical advertising. As the name implies, it suggests that advertising expenditures ought to be related to the business cycle in a counter rhythmic way. That is, when business conditions are depressed, more money ought to be spent for advertising, and when the business cycle is at its peak, less money should be spent. The logic of such a system is sound enough, yet in practice it contains certain deficiencies. It still suggests a known, predictable, determinate relationship between advertising and sales, a relationship (it has been shown) that does not exist. Timing would also be a critical factor, because in order to offset the decline in sales brought about by depressed business conditions, advertising and promotional expenditures should be accelerated somewhat in advance of the actual decline. Counter-cyclical advertising is a useful long-run philosophy for management, but as a year-to-year guide for determining the size of the appropriation, it has little practical value, especially in an economy that manifests great stability or near constant increases in demand brought about by expansion and other inflationary pressures.

The Task and Investment Methods. The task and the investment methods are yet other ways of determining the size of the advertising appropriation. Both methods are really names in search of an underlying supportive theory.

The task method suggests that the advertiser decide what he wants to accomplish (determine the nature of his task) and then appropriate an amount that will enable him to achieve this objective. Only in the most general of terms can such a procedure be very useful, for the reasons already proclaimed, i.e., the indeterminate nature of the advertising-sales response relationship.

The investment method suggests that advertising expenditures be viewed as a long-term investment and not a short-term current expense. This in turn would imply that advertising appropriations would be determined in much the same way as are all capital expenditures—an ideal that contains considerable merit.

After the total appropriation is decided upon, several important decisions remain to be made. The budget must then be broken down by seasons, months, weeks, and days. Furthermore, in addition to timing of expenditures, the question of prorating the budget over merchandise lines and departments must be considered. Usually, all of these questions are handled within the framework of what is known as the promotional or advertising calendar. Such a calendar is shown in Figure 17-4.

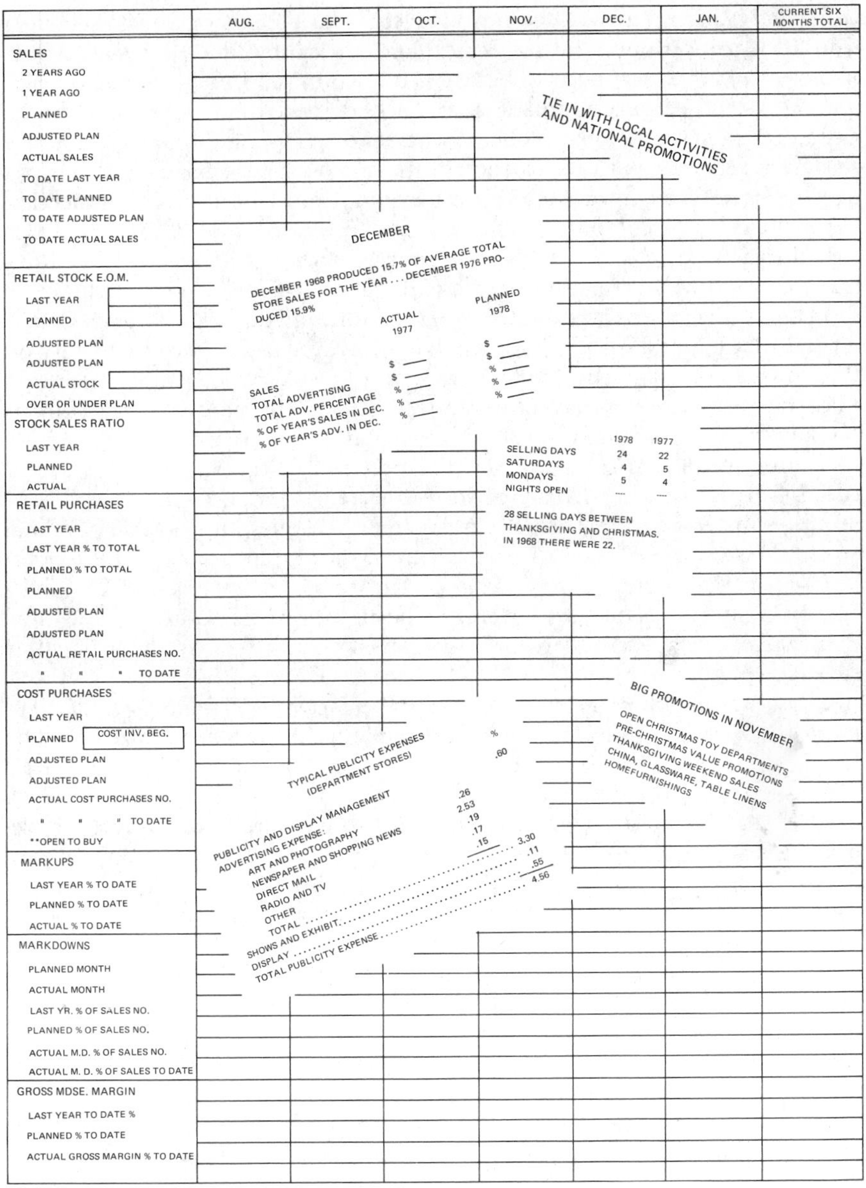

	AUG.	SEPT.	OCT.	NOV.	DEC.	JAN.	CURRENT SIX MONTHS TOTAL
SALES							
2 YEARS AGO							
1 YEAR AGO							
PLANNED							
ADJUSTED PLAN							
ACTUAL SALES							
TO DATE LAST YEAR							
TO DATE PLANNED							
TO DATE ADJUSTED PLAN							
TO DATE ACTUAL SALES							
RETAIL STOCK E.O.M.							
LAST YEAR							
PLANNED							
ADJUSTED PLAN							
ADJUSTED PLAN							
ACTUAL STOCK							
OVER OR UNDER PLAN							
STOCK SALES RATIO							
LAST YEAR							
PLANNED							
ACTUAL							
RETAIL PURCHASES							
LAST YEAR							
LAST YEAR % TO TOTAL							
PLANNED % TO TOTAL							
PLANNED							
ADJUSTED PLAN							
ADJUSTED PLAN							
ACTUAL RETAIL PURCHASES NO.							
" " " TO DATE							
COST PURCHASES							
LAST YEAR							
PLANNED [COST INV. BEG.]							
ADJUSTED PLAN							
ADJUSTED PLAN							
ACTUAL COST PURCHASES NO.							
" " " TO DATE							
**OPEN TO BUY							
MARKUPS							
LAST YEAR % TO DATE							
PLANNED % TO DATE							
ACTUAL % TO DATE							
MARKDOWNS							
PLANNED MONTH							
ACTUAL MONTH							
LAST YR. % OF SALES NO.							
PLANNED % OF SALES NO.							
ACTUAL M.D. % OF SALES NO.							
ACTUAL M.D. % OF SALES TO DATE							
GROSS MDSE. MARGIN							
LAST YEAR TO DATE %							
PLANNED % TO DATE							
ACTUAL GROSS MARGIN % TO DATE							

TIE IN WITH LOCAL ACTIVITIES AND NATIONAL PROMOTIONS

DECEMBER

DECEMBER 1968 PRODUCED 15.7% OF AVERAGE TOTAL STORE SALES FOR THE YEAR . . . DECEMBER 1976 PRODUCED 15.9%

ACTUAL 1977

PLANNED 1978

SALES
TOTAL ADVERTISING
TOTAL ADV. PERCENTAGE
% OF YEAR'S SALES IN DEC.
% OF YEAR'S ADV. IN DEC.

	1978	1977
SELLING DAYS	24	22
SATURDAYS	4	5
MONDAYS	5	4
NIGHTS OPEN	....	....

28 SELLING DAYS BETWEEN THANKSGIVING AND CHRISTMAS. IN 1968 THERE WERE 22.

BIG PROMOTIONS IN NOVEMBER
OPEN CHRISTMAS TOY DEPARTMENTS
PRE-CHRISTMAS VALUE PROMOTIONS
THANKSGIVING WEEKEND SALES
CHINA, GLASSWARE, TABLE LINENS
HOMEFURNISHINGS

TYPICAL PUBLICITY EXPENSES
(DEPARTMENT STORES)

PUBLICITY AND DISPLAY MANAGEMENT
ADVERTISING EXPENSE:
ART AND PHOTOGRAPHY .26
NEWSPAPER AND SHOPPING NEWS 2.53
DIRECT MAIL .19
RADIO AND TV .17
OTHER .15
TOTAL 3.30
SHOWS AND EXHIBIT .11
DISPLAY .55
TOTAL PUBLICITY EXPENSE 4.56

FIGURE 17-4 A merchandising planning chart.

Media Selection and Advertising Effectiveness

In recent years, advertising effectiveness has been enhanced somewhat by the development and use of what are called media models. Such models determine optimum schedule recommendations in terms of reach, frequency, and periodicity. The desire is to provide an optimum schedule of advertising activities in terms of the various media characteristics. Such a schedule would be conditioned by the rules laid down by the decision maker, namely, the buyer prospects to be reached, the desired frequency of exposure among all the prospect audiences, and the desired time intervals between exposures. The truly ideal model is one that attaches a dollar value to the optimum schedule, subject to the constraints of the decision maker. Most of these models are programming models and must be used in connection with an electronic computer.

Unfortunately, media models have generally been built for manufacturer-marketers selling on a national scale with considerable freedom of choice in terms of using alternative media. Such conditions do not characterize the typical retailer, and for these reasons, retailers generally continue to rely on their own media specialists to more or less subjectively determine the media question in relation to each store's advertising. Oftentimes, the question is not one of using printed advertising as opposed to radio or TV, though such questions do arise. But given the predominance of newspaper advertising that persists, in the case of stores located in large metropolitan communities served by more than one newspaper, the question is rather, "Which paper should be used?" or "To what extent should all or any of the papers be used?" Again the answer would hinge upon such factors as the characteristics of each paper, its coverage, the nature of its audience, and how these factors relate to the overall advertising objectives of the particular store.

The question of measuring advertising effectiveness remains a particularly sticky issue. Statistical and econometric techniques have proven to be extremely difficult and in many cases outright disappointments. Yet, retail managers continue their efforts to make their advertising dollars work harder. While they lack precise instruments to measure advertising effectiveness, they continue to experiment by using different advertising appeals, different media, by varying the size of the expenditure, and by varying the timing and positioning of their daily and weekly ads. Oftentimes, they learn that some appeals are more effective than others, and such knowledge therefore leads to increased effectiveness. The size of the ad (within given dimensions) might be found to have little impact on sales. For example, a two-page weekly food ad by a supermarket may be found to be no more effective than a single-page ad. Thus, again, such knowledge may lead to more effective advertising expenditures. Oftentimes, particular promotions or advertisements are found that produce generally predictable responses; therefore, such advertisements can be used whenever, positive and direct sales results are desired.

It might also be pointed out that advertising effectiveness can be measured in negative as well as positive ways. For instance, a retail store is likely to discover that its sales volume or market share is related in some fashion to its overall advertising activities. And if advertising expenditures are drastically curtailed or appeals markedly altered, then sales or market share (after some lagged period) are also likely to fall. Such a condition suggests that there is a causal relationship between advertising and sales results, even though the direct results of this relationship are not known with precision. What is more, it also suggests that some advertising by retailers is expected as normal retailing effort, and thus, some advertising might possibly be viewed as a part of the firm's defensive strategy. However, the astute retailing and advertising manager is one who views his efforts in the main as offensive and not as a puny and ineffectual reaction to forces that are largely beyond his control.

increasing the effectiveness
of retail advertising

The purposes of retail advertising in the final analysis are to increase store sales and to generate higher levels of profitability. Advertising attempts to do this by providing better or improved communication between the store and the consumer public. Retail advertising must be more than the typical drivel, sterile murmurings, or strident shoutings so frequently characteristic of the average store's ads. Retail advertising instead must communicate to prospective customers that they have bought wisely and in their best interests. Retail communications regardless of the media employed, tend to be more personal than national advertising. Therefore, each retail ad represents the voice of a local institution. Thus, the ads should convey something more than copy and illustrations which look like a catalogue—all brands and specifications with no human interest, no local color, no dynamic sense of excitement, no punch whatsoever.

If retail advertising is to communicate, the advertiser must learn to cope with and overcome the specific barriers to effective communication. In retailing, these barriers can often be recognized and specific management efforts made in order to eliminate them or to overcome their existence. These barriers are as follows:

1. Management makes no real commitment to advertising. In many instances, buyers and merchandise managers are concerned with buying and managing inventories to the point that they do not take advertising seriously. As a consequence, the advertising job is left to the copy writer, layout artist, and other advertising specialists, and there is too little involvement and coordination between the buyers and merchandising specialists and the advertising-promotional specialists.
2. Much retail advertising is an afterthought. Advertising is often viewed as a kind of necessary evil. Its results are not easily measured but, because others advertise, it seems like something each firm should do. Because of this casual approach, advertising is not taken too seriously and too many ads represent someone else's canned ideas. Retail ads often lack spontaneity, freshness, and sparkle, and thus the ads fail miserably to communicate positively to customers.
3. Retail advertisers often lack confidence. This lack of confidence is frequently related to inexperience. Retailers consider themselves knowledgeable, astute merchants—not necessarily advertisers. Advertising is seen as something beyond or different from merchandising, but it is not. Advertising is the most important extension of the firm's merchan-

dising strategy, and retail merchants must become more competent in applying effective advertising and communication principles.

4. Retail advertising is affected by the deadline compulsion. Because so much retail advertising involves newspapers, because there are usually favored days for running retail ads, and because newspapers have deadlines for submitting ads, there is often a near panic in many stores to meet deadlines. This panic and confusion often means that deliberate planning is omitted and expedient action substituted for sound managerial planning. Thus, what items to run in the ad, the ad size, layout, typeface, and choice of illustration become a kind of haphazard jumbled procedure. This inevitably means a diminution of the advertisement's effectiveness.

5. Finally, much retail advertising suffers from excessive puffery. Retail ads often lack the degree of desired credibility and hence effectiveness because they overdramatize and overstate their case. Statements such as "This 1975 model driven only 50,000 miles is virtually still like new"; "Best bargains this town has ever seen"; "Unbelievable reductions on every item in the store"; or "Visit our basement men's wear for perfectly tailored, perfect quality, perfectly fitting slacks." Such statements are worn out from overuse and they tax the customer's credibility and do little more than tarnish the store's overall image.

the ingredients of effective
retail advertising

Knowing who the audience is and relating your advertising to this specific market target are certainly the most critical factors in creating effective retail advertising.[21] According to the store's type of customer, whether in a large-scale price-oriented chain such as J. C. Penney or Sears or in a high-priced, independent, the merchandiser should search out the unique product advantages and promote those features in a unique way.

The best way to promote or advertise the unique product·features is through the effective use of layout, type, art, and copy. The layout becomes a kind of overall plan or blueprint and as such it becomes a guide or framework on which the ad will be built. Usually, a single illustration should dominate the ad in order to catch the reader's eye and thus direct him to the remainder of the artwork and copy. It is important to remember that people see first, then read, so it is important to make ads visually exciting. Through the use of copy, an attempt is made to communicate not only facts, but moods and tones of excitement. The illustration may rate more space in the advertisement, but it is the copy which drives home the advertising message. Because advertising copy is communication, the language of the copy should be conversational in tone and should be characteristic of the image of the store. Good, which of course means effective, retail advertising copy has in it the flavor of local communication and it uses to every

[21] See Steve Sohmer, "What Are the Ingredients of Good Retail Advertising?" *Editor & Publisher,* Vol. 104, No. 2 (January 9, 1971) , p. 52–53.

extent possible specific words. Specific language is unambiguous and effective.

Successful advertising copy writers almost always try for a personal and direct as well as a local tone. H. G. Wells is alleged to have once said that, "I write as simply as I can, just as I walk as straight as I can, because I want to get some place, and that's the easiest way to get there."

Many successful retail advertisements depend upon style. Style is a personal blend of tone, copy, and illustration into a combined image or personification of your store. It is style that differentiates one store from the other and which creates an easy identifiability. This is not only necessary, but essential if you are to carve out a special niche for your store in the community and to enable the firm to build sales volume in the face of the stringent competition of the late 1970s. By giving retail advertising image, character, personality, drama, and excitement you bring customers into the store and cause the cash registers to ring. After all, this is what retail advertising is intended to do.

In Chapter 18, the remaining aspects of retailing promotion—personal selling, store services, and retail credit—will be explored.

QUESTIONS FOR STUDY, REFLECTION, AND REVIEW

1. Discuss the major problem of good retailing communication. To what extent is good retailing communication necessary for effective retail promotion?
2. Discuss how the store's image or corporate style and communication are related to one another.
3. There are five basic *promotional* devices that work toward communication activities. Briefly describe these five promotional activities.
4. What are some of the factors necessary for a retail manager to develop an effective or successful advertising strategy?
5. Describe the advertising spiral and the stages of advertising within this concept.
6. To achieve many of the broad objectives, retail store advertising must be harmoniously related to the stages in the learning and consumer decision processes. Identify the consumer reaction models that were presented in the chapter.
7. Ernest Dichter argues that there are three prime purposes of displays, an awareness of which will make displays more effective in terms of increased sales and profits. What are these purposes?
8. What is advertising management? The objectives of advertising management must be in agreement with what other areas?
9. What is the fallacy in basing advertising expenditures upon the per cent of sales method (either past or forecasted sales)?
10. Describe the task method and the investment method of advertising appropriation.

18

personal selling, store services, and credit: extensions of the retailing promotional effort

The emphasis on promotional activities by retail stores is stark evidence of the increasing sophistication of our retailing and distributive systems and the increasing competition that is ever more the distinguishing hallmark of that system. In an era of widespread affluence when, concomitantly, needs and wants are increasing at a rate faster than incomes, when the merchandise carried by more and more stores is becoming increasingly similar, and when prices and price policies have become more and more alike, the need for enterprise differentiation becomes more and more acute. To achieve this differentiation, many firms resort to promotional activities such as advertising, personal selling, the greater extension of store services, and retail credit. As was stated in the previous chapter, what they strive for is a balanced and optimum promotion mix designed to generate store traffic, cement store-customer relationships, and enhance overall company profits. In this chapter, the discussion will deal with the issues and considerations involved in developing an optimum promotion mix, especially as it relates to the use of those factors just mentioned, personal selling, store services, and retail credit merchandising.

personal selling

In Chapter 17, personal selling was explained as a face-to-face confrontation between buyer and seller. This factor underlines the extreme importance of personal selling activities in retail management systems. Sales personnel are *the personnel* most frequently seen by the store's customers. It is therefore not at all surprising that to some great extent the typical customer's impression of the retail store is her impression of the retail store's sales personnel. For this reason alone, retail store systems ought to be extremely mindful of the ambassadorial role of its retail sales personnel; efforts to recruit, train, and maintain an effective store selling force should receive top management level priority. The face-to-face nature of retail store selling is an exceedingly important form of retail store communication.

Personal selling is therefore communication and part of the overall system's promotional and merchandising effort. When used in conjunction with sound merchandising and assortment policies, effective layout and organizational arrangements, and tempered with effective policies relating to the management of personnel generally, it is a valuable adjunct to the total effort put forth to satisfactorily tap a perceived market opportunity.

The Role of Personal Selling

In terms of the total retail merchandising strategy, the role and importance of personal selling will vary considerably from one store type to another and from one merchandise line to another. There is no question that the role and importance of personal selling has declined generally in most retailing systems. The rising wage rates of the recent era and the continuing spiral of the wage bill as a per cent of total store sales has brought about a marked movement toward less personal selling effort, centered around self-service and simplified selling approaches. The changing emphasis of many resellers toward pull versus push merchandising strategies has in some instances tended to accelerate this movement, as have the many changes in customer buying habits.

Nonetheless, there still remains in virtually all kinds of retail stores the necessity for some level of personal selling activity. In some stores, limited personal selling activities have been assumed by the personnel in the cashier-wrap stations, who answer questions and provide limited assistance when requested. However, their principal role is that of consummating or completing the sales transaction after the customer has already searched out the merchandise and decided to make the purchase. In some departments, even where self-service is the general rule, a great amount of personal selling effort is extended. Sporting goods departments, household furnishings, watches, jewelry, and appliance departments even in what are called discount department stores generally offer large amounts of personal selling services. Merchandise in these categories is seldom ever completely *presold* to the point where customers will enter the store and take the merchandise off the shelves without being told of the relative merits of the various models, styles, and so forth. In the supermarket, personal selling efforts are extended in many departments, especially meats, produce, and bakery.

Heavy emphasis on personal selling continues to be an integral part of the merchandising and promotional efforts of such famous retailing institutions as Brooks Brothers, Tiffany's, and Neiman-Marcus. Personal selling in retail stores is therefore not dead; it is only different. The use of personal selling as a promotional tool has changed. So, too, have personal selling appeals and approaches. Many of these changes stem from our increased understanding of the personal selling function.

In general, personal selling is considered vital when the product has substance (importance) because of its size or cost, or in cases where the buyer is likely to have a relatively high degree of uncertainty about what he needs or wants, and in all cases in which specialized requirements need to be fulfilled. Advertising may be exceedingly valuable in encouraging the consumer's initial interest for new products and services, but personal selling is often required to convince the customer of the merits of the goods or services in light of other alternatives. A good salesperson can add a strong measure of integrity and value to the product-purchase situation, and he is a valuable source of information for the problem-solving consumer who has a considerable need for knowledge and information on which to base his purchase decision.

Personal selling can be relegated to one or two categories. The first might be called *low-level selling,* as contrasted with the second category, *high-level selling.*

Low-level selling involves consummating a sale to a customer who has already made up his mind to buy and who knows, at least approximately, what he wants. Its purpose is to supply the prospective customer with information that will enable him to arrive at a decision to purchase.

High-level selling involves the process of arousing demand for new products or new brands or models of products, or influencing changes in patronage from one source of supply to another . . . In creative selling, people are persuaded to do what they had not intended to do, despite basically existing wants warranting contrary reactions.

In most retail store selling situations, low-level selling is more predominant. However, low-level selling can be done in an enterprising and creative fashion; low-level selling does not call for low-level selling tactics.

Matching the Personal Selling Effort to the Total Store Strategy

The communication of information via advertising and personal selling is a means of enhancing the total output of the retailing system. Although the system does create time, place, and possession utilities, the central task is to *inform* potential customers of the time, place, and possession implications of the firm's behavior in relation to customer needs and wants. In effect, the firm's output is a stream (bundle) of satisfactions designed to satisfy customer inputs of needs and wants. The results amount to what one writer has called *matched parallelism.*

The function of the retailing management system is to produce matched parallelism—to coordinate and match the many wants of consumers with those available goods and services that will satisfy those wants. Matched parallelism suggests that just as it is important for a company to match its product offering, its store design, layout, and other factors to its customer characteristics, it is equally important for the store to match the characteristics of its sales personnel to the characteristics of its market targets (customers).

The moral is rather simple. All the store's efforts at attracting customers must be reasonably congruent. A lackadaisical, impertinent, flippant sales person can easily drive away customers that have been attracted as a result of other sound merchandising efforts. Contrariwise, sales personnel possessing all the desired characteristics of mankind would not be enough to compensate for poor-quality merchandise, unreasonable prices, poor location, or other deficient aspects of promotion.

Understanding the Selling Situation

To understand the selling situation is to understand its many dimensions, such as the changing nature of retail selling and the different kinds of selling to be found in various kinds of retail selling situations. Other dimensions of the selling situation would include such factors as the nature of the goods being sold, the kinds of customers patronizing the store, and the total bundle of store services being extended. Needless to say, what may be an ideal sales approach for one classification of goods, one department, or even a total store can be detrimental or even self-defeating in another. And as would be imagined, the proper choice of the most effective selling method will determine in part the degree of success of the total retailing effort.

In many parts of the world, selling at nearly all levels strongly implies pushing unwanted goods on unwilling buyers. For many years, this philosophy prevailed in the United States, too; even today vestiges of this outworn practice remain in some small circles of retail selling. By and large, however, such high-pressure, salesman-oriented selling is gradually giving way to a newer kind of selling situation—one that is oriented toward the customer and is based upon insights gleaned from research and directed along social-psychological-economic lines of inquiry into customer motivation and behavior. In an earlier day, the selling of goods was guided by the legal doctrine of *caveat emptor,* a latin phrase that means, "let the buyer beware." Such a philosophy suggested that in selling, just about anything goes. Merchants often puffed their wares beyond the maximum limits of propriety. Goods were misrepresented, mislabeled, and willfully overpriced, in order that liberal price concessions could be granted. Customers in many instances were literally pulled in off the sidewalk as they passed a merchant's place of business and subjected to haranguing sales pitches. When one salesman had exhausted himself, customers were T.O.'ed, which meant turned over to another salesman whose energies were fresh and who repeated the efforts to wear down the customers' resistance. This kind of selling was referred to as "barrier selling," and the philosophy was that the customer represented a set of barriers that were to be worn or knocked down by the incessant and continuing onslaught of the salesmen. To facilitate this reigning philosophy, considerable emphasis was often placed on "sales psychology." During this period, sales psychology could most aptly be described as "a set of tricks for fooling the customer."

Another changing dimension of selling in the United States is the de-emphasis on price haggling. Almost invariably the one price policy prevails in most retail establishments, especially those selling convenience and shopping goods. This means that sales personnel no longer must be wholly familiar with merchandise costs in order to bargain effectively, but that they can, instead, focus and direct their selling efforts toward product attributes, uses, advantages, and so on. However, the degree of price haggling varies almost directly with the unit price of the commodity. Big ticket items such as appliances, home furnishings, and automobiles almost always involve some bargaining and negotiation over price, and therefore effective selling for these items must include a mutual sharing or understanding relating to merchandise value and price.

For all practical purposes, *caveat emptor* is dead. Yet, selling is very much alive and a viable part of the retail firm's promotional activities. The marketing concept and customer orientation have replaced *caveat emptor,* and consequently these newer concepts have brought with them newer approaches to the entire selling situation.[1]

From Salesmen to Buyer-Oriented selling. A vast body of knowledge relating to the social sciences (psychology, sociology, anthropology, and so on), marketing, and management is available today, and its presence has reshaped much of the thinking pertaining to the selling situation. The predominant and egotistical phase of salesmen-oriented selling (example: "How can I trick the customer into committing himself?") has given way to new modes of viewing the selling situation. The principal difference to occur is that successful selling has come to be essentially "customer oriented." Many sales authorities referred to this phenomenon as developing the "You" (as opposed to "I") attitude. Selling, therefore, is simply an extension of the retail firm's total effort to facilitate the consumer's need to solve problems. The retail salesman can be a unique and influential force in differentiating his store's products and services. But in light of the newer approaches to retail selling, he will go one step beyond what was earlier considered the normal selling procedure. Retail salesmen today are *problem solvers.* Thompson defines problem solving in selling as including, but not restricted to "'benefitizing' or interpreting the qualities of the product [or service] in terms of what it will do for the buyer."[2] Notice that selling as problem solving necessarily focuses on the buyer, not on the seller; it begins with the basic proposition that men (buyers) have a needs-wants hierarchy ranging from basic physiological needs through social, esteem, and self-actualization needs and that selling contributes to the buyer's ability to satisfy this range of needs.[3]

Selling as problem solving assumes that purchases are made to satisfy needs and wants. Consequently, in order to make a sale, the salesperson

---

[1] For more discussion on this point, see Seymour Banks, "Trends Affecting the Implementation of Advertising and Promotion," *Journal of Marketing,* Vol. 37 (January 1973), pp. 19–28.

[2] Joseph W. Thompson, *Selling: A Behavioral Approach,* McGraw-Hill Book Company, New York, 1966, p. 17.

[3] See A. H. Maslow, "A Theory of Human Motivation," *Psychological Review,* Vol. 50 (1943), pp. 370–396.

must discover or discern the customer's needs and demonstrate how his products or services will best fill those needs. The problem-solving approach to retail selling will vary from merchandise line to line and from department to department. In many cases the problem to be solved by the customer will consist simply of finding the product that *she* has already decided to purchase. The salesperson's role in such a situation could be characterized as *facilitating* the customer's problem-solving situation. In other instances, customers may be less aware of the nature of their problem and less directed in terms of possible solutions. In such cases the salesperson's role becomes more *instrumental* in that he may take a greater initiative in terms of diagnosing the customer's needs and of helping to suggest ways and means of contributing toward the solution of the problem(s).

Dyadic Interaction and Retail Selling. Retail selling involves a great deal of human interaction. Broadly defined, interaction refers to the fact that the response—gesture, word, or movement—of one individual is the stimulus to another, who in turn responds to the first. The basic model is the dyad $A \rightleftharpoons B$ in a recurring condition of interstimulation and response contact. For example, the generalized selling model could be shown as $S \rightleftharpoons C$, a dyadic relationship between S, the salesperson, and C, the customer, whereby each in turn is affected by the actions and behavior of the other.

Evans has suggested that a sale is "a product [the result] of the particular interaction situation of a given salesman and prospect rather than a result of the specific qualities of either alone." [4] The results of research into the dyadic nature of selling suggest that customers who purchase from given salesmen know more about the salesman and his firm and feel more positively toward them than prospects who do not buy. Furthermore, the more alike the salesman and his prospect are, the greater the likelihood for a sale to result. This has been found to be true for physical characteristics (age, height), other objective factors (income, religion, education), and variables that may be related to personality factors (politics, smoking). In short, a similarity of attributes within the dyad appears to increase the likelihood of a sale.

Other approaches to analyzing and understanding the selling situation have been undertaken. In a study of 621 consumers by the *Chicago Tribune* two types of shoppers (the independent and the dependent) were isolated and described. In the case of the dependent shopper:

> Shopping is pleasant if the salespeople are nice and unpleasant if they are not. The store is good if the clerks are warm, interested and courteous. She is apt to be a food loving and company loving person: she likes to go shopping with her friends, enjoys their company, and likes to eat lunch with them.[5]

[4] F. B. Evans, "Selling as a Dyadic Relationship—A New Approach," *The American Behavioral Scientist,* Division of Sage Publications, Vol. VI (May 1963), p. 76.

[5] "Psychological Aspects of Shopping," *The Chicago Tribune,* Research Division, Chicago, 1957, p. 285.

The dependent shopper is further characterized as being highly dependent on the opinions of others such as friends and sales personnel. The independent shopper is briefly characterized as "a rare shopper, sure of her tastes and of herself and who enjoys shopping."[6]

Gregory Stone classified shoppers according to the psychological needs that influenced their selection of a particular store.[7] He found four types of shoppers: (1) economic shoppers, (2) apathetic shoppers, (3) personalizing shoppers, and (4) ethical shoppers. It should be pointed out that Stone's "economic shopper" closely resembles the *Tribune's* dependent shopper.

The point is that all these studies indicate that the behavior of customers in terms of merchandise selection and choice of store is influenced by the behavior of the sales personnel.

Stafford and Greer, in an exploratory study, have attempted to relate customer preference for types of salesmen to conditions of customer independence and dependence traits.[8] Their findings suggest that there is a significant difference between independent and dependent persons in their preferences for salespersons with varying characteristics, with the dependent subjects preferring more aggressive salesmen. Quite obviously, the nature of the interactional process is such that (for yet undetermined reasons) dependent persons are those who may manifest the greatest need for assistance in their problem-solving purchase behavior and are more likely to respond favorably to salespersons who aggressively assert their willingness to provide this assistance. This would square well with the finding that consumers expect a certain degree of aggressiveness in a salesperson, depending on the product being sold, but that they do not like a salesperson to be over-aggressive.

The Selling Process. Most successful retail selling programs are now committed to the point of view that selling ought to be problem and customer centered rather than salesperson or firm centered. The selling situation in its broadest dimension considers the interactive nature of the salesperson, firm, product, and customer situation. The selling processes or approaches to the customer-salesperson dyad that are emphasized in retail store situations will vary from situation to situation. As discussed earlier, the nature of the actual sales processes or approaches used in any particular store will depend upon the nature of the circumstances surrounding that store, such as the type of merchandise being sold and the characteristics of the store's clientele. Some situations will naturally demand a high-level, creative type of selling. Other situations will require only a casual, low-key, order-taking kind of activity. Thus, a range of selling processes exists in

[6] Ibid.

[7] G. P. Stone, "City Shoppers and Urban Identification: Observations on the Social Psychology of City Life," *American Journal of Sociology,* LX (July 1954), pp. 36–45. See the followup study by David L. Kurtz, James C. Johnson, and John Bonno, "City Shoppers and Urban Identification—Revisited," *Journal of Marketing,* Vol. 38, No. 3 (July 1974), pp. 67–69. Also see Edward M. Tauber, "Why Do People Shop?" *Journal of Marketing,* Vol. 36, No. 4 (October 1972), pp. 46–50.

[8] James E. Stafford and Thomas V. Greer, "Consumer Preferences for Types of Salesmen: A Study of Independence-Dependence Characteristics," *Journal of Retailing,* Vol. 41, No. 2 (Summer 1965), pp. 27–33 and 47.

order to serve the range of selling needs likely to manifest themselves in a given retail selling situation. This range of selling processes can be characterized as three approaches that in turn represent the three distinct levels of selling activity likely to be found in retail selling situations. These three approaches (levels) are (1) stimulus-response selling, (2) formula selling, and (3) situation-management. Each will be briefly discussed.

Stimulus-Response (S-R) Selling. Stimulus-response selling is a low-level selling approach that is directed toward conditioning (training) a subject in new patterns of behavior or reaction. The subject or customer is assumed to be rather passive and his behavior change (favorable reaction to selling suggestions—the stimulus) is controlled by manipulating external forces.

Stimulus-response selling is somewhat less flexible than either formula selling or situation-management. In the S-R approach to retail selling, the salesman needs to have a whole repertoire of things to say, gestures to make and perform (stimuli), in order to bring about the desired buying response. It is somewhat mechanical, because it presumes that the right stimuli will always elicit the right response. Stimulus-response selling is a kind of routinized habit level behavior that may have some place in the retail selling situation, especially where the unit of sale is low and the time that can be devoted to each transaction is very limited. However, as most people know who have had any experience in dealing with people, a stimulus that brings about a desired response in one subject may bring about a completely different and undesired response in another subject. However, in some situations, stimulus-response selling may prove to be an adequate means of meeting the minimum demands of the retail selling situation.

Formula Selling. Formula selling might be characterized as the half-way point between stimulus-response selling and situation-management. It is at least an initial recognition that selling is problem-solving activity, but it is still largely a canned, mechanical approach to the problem of salesperson-customer interaction. The basic assumption that underlies formula selling is that about all customers are basically alike. Therefore, emphasis is placed on leading the customer through a sequential (formulalike) series of mental states, the typical approach being related to the AIDA formula, mentioned in Chapter 17. Recall that the AIDA formula suggests that in persuading or communicating effectively to customers, the message sender (advertiser or salesman) must first secure *attention,* then build *interest* and *desire,* and then make a positive bid for *action.* In the case of selling, the latter would mean a request for the order. The formula approach to selling has also viewed the selling process as a series of activities that must be performed by the salesman in order to effectuate the sale. Much of the actual sales training in retail systems has been directed along the lines of improving performance in the process or sequence. For example, emphasis is placed upon such activities as (1) the sales approach and greeting, (2) sizing up the customer, (3) asking questions, (4) meeting objections, and (5) closing the sale.

Such an emphasis is never without serious shortcomings. Far too often it is too salesman-oriented and not enough customer-oriented. Often, the individuality of the particular customer and her thoughts and impressions are ignored. The approach assumes that the transition from one mental state, say, attention, moves smoothly and progressively to each subsequent state. This is a condition (considering the factor of individual differences) that is not at all likely. Some customers may move rapidly from attention to action, whereas others may never move out of the attention stage.

However, formula selling is a rather efficient way of training sales personnel for low to medium level kinds of retail selling situations.[9] It is efficient, because it can indoctrinate and train (at relatively low cost in a brief period of time) sales personnel in the superficial aspects of retail store selling. It encourages some customer orientation, a friendly and pleasant personality for selling, and a degree of product knowledge. Nevertheless, this approach runs into difficulty when the customer wants to get the answer to a specific question. If the salesman fails to perceive this, he continues to make his presentation and may therefore literally talk himself out of a sale, annoy the customer, and cause her to shift her patronage to another store.

Situation Management. The situation management approach to retail selling considers the interactive nature of the retail selling situation and views it as a part of the communication process. Furthermore, it is customer-oriented in its philosophy rather than salesman-oriented. Situation management selling is high-level, creative selling which views each potential customer as a unique individual, thus restricting the tendency to stereotype customers. This approach emphasizes the accomplishment of desired results through human interaction. The results sought, of course, are satisfied customers whose problems have been analyzed and evaluated with a view toward effective solution of those problems. Human interaction means that the sales situation will be affected by the values, attitudes, and general cognitive structure of the individuals who are parties to the situation, namely, the salesperson and the customer. Thus, there is an awareness of the necessity for having sales personnel in various departments and merchandise lines with characteristics that are congruent with those demanded by the circumstances. Situation management implies an adaptive, accommodative, flexible form of behavior on the part of retail sales personnel. They are responsible for managing and coping with a wide range of sales situations. Sales personnel who attempt to adopt the situation management approach to retail selling place salesmanship on a high ethical plane. They do not attempt to manipulate or mislead. They fully adopt a "you" attitude in their selling behavior. They place great pride in their knowledge and understanding of people, and, moreover, in their continuing interest in learning more.

Such sales persons attempt to learn how all approaches and techniques of selling may be incorporated into managing sales situations. This approach develops an awareness of the personal, emotional, social, and status needs of the customer so that the salesman can adjust his behavior to cope with

---

[9] Marvin A. Jolson, "The Underestimated Potential of the Canned Sales Presentation," *Journal of Marketing,* Vol. 39, No. 1 (January 1975) , pp. 75–79.

these needs. The seller, furthermore, is aware of the distinction between these and the needs of the individual as a user of the salesman's product. Finally, sales situation managers understand the decision-making process that each buyer goes through in making purchase decisions.

managing the personal selling function

Understanding the retail selling situation can lead to greater success in *managing* that situation. From understanding flows a knowledge of processes, and requirements, and insight as to how to effectively plan, organize, and control these processes. Such is the case with retail selling. Managing the personal selling effort consists essentially of recruiting, selecting, training, and maintaining an effective retail selling force. Such management efforts and the impact of personnel management on the total system's performance have already been covered in earlier chapters on organization. They will therefore not be discussed again extensively in this section. However, there are some conditions relating to personal selling and the management of the personal selling function that will warrant additional consideration because of the uniqueness of their character. The discussion that follows will therefore focus on the principal management tasks relating to the personal selling effort, namely, (1) recruiting, selecting, and training; (2) staffing the personal selling effort; and (3) controlling the selling function.

Recruiting, Selecting, and Training
Retail Sales Personnel

The nature of the retail selling situation will affect the firm's efforts in terms of recruiting, selection, and training. Moreover, the problem of hiring and recruiting effective retail sales personnel is considerably hampered by several factors. Foremost are the low wage rates that prevail in retail store selling opportunities. This problem is a formidable obstacle that retail management must either overcome or live with. However, another nearly unmanageable problem also exists, and this is the problem of how to recognize or foretell who has the capabilities to become a successful retail salesperson. Efforts in this respect to date have met with relatively little success. The attempts have centered around approaches aimed at identifying personality characteristics that make for effective sales performance. Three approaches are common to such efforts. As described by Evans, they are[10]

1. *The Sales Personality.* What the salesman must or ought to be (mentally tough, diplomatic, poised) or how he must act (like to meet people, ambitious, self-confident and assured).
2. *The Persuasive Salesman.* How to persuade or manipulate prospects (understand people, dominate the social situation, be persistent and assertive).

[10] Evans, op. cit., pp. 76–77.

3. *The Adaptable Salesman.* Be whatever the prospects want, a chameleon, cultivate a supple spine, accommodate himself to everyone.

Unfortunately, the *descriptive* approach is rather meaningless as a *predictor* of sales success. The truth is that there are no really satisfactory ways of pinpointing persons with high sales ability potential, especially in the retail selling situation. The sales personality, the persuasive salesman, the adaptable sales person, or any other type is a rather elusive entity when it comes to pinpointing possible candidates for recruitment and selection. At this point, it may be well to consider in rather general terms the major conclusions that social scientists have reached in regard to the social and psychological characteristics of sales personnel.[11]

1. There is no significant relation between intelligence test scores and sales success.
2. No significant relationship has been found between independent measures of personality traits and sales success.
3. No correlation exists between age and sales success.
4. There is no correlation between measurable character traits and sales success.
5. There is no significant correlation between level of education and sales success.
6. No significant correlation exists between level of sales activity and sales success among individual salesmen.
7. The above factors have significance when studied in relation to all the others, in individual salesmen.
8. Salespersons are more likely to succeed when chosen with regard to the kinds of customers they will deal with than in terms of the types of products sold.

Although space will not permit a discussion of the full implications of each of these findings, the last generalization certainly appears to bear out what was said earlier in relation to the value of the interactive nature of the sales situation. Furthermore, generalization (7) suggests an important consideration, namely, that while no one of the cited factors, age, education, personality, level of activity, and so forth appears to have much singular predictive significance, research indicates that when such social and psychological variables are studied in relation to one another, the resulting profiles become valuable guides for the selection of people who are *likely* to become successful retail sales personnel. Salespeople are made. They are not born. Some evidence does exist to suggest that salespersons differ from non-salespersons in that[12]

1. Salespeople are persuasive rather than critical.
2. Salespeople are intuitive rather than analytical.
3. Salespeople have a higher average energy level.

[11] Samuel N. Stevens, "The Application of Social Science Findings to Selling and the Salesman," *Aspects of Modern Marketing*, AMA Report No. 15, American Management Association, New York, 1958, pp. 85–94.

[12] Ibid., p. 88.

4. Salespeople have a higher motivation for status achievement, power, prestige, and so forth.

Undoubtedly there are personality types who lend themselves better to retail store selling than others. Personality, intelligence, and aptitude tests along with the application blank and the personal interview may produce a profile of sales personalities manifesting the greatest tendency toward successful retail store selling. However, actual sales success is also a function of the environmental forces at work. Most of the traits manifested by the successful retail sales person are *acquired characteristics,* which means that sales ability and performance can be improved by in-store sales training. There is much evidence to suggest that retail selling personnel are doing only a fraction of the things they might do to induce more sales.[13] The poor quality of sales personnel is the reason offered by many retail managers. However, poor training or complete lack of training may be a more reasonable answer. New sales personnel are almost always never trained in better ways of selling. What training is provided is focused upon such things as filling out sales slips, operating the cash register, and other factors related to store systems and processes. However, some store groups (Allied Stores) have experimented with programmed sales training efforts involving the use of self-instructional manuals in courtesy and suggestion selling. Thus far, reported results are encouraging, with the programmed training group reporting sales-dollar revenue per hour increases of 25 per cent over the not-so-trained control group.[14] Generally, because of the high labor turnover and other considerations, retail stores have been reluctant to implement costly training programs in the face of uncertain returns.

Staffing the Personal Selling Effort

Staffing the personal selling effort is one of the most important aspects of managing the retail personal selling function. Staffing is concerned principally with the problem of having a balanced number of sales personnel to meet expected customer demand and to supply that demand with a level of service consistent with customer needs and store expense and profit constraints. Too many salespeople would mean too much idle time, thus raising wage rates as a per cent of sales. On the other hand, too few salespeople would mean limiting customer service levels. Customers who have to wait too long for a salesperson often walk out; this results in loss of sales and customer patronage.

Sales labor wages constitute the largest single operating expense item on the average retail store's operating statement. During a recent five-year period, hourly earnings of retail employees generally rose 16 per cent, while prices of department store merchandise rose by only 6 per cent. The persistent wage-margin spiral has necessitated much more careful control over retail selling costs. Of the total payroll expense in the average department

[13] Allen F. Jung, "Are Retail Salesmen Selling?" *Journal of Retailing,* Vol. 39, No. 2 (Summer 1962), pp. 9–14.

[14] See Frederick Finegan, "Programmed Sales Training," *Department Store Economist* (April 1963), pp. 33–34.

store, over one third is attributable to sales personnel wages. These payroll costs in department stores are approaching 8 per cent of sales. The need for continuous effort toward the effective management of the staffing function is therefore readily apparent.

Many retail stores approach the staffing function in a rather conventional way. They posit a given level for selling expenses and then add sales personnel up to the maximum limits set by this level. For example, assume that for a new department in an existing department store, sales expenses are budgeted at 8 per cent of sales. If forecasted sales for the new department are $220,000 per year, then at 8 per cent, the permissible level of sales expense would be $17,600. Now, if the prevailing wage rate is $3.00 per hour and the length of the average work week is 40 hours, this means that each salesperson would earn $120 per week, or $6,000 per year. Dividing $17,600 (the sales expense budget) by $6,000 (the average earnings per sales employee per year) gives a result of 2.9, or very nearly 3. In effect, the likely result would be that two full-time salespeople would be hired and at least one or possibly several part-time salespeople to handle peak loads during special sales, Saturdays, or to fill in during lunch hours, illnesses, or vacation periods. Retail sales personnel most often are compensated on a salary rather than a commission basis. This means that selling costs are a function of wages paid and sales produced. If sales fall below forecasted levels, the usual result is an increase in selling cost as a per cent of sales. However, in many merchandise lines such as furniture and appliances and automobiles, salespeople work on straight commission, and in such cases selling costs always remain a fixed percentage of sales. Commission payment plans suffer from several deficiencies. First of all, many retail sales personnel dislike the insecurity and uncertainty of working on a commission basis, and second, commission plans do not reward sales personnel for the typical large amounts of nonselling duties such as store housekeeping, merchandise maintenance, stock keeping, and display, which accompany the usual retail selling situation.

Several more scientific approaches to the staffing problem are currently being explored. The difficulty with the conventional approach is that it posits a given selling expense level and hopes that the service provided at this level will be sufficient to effectively satisfy the demand that presents itself. The newer, systems-oriented approaches begin by scientifically determining the level of sales personnel service that will maximize sales and profits and work from this figure to forecast selling expense.

Based upon a careful analysis of store and departmental goals, the variables that affect the staffing problem—customer arrivals, contacts, transactions, and sales clerk capacity—are incorporated into a queuing theory model so that in the process sales budgets are determined.[15] As a matter of fact, staffing and the sales budget both become outputs of the model. In addition, there are several further byproducts of the systems approach incorporated by queuing theory. These are

[15] For more discussion and a more formal treatment of this concept, see Robert J. Paul, "The Retail Store as a Waiting Line Model," *Journal of Retailing*, Vol. 48, No. 2 (Summer 1972), pp. 3–16.

1. A sound basis for staffing is obtained.
2. A basis for allocating total salesperson man-hours into permanent and part-time help is obtained.
3. It reduces employee turnover and makes for better work assignment possibilities.

Finally, such approaches give top management a useful and valuable set of tools for effecting and supporting suggested changes in merchandise classifications, layout, and other proposed systems changes.

Controlling the Selling Function

The corollary of effective planning is a well-designed set of control procedures. Control is a kind of follow-up that is a check on the efficacy of our planning and organizing efforts. Control (as we have learned previously) is concerned with establishing standards, evaluating performance, and taking corrective action. The retail personal selling function certainly warrants both careful planning and control procedures. As a part of the total retail management system effort, it is imperative that there be an optimum amount of productivity from the personal selling function. If productivity is low or below optimum, it would appear nothing less than prudent that efforts be made to improve selling productivity. Because productivity as applied to retail selling is defined as gross sales transactions per salesperson hour worked, there are only three ways to increase the productivity of salespeople: (1) increase the number of sales transactions that salespeople generate, (2) curtail the number of hours worked by salespeople, or (3) do both concomitantly.

To accomplish these ends requires effective personal selling planning, but as a parallel to these planning efforts, sound control procedures must also be implemented. Many stores, especially smaller ones, neglect the control aspects of managing the personal selling function. As a matter of fact, with the exception of efforts to hold down selling costs, these stores make little effort to implement standards or to evaluate the performance of retail sales personnel.

One study attempted to discover (1) how large departmentized stores measure the productivity of salespeople, (2) how they appraise their methods, and (3) what steps they are taking to improve their methods.[16] The study revealed that few stores depart significantly from the established methods of measuring productivity of salespeople. Furthermore, it revealed that the most frequently used standard for evaluating performance is selling cost, and that the unit assigned the control responsibility in connection with sales personnel performance is usually the personnel division.

There is little question that more and better control procedures would lead to improved sales performance productivity. There currently exist many standards by which retail sales performance can be gauged. For example, it is possible to relate the percentage of walkouts to total store or

[16] David J. Rachman and Robert Robichaud, "How Large Stores Measure Employee Sales Productivity," *Journal of Retailing,* Vol. 37, No. 1 (Spring 1961), pp. 1–5.

departmental traffic shopping. Such results are usually obtained by interviewing customers who have not made a purchase, as they leave the department or store. Many ratios for evaluating sales performance are also available for use. For example:

$$\frac{\text{Transactions}}{\text{Traffic}} = \text{Per cent of traffic sold (The complement of which is walkouts.)}$$

$$\frac{\text{Units sold}}{\text{Total traffic}} = \text{Traffic productivity ratio}$$

$$\frac{\text{Planned traffic}}{\text{Traffic sales}} = \text{Planned volume}$$

$$\frac{\text{Units sold}}{\text{Transactions}} = \text{Units sold per customer}$$

$$\frac{\text{Total transactions}}{\text{Hours worked}} = \text{Transactions per hour}$$

The use of such ratios by personnel and department managers can lead to a greater understanding of the factors that affect retail sales performance productivity. Such standards are criteria against which performance is compared in order to determine the relative merit or value of that performance.

Retail selling performance standards have been approached by analyzing three factors. The first of these is a count of the number of transactions accomplished by each salesperson. The second involves rating the salesperson, or attempting to evaluate the speed or tempo at which an individual is working during the study. Third and finally, the allowances (time away from the actual performance of duties) must be established.

Paul suggests that once such performance standards are established for sales personnel, their actual performance should be compared against them. If significant deviations between actual performance and standards are discovered, the reasons should be determined and corrective action undertaken.[17] When such an approach was employed in actual field conditions, sales personnel activities in terms of actual performance broke down as follows:[18]

Selling	25 per cent
Stock work	12 per cent
Miscellaneous work	14 per cent
Awaiting arrivals	34 per cent
Absent	15 per cent

Such approaches underline the conviction that it is possible to establish accurate and relatively low-cost standards for evaluating sales performance

[17] Robert J. Paul, "Scientific Determination of Performance Standards for Non-repetitive Duties," *Journal of Retailing*, Vol. 43, No. 3 (Fall 1967), pp. 50–56 and 74.
[18] Ibid.

activities and that when such scientific approaches are employed, the results most typically reveal a wide range of findings, namely:[19]

1. There is a significant difference in the manner in which highest-dollar-volume and lowest-dollar-volume salespeople spend their time.
2. The activity status difference is greatest in the "selling" and "idle time" categories.
3. Highest-dollar-volume salespeople spend a higher percentage of the work period doing stock work and miscellaneous activities than lowest-dollar-volume salespeople.
4. Higher-dollar-volume salespeople tend to work at a faster pace than lowest-dollar-volume salespeople.
5. Higher-volume salespeople are absent from their departments significantly less than low-dollar-volume personnel.

There are many ways other than the slide rule, stopwatch approach to controlling and improving retail sales performances. Better training methods, improved departmental layouts, more self-selection, the streamlined processing of sales transactions, and improved time schedules for selling employees all offer possibilities for improving performance and therefore producing increased sales and profits.[20]

promoting and managing store services

The retailing firm attempts to generate a bundle of satisfactions or expectations in order to both attract and hold patronage. The complex of satisfactions generated consists of merchandise, the store facility itself, the layout, style, and design of the building, and the promotional strategy, *all of which are usually complemented by a bundle of service activities whose purpose is to facilitate and promote the store's total offering*. As a matter of fact, the bundle of satisfactions and expectations generated by each store is just that—a mix of goods; facilities; activities such as pricing, promotion, merchandise selection, and assortment; and services such as wrapping, delivery, the handling of complaints, store hour adjustments, credit, and a continually exploding range of other consumer services.

Furthermore, it must be borne in mind that each store will attempt to generate a total bundle of expectations that is in keeping with its perceived market opportunity. As the range of market opportunities—through the continuing increase and development of new market segments—continues to grow, so will the range in the firm's generated bundle of expectations grow also. Not all firms will attempt to generate the same bundle of expectations. In the pursuit of enterprise differentiation, each firm will attempt to create a total market offering that is in keeping with the store's

---

[19] These findings are part of a larger set of findings reported by Robert J. Paul and Robert W. Bell, "Evaluating the Retail Salesmen," *Journal of Retailing*, Vol. 44, No. 2 (Summer 1968), pp. 20–21.

[20] For a review of these additional factors, see R. Dale Vonriesen, "Toward Staffing Optimality," *Journal of Retailing* (Winter 1973–1974), pp. 39–47.

philosophy and style, its market opportunity, and the behavior of its competitors.[21]

Most firms attempt to do more than just sell goods. Firms sell solutions to consumer problems. To do so often means that the goods sold must be embellished and packaged in a wide range of store services. In other instances, it may mean that consumers want only goods with a limited complement of additional store services.

What Are Services?

Store services must be promoted and managed. But just what is meant by services? A considerable amount of confusion exists to cloud this issue. *Services* have been defined as "activities, benefits, or satisfactions which are offered for sale, or are provided in connection with the sale of goods."[22] Such a definition suggests further elaboration. Services could represent intangibles that yield direct satisfaction, tangibles that yield satisfaction directly, or intangibles yielding satisfaction jointly when purchased either with commodities or other services. Examples of the first situation would be insurance; the second, transportation and housing; and the third, credit and delivery. There has been considerable dissatisfaction with the way services are described and classified. One writer has suggested that a distinction be made between (1) rented goods services; (2) owned goods services; and (3) nongoods services.[23]

The purchased right to possess and use a product is a rented goods service. Custom creation of, repair of, or improvement of a product is an owned goods service. Nongoods services involve no product elements, but rather are an experience or activity that facilitates possession and ownership. You will recognize at once that retail stores engage in the generation of all three kinds of service activities. However, our primary interest here will focus on category (3), nongoods services. Most assuredly you should recognize that many retail stores are moving heavily into the merchandising of both rented goods services and owned goods services, in order to further expand their market opportunity. The growth in these two categories of service merchandising results from the fact that the marginal attraction of services is increasing faster than that for more goods, and that such patterns of growth serve to underline more pointedly the essence of Ernst Engel's law, stated in 1857—one part of which stated that as income increases, the percentage spent for sundries increases rapidly.

[21] These themes are supported extensively in the following articles: Jerry Williams and Rachel Dardis, "Selected Personal Services: Consumer Reactions," and W. Thomas Anderson, Jr., "Convenience Orientation and Consumption Behavior," *Journal of Retailing*, Vol. 48, No. 3 (Fall 1972), pp. 42–49 and pp. 49–72, respectively.

[22] *Marketing Definitions, A Glossary of Marketing Terms*, Committee on Definitions of The American Marketing Association, American Marketing Association, Chicago, 1960, p. 21.

[23] See Robert C. Judd, "The Case for Redefining Services," *Journal of Marketing*, Vol. 28 (January 1964), pp. 58–59; and John M. Rathmul, "What Is Meant by Services?" *Journal of Marketing*, Vol. 30 (October 1966), pp. 32–36.

Services as Promotion

Nongoods services are usually offered by retailers as an extension of the firm's merchandising and promotional strategy. Such nongoods services as credit, delivery, store hours adjustment, wrapping, and customer complaints and adjustments are activities whose purpose is to attract and hold more customers, in order to increase the firm's profitability. The utilities of time, place, and possession delivered by the retailer yield increased satisfaction when accompanied by the performance of nongoods services (i.e., services provided in connection with the sale of goods). A new appliance has utility for its owner-user only when properly delivered and installed in her home, and after she has been fully instructed in its use. A store is satisfactory for a given customer or customer segment if it is conveniently located and has store hours that are coordinated to the shopping hours of its customers. Goods have value in use. A credit plan that affords customers the opportunity to possess the merchandise and its benefits now and to pay later is a valuable store service for many customers. *It would appear somewhat self-evident, therefore, that the store's bundle of nongoods services is a means of promoting its physical goods, plus its rented goods and owned goods mix.*

The store's nongoods service mix will vary widely as a result of customer demand and expectations, competitive offerings, costs, and other relevant considerations. The normal range of nongoods services includes such activities as store hours, the handling of customer complaints and merchandise corrections, delivery services offered, product alterations, workroom activities, and wrapping services.

Store services are the activities provided by the store for the customer in connection with the sale of goods and must be managed effectively. That is, the range of store services to be offered must be carefully considered within much the same framework as other store merchandising considerations. Sound management would dictate the careful planning and coordination of store services in a manner consistent with the overall corporate philosophy of the system as a whole. Prudent management would further suggest that policies designed to effectively control store service activities be soundly considered. The ultimate aim of a retail store is to produce or generate a balanced and desired blend of value-satisfying utilities. To the end that store services contribute to this blend, they must be planned, organized, coordinated, and controlled, in order to assure the attainment of their optimum contribution.

The Level of Store Services and Customer Costs

Are store services free? The answer is, No! Not in the sense in which *free* is usually interpreted. The offering of store nongoods services is a form of nonprice competitive activity. Such activity is designed usually to shift a firm's demand curve upward and to the right. It is an effort to affect total revenues without manipulating the price variable. Nonprice competitive activity is such that to undertake it is to incur costs. When a store advertises, it hopes to shift its demand curve (or in the face of competition to hold its demand curve steady). But in order to advertise, the firm must expend resources, namely, money. Store services are therefore no more free than is advertising. Quite frankly, in the final analysis, the ultimate consumer pays for all forms of promotion and nonprice competitive activity. The costs of advertising and providing nongoods services are reflected in the gross margin of the retail store and other parts of the distribution channel. However, the important point to be considered is, "Are customer prices higher as a result of nonprice competitive activity such as store services?" This question is not so easily answered. An answer based upon reflection would hedge by saying that it depends on certain considerations. Whether the customer pays more depends upon the cost structure of the firm in question. Does the nonprice competitive activity attract appreciably more customers? What are the costs of the nonprice activity? How might management choose to divide or share any differences between added costs for services and added revenues generated by the service offering? In an expanding market situation, added service offerings might successfully attract more patrons, and the increased business could be spread over the existing fixed costs, thus resulting in lower total average costs. This was likely the situation for many years. However, as market areas and trading networks began to be filled up, the firm's ability to generate extra or marginal business as a result of expanded store services declined. Too, when all firms are offering essentially the same bundle of service satisfactions, the competitive advantage for any single store is largely eliminated. Providing that service thus adds to operating costs that must be covered in the gross margin. The result is that either the customer pays for the service, or the store pays for it by taking less profit. With some ceiling imposed on rising prices by direct price competition and a constantly rising operating expense ratio brought about (at least in part) by continually rising levels of nongoods service offerings, many retail stores have been forced to reconsider these services, both in terms of the extent of the offering and whether to charge extra for their services.[24]

Furthermore, the success of many stores with limited nongoods offerings such as discount stores has been rather convincing evidence that some customer segments would prefer lower merchandise costs at the expense of foregoing many of the services frequently offered. To compete successfully with these newer outlets, many stores, especially department stores, have initiated a plan of nongoods service merchandising embracing the user-pay principle. A limited number of nongoods services continue to be offered free in the sense that their cost is absorbed in the total margin. Other services (workroom costs such as alterations, delivery and installation, and service and maintenance) are offered only on the basis that the customer is charged extra for them. Some stores charge full or average costs for these services, whereas others attempt to assay and charge only the marginal or incremental costs incurred. From the point of view of the firm, the guiding

---

[24] See James M. Carman, "Selection of Retailing Services by New Arrivals," *Journal of Retailing*, Vol. 50, No. 2 (Summer 1974), pp. 11–23.

principle related to whether or not to charge for nongoods services must be, "Does the provision of that service add more to revenues than it does to cost?" If it does, it may be absorbed in the margin. If it does not, then store profits are being seriously affected, and some consideration must be given to correcting the situation, either by eliminating the service, improving the efficiency with which it is being performed, or by adding an extra charge to the customer's bill to either totally or partially defray the added expense.

retail credit

Undoubtedly, retail credit is one of the most important nongoods services offered to their customers by retail stores. Ours is largely a credit economy and stores that fail to offer this important service are often falling far short in their effort to attain full market opportunity. In order to satisfy the demands of many shoppers, it is now imperative that stores offer not just limited, but a wide variety of customer credit services. Credit and credit services have become additional and important means of differentiating the store's total assortment offering and for generating additional revenues and profits. Credit is a nongoods service offering and has been found furthermore to be an important device for building and cementing the patronage of many customers. Customers are bound more closely to a given store, *if* they have established credit at that store. Credit is a means of attracting not only a more loyal class of customers, but a higher class of clientele. Credit customers buy more expensive merchandise, and they usually buy more of it than does the strictly cash customer. Credit offerings also have the advantage of smoothing out the erratic bunching of sales volume that tends to occur with the noncredit customer by spreading purchases throughout the month. When credit is available, the customer can purchase goods as the need arises and pay later. Finally, credit customers constitute an ideal mailing list for the store's special promotions and for its regular mailing pieces.

Consumer credit offered by retail stores is thus an important service—an identifiable value that facilitates and enhances the possession utility of the product.[25] What is more, credit extension is a valuable adjunct to the store's overall promotional activities.

The Extent of Retail Credit

Buying on credit is a widely accepted practice among consumers today. Of all retail stores, nearly one third offer some form of consumer credit. Quite naturally, the extent to which credit is offered and the kinds of credit offered will vary from store to store depending upon the kind of store, merchandise lines carried, the nature of competition, and the price of the merchandise. At one time, a large proportion of the retail food stores in the United States sold much of their output on a credit basis. Today, however,

[25] See Michael J. Etzel and James H. Donnelly, Jr., "Consumer Perceptions of Alternative Retail Credit Plans," *Journal of Marketing*, Vol. 48, No. 2 (Summer 1972) , pp. 67–74.

TABLE 18-1   The Changing Importance of Retail Charge Account Credit

YEAR	TOTAL VOLUME OF CHARGE ACCOUNT CREDIT	TOTAL VOLUME OF CONSUMER CREDIT	CHARGE ACCOUNT CREDIT AS A PER CENT OF TOTAL CONSUMER CREDIT
1965	$ 6,430[a]	$ 89,883[a]	7.2%
1966	6,686	96,239	6.9
1967	7,070	100,783	7.0
1968	7,193	111,770	6.4
1969	7,373	121,146	6.0
1970	7,968	127,163	6.3
1971	8,350	138,394	6.0
1972	9,002	157,564	5.7
1973	9,829	180,486	5.4
1974	10,134	190,121	5.3

[a] 000 omitted in dollar columns.

SOURCE: Compiled from Federal Reserve Bulletins, Board of Governors of the Federal Reserve System.

given the advent of the giant self-service supermarket, only a limited number of food markets offer any form of credit. Furniture and appliance stores would find it very difficult to carry on a successful merchandising program without offering credit services; so, too, would automobile and other big ticket item dealers. Among merchandise outlets such as fur and jewelry stores, far more than 50 per cent of their sales volume is attributed to credit accounts, and hardware stores do almost 50 per cent of their volume on a credit basis. Even discount houses, variety stores, and low-end general merchandise stores are rapidly extending the amount and range of their credit service offerings.

The large national mass merchandising chains such as Sears, Roebuck and Co., and Montgomery Ward aggressively promote their credit facilities to the extent that credit sales account for approximately 56 per cent of Ward's total sales, and 64 per cent of Sears'.[26] Even J. C. Penney, whose merchandising slogan for many years was "cash on the barrelhead," has now got on the credit bandwagon. Tables 18-1 and 18-2 show trends in consumer credit for 1965 through 1974.

Observe that retail charge account credit (while increasing in terms of absolute numbers) has been decreasing as a per cent of total consumer credit during the period 1965–1974. Several reasons are offered for this decline. The most important factor is not that consumer credit per se is declining, for it is not. Rather, charge account credit is declining because of the relatively increasing importance of other forms of consumer credit, namely, installment credit and revolving credit. Table 18-2 reports the volume of installment credit broken down into two categories, automobile

[26] Such information is available from the companies' annual reports to stockholders.

TABLE 18-2   Volume of Installment Credit, Automobile Paper, and Other
Consumer Goods Credit

YEAR	TOTAL INSTALL- MENT CREDIT	AUTOMOBILE PAPER	OTHER CONSUMER GOODS CREDIT
1965	$ 70,893[a]	$28,437[a]	$18,483[a]
1966	76,245	30,010	20,732
1967	79,428	29,796	22,389
1968	87,745	32,948	24,626
1969	97,105	35,527	28,312
1970	102,064	35,184	31,465
1971	111,295	38,664	34,353
1972	127,332	44,129	40,080
1973	147,437	51,130	47,530
1974	156,124	51,689	52,009

[a] 000 omitted in dollar columns.
SOURCE: Compiled from Federal Reserve Bulletins, Board of Governors of the Federal Reserve System.

paper and other forms of consumer goods credit. Note that columns (2) and (3) do not total to column (1) because of the omission of repair and modernization loans and personal loans, which are not considered as a part of retail store nongoods credit services.

Kinds of Consumer Credit

The preceding tables will become more meaningful when examined in light of the three main types of consumer credit services offered by retail stores—charge account services, installment account services, and revolving account services. The role and importance of each will be briefly explained. Retail credit is a medium of exchange much like money. It involves essentially a situation wherein consumers receive goods now in exchange for a promise to pay later. The various kinds of retail credit are simply devices for circumscribing the terms under which credit will be granted.

Charge Account Credit.   Charge account credit (or open book credit as it has sometimes been called) is a form of short-term consumer credit. After the credit worthiness of the customer has been established, the customer is permitted to charge items up to some usually predetermined limit. The customer receives the goods immediately and promises to pay for them within 30 days. The 30-day period is usually 30 days after the receipt of the billed invoice. There is no added interest or service charge for this service. Several different items can be charged at any one time or over a period of time so long as the agreed upon credit limit is not exceeded. For many years, the charge account was the principal type of retail credit offered by most stores. Today, however, given the breakdown in resistance to installment and installment type credit, charge account credit as a percentage of total retail credit is declining.

Installment Credit. Installment credit usually involves a more formal agreement between seller and buyer. The merchandise is purchased and a stated down payment is agreed upon, as is the period over which the remaining balance of the contract will be amortized. An interest charge (service charge) is added to the unpaid balance, and the total is then divided into weekly or monthly payment periods. The merchandise ownership may pass with the sale of the item to the buyer, in which case it is secured by a *chattel mortgage;* or title may remain with the seller under a *conditional sales contract* arrangement until final payment is made. Installment credit has made the ownership of durable goods such as automobiles, appliances, furnishings, and other big ticket items much easier. Many purchasers of such items view the payments associated with their ownership as a means of forced savings.

Revolving Credit. One of the newer forms of retail store credit is revolving credit. It was introduced in the early 1930s, but only became widely adopted after its successful promotion by Sears, beginning in the early 1950s. Under the more common types of revolving credit, the customer is allowed to purchase goods up to a predetermined amount and in return agrees to pay for the merchandise (or service) in 30 days without any carrying charge. To this point, the revolving credit plan is much like the charge account plan. However, if full payment is not made in 30 days, the customer must agree to pay a regular monthly payment, which includes a service charge (normally $1\frac{1}{2}$ per cent per month on the unpaid balance) for the privilege of using the credit extended. For example, if a credit limit of $300 is established, and $300 is purchased, then at the end of 30 days, the customer must either pay the entire $300 with no service charge, or make a payment, usually of at least 10 per cent of the outstanding balance, or $10, whichever is larger. The normal period for complete repayment is six months, but in some instances it is extended to twelve months. As long as the customer's unpaid balance is less than $300 (her maximum credit limit), she is open to buy up to this limit. Of all consumer credit plans used by retail stores, the revolving plan is growing fastest in importance.

Trends in Credit Offerings

Today the tendency in credit merchandising is to build as much flexibility into the credit plan as possible. To attain this end, many stores are offering what is called the option-terms plan. Such a plan is considered a flexible (all purpose) approach to retail credit service offerings. Under such an arrangement, all credit customers have the regular 30-day charge account privilege, but when the need arises in connection with large item purchases, the customer has the option of using an installment payment plan over a period of time and paying for this service through a service charge or interest charge each month on the unpaid balance.

Many retail stores and especially the smaller ones have avoided the necessity of offering any form of retail credit to their customers by encouraging them to use bank credit cards or the services of small loan finance companies. The bank credit card is considerably more fashionable than the latter. Prior to 1950, bank credit cards received very little mention, but during the 1960s they had a remarkable growth. Such plans enable the retailer to increase his sales, convert his charge accounts into cash, and to do these things without the cost and management responsibilities associated with operating a credit department. However, such a plan usually costs the individual retailer approximately 7 per cent of sales and some loss in store traffic.[27]

For the future, such farsighted ideas as a cashless-checkless society have been envisaged to facilitate shopping. Technically speaking, the checkless society is feasible now. All the computer hardware is available and readily capable to perform the task. The major obstacles now are in designing the system, coming up with the finances to implement it, and gaining the acceptance of the financial and merchandising community. Of course, as in most innovations, ultimate success rests with consumer acceptability. Such a plan would result in a nationwide integrated payment system that would embrace retailers and consumers and would facilitate the consumers' desire for the immediate and near effortless attainment of goods.

Credit Costs and Benefits

The benefits and advantages of using credit, from the point of view of both customers and retail stores, have been briefly mentioned before. Stores use credit because it is an effective means of increasing sales, expanding the scope of their market opportunities, evening out their sales performance curves, and generating customer mailing lists. Customers use credit because as an alternative medium of exchange it enables them to secure goods now and to pay for them later. Credit allows customers to shorten the period of postponement that usually develops between the time a merchandise item or service is wanted or needed and the time when the consumer would have the cash wherewithal in order to purchase the item. Credit tends to enable the consumer to expedite and accelerate his acquisition of goods.

Thus, consumer credit services extended by retail stores have mutual benefits for store and customer alike. But, what about the costs of credit? Credit, like other nonprice competitive or promotional activities, is not free. There are costs associated with both the extension of credit by retail stores and the use of credit by retail store customers.

Retail Store Management Costs. It costs the retail store considerable sums of money to extend credit. Additional personnel are usually required in order to manage and coordinate the credit activities with overall store merchandising strategies. Extending credit means using additional working capital. Funds which might otherwise exist either in the form of cash or

---

[27] Costs vary from store to store, depending on size and volume considerations. See Michael J. Etzel, "How Much Does Credit Cost the Small Merchant?" *Journal of Retailing*, Vol. 47, No. 2 (Summer 1971), pp. 52–60.

merchandise are tied up in another current asset, accounts receivable. The overall capital budgeting needs of the retail firm will therefore be affected by extending credit. Service charges in connection with credit extension will usually help to defray some or all of the added costs of extending credit. Nonetheless, credit extension is still not always a costless opportunity for the retail firm.

More progressive retail managers (including credit managers) are viewing the credit operations of the store as additional profit centers whose successful management implies the assumption of *reasonable amounts of risks and costs in order to build sales and profits.* The reigning philosophy of such operations is that when consumer credit is extended, the firm is committing some of its resources to support receivables. This amounts to an investment of firm funds to earn a profit, like the investment in inventory, buildings, or other equipment. Extending credit has its initial impact on company sales, but the ultimate goal is to increase profits. Thus, credit managers would continue to expand the investment in receivables to the point where the added demand for the firm's goods and services ceases to provide as much revenue as the costs incurred. Furthermore, an effort to increase net revenues by reducing costs through credit operations is emphasized. *Such an approach is literally labeled credit management.*

Customer Credit Costs. The use of credit is not free. In the case of short-term charge account credit where a service charge or interest cost is not added, the true net costs are reflected in the store's overall operating expense ratio and its gross margin. Whether the customer pays more for using such credit could only be answered within the same framework as was developed for handling the question of free services in the previous section.

There is no question that the consumer pays more for merchandise purchased on longer-run credit plans, such as revolving and installment credit services. The cash price and the credit price difference will vary considerably, depending principally upon the rate of interest or service charges added and the length of time for which credit is extended. The real question is, "Does the cash price and credit price difference represent a real value to the consumer?" All things considered, the answer is probably, Yes! If the consumer could afford to pay cash in all instances, she could conceivably reduce her economic costs of marketing. However, it has been well stated that "economy is a luxury of the rich." For too many of us, our consumption patterns and standards of living would suffer markedly if we were forced to forego purchasing for lack of sufficient credit. The consumer in his anxiety to acquire goods is often tempted to overlook the cost of credit. A charge of $1\frac{1}{2}$ per cent per month seems considerably less than 18 per cent per year. When purchased on a twelve-month contract, with a $50 down payment and a 10 per cent service charge, a major appliance with a cash price of $350 costs the consumer $380. Consumers often fail to consider that a contract to pay one twelfth of a given sum at the end of each month for 12 months is equivalent to a contract to pay the entire amount at the expiration of six and one half months. Thus, the nominal annual rate of 10 per cent in the earlier example becomes a true annual rate of 18.4 per cent.[28]

The costs of retail credit involving installment or revolving credit plans can be expressed in several ways: as a percentage carrying charge, as a dollar-and-cents carrying charge, or as the difference between credit and cash prices.[29] For some years, there has existed a considerable amount of agitation in Congress for a truth-in-lending bill, which would require that all credit charges be stated both in dollars and as an annual interest rate in percentage terms. Retail merchants generally have lobbied most forcibly against this bill. However, on July 1, 1969, a mild version of the truth-in-lending or Douglas bill was implemented. Its impact on retail credit services and merchandising is just now being assessed.[30]

The planning and organizing activities related to the whole spectrum of retail merchandising strategies involving location, product assortments, pricing, and promotion have now been discussed. In Part Eight, control activities and especially accounting control processes will be examined and their roles in the retail management system analyzed.

QUESTIONS FOR STUDY, REFLECTION, AND REVIEW

1. What are the two categories of personal selling, and how do they differ?
2. What has been the general change in the attitude and/or approach in retail salesmanship over the years?
3. Selling is a form of problem solving and focuses on the buyer, not on the seller. What is the basic proposition about man with which retail selling begins?
4. What are the broad dimensions of the selling situation, and what approach presently leads to the most successful retail selling program?
5. Discuss formula-selling and point out the basis for its approach, its limitations, and areas of benefit.

[28] This conversion is accomplished by the following formula developed by T. H. Beckman, op. cit., p. 138:

$$R = \frac{r(2n)}{(n+1)}$$

where: R = actual annual rate charged
r = nominal rate of charge per annum
n = number of installments required to pay the contract

Solving for R, we find

$$R = \frac{10\%(2 \times 12)}{(12 + 1)} = \frac{2.40}{13} = 18.4\%$$

[29] See Jan Robert Williams, "The Impact of Variable Billing Techniques on True Annual Finance Charge Rates on Revolving Credit," *Journal of Retailing*, Vol. 47, No. 3 (Fall 1971), pp. 3–15.

[30] See the following articles: Richard F. Sauter and Orville C. Walker, Jr., "Retailers' Reactions to Interest Limitation Laws—Additional Evidence," *Journal of Marketing*, Vol. 36, No. 2 (April 1972), pp. 58–61. Also, John J. Wheatley and Guy G. Gordon, "Regulating the Price of Consumer Credit," *Journal of Marketing*, Vol. 35, No. 4 (October 1971), pp. 21–28.

6. The retail firm attempts to generate a bundle of satisfactions or expectations in order to both attract and hold patronage. What is this bundle of satisfactions or expectations made up of, and how does it relate to market opportunity?
7. What are services?
8. Describe charge account credit.
9. Explain revolving credit.
10. Credit policies for retail stores are not only beneficial; they are also associated with costs. What are these cost drawbacks in extending retail credit plans?

EIGHT

RETAILING AND MANAGEMENT CONTROL PROCESSES

19

retailing management
and control procedures

Throughout most of this book, at least to this juncture, the emphasis has been placed upon analyzing and understanding the planning, organization, motivation, and, to some extent, the control of the retail management system or firm. This has been attempted by focusing upon the decision-making responsibilities of retail managers and by examining (1) the kinds of decisions demanded by the nature of the retailing firm—product, promotion, pricing, and place considerations; and (2) the approaches used by retail managers in handling the various kinds of decisions—problem solving, models, experience, and so on. Throughout, considerable attention has been directed to the critical need for *planning* in relation to decision making; that is, the need to anticipate and forecast probable conditions and to adjust the firm's behavior or response to the anticipated or forecasted conditions. The past several chapters have dealt with the retail decision maker's effort to anticipate his environment and then to devise a meaningful set of organizational inputs that would generate a set of desired results or outputs. *The objective of the retail management firm is to perform a desired, specified function.* Most of the activities discussed in the preceding chapters of this book have dealt with cost-generating activities. It costs money to create or establish retailing facilities. It costs money to aggregate balanced assortments of goods, to promote, display, and sell these goods. The point is, *the retail manager must control as well as plan these activities, and he must give careful and deliberate attention to controlling the costs associated with the performance of these tasks.*

Control is the necessary corollary to planning; without control, planning becomes meaningless and perfunctory. Control is also a vital part of decision making. Unless the effects of plans are known and attempts made to modify or control plans via feedback are implemented, planning performance will seldom improve. Quite literally, it is our mistakes that lead to further learning, and so it is with the firm. This chapter and Chapter 20 will place special emphasis on the role of control in managing retailing activities. The nature of control processes will be dealt with and the special role of accounting in *controlling* expenses associated with the operations of the retailing firm will be treated at length. In Chapter 20, some additional accounting techniques related to financial reporting will be presented, as well as some treatment of merchandise management accounting.

the general nature of control

Few, if any, merchandising institutions run well by themselves. They require constant attention, direction, and effort, and to control is to exercise directing, guidance, and restraining power over people, events, or systems. The objective of control is, of course, to improve performance. Thus, control is a means of instituting additional effort, constraints, or corrective action when sought after objectives or goals are missed by levels of performance that are deemed unsatisfactory by management. Kotler defines control as "the process of taking steps to bring actual results and desired results closer together."[1]

Newman and Summer apply the concept of control to the management of business firms such as retail management systems in the following manner:[2]

1. Standards that represent desired performance. These standards may be tangible or intangible, vague or specific, but until everyone concerned understands what results are desired, control will create confusion.
2. A comparison of actual results against the standard. This evaluation must be reported to the people who can do something about it.
3. Corrective action. Control measurements and reports serve little purpose unless corrective action is taken when it is discovered that current activities are not leading to desired results.

Control subsumes that conditions and operations can be changed and, when performance is unsatisfactory in terms of desired results, that efforts will be made to change (1) either the operation of the system, (2) the goals and standards upon which the system's operation have been evaluated, or (3) some condition in the external environment that has affected either goals or system operation.

The Elements of Control

Management authorities generally agree that in every control system essentially there exist four elements that occur in a constant or fixed sequence and have the same relationship to each other. These elements are

---

[1] Philip Kotler, *Marketing Management: Analysis, Planning and Control,* 2nd. ed., Prentice-Hall, Inc., Englewood Cliffs, N.J., 1972, pp. 751–752.
[2] William H. Newman and Charles E. Summer, Jr., *The Process of Management,* Prentice-Hall, Inc., Englewood Cliffs, N.J., 1961, pp. 561–562.

1. A controlled characteristic or condition.
2. A sensory device or method for measuring the characteristic or condition.
3. A control group, unit, or equipment which will compare measured data with planned performance and direct a correcting mechanism in response to need.
4. An activating group or mechanism which is capable of bringing about a change in the operating system.[3]

Figure 19-1 shows a schematic illustration of the control process. Observe that the four elements in the control process are shown in terms of the sequence of their behavior. The first element is the retailing management system and the management efforts which flow into this system. It is assumed that management efforts require control activities. The second

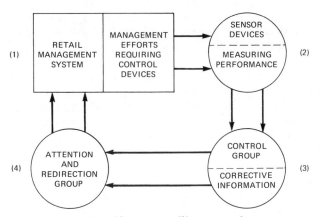

FIGURE 19-1 A retailing control system.

element is the sensor devices that are those aspects of the system that monitor and measure performance. For example, suppose operating expenses are being scrutinized. Management generates these expenses in an effort to activate the system. The sensory device (i.e., expense control procedures managed by the comptroller's office) monitors, and measures these expenses that are generated, in relation to predetermined expense budgets and schedules. The third element is the control group and it will react to the behavior of the sensory monitoring devices and report a stream of information. That is, the system's expense will be either in-budget or out-of-budget. If out-of-budget and beyond the acceptable limits set by standards, the fourth element (the attention and redirection group) will signal this behavior to management, who must then decide on the need for corrective action.

---

[3] See Fremont E. Kast and James E. Rosenzweig, *Organization and Management: A Systems Approach,* McGraw-Hill Book Company, New York, 1970, p. 70.

What Is Controlled?

The question arises, what is controlled, or needs to be controlled, in the retail firm's operations? The answer is rather simple. All effort put into the system needs to be controlled in order to assure that the effort is wisely and effectively utilized. However, in order to shape management's thinking about control activities and to direct control efforts to their most meaningful end, it might be wise to view the question of what to control from the standpoint of the major determinants of the firm's operation. Recall that this operation can be viewed as

$$\text{Sales} - \text{Cost of goods} = \text{Gross margin}$$
and
$$\text{Gross margin} - \text{Expenses} = \text{Profits}$$

Control efforts might therefore be most effectively directed at those activities or functions that bear heavily upon the residual effect of operations—profits. All activities that demand a manager's attention in terms of planning will require corresponding efforts directed toward controlling. As a matter of fact, our analysis thus far of such factors as sales planning and forecasting, merchandise assortment planning, pricing, advertising, personal selling, store design and layout, and location all emphasized the role of planning; but our consideration did not preclude the necessity of careful follow-up and control procedures relating to all these activities. Thus, the question of what needs to be controlled in a retailing operation is answered by the response—everything that requires or is subject to planning.

However, two important areas that greatly affect retail store operations and which are controlled in part as a result of sound accounting practices and techniques are (1) cost of goods and (2) operating expenses. Cost of goods is concerned in great measure with methods for evaluating retail inventories (the subject, in part, of Chapter 20), and operating expenses are controlled largely through techniques related to management accounting, expense center accounting, and production unit accounting, which are the central focus of the major portion of this chapter.

Several conditions are making retail managers increasingly conscious of the role that control can play in bringing about improved performance, especially profit performance. First of all is the realization that markets are not all infinitely expandable. The trading area network is becoming more and more complete. And as it is, the ability to reap increased profits through an enlarged and expanded volume of sales is diminished. More and more merchants are discovering that the costs involved in expanding sales are frequently such that the profits from those added sales are washed away. Furthermore, many retailing managers have come to realize that expense management and control is the last remaining—near virgin—territory subject to the extensive management processes that can lead to expense reduction and ultimately better profits. As buying economies for all retail stores become similar, and as operating procedures and policies all tend to converge toward some modal pattern of operation, the retail manager's last remaining hope for improving his profit showing often lies with tightening up his control efforts over operating expenses.

Other factors are forcing retail managers to give increased attention to control efforts also. The external environment within which the retail management system operates is becoming increasingly complex: the number and size of competitors is increasing, consumers are better informed, more alert, and more sensitive to changing conditions. These and other factors have led one authority to conjecture that in surroundings of increasing complexity and uncertainty, accurate planning becomes less easy, and thus forces management to shift much of its effort to control—an activity in which there is an increasing reliance on sensoring and monitoring mechanisms and more program flexibility.[4]

Finally, control is more important today in many retail firms because there is *more* to manage and control. Retail firms are larger and more complex. Many are multiunit operations encompassing a several state area. Even local or regional operations with branch units are faced with the necessity of integrating and controlling the *entire* system. There is an increasing need in complex multifaceted systems for more and better standards of performance, better and more rapid sensoring and monitoring devices, more rapid communication and feedback of results, and a shorter lead time for implementing corrective measures into the system.

information processing and control procedures

Control processes are closely related to the ways in which firms process and utilize information. Without information flows there can be no control. Norbert Weiner has stated, "Control . . . is nothing but the sending of messages which effectively change the behavior of the recipient. . . ."[5]

Control is concerned with improving performance. It is a process of recording variances between planned results and actual results. To be effectively utilized, all control procedures must be essentially systems for processing information.

An old military adage used to state that "an army moves on its stomach." The implication was that supply lines and logistic systems for moving supplies and food were necessary to keep men in the field and to win battles. However, any military man operating in a modern setting will tell you that military success today depends upon intelligence systems, i.e., information, and effective channels for receiving and transmitting information. Business firms are no exception. For both planning and control purposes they depend on information flows. The retailing executive largely fails or succeeds on the basis of his information. But there are many complaints voiced about the availability and the reliability of this information. It is criticized for at least the following reasons:

1. There is too much information of the wrong kind.
2. There is too little information of the right kind.

[4] Kotler, op. cit., p. 752.

[5] Norbert Weiner, *The Human Use of Human Beings,* Houghton Mifflin Company, Boston, 1950, p. 124.

3. Information is too decentralized.
4. Information is suppressed.
5. Information comes late.
6. Information is unverified.[6]

The nature of these complaints hardly warrants further elaboration. The usual problem is not lack of information per se but rather the lack of accurate, timely, meaningful information on which to base executive decisions relating to planning and control.

Several rapid generalizations need to be made at this point. Both the nature and size of the retail management system will affect the flow of information within the system and the control procedures necessary to maintain a satisfactory level of system performance. Highly bureaucratic but centralized management systems will likely call forth a different set of control responses than more decentralized and less autocratic systems. Paradoxically, the more decentralized and less autocratic system will more likely demand a more sophisticated information system and more elaborate control procedures. Small firms by virtue of their smallness and the nature of their operations are likely to have relatively unsophisticated information processing systems and much less elaborate control activities. Invariably it appears that increased size of firm, increased specialization, and complexity of operations call forth a necessary increase in the complexity of information or reporting systems and control procedures for monitoring and correcting the systems.

management accounting as
an information system

The retail firm's accounting system is an important part of its total information system. For many years, accounting information was generated within the firm primarily for the purpose of external reporting. Such reporting systems were referred to as financial accounting. However, in more recent years another kind of accounting practice and reporting system has evolved and is referred to as *management accounting*. It has been gaining increasing popularity in retail stores and other businesses. Management accounting is not designed to reduce or eliminate the need for financial accounting, i.e., the information required by stockholders, investors, government agencies, and others, but instead it is a means of bringing into closer balance the dual objectives that every accounting system should attempt to meet. Management accounting is responsible for the generation, processing, and flow of accounting information for internal decision making. Today's emphasis on management decision making and the need for relevant accurate information on which to base management decisions has tended to accelerate the necessity for sound management accounting systems that are the major information systems in almost every business organization. Concisely, therefore, management accounting is a kind of

[6] Kotler, op. cit., pp. 294–295.

internal accounting information reporting on which to base management and operating decisions. To be of maximum use to management, control considerations should be built into every phase of the design of the system. Accounting reports often furnish the very foundation upon which control procedures are established. Furthermore, the form and substance in which final information is desired will determine what data and how much data should be introduced into the system. For example, consider the matter of returns and allowances in the retail store. The total amount of returns and allowances at the end of any operating period offers some basis to management for exercising control efforts. An excessive amount is some indication of faulty merchandising practices and perhaps suggests unsatisfactory merchandise, overselling, failure to analyze carefully customer requirements, shipping department errors, or too liberal a returns and allowances policy. Because there is such a range of possible causes, effective control can be facilitated, if returns and allowances are broken down by causes and the causes analyzed for manageability. Such an analysis would then be followed by the establishment of better standards or revisions of operating practices based upon the preceding analysis.

Some Aspects of Management Accounting

Having thus described at some length the concept of management accounting, its role in information systems and something about its function as a control element in retailing management, suppose we look now at some of the more subtle and more important aspects of this concept.

Responsibility Reporting. Responsibility reporting (or responsibility accounting, as it is sometimes called) is a recognition on the part of managers and accountants that firms like retailing organizations are complex coalitions of subunits, each a viable and meaningful entity within itself. A retailing firm is a composite (aggregation) of subsystems, i.e., a goods and service mix or subsystem, a promotional mix, or a physical distribution mix, just to mention a few. The goal and logic of responsibility accounting is that management accounting systems should be adapted to report accurately the performance and needs of each of the responsible subsystems (entities) within the overall organizational structure and framework. The subsystems would be considered such entities as merchandising departments; workrooms such as receiving, marking, shipping, and alteration rooms; promotional departments such as advertising, store display, and public relations; personnel departments; and other operations such as credit, internal reporting agencies, such as electronic data processing, and others.

The most useful management accounting systems for purposes of both planning and control are those that attempt to ascertain what feedback or other information is desired by management. That is, only by meeting the retailing manager's needs can the accounting system be considered truly successful. For these reasons, information in operating reports prepared for management should be classified in two ways, by *responsibility* and by *object*. Because the control of business operations is accomplished through human effort, the results of operations are most usually reported in relation to those people who are *responsible* for the operations and whose behavior is related to the success or failure of the activity. Responsibility accounting is intended as a device whereby each person in the organization should be able to determine how successfully he has controlled the activities for which he is responsible. On the other hand, superiors should be able in turn to use this same responsibility reporting to judge the effectiveness of each person in carrying out the responsibilities delegated to him. Because reporting requirements dictate the details of the classification of budgeted account items, the company organization chart dictates the routes and the details of how and to whom information should be reported. At the lowest level of authority, operating results are usually reported in the fullest detail, and these details relating to each person's responsibilities are summarized in the report at the next higher level of authority.

If information ought to be reported in terms of responsibility, it needs also to be reported in terms of *object*. Information on expenditures is meaningful only in terms of what the money was spent for. Thus, the object of the expenditure must also be classified if meaningful control activities are to be undertaken. Every retailing transaction must be analyzed on an object basis, and conversely, object accounts must be further subclassified on the basis of responsibility, if effective control is to be exercised over the expenditures. For example, long distance telephone calls are a classic case that illustrates the point. Basically, such expenses are classified by object as telephone and telegraph expense. But to effectively control such costs, they must be further classified in terms of responsibility, at least by department, and preferably by individuals. If the cost of such calls is reported as part of the operating results for which the person is responsible, then each call will be weighed against the likely benefits and the cost of alternatives such as a letter or telegram.

Where responsibility accounting has been implemented, responsible members of the organization, e.g., decision makers and those who spend money or expend other resources, are provided with (1) a level of work performance or output for which they are instructed to perform and (2) a monetary budget that specifies the activity limits within which their performance range is expected to fall; (3) they are charged with the responsibility for reporting their performance as stipulated by the dictates of (1) and (2). Responsibility accounting when combined with expense center accounting (soon to be discussed) offers several possibilities for improved retail management decision making and control, at least in these respects:

1. It improves the availability of information for decision units.
2. It assures each decision unit that they will be evaluated and judged on the basis of relevant information in relation to control decisions.
3. It improves the accuracy and speed of reports to decision makers.
4. Because of the increased significance of management accounting reports, executives are more readily motivated to read these reports.

Organizational Needs and Management Accounting. Management accounting ought to provide the kind of information needed to handle operating problems posed by the nature of the organization, its size, and its characteristics. Furthermore, the management accounting system ought to provide the information needed throughout the various levels of the organization that harbor decision making and control processes of varying complexity. There are two basic needs in every control process and these are (1) information for measuring performance and (2) information that signals when the system is out of control or deviates from the standard.

In the case of the retail firm, such research would focus upon the store manager, the general merchandise managers, the division merchandise managers, the department heads and buyers, and others with authority and decision making responsibility. In the case of one study, the research team found that there were three types of information (each serving a different purpose, often at various management levels) that raise and help answer three different basic questions:[7]

1. Score-card questions. "Am I doing well or badly?"
2. Attention-directing questions. "What problems should I look into?"
3. Problem-solving questions. "Of the several ways of doing the job, which is the best?"

Score Card and Attention-Directing Questions. Questions in these two categories are quite closely related and the same management accounting data might very well be used for both. The same data might serve as a score card function for a retail buyer and an attention-directing function for the divisional merchandise manager. The nature of management accounting is such that these systems often provide performance reports with which actual results are compared to predetermined budgets or standards, for example, the general merchandise budget or the sales expense budget. In these cases, such performance reports often help to answer score card questions and attention-directing questions concomitantly.

Problem-Solving Questions. Problem-solving questions demand the kinds of management accounting data needed to handle nonprogrammed or special nonrecurring decisions and problems related to long-range planning. Examples of such situations would include problems related to the retail firm's market opportunity, the changing nature of the consumer, shifting trading areas, store design and new layout, and such major contemplated changes in merchandising strategies as new product lines or the opening of branch stores. Decisions such as these and others usually require expert advice from specialists such as economic forecasters and business analysts, layout and design engineers, budgetary accountants, and statisticians. The management accounting system must weigh and evaluate all proposed actions in terms of their potential impact on the store's profitability.

Relation Between Management Accounting Controls and Store System Planning. To conclude this section, one further important idea needs to be projected. The usual treatment of planning and control generally sug-

[7] Reported in H. A. Simon, *Administrative Behavior*, 2nd ed., Macmillan Publishing Co., Inc., New York, 1957, p. 20. The complete study is found in H. A. Simon, H Guetzkov, G. Kozmetsky, and G. Tyndall, *Centralization Vs. Decentralization in Organizing the Controller's Department*, Controllership Foundation, New York, 1954.

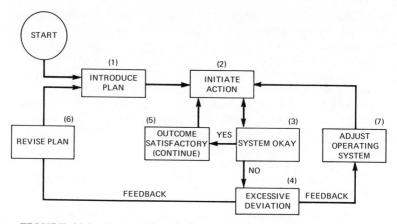

FIGURE 19-2 Control data feedback as planning inputs.

SOURCE: *Marcus Alexis and Charles Z. Wilson,* Organizational Decision Making *(Englewood Cliffs, N.J.: Prentice-Hall, Inc., 1967), p. 324.*

gests that control is a kind of follow-up activity in relation to planning. And this is largely correct, though it is certainly not the only permissible sequence. Because planning decisions are the basis primarily for controlling, why not learn how to plan more effectively from the results of control systems? This proposition considers using feedback from the control system as information for planning decisions. Thus the sequence between planning and control is no longer as one-sided as it is interdependent.

What this suggests is that the actual results collected can help fulfill not only control purposes but also the traditional needs for planning inputs. The answering of score card questions that mainly involves collection, classification, and reporting is an important aspect of management accounting for control purposes, but it also becomes the basis for sound organizational planning. An example of a *feedback* basis for planning activity is shown in Figure 19-2. Such a schematic model shows that the basis of control is the initiation of some *plan of action.* However, it also shows that, for continuing planning purposes the performance of the system depends upon the information provided by the budget and accounting data generated in the score card and attention-directing questions relating to items (3), (4), and (5). However, two further implications need to be pointed out. First, by sensoring and auditing the control system, useful feedback (score card and attention-directing questions) is obtained, and this feedback is used as the basis for correcting and reorienting future organization plans. Second, the information that flows out of such a feedback model is at least in part the data generated by management accounting systems.

controlling retailing expenses

One of the principal features of management accounting is its emphasis on *controlling* retailing expenses. Much has been written on the shrinking profit margins of retailing institutions. In order to stem this tide, many retailing managers have turned increasingly to improved efforts of expense management. The operating expenses associated with retailing firms in no way ought to be considered as given, or fixed, especially in the sense that they are not subject to manipulation or management. Quite the contrary, the retail store as an operating system suggests that expenses as inputs or fuel are necessary to provide the motive power to the system, but it also implies that these inputs must be managed and balanced in relation to the outputs generated. In the usual case, if the level of expense inputs can be lessened through better management controls, the result is higher profits, assuming that the efforts to lessen expenses did not dampen the system's ability to generate the same level of sales or gross margin.

Management accounting is a part of the internal information system of the firm and is responsible for generating meaningful approaches to better decision making through sound accounting practices. A major part of this effort is directed toward controlling retail operating expenses. One important point needs very special emphasis, however. Expense control is subject to several countervailing philosophies. One is conservative, niggardly, narrowminded, and—it should probably be added—considerably outmoded. Such a viewpoint emphasizes the reduction or elimination aspects of expenses. Expenses are considered as outlays to be eliminated or reduced. Each suggestion from responsibility centers to increase expenditures for promotion or wages for increased personnel and to broaden merchandise lines or other outlays is zealously challenged by the financial officer. The usual effect of this type of philosophy is that the growth and profitable operation of the firm are seriously constricted. Such an attitude is myopic—shortsighted, because it views expenses in the wrong light. The more modern viewpoint regarding expense control in retailing systems is that expenses are not necessary evils, but that expenses are willingly and enthusiastically incurred in order to generate sales, satisfied customers, large amounts of store traffic, and a favorable store image on the part of customers and potential customers. In an enlightened economic sense, such a set of attitudes suggests that the firm is willing and anxious to expend additional dollars for expense-incurring behavior, as long as the last dollar spent returns a dollar of sales revenue. Therefore, instead of eliminating expenses, the prudent manager may realize that it is necessary to increase expenditures and that effective expense control is concerned primarily with paring down or eliminating those expenses that (after careful deliberation and analysis) are shown to be unproductive in terms of the store's ability to maintain its desired level of sales and service objectives.

Expense control is therefore a means for reducing expenses or managing expenses that are unproductive; that is, expenses for which the firm gets no meaningful measure of needed response. Such a measure is usually evaluated within the framework of the following decision rule: "If an incurred expense adds as much or more to total revenue in dollars as it does to total cost, it is justified." Admittedly, such a decision rule is not always easy to apply in regard to expense control decisions. However, to be successful and to add to the profitability of the retail system, expense control must embrace at least these major aspects:

1. *Expense classification.* Only with the careful analysis of expenses by properly drawn classifications can meaningful expense management begin.
2. *Expense distribution.* After expenses have been broken down and analyzed by classification, they must then be allocated to those units responsible for their occurrence. This is related to the concept of responsibility reporting discussed earlier.
3. *Expense budgeting.* Steps (1) and (2) lead to and form the basis for effective expense planning, namely, the expense budget—a forecast of reasonable expense disbursements needed to support given levels of merchandising and total store activities.

The remaining sections of this chapter will treat these three aspects of expense management and control in considerable detail.

Classifying Retailing Expenses

Almost all retail stores of any consequence make some effort to classify their operating expenses. Expense classification is concerned simply with the grouping of all expenses into standardized classes according to some definite prearranged plan. This classification really is nothing more than partitioning a set, when the set is operating expenses and the partitioning shows the various standardized groups or classes of expenses. The value of expense classification is that it permits the continuing observation and analysis of expenses within a standardized framework. Such a framework in turn permits the analysis and comparison of a particular store's expenses on a time series basis; thus trends and changes in the various categories of expense can be more accurately observed, and better procedures for monitoring and managing these expenses can be implemented. Furthermore, these efforts make possible the comparison of expense classifications (centers) on both an inter-store and an intra-store basis. Of course, this has several obvious advantages. On an intra-store basis, it presents the opportunity to compare operations in one department with those of other departments. Thus, managers can be appraised and evaluated in terms of the assets at their disposal, the level of expenses incurred, and the resulting profits (contribution margin) that they have been able to generate. However, it should be pointed out that not all departments or expense centers in a store directly generate revenues, and when this is the case, the departments cannot be viewed as profit centers.

Expense classification also makes possible inter-store comparisons. It is often deemed advisable to compare a given store's operation with an average or median store reporting to a trade association group. In such a case the median figures of the reporting store become the benchmark (standard) to which other stores compare their operations. Such practices are encouraged in a number of retail trade groups, for example, the National Retail Furniture Association, the National Retail Hardware Association, and, of course, the National Retail Merchants Association. The following discussion will be patterned closely along lines suggested by the latter association.[8]

There are essentially two major types of expense classifications in retail stores. To put it another way, expenses are generally mapped or partitioned in two ways: First, there are what are called "natural expense classifications," and second is a classification referred to as "functional expense classifications." Each will be discussed in turn.

Natural Expenses. Natural expenses, as the name suggests, refer to a *natural* classification based upon the nature or kind of expense, regardless of its function. Such expenses as rent, supplies, payroll, and taxes are examples of natural expense classifications. The number and exact designation of such natural expense classifications will vary with the size and complexity of the retail store. Given that a natural expense is one "based upon the nature of the service realized from the outlay rather than upon the function of the business for which the outlay is made,"[9] the seventeen natural divisions of expenses historically used by business firms are as follows:

1. Payroll.
2. Property rentals and other real estate costs.
3. Advertising media costs.
4. Taxes.
5. Imputed interest.
6. Supplies.
7. Services purchased.
8. Unclassified.
9. Traveling.
10. Communication.
11. Pensions.
12. Insurance.
13. Depreciation.
14. Professional services.
15. Donations.
16. Losses from bad debt.
17. Equipment rentals.

Effective expense management and control, however, demands more than a simple classification of expenses into natural accounts. These expenses also need to be cross classified into functional groupings.

Functional Expenses. Expenses can also be classified in terms of the function for which they were incurred. Such classification means that the primary criterion for classification is related to the basic *activity* for which

[8] The reader is urged to examine and study carefully the *Retail Accounting Manual*, Controllers Congress, Sam Flanel (ed.), National Retail Merchants Association, New York, 1962.

[9] John W. Wingate, Elmer O. Schaller, and Irving Goldenthal, *Problems in Retail Merchandising*, Prentice-Hall, Inc., Englewood Cliffs, N.J., 1961, p. 260.

the expenditure is laid out, rather than the nature of the expenditure itself. Characteristically, retail stores have been concerned with five basic functional expense classifications:

1. *Administrative.* The general administrative expenses of the store as a whole that are not chargeable directly to any one division of the store.
2. *Occupancy.* All expenses arising from the use and upkeep of store buildings, fixtures, and equipment.
3. *Buying.* All the expenses incurred in the acquisition of goods for the store's assortment mix.
4. *Publicity.* Promotion expenses relating to advertising and window display.
5. *Selling.* Includes these general categories: compensation of sales-people, general selling expenses, and delivery expenses.

Sound expense management and control are therefore concerned with the classification, control, and budgeting of store expenses on both the basis of functional and natural expense categories. Table 19-1 shows how expenses would likely be mapped or partitioned on the basis of these classifications.

With such a procedure for cross classification, each of the functional expense classifications in turn is made up of as many of the 17 natural expenses as are pertinent to each functional or subfunctional group.

To further illustrate, look at the first natural expense item, payroll. It can now be seen that expenses for payroll can be allocated to any of the five major functional activities undertaken in the store. That is, payroll or salaries can be dispersed to general administrative officers, to a real estate manager, to buyers, to those engaged in advertising and other forms of promotion, and to those responsible directly for selling activities. Similarly, the natural expense item, supplies, can also be broken down by functional uses. Such a breakdown is a primary prerequisite to expense management

TABLE 19-1   A Natural and Functional Classification of Retail Expenses

FUNCTIONAL / NATURAL	ADMINISTRATIVE	OCCUPANCY	BUYING	PUBLICITY	SELLING
Payroll					
Property rental					
Advertising media costs					
Taxes					
Supplies					
Et cetera					

and control. The method or technique is infinitely flexible, inasmuch as it can be used in its most rudimentary form for smaller stores and can be fanned out to extremely complex dimensions for larger, more sophisticated stores, or multiunit systems.

Expense Center Accounting. The Controllers Congress of the National Retail Merchants Association has long been concerned with a system of expense classification and control that they called *expense center accounting*. Their system is based on the fundamental premise that expenditures should be assigned to the specific job of work that incurs the expense. To facilitate expense control and efficient administration, the accounts selected are those that represent the minimum number of major areas of responsibility that should be reflected and identified in accounting information. Such accounts are called *expense centers.*

The expense center accounting system advocated by the NRMA utilizes 20 expense accounts, each of which is descriptive of a major item of expense. These 20 centers closely parallel the 17 natural expense classifications shown earlier, with the major exception that imputed interest has been dropped as an expense category.

All expense centers under this new system are aggregates of controllable costs that are related to a particular job of work or store service. In other words, the functional expense categories have been replaced by a more meaningful and less abstract classification of work units or expense centers.

You will observe that the expense centers are listed across the top of Table 19-2 and that some centers involve a special or particular kind of work performed by specialized personnel in particular offices or locations. Others are concerned with particular kinds of work done in many different places throughout the system, whether it be a single or multiunit firm. Finally, some centers involve only a general type of service necessary to assist the operation of the business as a whole.

Expense Center Accounting and Responsibility Reporting. It is important to point out that expense center accounting is more concerned with controllable cost reporting, rather than the determination of the complete cost of the work or activity represented by each expense center. Only the costs controllable by the person responsible for the function are reported. This would square well with the logic and philosophy of responsibility reporting as a part of management accounting efforts to provide data for managerial decisions. As a matter of fact, expense center accounting becomes most useful to top management when applied and implemented within the following guidelines:

1. Top management should only see key elements of information that point out problem areas. The details concerning the problem area should be presented to the subordinates responsible for correcting the problem.
2. In reporting any information, the organization structure must be considered, so that top management knows who is responsible for the results shown on the report and so that subordinates receive only information pertaining to their particular area of responsibility.

TABLE 19-2 The NRMA Chart of Expense Accounts

	PAYROLL	FRINGE BENEFITS	ADVERTISING	TAXES	SUPPLIES	SERVICES PURCHASED	UNCLASSIFIED	TRAVELING	COMMUNICATIONS	PENSIONS	INSURANCE	DEPRECIATION	PROFESSIONAL SERVICES	DONATIONS	BAD DEBTS	EQUIPMENT COSTS	REAL PROPERTY RENTALS	EXPENSE TRANSFERS	OUTSIDE REVENUE & OTHER CREDITS	MULTISTORE DISTRIBUTION
110—Management	01	S		04	06	07	08	09			12		14	15						99
120—Property and Equipment		E E		04							12	13				17	20	91	92	99
210—Accounting and Data Processing	01				06	07	08	09	10				14			17		91	92	99
310—Accounts Receivable	01	S P			06	07	08		10							17		91		99
320—Credit and Collections	01	E C			06	07	08	09							16	17		91	92	99
410—Sales Promotion	01	I	03	04	06	07	08	09	10				14					91	92	99
510—Service and Operations	01	A L			06	07	08	09					14							99
550—Telephone and Other Utilities	01				06		08		10									91		99

Account	01	EXPLANATION	06	07	08	09	10	11	12	13	14	17	91	92	99
570—Cleaning	01		06	07	08							17		92	99
580—Maintenance and Repairs	01		06	07	08								91	92	99
610—Personnel	01		06	07	08	09					14				99
630—Supplementary Benefits	01	04	06	07	08			11	12		14		91	92	99
720—Maintenance of Reserve Stock	01		06		08							17			99
740—Receiving and Marketing	01		06	07	08							17	91		99
750—Shuttle Service	01		06	07	08							17			99
810—Selling Supervision	01	48	06		08										
820—Direct Selling	01		06		08	09							91	92	
830—Customer Services	01		06	07	08	09	10					17	91	92	99
860—Wrapping and Packing	01		06		08	09								92	99
880—Delivery	01	04	06	07	08	09			12	13		17	91	92	99
910—Merchandising	01		06	07	08	09					14				99
920—Buying	01		06		08	09									99
930—Merchandise Control	01		06		08								91		99

SOURCE: *Retail Accounting Manual*, Controllers Congress, NRMA, Sam Flanel (ed.), The National Retail Merchants Association, New York, 1962, p. iv–1.

3. Wherever possible, the reports should show amounts rounded to the nearest significant digit. For example, amounts can often be rounded to the nearest thousand without impairing the usefulness of the information.

4. Wherever possible, results should be presented in trend form as opposed, for example, to showing only the results for the current period.[10]

The expense center management approach to expense control advocated by the NRMA represents a sound and effective step toward meaningful expense management. As more and more stores tend to adopt this system, it seems likely that retail store expense classification will become considerably more standardized. Furthermore, the experience gained from such standardized expense classification and control procedures will lead to even more scientific approaches to expense management and greater retail store profitability.

Management Accounting and Expense Allocation

Another important function of management accounting in the retailing firm is that it aids in the important task of *expense allocation*. Given the complexity and multidepartment nature of most stores, it is usually necessary for management to analyze the operations of each of these departments in terms of their gross margin contribution. Furthermore, management often feels compelled to also evaluate each department's efforts in terms of other performance measures such as contribution margin and net profit. In the usual case, gross margin for a particular department is not too difficult to determine. However, several problems usually arise, when an attempt is made to allocate the operating costs that should be assigned to each department for the purpose of determining either (1) the department's contribution margin or (2) its net profit. To understand the nature of these problems it is necessary once again to review briefly some considerations relating to costs. Recall the abbreviated operating statement of a retail store, where

> Sales − Cost of goods = *Gross margin*
> Gross margin − Direct expenses = *Contribution margin*
> Contribution margin − Indirect allocated expenses = *Net Profit*

Such a set of statements shows the three measures of store or departmental performance: (1) gross margin, (2) contribution margin, and (3) net profit. Each has some merit in judging the departmental performance. Gross margin is the difference between sales revenue and cost of goods and is an important indicator of high-profit potential merchandise lines. Gross margin can be used meaningfully as an index of what products to select and promote, and for rapidly estimating the likely effects of changes in the assortment mix. Contribution margin is an even more meaningful

[10] Quoted from the *Retail Accounting Manual*, op. cit., pp. vii–1.

index, however, because it considers the direct costs that must be incurred in selling the particular lines which constitute the operating department. Net profit is a most useful concept from the standpoint of the entire retailing management system but is fraught with many ambiguities and difficulties when an attempt is made to apply it to the operations of an individual department. The impracticality of allocating the entire system's *indirect costs* to the individual departments makes it considerably less than an optimum measure of a department's worth or management's effectiveness.

Expense Allocation and Costs. The nature of the various costs or expenses incurred in a retail store was discussed at some length in Chapter 4. Some brief review of these concepts would appear in order, especially as they relate to the task of expense allocation, expense control, and budgeting.

In terms of expense management, there are several relevant expense concepts (different kinds of costs). One of the more frequent and easily dealt with cost concepts is that of *direct costs,* or those costs that are linked directly to a given department's operation. For example, the direct costs in a men's wear department are the department manager's salary and the salaries of the sales personnel within that department, as well as the other costs of directly operating the men's wear department. Such costs are also referred to as *escapable* costs, because if that particular department were eliminated then the direct expenses that it generates would be eliminated also, and they are therefore escapable. Expenses incurred as a result of operating the entire system are *indirect costs.* Indirect expenses are therefore incurred by several departments jointly, or by the store as a whole. For example, the salaries of top management, the salaries and expenses of the accounting office, or the electronic data processing department all must be prorated among the various departments on some equitable basis. Indirect expenses are viewed as *inescapable,* because unless the function or activity is completely eliminated from the entire operating system the expense cannot be eliminated.

Another interesting method has considerable relevance to the problem of cost allocation, namely, to divide costs into *controllable,* as opposed to *noncontrollable,* categories. Controllable costs are subject to the authority and management of the decision maker at a given operating level. For example, department managers are usually responsible for payroll costs for their departments. Such costs are therefore direct and controllable. On the other hand, those costs which are related (or allocated) to an operating unit but over which the manager of that unit can exercise little or no authority are noncontrollable costs.

Allocating Expenses. In most retail stores, in order to evaluate department operations, develop priorities, and assess management effectiveness, it becomes necessary to decide upon what criteria will be used for such assessment; i.e., gross margin, contribution, or net profit, and to wrestle with the problem of equitable expense allocation. Two commonly used criteria are (1) the contribution plan and (2) the net profit plan.

Contribution Plan. The contribution plan evaluates a department's operation and its management in terms of its contribution margin or the *difference* between gross margin and direct expenses. Such a plan[11] has much to recommend it. In the first place, only *direct* and *controllable* expenses are considered in the evaluation. This is in keeping with the basic tenets of management accounting and responsibility reporting, which hold that the only costs relevant for decision making are those affected by the decision. Such is the case in the contribution plan of expense control.

Net Profit Plan. The net profit plan holds that all store expenses must eventually be borne by some part of the operation; therefore, each department is given a prorated share of all indirect store expenses, and the final measure of its effort is judged in terms of its net profit before taxes. Many problems arise in relation to questions of the equitableness of the prorating method. Quite often department managers resent the net profit plan, arguing that it makes them responsible for costs over which they have no effective means of control.

Another frequently voiced complaint regarding this plan is the basis on which indirect costs are allocated. Volume of sales of the various departments often becomes the basis of allocation; however, in the case of many expenses, a better basis can be found. Rental expenses are often prorated over the amount of space used and the location of that space, that is, the floor on which the department is located or the relationship of the department to main traffic aisles, escalators, elevators, or other high traffic drawing departments. Table 19-3 illustrates the proration basis suggested by one large retailers' association.

Table 19-4 contrasts a merchandising department's operation in terms of the net profit plan and the contribution plan.

As can be seen in Table 19-4, the contribution plan reports the department's operation and its merit in terms of the total store's operation in a much more favorable light than does the net profit plan. Sound economic store practice often dictates that departments be continued even though on the basis of the net profit plan they are not actually showing any real profit. The general decision rule is that a department would be continued (provided no more favorable alternative presented itself) as long as the gross margin generated by the department at least covered its direct (escapable) expenses.

The usual practice in many stores today is that both the net profit plan and the contribution plan are employed as evaluative and control techniques. Because all the expenses of a retailing management system must eventually be covered and allocated to some operating department, the net profit plan is used for preparing operating statements and for budgeting purposes relating to the entire systems operation. For the purpose of evaluating the merchandising effectiveness of the individual departments and department managers, the contribution plan is preferred and more

[11] The contribution (reservoir) plan was originated by C. B. Clark and first presented in a speech at the National Retail Dry Goods Association convention in January 1934.

TABLE 19-3   Bases for Expense Distribution

EXPENSE CENTERS	BASIS OF PRORATION
General Management.....................	Net sales
Real Estate Costs........................	Weighted floor space
Furniture, Fixture, and Equipment Costs......	Weighted floor space
Other Fixed and Policy Expenses...........	Net sales
Control and Office Management...........	Net sales
Accounting and Payroll...................	Net sales
Accounts Payable.......................	Number of invoices
Cash Office............................	Net sales
Sales Audit............................	Gross sales transactions
Credit.................................	Gross credit sales transactions
Accounts Receivable......................	Gross credit sales transactions
Publicity and Display Management.........	Column Inches of advertising
Advertising.............................	Direct
Shows and Exhibits......................	Direct
Display................................	Direct
Service and Operations Management.......	Net sales
General Telephone Service................	Net sales
Protection..............................	Weighted floor space
Miscellaneous Customer Services...........	Net sales
Escalators and Elevators..................	Net sales
Cleaning...............................	Weighted floor space
Maintenance of Properties and Utilities......	Weighted floor space
Personnel..............................	Number of employees (full-time equivalent)
Employee Welfare......................	Number of employees (full-time equivalent)
Supplementary Benefits...................	Payroll dollars
Receiving and Returns to Vendors...........	Dollars of merchandise received
Checking and Marking...................	Number of pieces marked
Transfer Hauling........................	Net sales
Delivery...............................	Pieces delivered
Direct Selling—Owned Departments........	Direct
Other Direct and General Selling...........	Net sales
Maintenance of Stock....................	Direct
Selling Supervision.......................	Direct
Selling Service..........................	Net sales
Merchandise Management................	Direct
Buying.................................	Direct
Domestic and Foreign Buying Offices........	Net sales

SOURCE: *Standard Expense Center Accounting Manual,* Controllers Congress, The National Retail Merchants Association, New York, 1957, pp. 8–9 and 150–151.

frequently used. There is nothing which should preclude the use of both methods as far as sound management and control are concerned.

Allocating Expenses in the Multistore System. The problem of allocating expenses is not limited to single store operations. In the case of multiunit stores, the problem becomes even more paramount. There exist

TABLE 19-4   Operating Statement of a Merchandising Department Contrasting the Results of Evaluation on the Basis of Net Profit Plan and the Contribution Plan

NET PROFIT PLAN		CONTRIBUTION PLAN	
Net sales	$348,773 (100.0%)	Net sales	$348,773 (100.0%)
Cost of sales	207,458 (59.5%)	Cost of sales	207,458 (59.5%)
Gross margin	$141,315 (40.5%)	Gross margin	$141,315 (40.5%)
Less prorated expense:		Less direct expense:	
Administration $17,183		Administration $ 4,080	
Occupancy 61,358		Occupancy 855	
Publicity 23,130		Publicity 20,790	
Buying 13,313		Buying 5,978	
Selling 49,080		Selling 43,155	
Total charged expense:	$164,064 (47.0%)	Total direct expense:	$ 74,858 (21.5%)
		Department's	
Net loss	$ 22,749 (6.5%)	contribution	$ 66,457 (19.0%)

five commonly used methods for handling the expense distribution problem in the multistore operation:

1. Branch stores charged with direct operating expenses only.
2. Branch stores charged with direct operating expenses plus incremental expenses.
3. Branch stores charged with direct operating expenses plus overhead computed as a percentage of sales.
4. Branch stores charged with direct operating expenses plus overhead based upon work load.
5. The multistore approach to expense distribution.

You will observe that methods (1) and (2) closely resemble the contribution plan discussed earlier, and that methods (3) and (4) parallel the net profit plan. In the first four methods, the prevailing philosophy is that branch stores are appendages serviced by personnel and facilities whose fundamental tasks are those of operating the main store. Using method (5) each store unit (including the downtown store) is treated as a subsystem within the total system operation, and as such is charged with its own operating expenses. The remaining expenses (i.e., the central organization expenses) are accumulated in appropriate expense centers and later allocated throughout the various units of the system. Such an approach recognizes that for the individual unit, the contribution figure is the most meaningful single control figure, and such figures are derived most realistically under method (5). Furthermore, the multistore approach clearly isolates the true operating figures for the main store and therefore facilitates management's desire to better evaluate the profitability of the various aspects of the total operation, namely, the downtown or central headquarters store and the satellite stores which surround it. Such a procedure also assures the fulfillment of another management need, which is the desire for accurate, relevant, and meaningful accounting information based upon industrywide figures for exchange purposes.

expense budgeting

An expense budget is a formal and systematic means of expressing the operating objectives of management in quantitative terms. The nature and role of budgets were described much earlier, in relation to the merchandise budget: A budget relates to plans and expectations and it is specifically designed to aid in the control processes as they relate to plans, goals, objectives, and organizational expectations. The value of budgets is that they help to identify the consequences of alternative contemplated actions. Budgets most often become the basis for control procedures, inasmuch as they relate standards or norms against which actual results are compared.

Most retail stores today usually consider it necessary to prepare expense budgets for six-month operating periods. Such budgets are most effectively used in direct conjunction with the merchandise budget. It would go without saying that the value of the budget is directly related to the efficacy of the store's accounting system. Budgets based upon crude inaccurate figures and sloppy accounting techniques cannot be anything but crude, inaccurate, and sloppy.

Most budgets are based upon historical operating figures, and to the degree that future conditions will be similar to past operating conditions, such an approach has merit. However, past figures and past conditions must always be tempered with the decision maker's expectations regarding the future. Only then will budgets reflect the necessary reality for effective, sound decision making. Budgets, then, are the basis for generating sound data for purposes of intra-industry reporting.

Expense budgets have several important features that facilitate retail management decision making. First, the expense budget requires the planning and control of expenses before they occur, which permits management action rather than simply reaction. The expense budget plans the expenses necessary to generate desired levels of behavior and is an effective record with which to compare actual expenses. Second, budgeting expenses is a means of coordinating and integrating the activities and behavior of the many diverse divisions of the store. Third, and finally, the expense budget is a means of assigning definite responsibility for the various expenses incurred.

Expense budgets are usually determined both on the basis of percentage of sales and also as fixed dollar amounts. In order to provide meaningful standards for expenses, it is necessary to construct flexible budgets which relate the level of expenses to various levels of activities. The basis for flexible expense budgeting involves at least the following considerations:

1. *A measurable unit of activity.* Such a unit effectively indicates the work load of the area being budgeted.

CENTRAL ORG.	X	SUPERVISOR		EXPENSE CENTER		ACTIVITY UNIT		
STORE		H. JONES		225 – PAYROLL		PAYMENTS MADE		
(CHECK ONE)								

NATURAL EXPENSE DIVISION	800	900	1,000	1,100	1,200	1,300	1,400	1,500
					LEVEL OF ACTIVITY			
			EXPENSE BUDGET FOR PERIOD					
01 PAYROLL	2,100	2,100	2,350	2,350	2,900	2,900	3,150	3,150
02 FRINGE BENEFITS	210	210	235	235	290	290	315	315
03 ADVERTISING								
04 TAXES								
06 SUPPLIES	80	90	100	110	120	130	140	150
07 SERVICES PURCHASED	120	135	150	165	180	195	210	225
08 UNCLASSIFIED	40	45	50	55	60	65	70	75
09 TRAVEL								
10 COMMUNICATIONS								
11 PENSIONS								
12 INSURANCE								
13 DEPRECIATION								
14 PROFESSIONAL SERVICES								
15 DONATIONS								
16 BAD DEBTS								
17 OUTSIDE EQUIPMENT COSTS								
20 PROPERTY RENTALS								
91 EXPENSE TRANSFERS								
92 OUTSIDE REVENUE AND OTHER CREDITS								
TOTALS	2,550	2,580	2,885	2,915	3,550	3,580	3,885	3,915

PAYROLL DETAIL

JOB FUNCTION	SALARY FOR PERIOD	NO.	AMOUNT	NO.	AMOUNT	NO.	AMOUNT	NO.	AMOUNT	NO.	AMOUNT	NO.	AMOUNT	NO.	AMOUNT	NO.	AMOUNT
SUPERVISOR	$500	1	500	1	500	1	500	1	500	1	500	1	500	1	500	1	500
MCH. OPERATOR	300	2	600	2	600	2	600	2	600	3	900	3	900	3	900	3	900
GEN'L. CLERK	250	4	1,000	4	1,000	5	1,250	5	1,250	6	1,500	6	1,500	7	1,750	7	1,750
TOTALS			2,100		2,100		2,350		2,350		2,900		2,900		3,150		3,150

SUMMARY

BUDGETED VARIABLE EXPENSE RATE	$2.33	PER ACTIVITY UNIT	Howard N. Jones	5-17-77
			SUPERVISOR'S SIGNATURE	DATE

FIGURE 19-3   A flexible budget.

SOURCE: Sam Flanel (ed.), Retail Accounting Manual, Controllers Congress, National Retail Merchants Association (1962), pp. viii-17.

2. *A sound analysis of expense behavior.* Such an analysis determines the way in which each element of expense being budgeted should vary with activity. It is the usual case that some expenses have both a fixed and a variable element.

3. *Agreement with the budget.* Such a condition stipulates that the individuals responsible for the expenses budgeted be in sympathy and accord with the budget to which they must conform.

Figure 19-3 provides a suggested form for preparing a flexible budget for an expense center. The natural expense divisions are listed vertically on the left-hand side of the form while space is provided across the top for indicating various levels of activities. The preparation of a flexible expense budget requires that the activity unit used to measure the level of activity must be one that reflects the work load of the expense center and that can be measured without undue difficulty.

The budgeted variable expense rate should be indicated at the bottom of the form. At the end of the operating period, this rate will be applied against the activity units created by each store or each selling unit, in order to determine the amount of indirect variable expense to be charged to them.

The total of all flexible expense budgets for all expense centers constitutes the expense budget for the entire retailing management system for a given operating period. The final total expense budget is also used as a basis for planning future expenses and merchandising operations, and for the formal profit-planning program. It has even been suggested that budgets can play an important motivational role in the organization and that the desired performance level of budgets can be differentiated to reflect the aspirations and motivational levels of the managers and operatives to be controlled.

QUESTIONS FOR STUDY, REFLECTION, AND REVIEW

1. Why are retail managers giving more attention to control efforts?
2. Responsibility accounting when combined with expense center accounting offers several possibilities for improved retail management decision making and control. Point out some of these benefits.
3. The management accounting system of any retail organization must at least meet the two basic needs of every control process. What are these two basic needs?
4. What is the more modern viewpoint regarding expense control in retailing systems, and how is the level of expenses evaluated?
5. To be successful and to add to the profitability of the retail system, expense control must embrace at least three major aspects. What are they?
6. Discuss net profit as a management decision tool. Point out its applicability and limitations.
7. What is the relationship between *direct* expenses and *controllable* expenses, and for what purpose would you classify expenses into such categories?

8. Explain how the *contribution plan* is used to evaluate a department's operation and its management.
9. Explain how the net profit plan evaluates a department's operation and its management. What are some criticisms of the net profit plan?
10. What features of the expense budget facilitate retail management decision making?

20

---

retail control through additional accounting techniques

We learned in Chapter 19 that the accounting system within the retailing organization is the major formal information system. Furthermore, the scope of the accounting system within the retailing organization is very broad. At one and the same time, the accounting system must provide information for three general purposes: (1) external reporting to stockholders, governmental agencies, and other concerned outside parties; (2) internal reporting to managers for the purpose of planning and controlling current operations; and (3) internal reporting to managers and other decision makers for the purpose of formulating long-range plans. Quite naturally, retailing managers are interested in all three aspects of the firm's accounting system, but the emphasis of financial accounting and management accounting differs. As pointed out by Horngren, financial accounting has been mainly concerned with the first purpose and has historically been oriented toward the stewardship aspects of external reporting.[1] The distinguishing feature of management accounting is its emphasis on the second and third purposes, and it is these purposes (i.e., short-run and long-run planning and control processes) that have been the central focus of this book.

Retailing managers are decision makers, and decision makers must have information. Therefore, the retailing manager looks to the accounting system as a source of meaningful, relevant, timely, and accurate information on which to base decisions.

---

[1] Charles T. Horngren, "Choosing Accounting Practices for Reporting to Management," *National Association of Accountants Bulletin,* Vol. 44, No. 1 (September 1962) , pp. 3–16.

But what, really, is an *accounting system?* One pair of writers has described what they mean by the term:

> The accounting system is a means by which the management of an entity accomplishes the collecting, processing and reporting of the essential data that reflect the results of the operations carried out under its direction and supervision. The accounting system includes the forms, records, procedures and devices utilized in recording, summarizing, and reporting the operating and financial data required by management for its own use in controlling the activities for which it is responsible and for presentation to interested parties outside the business entity.[2]

That statement reflects at least two important implications about an accounting system:

1. It is a means (process) for reporting meaningful information pertaining to the firm's behavior.
2. It consists of a series of forms, records, procedures, devices, and techniques utilized to accomplish (1).

The purpose of this discussion is to point out that two chapters of this book give considerable attention to the retail firm's accounting system and to the records, procedures, and techniques for processing meaningful information for purposes of decision making. In Chapter 3, the overall problems of financial analysis and retail management decision making were explored. The reader was introduced to such concepts as the operating statement, the balance sheet, the Dupont Schematic, and many other important financial management devices. In Chapter 19, certain management accounting devices were introduced as they pertained to the important problems of expense budgeting and control. For example, expense classification, expense center accounting, and expense budgeting are important concepts related to controlling or managing retail store expenses. Our discussion of control processes based upon accounting techniques will be concluded in this chapter as we proceed to analyze some additional accounting concepts, namely, the cost method of accounting, the retail method of accounting, and merchandise management accounting. A special word of explanation would appear warranted at this point, however.

The cost method and retail method of accounting are both misnomers. *Neither the retail method of accounting nor the cost method of accounting are accounting systems as such, but instead are special accounting techniques used for the purpose of valuing merchandise inventories in retailing management systems.* The cost method of accounting should not be confused with "cost accounting," which is another special accounting technique utilized most frequently in manufacturing enterprises. Merchandise management accounting is a technique that attempts to supply better information about selling and merchandising costs in order to permit better pricing decisions. Thus, accounting techniques are an important set of tools and

[2] Francis E. Moore and Howard F. Stettler, *Accounting Systems for Management Control,* Richard D. Irwin, Inc., Homewood, Ill., 1963, p. 4.

TABLE 20-1   Retailing Operations and Management Accounting Techniques

ABBREVIATED OPERATING STATEMENT	MANAGEMENT ACCOUNTING TECHNIQUES
Sales	Merchandise management accounting
— Cost of goods sold	
(Cost of goods sold = Beginning	Cost method and retail method
inventory + Purchases	FIFO and LIFO
— Ending inventory)	
= Gross margin	
— Direct expenses	Expense classification
= Controllable profit	Expense center accounting
— Indirect (allocated) expenses	Expense budgeting
= Net profit	Production unit accounting
	Merchandise management accounting

devices used for management decision making within the retail firm. Table 20-1 attempts to show something of the scope of these tools in relation to particular aspects of retail operations as depicted by elements of the operating statement.

Observe that the management accounting techniques treated in Chapter 19 were related to managing and controlling operating expenses, in an attempt to create a more profitable operation. The retail and cost methods of accounting relate to the values placed upon opening and closing inventories, and thus affect cost of goods sold. Merchandise management accounting relates to the *sales* or total revenue figure, and to methods for treating certain selling or merchandising costs. Each of these concepts will be treated in some detail.

the cost method of inventory valuation

The beginning student of retailing (as well as the seasoned, experienced merchant) must understand the importance of correctly valuing the merchandise inventory. This evaluation has a direct bearing on the firm's *cost of goods sold,* which in turn will bear directly on gross margin and profits. To illustrate, consider the following brief operating statement:

1. Net sales		$200,000
2. Total merchandise available for sale	$210,000	
3. (less) Closing inventory at cost	90,000	
4. (equals) Cost of goods sold		120,000
5. Gross margin		$ 80,000
6. (less) Operating expenses		70,000
7. (equals) Net operating income before taxes		$ 10,000

From the above illustration, the reader can observe that cost of goods sold (4) was found by subtracting the closing inventory at cost value (3) from total merchandise available for sale (2). These relationships become somewhat clearer by examining the following, more elaborate "blow up" of the cost of goods sold factors:

Opening inventory at cost	$ 60,000
(plus) Purchases at billed cost, delivered	150,000
(equals) Total merchandise available for sale	$210,000
(less) Closing inventory at cost	90,000
(equals) Cost of goods sold	$120,000

To facilitate the discussion, one additional set of concepts needs to be presented relating to the treatment of certain factors in determining the "Purchases at billed cost, delivered" figure just shown.

Total purchases at billed cost	$160,000
(less) Returns and allowances from suppliers	14,000
(equals) Net purchases	$146,000
(plus) Transportation charges	4,000
(equals) Total billed cost of purchases, delivered	$150,000

The original abbreviated operating statement has now become somewhat more sophisticated and considerably more detailed. Several observations would now appear justified.

Total merchandise available for sale is the summation of the opening inventory for the period plus the purchases or additions to inventory made during the period.

Purchases at billed cost, delivered, is the total invoice cost of all the goods purchased during the period, less the invoice cost of the goods returned to the various suppliers (because they were unsatisfactory, arrived too late to meet seasonal demands, or other reasons), and allowances from suppliers (reductions in invoice cost because of damage in transit, and so on), plus the transportation (freight charges) that are paid by the buyer to get the goods into the store. One additional comment should be made. Notice that cash discounts earned on purchases are not deducted from the invoice cost of the purchases, at least not at this point.[3]

The opening inventory at cost is the cost value of the merchandise inventory on hand at the beginning of a selling period. The opening inventory is the same as the closing inventory of the previous merchandising period.

Now, to return to the major point: the value placed on the closing inventory affects the firm's gross margin and its profit showing. To illustrate, consider the earlier example under three conditions: (1) as earlier illus-

---

[3] Cash discounts are usually treated as "other income" and are not considered in determining the department's initial markup or the gross margin. The usual explanation offered for this treatment is that the buyer has little or no control over the payment of the merchandise invoices and that cash discounts are not a part of the selling department's income earned from operations.

	(1)	(2)	(3)
Net sales	$200,000	$200,000	$200,000
(less) Cost of goods sold:			
Total merchandise available for sale at cost	$210,000	$210,000	$210,000
(less) Closing inventory at cost	90,000	100,000	80,000
(equals) Cost of goods sold	120,000	110,000	130,000
(equals) Gross margin	$ 80,000	$ 90,000	$ 70,000
(less) Operating expenses	70,000	70,000	70,000
(equals) Net profit	$ 10,000	$ 20,000	$ (0000)

trated, (2) with an overvalued inventory, and (3) with an undervalued inventory.

In column (1) it is assumed that the $90,000 at which the closing inventory is valued reflects the true cost value of the inventory. In columns (2) and (3), the inventory has been overvalued and undervalued, respectively. The results are readily apparent. In column (2), where the cost of the merchandise inventory has been overvalued, the effect is to *decrease* the cost of goods, *increase* the gross margin, and correspondingly to *increase* the net profit. Conversely, in column (3), where the cost of the closing inventory has been undervalued, the effect is to *increase* the cost of goods, *decrease* the gross margin, and *decrease* the net profit. More simply stated, the general effect of overstating or understating the value of the closing inventory is as follows:

1. If the closing value of the inventory is overstated, the general effect is to overstate profits for the current year.
2. If the closing value of the inventory is understated, the general effect is to understate profits for the current year.

An error in ending inventory valuation in the current year with the resultant effect of over- or understating net income for the year also automatically results in an offsetting error in the net income for the following year.

The ending inventory of one period becomes the beginning inventory of the next period, and because cost of goods sold (CGS) is derived from the summation of beginning inventory and purchases, less ending inventory, an error in either beginning or ending inventory creates an error in CGS.

Example: If the ending inventory in Year 1, with an actual value of $15,000 is incorrectly recorded at $20,000, the cost of goods sold will be understated by $5,000 in Year 1 and overstated by $5,000 in Year 2.

	YR. 1		YR. 2	
	INCORRECT	CORRECT	INCORRECT	CORRECT
Beginning inventory	$10,000	$10,000	$20,000	$15,000
+ purchases	50,000	50,000	50,000	50, 000
= GAS	60,000	60,000	70,000	65,000
− ending inventory	20,000	15,000	15,000	15,000
= CGS	$40,000	$45,000	$55,000	$50,000

Because CGS is a deduction from revenues in arriving at net income (NI), an understatement of CGS results in an overstatement of NI, and conversely, an overstatement of CGS results in an understatement of NI.

In order effectively to evaluate the firm's overall merchandising activities, it is therefore imperative that inventories be fairly and accurately valued so that profits will be neither understated nor overstated. Furthermore, only if inventories are properly valued can they constitute the basis for additional planning relating to buying and merchandise management.

the decision rule
for inventory valuation

Under certain circumstances, it is acceptable to depart from valuing merchandise inventory at original cost (billed cost, delivered) when the current replacement cost of merchandise is less than the cost at which it was purchased. Businessmen generally agree that the inventory value should be reduced to this current replacement cost (current market price). Justification for the inventory revaluation lies in the implicit assumption that selling prices decrease in direct proportion to decreases in replacement cost, and that there has, therefore, been a real decline in the value of the inventory. Thus, the general decision rule to guide the retail merchant is to value all items in the merchandise inventory at *cost or market, whichever is lower.*

For example, assume that a merchant purchased at cost a quantity (144) of men's shirts at the delivered price of $3.75 each. He is now taking a physical inventory and discovers that he has 100 of these shirts remaining, but in checking vendor prices for this item, he learns that the cost has now risen to $4.00. In line with the decision rule listed previously, the 100 shirts would be listed at the $3.75 price instead of the higher market price of $4.00. Such a rule is conservative in the sense that it forces the retailer to anticipate losses, but not gains. To have listed the shirts at the higher market price of $4.00 would have meant anticipated paper profits of $.25 per shirt. Conversely, however, still considering the same example, suppose the market price has declined to $3.50. The rule "cost or market, whichever is lower" now stipulates that the 100 shirts be listed at $3.50 instead of the original cost price of $3.75, and the effect is to write down the value of the inventory by $.25 on each shirt. Losses are thus anticipated, whereas profits are not. Quite obviously, those merchants who are replenishing their stock of this item will pay the lower market price of $3.50, and to compete successfully, it would probably mean that our merchant ought to value his inventory on the basis of the lower cost, also.

The Cost Method and the Closing Inventory

The cost method of accounting is therefore only a method of valuing retail inventories. It requires that the retailer record the cost of all items entering the store, and usually this cost information is encoded on the price ticket attached to the merchandise. The cost method of inventory valuation also requires that the physical inventory be taken on a cost basis with the necessary adjustments, so that it will reflect a valuation based upon the decision rule "cost or market, whichever is lower."

The Physical Inventory. The various types of inventory records were discussed earlier in the chapters on merchandise management. Two principal types were discussed, the physical inventory and the perpetual (book) inventory. Under the cost method of inventory valuation where it is necessary to take the physical inventory at cost or market price, whichever is lower, certain difficulties arise.

First, in large stores with multiple product lines and broad and deep merchandise inventories, it is virtually impossible to maintain a perpetual inventory system.[4] And without a perpetual inventory system, it is impossible to determine profits at any point in time without a physical or actual counting of the inventory and an evaluation of each article on the basis of cost or market, whichever is lower. In smaller stores, or in stores specializing in the sale of big ticket items such as furniture stores or automobile dealers, it is considerably more feasible to maintain a meaningful perpetual inventory with which to determine profits at any point in time. However, it is important to realize that without a perpetual inventory or an actual physical inventory the cost of goods cannot be determined, and without cost of goods gross margin cannot be determined, and so on. One other point relating to the cost method of inventory valuation and the physical inventory needs to be made. When the physical inventory is taken, two things must be noted in regard to each item: (1) its purchase price and (2) its current market price.[5] It has already been mentioned that the purchase or cost price is usually encoded on the price ticket placed on the item. However, if the price ticket has been removed or is lost, it becomes necessary to look up the original purchase price. In addition, the merchant must also seek to find out the current market price so that the item can be listed on the inventory sheet at cost or market, whichever is lower. Quite obviously, the taking of a physical inventory under these conditions presents considerable difficulties and involves large amounts of time and effort. Such a procedure usually dictates that the merchant have at his disposal vast amounts of information about current market prices, or that he use some judgment methods, such

[4] Electronic Data Processing is of some aid in this regard.
[5] See A. Phillips, "Pricing Retail Inventories," *New York Certified Public Accountant,* Vol. 32 (November 1962) , pp. 732–737.

as aging his stock, subjectively appraising each item, or using a markdown method.

When stocks are aged, it means that values are written down in accordance with some arbitrary aging schedule. For example:

AGE OF MERCHANDISE (MONTHS)	REDUCTION FROM ORIGINAL VALUE (%)
0–4	0
5–7	25
8–12	50
Over	75–100

Thus, any item in stock six months would automatically be written down by 25 per cent. The markdown method is based upon the assumption that if the retail price of an item has been marked down, then it logically follows that its wholesale selling price would also have decreased. For example, if a woman's coat that sold for $60 and cost $40 has been marked down by 10 per cent, it is automatically assumed that the wholesale price would be reduced by 10 per cent also and would be listed at $36 instead of $40 in the physical inventory. Merchants sometimes simply use very arbitrary judgment methods to determine inventory values, and in the case where judgment or some loose rule of thumb such as the aging method or the markdown method is used in lieu of actual market figures, the results are likely to be spurious and result in either undervaluing or overvaluing the inventory with all the attendant shortcomings.

Criticisms of the Cost Method. The cost method of valuing retail merchandise inventories has been criticized on several counts.[6] As we mentioned, it is a time-consuming method, especially in relation to taking the physical inventory. In this regard, also, it is a technique that requires considerable record keeping of information relating to cost data. Furthermore, when judgment methods for valuing inventory are used, the cost method is quite arbitrary and whether merchandise is truly valued at cost or market, whichever is lower is highly problematic.

However, the cost method continues to remain the most widely adopted method of inventory valuation among smaller and medium-sized retail institutions. It should be added that many stores, especially those that engage in large amounts of workroom activity or in the actual alteration or change in form of commodities—such as furniture stores, upholstery shops, automobile agencies, drugstores or pharmacies—must of necessity use the cost method of inventory valuation. For that matter, there are no sound reasons why larger stores cannot use both the cost and the retail methods of inventory valuation in different departments of their total operation. The fact is, of course, that many do.

---

[6] See H. F. Bell and L. Moscarello, *Retail Merchandise Accounting*, 3rd ed., The Ronald Press Company, New York, 1961.

the retail method
of inventory valuation

It must be remembered that retail managers need information for decision making that is both accurate and timely, and where the cost method of inventory valuation is used, it is very time-consuming to obtain accurate data about the inventory. And without an accurate inventory valuation, it is impossible to derive cost of goods sold, or gross margin, or inventory turnover information, all of which are essential ingredients in the management decision making process.

In an attempt to overcome this problem, the retail method of inventory valuation, which is essentially a procedure for estimating the inventory value at any time, has been widely adopted by retail stores, particularly department stores which sell a diversity of items. The essential feature of retailing institutions that makes the retail method of inventory valuation possible is that merchandise purchases are immediately priced for resale. The emphasis is on selling price; i.e., retailers relate markups, analyses, budgets, estimates, markdowns, and so forth to sales price rather than to cost price, and income statements are traditionally broken down as percentages of sales. So, it is a natural tendency to think of the inventory value in terms of retail prices also.

Application of the retail method requires keeping records that show the following data:

1. Beginning inventory valued at cost and retail.
2. Purchases valued at cost and retail.
3. Adjustments to the original retail price such as additional markups, markup cancellations, markdowns, and markdown cancellations.
4. Sales at retail.

The computation of the final inventory at cost is based on the ratio of cost to selling price, or the cost ratio, which is computed by dividing goods available for sale at cost by goods available for sale at retail.

Often, neither formulas nor written descriptions are as explanatory as a numerical illustration. Therefore, in order to explain the retail method of inventory valuation, Table 20-2 is presented in the form of a matrix with easily identifiable rows and columns. Each item will be explained in order to assure a full understanding of the technique.

Row 1 shows the beginning inventory at both cost and retail figures. It should be pointed out that when using the retail method, it is necessary to record all purchases and all additions to and subtractions from stock, at both retail and cost. The difference between the retail value of the inventory and the cost value is the markup. This is in keeping with the statement that Retail = Cost + Markup.

Row 2 records purchases at both cost and retail, and once again the difference is recorded as markup, both in dollars and as a markup percentage.

Row 3 treats transportation as an additional cost of acquiring merchan-

TABLE 20-2   Retail Method of Inventory Valuation Matrix

		(1)	(2)	(3)	(4)
ROW	ITEM	COST	RETAIL	MARKUP ($)	MARKUP (%)
1	Beginning inventory[a]	$ 8,000	$12,000	$ 4,000	33.30%
2	Purchases	12,000	20,000	8,000	40.00
3	Transportation-in	240			
4	Additional markups, less Additional markup cancellations		300		
5	Inventory total, plus Additions	$20,240	$32,300	$12,060	37.34%
6	Net sales		$19,740		
7	Markdowns, less Markdown cancellations		1,200		
8	Total retail deductions		$20,940		
9	Ending inventory at retail Row 5 ($32,300) — Row 8 ($20,940)		$11,360		
10	Calculation of cost percentage Retail = Cost + Markup 100% = x + 37.34[b] x = 62.66, the cost percentage				
11	Ending inventory at cost Row 9 ($11,360) × Row 10 (62.66%)	$ 7,118			
12	Cost of goods sold Row 5 ($20,240) — Row 11 ($7,118)	$13,122			

[a] The beginning inventory would be Rows 9 and 11 of the preceding inventory.

[b] The 37.34% is the cumulative markup percentage and is found by subtracting $20,240 from $32,300 = $12,060. $\dfrac{\$12,060}{\$32,300} = 37.34\%$.

dise to sell. The $240 figure for transportation is added to the cost column only, as it does not affect the retail column.

Row 4 reflects that there have been additional markups taken during this period and that these additional markups affect the total retail value of the inventory. In some cases, markup cancellations occur. For example, suppose a buyer orders a quantity of merchandise to sell for $4.00 per unit, but the price marker incorrectly marks the item at $5.00. When the buyer discovers the mistake, the markup is written down to the $4.00 intended price. This would tend to alter the retail value of the inventory and thus the cumulative markup percentage. Most stores exercise stringent controls over policies relating to markup cancellations. Otherwise, the buyer would have unusual discretion to willfully cancel buying errors, and not just price marking errors.

Row 5 now shows total inventory figures at both cost and retail values, the dollar and the percentage cumulative markup figures. The latter is a very important figure because its reciprocal—the cost percentage—is the essential figure for finally determining the cost value of the closing inventory.

Row 6 shows only net sales, as would be logical, because net sales are always reported at retail values.

Row 7 shows markdowns less markdown cancellations. This may warrant a brief explanation. You will observe that when added to net sales this item equals total retail deductions. And herein lies the explanation: a markdown does tend to subtract or diminish the value of the store's inventory; therefore, markdowns must be added to net sales and considered as a reduction from the total value of the merchandise inventory. Observe that what has occurred is that a value at cost for the ending inventory at retail (Row 9) has been obtained by multiplying this figure by the cost percentage (62.66%). The cost percentage, Row 10, is simply the reciprocal of the cumulative markup percentage. For example, if sales = 100% and the cumulative markup = 37.34%, then the cost percentage must be 62.66% (100% − 37.34%). The important generalization to be derived from all this discussion is that *the closing value of the merchandise inventory at cost is found by multiplying the cost percentage times the value of the merchandise inventory at retail.* In the following pages, the importance of this generalization will be underscored and further explained.

Adopting the Retail Method of Inventory Valuation

The first question that may strike you is, "Why should a retail firm adopt the retail method as opposed to the cost method of inventory valuation?" There are several answers to this question. Perhaps the major reason lies with the nature of the retail method itself. It is an extremely logical, internally consistent, and well-conceived concept that ties all figures together, with net sales as the common denominator. The method is relatively easy to install and master, and when this is accomplished, it provides an excellent basis for gathering historical data and for the interpretation and analysis of this data. Merchandise management through book (perpetual inventory) systems is greatly facilitated with this method. The actual taking of the physical inventory is also greatly facilitated, as is the provision of a gross margin figure without the necessity of taking a physical inventory. Finally, the way in which the retail method automatically depreciates inventory values in accordance with retail price reductions is a most noteworthy and esteemed feature of the technique. In short, the retail method does two important and vital tasks perhaps better than does the cost method. On the one hand, it permits the more extensive use of perpetual book inventories, which makes it possible to determine the profitability of any period's operations without taking a physical inventory.

Second, when the physical inventory is taken, it is a much easier process since the inventory is actually made in terms of retail prices and then reduced to a cost basis via the use of the cumulative markup figure and its complement, the cost percentage. Each of these ideas warrants further amplification.

The Physical Inventory. Only a physical inventory, an actual counting of goods in stock, can truly reveal the nature and character of a merchant's stock of goods. However, in most stores taking inventory is a costly and time-consuming process, and for these reasons, an actual physical inventory is usually taken only once or twice a year. However, when a firm has adopted the retail method of valuation, it is necessary that the inventory be taken only in terms of retail prices. Thus, the laborious effort required to take the physical inventory (i.e., the exhaustive listing of each item on the basis of cost or market, whichever is lower, where the cost method is employed) is largely eliminated. When the physical inventory is completed, the total value of retail stock is compared with the book inventory, and any difference is recorded as either a merchandise shortage or overage. A *shortage* occurs when the physical inventory is less than the book inventory, and an *overage* occurs when the physical inventory is larger than the book inventory. A shortage suggests either merchandise shrinkage through thievery or clerical errors in manipulating the inventory system. An overage suggests only clerical errors.

Conservative Valuation. The retail method, it has been stated, provides for an automatic conservative valuation of merchandise inventories in accordance with the decision rule, cost or market, whichever is lower. The retail method has as an underlying assumption the idea that, in terms of retail prices, any item in an inventory collection is worth only what it will bring in the market place. Consider the following example.

A department buyer in a men's clothing store has a quantity of windbreakers. They are currently priced at $24.95, but are not turning over very rapidly. Upon examination, the buyer discovers that his competitor is selling the same item for $22.95, and that it is nearing the end of the selling season for such items. Consequently, he marks his windbreakers down to $19.95. What is their value for inventory purposes? In retail prices, they would be listed at their current market price of $19.95. Thus, the market becomes the determiner of value, not original price or even cost. But what about the cost value? This is determined by multiplying the market value by the cost percentage. That is, if the typical or average cumulative markup in this department equalled 40 per cent, then the cost percentage would equal 60 per cent and the cost value of the windbreaker would be ($19.95 × .60) or $11.94. To reiterate, the retail method of inventory valuation is conservative, at least in the sense that it allows the market (or the decision maker's interpretation of the market) to be the arbiter of value.

Requirements for Implementing the Retail Method

The retail method of inventory valuation is relatively easy to implement in most any size or type of retailing operation, provided that certain fundamental groundwork is undertaken. Keeping in mind that the retail method depends upon accurate and meaningful records and data for its successful implementation, the first step toward adopting this method must therefore focus upon the development of a system of inventory records designed purposely to facilitate this end. The retail method is a somewhat arbitrary method of inventory valuation in the sense that it is a method concerned with average values. The implication of this will be explained more fully, subsequently. Suffice it to say at this juncture, that in order successfully to adopt the retail method of inventory, it is essential that the merchandise be categorized or departmentalized in terms of similarity of markups and turnover rates. If this is not done, the average cumulative markup percentage that constitutes the real basis for costing the final inventory figure will not necessarily be representative of the wide range of markups and turnover to be found throughout the entire store.

The next step in adopting and implementing the retail method is that a complete physical inventory at both cost and retail prices must be undertaken. The reason for such a requirement becomes apparent when Table 20-2 is re-examined. Notice that Row 1 and columns (1), (2), (3), and (4) would all be determined at the outset by such an inventory. This procedure therefore establishes the basis for the retail method.

Finally, as was said earlier, the retail method rests on a foundation of collected, classified, and interpreted data. This means that a continuous flow of this information is needed, relating to all purchases at both cost and retail value, all markup cancellations, all markdowns and markdown cancellations, all transfers into and out of stock for a given department, freight-in, and discounts to customers and employees. The retail method is so heavily oriented toward record keeping and bookkeeping that without this effort it cannot at all be successfully employed. Yet, in spite of the necessity for all this record keeping, the retail method is highly successful and widely adopted by many stores, especially the medium to larger-sized department stores and departmentized specialty stores. The adoption of this method has made possible financial standards and ratio comparisons on both an area and a nationwide basis, simply because the data is presented in a similar format that shows all figures as a percentage relationship to net sales. The collection and dissemination of such information has been a boon to retail firms seeking better standards and criteria for both planning and control. One authoritative source wrote about the retail method, stating:

> The whole retail system of accounting should provide an appropriate framework within which managers should be able to appraise demand, select suitable merchandise, price it to yield optimum dollars of gross margin, and manage promotion and expenses so as to maximize profits.[7]

In theory this all sounds very well. But the fact is there are several important factors that limit the effectiveness of the retail method, and that in turn tend to limit its adoption. As we saw in Chapter 17, the retail method is a method of averages that focuses the manager's attention on gross margin and the planned markon percentage, and pays practically no attention to differences in the costs generated by particular items. In short, attention is focused on ratios to sales, rather than on actual dollars or the contribu-

[7] Malcolm P. McNair and Eleanor G. May, "Pricing for Profit," *Harvard Business Review,* Vol. 35 (May–June 1957), p. 107.

tion dollars concept. Attempts at overcoming these shortcomings via the use of merchandise management accounting will be discussed in the latter part of this chapter.

The retail method is not usually adopted by smaller stores. Even some larger stores complain that it poses certain operational difficulties, because it is not easily understood. The manager/decision maker is forced to think in terms of retail prices and derived costs, rather than in actual purchase or acquisition costs of articles. Finally, perhaps the greatest disadvantage that the retail method has is the fact that it is a method of averages, and to be used successfully it must be matched to department or merchandise classifications in which turnover rates and markup percentages are very nearly uniform. Table 20-3 is provided to illustrate this point. These figures show the effect of different markups and rates of sale on the cumulative markup percentage and its effect on inventory valuation. Row 1 shows that beginning inventory at cost and retail was $36,000 and $60,000 respectively. This provides a dollar markup of $24,000 and a percentage markup of 40 per cent. To this beginning inventory are added purchases over three periods. In period A_1, purchases at cost and retail were $16,000 and $20,000, respectively, and this merchandise carried a markup of only 20 per cent. Purchases in period A_2 were high markup goods and resulted in a percentage markup of 50 per cent. In period A_3, another quantity of goods was purchased, and these, too, were relatively low markup items. However, observe that the total cumulative markup percentage is 38 per cent (Row 5) and that by using this cumulative markup per cent (Row 6), the closing value of the inventory at cost equals $31,000. The question is, is this a fair valuation? Whether it is or not depends actually on whether or not the items constituting the final inventory are representative of the purchases made during the three purchase periods. If they are not, the inventory is likely to be undervalued or overvalued. For example, the usual assumption

TABLE 20-3   The Retail Method and Diverse Merchandise Markups

		(1)	(2)	(3)	(4)
ROW	ITEM	COST	RETAIL	$ MARKUP	MARKUP %
1	Beginning inventory	$36,000	$60,000	$24,000	40%
2	Purchases				
	Period (A_1)	16,000	20,000	4,000	20%
	Period (A_2)	20,000	40,000	20,000	50%
	Period (A_3)	21,000	30,000	9,000	30%
3	Total merchandise handled	$93,000	$150,000		
4	Cumulative $ Markup = $150,000 − $93,000 = $57,000 Markup				
5	Cumulative percentage markup = $\dfrac{\$57,000}{\$150,000}$ = 38%				
6	If Closing inventory at retail = $50,000, then $50,000 × 38%, or $19,000, is the dollar markup. Retail ($50,000) − Markup ($19,000) = $31,000, the closing value of the inventory at cost.				

is that low markup items sell at a faster rate than higher markup items. If this were the case in the example just presented, then the final retail inventory would likely be composed mainly of the higher markup items purchased in period A_2 and the average cumulative markup would be higher than 38 per cent, thus the closing inventory at cost would be *overvalued*. Conversely, suppose the lower markup merchandise purchased was incompatible with the store's image and did not sell well, yet the higher markup merchandise sold out readily. In such a case, an opposite result would occur. The cumulative markup percentage would be actually lower than that reflected by the average and the closing value of the inventory at cost would be undervalued. This example dramatizes why it is essential that the retail method be adopted only after departmentation has occurred and where markup and rate of sale for the various merchandise lines within a given department tend to be very similar. One additional concept, known as LIFO, needs to be discussed at this point because it is sometimes adopted as a modification of the retail inventory method of accounting.

fifo and lifo valuations

With both the cost method and the retail method of inventory valuation, the merchant is concerned with a conservative, yet realistic appraisal of the final closing inventory. The reason is that he wants a fair and realistic determination of his cost of goods sold, which plays a determinate role in assessing gross margin and, ultimately, profits. As we learned earlier, if the closing inventory is overvalued, profits tend to be overstated; and, if the closing inventory is undervalued, profits are understated. Herein lies the dilemma. Fluctuations of supplier prices can greatly affect the profit showing of retailers, depending upon what particular prices they use to evaluate their merchandise inventory. For example, the usual procedure is that merchants evaluate their inventories on what is called a first-in, first-out basis, or FIFO. That is, the merchandise that is purchased first is considered to be that which is sold first and, therefore, moved out of the inventory assortment. The inventory valuation under FIFO conforms closely to the actual physical flow of merchandise through the store. Thus, when the inventory is taken and valued, the usual assumption is that the merchandise inventory is largely constituted of the merchandise more recently acquired, which approximates current replacement cost.

Consequently, during times of rising prices, the ending inventory value will be higher than that of the beginning inventory even if the quantities of the items in both inventories are approximately the same. And, the larger the value of the ending inventory, remember, the smaller is derived cost of goods sold, and consequently, the larger is reported net income.

Even though this may be a reasonable and accurate representation of actual operating results, an additional complication exists. Opponents of the FIFO method of inventory costing argue that the ending inventory value is artificially inflated. As retail prices rise in an inflationary period, the practice of deriving ending inventory at cost from an application of the average cost percentage existing during the period to ending inventory at retail results in an inflated ending inventory at cost and so on down to the bottom line of the income statement where an inflated net income figure results. And whether or not the income figure represents real profit or un- realized profit, the firm is required to pay taxes on the total amount of income reported. Consequently, after the World War II period when many retail firms began to anticipate that a period of considerable inflation was about to ensue, they began to agitate—largely through the National Retail Dry Goods Association (N.R.D.G.A., now the National Retail Merchants Association)—with the Bureau of Internal Revenue for the right to value inventories on the basis of LIFO, or last-in, first-out valuation.[8] For many years, manufacturers and material processors had attempted to gain the right to use LIFO techniques. It was not until section 22 (d) of the Revenue Act of 1939 was written, however, that the general use of the LIFO method, without restrictions as to type of industry, was permitted. Retailers were not permitted to use the LIFO method until after 1947, when the Tax Court of the United States, in the Hurtzler Brothers Case, decreed that "Congress provided in 1939 that the LIFO method of inventory might be used by any taxpayer."[9]

What Is LIFO?

LIFO is a concept that attempts to assess the true nature of retailing profits, those that reflect merchandising operations and not capital appre- ciation of inventories because of inflationary price increases.

LIFO is based upon the notion that a minimum inventory (a base stock) is vital to the continuing operation of the business. A further assumption is that current acquisition costs are incurred for the purpose of meeting cur- rent sales. In other words, it is in anticipation of sales that additional pur- chases are made, so as not to liquidate the base stock and create an out-of- stock situation. The major argument in favor of the LIFO method, then, is the attempt to match current revenues (sales) with the costs (current pur- chases) that must be incurred to produce them. Under this method the cost of the units remaining in inventory represents the oldest costs available.

Thus, the flow of costs is assumed to change to a last-in, first-out basis, even though the actual physical flow of the units in inventory is not affected. As is the case under any inventory costing procedure, the first goods pur- chased are usually the first goods sold. Consider the following greatly sim- plified illustration. A small boutique shoppe sells only men's hand-blocked silk ties. It had sales during a recent period of $100,000. This is a period of rising prices. The ties have normally been purchased at $6.25, but just re- cently went to $6.50. What is the effect of inventory valuation under FIFO and LIFO, given these circumstances? Consider Table 20-4.

---

[8] For a really intensive treatment of LIFO and FIFO techniques, the reader is urged to examine Malcolm P. McNair and Anita C. Hersum, *The Retail Inventory Method and LIFO,* McGraw-Hill Book Company, New York, 1952. See especially Chap. VIII, "The LIFO Concept: Basic Principles and Early Development." For another, far simpler, treat- ment, see "The Facts of LIFO," *Fortune* (December 1951) , p. 198.

[9] Brief for the Petitioner, p. 44.

TABLE 20-4   FIFO and LIFO Illustrated

	FIFO		LIFO
Sales	$100,000		$100,000
Cost of goods sold			
10,000 ties at $6.25	62,500	10,000 ties at $6.50	65,000
Net profit	$ 37,500		$ 35,000
(less) Income taxes at 50%	18,750		17,500
Net profit after taxes	$ 18,750		$ 17,500

You will observe that under FIFO, the cost of goods is determined by multiplying the ties sold, by their original purchase price; whereas under LIFO, cost of goods is determined by multiplying the ties sold by the new wholesale price of $6.50, even though none of the ties actually sold were purchased at the new higher price. The effect is to reduce the firm's profit before taxes and, consequently, to reduce the firm's actual tax liability.

Several generalizations about LIFO can now be made.

1. Under LIFO the cost of the most recently acquired goods is charged against sales.
2. If the quantity of goods in the ending inventory remains unchanged in terms of the quantity of goods in the beginning inventory, Cost of goods sold = Cost of purchases.
3. When using LIFO methods in a period of rising prices, the effect is to reduce gross margin and profits.
4. When using LIFO methods in a period of falling prices, the effect is to increase gross margin and profits.
5. If costs are stable over a relatively long period of time, there is no impact on either gross margin or profits as a result of using either LIFO or FIFO. In short, it does not matter which method is used.

Thus, the impact of LIFO is to reduce stated earnings to some degree in periods of rising prices, and on the other hand, to increase stated earnings in periods of falling prices. The usual case regarding FIFO is that profits tend to be higher in periods when wholesale prices are advancing and lower in periods of falling prices. In order to redress this effect, some merchants have adopted LIFO. Once again, the reader should grasp the notion that when profits are overstated, an overpayment of income taxes is the result.

The traditional retail method of inventory valuation may be adapted to approximate LIFO results by maintaining a distinction between the cost of the base stock layer and subsequent purchases. This is done by computing the ending inventory at retail in the traditional manner, except that the cost ratio is determined by excluding the beginning inventory and including both markups and markdowns. In addition a restatement to the cost basis requires the utilization of a price index deflator so that the base inventory layer and subsequent purchases can be compared in common dollars. A comprehensive explanation of the mechanics of the procedure can be found in most intermediate accounting textbooks.

LIFO is not widely used by retail firms, either large or small. The Bureau of Internal Revenue has ruled that although retail firms are entitled to use LIFO as an inventory valuation technique, those who do adopt it must continue to use it more or less permanently. This has given retailers considerable pause, because they would not like to adopt the technique, only to discover that a period of falling prices was about to ensue. If such were the case, financial statements would reflect higher profits and correspondingly larger income tax liabilities—a most untoward condition. It is not possible for the retailer to seek the best of all possible worlds. He cannot switch to LIFO during periods of rising prices and FIFO during periods of falling prices. As desirable as this might be from the retailer's point of view, the Bureau of Internal Revenue has foreclosed on such a utopian possibility.

There is an increasing trend for professional accounting firms and some large retailers to accept LIFO as a method of inventory valuation. However, in spite of the prolonged period of inflationary pressures that strengthen the argument in favor of LIFO, the majority of retail firms continue to use the more traditional retail method of inventory valuation that is based on the FIFO cost flow assumption.

merchandise management accounting

The cost method and the retail method of accounting are not complete accounting systems, as we have learned, but they are instead methods or approaches to the important problem of valuing inventories. Furthermore, as has also been repeatedly emphasized, the importance of properly valuing the retail inventory cannot be overstated. The value placed upon the retail inventory will affect the firm's gross margin and its reported profits.

The retail method and the cost method of accounting are simply extensions of the firm's overall management accounting activities. *Recall that management accounting is concerned with the information flows that stem from accounting efforts and are directed toward the end of providing useful, accurate, and reliable data on which to base the internal operating decisions related to problems of planning and control.* Thus, the concepts discussed in Chapter 19 (i.e., expense classification and expense center accounting) are management accounting techniques. *Merchandise management accounting is simply another management accounting technique—a device or set of practices used to generate useful information for merchandising decisions at the individual item level.*

It is most important to point out that merchandise management accounting is not a method for valuing inventories, but is instead a technique that builds upon the concepts of expense center accounting.[10]

The use of the term accounting should not be such that the concept is

---

[10] The point has been well stated by Kenneth P. Mages in his article, "M.M.A. Should Supplement Expense Center Accounting," *Journal of Retailing*, Vol. 34, No. 1 (Spring 1958), pp. 30, 32–37, and 52.

relegated to use only in the finance office of the firm. Recommendations for relabelling have been numerous. For example, the following descriptive labels have been suggested: merchandising cost analysis, controllable profit merchandising,[11] item costing, item contribution accounting,[12] and item profitability. Knowledge about item profitability can be extremely useful and lead to better decision making in at least the following areas:

1. The determination of product prices.
2. The selection of items to advertise and promote.
3. Determining stock quantities.
4. The determination to drop or add particular products.
5. Expense control.[13]

The truth of the matter is that merchandise management accounting is really more of a set of methods and approaches to decision making relating to the whole spectrum of merchandising and pricing than it is a form of accounting.

The Need for Merchandising Management Accounting

Merchandise management accounting has grown out of the need for retail merchants and decision makers to *reorient* themselves to a more proper and accurate criterion for decision making. The point is that the widespread use of the retail inventory method has tended to place too much emphasis on storewide gross margin percentages; furthermore, overall departmental expenses (both direct and allocated) are often treated as if they applied to all the goods sold in the department.

The most serious and profound indictment of the firm's inventory method of accounting and the results that stem from the abuse and lack of understanding of the retail method has been presented by McNair and May with quite forceful arguments:[14]

1. Merchandise managers and buyers, possibly not fully understanding the retail system, have focused on the gross margin percentage and the planned markon percentage as the major operating tools.
2. The planned markon percentage is used across the board departmentally with tacit assumption of applicability of average cost.
3. Practically no attention is paid to differences in the cost generated by particular items.
4. There is almost complete disregard of possible elasticities of demand.
5. No distinction is made between fixed and variable costs.
6. There is a purely mechanical retailing of orders, using either the

---

[11] Gordon B. Cross, "A Critical Analysis of Merchandise Management Accounting," *Journal of Retailing*, Vol. 34, No. 1 (Spring 1958), p. 22.

[12] McNair and May, op. cit., p. 111.

[13] Suggested by William H. Hoffman, Jr., and Donald E. Vaughn, "Departmental and Item Profitability," *Journal of Accounting* (August 1963), pp. 50–58.

[14] McNair and May, op. cit., p. 108.

manufacturer's suggested retail price or a traditional price line of the department.

7. There is a general acceptance of net sales as an appropriate basis of expense allocation.
8. Too much confidence is reposed in the final departmental net profit percentages after expense allocation.
9. There is a frequent tie-in of the gross margin percentage with the buyer's compensation in such a way as to make the buyer most reluctant to place any orders carrying a lower markon percentage than his planned figure.
10. In sum, attention is focused on ratios to sales rather than dollars, and the convenient percentages have become crutches.

In the light of such criticisms, merchandise management accounting was developed, with its basic aim being to improve dollar profits (rather than percentage profits) through a better interpretation and determination of costs by individual items, via the use of improved cost accounting techniques.

Such an approach has been slow to develop in retail store operations for many reasons.[15] For one, the exceedingly wide variety and number of products handled by most retailers have served to impede unit cost computation approaches. Still another reason, as has been mentioned, is that all too often emphasis has tended to be placed upon the calculation of departmental net profit or loss, rather than upon individual unit profit or loss calculations. Then, too, even when merchandising decisions at the item level are made, the usual procedure is to project costs based upon percentage figures derived from departmental averages. Finally, until more recent developments in expense center accounting, the grouping and affixing of responsibility for expenses has not always followed methods or procedures that stressed productivity and effective control.

Decision Making at the Action Level

Merchandise management accounting is at least in part an attempt to dissuade decision makers from slavishly using average gross margin figures as their principal criterion for decision making. In short, it is an effort to debase the percentage syndrome that appears to permeate so much of the thinking of retail decision makers. More positively stated, merchandise management accounting postulates that the important decision making area for managers is the individual item level and that there is characteristically a paucity of financial and accounting data at this level. The concept furthermore underscores the idea that the use of departmental or store-wide percentage relationships tends to obscure the variations in the cost and profit of individual items, and thus to mislead management. Finally, merchandise management accounting acknowledges and supports several previously made contentions of this text. Real profit must be viewed as a return on merchandise investment or earnings on total invested capital. Further-

[15] Hoffman and Vaughn, op. cit., p. 50.

more, merchandise management accounting dictates that profitability and pricing must be combined with a turnover factor in order to accomplish this objective.

Merchandise management accounting is essentially, then, the application of cost accounting methods at the item level with the purpose of obtaining meaningful accounting and financial data on which to base merchandising decisions. The technique of merchandise management accounting rests on several important concepts, each of which will be explained in some detail.

The Concept of Controllable Profit. One of the foremost concepts of merchandise management accounting is that of controllable profit. This is not a new concept, inasmuch as it has been discussed throughout several chapters of this text. The concept of controllable profit is closely related to the "contribution plan" of expense allocation discussed in Chapter 19. *Controllable profit defined* is

Sales — Cost of goods = Gross margin
Gross margin — Direct expenses = Controllable profits.

The controllable profit concept requires that expenses be classified into direct and indirect categories, but the terms direct and indirect have no meaning unless they are related to the item under consideration. The word direct refers to the *obvious physical tracing* of cost to a particular product, or department, as the case may be, whereas an indirect expense is one that is incurred as a result of other factors than the existence of the object in question. In other words, the direct cost of salesclerks' salaries in a department would be eliminated if the department were eliminated, but the indirect rental cost allocated to that department would continue. At the individual department level we can then assume for simplicity that most variable expenses are direct and most fixed expenses are indirect. You will recall that fixed expenses are those expenses that are incurred as a result of being in business, regardless of whether or not a specific item is sold. Variable expenses are costs incurred as a result of selling a particular item. In terms of responsibility accounting, the direct expenses of a given operation are those over which the manager of that operation can exercise some control. In other words, a direct or controllable expense can be altered by the department manager's decisions. In retailing operations, though, there are many exceptions, inasmuch as a variable expense may sometimes become a fixed expense, and vice versa. Variable expenses usually include such items as receiving, warehousing, delivery, selling, advertising, wrapping, alterations, sales audit, and accounts payable. Fixed expenses normally would include such items as real estate costs, furniture, fixture and equipment costs, superintending and building operations, personnel, professional services, employee programs, and personal selling management. The implementation of a concept of controllable profit at the departmental level usually leads to a procedure where only those expenses under the control of the department manager are assigned to his operation. As one writer on the subject commented, "Most important of all, introducing controllable

**TABLE 20-5   Major Appliance Department
Statement of Income and Expense**

	AMOUNT
Net sales	$2,000,000
Initial markon	$ 544,000
Variable expenses	
Markdowns	59,400
Selling	124,000
Receiving and marking	14,000
Delivery	46,000
Installation and warranty	80,000
Inventory shortage	4,600
Advertising	50,000
Carrying charge income	(50,000)
Credit department expenses	40,000
Imputed interest	10,000
Warehousing	40,000
	$ 418,000
Controllable profit	$ 126,000
Fixed expenses	
Buying	70,000
Occupancy	40,000
Administrative	66,000
	$ 176,000
Net loss before income taxes	($ 50,000)

SOURCE: Harvey E. Kapnick, Jr., "Merchandise Management
Accounting," in Frank M. Bass (ed.), Frontiers of Marketing Thought
and Science, American Marketing Association, Chicago, 1958,
p. 123.

profit at the departmental level formulates the predicate necessary for placing increased emphasis upon the individual product."[16]

Table 20-5 shows the operating statement of a major appliance department and the expense breakdown into variable and fixed components.[17] Observe that after subtracting all the variable expenses from initial markon, a controllable profit figure is obtained.

The Concept of Cost Patterns.   The idea of cost patterns is another of the important concepts upon which merchandising management accounting rests. It stresses that by using cost accounting techniques that have been used for many years in other industries, individual unit cost, by item, can be determined. It should be pointed out most explicitly that it is not neces-

[16] Ibid., p. 53.

[17] The illustrations and figures used in discussing merchandise management accounting are those of Harvey E. Kapnick, Jr., taken from his article, "Merchandise Management Accounting," in Frank M. Bass (ed.), Frontiers of Marketing Thought and Science, American Marketing Association, Chicago, 1958, pp. 120–134.

sary to apply merchandise management accounting costing methods to all items in the departmental or store assortment. Such a widespread application would undoubtedly be extremely time consuming and costly. Instead, the technique is usually implemented only in the higher priced and critical merchandise lines. It should be added, however, that with the more widespread application of electronic data processing in inventory management and management accounting, a nearly universal or storewide application of the concept is considerably more feasible.

The concept of cost patterns suggests that the cost for performing different merchandising and expense-inducing functions necessary to sell goods are likely to fall into a series of clusters or patterns. Furthermore, these variable costs are likely to be either *flat costs* (i.e., varying with the necessity of performing the function) or *percentage costs* (i.e., varying directly with the selling prices). A brief example will help to clarify this point. Suppose that in a men's clothing store a $75 sport coat is sold. If salesmen are compensated on the basis of commissions at the rate of 10 per cent, the direct selling cost is $7.50, and this cost varies directly with the selling price. If the item is delivered, cost accounting analysis of delivery cost is likely to reveal that the wrapping and delivery cost for sport coats amounts to $5 per unit, which is a flat cost. Now, if a $50 sport coat is sold, the selling cost (which is a percentage cost) would be $5. Yet the delivery cost (which is a flat cost) would remain at $5. The direct costs—both percentage costs and flat costs—for various categories of goods are derived from accounting data resulting from expense center and production unit accounting efforts. By applying cost accounting techniques in a major appliance department, it was found that several unit costs could be recognized for each type of expense because of various methods of handling, the physical characteristics, such as size and weight, and so on, and certain other store policies and practices. Table 20-6 shows these patterns.

TABLE 20-6   Major Appliance Department

VARIABLE COST CENTERS	UNIT COMPUTATIONS					
Receiving	$ .37	$ .50	$ .65	$ .78	$ .92	
Warehousing	$ .75	$1.19	$1.45	$1.80	$2.25	
Selling	6.0%					
Advertising	2.5%					
Carrying charges	(1.05%)	(1.95%)	(2.75%)	(3.77%)	(4.90%)	(8.25%)
Credit expense	$1.35	$1.60	$2.00	$2.40	$2.90	$4.25
Delivery	$1.40	$2.20	$2.95	$3.63	$4.40	$5.10
Installation	$3.50	$5.10	$5.50	$6.40	$7.25	a
Warranty	$ .75	$1.20	$1.82	$2.10	$2.95	$5.25
Markdowns	3.50%	4.00%	4.50%	10.00%		
Other costs	.70%	.90%	1.17%			

a Customer pays.

SOURCE: Adapted from Harvey E. Kapnick, Jr., "Merchandise Management Accounting," in Frank M. Bass (ed.), Frontiers of Marketing Thought and Science, American Marketing Association, Chicago, 1958, p. 124.

Notice that the variable costs are shown either as flat costs or as percentage costs. This cost data is then evaluated in terms of the anticipated future expenses for such costs, and if it is determined that the data is relevant (the historical past costs will be similar to anticipated future costs), they can then be used for making decisions that will affect future profits. By securing such information, a new basis for decision making—the minimum cost incurred in merchandising the particular item—is underscored. For example, in the Major Appliance Department (in Table 20-6), one particular item incurred a receiving cost of 65 cents, a warehousing cost of $1.45, a selling cost of 6 per cent, an advertising cost of 2.5 per cent, and other specific costs for each expense center. Table 20-6 shows cost patterns for six different category items. Assuming now a selling price of $200 and a 30 per cent markup, and given the various costs incurred to sell this item, what would be its controllable profit? Figure 20-1 relates the relevant factors of this particular problem.

The flat costs and the percentage costs have been shown separately. Notice that those costs that are percentage costs total 10.92 per cent of the selling price, which, given a selling price of $200, equals $21.84. The flat costs total $13.33; therefore, total direct costs equal $35.17. With a 30 per cent markup, gross margin would equal $60, and controllable profit ($60.00 − $35.17) would therefore equal $24.83. Controllable profit as a per cent of the sales price thus equals 12.41 per cent.

The combined use of the concept of controllable profit and the concept of cost patterns is very useful for many merchandising decisions. For example, assume that the price of the major appliance used in the illustration above had not yet been determined. The manager of this department might like to speculate on the effects of alternative pricing strategies.

For example, assume:

	(1)		(2)
Retail price of appliance	$225.00		$185.00
Cost	140.00		140.00
Gross margin	$ 85.00		$ 45.00
Flat costs	$ 13.33		$ 13.33
Percentage costs			
(.1092 × $225.00) =	24.75	(.1092 × $185.00) =	20.35
Total variable costs	$ 38.08		$ 33.68
	$ 85.00		$ 45.00
	38.08		33.68
Contribution to overhead and profit			
(Controllable profit)	$ 46.92		$ 11.32

Notice that even at a price of $185.00, a controllable profit of $11.32 is returned. Such findings support arguments long advocated by many progressive merchants, namely, that all items do not necessarily have to make a significant contribution to controllable profits. Items are often carried and merchandised at a low price, because they are needed in order (1) to build

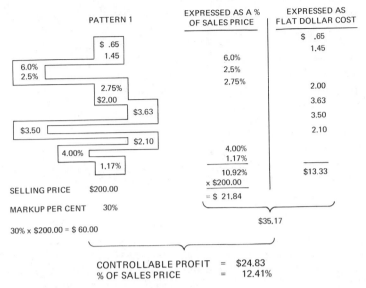

FIGURE 20-1 Patterns of flat and percentage costs.

SOURCE: Harvey E. Kapnick, Jr., "Merchandise Management Accounting," in Frank M. Bass (ed.), Frontiers of Marketing Thought and Science (Chicago: American Marketing Association, 1958), p. 126.

traffic, (2) to match competitive offerings, or (3) to round out merchandise assortments.

   The Concept of Turnover.   The role of turnover as it relates to profitability in merchandising and pricing decisions has been discussed in nearly infinite detail in earlier parts of this text. It needs only to be pointed out in this section that merchandise management accounting procedures are strongly oriented to the concept of merchandise turnover. That is, merchandise management accounting emphasizes to the decision maker that *demand* for a good will affect *price. Price* in turn will affect *demand. Demand* will affect *costs* and, finally, in near circular fashion, *costs* will affect *price.* Once again, consider the example involving the major appliance. Suppose that pricing at $200, the department sells only four units per year. A more stringent competitor, however, prices the same item at $185 each and increases the number of units sold to 12. If each has an average investment in inventory of this item of two units, the turnover at the $200 price will be two, and at the $185 price, six.

   The significance of merchandise turnover cannot be overemphasized as a guide for merchandising decisions. To be truly meaningful, merchandise turnover ought to be related to item profitability and the sales velocity of the item. For many years an oversight in this respect caused department stores and other higher margin stores to lose significant amounts of volume in major and traffic appliance lines to discounters and others who were willing to sacrifice some margin in order to increase their rate of sales, and in the process generate a large number of absolute profit dollars. By selling four units of the major appliance at the $200 retail price, a controllable profit of $99.32 is generated (4 × $24.83—the controllable profit per unit). Yet, at the $185 selling price with a turnover of six (12 units are sold), a controllable profit of $135.84 is generated (12 × $11.32—the controllable profit per unit), which is clearly a better showing than the $200 price affords.

Return on Merchandise Investment. Another concept related to merchandise management accounting is that of profit, or return on merchandise investment. Merchandise management accounting stipulates that the most meaningful criterion for decision making is controllable profit as a return on merchandise investment.

Again, to use our previous example—at the $200 retail price with a turnover of two, four units were sold and the controllable profit generated was $99.32. The average investment at retail was $200 per unit, or $400. Thus, the return on merchandise investment was 24.83 per cent ($99.32 ÷ $400). At the $185 price, a controllable profit of $135.84 is generated on an average merchandise investment of $370. The return on merchandise investment is thus 36.71 per cent, which is a better return than that afforded by the $200 price.

Such a measure of profitability makes it possible to move easily to return on investment as a criterion for decision making, as discussed in Chapter 4. For example, assume that an item with an average investment of $40 carries a $12 contribution. This would be a 30 per cent return on merchandise investment. Assume, further, that the accounting records reveal that for every dollar in inventory investment, two additional dollars are required for other assets. Thus, $120 in investment is required. If the contribution margin of $12 is earned on $120, this is a 10 per cent return on total investment.

Merchandise management accounting is an attempt to formally incorporate many well-known and accepted retail management concepts into an overall framework for decision making at the item level. The adoption of the concept is alleged to produce important improvements in merchandising decision making and retail management thinking. Foremost among these changes are the following:

1. The gross margin concept is now completely removed.
2. Emphasis is thrown on dollar contribution and return on investment.
3. The use of percentages at the departmental level is greatly minimized, and the buyer is encouraged to think primarily in terms of dollar cost and dollar contribution.
4. Instead of merchandising principally to the tune of department-wide historical percentages, the buyer focuses his attention on the profit possibilities of individual items.
5. Comprehension of retail problems on the part of suppliers and on the part of the general public is enhanced.[18]

---

[18] McNair and May, op. cit., p. 122.

The Future of Merchandise
Management Accounting

At the time of its inception and early development in the mid 1950s, merchandise management accounting was highly touted as a near panacea for handling a vast range of merchandise management decisions, and especially pricing decisions at the item level. Here at long last, it was argued, was a set of techniques based upon sound management accounting logic that ought to produce more scientific retail management decisions. However, in terms of actual practice and adoption, merchandise management accounting appears to have offered more promise than substance. The concept has never been widely adopted. The scale of its actual usage has been extremely limited; even in several larger retail management systems where it was adopted early, considerable dissatisfaction arose in connection with its usage. Today, it is viewed by the typical practitioner as one of those interesting and desirable theoretical concepts, which in actual practice does not really deliver the results expected from its implementation and application.

Merchandise management accounting has intrigued the imagination of the academician since its earliest inception. The ideas of controllable profit, cost patterns, and turnover are economically and managerially sound. Such an approach appeared at long last to offer the decision maker the vehicle for marginal cost pricing and other applications of marginalistic decision making in the retail firm. Yet, actual experience has not, to any significant degree, borne out these expectations.[19]

Specific Criticisms of Merchandise Management Accounting. The major criticism of merchandise management accounting is that it is difficult to implement and practice in retail stores. The major argument persists that it involves far too much data and bookkeeping and that the results obtained (in lieu of more conventional methods of decision making) do not justify these added efforts and costs.

Merchandise management accounting does require considerable data and calculations, and it does necessitate the use of both expense center accounting and production unit accounting. Perhaps with a greater substitution of electronic methods of calculation for more human and physical methods, this argument will no longer seem so important. However, there is much argument to the effect that it is not the time, effort, nor difficulty of implementing merchandise management accounting that is its major drawback. Rather, some contend that there are inherent deficiencies in the concept that limit its usefulness and application.[20] These deficiencies fall into several categories. One of the major deficiencies of merchandise management accounting is its dependence upon cost patterns. Some have argued that the cost pattern is not an accurate cost compilation. One critic has argued that

---

[19] See Roger Dickinson, "Marginalism in Retailing: The Lessons of a Failure," *Journal of Business*, Vol. XXXIX, No. 3 (July 1966), pp. 353–358; and Peggy Heim, "Merchandise Management Accounting: A Retailing Experiment in Explicit Marginal Calculation," *Quarterly Journal of Economics*, Vol. 77, No. 4 (November 1963), pp. 671–675.

[20] Cross, op. cit., pp. 21–29.

the use of these patterns, is "analogous to measuring tree trunks with micrometers: an interesting but costly procedure with somewhat dubious prognosis for practical application of the results."[21] This is simply a way of saying that because of the difficulties of computing them, cost patterns are not likely to reflect the accuracy and validity needed for exceedingly "fine tuned" decisions. It is argued that users of merchandise management accounting must be careful to investigate the derivation of the individual costs in each pattern and also to consider carefully the adaptability of the patterns to unique merchandising problems. Too often, it is argued, there is the danger that once cost patterns have been determined and accepted they will be slavishly seized upon and used in perpetuity, never to be challenged again.

Another weakness of merchandise management accounting (according to its critics) is that it ignores the *time element* in merchandising. This is not a strong argument. When used prudently, merchandise management accounting emphasizes three important dimensions of retail merchandising: *time, cost,* and *volume.* Volume itself implicitly recognizes the time dimension, as does the turnover concept. It is true that the secret of a price-cutting operation is not necessarily involved with cost, though this is certainly important, but rather with cost incurred per unit of time. Another important weakness of merchandise management accounting is that it tends to neglect some important implicit costs, especially in price line analysis. For example, profitability studies based upon merchandise management accounting techniques applied to different price lines generally tend to reflect that higher price lines are more profitable than lower price lines. However, merchandise management accounting does not impute space costs to the various lines and, given the tendency to allow (1) more space for higher price lines and (2) better quality space to higher price lines, these findings are not too unlikely. Techniques other than merchandise management accounting place a greater emphasis on space expense and rate of sale and are likely to produce more meaningful merchandising results.[22]

Merchandise management accounting has also been criticized because it suggests the substitution of one benchmark—controllable profit as a return on merchandise investment—for another benchmark—profit as a per cent of sales. Thus, one critic has stated, "whenever an average is used as a guidepost, there is a tendency for the merchant to accept only those items above average in contribution and to reject those below average. This has the effect of raising the average and thus starting a cycle that continues to spiral upward until the goals become unattainable."[23] Two comments would appear warranted. First, the above statement is a value judgment and not necessarily true. For competitive reasons, merchants can hardly afford to indulge themselves in such luxury. On the other hand, previous goals in practical operations often become standards by which to evaluate performance. The retail merchant's grasp often exceeds his reach, but he is inces-

[21] Joseph S. Freidlander, "Perspectives on Merchandise Management Accounting," *The New York Retailer*, Vol. 10, No. 5 (December 1957), p. 31.

[22] See Appendix D in John W. Wingate and E. O. Schaller, *Techniques of Retail Merchandising*, Prentice-Hall, Inc., Englewood Cliffs, N.J., 1950.

[23] Cross, op. cit., p. 28.

santly trying to improve his operation by beating last year's figures, improving his sales per square foot, his merchandise turnover, and so on. Why not also try to improve his performance, measured by controllable profit as a return on merchandise investment?

Finally, and not to be dismissed so lightly, is the charge that merchandise management accounting is just another cost oriented pricing approach. It certainly rests heavily on a cost basis and decision making utilizing this concept is heavily cost oriented. Therefore, decision making that focuses on merchandise management accounting concepts may lean so heavily on costs that demand might scarcely be considered. Demand becomes an integral part of price and merchandising decisions only when the decision maker begins thinking about possible alternative levels of sales that might be generated at different cost and volume levels. Merchandise management accounting should not lead the decision maker to place an overemphasis on the cost side of the demand-supply equation. The astute manager should always consider the effects of his price and merchandising decisions on consumer reaction, the motive force in any demand consideration.

It may be safe to conclude that merchandise management accounting is still a potent weapon in the retail manager's strategic arsenal. This writer, for one, would argue that it really never got a sufficient and prolonged trial. The fact is that the concept may have emerged prematurely—that is, before our technological and electronic devices were sufficiently developed to handle a concept requiring so much data manipulation and record keeping. The concept has not been abandoned and discarded completely. At the moment, it remains somewhat dormant, waiting to be rediscovered and refined.

In summary, management accounting concepts such as expense classification, expense center accounting, production unit accounting, and merchandise management accounting have as their aim the objective of improving the overall performance profitability and efficiency of the retail management system. These objectives will be accomplished, at least in part, by adopting some method of expense classification and establishing expense centers with definite clear-cut lines of authority and responsibility. To these concepts must be added the techniques which formulate units of measurement with which to evaluate the productivity of expense generating centers. Sound control requires that only those expenses within the regulation of revenue producing departments should be assigned to those departments; that criteria for effective merchandising decisions be implemented whenever possible at the item level; and that key management decisions be oriented to this level and evaluated on the basis of return on merchandise investment or other, broader, return on investment concepts.

QUESTIONS FOR STUDY, REFLECTION, AND REVIEW

1. Name the three general purposes that an accounting system must serve and point out which areas are emphasized by managerial accounting.
2. What effect does the evaluation of closing inventory have upon net profits in the current accounting period and the next accounting period, when the closing inventory is understated and then overstated?

3. What is the desired way to value closing inventory and what is the general decision rule to follow?
4. Why should a retail firm adopt the retail method as opposed to the cost method of inventory valuation?
5. Briefly describe merchandise management accounting.
6. Explain how or why merchandise management accounting has grown out of the need for retail merchants and decision makers to *reorient* their decision making.
7. If the basic aim of merchandise management accounting is to improve dollar profits through a better interpretation and determination of costs, why has it been slow to develop?
8. How is the *turnover* concept related to merchandise management accounting, and how does it aid merchandising decisions?
9. What are the alleged important improvements in merchandising decision making and retail management thinking caused by the adoption of the merchandise management accounting concept?
10. Briefly, what is the objective of management accounting concepts?

NINE

RETAILING: INDUSTRY OF FERMENT AND CHANGE

21

the changing nature of retail merchandising

Retail merchandising is one of the most dynamic and responsive of industries. It is in a near constant state of change, adaptation, and accommodation. Retailing in many respects is a reactive industry—it reacts and accommodates to all kinds of wide-ranging social and economic changes—population growth in certain age groups, mobility of people, suburban living, changes in personal income, consumer credit uses, and many others. Furthermore, retailing is responsive and must accommodate to changes in technology and changes in the general culture of our society—energy shortages, urban renewal, equal opportunity, women's liberation, changing modes of travel and of living.

The retailer's general responses to such pressures and changes in the environment can be readily traced throughout the recent history of retail merchandising. For example, consider the following:

1. Stores are being relocated throughout various geographic locations, some in suburban and outlying areas, but also many are being reestablished in the downtown central business district. Whenever there are shifts in people's location, their places of residence, work, and wherever people congregate for almost any purpose, there will be retail facilities to serve them.
2. There has been a recent double-barreled trend toward both the establishment of larger and smaller stores. The larger stores are usually department stores or branches, general merchandise stores, or large super-supermarkets, sometimes called family centers. The smaller stores are often specialty and limited-line stores, which are sometimes called boutique (boo-tĕk) stores, and which emphasize thematic merchandising or merchandising to a theme.

3. There has been a constant tendency toward store improvement, modernization, revitalization, and the recycling of older buildings in order to update them to meet the high aesthetic demands of today's critical shopper.
4. All kinds of changes and restructuring of organizations have been undertaken in retailing to make the administrative and operating organization more responsive to both the rising level of retail customers' and retail employees' expectations.
5. Convulsive changes in styles of operation for retail stores have been witnessed. Hours of work, flexibility scheduling, and night and Sunday openings have been adopted by many merchandisers.
6. The frenetic effort to find new, exciting merchandise lines to meet the widening expectations of today's affluent consumer goes on with an increasing emphasis on leisure time merchandise, antiques, art objects, and a wide range of quality imported items. All this tends to swell the already well-established tendency toward broadened merchandise lines and scrambled merchandising.
7. The rising level of operating expense ratios and decreasing gross margins and profit levels have caused retailers to respond by a more widespread application of new technology to control inventory shortages and to better manage and control overall inventory levels by the use of closed circuit monitoring devices and information retrieval and information processing equipment.
8. Finally, countless new forms of organization such as franchising have emerged to meet the capital needs of those wishing to grow and expand rapidly and the needs of the smaller manager-entrepreneur. The increasing development of nonstore retailing, telephone and catalog selling, mail-order merchandising, and vending machine selling are all responses, answers, if you will, to the increasing and changing demands of today's aware and affluent consumer.

what does it mean?

What it means is that retailing changes, and the reason it changes is because it responds, reacts, and accommodates to changes in the environment in which it operates. This environment consists of people; the customers of retailing organizations; the technological, social, economic, and demographic forces which bear upon people's lives and ultimately affect the range and nature of their choices—where they work, what they do, how they play, where they shop, and what they buy. Retailing changes, but in one respect, no matter how much it changes, it remains the same. How? By being ever ready, as it has throughout its history, to serve its customers, and by being perpetually that important link which connects manufacturing and production enterprises with the consumer. Retailing has persistently been the means whereby America was democratized by stylish, yet low-cost clothing. Retailing institutions are consumer palaces in which millions of nationwide customers can continue to fill their needs for the ever-widening range of demanded and sought-after commodities. As these needs change, so too will retail merchandising.

an industry of contrasts

It is not easy to generalize about retail merchandising. Retailing is an industry of contrasts. These contrasts are related to size, location, management style, and organization arrangement. Some stores are independents, some chains, some franchised operations which are a kind of hybrid, possessing qualities of both the chain and independent. Some stores are very small, highly specialized, and limited in scope. Others are merchandising giants covering acres of ground, employing multitudes of people, specialists in all areas. Some retailing does not even involve a retail store. Increasingly, a larger and larger portion of retail sales are being made not through retail stores but through direct-selling organizations, by mail-order, by catalog, and perhaps in the very near future by video-data phones or by cable television piped directly into the consumer's home. A part of the contrasts in retailing must be explained in terms of the dispersion of methods of retail selling. Fixed location stores selling over the counter will remain unquestionably the most important method of retail distribution, but changes already discussed will accelerate the growth and development of much nonstore retailing.

The student of retailing must never overlook the importance of diversity. Diversity on the demand side of the marketing equation calls forth and necessitates diversity on the supply side. Different market segments, each with a different set of demand characteristics, will call forth different kinds of retail distribution facilities, and such a condition demands careful management analysis and decisions concerning the market positioning of a particular store. Some of this demand diversity will call for increased depersonalization of retailing. A busy, active, mobile, overstressed population will in part demand an increase in nonstore retailing. Many will be reluctant to leave the sanctuary of the home, the office, or the subway to visit a retail store. Instead, they may choose to shop by catalog, by mail, or by telephone, or to have a salesperson call on them directly at home or at their office. Others may be more price-oriented and thus seek the mass instore merchandiser or maybe prefer the catalog order house. Still others may shun the nonstore methods and seek out the novel, the new, the exciting and stimulating shopping places of the community. For them, style, fashion, personal attention, and consultative advice by the sales personnel, are much more reinforcing than the plastic artificial sameness, the Sominex atmosphere, of so many mass merchandising institutions.

scope of chapter

Now that we have dramatized the importance of change and underscored it in terms of contrast, dispersion, and diversity, let us examine in this chapter some of the important elements of change that are characteristic of retail merchandising in the late 1970s and those which are likely to affect and shape the destiny of retailing well into the early period of the 1980s. We shall explore, therefore, three major and significant trends which are largely operational in nature. These are (1) franchising, which is both operational and organizational; (2) nonstore retailing, which is concerned with a whole range of both older and newer approaches to retail distribution; and (3) thematic merchandising, which looks at the tendency of some retailers to generate important and significant consumer responses by merchandising to special categories of consumers in terms of *themes*. These themes almost always have certain style and fashion implications and involve generally high price/quality relationships.

franchising operations

Throughout the late 1960s and early 1970s there was a virtual groundswell of retailing activity and expansion of franchised operations. Franchising is in some respects a rather simple and yet complicated organizational and operating arrangement. Franchising involves a legal contractual agreement between two parties, one known as a *franchisor* and the other as a *franchisee*. The franchisor for certain monetary considerations licenses the franchisee to carry on certain activities. Let us look at a simple, though not unrealistic, example. Suppose Joe McIver, a mythical student at Pacific Northwestern University, decides to go into business for himself by opening up a hamburger, fries, and shake shoppe. He opens his establishment, streamlines the production of hamburgers, creates a special, secret-recipe sauce, learns a new way of creating crisp, nonsoggy French fries, packages his commodities uniquely for carryout sales, and widely and successfully promotes the name of his firm and his principal product, the "Fantastic McI. Hamburger" along the theme, "You deserve to try the Fantastic McI." Flushed with success, McIver wishes to expand. However, in spite of his success, he suffers both a capital shortage and a lack of a highly motivated, trustworthy, experienced person to run his next unit. What can he do? He can sell a franchise to an interested person with sufficient capital, whom McIver and his existing staff can train. The next unit is a carbon copy of the first, and situated in a strategic location. It is completely standardized in terms of appearance, style and method of operation, and uniformity of product. The new franchise is sold to and operated by Joe Davis. McIver is the *franchisor* and Davis is the *franchisee*. What McIver sold Davis is a franchise and all that is entailed in a franchised operation.

Franchising Defined

Put more formally, franchising is a method of organizing and doing business which permits the rather rapid expansion of a successful venture without the necessity of investing large sums of money and without the necessity of going to a strictly chain store type of operation. The franchisee is in part a semi-independent business person who puts up his money in return for technical assistance and operating know-how, provided by the franchisor. The franchisor receives for his technical assistance and operating know-how remuneration in several forms. He also receives or expects to receive a highly devoted, motivated, and committed individual who in his own self-interest and the possibility of economic reward will work to promote the welfare of the business so that both franchisor and franchisee mutually benefit. Franchising is one of those delightful situations whereby, through a kind of mutual cooperation or transactional process, both parties come out ahead. It doesn't always work that way, but again, oftentimes it does.

Franchising as a method of business operation is a situation whereby a continuing transactional relationship is created in which a franchisor provides both a licensed right to do business and supporting assistance in operations, such as merchandising, management, organization, training and control, in exchange for a monetary consideration from the franchisee.

The History and Development of Franchising

Franchising, although it has undergone a recent mushrooming of growth, has as an organizational and operating form been around for a long time, supposedly since the Middle Ages.[1] It emerged in the United States just after the Civil War when the Singer Sewing Machine Company used franchising as a way of expanding sales facilities and as a means of controlling the behavior of the operators of these outlets. Franchising has been extremely popular in the United States in the sale and distribution of automobiles through franchised dealers or agencies, and petroleum companies have used franchising extensively in the sale and distribution of gasoline and related commodities.

Vertical vs. Horizontal Franchising

The kind of franchising described and used by the automobile manufacturers and the large petroleum refiners is a form of *vertical franchising*. It is called vertical because it involves operations on two or more different planes or levels of distribution. For example, the manufacturer of the automobile seeks retail outlets and what is franchised is the right to sell the manufacturer's products, not to produce them. However, more recently franchising has expanded through a form of *horizontal franchising* whereby retail sellers of products and services license or franchise others on the same plane or level of distribution to duplicate these services in some other geographical region or territory. This kind of franchising is known as a *service-sponsor-retailer franchise* in which the *franchisor,* who is the service-sponsor, sells and licenses the franchisee an established method for operating a retail business. It is in this area of service-sponsor-retailer franchise or horizontal franchising that recent growth and expansion has been

---

[1] Ernest Henderson, Sr., "Franchising Yesterday," in *Franchising Today,* Matthew Bender, Albany, N.Y., 1966–1967, p. 239.

so phenomenal. Much of this expansion of franchising has occurred in non-traditional areas such as the following:

1. Coin-operated laundries and self-service dry cleaning establishments.
2. Part-time manpower and assistance agencies.
3. Specialty food and beverage retailing.
4. Ready-to-eat carryout food facilities.
5. Tool and equipment rental.
6. Automobile, truck, and trailer rental units.
7. Carpet, upholstery, and general cleaning services.

The American consumer may drive a car rented from a franchised outlet, move across country in a truck which is rented from a franchised agent, eat his meals in franchised restaurants, and stay in a hotel or motel operated as a franchised unit. The range of products and the retail outlets that serve consumers may increasingly be franchised operations. To a great extent, the increasing success of franchising may well be linked to the increased mobility, restlessness, and changing life styles of American consumers—highly dependent on automobile travel and utilization, activity-oriented, on the move and on the go, who desire quick service and instant response to needs related to cleaning, eating, travel, leisure, sleeping, and a wide range of other activities. Franchising may owe its success in part to the increased emphasis on customer services rather than on goods, and to a diminishing interest in ownership of goods as opposed to simple utilization of goods. Ownership often means more responsibility. Utilization may mean having all the amenities of ownership without ownership commitment, such as long-term payments, repair, maintenance, and depreciation.

Current Significance

According to projected figures, sales of products and services through franchising reached $155 billion in 1975, up over 30 per cent from 1970 figures.[2] There were in 1975 approximately 500,000 franchised outlets, an increase of nearly 10 per cent over 1970. Over 1,200 corporations had franchised operations in 1975, and franchising was being conducted in nearly 100 Standard Industrial Classifications (SIC). Franchising exists in many forms and in many areas of product and service distribution. McDonald's, A & W Rootbeer, K O America Campgrounds, Holiday Inns, and Shakey's Pizza Parlors are franchised operations with which students are likely to be most familiar. As we shall learn, franchising has impacted significantly not only on consumers generally, but is also playing a significant role in the operations of many retail firms and their methods of doing business. It is a unique form of organization and ownership with a strong appeal to both developers of business ideas and to those who would like to participate

[2] These figures are the author's projections, based upon statistics found in *Franchising in the Economy*, 1972–1974, United States Department of Commerce, Washington, D.C., 1974, p. 1.

as semi-independent owner/operators of individual units as part of a larger franchised system.

The Range of Service-Sponsor Retailer Franchises

There exists a wide range of business opportunities for the aspiring franchisee. Depending upon a person's ambitions, the amount of his capital, and other factors, he can find a wide range of franchising opportunities. Table 21-1 depicts several of these various kinds of opportunities, and shows the capital requirements likely to be involved and some of the main elements of the franchisor's package of service.

As can be seen from Table 21-1, there is a wide range of franchising op-

TABLE 21-1   Franchising Opportunities—Franchisee Requirements and Franchisor's Package of Service

FRANCHISE OFFERING TO CUSTOMERS	ITEMS IN THE FRANCHISE PACKAGE	FINANCIAL REQUIREMENTS
Holiday Inn: Food and hospitality services	Training for management and key employees, workshops and retraining conferences, promotional and operational services.	Total investment, approximately $1,500,000. Royalty payments of 3% of gross room service.
Shakey's Pizza Parlor: Pizza, beer, entertainment	Complete training and instruction by Shakey's Corporate Training Personnel at Shakey's University. All skills needed to create and operate Shakey's Pizza Parlor. Promotional and total operating services.	Total investment, $220,000. For full-scale operation, approximately $35,000 cash requirements. Franchise royalty payment of 5½% of monthly food sales.
McDonald's Hamburgers: Fast food, French fries	Training at Hamburger University. Follow-up retraining and update seminars—complete, comprehensive operations manual, broad training materials by field service staff.	Total investment, $140,000 including $75,000 cash requirement. Service fee of 3% monthly of net gross sales, and rental of 8.5% of monthly gross sales.
Rent-All stores and United Rent-All	Management training, inventory and control planning, merchandising, and accounting consulting service. Comprehensive manual of operations.	$25,000 to $50,000. Total investment, with $10,000 to $15,000 cash requirement. Royalty payment of 4% to 5% on monthly sales.
Management or help assistance agencies—Kelly Girl	Personnel selection assistance service, training and procedural assistance. Advertising and promotional assistance. Accounting methods and tax assistance.	$10,000 to $25,000 investment. Usually no more than $10,000 cash requirement. Sign rental and royalty fee of 5% of monthly billings.

portunities—something for nearly everyone. Certainly franchising creates a retailing possibility which combines in an unusual way the know-how and expertise supplied by the franchisor and the eager willingness to work hard and the desire for a profitable growth and self-employment opportunity supplied by the franchisee. Such a combined business system can produce good results for both members of the franchising team. In franchising the dual ideas of democracy and free enterprise come together very closely, and franchising makes it more possible for a number of enterprising business persons to become independent and self-sufficient.

The Franchisee's Success

From the franchisee's point of view, franchising offers help. What he receives is almost a total merchandising operations support system. Most who contemplate undertaking a franchise are looking for a way to have their own business, but they may feel either managerially or financially deficient. Franchisees are looking for opportunities to do better financially, to be on their own and to manage their own affairs, to be freer and more independent. They attain these objectives only in part. In many instances, the constraints and controls imposed by the franchise contract rule out anything approaching total autonomy, and in some instances the written franchise agreement favors a franchisor much more than the franchisee. However, there exists a degree of distributive justice between franchisor and franchisee. Each benefits from the association.

In many instances, businesses begun under franchised arrangements are more successful and have a lower mortality rate than their independent counterparts. Small businesses usually fail for two major reasons: (1) Inept management and (2) lack of financial resources. Franchisors provide the management skill and they are loathe to accept franchisees whose capital resources are inadequate. The success of the franchise is therefore a function of two factors: (1) the support facilities provided by the franchisor; and (2) the skill, drive, motivation, and effectiveness of the franchisee.

A franchisee's success is never assured, but the risks are minimized by the franchisor's contribution toward such critical decision areas as outlet location, based upon adequate demand analysis; the franchisor's assessment of a given franchisee's management potential; the sophisticated, in-depth technical training and assistance provided by the franchisor; and the long-range continuing management assistance and audits provided by parent company personnel.

To attain these support facilities the franchisee must submit himself and his outlet to rigorous examinations, on-site visits, accounting and general management audits, and a tight degree of overall regimentation.

The Point of View of the Franchisor

The franchisor as well as the franchisee has profit expectations. The franchisor's revenue is generated by payments made by the franchisee. These payments vary in kind, but often consist of an initial, nonrefundable fee. However, sometimes the fee is refunded over time if a unit is highly successful and well managed. This initial fee is oftentimes as much as $10,000, and given its magnitude, it tends to discourage all but the truly interested and well-financed applicant. Franchisors also receive rental fees for the use of equipment, supplies, and materials, and of course, rental income when the building and land are owned by the parent company. Of course, the main income generated by the franchisor is from royalty payments that the franchisee makes for the use of the company name, advertising, logos on supplies, etc. Sometimes franchisors receive other forms of income from the franchisee for the sale of territorial rights, and increasingly, many franchisors are sharing more directly in the profits of the franchisee through part-ownership of the franchised unit.[3]

Clearly then, the perceived advantages of franchising from the franchisor's point of view are concerned with his ability to expand rapidly and thus exploit a well-developed market opportunity and a differentiated enterprise. A franchisor can often make more money by franchising his units rather than by direct ownership, because the operating expenses and other capital costs are borne by the franchisee and further revenues are generated through franchising fees, royalties, and other payments. Finally, a critical advantage from the franchisor's perspective is that a better quality, higher caliber, more strongly motivated unit manager is obtained because the managers are also the owners of the business and their semi-independent status usually means a better performance through self-interest.

The Future of Franchising

Franchising is not a panacea. Nothing is perfect and even though success breeds success, it sometimes breeds and sows the seeds of its own demise. The rapid period of franchise growth may have already tapered off. Many who entered franchising, both franchisee and franchisor, have failed. Some industries and some communities are already saturated with too many franchised units. A steady-state economy will only support so many of any given kind of institution whether franchised, chain, or independent. Franchising has not been without its "rip off" artists or its financial charlatans whose sole purpose was to make a fast buck by fraudulently misrepresenting the profitability or the financial requirements of operating a franchise unit. Some developers were glib talk artists who built quick fortunes on a paper empire, unsupported by either physical assets or managerial know-how. It is to be hoped, however, that this period of exploitation has passed. Many strong relationships have now been forged between the franchisor and the franchisee, each recognizing the interdependent nature of the other's contribution and cooperation.

In the future, two factors may tend to depress the continued growth and development of the retailing franchise industry. First, there is some possibility that the courts may interpret a franchised operation to mean that the franchisee is the legal agent of the franchisor. For the franchisor, this would

---

[3] Milton Wall, "Sources of Revenue to the Franchisor and Their Strategic Implications," *Journal of Retailing*, Vol. 44, No. 4 (Winter 1968–1969), pp. 14–20. (Author's note: This entire issue of the *Journal of Retailing* is devoted exclusively to franchising.)

have staggering and far-reaching financial and legal implications, the nature of which could literally spell disaster for the future of franchising. Already, the courts and many state legislatures are working to tilt the balance of advantage via the franchise agreement more to the franchisee and less to the franchisor. Should this continue, a point may be reached whereby franchising loses its strong appeal as both a form of organization and operation. Second, franchising has been too successful in some respects to the point that the franchisor is willing to buy back the franchise and operate the outlet as a wholly owned unit. Should this trend continue, franchisors will more and more become companies which own and operate their own chain units. In some systems already, income from the small number of units either partially or wholly owned exceeds the income generated from a much larger number of franchised outlets. Primarily, franchisors are motivated toward becoming wholly owned chains by a desire for greater profits and a wish to use more directly the management skills, technical assistance, and operating expertise which they have acquired.

Whatever franchising's specific future, its development has already had a strong impact on retail merchandising. The quality of operation of many smaller-scale retail enterprises has been improved through franchising, and the high quality of service and operating efficiency of many franchises have caused smaller independents to emulate their methods of operation. Even the larger chain organizations have, given the competitive nature of some franchised operations, been forced to update their facilities and to improve the overall nature of their operations in order to remain competitive.

nonstore retailing

Somehow, retailing always seems to create the notion of the retail store. The supermarket, the department store, the men's or women's specialty shoppes are the retailing institutions upon which our basic images and perceptions concerning retailing are focused. Yet, nonstore retailing—merchandising directly to ultimate consumers without the benefit or the intermediary physical store facility—is an increasingly important way of doing business for many retailers. Our changing life styles, increased mobility, and hyperactive nature are bringing about important changes in consumer shopping and purchasing habits and patterns. A response to these changes by retailers, in part at least, is a number of alternative shopping-purchase options, many of which lie in the realm of nonstore retailing.

Important new growth and profit opportunities are being discovered each day by enterprising and imaginative people who find new ways of satisfying customer shopping needs. It is important to understand that a person can go shopping without necessarily visiting a retail store. Merchandise can be ordered by telephone, a catalog can be examined, merchandise can be displayed on closed-circuit television, a salesperson can visit the customer at his home or office, or merchandise can be purchased directly from a machine by paying cash, and maybe very soon now by inserting one's bank credit card.

In-store, over-the-counter retailing still remains the principal means by which goods are sold at retail—well over 90 per cent of the total dollar volume of goods is distributed through retail stores. Yet nonstore retailing, involving the alternatives just mentioned, is growing in importance and constitutes an important dimension of retail merchandising which must not be overlooked.

The distinction between in-store and nonstore retailing is not as tidy as one might desire. Much merchandise is sold, for example, by telephone and mail-order from the retail store premises. Thus, we must be careful not to push the distinction between store and nonstore merchandising too far. Conceptually, the distinction is shown in Figure 21-1.

As Figure 21-1 shows, nonstore retailing takes two major forms: personal nonstore selling and nonpersonal nonstore selling. As you would surmise, the basic difference between these two forms of nonstore selling is the minimal personal, face-to-face, or oral contact between seller and buyer in the nonpersonal, nonstore retailing category.

Again to illustrate the untidy distinction between store and nonstore retailing, consider the illustration contained in Table 21-2.

Table 21-2 shows a matrix of combined selling techniques which may be employed in either or both in-store or nonstore environments. For example, a salesperson in a retail store during periods of slack business activity may be instructed to call prospective customers and suggest items which may be featured at a discounted or a sale price. There are also situations whereby trained telephone salespeople sell products and services directly to customers without having a retail store facility. Another illustration should suffice to make our point. Salespersons are sometimes asked to make direct visits and canvass sales on a door-to-door basis, even though their work is traditionally and customarily cast in the framework of in-store selling services. Other direct selling organizations have no retail facilities at all—only a sales organization and warehouses out of which purchased merchandise is shipped.

In the next several pages, we shall explore this often overlooked dimen-

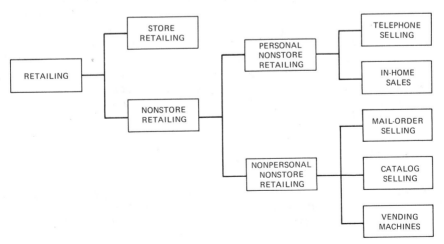

FIGURE 21-1 Conceptual distinction between store and nonstore retailing.

TABLE 21-2 A Matrix of Techniques Involved in Both Store and Nonstore Retailing

SELLING TECHNIQUES	NONSTORE/ PERSONAL	NONSTORE/ NONPERSONAL	IN-STORE
Telephone selling	✓		✓
In-home sales	✓		✓
Mail-order		✓	✓
Catalog sales		✓	✓
Vending machines		✓	✓

sion of retail merchandising along the lines suggested by the diagram in Figure 21-1.

Personal, Nonstore Retailing

Personal, nonstore retailing is of two major types, telephone sales and direct selling in the customer's home or office. Once again, it should be emphasized that *personal* connotes either a face-to-face or oral transactional process.

Telephone Selling. Telephone selling may involve either selling from a retail store, or from a firm which has no store itself but acts in behalf of a store, or it may involve simply a person or persons who attempt to sell merchandise via telephone, and when purchases are made the items of merchandise are delivered from a central storage or warehouse facility.

Telephone selling which does not involve a store facility has not yet come of age, and thus accounts for only a very small volume of retail sales. However, telephone selling in conjunction with a retail store facility is a rapidly growing merchandising activity. The telephone is a most effective sales tool. Increasingly, retail firms are planning to make the telephone as much a medium of advertising and selling as are newspapers, radios, television, and billboards. Telephone selling is increasing for a number of reasons. For example, direct mail costs have soared and the price of personal selling in retail stores has risen rapidly. Yet the telephone is a relatively low-cost medium and it is very personal. The telephone is becoming a major marketing tool. Sears, Roebuck and Co., for example, has had a phone operation for nearly two decades to remind people to use their catalogs or to visit their retail stores. Telephone selling thus complements Sears' other forms of merchandising activity. Sears has over 700 operators who call regular charge customers and inform them of coming sales and special price discounts in featured commodities.[4] Sears executives report

---

[4] "Selling by Phone Is Ringing the Bell," *Business Week*, November 11, 1972, p. 159.

that in-home customers appreciate the suggestions and consider the calls a special service. Items that sell well to women over the phone are children's wear, linens, curtains, and cookware. Men respond to such items as tires, automobile accessories, batteries, tools, and sporting goods.

Why Customers Respond. Customers respond to telephone selling or solicitation for a number of reasons. In some cases, they may have already been alerted to a purchase possibility by the firm's catalog, by a direct mailing piece, or by other print or electronic media advertising. Given their higher state of awareness they may be receptive to suggestion or reminder selling by telephone, especially if the telephone user is well trained in the procedure.

Many customers consider the telephone a highly effective device for personal communication and as a means of transacting business. Some customers, because of illness or disability, simply are not mobile and cannot visit the store and thereby rely heavily on the telephone. Other customers lack transportation, do not like to drive to a trading center or dislike the congestion related to parking or driving. Others simply dislike store crowds or dealing with salespersons. Some customers, not too surprisingly, feel threatened by aggressive sales personnel and like the comfort and convenience of shopping from their home by telephone.

Retailers increasingly are moving toward more telephone solicitation. It is an effective way of increasing the efficiency of their in-store sales personnel. Each day there are usually slack periods when customer in-store traffic is slow and when housekeeping and merchandise inventory chores are caught up. These are the periods that can be filled effectively by shifting efforts to telephone solicitation. Furthermore, each telephone sale or store visit that is added as a result of such effort is an incremental merchandising plus. Each sale thus obtained is added or plus revenue and, of course, plus profit. It may be a significant profit too, especially if such a sale does not add appreciably to the direct costs of attaining it. Telephone solicitation is an important means of complementing the firm's advertising and its overall promotional effort. A well-trained telephone salesperson is a means of making friends and customers for the store, another important support system and a response to changing customer needs and expectations.

Developing Effective Telephone Selling Strategy. There are a few simple rules which retail firms follow in establishing a telephone selling program and, it should be pointed out, such a program must be coordinated with all the other aspects of the firm's merchandising strategy if optimal effectiveness is to be attained. Here are a few guidelines which have proved to be effective:[5]

1. *Develop a telephone program.* Such a program is a schedule of activities or an advance plan concerned with exactly which accounts will be called and with what frequency.

[5] These suggestions are adapted from John H. Rosenheim, "For Openers, Try the Telephone," *The Marketing Magazine,* Vol. 109, No. 19 (October 1972) , p. 9.

2. *Set telephone sales objectives.* Be sure that a well-conceived plan of what you plan to do is established before the call is made. Upon reaching your party:
   a. *Clear time to talk.* Ask if it is convenient for the person to talk now. If not, courteously dismiss yourself and call back later.
   b. *Find a need.* Try to uncover the customer's need. If you open with a message about an item and no interest is shown, ask the customer if there is any commodity she may be planning to buy about which you could offer her some information.
   c. *Build desire.* Remember the call is to open the sale. Offer the customer a means to satisfy needs. Talk about your credit terms or about special sale prices or special purchase merchandise.
   d. *Closure.* Make something positive happen. Ask the customer to give you an order or ask to send the merchandise out on approval or at least ask the customer to visit your store the next time she is in your shopping neighborhood. Beware of using pressure, but be ready to offer help and general assistance that is cheerful, positive, and upbeat.
3. *Plan follow-up activities.* Some phone calls, especially for big ticket items such as appliances, televisions, stereo components, or automobiles, should be followed up by visits by personal salesmen or at least by a direct mailing piece.
4. *Finally, periodically evaluate your telephone selling results.* Results should be evaluated not only in terms of sales contracts written, but in good will generated. Admittedly, this latter criterion is difficult to evaluate.

In-Home Selling. The home has characteristically been an important point-of-purchase throughout the history of retail merchandising. Earlier in our society, direct selling or door-to-door selling, as it is sometimes called, accounted for a significant portion of total retail sales. A wide spectrum of products was sold: fresh fruits and vegetables; milk and dairy products; bread and pastries; patent medicines such as salves, ointments, and other nostrums; clothing, tools, appliances, furniture; insurance, and many other commodities. Today, door-to-door selling continues as an important means of distributing some goods, but the frequency, range of goods, and general success of door-to-door selling as a per cent of total retail sales has diminished somewhat in importance, especially in relation to earlier periods.

However, the home is a desirable atmosphere for the buying and selling of services and commodities. It is a reinforcing and familiar environment for the customer-buyer and consequently such customers often feel less threatened and intimidated by an aggressive seller. Many customers are quite willing to have sellers call and visit with them in their home for the purpose of conducting a sales transaction. There are several reasons which support their inclination.[6] First, such direct-in-the-home selling situations mean that when other family members are present they too can be consulted about the merits of the proposed product. Second, some customers contend that because of their personal reluctance they would not neces-

---

[6] Marvin A. Jolson, "Direct Selling: Consumer vs. Salesman," *Business Horizons* (October 1972), pp. 87–96.

sarily have bought a given product had it not been brought to their homes and persuasively and effectively demonstrated by the salesman. Third, many customers prefer to try out the product and actually use it in the home before making the purchase commitment. Direct-in-the-home buying permits this kind of product use and evaluation. Finally, many customer-buyers see the home as an unhurried, casual shopping environment where they control what is happening. The home, for these customers, is a shopping-buying facility in which they can save time, money, and expense. The retail store, for some shoppers, is seen as an aversive place, a place to be shunned and avoided, a place where one encounters unfriendly, discourteous, and poorly trained sales personnel. The better-trained direct salesperson who calls upon the customer in her own familiar territory is perceived as a desirable alternative.

Seller Advantages. Direct-in-the-home selling may be a relatively low-cost form of retail distribution. Overhead and operating expenses associated with in-store selling are sometimes eliminated if not reduced. However, selling costs are often very high and considering other added costs of training, recruiting, and maintaining a staff of salespersons, direct-in-the-home selling sometimes can be costly to the point that operating expenses represent a substantial proportion of sales revenues. Nonetheless, many direct-selling companies still exist, and direct-in-the-home selling offers a desirable and often more profitable alternative to other means of retail distribution. There are few significant qualifications for entry, which means that not too many who desire to enter this field are deterred. Capital requirements are also not too formidable, and direct-in-the-home selling sometimes offers an opportunity for the salesman to work as little or as much as he wishes because the income is usually directly geared to produced results.

Direct selling has always had a somewhat tainted image; a reputation as a form of distribution in which the customer might best be reminded of the admonishment, *caveat emptor.* However, direct-in-the-home selling has cleaned up its image considerably in recent years, and through concerted efforts by direct-selling organizations to recruit and train a higher caliber salesperson, this form of distribution continues to be both valued and well received by many customers.

Forms of Direct Selling

Direct selling takes two major forms. One of these is called *route selling;* the other is *party selling.*

Route Selling. Route selling means selling to customers directly along a well-established delivery route. Such items as bread, milk and dairy products, or laundry and dry cleaning services are the most popular and well-recognized kinds of route selling. In some rural parts of the country, wagon distributors still operate so that a wide range of specialty products, general merchandise lines, and some dry groceries are sold along an established route directly to in-home customers. However, this kind of selling is a rapidly vanishing part of America. On the other hand, in some metropolitan areas, milk truck driver salesmen are increasing their earnings by placing general merchandise or specialty catalogs with their customers, and then picking up and delivering their customers' orders.

Party Selling. Party selling has been successfully employed as a form of in-home selling by such firms as Tupperware and Stanley Home Products. Goods sold by party plan sellers range from women's apparel and cosmetics to vacuum cleaners and mops. Beeline Fashions, for example, sells through fashion parties where sample wearing apparel is brought into the home on a portable clothing rack and shown informally. Health-More makes and sells a vacuum cleaner that is merchandised largely on an in-home party plan basis. Wigs, cosmetics, and many other products are successfully merchandised in this manner.

Avon, of course, is the leader in door-to-door selling of cosmetics and toiletries with annual company sales over \$1 billion. Avon uses some party plan arrangements through demonstrations in customers' homes.

The Future of Door-to-Door Selling

Door-to-door or direct-to-home selling is seriously affected by economic slumps. Because women are often the principal customers, increased levels in the general household budget usually mean a cutback by the housewife in these discretionary expenditures for cosmetic and toiletry goods. Furthermore, recent sociological changes may bode ill for in-home selling. More women are working and out of the house during the day. Then too, fewer women want to go out alone at night to work as salespersons and even more do not want to open their doors in the evening even to an Avon lady. Until recently, Avon had been generating nearly a 15 per cent per year annual increase in its sales volume. Now that increase has fallen just slightly below 8 per cent per year.

There is another aspect to be considered, however. Economic slumps and their resulting unemployment often make more full-time and part-time manpower available for direct-to-home selling. Even though crime is a deterrent, more women seeking employment can mean more women working in the direct-to-home selling occupation. Because sales volume is a linearly increasing function of the number of active salespeople, more people thus mean more potential volume.

Nonpersonal Nonstore Retailing

We shall discuss briefly three forms of nonpersonal nonstore retailing: mail-order retailing, catalog selling, and vending machines.

Mail-Order Selling. Many retailing organizations use direct-mail advertising, but this form of promotion should not be mistaken for mail-order selling. Direct-mail advertising is often employed by retail stores as a means of attracting customers to the store to purchase and shop, and it is used to encourage customers to order items by mail *from the store*. However, for our purposes we are discussing a form of selling and retail distribution which uses direct-mail to sell merchandise directly to consumers *by mail* and in which there is no retail store facility as such.

There are several reasons why mail-order selling has much general customer appeal. More important among these reasons are the following:

1. *Lower Prices.* Mail-order selling as a form of direct distribution can sometimes be an efficient, streamlined, and low-cost method of selling. Customers are often stimulated by the low selling prices which are, in many instances, the result of low overhead and low operating expense ratios.

2. *Uniqueness.* Many mail-order items that are merchandised successfully can attribute their success, in part at least, to the novelty of the item and the curiosity of the shopper. Items that are successfully merchandised by mail are often unique articles with unusual, reinforcing qualities and, in the case of some personal items, those which customers might desire but which might cause some embarrassment to buy in a conventional retail store.

3. *Convenience.* The foregoing statement underscores the importance of convenience. Many buyers, for reasons that are obvious and that have already been explained, wish to shop, buy, pay for, and use items in the privacy of the home environment. This eliminates all the problems associated with visiting and shopping in a store.

Problems of Mail-Order Selling. Mail-order selling continues to grow in popularity and in overall success in spite of some serious overriding problems.

One of these major problems is related to the mail service itself. The mails are increasingly getting the reputation of being slow and unreliable. It can take a week to ten days for a letter to get from one side of the city to another. Letters and packages are often lost or arrive damaged in transit.

It is also difficult for a buyer to return items which he has purchased by mail, and other adjustments are equally difficult. There have been some problems with fraud and misrepresentation, such as an ad which read, "Complete sewing machine kit $3.98" but turned out to be a needle, thread, and thimble.

Mail costs have soared during the past 5 years and are likely to increase even more in the future. This will raise operating costs and, of course, the selling price of the commodities sold.

Finally, mail-order selling is a more sophisticated kind of merchandising effort. The products themselves must be promotable by mail, and must be mailable, dependable, reliable, and somewhat exclusive. The control feature of success concerning mail-order selling is the design of the advertisement itself. The ad must do the complete selling job, which means it must create awareness, build interest, desire, conviction, and make the sale. Furthermore, there are the attendant problems of placing the ad in the right media—either sending it direct to the ultimate customer, which means the seller must either build for himself or purchase his mailing list, or knowing what other media, such as radio, television, newspapers, or magazines to employ.

Catalog Sales. Catalogs have often been alluded to by customers as *wish books* and well they are for many users. Sears, Montgomery Ward, J. C. Penney, and many others have successfully combined catalog selling with their in-store merchandising activity. Sears, for example, prints and distributes nearly 17 million catalogs a year.

There are various forms of catalog selling. Some combine direct selling with in-store merchandising. Some retailers are successful merchandisers without benefit of stores at all. And finally, a recent development that is gaining widespread merchandising acclaim is the catalog store, which we shall examine in some detail.

Catalog selling without a corresponding store operation or with limited store facilities is widespread in many lines of distribution. Herter's and Cabela's in the sporting goods field are well known. There are other firms in the general merchandise categories such as Great Western Distributors, and many others.

Catalog selling is successful to the extent it is for primarily the same reasons that contribute to the success of mail-order selling. Catalog selling and mail-order selling are similar in many respects. It should be no surprise to students of retailing that merchandise has strong reinforcing qualities and the catalog is an effective way of illustrating and dramatizing the significance of certain goods.

From the standpoint of the seller, catalog selling offers an excellent opportunity to create sales and profits without benefit of sales personnel, store facilities, and physical assortments and displays of merchandise. Catalog selling is a means of getting plus business. For example, United Airlines has arranged a tie-in agreement with a catalog merchandiser. United dispenses to passengers an elaborate, 24-page, full-color, illustrated, slick paper, high-quality catalog, which United calls its *Friendship Store-Shopping Service*. Items are chosen in accordance with their fit with the socio-economic life style characteristics of passengers. Another firm, the House of Webster, which specializes in what they call *old-fashioned gifts* and replicas of early American household appliances and tools, distributes its catalog, called a *scrapbook,* throughout the major air terminals of the United States.

Catalog selling will undoubtedly continue to grow. The sophistication and techniques for creating highly attractive and successful catalog merchandising opportunities grow apace. Its growth in turn is related to the increasing selectivity and preference of many emerging market targets. Catalogs are convenient to shop and such shopping can be done at the convenience of the buyer, wherever he or she may be—at home, at the office, traveling across country on a Boeing 747, or commuting to work on the California BART system.

There is little question that some significant number of consumers prefers by actual choice, nonpersonal, nonstore methods of distribution. Catalog selling is for them, therefore, a significant merchandising response to an explicit manifest consumer need.

Catalog Stores. Though somewhat out of place, it would appear necessary that some limited treatment of catalog stores be included in this chapter. Catalog stores are a blend of catalog selling techniques and in-store merchandising of a novel and nonconventional order. Catalog stores are sometimes called *catalog showrooms.* They combine the atmosphere and service of a general merchandise operation with the convenience of a catalog and the savings of a discount store.

Conservative estimates place annual catalog-showroom sales at approximately $3 billion in 1975, and estimates are that such sales may reach $15 billion by 1980.[7] Historically such stores were the bastion of the mail-order houses, discount firms, department stores, and the premium stamp companies. However, during the mid 1970s such firms as the May Company department stores and such giant food supermarket chains as Grand Union, Pathmark, and Giant Food have joined the catalog store stampede.

Most of these stores are free standing units, are dressed in eye-pleasing color schemes, plushly decorated with full carpeting, and expensive fixtures. Well-managed catalog showrooms are recording profits of 5 to 10 per cent of sales based upon 25 to 30 per cent margins. Sales per square foot range from $85 to $200 per square foot. Operating costs are lower than the average supermarket, averaging 15 to 20 per cent.

Catalog stores are basically order houses whereby customers shop from 400-page catalogs that include some 8,000 different items. Only one or two of each item are displayed in the store. When a selection is made, the order is filled from the store's warehouse stock. Such stores have several operating advantages:

1. Using the catalog as a shopping guide reduces the need for a large number of clerks.
2. Display of descriptively price ticketed, one-of-a-kind merchandise reduces showroom pilferage to about 1 per cent of sales.
3. Direct take-home of purchased items by customers nearly eliminates delivery costs.
4. The pulling power of the attractively displayed, low-priced discounted merchandise allows showrooms to be located on less expensive land and in low-rental areas.
5. Payment in cash or customer's bank credit card lowers the cost of credit.
6. The use of a catalog as the primary advertising medium keeps promotional costs to a bare minimum.

Thus, by the end of the 1970s there may be as many as 2,500 of these new outlets. Just how significant this new special breed of retailers will become is uncertain. However, catalog selling in especially attractive surroundings in stores, as well as in the customers' homes, appears destined to be an important and significant part of retailing for the future.

[7] See Don L. James, Bruce Walker, and Michael J. Etzel, *Retailing Today: An Introduction,* Harcourt Brace Jovanovich, Inc., New York, 1975, pp. 619–620.

Vending Machine Selling. The ultimate, in many respects, of nonstore, nonpersonal retailing is the automatic vending machine. Given our highly automatic, almost cybernetic society, selling by machines offers exciting prospects for both buyer and seller. Machines do not go on strike; they do not require coffee breaks and rest periods, or ask for salary increases, or pilfer merchandise. From the customer's perspective, they do not slur nor insult. They are perennially available and do not talk back. Neither are they overly persistent or aggressive. They do not sell unwanted merchandise to reluctant customers. Given all these desirable features, it is small wonder that so many cast such a rosy future for machine selling during the 1960s. Yet, sales from automatic vending machines have reached only about $300 million by mid-1970, and the prospects for future growth seem somewhat dim.

Automatic machine vending is ideally suited for many convenience items of low unit value. Machines for off-hour selling of bread, milk, and other fill-in items were installed in supermarket parking lots with very marginal success during the 1960s. Problems of pilferage and malfunction have been the greatest impairments to more successful utilization. Machine selling is common at bus terminals, air terminals, college and university locations outside classrooms and in dormitories, factories, offices, and almost all places where people congregate and need snacks, beverages, or personal care items.

During the 1960s several new technological breakthroughs were witnessed; change makers, paper money machines, machines that not only dispensed but produced items (brewed coffee, tea, or hot chocolate), machines that heated commodities or kept them chilled or refrigerated, all were introduced—some with great success, and others with more modest records of success. Yet, during the 1970s no really new technological breakthroughs were witnessed, and vending machine selling has just about kept pace with food and beverage production and the increases in the total population. This record of growth can be seen more explicitly in Figure 21-2.

In the early 1960s, when these innovations were being introduced, sales from vending machines increased dramatically as much as 42 per cent in 1961 over 1960. However, since about 1970, sales have suffered because the industry seems to have run out of technological innovation. Furthermore, the market or the overall demand for machine vending appears to have reached a point of near saturation. There is an equipment surplus and the rapidly rising price levels of the 1970s have generated real merchandising difficulties, especially in the area of pricing. However, there are factors which tend to bolster machine selling. Americans are hedonistic in their use of snacks and coffee breaks. Such practices are now an accepted part of the core culture of our society.

Our mobile population supports the need for quick snacks and the replenishment of personal items as people travel, seek leisure, go to work or school, and generally move about. Our society, in spite of inflation and high rates of unemployment, is still largely affluent, and many consumers are hardly hesitant about dropping a few coins into a machine to buy an item which they perceive as satisfying or amusing. There may even be new technological breakthroughs in the future relating to the machines or in the area of packaging that would tend to accelerate sales. Vending ma-

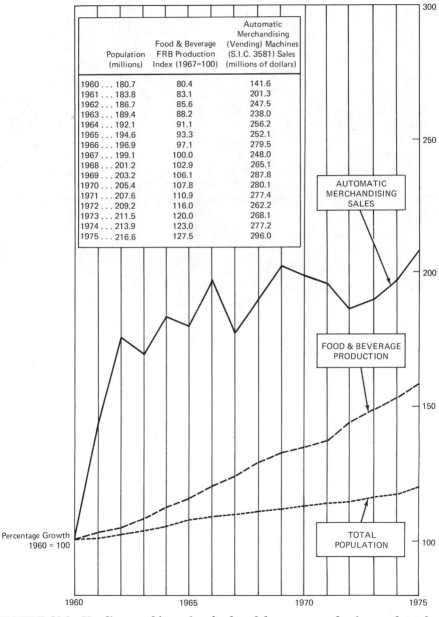

	Population (millions)	Food & Beverage FRB Production Index (1967=100)	Automatic Merchandising (Vending) Machines (S.I.C. 3581) Sales (millions of dollars)
1960 ...	180.7	80.4	141.6
1961 ...	183.8	83.1	201.3
1962 ...	186.7	85.6	247.5
1963 ...	189.4	88.2	238.0
1964 ...	192.1	91.1	256.2
1965 ...	194.6	93.3	252.1
1966 ...	196.9	97.1	279.5
1967 ...	199.1	100.0	248.0
1968 ...	201.2	102.9	265.1
1969 ...	203.2	106.1	287.8
1970 ...	205.4	107.8	280.1
1971 ...	207.6	110.9	277.4
1972 ...	209.2	116.0	262.2
1973 ...	211.5	120.0	268.1
1974 ...	213.9	123.0	277.2
1975 ...	216.6	127.5	296.0

AUTOMATIC MERCHANDISING SALES

FOOD & BEVERAGE PRODUCTION

TOTAL POPULATION

Percentage Growth 1960 = 100

FIGURE 21-2 Vending machine sales, food and beverage production, and total population, 1960–1975.

SOURCE: Industry Week: Trends and Forecast, Vol. 170, No. 4 (July 26, 1971), pp. 53–54.

chines are highly dependent for their success on eye-catching appeal, which leads to impulse and reminder buying. Without eye-catching packaging and machine design, plus good locations, the success of machine vending is at best a speculative merchandising venture.

thematic merchandising

American merchandising has always had its themes—the central scripts and settings which cast a given store into some kind of alliance with its target customers. The overwhelming theme of retailing in the United States has generally focused upon the central or core theme, mass merchandising. Here the emphasis is usually on price, good quality, undifferentiated facilities and services. In some respects this generates a kind of sameness, a blandness, with a capacity for satiation and dullness. Given the increasing diversity of the American market, this mass merchandising theme is not satisfactory for all market segments. Some customer groups, because of vastly different socio-economic characteristics which support different interests, activities, and overall different life styles, prefer different themes— hence, the concept of *thematic merchandising*. These themes are as varied as the customer segments which support them: leisure, youth, travel, recreation, hobbies, sports, education, epicurean, ecological and environmental, wealth, and luxury. Almost every special interest of any magnitude can in turn both generate and support merchandising institutions which cater to these interests.

America, all the folklore notwithstanding, is not a melting pot nor a great egalitarian society. Not everyone wishes to eat in stainless steel buildings and dine on plastic hamburgers and rubber chicken. Sears is not a mecca or a consumption palace for all consumers. For many, price is not a relevant consideration—what is important to some is to shop in settings that are rewarding and reinforcing to a given customer's self-interest, or to have assistance from knowledgeable salespersons who are consumption consultants. For some, price is never relevant. What is relevant may be style, color, reputation of manufacturers and/or seller, or the uniqueness of the product itself.

Americans are beginning to discover their heritage. There is a longing on the part of some customers for things that are real, that link people to their past, that remind them not everything is discarded after a few years' service. To some extent this is a rebellion against the waste and profligacy of the throw-away culture.

Nostalgia Sells

It would be impossible to track and detail each of these emerging merchandising trends. However, we will explain a few of the more prominent ones which seem to be affecting modern retail merchandising. In addition to nostalgia, luxury and boutique merchandising will be briefly detailed.

Across the country, many of the old, abandoned monuments to America's past are being recycled, rejuvenated, and reinitiated into new uses. These include the red brick firehouses, rococo waterworks, old marble banks, abandoned railroad stations and warehouses—even the lowly gasoline service stations are being converted to new retail merchandising facilities with great success. If there is any explanation for consumer reaction to these developments, it would have to be novelty. Such spaces have desirable, rewarding, and reinforcing qualities. Why? Perhaps because many of these are such solid, real structures. Brick, old oak, solid beams, heavy girded structures, massive size and scale remind people of an era that was not all plastic and new. These facilities link people to a solid past —a past which in retrospect and perhaps in fantasy seemed more secure, more lasting, more solidly tough old Yankee American.

One of the most substantial of the new thematic restaurants is the Last National Bank Restaurant in Hartford, Connecticut, occupying a building that once housed the Hartford National Bank and Trust Company. Diners eat behind 30-ton vault doors. Ancient, glass-covered safe doors serve as tables, wine lists arrive in zippered money bags, and place mats are blown-up replicas of $1,000 bills.

Another example of recycled thematic elegance is the Terry Avenue Freight House Restaurant in Seattle. This restaurant is a converted LCL (less than carload lot) freight house. It includes a seven-foot high round-house stove, headlights from old engines, and scales built in 1914 with Corinthian columns supporting the balance beam. The restaurant is furnished with 1900–1920 vintage railroad benches and chairs. The bar is made from a 35-foot flat car with the center I-beam and structure cut away. The car resting on its wheels serves as a stand-up bar. The restaurant itself will accommodate up to 550 patrons.

In Nappanee, Indiana, one merchandiser has fulfilled a need and tapped a market opportunity by opening a women's dress shop and apparel store in an early-1900 Victorian household, called "The House Across the Street." The store is completely fitted out in period furniture and accessories to match the period and style of the house. The merchandise, however, is completely modern and up to date, and the period setting makes a dramatic contrast to the contemporary and casual clothing lines.

Classic restaurants, bars, and clothing stores are blooming around such nostalgic themes as railroading and old automobiles. In Portland, Oregon, a very successful men's wear store, called "The Depot," has been developed in what was once the waiting room of a railroad station. The store features high-quality men's wear for the successful, upward mobile young executive. In Detroit, diners eat in old luxury automobiles in a restaurant called "Doug's Body Shop."

In Spokane, an old flour mill has been converted into a series of merchandising establishments, all of which stress the recycled nature of the facility and emphasize nostalgia by displaying large, blown-up prints of the old mill in its original use.

Luxury

While most of us, admittedly, have strong identification with the middle class, there is a very sizable luxury or carriage trade market segment in the United States.

During the depths of the 1974–1975 recession, for example, Tiffany's sales were up 25 per cent. Gumps in San Francisco, Sakowitz in Houston, J. E. Caldwell's in Philadelphia, Charles Willis, Inc., in Atlanta, and Moyer's Jewelers in Miami *all* reported maintaining the same level of sales volume or increases in sales volume during 1974, a year of depressed retail sales generally.

It is difficult for us to imagine that there are customers in large numbers who buy rubies, diamonds, emeralds, and sapphires with little thought to price. Big spending goes on for many high-priced items—not just jewelry. Luxury boats, cars, motorcycles, airplanes, houses, clothing, and even food are areas that have large or relatively large demand segments.

Whenever there is a return to the classic, more elegant look in fashion, the desire for better merchandise seems to increase. For example, in 1975 such classic items as $450 cashmere sport coats and $1,895 ranch mink coats became popular items. For the gourmet, one luxury store offered a complete side of corn-fed beef that a customer could select on the spot in the cattle feed lot. As absurd as it appears, one store successfully merchandised a combination office and luxury apartment inside a Boeing 727 at $9.2 million.

Bowls, Chinese porcelain vases, statues, and lamps were popular items in San Francisco during 1975. At what price ranges? In the luxury stores, prices usually started at $500 and went as high as $3,000 for a pair of Burmese jadeite birds. One firm introduced a popular luxury item in early 1975, a men's toilet kit that retailed for only $2,000.

The actual size and the dollar magnitude of the luxury market are not easy to estimate, but they are significant. And it is important as students of retailing that we recognize the existence of this market and understand the basis of its existence. In a country where success is usually attained by unusual merit in some endeavor and where such success is measured in dollars, the presence of large numbers of energetic, successful people with large incomes will spawn a luxury market segment.

Boutique Merchandising

A boutique store is a shop-within-a-shop. The essence of the boutique is individuality. Boutique merchandising is the essence also of theme-oriented retailing. Atmosphere is exceedingly important, and most boutiques, although not necessarily in the luxury category, are certainly not price-oriented. Boutiques are for a special group or groups of people with a special point of view about fashion or special product needs. Identifying a special customer group becomes the first step to success in boutique merchandising, and the second most important step is creating special identification or individuality through merchandise assortment, atmosphere, and store image. Boutique assortments often include a large number of relatively unusual, handcrafted items of clothing, gifts, jewelry, crafts, and furnishings. As a matter of fact, a boutique means the opposite of plenty of everything; it means a few of different things.

Boutique merchandising emphasizes cluster selling; showing customers how to complement different items of purchases; showing customers how they will look when two or more items are combined. Boutiques often stress what they call the "synergistic look," putting the parts together to make a complete whole, the total effect of which is dramatic or eye-catching.

Boutiques consider the hallmarks of their operation to be exclusivity and specialness combined sometimes with a touch of audacity and theater. The decor of the boutique becomes a kind of managed stage setting in which the line between merchandise and furnishings is often blurred. Items that are considered only decor are often requested by and sold to customers.

Boutique merchandising is another example of retailing response to meet particular and special needs. As giant retailers are expanding, fashion has tended to become more uniform. However, there are always those who resist uniformity and who will pay for something different. The major advantage of the boutique is that it helps to personalize. This advantage is important to many customers who feel lost when they walk into a large store. Boutiques attempt to make a specialty of catering to particular customers' preferences.

Boutiques as independent free-standing units usually attempt to create layouts that can carry 30–35 per cent more merchandise than conventional specialty stores and to boost their sales per square foot to as much as $250. They are highly streamlined atmosphere-oriented shoppes that constitute an all-out assault on the sensory perceptions of their customers. They are located everywhere that people congregate in sufficient numbers—downtown, suburbs, and other places of high foot traffic and customer density. Air terminals have become highly successful as location points for boutiques.

Many department stores are now attempting to emulate the successful independent boutiques by establishing their own shops-within-a-shop. The next decade may see many more department stores opening boutiques.

Perhaps we have treated the subject of "The Changing Nature of Retail Merchandising" sufficiently to have projected something of the atmosphere and the psychology of these changes. Retailing, in our culture at least, is almost never static. In the following and concluding chapter we shall examine the larger environment in which retailing is embedded and thus perhaps serve a better understanding of those things that augur to create change.

QUESTIONS FOR STUDY, REFLECTION, AND REVIEW

1. Explain why retailing appears to be in a near constant state of change.
2. Retailing is an industry of great contrasts. Why? What role does diversity play in creating retailing contrasts?
3. What are the major appeals of franchising to the franchisee? The franchisor?
4. What is the difference between vertical and horizontal franchising?
5. What is meant by nonstore retailing? List and discuss the major kinds of nonstore retailing.
6. Why do customers respond to nonstore merchandising strategies?
7. In your assessment, what does the future hold for door-to-door selling?

8. What is meant by thematic merchandising? What in your judgment is responsible for its emergence?
9. What is a boutique shoppe? What is basically featured in boutique selling?
10. What accounts for the emergence of such retailing developments as thematic merchandising and boutique selling?

22

retailing: what lies ahead

Retailing is a relatively fast-paced, dynamic industry. The industry and the many individual firms that make it up are in a near constant state of accommodation with the environment. Most of the changes witnessed in retailing institutions come about not because of any inherent tendencies of the institutions to change, but because of needs and stresses in the external environment within which retailing operates. It is for this reason that we examined in earlier chapters the changes that were taking place in this environment—changes related to economic, demographic, social-cultural and psychographic dimensions.

Most changes that occur in retailing are changes that relate to consumer needs. Yet these needs, in turn, are affected by a large number of considerations, as we have already learned. Retailing, you can be assured, will be different in 1985 than it was in 1975. It will be even more different in 1995. Such is the dynamic nature of the industry. New needs will emerge, and new stores and new methods of retail distribution will emerge to accommodate those needs. Some forms of retail distribution will likely fade out of existence altogether, but by and large, most existing forms will show enough tolerance and flexibility to meet the new requirements of future market conditions.

No one can completely foretell the future. We have few seers or retailing soothsayers. Yet astute retail practitioners, managers, and all those who study and research the area of retail merchandising can, on the basis of current developments, predict with reasonable success what forces are likely to shape the destiny of retailing in the years ahead. Such forecasts invariably lack the detail and specificity of a description of current retailing events. They are instead, in most instances, rather large sweeping generalizations concerning major trends that are likely to impact with current retailing practices, and thus become the motive force for future changes in the industry.

Although it is true that no one can foretell the future, nonetheless, people who exercise leadership and who have the capacity to act in any field of endeavor are in an ideal position to translate their own assumptions about the shape of the future into decisions and behavior that, in turn, shape and affect the future course of events.

industry leaders plot the future

Recently a host of retailing industry leaders made a purposeful effort to plot the future destiny of retail merchandising. The effort was a study conducted by a management research firm and sponsored by the Bureau of Advertising and the National Retail Merchants Association. This study was designed to pinpoint trends and developments in retail merchandising between the present and the year 2000. The Delphi technique was used in making the survey. The Delphi technique is based upon the process of asking experts to make guesses concerning the probability or likelihood of certain events taking place. The initial predictions were fed into a computer, and the results were then presented for analysis to a panel of 105 retailers. After further discussion, the results were again programmed into the computer, correlated, and a final set of generalizations and the probability of their occurrence were written up into a major report.[1] The major highlights of this report will be presented here, and in subsequent sections of this concluding chapter we shall build upon specific items within the report to conjecture in our own way concerning the future of retail merchandising.

Retailing Leaders Express Fear and Optimism

Like most industries, retailing has a mixed future. There is a growing concern with a number of current problems that must be faced. These will come as no great surprise to you. In our previous discussions throughout the text, these problems have largely been acknowledged and analyzed. Retailers are fearful of three major current problems that must be addressed in order to create a secure and optimistic future.

1. Retailers must curtail rapidly rising operating expense ratios and reverse shrinking profit margins. They anticipate accomplishing this by increasing productivity via the increased implementation of person/machine systems within their operations.
2. Retailers must readily accommodate to the already manifest trend of society toward an increasing service-oriented demand. They will ac-

---

[1] Only the summary highlights will be reported here. For more detailed discussions concerning both the methodology and the results, see Leo Bogart, "The Future of Retailing," *Harvard Business Review* (November–December 1973), pp. 16–32.

complish this in large part by developing more emphasis on specialty stores, boutiques, and expanded customer services.

3. Department store retailers are perplexed and anxious concerning the steady increase in the competition they face from discounters, from the ever-aggressive specialty stores, from food and drug chains, and from direct-to-customer warehouse furniture outlets, catalog showroom stores, and other competitors. Department stores, in order to cope with these competitors, will themselves demonstrate a higher level of merchandising aggressiveness and innovation. Department stores will survive, but will place greater emphasis on store image, and will work to streamline merchandise assortments and reshuffle merchandising efforts in order to do so.

Retailing in the Larger Context

The future of retailing in all its dimensions—the downtown flagship department store, the vitality of central-city shopping, the threat to continued expansion of suburban living, the near total absence of mass transit systems—depend upon our society's willingness and ability to solve the major social and economic problems existing in the larger environment within which retailing is embedded. Basically, retailing leaders are optimistic that these problems—poverty, crime, economic debilitation of cities, transportation, and energy shortages—can be solved. And by and large the major social, economic, and demographic forces that affect retailing will manifest themselves in such a way as to be a positive uplifting force for retail merchandising in the future. Let us review briefly these forces and assess their impact on retail merchandising.

Economic Forces. Most retail industry leaders are confident and optimistic concerning the economy of the United States. Most believe the market will keep growing in terms of actual numbers of consumers in spite of the current decline in the birth rate. Incomes are also expected to continue to increase dramatically. Many leaders forecast that 60 per cent of the households in the United States will have incomes of $15,000 or more (in 1972 dollars) by the year 2000, compared to 25 per cent in 1973. Almost everyone will be able to participate in the consumption ethic. Poverty will be virtually eliminated by a negative income tax or some other federal program. Consumers, it is forecast, will continue to become better educated. Fifty per cent of men aged 30–34 will have had some college education, compared to 33 per cent today. Increased education will presumably lead to increased awareness and greater discernment in purchase consumption decisions, especially those related to their effect on the environment.

Social Forces. Most industry leaders believe that solutions will be found for a number of our contemporary social ills. For example, teen-age unemployment in ghetto areas will be eliminated. They further believe that massive government aid will largely revive central cities and that consequently, large numbers of middle-class people will return to live in these areas. If this happens, the consequences for retailing and the location and structure of retail distribution will be significantly altered. Leaders also predict that our society will remain highly mobile, with all that this implies for retailing. As a matter of fact, retail leaders predict even higher levels of mobility, suggesting that 25 per cent of the population will move each year by the year 2000, compared to today's figure of 18 per cent.

Employment Patterns. The work ethic is predicted to continue toward its eclipse. By 1980, retailing experts predict the advent of the 4-day work week, and they further suggest that this will have rather profound implications on such factors as store hours and other personnel matters. Another item forecast is that 65 per cent of the women aged 18 to 64 will be gainfully employed by the year 1987. This, they believe, will tend to upgrade women's fashions and encourage longer store hours. It may also tend to change existing patterns relating directly to the customer retail selling and store advertising procedures. It is forecast that Sunday openings will be legal in 95 per cent of the country by the year 2000. Few retail leaders believe, however, that there is much likelihood of such factors as 24-hour, 7-day-a-week store openings. Neither are they inclined to predict much of a downturn in employee turnover or much reduction in employee labor costs. Yet, they are nearly unanimous in their contention that these problems must be attacked aggressively if retail stores are to remain profitable.

Technological Changes. Retail industry leaders predict that technological changes will drastically affect retailing processes and procedures. By the year 2000, 50 per cent of all American households will be linked to cable television (CATV). This linkage will bring with it two-way television communication capability, and by the early 1990s will trigger revolutionary changes in merchandising and sales methods. Furthermore, almost all predictions embrace forecasts of increased and better use of computerized information at lower operating levels within the organization. This will permit increased emphasis on decentralized management and permit greater buyer and branch manager autonomy. Continued improvement in the application of person/machine systems will reduce transaction time and customer frustration and anxiety. Industry experts also predict that by the late 1980s, individual credit accounts will be eliminated and replaced by some form of national credit and banking system. In other words, retail merchandising will become a part of the cashless or checkless society of the future. Some fear is manifested by industry leaders that this may lead to some withering of store loyalty, but they are buoyed in their optimism concerning this development by the distinct possibility of marked reductions in store operating expenses. Finally, because of the continuing emphasis on mass merchandising and the need to bring forth a continuing supply of needed goods to meet tastes, not only of the mass market, but of special needs as well, central buying offices will continue to grow in importance. By 1986, most agree that central buying offices will account for three quarters of the general merchandise purchased.

Store Operations. Retail leaders predict that the number of items carried per store will continue at about the same level. However, they do comment that retailers ought to examine this issue carefully. They also predict an increase in sales per square foot of selling space. They anticipate accomplishing this increase by greater utilization of self-service merchandising racks and greater merchandising density within available space confines. They believe that greater sales per square foot will further affect shrinkage controls, store layout procedures, and fixturization. The experts predict that there will be a 50 per cent increase in sales of items sold in standardized packaging.

About the same distribution of selling space for fashion items is predicted for the future, but also forecast is the tendency to set aside more floor space for free and flexible swing areas. Branch stores are expected to become specialty stores rather than full-line department stores. And once again, profit margins on staple utilitarian items are predicted to shrink. In an effort to offset shrinking profit margins generally, the members of the panel of experts forecast that, by as early as 1981, retail stores generally will discontinue free home delivery. One final interesting prediction in this category: Retail experts seem to believe that the ratio of store units to general population has about reached an equilibrium point and that the total number of retail units servicing today's volume base will remain about the same in the future.

Competition. Retailers predict a continuing stringent competitive picture for the future with aggressive new competitors and continuing severe competitive pressure from nearly all store and merchandising types. For example, one third of all general merchandise sales will be attained outside the store; furniture warehouse selling will increase its share of the market fourfold. Discount stores, it is predicted, will account for 25 per cent of the general merchandise volume by the year 2000. They currently account for 15 per cent of this trade. The future will witness an increased emphasis on boutiques, specialty shops, and other life-style oriented merchandisers. Specialty stores are expected to increase their market share by 20 per cent.

Large stores will seek to create a sense of shopping excitement at new suburban locations as well as within the downtown urban core. Most stores will continue to promote and create a renewed emphasis on the pleasurable and social aspects of shopping, and will work to continue the tradition of excitement in the market place.

Services, Promotion, Merchandise. One of the most pronounced predictions is that leasing of consumer durable goods will increase 50 per cent by the year 2000. Fifty per cent of the general merchandise sold will be under private or reseller label and this, it is expected, will bode well for high-acceptance retail stores. There will be more aggressive efforts toward increased individualization of store images to appeal to the growing number of distinct market segments. This leads to the further forecast that one third of retail advertising will be pinpointed to specific consumer targets. It is projected that consumers will become more and more service-oriented and that services will represent 40 per cent of all personal consumption expenditures by the late 1990s. As would be expected, consumers will pay higher markups for more personal services.

Retailers thus stand ready to face the future. Few businesses or industries have shown more tolerance or plasticity for meeting the challenge of the future. Almost no business is more action- and strategy-oriented than retailing. Each day presents retailers with new challenges and with a fresh set of consumer demands and competitive pressures. Each store, if it is to survive, must tread its way cautiously from today to tomorrow. As today's students of retailing, you will likely be among tomorrow's managers. Hence, this future and the conditions that have been described are the conditions and the environment within which you must operate.

In the next section, we shall explore in somewhat greater detail some of these forecasted conditions and the consequences that they are likely to render on the retail merchandising of the future.

retailing in the post-industrial society

The world is not as simple as it once was. There are tremendous global forces at work that are challenging beliefs and practices held to be immutable only a short while ago. Within the United States particularly, and in other developed countries as well, there are large-scale changes in the family, the nature of work, the roles of men and women, and the relationship of society to the individual. These changes are manifested in such welfare programs as federal health care, consumerism, power-sharing in organizations, and a steady unrelenting momentum in the growing psychology of entitlement. These changes are important, disturbing to many, and in all likelihood, destined to both last and have far-reaching implications for nearly all kinds of economic processes. In short, we are in a time of change, a transition era between one period and another. We are perhaps about midpoint between the industrial and post-industrial period. Retailing, it must be pointed out, the complex process of informing and bringing products and services to customers, will both affect and be affected by these enormous waves of change.

Table 22-1 contrasts what may be the major differences between the industrial and post-industrial society. Economic activity, including retailing, has been dominated by the industrial society ethic for at least the last 50 years. Now as we move closer to the post-industrial period, the characteristics of this period will more and more become the underlying ethic and value system that will guide economic endeavor. If you will recall many of the predictions and forecasts of the retailing experts reviewed in the previous section, you will no doubt be impressed with the extent to which they appear to be based upon trends and conditions that are an endemic part of the post-industrial society. Evidence concerning the transition from the industrial to the post-industrial society is largely anecdotal and conjectural, but it does appear that vast changes in the sociocultural forces of our society are under way. We have already discussed briefly some of these developments, and we shall not discuss each of the changes shown in Table 22-1. We will, however, discuss at some length several developments that are likely to markedly affect the atmosphere or environment of retailing in the future.

TABLE 22-1   Characteristics of the Industrial Versus the Post-Industrial Society

CHARACTERISTICS	INDUSTRIAL	POST-INDUSTRIAL
Demographic and income levels	Extensive urban development, high rate of population increase, longer-lived citizens. Rising per capita income.	Dense population. High per capita income. Interest in stable population. Less desire for income growth.
Knowledge, Science, Technology	Deeply, almost naively, respected. Mandatory primary and secondary education. Extensive public support for higher education. Extensive organized basic and applied research.	Highly educated population. Ecological orientation. Recognition of second order effects of scientific progress. Interests in ethical and human dimensions of science.
Values	Materialistic society: Nature an enemy to be subdued. Competition. Consumer sovereignty. Hedonism-Secularism, The Organization Man.	Aesthetically oriented society: Nature a force to be co-operated with—Humanism—individual dignity. Basic needs of all satisfied.
Social structure	Complex: Many influences, nuclear family relationships. Open class structure. Leaders: Businessmen, politicians, opinion leaders in various fields.	More open and free structure—temporary familial group-ings. Less noticeable class structure. Leaders: Philosophers, artists, in-tellectuals.

SOURCE: Adapted from Marketing Principles: The Management Process, by Ben M. Enis, p. 59. Copyright © 1974 by Goodyear Publishing Co. Reprinted by permission.

Technology

The United States has become more than just a gadget-oriented society. Machines, especially electronic machines, stand ready now largely to revolutionize much of retail merchandising. These technological devices are most evident now in terms of point-of-sale terminals, credit verification procedures, and automated check-out devices.

Point-of-sale terminals will eventually, in all but the smallest retail stores, replace the conventional cash register. Information about the transaction is recorded and transmitted to a central computer that performs a host of complex functions, including inventory control, statistical reporting on the sales velocity of goods, determination of the effectiveness of advertising, and tracking the characteristics of the store's clientele. Automatic check-out can be hooked up to point-of-sale (POS) terminals. These devices can scan product codes printed on labels or packages and feed this information into check-out and cost-accounting systems. Typically the product code is a series of concentric rings or a series of bars that, when passed over by an electrically applied scanner, generate a series of digital pulses. Errors by check-out personnel are virtually eliminated by this person/machine system.

Point-of-sale equipment is expensive but should eventually more than off-set its higher initial capital costs by lower operating expenses. Many large merchandisers are already converting to POS systems. Firms such as J. C. Penney, Sears, and Montgomery Ward have already installed over 50,000 terminals, valued at nearly $190 million. Even more complex and expensive systems have been developed for the food industry. An installation of POS equipment in an 8–10 check-out station supermarket currently costs about $125,000, compared to $45,000 for more conventional cash registers. Super-market management is anxious to install this equipment on a widespread basis in order to reduce high labor costs at the check-out station. Such systems permit a 45 per cent reduction in check-out time and this in turn would permit nearly halving the number of check-out stations required to service a given volume of sales.

Other electronic-oriented technologies now make possible accurate and speedy credit authorization of customers. This capability has a great utilitarian value to merchants when it is recognized that credit fraud alone amounts to an annual $500 million loss to the retailing community. Once such systems are installed, a retailer's credit losses drop quickly.

Most significant perhaps of the new check-out and POS systems is that stores will have complete information about who buys what and how. This information will have a truly profound impact on advertising, will lead to more precise inventory management, planning, and control, and will en-able retailers perhaps, at last, to do some significant market research based upon a much more extensive and exact data base. Retail stores, based upon more extensive market research and customer analyses, should be able to better align their own store images with their customer clientele and hence better position themselves in the total competitive alignment.

Such technological marvels will characterize the future of retailing. Most of this capability exists now and waits only to be implemented. The results will be far-reaching and will include rapid feedback about what products are selling best and where, a better correlation of advertising expenditures and sales, accurate estimates of price elasticity, the effect of packaging and shelf placement, more complete demographic and economic profiles of consumers, and other subtle but rich and vital pieces of retailing informa-tion.

Consumer Affluence

We have detailed the rising economic prospects of the American con-sumer in an earlier chapter and in this present treatment. Perhaps we should not overly belabor the point, but it must be underscored. The American consumer, by nearly all standards of measurement, is affluent—rich almost to the point of overindulgence. This fact will not likely change in the future. The economic futures of the American consumer will increase in the years ahead. The growing psychology of entitlement will also increase. This psychology of entitlement is the belief that all should share in the good life, not just in satisfying the basic needs, but in the entire spectrum of the needs-wants hierarchy.

The values of the industrial society, which extols materialism, consumer sovereignty, hedonism, and instant gratification, will die slowly, if at all. The American consumer is shaped by his culture to want, to seek, to strive for, and to use vast amounts of goods and services. Goods are psychologically reinforcing and the American consumer will be loathe to relinquish his consumption culture.

With the prospects of future increases in individual and family incomes, retailers feel that consumers will demand better quality and more specialty merchandise, and that stores will be required to stock and maintain better assortments. Customers, it is believed, will insist upon better service and higher-quality sales personnel.

More affluence will mean changes in the structure and in the behavior of the mass market and the continuing emergence of new, high-quality, special-need market segments. New markets and special merchandising efforts will emerge to meet the needs of the more affluent, the better educated, the more mobile, the increasingly leisure- and recreation-oriented, the liberated women, the working wives, and many others whose needs will demand and generate important retailing responses.

The society of the future may continue as at present to be a society of scarcity. Goods will continue to be in great demand. Inflation and energy shortages are likely to be chronic problems of the future. Yet unless these problems become significantly more serious, the American consumer is not likely to de-escalate his levels of consumption. It would be a heroic task to get people to modify their habits. The American consumer does not have a flawed character. He has been taught from birth, shaped and socialized by the culture, to waste resources rather than to conserve them. To change this consumption, throwaway ethic would require basic modifications in the American core culture. The American consumer, to spend less and consume less, would have to be indoctrinated to the notion that this was not only proper behavior, but socially desirable and necessary for survival. This is not a situation likely to develop, at least within the near future.

Consumerism

The consumer of the future will not only be more affluent, he will also be better educated, and he is likely to be more aware. The consumer's increased awareness will reflect itself in his general insistence that he be treated fairly, and when he is not his response will likely be either an individual or a group reaction to seek redress of his grievances. Consumerism is a form of psychological projection engaged in by consumers who have accumulated negative attitudes toward marketers.

Retailing is an important part of a socioeconomic exchange process. Consumers seek retailing facilities because these facilities are perceived by them as a means of attaining sought-after and desired goods and services. Thus, retailing is a part of a social system. This social system is (1) comprised of a set of interrelated groups of people, (2) engaged in reaching a shared goal, and (3) having patterned relationships with one another.[2] Implicit in this view is a definition of retailing as the process in which exchanges occur among persons and social groups. When consumers perceive that they have been treated unfairly or "ripped off" by corner cutting, deceptive, or fraudulent practices, they witness a behavioral phenomenon known as the frustration-aggression syndrome. When a customer of a retail store does not receive the satisfaction or reward he expected from a purchase or receives punishment he did not expect, he will be angry. Being angry and frustrated, he becomes more likely to exhibit aggressive behavior, and the results of such behavior become more valuable to him. In other words, when the customer of a retail store gets less than he perceives he bargained for, he reacts militantly and aggressively, and this aggressive behavior itself has satisfying and reinforcing qualities.

Consumerism is caused by discontent. Discontent comes about from advancing incomes, advancing technology, advancing education, or advancing exploitation of the environment. These factors create a concern for the quality of life, and as we seek the qualities of life, we become discontented when we find economic, social, ecological, political, or marketing conditions that are less than satisfactory. Our degree of discontentment depends upon how we perceive the situation. Discontentment over a minor condition may be passed off with a shrug, but discontentment over several minor conditions or a few major conditions may be disconcerting enough to trigger angry consumer reactions. Consumers are often promised much but receive very little. Virginia Knauer, the White House Special Assistant for Consumer Affairs, receives thousands of letters yearly, each echoing the problem. She comments that nearly all the letters adhere to an instinctive and universal form:[3]

> On a specific date I bought a particular product at a certain store. It either didn't work from the start or it soon broke down, and when I took it back or called the store's servicemen, they either couldn't fix it, or after they had fixed it, it still didn't work. The warranty was not honored. The store wouldn't stand back of its merchandise, and letters to the editor accomplished nothing.

The credibility of many merchants is in serious jeopardy. Retailing in the years ahead will be forced to cope with an increasing customer skepticism and a continuing rising tide of consumerism. This skepticism and its resulting militancy are a part of the growing alienation of people with institutions generally, with politicians, with government, with educators and all those who wield influence over other people's lives. Retailers will be forced by this skepticism and militant consumerism to become more open institutions, to share more fully with their customers the facts concerning transactions, to be more receptive to consumer complaints, more

[2] See Sidney J. Levy and Gerald Zaltman, *Marketing, Society, and Conflict,* Prentice Hall, Inc., Englewood Cliffs, N.J., 1975, p. 26.

[3] David Sanford, *Who Put the Con in Consumer?* Liveright, New York, 1972, p. 122.

responsive to consumer demands, and to broaden the range of their social responsibilities.[4] As we linger on in what may be the terminal stages of the industrial society—a period best characterized as overanxious, overstressed, overrushed, and overly demanding, these conditions will continue to trigger consumer behavior characterized as aggressive and militant. The transitional period from an industrial society to a post-industrial society is obviously a period of instability, conflict, and discontent. An essential part of this transitional period is an attempt to shift from a reactive form of public decision making, in which we respond to problems as they are forced upon us, to an anticipatory form in which we try either to avoid problems or prepare to deal with them as they emerge. Such would be the ideal atmosphere or environment of retailing and retail decision making of the future.

the coming era of retail
store positioning

Thus far in this concluding chapter, we have examined a number of significant factors that are likely to affect retailing in the future. We have looked extensively at what industry leaders, retailing experts, believe to be the significant developments that will affect retailing operations between now and the year 2000. We have amplified on some of these factors with a further discussion of what is called the post-industrial society. Most significantly, we have learned that many of the values, beliefs, and practices of our current culture are changing and that, culturally speaking, we are in a period of transition. The new cultural values which are emerging will undoubtedly affect retail merchandising in the years ahead.

In this final section, we shall examine how these developments will specifically affect retailing strategy and lead to what may become the single most significant development to emerge in retailing since the concept of store image—the notion of *store positioning*.

Future Retailing Strategy

Will retailing meet the challenges of the 1980s, the 1990s, and beyond? The answer of course is yes! Not all retailers will survive the tests and challenges of the future. Many will fall by the wayside and become statistics that will bloat the Dun and Bradstreet failure rates. Retailing, however, will not only survive but it will likely prosper, and those stores and institutions that will make it, will do so by adopting and implementing a retailing strategy based upon their assessment of what is likely to happen in the future. These strategies, comprehensive plans of action based upon long- and short-run planning programs, incorporate elaborate control procedures for keeping the firm aligned toward its goals and objectives.

Further retailing strategies will be oriented around the basic ingredients

[4] For a more extended treatment of consumerism, see Boris W. Becker, "Consumerism: A Challenge or a Threat?" *Journal of Retailing*, Vol. 48, No. 2 (Summer 1972), pp. 16–29. Also, see Robert Kahn, "Present Retailer Reaction to Consumerism—Death or Hope?" *Journal of Retailing*, Vol. 49, No. 1 (Spring 1973), pp. 3–9.

of past strategy—planning, organization, and control—but the essential difference is that future strategies will of necessity be based upon an assessment of conditions that are likely to prevail in the future. All really effective strategies are anticipatory. Successful managers and strategists are those who can anticipate the future and shape their organizations to the emerging needs and conditions of the market place.

With the background already developed in the previous sections of this chapter, as well as the many other chapters throughout the text, let us consider now what might be some important guidelines or signals that will affect future strategy considerations.

Be Flexible

The American economy and the entire American culture are in a period of transition. When things are changing, flexibility is a must. It permits accommodation and hence survival. Retailers must recognize and incorporate into their strategic thinking that our economy has reached the end of what might be called the *cowboy economy* or the open frontier psychology which has prevailed so long in our thinking. This thinking or attitude embraced the notion that there was always a new retailing frontier, plenty of new business, and new untapped territories available for the taking. We must think now and in the future in terms of a *space ship mode* in which we recognize that resources are limited, most available space is taken up and, from the standpoint of opportunity, the existing network of retail stores, although not optimum, is such that there are no longer vast untapped territories for new stores. These facts pose a specific and unique challenge to retailers in the future from the standpoint of strategy considerations. Retailers face a serious marketing challenge. Stores can no longer expect automatic growth simply by holding on to their share of a growing population. To do so may assure some success, but the really successful merchants of the future will understand that significant success will have to come from increases in their share of the market. In other words, some retailer's gains will come at the expense of other's losses, and strategy will demand aggressive, competitive behavior. Each retail store in the future must have a clear, distinct reason for justifying its existence and being in the marketplace—i.e., the reason must be clear or identifiable from the customer's point of view if the retailer expects to attract and sell customers, and most importantly, to change consumers into customers.

Identify Your Market

Successful retail strategies of the future will demand that each store clearly identify the market segment to which it hopes to appeal. There may be, in an increasing age of specialization, little room for "me too" kinds of stores that attempt to appeal to a broad spectrum of customer groups or clusters. Retail market segments are not all that easy to identify, nor will they be in the future. The distinction between mass and class markets is fuzzy. Many customers of class stores are also customers of mass merchandising stores for some items. Today's and tomorrow's customers have many complex and specialized needs. These needs are the outgrowth of new life styles and novel living patterns. Market segmentation has produced an abundance of specialized stores, and even further refinements in segmentation techniques will produce even more specialized stores of the future. However, diversity among consumer groups permits a great range of diversity or store types among retailers. Mass merchandising has great appeal to many buyers and will continue to be appealing to many in the future.

To be successful in the future, each store will need to know what customers it is aiming for with its merchandise, with its advertising, and with its total promotional strategy. Each store will need to project a point of view and it will have to succeed in getting this point of view across to its defined market targets.

Retailing Is People-Oriented

Almost all our suggestions for retailing strategy are based upon the notion that things are changing. Things are changing! But what is changing most is people and it is people that are most important to retailing. People are changing, and the way people are living is changing, and these are the most significant challenges to retailing.

Retailers simply must understand these changes in society generally, but in people particularly, and incorporate these changes into their merchandising strategies. Retailers must assess the values, attitudes, and changes that are transpiring among all classes of consumers, blue-collar workers, the new emerging middle class, the super-rich, the poor, the over- and underprivileged consumers. It is time to abandon many of our stereotypes concerning different kinds of customer groupings. What people believe, the priorities they demonstrate for consumption, what they value and esteem, how they dress, how much they spend and for what—all these issues are no longer job-related.

Retailers, to survive in the future, will have to discard the taken-for-granted demographic profiles of customers. Such factors as age, income, job, and marital status are not very valid indices of purchase-consumption behavior. More important will be psychographic data—what are people's activities, what are their interests, what values and opinions they hold and express.

Discretionary income should become a more important criterion than simply income alone. Pooled incomes of persons living together, open marriages, new kinds of living arrangements—all these factors are likely to become more significant in the increasingly tolerant or promiscuous society of the future.

Retailers must recognize that tomorrow's customers will be demanding and impatient. They have been reinforced by a history of instant gratification. They won't wish to wait; out-of-stocks will be costly in terms of customer loyalty. As a matter of fact, customer loyalty itself may decline markedly in the future. In a period of transition, impermanence becomes a way of life. People are likely to have few long-term commitments to anything—marriages, houses, apartments, possessions, where they live, the jobs they hold—let alone the stores where they shop.

The Emphasis on Efficiency

In an expansive, buoyant economy, a rising tide lifts all ships. Stores that are less than efficient survive. In a steady-state economy, which is likely to be the characteristic mode of the future, the less efficient retailers will be eliminated quickly. Hence, intensive efforts and widespread innovativeness directed toward reducing operating expense ratios, especially in those major categories of expense such as selling costs and inventory management, will be undertaken aggressively.

Furthermore, scrambled merchandising, especially the pirating of high-demand, fast-moving items by one type of institution from another, will continue if not accelerate. Products fall basically into three major categories. The first category is *convenience goods.* Customers want to buy these products under ideal conditions of convenience and expend a minimum of effort to acquire them. The next category is *shopping goods.* They are purchases that the shopper considers carefully, going from store to store to make comparisons on the basis of price, quality, style, comfort, and other considerations. It is, in part, purchases of these kinds that make the buying experience exciting and interesting for the customer. However, it is from this category that items are in danger of being pulled away and into the convenience classification by such highly skilled marketing firms as supermarkets, with product categories such as magazines, cigarettes, panty hose, children's jeans and underwear, and even such items as transistor radios and television sets. Fighting this trend will be a major problem for department stores throughout the decade of the 1980s.[5]

The final category of goods is called *specialty products,* but a more accurate and meaningful label would be *life style products.* This category includes a host of different kinds of items: cameras, recreation equipment, autos, boats, some clothing, books, materials for arts and crafts, and other kinds of so-called self-actualizing activities. This category of goods is perhaps the fastest growing in our affluent, active, youth-oriented, self-invested culture.

The point is retailing and retailers must increasingly use clear and specific marketing thinking in order to coordinate their product assortments with their customer segments. And it may become, for reasons of efficiency, increasingly necessary for each retailer to examine his strategy from the perspective of these questions: Am I in the convenience goods business? The shopping goods business? The specialty goods business? Am I in all of them? How do I merchandise these different categories to different customer groups? Can I distribute and sell more than one category of goods efficiently? What balance should I strike in my merchandising efforts among the various categories? In almost all categories the efficient merchant will reap the rewards, but rewards go beyond efficiency alone; the rewards flow to the skillful, innovative merchant who is also efficient. In

[5] See *Department Store Retailing in an Era of Change,* U.S. Department of Commerce, Washington, D.C., 1975.

the future, because of inexorably rising expenses, every square foot of retailing space will be examined and challenged. Steadily rising operating costs, rentals, construction costs, wages, and energy and environmental considerations, plus the higher costs of borrowing and using money have all combined to put the investment of every dollar of space, merchandise inventory, or any other alternative under close and careful scrutiny.

Retail Store Positioning

A chapter on retailing's future ought perhaps to end on a slightly conjectural note. What much of this discussion points to as most likely to affect retail stores is an emerging trend that could best be labeled *store positioning*. The concept of store positioning may well be the key to successful retail merchandising strategy in the period that lies ahead. It was previously asserted that each retail store must have a clear reason for being in the market place. "Clear" was specified as meaning from the customer's point of view. This idea is the nucleus of the store positioning concept. It should be evident that stores that appear to be competitive may actually be serving different segments of the consuming market and serving them in somewhat different ways. In order to provide a basis for retail store strategy, the specific factors that distinguish store shoppers from nonshoppers and heavy shoppers from light or occasional shoppers need to be identified. The differentiation of stores by studying the ways their customers differ as well as how consumer perceptions of various stores differ we call store positioning. On the basis of simple and direct survey questions, consumers have been described in terms of their usage (shopping frequency) and their image of a given store as well as in terms of conventional demographics such as age, income, and size of family. However, more recent developments utilizing factor analysis have proved useful in identifying the differences between stores in relation to consumer preferences and purchases. We shall not worry about the methodology of store positioning but concern ourselves more with understanding the concept and its implications.

In our overstimulated and overcommunicated society, it is important that each store clearly signify to its customer segments exactly what it stands for, the merchandise it sells, the services it offers, and how the store plans to relate these to its customer population. This, too, is store positioning.

Retail merchandising has moved through two periods of its history and it is rapidly approaching and entering a third. Prior to and even including the 1950s, retail merchandising was in the *store attribute* period. These were the "good old days" when every merchant attempted to make his store "the better mousetrap." It was a time when retail advertising focused attention on store attributes, including such features as location, product assortments, prices, and customer shopping benefits. Advertising tended to focus upon unique selling propositions (USP). These (USP's) began, however, to come to an end with the fantastic growth of new firms when a virtual avalanche of "me-too" stores entered the market place. The store attribute period was thus replaced during the 1960s and 1970s by the *store image* period. Retail merchants discovered during this period that their store image—a total bundle of customer perceptions concerning their store

—was more salient from the standpoint of successful merchandising than simply promoting individual store attributes. The image period was an attempt to consolidate as many of the store's attributes into a total conceptualization as possible. Sometimes attributes that hardly existed at all were included or implied in the image. During the image period, all merchandising effort was considered as a long-term investment in the image of the store.

However, just as the "me-too" stores finished off the store attribute era, "me-too" firms are ending the image period. As so many retail firms scrambled for recognition and tried to establish identifiable images for themselves, the clamor and noise level became so high that only a few companies really succeeded. Many companies were quite successful in creating distinct and highly identifiable public store images. However, many retail firms missed the boat entirely, and the image period, while it will linger on for some time to come, is being replaced, at least in terms of many managers' and strategists' thinking, by the store positioning concept. Hence, store positioning may likely be the wave of the future.

Positioning has its roots and origins in the package goods business. It meant originally the product's form, package size, and price, compared to competition.[6]

For retail stores the positioning concept is similar, i.e., how do customers perceive your store, its physical and behavioral aspects, its prices, merchandise lines, location—the sum total of its attributes and characteristics, even its image—in relationship to that store's competitors. Even if a given store is perceived favorably, but ranks too far below the customer's recognition threshold or too low in relation to other competitive store facilities, it isn't going to be very successful. Why? Several reasons can be offered. First, customers-shoppers never think in terms of very many alternative stores. Even if customers are asked to list the major department stores or specialty shops at which they may shop, they usually can list only four or five. If a store isn't positioned in the customer's mind as a major alternative, that store is out of luck. Second, customers develop a kind of selective perception concerning incoming retailing messages. Again, if a store isn't one of those positioned high in the ranking hierarchy of alternatives, these customers simply tune out the advertising for that firm. Another interesting phenomenon related to positioning is that about 25 per cent of the people who read or watch advertising attribute the ad, not to the sponsoring firm, but to the competition. This means that the highly positioned store such as Sears or J. C. Penney gets credited positively with advertising and other merchandising activity that it doesn't even do.

This means that dominant firms that have attained a high degree of success are hard to knock out of their dominant position. Too many retail firms embark on merchandising strategies as if their competitor's position did not exist. They promote and merchandise in a vacuum and are disap-

---

[6] The author's thinking in terms of this concept has been shaped considerably by the work of Jack Trout and Al Ries, "The Positioning Era Cometh," *Advertising Age,* April 24, 1975, pp. 22–26.

pointed when sales and market share fail to increase. An understanding of the positioning concept would better equip them to understand that customers accept only information that matches prior knowledge, experience, or cognitions. They filter out or ignore everything else. Thus, witness the unhappy experience of National Cash Register, which advertised that "NCR means computers." Customers wouldn't buy that; they knew that IBM means computers. NCR means National Cash Register. Take a moment in your own mind to relate this to store positioning. Who and what and where in your mind is Sears? As opposed to Montgomery Ward? What is the major department store in your community? Are there more than three? Rank them. Compare your ranking with that of your associates.

The mind has a tendency to place objects such as stores on a ladder. On each step of the ladder there is a store. If a given store is too far down the ladder, it can move up only by dislodging a higher-ranked competitor. Avis tried this by attempting to dislodge Hertz, but it didn't work. J. C. Penney is making a direct assault on Sears and making some headway by a positioning strategy designed to create specific profiles for their stores throughout all parts of the country. By recognizing in part that Penney customers have no unique demographic requirements, Penney's is assuming that all department store customers are Penney customers. These customers may buy different things at other department stores, but they buy lots of specific things at J. C. Penney. Penney's positioning strategy is thus to cater to discerning customers who want good-quality merchandise at reasonable prices, but not to turn off the higher-income customer who may wish to buy some staple or utilitarian items from Penney's.

In the store positioning period, strategy is the keystone to successful merchandising. It incorporates the notion that your merchandising effort must be keyed not only to well-defined and delineated market targets, but that it also must be aligned and coordinated in accordance with your competitor's strategy as well. Positioning strategy suggests that attacking your competitor head-on may be a monumental merchandising mistake. A better approach, one that is the essence of positioning, suggests that you study the psychographic characteristics of your perceived customer segment and slide your merchandising effort in where deficiencies may exist. Such efforts call for a strong positioning idea. In the final analysis, this is the meaning of creative strategy.

Retail merchandising is an exciting, dynamic field of enterprise. Perhaps no textbook can really capture the excitement, the tension, the stress, the frustration, and the satisfaction of the endeavor. However, it is hoped that throughout these pages some of the drama of retailing and the flavor and scope of its activities have been conveyed. Retailing has an exciting future. Our standard of living and our style of life will require a fast-paced, responsive retail merchandising system. The United States system is up to this challenge. Far-sighted retailing executives are already anticipating the changes and forces that will shape the destiny of retail distribution, and at this moment, these very same retailers are converting their anticipations and visions of the future into realistic programs, strategies, and institutions that will serve these future needs.

QUESTIONS FOR STUDY, REFLECTION, AND REVIEW

1. Most changes that occur in retailing are changes that relate to consumer needs. Explain.
2. List and discuss five changes in retailing that are likely to emerge during the decade of the 1980s.
3. How do future changes in economic and social forces affect the future of retailing?
4. How would you characterize retailing in the post-industrial society?
5. Are consumers generally likely to be more or less affluent in the future? How will this affect retailing strategies?
6. Consumerism as a movement is likely to grow increasingly in the future. How will this affect retailing?
7. What is meant by retail store positioning?
8. How should decision makers attempt to position their retail stores? What guidelines would you suggest that they follow?
9. Retailing is often said to be a people-oriented enterprise. What does this imply concerning the "market concept"?
10. What role or relationship exists between the concepts of customer orientation, market segmentation, and store positioning?

index

a

Accounting
  cost method, 477–80
  decision rule for inventory valuation, 480–82
  FIFO method, 489–90, 491–92
  LIFO method, 490–92
  management, 454–58; *see also* Merchandise management accounting
  retail method of inventory valuation, 483–89
  role of, 475–76
  See also Accounting costs; Costs; Expense budgeting; Expense Center accounting; Financial analysis
Accounting costs
  differentiation from economic costs, 34
  Dupont Schematic and, 49–50
Accounts receivable, 58
Adaptable salesman, defined, 430
Administered pricing models, 359–62
Administrative expenses, 462
Adoption process, role of early buyer in, 283–84
Advanced dating, defined, 288
Advanced main store system, 232
Advertising
  consumer reaction to, 402–403, 404
  costs of, 399
  defined, 396
  effectiveness of, 415–19
  expenditures, 412–14
  in future, 547–58
  media for, 403–10
  organization and, 396–97
  role of, 397–99
  spiral 401–402

types of, 399–401
  See also Advertising management
Advertising management, 411–18
  decision making and, 411–12
  and determination of expenditures, 412–14
  media selection and, 415–17
Age
  market opportunity and, 98, 101–102
  of outshoppers, 170
  store image and, 81
  of supermarket shoppers, 138
AIDA model (Attention, Interest, Desire, and Action model), 403, 427
Algebraic interpretation in break-even point analysis, 56–57
Anticipation-selection, defined, 22
Arithmetic approach to break-even analysis, 53–55
Assets, ratio between current and fixed, 49; *see also* Inventory
Associated office, 292
Assortment mix, 270–92
  dropping items from, 272–74
  fashion cycle and, 277–84
  location of, *see* Store layout
  market segmentation and, 259
  pricing goals and, 254–55
  product life cycles and, 274–77
  profitability as criterion for, 271–72
  resident buying office and, 292–93
  unit control and, 316–18
  See also Merchandising; Planned stocks; Space allocation
Automobile
  community structure and, 152, 153
  expenditures on, 110, 113
  See also Parking facilities

Average cost pricing, 359–60, 369
  markup and, 362–67
  shortcomings of, 361–62
Average propensity to save, 107
Axial site, 186

b

Balance sheet, 46
  in ratio analysis, 64–70
Bank credit cards, 443
Bargain hunting, 81
Bargaining, buyer behavior and, 263
Basic main store system, 232–33
Basic stock method, 305, 306, 307
Beginning of the month stock, *see* B.O.M.
  stock
Big ticket items, perpetual inventory
  method and, 315
Birth rate, *see* Population growth
B.O.M. stock, determination of, 304–307
Bon Marche Department Store, 156
Bonuses, 244
Boutique merchandising, 530–31
Branch store organization, *see* Department store branch
Break-even point analysis, 50–58, 161–62,
  165–66
  algebraic interpretation of, 56–57
  arithmetic approach to, 53–55
  graphic approach to, 52–53
  limitations of, 57–58
  in space allocation theory, 217
Budgeting, *see* Accounting; Cash budgeting; Expense budgeting; Financial
  analysis; Merchandise budgeting
Bureaucracy
  buyer orientation and, 261–62
  buyer role and, 260–62
  information flow and, 454
Business cycle
  advertising expenditures and, 414
  number of retailing institutions and, 7
Buyer/seller dyad, 262–63
Buyers, 137
  behavior model of, 259–66
  branch store organization and, 233
  central activities of, 290–91
  consumer behavior and, 41
  as gaming strategists, 262–64
  as gatekeepers, 260–62
  interaction with vendors, 284–88
  purchase planning by, 307–309
  unit control and, 316
  vendor analysis and, 288–93
  See also Buying
Buyer's Fast Selling Book, 289
Buying
  assortment mix and, *see* Assortment
  mix
  chain store organization and, 235

defined, 264
errors, stock turnover and, 344
expenses, 462
of fashion goods, *see* Fashion cycle
importance of, 255–59
intentions, 41–42
process, 266–68
Buying Power Index, 172

c

Capital budgeting, 334–38
Capital turnover, profits and, 256–58
Cash balance, 63
Cash budgeting, 58–64
Cash disbursements, in cash budget, 61–63
Cash discounts, defined, 287
Cash flow, in merchandise budget, 295
Cash needs, planning for, 58–59
Cash receipts from sales, computation of,
  60–61
Cash registers, *see* Split total cash registers
Catalog sales, 524
Catalog stores, 525
Category shopping, *see* Shoppe concept
Central business district (CBD), 147
  core vs. frame concepts of, 178–80
Central buying offices, 290–91
Centralized system, marketing in, 17
Chain stores
  consumer needs and, 40–41
  organization of, 234–39
Channel control, 285
Charge account credit, 441–42
Chattel mortgage, 442
Check cashing and clearing operation, 169
Checkless society, 443
Christaller Hypothesis, 161
Christmas, work flow at, 240
Cities, *see* Community analysis
Civil Rights Act (1964), 247
Classification control activities, *see* Dissec-
  tion control activities
Clothing expenditures, 110, 112
Cluster selling, boutiques and, 530–31
College fashion boards, 90
College towns, 148–49
Colonial Stores, 239
Color scheme, in store design, 198
Commercial centers, in community analy-
  sis, 147–48; *see also* Downtown
  commercial areas
Commissions, 244
Communication
  consumer perception of, 126
  implementation of retailing strategy
  and, 395
  -information systems, 22
  mix, 28–29
  promotion as, 395–97
  See also Information systems

Community
  accommodation of store to, 174–91
  defined, 146
  functional classification of, 148–49
  See also Community analysis; Community structure
Community analysis
  functional classification of communities in, 148–49
  growth patterns of communities in, 149–50
  industry and, 146
  store location and, 145–55
  trading area analysis and, *see* Trading area, analysis of
  types of commercial centers in, 147–48
Community center, 181–82
Community leaders, community growth patterns and, 150
Community structure, 150–55
  concentric zone theory of, 150–52
  multiple nuclei theory of, 153–55
  sector theory of, 152–53
Company demand forecasting
  based on attitudes and impressions, 88–89
  based on observable behavior, 89–90
  based on past behavior, 90–92
Compatibility
  of assortment, 270
  of store location, 187–89
Competition
  advertising and, 397–98, 399, 402
  assortment mix and, 272
  buying and, 275–76
  dating process and, 287
  determination of, 299
  in future, 537
  increased capital turnover and, 257–58
  outshopping and, 170
  pricing and, 352, 353, 377–78
  retail management strategy and, 29–30
  store design and, 192–93
  store location and, 144–45
  See also Monopolistic competition
Complementary reinforcement, defined, 407
Composite method of company demand forecasting, 89
Computers
  in checkless society, 443
  in merchandise management, 344–48
  See also Electronic data processing; Programming
Concentrated variety, 18
Concentric zone theory of community structure, 150–52
Conditional sales contract, 442
Conservative valuation, defined, 486

Consumer (s)
  affluence, 39, 540–51
  attraction-repulsion principle and, 394
  concentrated variety and, 18
  cost of retailing activities and, 18–19
  credit costs, 444–45
  -oriented selling, 424–25
  resale price maintenance and, 387
  retail store image and, 79–82
  See also Consumer behavior; Customer shopping behavior; Market opportunity; Market segmentation; Markets
Consumer behavior
  advertising and, 388–89, 403–404
  changing shopping habits, 137–38
  consumer choice theories and, 122–25
  decision processes involved in, 138–39
  economic theories of, 122–23
  forecasts of company demand based on, 88–90
  heuristic problem solving and, 131
  importance of, 120–22
  industrial and family, 137
  integrated approach to, 134, 136
  motivation and, 3
  post-decision dissonance and, 131–32
  psychographic analysis of, 133–34
  retailing mix and, 28
  role of market research in, 138–39
  socio-psychological approach to, 123–30
  store design and, 199–201
  in supermarkets, 210–11
  telephone selling and, 519
  trading area size and shape and, 156
  See also Diffusion process; Family expenditures
Consumer experience group, 90
Consumer innovator, diffusion process and, 281–82
Consumer panels and fashion boards, 89–90
Consumer sovereignty, 18, 39, 40
Consumerism, 541–43
Consumption
  family expenditures for major categories of, 110–11, 112–13
  in income class market profiles, 117–19
Contests
  delineation of trading areas through, 169
  as promotional devices, 410–11
Continuous-purchase-record group, 90
Contribution margin, 466–67
Contribution plan for expense allocation, 468–71
Contribution pricing, 379
Control
  elements of, 450–51
  expense budgeting and, 471–73

Control (*cont.*)
  extent of, 452–53
  general nature of, 450–53
  governmental, *see* Government control
  information processing and, 453–54
  planning and, 449–50
  of retailing expenses, 458–71
  of selling function, 433–35
  See also Merchandise controls
Controllable profit, 495–96, 502–503
Convenience, defined, 22
Cook's Tour method of training, 243
Cooperative advertising, 400–401
Core, *see* Central business district core
Cost of goods sold, 60
Cost method accounting, 476–80
  closing inventory and, 481–82
  criticism of, 492
Costs
  in break-even point analysis, 50–58
  of credit, 443–45
  patterns of, 496–99
  physical tracing of, 495
  price and, 499
  of sales personnel, 431–42
  See also Expenses
Counter-cyclical advertising, 414
Credit, 45, 439–45
  costs and benefits of, 443–45
  extent of, 439–41
  kinds of, 441–42
  role of, 439
  trends in, 442–43
  See also Installment credit
Credit and collections function, 226
Credit record analysis, delineation of trading areas through, 169
Crescent Department Store, 156
Cues, consumer behavior and, 129
Cumulative attraction, store location and, 187–89
Customer convenience
  shopping centers and, 181
  store location and, 176–77
Customer shopping behavior
  department store location and, 207, 208
  factors perceived as important and, 255
  layout and, 201
  retail store image and, 81–82
Customer spotting, delineation of trading areas through, 168
Customer traffic, sequence of, 201–203

d

Datings, defined, 287–88
Decentralization of retailing, 180–82, 238–39

Decision making
  customer shopping behavior and, 82
  organization and, 224
  organizational goals and objectives and, 33–34
  profit as criterion for, 31–38
  uncontrollable variables in, 25
Decline stage in product life cycle, 277
Demand, 73–74
  decreased, 30–31
  forecasting, and analysis of, 85–88
  in monopolistic competition, 357–58
  price and, 499
  for services, increases in, 30–31
  trading area concept and gradients of, 157–60
Demand items, location of departments and, 209
Demographic factors
  compared with psychographic factors, 133–36
  market opportunities and, 99–102
  market segmentation based on, 102–104
Department stores, 41
  advertising by, 397
  boutiques in, 531
  development of, 5
  expense allocation and, 466–71
  future problems of, 535
  images of, 80–81
  intention surveys and, 88–89
  market opportunities of, 76
  organization of, 227–32
  price lining and, 382–83
  profitability of items in, 271–72
Departments, 201
  break-even point analysis for, 55–56
  location of, 207–209
  in store planning, design, and layout, 206–207
Dependent shopper, 425–26
Differential advantage, 26, 27–29
Diffusion process, fashion and, 280–84
Direct costs, 467
Direct mail, 407–408
Direct product profit (DPP), 272
Direct selling, 520–22
Discount houses, 5, 40
Discounts, 286–87
Disposable personal income, personal consumption expenditures as percentage of, 105–108
Dissection control activities, 313–14
Dissonance, *see* Post-decision dissonance
Disutility, consumer shopping behavior and, 175
Diversity, in theory of retail organization, 239
Division of labor, functional, 224–26
Dollar control systems, 312–18

Dollar margin pricing, *see* Contribution pricing
Door-to-door selling, *see* Direct selling
Downtown commercial areas, 147
deterioration of, 180
parking facilities for, 190
re-emergence of, 184–85
Drawing power, 174
cumulative, *see* Cumulative attraction
Driving time, shopping center customers and, 182
Drug chains, 41
Dupont Schematic, 69
financial analysis through, 45–50
stock turnover and, 340

e

Economic development, retailing and, 4–5
Economic forecasting, 85–88
Economic ordering quantity model, *see* E.O.Q. model
Economic utility, maximization of, 20
Economy
economic forecasting and, 85–86
franchising and, 515–16
future of retailing and, 535
market opportunity and, 104–107
propensity to save and consume and, 107
Efficiency, store layout and, 211–13
Electronic data processing, 345–48
merchandise control and, 318
Empirical method for delineation of trading areas, 168–69
Employees, *see* Retail employees
End of the month stocks, *see* E.O.M. dating
Energy crisis, suburban shopping centers and, 184
Engel's Law of Consumption, 110–11
Enterprise differentiation, 420
Environment
forecasting and, *see* Forecasting
relationship between retail stores and, 24–25
E.O.M. dating, defined, 288
E.O.Q. (Economic ordering quantity model) 326–34
graphic approach to, 330–31
by tabular determination, 329–30
Escapable costs, defined, 467
Expectations
goal object and, 129
price in terms of, 353
Expenditures
on advertising, *see* Advertising expenditures
for goods and services, teenage, 103
See also Costs; Expenses

Expense center accounting, 463, 464–65, 466
Expenses
budgeting, 460, 466–73
classification of, 460–66
control of, 458–71
distribution of, 460
See also Costs; Financial analysis
Explicit forecast, 83
Exterior appearance of store, 196–97
External site, 186
Extra dating, defined, 288

f

Fad cycle, *see* Fashion cycle
Family expenditures, for major categories of consumption, 110–11, 112–13
Family life cycle (FLC), 111, 114
Family purchase behavior, 137
in supermarkets, 138
Fashion appeal stores, 81
Fashion cycles
assortment mix and, 277–84
diffusion process and, 280–84
merchandising with, 280, 281
Fashion factor, 91
Federal Trade Commission Act, 386
FIFO (First-in, first-out accounting method), 489–90
Financial analysis
break-even point, 50–58
cash budgeting and, 58–64
Dupont Schematic and, 45–50
merchandising planning and, 48–50
ratio analysis and, 64–70
selection of profit measure for, 44–45
Financial requirements for franchises, 513
First-in, first-out basis, *see* FIFO
Fixed costs
in break-even point analysis, 53
contribution and, 52
Fixtures, in store design, 197–98
Flat costs, defined, 497–98
Flexibility
in retailing, 544
in store design, 196
Floor audit system, merchandise controls and, 313–14
Flow and stock data, 46
Follow-up activities in telephone selling, 520
Food budgets, changes in, 138
Food stores, 41
consumer behavior in, 137
See also Supermarkets
Forecasting, 82–93
of company demand, 87–88
data sources for, 85–86

Forecasting (*cont.*)
demand analysis and, 85–88
importance of, 83–84
measuring vs., 84–85
merchandise management and, 294
types of, 84
See also Sales forecasting
"Form follows function" concept
layout and, 201
store design and, 194–95
Formal organization, 224
Formula selling, 427–28
Frame, *see* Central business district frame
Franchising, 508, 510–16
defined, 510–11
future of, 515–16
history and development of, 511
impact of, 512–13
opportunities in, 513–14
pricing and, 385–86
profit expectations in, 514–15
range of service-sponsor-retailer franchises, 513
reasons for success of, 514
vertical vs. horizontal, 511–12
Free form pattern of store layout, 205–206
Free standing location, 178
Functional analysis
in department store organization, 227–32
small store organization and, 224–26
Functional approach to retailing, 11, 16–22
Functional expenses, defined, 461–63

g

Gaming, buyers and, 262–64
Gasoline shortage, supermarket shopping habits and, 138
Gatekeeper behavior, 260–61
General store, 146
Generalization, consumer behavior and, 130
Generative business, defined, 176, 177
Geriatrics, *see* Senior citizen market
GMROI, 338–39
Goal objectives, in consumer behavior, 129
Goods
classification of, 175–76
nature of, location of departments and, 209
Goods and services mix, 28
Government control
cooperative advertising and, 401
franchising and, 516
organizational, 245–47
pricing and, 385–88

Graphic approach to break-even analysis, 52–53
Gravitational approach, 165–67
Great Atlantic and Pacific Tea Company, organizational chart of, 235, 236, 238
Grid pattern of store layout, 205, 206
Grocery store, computerized, 346–47
Gross margin, 466
classification of goods and, 176
decreasing, 508
GMROI and, 339
Gross margin return on investment, *see* GMROI
Gross national product (GNP), seasonally adjusted annual rates, 105
Growth patterns of communities, 149–50
Growth stage in product life cycle, 276

h

Handbills, as advertising medium, 407–408
Heuristic approaches to space allocation, 214–16
Heuristic problem solving, consumer behavior and, 131
High fashion image, 81
Hiring of sales personnel, 429–31
Home inventory group, 90
Horizontal cooperative advertising, 401
Horizontal franchising, defined, 511
Households
changes in characteristics of, 97–98
growth of, 97
husband-wife, 98

i

Implicit forecast, 83
Impulse purchases
lighting and, 199
special displays and, 408
Incentives for retail employees, 244
Income
changing distribution of, 108–10
consumption and, 110, 111
life cycle concept and, 111, 114
market opportunity and, 104–16
market segments based on, 116–19
of outshoppers, 170
of senior citizens, 103–104
See also Disposable personal income
Income pyramid, changing, 109–10
In-home selling, *see* Direct selling
Indifference curves, 122–23
Industry, community analysis and, 146
Industry leaders, on future of retailing, 534–38
Inflation, 5–6
consumer expectations and, 39
supermarket shopping habits and, 138

Information systems
  control and, 453–54
  management accounting as, 454–59
Initial markup, 310
Innovation, 32, 129
  in advertising programs, 411
  by buyer, 261–62
  in vending machines, 526
  See also Diffusion process
Installment credit, 442
  volume of, 440–41
  See also Credit
Institutional advertising, 400
In-store promotional activities, 408
Interception, principle of, 186–87
Interior of store, 107; *see also* Store layout
Internal core approach, defined, 204
Internal site, 186
Inter-store comparison, expense classification and, 460–61
Inventories
  assortments, 294, 316–17
  in capital turnover calculations, 257–59
  carrying costs for, 331–32
  causes of problems with, 321–22
  classification of, 326–34
  cycles of, 323–25
  determination of value of, 314–15
  importance of, 297
  levels of, 323–25
  merchandise management and, 294
  nature of, 301–302
  ratios related to, 68–69
  See also Inventory valuation; Merchandise management; Stock turnover
Inventory management model, *see* E.O.Q. model
Inventory valuation
  cost method of, 477–80
  decision rule for, 480–82
  inventory classification and, 326–34
  retail method of, 483–89
Investment
  advertising expenditures and, 414
  profit as return of, 36–38, 255–58
  turnover, defined, 46–48

k

Key influentials, 129, 137

l

Last-in last-out valuation, *see* LIFO
Layout, *see* Store layout
Leader pricing policies, 383–84
Learning
  advertising and, 403
  consumer behavior and, 128–29
Learning curve, 128–29
Leases, type of, 190

License plate analysis, delineation of trading areas and, 168–69
Life cycle, 111, 114
  position of community in, 149–50
Life style
  market segmentation and, 115–16
  in psychographic analysis, 133–34
  retailing and, 3
LIFO, 490–92
Lighting, in store design, 198–99
Limited assortment discount food store, layout pattern of, 212, 213
Line organization, 224, 238
Linearity assumptions, in break-even point analysis, 57
Lines handled, classification of retail stores by, 8, 10
Liquidity and indebtedness ratios, 67–68
Location
  accommodation to trading area and community and, 174–91
  buying vs. leasing and, 190–91
  changes in, 507
  classification of retail stores by, 8, 10
  community analysis and, 145–55
  cumulative attraction and compatibility theory and, 187–89
  customer convenience and, 176–77
  decentralization of retailing and, 180–82
  delineation of trading area and, 164–70
  importance of, 143–44
  interception and, 186–87
  kind of, 178–80
  market opportunity and, 81
  parking facilities and, 189–90
  problems involved in, 144–45
  research objectives and, 191
  retailing mix and, 28
  for shopping centers, 182–85
  type of store and, 177–78
  See also Site selection; Suburbs; Trading areas; Urbanization
Logical flow models, 370
Loop, 151
Loss leaders, 384
Luxury market, 529–30

m

McGuire Act (1912), 387
Macy's Department Store, 380–81
Mail-order selling 522–24
Management, *see* Merchandise management; Personnel management; Retail management
Management accounting, 454–58
  controlling retailing expenses and, 458–71
  expense allocation and, 466–71
  organizational needs and, 456–59

Management accounting (*cont.*)
  responsibility reporting and, 455–56
  store system planning and, 457–58
  See also Merchandise management accounting
Marginal costs curve, in monopolistic competition, 357–58
Marginal revenue, in monopolistic competition, 357–58
Markdowns, 373–76
  markup requirements and, 310, 311
  in merchandise budget, 301–304
  as percentage of retail sales, 302–303
Market, defined, 38–39, 77
Market demand, 86; *see also* Demand
Market opportunity, 28
  buying decisions and, 255
  characteristics of households and, 97
  community analysis and, *see* Community analysis
  consumer mobility and, 101–102
  contraction and consolidation of, 144
  defined, 73–74
  demographic forces affecting, 94–102
  fallacy of population growth and, 104
  family expenditure patterns and, 110–11, 112–13
  forecasting of, *see* Forecasting
  growth of suburbs and, 98–101
  income and income-related factors affecting, 104–16
  indices reflecting nature of, 172–74
  life cycle concept and, 111, 114
  market segmentation and, 76–77, 102–104, 116–19
  merchandise management and, 294
  nature of markets and, 75–76
  number of households and, 97
  population growth and, 95–96
  retail store image and, 79–82
  selection of market target and, 25–26
  site evaluation and, 185–87
  size of investment turnover and, 48
  social class and, 114–15
  trading area and, 170–72
  See also Consumer behavior; Forecasting
Market research
  demographic vs. psychographic questionnaires in, 133–36
  role of, 138, 139
  utilizing sales tax expenditure data, 299
Market segments (Market segmentation), 76
  based on demographic characteristics, 102–104
  based on income, 116–19
  buyer knowledge of, 259
  criteria for, 77
  future, 544–45

life style and, 115–16
  luxury, 529–30
  social class and, 114–15
  See also Market target, selection of
Market share of trading area, defined, 174
Market system, defined, 17–18
Market target
  defined, 26
  selection of, 25–26
Marketing
  buyer behavior and, 259; *see also* Buyers; Buying
  defined, 16–17
  in department store organization, 230–31
  functions of, 17
  retail management strategy and, 38–42
Marketing managers, defined, 17
Marketing systems
  defined, 16–17
  differentiated from market system, 17
Markup
  average cost pricing and, 362–67
  percentage, 378–79
  requirements in merchandise budget, 309–12
  retail method and, 487–89
  See also Pricing
Married couples, *see* Husband-wife households
Mass market, growth of, 108–10
Mass media, diffusion process and, 283; *see also* Advertising
Matched parallelism, 21, 422–23
Matching and sorting process, 19, 132
  selection of market target and, 26
Matrix
  of techniques involved in both store and nonstore retailing, 518
  of retail method of inventory valuation, 483–85
Maturity stage in product life cycle, 276–77
Mazur Four-Functional Plan, 228–32
Measuring vs. forecasting, 84–85
Media models, advertising effectiveness and, 415–17
Merchandise
  cash disbursement for, 61, 62
  classification of, 300–301
  in future, 537–38
  new lines of, 508
  return on investment in, 500
  turnover, capital turnover and, 257–58
  See also Inventories
Merchandise assortments, *see* Assortment mix
Merchandise broker, defined, 292
Merchandise budget, 51, 295–312
  components of, 297

forecasting and, 83
markup requirements in, 309–12
nature of, 296–97
planned stocks and, 304–307
procedures, 297–312
purchase planning and, 307–309
in retail deductions, 301–303
sales forecasting in, 299–301
Merchandise controls
dissection control activities and, 313–14
dollar and unit systems, 312–18
Merchandise management
capital budgeting and, 334–38
classification of inventories and, 326–34
computers and, 344–48
defined, 294–95
GMROI and, 338–39
inventory levels and time considerations
in, 323–25
management-intuition approach to, 322
management science approach to, 322–23
merchandise budget and, 295–312
problems of, 321–38
stock turnover and, 339–44
Merchandise management accounting, 477
controllable profit in, 495–96
cost pattern and, 496–99
criticisms of, 501–503
decision making at action level and,
494–500
defined, 492–93
future of, 501–503
need for, 493–94
return on merchandise investment and,
500
turnover and, 499–500
Merchandise management models, 320–48
Merchandising
boutiques and, 530–31
in branches, 233
buyer behavior model and, 266–68
changing nature of, 507–31
defined, 253–54
development of policies for, 254–66
fashion cycle and, 280, 281
franchising operations and, see Franchising
importance of buying decisions in, 255–59
improved performance through increased stock turnover in, 343–44
as industry of contrasts, 509
nonstore, 516–28
store design, layout and space utilization in, 192–93
store image and, 80
in store positioning period, 547–49
thematic, 528–31
Merchandising cycle, profitable, 58

Miller-Tydings Act (1937), 386–87
Model stock procedure, 215–16
Monopolistic competition, pricing and,
356–58
Montgomery Ward and Company, organizational chart of, 237, 238
Motivation, in consumer behavior, 3, 127–28
Multiple correlation analysis, 92
Multiple nuclei theory, 153–55
Multistore system, expense allocation in,
469–71
Mutual reinforcement, defined, 407

n

National Labor Relations Act (1935),
246–47
Natural expenses, defined, 461
Needs, hierarchy of, 127–28
Negotiation process, 284–88
buyer behavior and, 263
defined, 284–85
terms of sale and, 285–88
Negotiative prices, 380
Neighborhood areas, defined, 178, 179
Neighborhood centers, 148, 181–82
Net profits
expense allocation and, 468–71
in monopolistic competition, 357–58
New products, advertising spiral and, 401–402
Newspaper advertising, 405–406
Noncontrollable costs, defined, 467
Nondurable goods, teenage market for,
103
Nongoods services, defined, 436; see also
Credit
Nonpersonal nonstore retailing, 522–28
Nonselling areas, see Service areas
Nonstore retailing, 516–28
Nostalgia, sales and, 528–29

o

Occupancy expenses, 462
Odd pricing, 380–82
Oligopoly model, 356
One-price pricing policies, 380
One-stop shopping, 31
Open book credit, see Charge account
credit
Open-to-buy concept, 308–309
Operating expenses
cash disbursement for, 61–63
markup requirements and, 311
ratios, rising level of, 508
sales and, 49
Operating statement items, in ratio analysis, 64–70
Opinion leaders, diffusion process and,
283

Opportunity costs, inventory and, 331–32
Opportunity earnings, 37
Option-terms plan, 442
Order costs, order size and, 331
Order cycling method, 327
Order size, order costs and, 331
Ordinary dating, defined, 287–88
Organization
  advertising and personal selling and, 396–97
  budget and, *see* Merchandise budget
  of chain store system, 234–39
  of department store, 227–32
  employee turnover rates and, 240–41
  expense center accounting and, 463
  goal and objectives of, 33–34
  government role in, 245–47
  larger store, 227–39
  management accounting and, 456–58
  new forms of, 508
  personnel management and, 241–48
  purpose of, 223
  small store, 224–26
  special problems affecting, 239–41
  unionization and, 247–48
  work flow and, 240
Organization charts, 235, 236, 237, 238
Out-of-stock merchandise, unit control system and, 318
Outshopping, in trading area analysis, 169–70
Overage, in physical inventory, 315
Owned goods services, defined, 436
Ownership
  classification of retail stores by, 8, 10
  vs. renting, 512

P

Packaging, defined, 396
Parking facilities, store location and, 189–90
Party selling, 522
Patronage
  kinds of, 176–77
  motives for, 127
  See also Consumer behavior
Per capita GNP, 104
Per capita income, in income class market profiles, 117–19
Per capita retail sales, 6, 8
Per cent of sales method, advertising expenditures and, 413–14
Percentage costs, 497–98
Percentage deviation method, 304–305
Perception
  consumer behavior and, 126
  price lining and, 382 *n.*
Perforated price tickets, unit control and, 317
Peripheral service concept, 204

Perpetual inventory method, 314–15, 318
Personal consumption expenditures, as percentage of disposable personal income, 107–108
Personal nonstore retailing, 518–21
Personal outlays, disposable personal income and, 106–107
Personal savings, 106–107
Personal selling, 420–35
  buyer-oriented, 424–25
  categories, 422
  defined, 396
  dyadic interaction and, 425–26
  management of, 424–35
  matching to total store strategy, 422–23
  nature of, 420–21
  organization and, 396–97
  process, 426–29
  role of, 421–22
  understanding sales situation and, 423–29
Personality characteristics, of sales personnel, 429–31
Personnel management, 241–48
  compensation in, 243–45
  development and training in, 242–43
  integration and maintenance in, 245
  legislation and, 245–47
  recruitment problems in, 241–42
  turnover rates in, 240–41
  unionization and, 245–48
  See also Sales personnel
Persuasive salesman, 429
Physical distribution mix, 29
Physical inventory, 315, 318
  in cost method of accounting, 481–82
  nongoods services and, 437
  in retail method of inventory valuation, 486
Pioneering stage, 402
Pivotal site, 186
Planned stocks, 304–307
Point-of-sale terminals, future, 539–40
Population
  growth, 95–96, 162–63
  by selected residence categories, 100–101
  shifts in location of, 98–102
  See also Demographic factors
Post-decision dissonance, 131–32
Predicasts, 86
Preference probability, 255
Premiums, as advertising medium, 409–10
Price (s)
  credit and, 444–45
  defined, 352–53
  promotional activities and, 410–11
  range of, 368
  retailing mix and, 28
  service costs and, 437–39
  turnover and, 499–500

-value relationship, customer behavior and, 255
Price appeal stores, 81
Price emulation, *see* Pricing at the market
Price-fixing agreements, horizontal, 385
Price leader, characteristics of, 384
Price lining, 382–83
Pricing, 351–88
  administered models for, 359–62
  costs and, 368–69
  economic models for, 355–56
  goals of, 354–62
  government constraints on, 385–88
  influences on, 353–54
  monopolistic competition and, 356–58
  policies, 377–85
  programmed, *see* Programmed pricing decisions
  role of, 351–52
  stock turnover and, 344
  uncertainties and, 355
  upper and lower bounds in, 358–59
  See also Average cost pricing; Target-rate-of-return pricing
Pricing at the market, defined, 377–78
Primary buying motives, 127
Probability contours, trading area concept and, 157–60
Product assortment, *see* Assortment mix
Product classification
  market classification by, 75–76
  small store organization and, 225
Products
  break-even point for, 55–56
  deletion of, 272–74
  life cycles of, 274–77
  retailing mix and, 28
  sales, shelf space and, 218
  unique features of, 418–19
  See also Assortment mix; Product classification
Profit (s)
  in absolute dollars, 35
  assortment decision process and, 271–72
  in break-even point analysis, 50–58
  in chain stores, 239
  control of retailing expenses and, 458–71
  definition of, 34–38
  expectations, in franchising, 514–15
  investment turnover and, 48
  leader pricing and, 383–84
  main elements contributing to, 35–36
  maximization of, as foremost organizational goal, 31
  as per cent of sales, 255–56, 502
  pricing and, 353–54
  ratios, 69
  as return on investment, 36–38, 255–58
  selection of measure of, 44–45

shortages and, 303
space allocation theory and, 216–17
store image and, 82
See also Financial analysis
Profit and loss statement, 46
Programming, 243
  markdowns and, 374, 375
  policies and, 376–77
  pricing and, 369–76
Promotion, 393, 419
  changing attitudes regarding, 411
  as communication, 395–97
  criticisms of, 397
  defined, 394
  in Dupont Schematic, 49
  in future, 537–38
  kinds of, 395–96
  personal selling and, 420–35
  role of, 393–94
  services as, 435–39
  stock turnover and, 344
  trading stamps and, 410–11
  See also Advertising
Promotional calendar, 414, 415
Psychographic analysis of consumer behavior, 133–34
Psychological pricing, 381–82
Publicity
  costs, 462
  defined, 396
  See also Advertising; Promotion
Pull strategy, 398
Push strategy, 398

q

Quality of merchandise, customer behavior and, 255
Quantity discounts, defined, 287

r

Radio advertising, 406–407
Record keeping, layout and, 201
Regional shopping center, defined, 181–82
Reilly's Law, 166, 167
Reinforcement
  advertising and, 406–407
  consumer behavior and, 130
Relations analysis, organization and, 224
Rented goods services, defined, 436
Reordering costs vs. inventory costs, 324–25
Replacement rate
  classification of goods and, 175
  location of departments and, 209
Resale price maintenance, 386–87
Resident buying offices, 291–93
Response, defined, 130
Responsibility reporting, 455–56
  expense center accounting and, 463, 466
Restaurants, thematic, 529

Retail employees, *see* Personnel management

Retail management, 21–22
buyers and, 263–64, 290–91
in chain store systems, 235
consumer behavior and, *see* Consumer behavior
evaluation of, 44
features of, 32–33
goals of, 33–34
matched parallelism in, 422–23
personal selling function in, 424–35
resale price maintenance in, 387
strategy, 24–34
unit control and, 316
See also Control; Inventories; Merchandise management; Organization; Personnel management

Retail method of accounting, 476

Retail method of inventory valuation, 483–89

Retail pricing, *see* Pricing

Retail store (s)
changes in size of, 507
classification of, 8–10
function of, 22
growth and development of, 4–6
image, 79–82
number of, 144
positioning, 543–49
relationship between environment and, 24–25
specialization in, 255
type, profit as percentage of sales and, 256
See also Location factors; Site selection; Store design; Store layout; Trading areas

Retailer, defined, 18

Retailing
competition in, 537
consumer affluence and, 540–41
consumerism and, 541–43
decentralization of, 180–82
defined, 3–4
economic forces and, 535
efficiency of, 546–47
flexibility in, 544
functional approach to, 11, 16–22
future of, 533–49
identification of market in, 544–45
people-oriented, 545–46
plans of industry leaders for, 534–38
in post-industrial society, 538–39
store design and, 195
strategy, 543–44
in systems framework, 20–22
technology and, 536, 539–40
transactional nature of, 3–4
value added by, 19–20

Retailing mix
defined, 27
effect of, 48–49
elements of, 28
submixes and, 28–29

Retailing system, 18–20
model of, 21

Retentive stage of advertising, 402–403

Return on investment
in Dupont Schematic, 46–50
investment turnover and, 47–48

Review stage of buyer decision making, 268

Revolving credit, 442

Right-angle approach to forecasting, 93

Robinson-Patman Act (1936), 401

Role-taking model of buyer behavior, 264–66

Route selling, 521–22

S

Safety stock, 325

Sales
advertising expenditures and, 412–14
break-even table for, 54
cash receipts from, 60–61, 62
of catalog-showrooms, 525
dollar and per capita volume of (1929–1972), 6
dollar volume of (1972), 19
forecasting, in merchandise budget, 299–301
by kind of business, 9
operating costs and, 49
parking facilities and, 189–90
per capita, market opportunity measurement and, 172
per square foot of selling space, market opportunity measurement and, 172
profit and loss comparisons for, 36
profit margin and investment turnover and, 48–49
profit as per cent of, 35
projections from, 91
promotion, *see* Promotion
vending machine, 527
volume, profit and, 36
volume per establishment (1929–1972), 7–8
See also Terms of sale

Sales personality, defined, 429

Sales personnel
characteristics of, 422–23
control of, 433–35
number of, 431–33
personality characteristics of, 429–31
recruiting, selecting, and training of, 424–31
See also Personnel management

Sales revenue, in break-even point analysis, 50–58

Sandwich approach, defined, 204

Satellite community, central business district of, 147

Saturation of trading area, 173–74

Savings vs. spending, 107

Score card, in management accounting, 457

Scrambled merchandising, 271

Search, in buying process, 268

Seasonality factors, 91
   location of departments and, 209

Secondary shopping area, 178, 179

Sector theory, 152–53

Selection, in buying process, 268

Selective buying motives, 127

Self-image
   consumer behavior and, 132
   of retail salespeople, 248

Self-service merchandising, 31
   shortage problem and, 303
   special displays and, 408

Selling
   chain store organization and, 235
   expenses, 462
   method, store layout and, 209–10
   performance standards, 433–35
   See also Sales; Sales personnel

Semi-variable costs, break-even point analysis and, 52

Seminar training, 243

Senior citizen market, 103–104

Service areas, location of, 203–204

Service-sponsor-retailer franchise, 511–12, 513–14

Services
   customer costs and, 437–39
   defined, 436
   in future, 537–38
   increased expenditures for, 30–31
   promoting and managing, 435–39

Shared business, 176, 177

Shelf space, product sales and, 218

Sherman Antitrust Act (1890), 386

Shoplifting, *see* Shortages

Shoppe concept, 209

Shopping centers, 31, 147, 178
   cumulative attraction and compatibility theory and, 187–89
   hypothetical effectiveness of, 182, 183
   parking facilities for, 189
   suburban, *see* Suburban shopping centers
   trading areas of, 181–82
   types of, 181–82

Shopping process, 130–39; *see also* Consumer behavior

Short-term forecasts, 83

Shortages
   causes of, 303
   markup requirements and, 310, 311
   in merchandise budget, 301–304
   in physical inventory, 315
   value of inventory and, 302

Sink or swim training method, 243

Site selection, 143–44
   shopping center location analysis and, 184
   site analysis and, 185–87
   See also Location; Trading areas

Situation management approach to selling, 428–29

Small business failures, 514

Social classes
   diffusion process and, 282–84
   market opportunity and, 114–15

Social-psychological approach, determinants of, 125–30

Sociological theories of consumer behavior, 124–25

Space allocation, 213–18
   heuristic approaches to, 214–16
   homogeneity of store space and, 218
   model stock procedure and, 215–16
   space productivity ratios and, 214–15
   theoretical approach to, 216–18
   See also Store layout

Space productivity ratios, 214–15

Special displays, 408–409

Split total cash registers, merchandise controls and, 313–14

Spokane, Wash., trading areas of, 156, 157–58

Sponsors, 242, 243

Standard Metropolitan Statistical Areas, 12–13, 100

Status, diffusion process and, 282–84

Stimulus-Response (S-R) selling, 427

Stock level, *see* Planned stock

Stock-sales ratio method, 304

Stock turnover
   GMROI and, 339
   increased, 343–44
   measures of, 340–42
   in merchandise accounting, 499–500
   merchandise planning and control and, 342–43
   merchandising management and, 339–44

Stock turnover index, 342–43

Stockouts, inventory levels and, 324–25

Stocks of assets, 46
   flows of income and, 47–48

Storage areas, in store layout, 204

Store attributes, 547
   in psychographic analysis, 133–34

Store design
   competition and, 192–93
   comprehensive planning of, 195–96

Store design (*cont.*)
consumer behavior and, 199–201
contemporary trends and influences in, 196–201
form follows function concept in, 194–95
retailing activities and, 195
role and importance of, 193–201
Store layout
approaches to, 201–203
basis for, 201–13
boutiques and, 531
defined, 201
departmentizing and, 206–207, 208–209
location of service areas and, 203–204
major patterns of, 204–206
merchandising sequence and, 201–203
operating efficiency and, 211–13
selling method and, 209–10
in supermarkets, 210–11
Store manager, *see* Retail management
String street developments, 178, 179
Submixes, activities in, 28–29
Suburban shopping center, 180–81
Suburbs
customer characteristics in, 81
market opportunity in, 98–101
Succession, in concentric zone theory, 151
Supermarkets
and changes in consumer shopping habits, 138
development of, 5
index of saturation and, 173–74
leader pricing in, 384
parking facilities for, 189–90
shelf space related to product sales in, 218
Suppliers, selection of, 276
Suscipient business, 176, 177
Syndicated office, 292
Systems approach, 32

t

Taft-Hartley Act, 246
Target-rate-of-return pricing, 360–61, 369
Task method, advertising expenditures and, 414
Teaching machines, 243
Technological changes, retailing and, 536, 539–40
Teenage market, 99, 103
Telephone interviews, delineation of trading areas through, 169
Telephone selling strategy, 519–20
Television advertising, 407
Tension reduction, consumer behavior and, 131
Termination dates, for merchandise budget, 299
Terms of sale, 285–88

Test marketing, 89
Thematic merchandising, 528–31
Time of consumption, classification of goods and, 176
Time series analysis, 90–91
Trade discounts, defined, 286–87
Trading area(s)
accommodation of store to, 174–91
analysis of, 155–63
definition of, 155–56
delineation of, 164–70
indices, 173–74
market opportunity and, 170
movement, 162–63
nature and scope of, 158–60
outshopping and, 169–70
of planned shopping centers, 181–82
saturation of, 173–74
size and shape of, 160–62
Trading stamps, 410–11
Traffic, leader pricing and, 384
Transportation facilities, dating provisions and, 287
Travel paths, in supermarkets, 210
Trend analysis, 64
Trickle effect, diffusion process and, 282–84
Turnover, *see* Stock turnover
Turnover and funds utilization ratio, 68–69
Turnover rates of employees, 240–41
Two-functional arrangements, 225

U

Uncertainty
buyer behavior and, 262–63
pricing and, 355
Underorganizing, 223
Understoring, 174
Unfair sales practices acts, 387–88
Unionization of retail employees, 245–48
Unit control, 312–18
Unit pricing, 384–85
Unit profit, 36
Unique selling propositions, 547
Urbanization, rate of, 97
Utility, consumer shopping behavior and, 175

V

Value added by retailing, 19–20
Variable costs, in break-even point analysis, 52
Variables
markup-related, 311
in merchandise budget, 297
psychographic, 133–34
uncontrollable, 25, 28, 83
Variety chains, 41
Vending machine selling, 526–28

Vendor-buyer interaction, 284–88
Vendors
   evaluation of behavior of, 289–90
   selection of, 288–93
Vertical cooperative advertising, 401
Vertical franchising, defined, 511
Vertical pricing, 385–87
Visibility in supermarkets, 210–11

w

Wages, for retail employees, 243–45
Washington State metropolitan areas,
   market opportunity in, 172

Weber's law, 382*n.*
Weeks' supply method, defined, 304
Wheel of retailing concept, 31–32
Wholesaler, defined, 18
Wilston's Men's Shoppe, merchandise
   budget for, 298–312
Women as heads of household, 97–98
Women, working, family and, 109
Work flow, organization and, 240

y

Youth market, *see* Teenage market